THE CURÉ D'ARS

St. John Baptist Vianney
The Curé d'Ars
1786-1859

THE CURÉ D'ARS

ST. JEAN-MARIE-BAPTISTE VIANNEY
(1786-1859)

According to the Acts of the Process of Canonization
And numerous hitherto unpublished documents.

by

Abbé Francis Trochu

Translated by

Dom Ernest Graf, O.S.B.

St. Mary's Abbey, Buckfast

TAN Books
Charlotte, North Carolina

Imprimatur:

Cum Opus cui titulus: "The Life of the Curé d'Ars" lingua gallica conscriptum atque a R. P. D. Ernesto Graf Monasterii Buckfastriensis Monacho in linguam anglicam versum Censor a Nobis deputatus rite recognoverit, nihilque in eo contra fidem et mores reprehenderit, Nos, quantum ad Nos attinet, imprimi permittimus.

Datum ex Asceterio S. Specus, die 5 Maii, 1927.

D. BENEDICTUS GARIADOR, O.S.B.,
Ab. gen.
D. HIERONYMUS HAULER,
Cons. a secr.

Nihil Obstat: Innocentius Apap, O.P., S.T.M.
Censor deputatus.

Imprimatur: ✠ Edm. Can. Surmont
Vicar General
Westmonasterii, September 5, 1927

In conformity with the decrees of Urban VIII, we declare that in using the qualifications *holy, venerable,* or when we speak of *intuitions, prophecies, miracles, visions,* and other facts of the supernatural order we only follow the received practice of the faithful and have no intention of anticipating the judgement of the Church.

Originally published in 1927 by Burns Oates & Washbourne

Reprinted by TAN Books and Publishers, in 1977 by arrangement with Burns & Oates, London. Retypeset by TAN in 2007.

ISBN: 978-0-89555-020-0

Cover design by Milo Persic, milo.persic@gmail.com.

Printed and bound in the United States of America.

TAN Books
Charlotte, North Carolina

1977

TRANSLATOR'S PREFACE

THE holy Curé d'Ars is one of the most remarkable figures of modern times. Not so very many years ago, his name was on the lips of countless thousands, and the events of the tiny village of Ars were of far greater interest to numberless souls than the political happenings of a period which was certainly neither dull nor uneventful. If, after perusing this volume, the reader still wishes to know something more of the life of this wonderful village parish priest, we would refer him to chapter five of Book IV of the *Imitation.* The nineteen verses of that admirable chapter might have been written after a study of the sublime priestly career of St. Jean-Baptiste Vianney.

M. Trochu's work is on strictly scientific lines. Instead of drawing on imagination or pious emotionalism—as too many would-be hagiographers have done—he drew on the most reliable of all historical sources—viz., the *Acts of the Process of Canonization.* The result is a book that shows us the holy man as he lived, thought, and spoke. There can be no doubt that the effect on the reader will be an increased sense of the reality of the supernatural, of reverence for the mysterious power of the Catholic priesthood, and of love for that Christian humility and abnegation which are the real secret of the saints.

The translator has thought it best to leave all French proper nouns untranslated, as well as certain titles with which all educated readers are familiar, such as "cure" "vicaire," etc.; one or two names of towns which are frequently mentioned have been spelled in the usual English fashion, and distances are given in kilometers. The late war and the daily papers have long ago familiarized us with the weights and measures of the metric system.

The translator has not judged it necessary to reproduce all the footnotes of the French text, the more so that these references are to texts to which the reader cannot hope to have access—viz., the Papers of the *Process.* However, the reference is invariably given when the importance of some statement made in the text seemed to demand that the source of the information be clearly indicated.

My thanks are due and hereby tendered to a friend who very kindly drew up the index to this second edition.

BUCKFAST ABBEY,
Candlemas Day, 1927.
July, 1930.

Bibliographical Introduction

THIS is the first *Life* of the Curé d'Ars compiled from the documents of the *Process of Beatification and Canonization.* Thanks to the kindness of Mgr. Manier, Bishop of Belley, to whom we once more tender an expression of our deepest gratitude, we have been able, in this work, to draw, not only on the *Informative Process* or the *Process of the Ordinary,* which was set up and did its work between 1862 and 1865, but likewise on three successive *Apostolic Processes* which were held under the direct control of the Holy See between the years 1874 and 1886.[1]

The depositions of the *Cause of Ars* were, in themselves, a source of documentation of the first order, one which, it would seem, should have sufficed to show in its true light the amazing and attractive personality of St. Jean-Marie-Baptiste Vianney. Here was an exceedingly rich mine, one that supplied the best guarantee of the authenticity and veracity of the facts contained in its pages. The volumes are made up of the depositions—collected by competent judges—of the persons who have best known the Curé d'Ars, such as his sister Marguerite, the playmates of his childhood, his fellow-students at the seminary, his parishioners, his brother priests, those who assisted him in his heroic toil. All these witnesses are worthy of belief, they are blinded neither by passion nor

---

1. In the last chapter of this book we give the history of the *Cause of Ars.* The *Process of the Ordinary* and the *Apostolic Processes* are contained in five volumes in-folio and comprise 4,560 pages.

The *Apostolic Process on the heroicity of the virtues* is held twice over. First there is the *Process* called *inchoative* (preliminary) *ne pereant Causa probationes,* during the course of which the tribunal hears the evidence of old men and others whose death is to be feared. Then there follows the *Continuative Process super virtutibus et miraculis in specie,* which is held at the date fixed by Canon Law, when those witnesses are heard who were able to wait until then. Between these two parts of the one *Process* there takes place the *Apostolic Process on the reputation for sanctity (super fama sanctitatis vitae, virtutum et miraculorum in genere).*

For the sake of simplifying references in the footnotes, we call *Procès apostolique ne pereant* the *inchoative Process,* and *Procès apostolique in genere* the *Process* on the reputation for sanctity.

interest; all of them are convinced Catholics and bound by a solemn oath taken on the Gospel. Nor was there a delay of twenty or thirty years before they were questioned; the great value of the *Cause of Ars* lies precisely in that it was begun immediately after M. Vianney's death. Hence, *Legend,* that too pretty waiting-maid of *History,* has not had time to transform and disfigure facts that were still fresh in the memory of those who had witnessed them.

In addition to the five in-folios of the *Process,* we were able, thanks to the courtesy of Mgr. Hippolyte Convert, fourth successor of the saint in the parish of Ars, to utilize freely numerous manuscripts preserved in the archives of Ars. They are:

1. Three successive editions of the *Petit mémoire sur M. Vianney,* written by Mlle. Catherine Lassagne, of Ars, the first between 1839-1855; the second in 1860; the last between 1862-1867.
2. Some undated *Notes,* collected by the Abbé Renard, of Ars.
3. A *Diary* kept during 1855 by M. l'Abbé Toccanier, the saint's assistant and future successor.
4. A fragmentary *Life* of the Curé d'Ars (193 pages in-folio) by M. Raymond, who acted officially as his vicaire from 1845 until 1853.
5. A collection of numerous inquiries made by Canon Ball (the saint's third successor) on the *facts of intuition* attributed to M. Vianney.
6. Two manuscript books of *Notes* in which Mgr. Convert set down, from 1889 to 1924, some oral traditions still lingering among aged inhabitants of Ars who had been the saint's parishioners.
7. Three *Mémoires sur M. Vianney, Curé d'Ars (Ain)* (1848-1855), due to the unskillful but sincere pen of an agriculturist of Cousance (Jura), Jean-Claude Viret.
8. A *Notice sur M. Balley, curé d'Ecully et premier professeur de Jean-Marie Vianney,* composed by M. Michy, at that time curé of Job (Puy-de-Dôme) and subsequently editor of *La Croix de Clermont.*

9. A *Notice historique sur la Providence d'Ars, oeuvre du bienheureux Vianney,* by Canon Béréziat, chaplain to the mother house of the Sisters of St. Joseph of Bourg.

10. Some *Notes sur le séjour de M. Vianney aux Noës* (Loire) taken from the reminiscences of the old people of that place and collected by two successive curés, MM. Perret and Monin-Veyret.

11. Numerous autograph *Letters* of M. Vianney and bearing his signature (about sixty in all); of the Vicomte d'Ars, Mme. Prosper des Garets, the Abbé Toccanier, etc.

We have also searched the *National Archives,* the *Municipal Archives* of Trévoux, and the *Episcopal Archives* of Lyons and Belley.

We have likewise consulted a long list of *Mémoires, Accounts, Letters* dealing with the extraordinary occurrences of Ars; also documents such as the *parish* and *municipal registers of Ars;* the *Livres de raison* of Mlle. Anne-Colombe des Garets, as well as the *estimates, accounts, receipts* in connection with work done on the church of Ars.

Our constant anxiety to go to sources in the composition of this history has not caused us to neglect the study of such books and pamphlets as might help us in our task. Especially did we examine the collection of *Sermons* of M. Vianney, the *Annales d'Ars,* and the various biographies of the holy Curé.

The *Annales d'Ars* began to appear in June, 1900. This small monthly review—in addition to a number of documents kept in the archives of Ars, anecdotes relating to the saint's life and the panegyrics delivered every year on August 4, the anniversary of his death and the saint's feast—published, at first anonymously, interesting monographs which, when they were published in book form, revealed the name of their venerable author, Mgr. Convert. The titles of those writings are: *Le bienheureux Curé d'Ars et le sacrement de Pénitence* (1920); *A l'école du bienheureux Curé d'Ars et Méditations eucharistiques tirées des écrits du bienheureux Curé d'Ars* (1921); *Notre-*

Dame d'Ars, méditations sur la Sainte Vierge tirées des écrits du bienheureux Curé d'Ars (1922); *Le bienheureux Curé d'Ars et la famille; Le bienheureux Curé d'Ars et les dons du Saint-Esprit* (1923).[1]

Of the various biographies of the saint which have appeared up to this day, only two have proved of real interest:

1. *Le Curé d'Ars, vie de M. Jean-Baptiste-Marie Vianney,* par M. l'Abbé Alfred Monnin, missionaire (2 vols. in 8vo, Paris, Douniol, 1861; and this original edition is the only one to which we refer).
2. *Le bienheureux Curé d'Ars* (1786-1859), par Joseph Vianney, Paris, Lecoffre, 1905.

The other biographies, popular works which aim purely at edification and so may have some merit, add nothing really fresh to the information contained in the above-quoted books. As for those which appeared during the lifetime of the saint, and which were circulated among the faithful notwithstanding his repeated protests—they are in a great measure exceedingly fanciful.

The *Life* by M. Monnin has had many editions.[2] For Catholic readers it is the most complete biography of the Curé d'Ars published until now. We are impressed, and rightly so, by the fact that M. Monnin personally knew the holy Curé. It was in 1855 that his relations with the saint began. "Before that date," he himself relates, "I had been twice to Ars out of curiosity. I then saw M. Vianney but did not speak to him. In my capacity as diocesan missionary I afterward stayed with him at various dates each year, making altogether about two or three months. This went on for five years."[3] Thus M. Monnin knew the Curé d'Ars in his old age, at a time when the ministry of the confessional absorbed his days. Nevertheless, each night, more or less, he enjoyed the exquisite privilege, with other priests, of accompanying the saint

1. All these books have been published by Vitte, Lyons-Paris.
2. There exists an English translation by Bertram Wolferstan, S.J., Sands and Co., London.
3. *Procès apostolique ne pereant,* p. 945. Deposition of the Abbé Monnin, then a Jesuit at Lyons (August 8, 1876).

when he returned to his room. In this way he had treasured up some precious memories. We know from other sources that he took notes and caused others to do the same about so extraordinary a man.

For all that, M. Monnin's book exhibits most of the features of a hasty and inadequate compilation. He felt compelled to write his book with great rapidity so as to publish it as soon as possible after the Curé's death, and, in order to get on more speedily, he even embodied in his own text many pages written by other hands, the authorship of which he refrained from acknowledging. Thus, in the first part, he borrowed in their entirety chapters eight and nine from the manuscript of M. Raymond, which we mentioned above; his chapter five was taken from the same source, except for a few slight alterations. He had in his hands the second edition of the *Petit mémoire* of Catherine Lassagne—written for him, as a matter of fact, but much shorter than the third edition—but he mentions only on rare occasions the contributions of others, even though he makes use of them. For this, no doubt, he had obtained the assent of Mlle. Lassagne and M. Raymond.

The work is incomplete because, as regards the facts anterior to 1855, the author has consulted very few witnesses.[4] Hence arise vagueness of statement and errors of chronology. True, M. Monnin has taken advantage of more than one interesting correspondence; but access to the most reliable and at the same time the most plentiful source of information was denied him—we mean the *Process of the Ordinary* and the *Apostolic Processes.* Nor did he take into account, together with other documents, the *Sermons* of the Curé d'Ars, which throw so much light upon the opening years of his ministry.

4. On June 7, 1863, the Abbé Gaffino, who signs his letter "Curé-doyen," wrote from Cette to the Abbé Toccanier: "How inadequate I find the *Life* by M. Monnin! Let someone make haste to write another more complete as regards the sayings and actions of the Curé d'Ars. Otherwise, the only known and authentic *Life* of a saint whom millions have seen or watched will be that written by M. Monnin! . . ."

M. Gaffino did not know as yet that the authorities of Belley were even then busy collecting the precious testimonies which, in themselves, contain a full *Life* of the holy Curé.

Moreover, the Abbé Monnin's work lacks perspective. He writes as one who saw in M. Vianney only the ascetic who has reached the summit of perfection, whose head is already encircled by the halo of the saints.

Even his style, which is almost consistently rhetorical, affects sonorous periods and harmonious redundances and stoops with reluctance to simple and matter-of-fact details. Most of his chapters are planned on the model of a sermon—that is, they have an introduction, moralizing mixed with the narrative of facts, and finally, a conclusion or peroration. In short, M. Monnin was too near the period to pass an unbiased judgement on men and events.

Nevertheless, however we may judge the work, it has certainly and most happily realized the end which its author sought—viz., the edification of the faithful. It was the great merit of the Abbé Monnin to have rendered eminently popular the most attractive personality of the Curé d'Ars.

Though he followed a different method, M. Joseph Vianney has pursued a like aim. The collection *Les Saints,* which includes his fine book, is intended to make the saints known to the people. M. Vianney was not on the lookout for anything new or original. In order to remain within the narrow limits assigned to him, he found himself compelled to touch rapidly on important facts and even wholly to omit some incidents in the saint's life.

The documents at our command have enabled us, we believe, to make quite clear certain episodes in the life of the holy Curé which up till now were somewhat vague and dim, such as the stay of Jean-Marie Vianney at Les Noës from 1809 till 1811; his passage through the seminary of Lyons in 1813-1814; the calumnies of which he was the victim during his first years at Ars; the moral transformation of his parish; the foundation and fall of the *Providence* of Ars; the contradictions to which he was subjected by some brother priests; the incident of La Salette; his "flight" to La Trappe of La Neylière; the last illness and death of the servant of God.

CONTENTS

Translator's Preface v
Bibliographical Introduction vii

PART I
THE YEARS OF PREPARATION
(1786-1818)

Chapter 1
FIRST YEARS
(1786-1793)

Benôit Labre at Pierre Vianney's—Gratitude of the holy mendicant—Matthieu Vianney and Marie Beluse—Birth of Jean-Marie—A Christian mother—A model of obedience—Beads and a statuette—First steps out of the common road—Before the altar 3

Chapter 2
A YOUNG SHEPHERD UNDER THE TERROR
(1793-1794)

The Vianneys at the Mass of the juror-priest—Indignation of Marie Vianney—Marie and the faithful priests—Mass in the attic—Fighting near Lyons—Dardilly and Chante-Merle—Prayers and rustic processions—Games and sermons—Jean-Marie Vianney and Marion Vincent—Jean-Marie and the wandering poor—Family life 12

Chapter 3
SCHOOL, FIRST CONFESSION, AND COMMUNION
(1794-1799)

The lessons of citizen Dumas—The exemplary pupil—Missionary priests: MM. Groboz and Balley—First Confession of Jean-Marie Vianney—The farm of Point-du-Jour at Ecully—A saint's first Communion 23

Chapter 4
LABORER AND VINE-DRESSER
(1799-1805)

Labor sanctified—Sneers of his comrades—The Concordat of 1802—Reestablishment of public worship at Dardilly—Thoughts of the priesthood—First confidences and difficulties—Acceptance by M. Balley 29

Chapter 5
A LATE VOCATION
(1805-1809)

Jean-Marie at the age of nineteen—Among the children—A vision—Pilgrimage to La Louvesc—A troublesome vow—Conscription—Visitation of the Cardinal-Archbishop—Confirmation of Jean-Marie-Baptiste Vianney—*Marching orders* 41

Chapter 6
THE DEFAULTER OF LES NOËS
(1809-1811)

The levy of 1809—Called up though exempt—At the Military Hospital of Lyons and the General Hospital of Roanne—On the road to Renaison—With Guy the defaulter—At the house of the mayor of Les Noës—Jérôme Vincent under the roof of Claudine Fayot—The sorrows and consolations of his exile—Alarms—*Mère* Fayot at Dardilly—Amnesty—Farewell to Les Noës and joy of the return—Death of his mother—What the saint thought of his having hidden himself at Les Noës and how we should judge his conduct 51

Chapter 7
THE YEAR OF PHILOSOPHY AT VERRIÈRES
(1812-1813)

At the presbytery of Ecully—First tonsure—The lessons and examples of M. Balley—The house of Verrières—A "philosopher" of twenty-six—Friends and enemies—Marcellin Champagnat—The marks of a future saint . . 73

Chapter 8
AT THE GRAND SÉMINAIRE OF LYONS
(1813-1814)

Happy vacation of 1813—The seminary of Saint-Irénée—Admirable virtue—A rebellious mind—Dismissed!—A visit to the novitiate of the Christian Brothers—Examination at the presbytery of Ecully—Decision of M. Courbon, the Vicar-General 81

Chapter 9
SUBDIACONATE, DIACONATE, PRIESTHOOD
(1814-1815)

The subdiaconate—Presentiments of the Abbé Mellon—Politics at the Grand Séminaire—The diaconate—Canonical examination before the priesthood—Testimonial letters—Ordination to the priesthood—Impressions of August 13, 1815 90

Chapter 10
VICAIRE AT ECULLY
(1815-1818)

Rejoicings at Ecully, Dardilly, and Les Noës—M. Vianney's first penitent—Beginnings in the sacred ministry—"He gives away all he has"—At the school of a saint—Visit of *Mère* Fayot—Pauline Jaricot and St. Philomena—Intimacies of the presbytery—Illness and death of M. Balley—Inheritance and memories—M. Tripier and his vicaire—The chaplaincy of Ars 97

PART II
PASTORATE OF ARS
(1818-1859)

Chapter 1
ARRIVAL AT ARS AND FIRST CONTACT WITH HIS PARISH

The village of Ars—M. Vianney and young Givre—A vision of the future—Ars as a Christian parish in the eighteenth century—The Revolution: faithful and apostate priests—A reawakening—Ars in 1818—The lady of the manor—Programme of the new pastor—Ceremony of installation—Furnishing the presbytery—House to house visitation 111

Chapter 2
THE CONVERSION OF ARS
I. Prayer and Penance

Prayer in Church—Through fields and meadows—Sleeping on the ground—The discipline—M. Vianney's first Lent at Ars—The bread of the poor—The potato-pot—The secret of his first conquests 125

Chapter 3
THE CONVERSION OF ARS *(continued)*
II. War against Religious Ignorance

M. Vianney's efforts to render the church more attractive—The sin of ignorance—He catechizes the children—Instructions for adults—An heroic preacher—Favorite topics of the Curé d'Ars—The altar and the Eucharist—Exhortations on the occasion of great feasts 134

Chapter 4
THE CONVERSION OF ARS *(continued)*
III. Fight against the Profanation of the Sunday, against Taverns and Blasphemies

Profanation of the Lord's Day—Drinking and dancing after Sunday work—

The Curé's resolutions—Anathema on taverns—Their disappearance—The hostelries of Ars—Suppression of blasphemy and Sunday work—No dispensations! 146

Chapter 5
THE CONVERSION OF ARS *(continued)*
IV. Campaign against Dancing

A matter of principle: duty to flee from the occasion of sin—Fight against the vice of impurity—Ten years' preaching—Direct action—First fruits—Refusal of absolution to frequenters of balls—Equal treatment for all—Parents held responsible—A dearly bought victory—Invectives against immodest dress—The Curé d'Ars as arbiter of fashions—Décolletage and crinolines 154

Chapter 6
RESTORATION OF THE OLD CHURCH OF ARS

New projects—Appointment to the parish of Salles-en-Beaujolais—The chaplaincy of Ars is erected into a parish—Reconstruction of the bell tower—Erection of new altars—Decoration of the nave and chancel—Liberality of the Vicomte d'Ars—The Pilgrimage 167

Chapter 7
GREAT TRIALS OF THE FIRST YEARS:
CALUMNIES AND TEMPTATIONS

The inevitable trial of an apostle—*"Ingrat"*—Complaints and criticisms—M. Vianney summoned to leave the parish—The calumnies of libertines—Inquiry by the curé of Trévoux—Attitude of the saint under calumny—A stainless reputation—Retaliation by honest people—The end of the storm—Fear of God's judgements—Love of the cross—Weariness and longing for a change—Appointment to the parish of Fareins 181

Chapter 8
THE TRIUMPH OF GOODNESS:
APOSTOLIC LABORS

The influence of an *élite*—"Jansenism" of Mlle. d'Ars—Worshippers of the first hour—*Père* Chaffangeon—Efforts to win the youths: Guild of the Blessed Sacrament—Christianizing the home: prayer in common, good reading, examination of conscience—Teaching peasants the secret of the interior life 195

Chapter 9
THE "PROVIDENCE" OF ARS

Plan for a girls' school—The youthful teachers—Installation and first beginnings—Creation of a house of *Providence—The* Curé d'Ars on a begging tour—Critical hours—The miracle of the attic—The miracle of the kneading trough—The *Providence,* a charitable institution of primary importance—The little one and her doll—Some admirable deathbeds—An uncommon school—"A model of popular education"—The saint's favorite work—Catechism at the *Providence*—A new chapel and thoughts of retirement . 209

Chapter 10
ARS TRANSFORMED

After five years' work—Pilgrimage to Fourvière—The mission of 1827—A cry of victory—Sanctification of work and Christian habits of life—Regeneration of the family—Exemplary conduct of the villagers—M. Vianney's attachment to his people—The fine families of Ars—A Sunday at Ars—The truce of God—Feasts of devotion—Frequent reception of the Sacraments—Splendor of the ceremonies—The saint's liturgical mind—Corpus Christi at Ars—Edifying lives and holy deaths—Ars protected from scourges—Sorrowful partings 227

Chapter 11
THE CURÉ D'ARS AND THE DEVIL

The devil's object in his persecutions—First nocturnal attacks—André Verchère and his gun—Identity of the mysterious assailant—"He is angry. So much the better!"—Hours of combat and sleeplessness—The *grappin* annoys the Curé and rages against him—A hellish escort on the road to Saint-Trivier—Eye and ear witnesses—The burned bed—A sleepless night at the presbytery of Montmerle—The disturber disturbed—Power of the Curé d'Ars over the evil spirits—Cases of liberation of possessed persons—A fantastic scene—Opposition to occultism and spiritualism—The adventure of Comte Jules de Maubou—In the room of Capitaine de Montluisant—The end of diabolical obsessions—Satan's defeat 250

Chapter 12
THE PILGRIMAGE TO ARS
I. The Beginning—St. Philomena

Lowly beginnings of a world-wide fame—After the mission of Trévoux—Cause of the attraction to Ars—First rumors of miracles—Under the shadow of "dear little St. Philomena"—Brief story of *Filumena*—The heavenly friend 274

Chapter 13
THE PILGRIMAGE TO ARS *(continued)*
II. The Contradictions of the Clergy

Criticisms—Neglect of external appearance—"Consulting that ignorant man!"—Was the Curé d'Ars ignorant?—Priestly knowledge—The "wasps" of the Pilgrimage—"I do not tell them to come"—Opponents become admirers—A letter that hurt and the Curé's reply—Denunciations to the Bishop—Inquiry by the Vicar-General and decision of the Bishop—Unanimous feelings of the clergy towards the Curé d'Ars 281

Chapter 14
THE PILGRIMAGE TO ARS *(continued)*
III. The Curé d'Ars as a Confessor

On the road to Ars—Lodgings—At the door of the church—Endless waiting—Preferences—Sinners seized "on the wing"—Telling words—Tears that convert—The men's confessional—The great miracle of the Curé d'Ars: the conversion of sinners—Conditions before absolution—Short penances—Medicinal penances—A few accounts of conversions 298

Chapter 15
THE PILGRIMAGE TO ARS *(continued)*
IV. The Curé d'Ars as a Spiritual Director

Giving to each soul the necessary time—Wisdom of his decisions—Souls that were urged on by the holy Curé—Souls held back by him—Devotions recommended by him—First, that which is of obligation—Duties of married people—Direction of priests—Dealing with the scrupulous—Frequentation of the Sacraments—Preparation required by him—Frequent Communion and the requisite understanding—"Go oftener to Holy Communion"—The radiant influence of a saint 326

Chapter 16
THE PILGRIMAGE TO ARS *(continued)*
V. A Typical Day of the Curé d'Ars—His Interior Life

Confessions at the end of the *veillées*—Rising at midnight—Confessions of women—The Mass of the Curé d'Ars—Thanksgiving—Audiences to pilgrims in the sacristy—Recitation of the *Little Hours* of the Breviary—The famous eleven o'clock *catechism*—After the catechism—On his way from the church to the presbytery—A hurried meal—Sick calls—A visit to the *Providence*—Resumption of Confessions and night prayers—The first hours of the night—Role of the inner life in the day of a parish priest—Prayer of simplicity—Joy of the presence of God 340

Chapter 17
THE CURÉ D'ARS' YEARNING FOR SOLITUDE—
GRAVE ILLNESS AND FLIGHT OF 1843

Fear of dying as curé—A resignation always offered and always refused—A subtle temptation—Solitude and apostolate, and the contradictory attractions of his soul—A first attempt at flight—Alone to carry out an overwhelming task—Grave illness of May, 1843—Distress of the parish—Between life and death—Cure attributed to St. Philomena—Need of rest and growing desire for solitude—Flight of September 12—Ars without pilgrims—Exodus to Dardilly—M. Raymond's message—Journey to Notre-Dame de Beaumont—Triumphant return 364

Chapter 18
INCIDENTS OF THE LAST YEARS:
I. Suppression of the Orphanage—Foundation of the

Day School and of the Boarding School of the Brothers —Decennial Missions

A conspiracy that is no conspiracy—Complaints and fears concerning the girls' orphanage—M. Vianney's arrangements with Mère Saint-Claude—A previous liquidation—Sorrow and resignation of the holy Curé—The Sisters of St. Joseph and the former directresses of the *Providence*—Attitude of the Curé d'Ars—The boys' school of the commune entrusted to the Brothers of the Holy Family—M. Vianney's zeal for the education of children—The work of decennial missions—Whence the resources?—A "miser" of a novel kind—Foundation of Masses in perpetuity 388

Chapter 19
INCIDENTS OF THE LAST YEARS *(continued)*
II. La Salette

Arrival of Maximin Giraud—M. Vianney's immediate faith in the apparition of La Salette—Maximin's companions and the real object of their visit—M. Raymond's remarks on receiving them—Maximin's interview with the Curé d'Ars—M. Vianney takes up a new attitude with regard to La Salette—The anguish of a holy soul—The end of the trial—The act of faith that restored peace 404

Chapter 20
INCIDENTS OF THE LAST YEARS *(continued)*
III. The Curé d'Ars a Canon of Belley and Chevalier of the Légion d'Honneur—The Feast of December 8, 1854

A canonry imposed by surprise—Sale of the mozetta—M. Vianney proposed for the Légion d'honneur—Reflections of the new chevalier—The investiture—The Curé d'Ars and our Blessed Lady—December 8 in the village of Ars 415

Chapter 21
INCIDENTS OF THE LAST YEARS *(continued)*
IV. Towards "La Trappe" of La Neylière

M. Vianney a tertiary of St. Francis—M. Vianney and Pere Colin—La Trappe of La Neylière—A new Bishop of Belley—M. Toccanier, missionary of Pont-d'Ain, is appointed auxiliary to the Curé d'Ars—Plans of retirement—A well-kept secret!—On the bank of the Fontblin—Return to the presbytery—The improvidence of a saint—An ill-concerted plan—Trial and temptation—Endeavors of the people of Dardilly—Illness and death of François l'ainé 427

Chapter 22
PHYSICAL AND MORAL PORTRAIT

A first impression—The saint's features and expression—In old age—Simplicity and courtesy—Anecdotes worthy of St. Francis de Sales—Gentleness and strength—The Curé's tenderness of heart—His attraction towards pure souls—A *liquid* heart—His refined gratitude—The Curé d'Ars and the sorrowful—Some of those whom he comforted—Sorrowing mothers—His mail bag—Some of his letters—His exquisite tact and judgement—The absence of all selfishness—Good-natured irony—His horror of sins of the tongue 443

Chapter 23
AT THE HEIGHT OF SANCTITY
I. Testimonies

The way of perfection: Reputation for sanctity of the Curé d'Ars in his immediate entourage—Testimonies of his confessor, Catherine Lassagne, Mgr. Devie, and of priests, friends of M. Vianney—The opinion of lay people: Dr. Saunier, pilgrims, and inhabitants of Ars—The verdict of the crowd—Unanimous encomiums—What the majority saw in the Curé d'Ars . 467

Chapter 24
AT THE HEIGHT OF SANCTITY *(continued)*
II. Heroic Virtues: Humility, Love of Poverty and of the Poor

Heroic virtues that distinguished the Curé d'Ars. *Humility:* Applauded by the crowd—The source of his great humility—Hatred of praise—"What misguided devotion"—M. Vianney and his *carnaval*—The story of a wax bust—The Curé d'Ars and Lacordaire—Thoughts of the saint on humility. *Love of Poverty and of the Poor:* The wardrobe of the Curé d'Ars—His presbytery—His contempt for earthly goods—M. Vianney and the unfortunate—Ars the rendezvous of all miseries—Esteem of the saint for the poor 478

Chapter 25
AT THE HEIGHT OF SANCTITY *(continued)*
III. Heroic Virtues: Patience and Mortification

Patience: The most astonishing virtue of the Curé d'Ars—Subjected to insults—In the midst of the importunities of the crowd—M. Vianney and M. Raymond—Patience and bodily infirmities. *Mortification:* "More admirable than imitable"—The most terrifying instrument of penance: the confessional of the saint—Total self-immolation—Disciplines, iron cincture, the hair-shirt—Fasts of the Curé d'Ars—How he treated his guests—The homage of a Carthusian 500

Chapter 26
INTUITIONS AND PREDICTIONS OF THE CURÉ D'ARS

The eyes of a seer—Supernatural gift of intuition—How did the Curé d'Ars see and know?—Examples of intuitions and predictions: of a call to the married state or the religious life; of happy or unhappy events to come—Instances of his visions of distant events—Reading the consciences of men—The Curé d'Ars and the destiny of religious communities and undertakings—Did the Curé d'Ars foretell great events, persecutions, wars?—His predictions concerning Pius IX, Napoleon III, the Prince Imperial—The future destiny of the Society of Jesus and the conversion of England—Is there a prophecy concerning the future of Ars? 518

Chapter 27
THE MIRACLES OF THE CURÉ D'ARS

In the shadow of St. Philomena—Miracles in conjunction with St. Philomena—Miracles of his own—Where suffering patiently borne is better than a cure—Faith the first requisite for a miracle and a tangible proof of the supernatural. 551

Chapter 28
THE GREAT MYSTICAL EXPERIENCES OF THE CURÉ D'ARS

The silence of humility or of wonderment—The saint's Mass—Ecstasies and visions—Glimpses of Purgatory, Hell, and Heaven—The gift of tears, levitation, aureola—Mystical ring 565

Chapter 29
THE LAST YEAR OF THE SAINT'S LIFE (1858-1859)

More pilgrims than ever—Growing exhaustion of the Curé d'Ars—He still takes the discipline—Sleepless nights—A sublime dialogue—"Ah! really, this is laughable!"—Plan for a new church—Evening calm—A visit of Pauline-Marie Jaricot 586

Chapter 30
LAST ILLNESS AND DEATH

Presentiment of approaching death—The day when he collapsed—"This is my poor end"—Complete exhaustion—The people's leave-taking of their old parish priest—Attempts to save him—The calm of ecstasy—Viaticum and Extreme Unction—The last will of the Curé d'Ars—Visit of Mgr. de Langalerie—Death—Funeral knell from every steeple of the neighboring villages 595

Chapter 31
IN GLORY

Homage to the body of the Curé d'Ars—Triumphal funeral—First requests for relics—The glorious tomb—The Process of Beatification—Two miracles examined by Rome—The joyous assent of Pius X—Solemn Beatification at St. Peter's, Rome—Love for love—In the village of Ars—Crowning honors: Canonization 610

Index 629

LIST OF ILLUSTRATIONS

AUTHENTIC PORTRAIT OF THE CURÉ D'ARS .... *Frontispiece*

BASILICA AND OLD CHURCH OF ARS 171

INTERIOR OF THE CURÉ D'ARS' ROOM 171

THE CHURCH OF ARS (1818-1859) 172

THE PRESBYTERY AT ARS (1818-1859) 172

SHRINE OF ST. PHILOMENA 361

THE CURÉ D'ARS AMONG THE SICK 362

THE CURÉ D'ARS CALLING PENITENTS TO THE CONFESSIONAL 362

THE NEW CHURCH AT ARS—INTERIOR 497

THE CURÉ D'ARS ON HIS DEATHBED 498

THE SHRINE OF THE CURÉ D'ARS 603

PART 1

THE YEARS OF PREPARATION
(1786-1818)

Chapter 1

FIRST YEARS (1786-1793)

THE VILLAGE of Dardilly[1] is set among the low hills that rise in the neighborhood of Lyons. One of its inhabitants was Pierre Vianney, husband of Marie Charavay.[2] Besides being a prosperous farmer, he was likewise a man of faith, and much given to the practice of the Christian virtue of charity. In July, 1770, the fame of his good works brought to his door a mendicant who was also a saint.

Tortured by scruples, Benoît Labre had just left the Trappist monastery of Sept-Fonds, where he had been a novice under the name of Brother Urban. He had now acquired a certainty that his vocation was to be a wayfarer for the remainder of his life, so he set out for Rome.

---

1. Dardilly, a commune of 1,100 souls, is situate some eight kilometers to the northwest of Lyons.
2. In *La Semaine religieuse de Grenoble* (November 30, 1905) there appeared an article by Mgr. Devaux, rector of the Catholic Faculty of Lyons, on the surname of Vianney, which he thinks originates from the Dauphiné. According to the learned rector, the primitive form *Vianeis* or *Vianneis* was a corruption of *Viennensis,* that is, a citizen of Vienne in Dauphiné. Hence it would seem that *Vianneis* and *Viennois* are synonymous.

   The registers of Dardilly date back only to the year 1617. In that year, however, we find a record of the Baptism of Madeleine Vianey, daughter of Barthélemy Vianey and of Claudine Beluze. Authentic documents furnish us with a list of the ancestors in the direct line of the Curé d'Ars. They are: Pierre Vianey (great-great-great grandfather); Pierre (great-great-grandfather), born in 1655; Pierre (great-grandfather), born in 1689; Pierre (grandfather, mentioned at the beginning of this book), born in 1716; finally, Matthieu (father of our saint), born in 1753. All these were baptized in the church of Dardilly.

   As regards the spelling of the name, though the ancestors of the saint wrote *Vianey,* we have no hesitation in spelling it *Vianney,* as he did himself. His younger sister, Marguerite, spelled the name in this manner when signing the process of canonization.

   Various episcopal documents spell the name indiscriminately *Vianay* or *Viannay, Vianey* or *Vianney;* thus the dimissorial letters for the sub-diaconate have *Vianey;* those for the diaconate, *Vianay;* those for the priesthood, *Viannay;* faculty papers of 1832, *Vianney;* papers of 1853, *Viannay.*

His first halt was at Paray-le-Monial, where he paid long visits to the chapel of the Apparitions. From Paray he journeyed to Lyons, but rather than enter the city at nightfall he chose to spend the night at Dardilly. On observing a number of poor persons going to the house of Pierre Vianney, he went along with them.[3]

Benoît Labre was strangely attired. He wore the novice's tunic, which he had been permitted to retain on leaving the monastery. A wallet was suspended from his shoulders, a rosary hung round his neck, and a brass crucifix shone on his breast. A breviary, an *Imitation,* and the book of the Gospels constituted his luggage.

In these weird accoutrements he entered the small enclosure in front of the low-roofed house of the Vianneys.[4] The master of the house received him as he received all destitute persons. The children gazed with pity at the hapless man in whom their parents had taught them to see Jesus Christ himself. Matthieu, one of the five boys, was there. Little did he guess, as he contemplated this youthful mendicant, so pale and so meek, who was telling his beads all the time, that one day he himself would be the father of a saint. In the vast kitchen, near the hearth, where, sixteen years later, the child of predestination would warm his little bare feet, Benoît Labre and his companions in distress sat down with the Vianneys before plates of steaming soup, followed by meat and vegetables. After grace and night prayers, the guests were shown a place over the bakehouse, where they were to sleep, and where a thick layer of straw was to be their bed. On the morrow, ere they departed, one and all thanked their hosts, but the refined, gentle youth expressed his gratitude in terms which plainly showed that he was no common beggar.

Great was the surprise of Pierre Vianney when, a little later, he received a letter from the poor pilgrim.[5] Benoît

3. J. Mantenay, *St. Benoît Labre,* Paris, Gabalda, 1908, p. 27, *passim.*
4. The old farmhouse, with its two entrance doors facing the yard, has since had another storey added to it.
5. "The Curé d'Ars often spoke of this letter. He made a present of it to someone who asked him for it." (Frère Jérôme, *Procès de l'Ordinaire,* p. 533).

Labre wrote but seldom; the hospitality of Dardilly must have touched him deeply; perhaps God had vouchsafed to give him a presentiment of the child of benediction, who was one day to shed undying luster upon this house.

Eight years after this event, on February 11, 1778, at Ecully, a village barely a league from Dardilly, Matthieu Vianney married Marie Beluse. If Matthieu was a good Christian, so also was his young wife, who brought him as the most precious of dowries a keen and enlightened faith.

Their union was blessed by God. They had six children, all of whom, as was the touching custom of the time, were consecrated to our Lady even before their birth. The children's names were: Catherine, who married at an early age and died shortly after her marriage; Jeanne-Marie, who departed to a better world when about five years old; François, the heir to the ancestral home; Jean-Marie, now scarcely known by any other name than that of "the Curé d'Ars"; Marguerite, the only one of the six to survive, and that by several years, her holy brother;[6] lastly, another François, called Cadet, who, on joining the army, left Dardilly never again to return.

Jean-Marie was born about midnight on May 8, 1786, and baptized that same day.[7] His godfather and godmother were an uncle and aunt—namely, Jean-Marie Vianney, a younger brother of his father, and his wife Françoise Martinon. The godfather, without looking further afield, was content simply to give his own name to his godson.[8]

---

6. Marguerite Vianney, widow of Laurent Guérin, died at Bois-Dieu, in the parish of Lissieu, on April 8, 1877, at the age of ninety-one years.

7. The ceremony did not take place in the present church of Dardilly. The font used at the baptism of Jean-Marie Vianney has been enshrined in a new font adorned with mosaics, in keeping with the style of the new church. It bears the following inscription:

EX HOC FONTE IN XTO NATUS J. M. VIANNEY, 8 MAII 1786.

8. Extract from the register of the parish of Dardilly: "Jean-Marie Vianey fils légitime de Matthieu Vianey et de Marie Beluse sa femme né le huit may mil sept cent quatre vingt six a été batisé le même jour par moi vicaire soussigné: son parrain a été Jean-Marie Vianey son oncle paternel habitant de Dardilly et sa marraine Françoise Martinon femme dudit Jean-Marie Vianey tous deux ilitérés de ce enquis. BLACHON. vicaire."

So soon as the last comer, a favorite apparently from the start, began to notice things, his mother took pleasure in pointing out to him the crucifix and the pious pictures that adorned the rooms of the farmhouse. When the little arms became strong enough to move with some ease, she guided the tiny hand from the forehead to the breast and from the breast to the shoulders. The child soon grew into the habit of doing this, so that one day—he was then about fifteen months old—his mother having forgotten to help him to make the Sign of the Cross before giving him his food, the little one refused to open his mouth, at the same time vigorously shaking his head. Marie Vianney guessed what he meant, and as soon as she had helped the tiny hand the pursed-up lips opened spontaneously.

Are we to conclude that even from the cradle Jean-Marie Vianney gave unequivocal proofs of future holiness, such as we read of in the lives of St. Raymond Nonnatus, St. Cajetan, St. Alphonsus Liguori, St. Rose of Lima, and many others? Not one of the existing documents suggests such a phenomenon. However, in all that had to do with religion he was a precocious child, and responded much more readily than his brothers and sisters to the solicitude of his admirable mother. His was one of those dispositions that are easily directed towards God. From the age of eighteen months, when the family met for night prayers, he would, of his own accord, kneel down with them—maybe merely from natural imitativeness—and he knew quite well how to join his little hands in prayer.

Prayers ended, his pious mother put him to bed, and, before a final embrace, she bent over him, talking to him of Jesus, of Mary, of his Guardian Angel. In this way did the fond mother lull the child to sleep.

So soon as he could stand on his feet, he was to be found all over the house, though he did not stray far from the threshold, because, on the far side of the yard in the direction of the garden, there was a deep trough where the cattle used to drink. For this reason Jean-Marie hardly ever left his mother's side, busy as she was; on her part, she began the task of her little son's education whilst doing her housework, teaching him in a manner that could be readily grasped by his childish mind. In this way she taught him the "Our Father" and the "Hail Mary" together with some elementary notions of God and of the soul.

The little one, who was very wide awake for his age, would himself ask naive questions. What interested him most was the sweet mystery of Our Lord's birth at Bethlehem and the story of the manger and the shepherds.

These familiar talks were sometimes prolonged far into the night. For the sake of hearing the story of the Bible, Jean-Marie was willing to sit up late with his mother and Catherine, the most devout of his sisters.[9] Sometimes he even knelt on the stone floor, folding his hands and putting them within those of his mother.

In fine weather Matthieu Vianney set out very early for the fields, where his wife and the children came to join him in the course of the morning. Catherine and the elder François walked ahead, stick in hand, driving the sheep and cows. A donkey brought up the rear, carrying on his back Jean-Marie and Marguerite, whose pet name was Gothon. On arriving at the fields, the children played on the sward or tended the grazing flock. Jean-Marie was a bright and lively boy, who could put endless zest into their games. Contrary to the assertion of his first biographer, he was very far from being one of those youthful prodigies who have none of the charm and vivacity of their age.[10] This brown-haired, blue-eyed boy, with his pale complexion and expressive countenance, did not lack a certain petulance, even though his piety was far in advance of his years. "He was born with an impetuous nature"; his perfect meekness was the fruit of prolonged and meritorious efforts. But from his tenderest years the

9. Catherine was wont to gather her youthful companions at the house of her parents, in order to read to them out of some pious book (François Duclos of Dardilly, *Procès de l'Ordinaire,* p. 1,000).

10. "He was never seen to take part in a game," says the Abbé Monnin. The saint's three playmates assert the contrary in their depositions in the process of canonization.

sensitive and nervous child studied the art of self-conquest. His mother, fully aware of the power of example, often held him up as a pattern to his brothers and sisters: "See," she would say, when they refused to obey promptly, "Jean-Marie is much more obedient than you; he does at once what he is told."

However, once, at least, there were tears. The boy had a rosary which he greatly prized. Gothon, who was eighteen months younger, took a fancy to her brother's beads, and, of course, wished to get possession of them. It came to a scene between brother and sister; there was screaming, stamping of feet, and even a preliminary skirmish, when suddenly, full of grief, the poor child ran to his mother. Gently, but firmly, she bade him give the beads to Gothon: "Yes, my darling, give them to her for love of the good God." Jean-Marie, though bathed in tears, immediately surrendered his precious rosary. For a child of four this was surely no mean sacrifice! Instead of petting and fondling the child with a view to drying his tears, his mother gave him a small wooden statue of Our Lady. The rude image had long stood on the mantelpiece of the kitchen chimney, and the little one had often wished to possess it. At last it was his, really his! What joy! "Oh! how I loved that statue," he confessed seventy years later; "neither by day nor by night would I be parted from it. I should not have slept had I not had it beside me in my little bed . . . the Blessed Virgin was the object of my earliest affections; I loved her even before I knew her."

Some of his contemporaries, his sister Marguerite in particular, have related how, at the first sound of the *Angelus,* he was on his knees before anybody else. At other times he might be found in a corner of the house kneeling before the image of Our Lady, which he had placed on a chair.

Children do not fall victims to the foolish disease called human respect. Wherever he happened to be, whether at home, in the garden, in the street, Jean-Marie, following the example of his mother, was in the habit of "blessing the hour"—that is, so soon as he heard the clock strike the hour, he would cross himself and recite a "Hail Mary," ending with another Sign of the Cross. A neighbor who one day saw him carry out this practice, remarked to Matthieu Vianney: "I believe that little brown-haired fellow of yours takes me for the devil." When Matthieu related the incident, the boy's mother asked him for an explanation: "I did not know our neighbor was looking," was the reply, "but do we not cross ourselves before and after prayers?"

Some women of the neighborhood, hearing the child praying aloud, said to his parents: "He knows his litanies well. You will have to make him either a priest or a *Brother.*"

Marie Vianney may not have had any inkling of the wonderful future of her favorite child; nonetheless, the beauty of his soul was precious in her eyes, and she spared no pains to keep from him the very shadow of sin: "See, *mon Jean,*" she used to say, "if your brothers and sisters were to offend the good God, it would indeed cause me much pain, but I should be far sorrier were you to offend Him."

Her Jean-Marie was no ordinary child. Even before the powers of his mind had reached their full development, the privileged child of grace had made the first step out of the common way, for this seems to be the true explanation of the following occurrence.

One evening—he was then about four years old—Jean-Marie left the house unnoticed. As soon as his mother became aware of his absence she called to him by his name, but no answer came. With ever-increasing anxiety she looked for him in the yard, behind the straw rick and the piles of timber. The little one was not to be found. Yet he never failed to answer the very first call. As she proceeded in the direction of the stable where he might be hiding, the distracted mother suddenly remembered with horror that deep pond full of murky water, from which the cattle were wont to drink! But what was her surprise when she beheld the spectacle that now presented itself to her eyes? There, in a corner of the stable, among the cattle peacefully chewing the cud, was her boy on his knees, praying with folded hands before his little statue of Our Lady. In an instant she had caught him in her arms, and, pressing him to her heart: "Oh! my darling, you were here!" she cried, in a flood of tears. "Why hide yourself when you want to pray? You know we all say our prayers together."

The child, unable to think of anything but his mother's grief, exclaimed: "Forgive me, *maman,* I did not think; I will not do it again."

Whilst these homely scenes were being enacted in a small and obscure hamlet, events of an appalling nature had taken place in France. However, neither the pillage of Saint Lazare and the taking of the Bastille (July 13 and 14, 1789); nor the decree depriving the clergy of their benefices (November 2); nor that which suppressed the monasteries and the vows of religion (February 13, 1790), appear to have affected the good country folk: they were either ill-informed or unable to grasp the significance of these events. Hence, their peace of mind was not perturbed until the day when, by the civil constitution of the clergy, the Revolution threatened their priests and their altars (November 26, 1790).

Mme. Vianney was a woman of "eminent piety." If at all possible, she would go to daily Mass. Catherine, her eldest daughter, accompanied her as a rule, but soon her favorite companion came to be the little four-year-old, whose precocious piety caused him to relish the things of God. Whenever the bells of the church nearby announced that Mass was about to be said, Jean-Marie entreated his mother to let him go with her. The request was granted. She placed him before her in the family pew, and explained to him what the priest was doing at the altar. The child soon developed a love for the sacred ceremonies. However, his attention was divided: the embroidered vestment of the celebrant entranced him, whilst he was wholly overcome with admiration for the red cassock and white rochet of the altar boy. He, too, would have liked to serve at the altar, but how could his frail arms lift that heavy Missal? From time to time he turned to his mother; it was an inspiration merely to see her so absorbed in prayer, and as it were transfigured by an interior fire.

In subsequent years, when people congratulated him on his early love for prayer and the Church, he used to say with many tears: "After God, I owe it to my mother; she was so good! Virtue passes readily from the heart of a mother into that of her children. A child that has the happiness of having a good mother should never look at her or think of her without tears."

Chapter 2

A YOUNG SHEPHERD UNDER THE TERROR (1793-1794)

IN JANUARY, 1791, the civil constitution of the clergy began to be enforced in the province of Lyons. Jean-Marie had not yet completed his fifth year. Messire Jacques Rey, curé of Dardilly during the past thirty-nine years, was weak enough to take the schismatical oath. However, if we may believe local traditions, enlightened by the example of his curate and the neighboring clergy, who refused the oath, he soon came to understand and disavow his fault. He continued for a time to reside in his parish, saying Mass in a private house. Eventually he retired to Lyons, and from there he went to Italy.[1] The disappearance of M. Rey did not pass unnoticed, yet Dardilly was not as much upset as might have been expected. The church remained open because another curé was sent by the new bishop of Lyons, M. Lamourette, a friend of Mirabeau's, who, without any brief from Rome, had been installed by the Constituent Assembly, in succession to the venerable Mgr. de Marbeuf. The new parish priest, like the new bishop, had duly taken the oath. But how were the good folk of Dardilly to suspect that the civil constitution, of which, perhaps, they did not so much as know the name, would lead to schism and heresy? There was no outward change in the ceremonies and customs with which they had so long been familiar. For a time, at least, these simple people did not scruple to assist at

1. Such are the traditions of Dardilly. The parochial registers only show that Messire Jacques Rey, doctor of the Sorbonne, curé of Dardilly since February 1753, was replaced on July 7, 1803, by M. Jacques Tournier, and that he died in the parish of Vaise, Lyons, on October 22, 1804.

the Mass of the juror-priest. Matthieu Vianney and his family acted thus in all good faith.[2]

After a while, however, their eyes were opened to realities. Though barely twelve years old at the time, Catherine, the eldest of the girls, was the first to scent danger. In the pulpit the new pastor did not speak quite like M. Rey, nor on the same topics. His sermons were interlarded with the words *citizen, civism,* and *constitution.* He so far forgot himself as to criticize his predecessors.[3] The congregation was more promiscuous and scantier than of yore: persons who were noted for their fervor were no longer seen in church—where did they go to Mass on Sundays?—others, on the contrary, were there and occupied the best seats, who previously had hardly ever darkened the threshold of the sacred edifice. Catherine felt anxious, and she confided her secret fears to her mother.

In the meantime, a relative living at Ecully paid a visit to the Vianneys. "What are you doing?" she exclaimed on hearing that they attended the Mass of the juror; "all good priests have refused the oath, and in consequence are being hunted and persecuted and driven into exile. Happily at Ecully we still have some good priests. It is to these you must go. By taking the oath your new parish priest has separated himself from the Catholic Church; he is not your true shepherd and you cannot make yourselves his abettors."

This staggering revelation drove Mme. Vianney almost frantic. She did not hesitate to speak to the unfortunate priest, reproaching him with having severed himself from the true Church. When she reminded him of the saying of the Gospel that the branch that is cut off from the vine shall be cast into the fire, the priest owned to the truth of her words: "True, madam, the vine is better than the branch."[4]

2. In many parishes the transition from Catholic to schismatical worship was effected without the least disturbance. *Cf.* P. de la Gorce, *Histoire religieuse de la Révolution,* Paris, Plon, 1909, I, p. 414 ss.

3. "These people," he used to say, "are no more parish priests than my shoe!" (Abbé Vignon, curé of Dardilly, *Procès apostolique in genere,* p. 368).

4. "C'est vrai, Madame, le cep vaut mieux que le sarment." (Abbé Vignon, *Procès apostolique in genere,* p. 368).

Marie Vianney must have informed her family of the state of affairs, because we are told that little Jean-Marie "showed his horror of sin from the day when he began to avoid the juror-priest." From that moment the Vianneys ceased to attend the parish church, though it held for them so many tender associations, since within its walls the parents had been married and the children baptized. In point of fact, the sacred edifice was soon closed altogether.

A cruel persecution was now raging. Priests who had refused the oath ran the risk of arrest and execution, without the possibility of an appeal—within twenty-four hours. A reward of 100 livres (100 francs) was paid to anyone denouncing the proscribed, whereas deportation was the punishment of all persons harboring a priest. Such were some of the enactments of laws passed on April 24, September 17, and October 20, 1793. Notwithstanding these terrible threats, a few faithful priests were still moving about in the district of Dardilly, and one after another found shelter in the home of the Vianneys. On occasion they even said Mass there. Only a miracle preserved the good farmer from paying with his head for his holy daring, for he did not escape the suspicions of the Jacobins. However, the greater number of these confessors of the faith found an asylum either in Lyons itself, or in the outskirts of the city.

On certain days trusty messengers would arrive from Ecully and call on Catholic households. They brought information of the secret spot where, on the following night, the Holy Mysteries would be celebrated. As soon as darkness fell, the Vianneys set out in deepest silence. In his happiness at being allowed to accompany his parents, Jean-Marie stepped out bravely. "His brothers and sisters grumbled at times, thinking the distance too great; then their mother would say: 'Can you not be like Jean-Marie, who is always the keenest of all?'"

When they reached the appointed place they were led into a barn or some retired room, where hardly a light was allowed. They saw kneeling at a plain table a tired-looking stranger of gentle mien. The stranger met the newcomers with outstretched hand. Then, in the farthest corner of the room, behind an improvised partition, the good priest, speaking in whispers, exercised his ministry of counsel, comfort, and pardon. Sometimes he would also have to bless marriages. And then followed the Mass, the Mass so keenly longed for by young and old.

The priest placed on the table the altar stone he had brought, the Missal, the chalice, and several small altar breads, for tonight he would not be the only communicant. Quickly he donned the sacred vestments, faded and crumpled in consequence of much hasty folding. Amid deep silence he began the prayers of the Liturgy: *Introibo ad altare Dei.* What fervor there was in his voice, what recollection, what emotion in the congregation! Sobs mingled with the prayers. It was like being at Mass in the Roman Catacombs, before arrest and martyrdom.

These were unforgettable moments for little Vianney, moments of deepest emotion. Kneeling between his mother and his sister, he prayed like an angel, mingling his tears with the sobs of the others. Though unable to understand everything, he listened with the utmost gravity to the exhortations of the proscribed man, who, for love of souls, daily risked his life. Maybe it was during these nocturnal gatherings that he felt the first call to the priesthood.

The year 1793 saw the reign of Terror. At Lyons blood flowed in torrents; in the Place des Terreaux the guillotine did its hideous work without interruption. The "proconsul" Chalier had the names of twenty thousand persons on his lists of proscription. A rising of the populace, led by de Précy, brought the tyrant himself to the scaffold. The hopes of Catholics were reviving when an army of the Convention, under Couthon and Dubois-Crancé, laid siege to the city. From August 8 until October 9 de Précy offered a bold resistance, but famine compelled him at last to surrender.

Events such as these were beyond the understanding of a boy of seven. From his father's fields he listened to the noise of battle. Dubois-Crancé was encamped round

Limonest, a few kilometers to the north of Dardilly, so that the soldiers of the Revolution were often seen in the village. And yet the continued silence of the bells was much more distressing to the pious boy than the sounds of battle. The church remained closed. Men had been sent from Lyons to destroy the wayside shrines, so that only the pedestals of the crosses remained.[5] Even at home crucifixes, statues, and other pious objects had to be carefully hidden. Alone the sanctuary of loyal hearts remained inviolable. Jean-Marie, however, clung to his statuette of Our Lady; he treasured it more than ever, and when he went into the fields he invariably carried it in a pocket of his blouse.

Children are quick to forget, and are easily comforted: they want so little to make them happy! Whilst the Revolution drenched France with blood, in the fields of Dardilly the birds sang and the lambs skipped as if nothing unusual were happening. During those terrible months Jean-Marie spent long hours amid the tranquil scenes of Nature, where nothing had as yet marred the handiwork of God.

Dardilly offers wide and pleasing prospects. The village rises in tiers on the side of a rocky eminence, which slopes down in the direction of Lyons. The Mont-d'Or, the heights of Fourvière seem quite near. Jean-Marie took little notice of them; he preferred the familiar meadows which spread like green carpets in dales and hollows with the most fascinating names, such as Pré-Cusin, Chêne-Rond, and Chante-Merle. Here were the grazing lands belonging to his father's farm.

On May 8, 1793, the child attained his seventh year. He was then big enough to make himself useful. His principal task was to tend the flocks. Twice daily he drove out the donkey, the cows, and the sheep to graze, leading by the hand his little sister Gothon, for the paths

---

5. By a decree of November 8, 1793, Fouché ordered the removal, throughout the province of Lyons, of all religious emblems to be found along the roads, in public places, or on public buildings.

leading into the vale were steep and strewn with rough pebbles. Both children had promised to be very good; and, moreover, there was work for them to do, for they took with them their knitting wool, since it was the custom for the shepherds of both sexes to make stockings whilst looking after the cattle.

The vale of Chante-Merle has lost, with its shady groves of old, its peace and solitude. But even today it charms the visitor by its rivulet of the Planches, the course of which is marked by eglantine, alders and aspens. Singing birds abound in this peaceful retreat, whence its name. Jean-Marie loved this fair corner of earth; all his life he loved to think of it. When admiring crowds surged around him, he was heard to sigh for those fields of his childhood where he had been so happy, because then "he found time to pray to the good God and to think of his soul."

On reaching the meadow, brother and sister, obedient to their mother's advice, went down upon their knees in order to dedicate to God the task they were about to perform. After that they gave their undivided attention to the flock, careful lest the cows damage the crops of the neighbors.

No doubt Gothon would have loved to spend the time talking to her brother, who had a gift for story-telling. Jean-Marie told her stories out of the Old and New Testament; he also taught her her prayers and gave her sundry spiritual counsels: "See, Gothon," he would say, "when you are at Mass you must behave with the utmost modesty"; and he showed her what he wished her to do. As for himself, he who had been discovered in a cattle shed rapt in contemplation, continuously experienced that yearning for God which is the pain and the bliss of holy souls: "Knit my stocking," he used to say to Marguerite, "I must go and pray down there beside the brook."

On the bank of the stream there stood a willow tree, old and worm-eaten. In a hollow of the trunk Jean-Marie sometimes placed his little statue, and after surrounding it with moss, branches of trees and flowers, he knelt down to say his Rosary. Thus did the river bank take the place of the church to which people no longer went to pray.

At other times he erected a kind of shrine for his statue. With clay from the river bank he constructed diminutive chapels or molded effigies of saints and priests. He possessed a natural deftness which might have been greatly developed by tuition. In this way he made a statue of the Blessed Virgin, which was judged quite good; in fact, his father had it hardened in the oven, and it was long kept at the Vianneys' house. As soon as the altar was ready, he and Gothon, with vague memories of processions and festivals now suppressed, sang together what snatches of religious canticles they could remember.

Other young shepherds tended their flocks in the same district, and not all of them were suitable companions for well brought-up children. Some of these occasionally passed over to the Vianneys' meadow to look at the shrine. Jean-Marie replied to their questions without either embarrassment or annoyance. But how was it that these children, who were of the same age as our saint, were yet ignorant of the meaning of those images? Alas! less devout and attentive, they had already forgotten the beautiful ceremonies of Sundays and holidays. All unawares little Vianney became the teacher of these poor children. He constituted himself their catechist. Taking his stand before the rustic altar, he gave utterance to the thoughts that came to his mind in the silent hours of the night, and taught them the prayers he had learned at his mother's knee. "A child," he would say, "must never disobey its parents, nor utter blasphemous or coarse words." With all gravity he would add, by way of peroration: "Well, children, be very good and love the good God very much." A priestly vocation had sprung up in the peaceful vale of Chante-Merle!

The "congregation" proving somewhat restless, the sermon had of necessity to be short. But the youthful preacher bethought himself of other means by which he hoped to retain his audience. He organized processions. Thus it came about that in this unknown dale, whilst throughout France religious ceremonies were being suppressed, a band of children might have been seen walking in procession behind a cross formed of two sticks. The Rosary was recited, and childish hymns were sung: "It was nearly always I who acted as curé," Jean-Marie Vianney used to say, not without a touch of gentle pride, at a time of life when his fair dreams had become a blessed reality.

These pious games excepted, the little preacher did not much relish the companionship of other children. Their rough and noisy games, and at times their language, were distasteful to him. However, to please them, he occasionally agreed to play with them at quoits. André Provin, a playmate of the saint but two years younger, declared seventy years later that "he was very good at the game and won with ease. When we lost we were sad, and he, seeing our depression, would say: 'Well, you should not have played,' then to comfort us he gave back what he had won, always adding a *sou* over and above."

He often took a huge chunk of bread to Chante-Merle to divide among the poorer children. These kindnesses made him claim and use the right to rebuke the wilder spirits who, when angry, were in the habit of striking their playmates or their beasts: "You must not do that," he pleaded, "it is a sin." As a rule they listened to him, but more than once it happened that the rebuke was not to the liking of a cowardly lad much bigger than Vianney. This boy struck Jean-Marie on the legs, assured that he need fear no retaliation.

Happily, among that childish band there were those who were refined and well bred; such were François Duclos, André Provin, and Jean Dumond.[6]

On days when Gothon could not accompany her brother, Jean-Marie was allowed by his father to take with him André, Jean, or François. "Come along with me," young Vianney would say to little Duclos, "come with me, I have

6. François Duclos and André Provin were natives of Dardilly. Jean Dumond, who joined the Brothers of the Christian Schools, came originally from Larajasse (Rhône), and lived with an uncle at Dardilly. Born in 1787, he was a year younger than his friend Vianney.

something good to eat—we will go shares."

One day Jean-Marie hid himself among the willows, which formed a silver fringe to the river Planches, in order to pray undisturbed. "Where can he have gone to?" asked the young shepherds in the adjoining meadows. François Duclos pointed a traitorous finger towards the hiding-place of the little hermit; so they all went and looked among the trees where they discovered him on his knees praying.

One summer's afternoon the boy set out with his donkey laden with corn, which he was to take to the mill at Saint-Didier. Marion Vincent, the little daughter of some neighbors, who was the same age as Jean-Marie, begged for permission to accompany him. The parents of both children readily agreed. So the two set out in the heat of the early afternoon. After some time they decided to rest awhile in the shade of a tree. The hour seemed favorable to an exchange of confidences. Marion liked this quiet, gentle lad: "Jean-Marie," she said naively, "if our parents were willing, we two would be well matched." "Oh! no, never," the other replied with a vivacity which testified to his surprise; "no, Marion, do not let us talk of this."[7] Presently he rose, urged on his donkey, and the two children trudged together in the direction of the mill.

Sixty years later Marion Vincent, seated with her distaff on the threshold of her cottage, used to relate without bitterness, but not without tender emotion, this charming idyll, the sweetest and, maybe, the only one of her life.

Already Jean-Marie displayed that reserve, that innate delicacy, which caused him to shrink from even the purest and most legitimate demonstrations of love: "I know perfectly well that it is lawful," he said, later on, "and yet at times I would not even embrace my poor mother."

In closing the churches the Convention had sought to destroy divine worship; but it was unable to repress one

7. "Jean-Marie, si nos parents voulaient, on s'accorderait bien." "Oh! non, jamais; non, ne parlons pas de ça, Marion."

of the most touching manifestations of religion—charity. In the home of the Vianneys this virtue continued to flourish, for it was like a family heirloom and our saint constituted himself the apostle of this truly divine virtue.

André Provin, one of his playmates of Dardilly, testifies to having seen him visiting the houses of the poor with his little grey donkey laden with firewood. Jean-Marie was radiant: "Take two or three big logs," his father would say at first, but after a moment he would add: "Take as many as the donkey can carry."

Vagrants also found an ever-ready asylum at Dardilly. The Vincent family—Marion's parents—struck a bargain with the Vianneys, which bears eloquent testimony both to their neighborliness and to the delicacy of their Christian sentiments: it was agreed that the women should receive hospitality at the Vincents', whilst the men were to go to the Vianneys'. Jean-Marie eagerly directed these poor people to his father's house. Some of the travelers—all on foot as a matter of course—were accompanied by little children. Jean-Marie would be moved to tears at sight of their misfortune, and he would hasten to take the little ones by the hand and to plead with his mother in their behalf. One needed clogs, another a vest or some other garment. It was not difficult to persuade Mme. Vianney: the boy was soon gladdened by the sight of the various gifts which were being produced from the big cupboard. The poor sat at the same table as their hosts and were the first to be waited upon. One night Providence sent the Vianneys as many as twenty such guests. "There is not enough broth for all," the farmer's wife sometimes said to her husband. "Very well, I will go without," was that good man's reply.

It must occasionally have happened that among these wanderers there were proscribed priests, and at other times miscreants who had imbibed the ideas which were then prevalent. By a special protection of God, the Vianneys were never betrayed, though they took many risks. Supper over, and the door having been locked, the guests were invited to go on their knees. Then the fresh and limpid voice of a child would be heard, for Jean-Marie recited night prayers in the name of all. After prayers he and his brothers showed the visitors to the barn, or to a room above the bakehouse, where thick beds of straw awaited them. The whole house would soon be asleep under the watchful eye of God.

Before retiring for the night, Jean-Marie did what he had seen his father do, what had likewise been done by his grandfather, Pierre Vianney. He swept the corner by the fireside, where the ragged travellers had sat in front of the dying embers, drying their worn and rain-soaked outer garments. All the while he conversed on some religious topic with his mother or his elder sister, for his piety was growing steadily. Finally the whole family recited a few "Our Fathers" and "Hail Marys" for deceased relations—for, are not the souls in Purgatory mendicants of another world? Only then did they wish each other good-night.

Jean-Marie, even in those early days, had a devotion to the Holy Souls. "In the course of 1793, one of our aunts died," Marguerite relates. "'How tiresome!' we said among ourselves, 'we shall have to add another "Our Father" and "Hail Mary" to the many we already say.' Jean-Marie, who was about seven years old at that time, exclaimed: 'Well, what is one more "Our Father" and "Hail Mary"? They are soon said.'"

At an early date our saint—who was no spoiled child, indeed—was made to sleep in a corner of the stable, as was the custom of the peasantry, in a bed prepared for him and François: "Let us be very good," he used to say to his elder brother; "let us be very good, so that we may not be taken by surprise, like the wicked."

Chapter 3

SCHOOL, FIRST CONFESSION, AND COMMUNION (1794-1799)

TO JUDGE by divers incidents, the reasoning powers of little Vianney asserted themselves at an early date, for he was not by any means a dull boy. But it must be confessed that when he reached his ninth year, beyond religious subjects, he was almost wholly devoid of human learning. True, Catherine, his elder sister, had taught him to read and write, and he could spell the words of a Prayer-Book. For all that it was high time he went to school. Unfortunately Dardilly could boast a school no longer.

The law of December 19, 1793 (2 frimaire, year II), ordained that on reaching their sixth, or, at latest, their eighth year, all children should frequent the public schools during three consecutive years under threat, for their parents, of a fine equal to a fourth of the sum of the taxes paid by them. All were to receive an identical and compulsory education. By this means the Convention hoped to reach even the humblest villages. But the scheme was an empty dream because the Revolution had choked the springs of learning. The first paragraph of the law of 29 frimaire declared that "education is free," yet no one was to be permitted to teach unless he had taken the oath and secured a certificate of what in the revolutionary jargon was called *civism.* The office of schoolmaster could not be exercised either by a priest or a former member of a religious congregation. Everywhere there was a dearth of Jacobin teachers. Thus it came to pass that on the death of the worthy Catholic man who had kept the small school of Dardilly, that establishment was closed for good.

However, even in the sphere of elementary education the fall of Robespierre (July 27, 1794, 9 thermidor, year II) brought about a happy reaction. The Convention abolished the oath of *civism* previously required from teachers and extended to all citizens the right to teach (November 17, 1794, 27 brumaire, year III). Thanks to this toleration, early in 1795, citizen Dumas opened a school at Dardilly. It was winter, when children were not needed in the fields, so the new master, an excellent man withal, saw himself surrounded by a crowd of pupils to whom, besides reading, he taught writing, arithmetic, history, and geography. Jean-Marie drew attention to himself by his excellent conduct and his application. "M. Dumas," Marguerite relates, "was very satisfied with him, and often said to the others: 'Oh! if only you were like little Vianney!'" In point of fact, the boy must have made fair progress, and during the long winter evenings he could be seen learning his catechism or teaching it to his younger sister Gothon, or reading aloud the lives of the saints, when he would be devoutly listened to both by his parents and their guests, the poor.

The church, alas! remained closed. At the death of Robespierre hope momentarily revived, and indeed the persecution became less violent. The *décret de ventôse* (February 21, 1795, 3 ventôse, year III) abrogated the worship of the Supreme Being which had been established by the Convention and likewise suppressed the civil constitution of the clergy. Three months later, however, on the 11th prairial (May 30), a fresh decree declared that "no one could exercise any religious functions in whatever churches might be reopened, unless he had previously made an act of submission to the laws of the Republic." The former curé of Dardilly, M. Rey, did not reappear, and from among the priests who had refused the oath no one presented himself to claim his church. The Vianneys, who would in any case have refused to acknowledge a priest who had complied with the decree of the 11th prairial, continued to hear Mass in private houses.

Until the close of 1794 some thirty Catholic priests who, at the risk of their lives, had remained in the province of Lyons, ministered to the needs of the faithful, but in a desultory fashion; they were now here, now there, a fixed abode being altogether out of the question. France was now a missionary country; in some respects she was worse off than that. The need of some sort of organization was painfully felt. Mgr. de Marbeuf had indeed deemed himself justified in leaving the country, but M. Linsolas, his Vicar-General, disguised and in hiding, would not leave his post. In the spring of 1794 he divided the diocese into groups of parishes, each group being entrusted to missionary priests who were in their turn assisted by lay catechists. Ecully became such a centre and Dardilly was attached to it. We know the names of the confessors of the faith who heroically exercised their ministry in the district; they were, in the first place, two Sulpicians, M. Royer and M. Chaillon, both former rectors of the grand séminaire. Next there was a religious whom the storm had driven from his monastery, M. Balley, whom we shall meet again, and finally M. Groboz, vicaire in the parish of Sainte-Croix, who at first fled into Italy but recrossed the Alps in order to take the place of his many martyred colleagues.

All these priests lived at Ecully, lodging in separate houses, and by way of additional precaution they took up some trade, even though they may not have been keen in its pursuit. Thus M. Balley acted as a carpenter and M. Groboz as a cook. Their tools and implements furnished a plausible explanation of their movements. Moreover, they only went abroad at nightfall and avoided the highway when going to the house which had been selected for the celebration of Mass.

With what emotion and reverence did not little Vianney look up to these men as they stood at the altar? They had grown old before their time, and their faces bore the telltale traces of the labors and privations which they had endured for the love of souls. The priests themselves ended by noticing the bright-eyed lad whose fervor and recollection were so manifest. One day, in the year 1797, M. Groboz came to the village of Dardilly and called at the house of the Vianneys. After blessing the children one by one, he asked Jean-Marie: "How old are you?"

"Eleven."

"How long is it since you last went to Confession?"

"I have never yet been to Confession," the boy replied.

"Well, let us set right this omission at once."

So Jean-Marie and the priest were left alone together, and the lad began his first Confession. "I remember it well," the saint related in later life, "it was at home, at the foot of our clock." What could he have to confess? The priest, to be sure, must have marvelled at the whiteness of this beautiful soul. However, the boy was in need of further instruction. This he could receive from the lady catechists who had been secretly established at Ecully. M. Groboz experienced no difficulty in convincing the parents; they saw no reason why Jean-Marie should not spend a few months in a village that was quite near and in the house of Marguerite Beluse, his aunt, who was the wife of François Humbert.

For some reason or other—probably the need of further schooling at the hands of M. Dumas—the plan remained in abeyance for a whole year. At last, about May, 1798, Marie Vianney took her favorite son to Ecully. It was agreed that he should lodge with his aunt Marguerite, his parents providing his food and clothing. Thanks to this arrangement, Jean-Marie often saw his parents, brothers and sisters, at the farm of Point-du-Jour—for this was the charming name of the house.

Two Sisters of St. Charles, Sisters Combes and Deville, after the suppression of their convent, had found a refuge at Ecully. To their zeal the missionaries entrusted the preparation of the children for their first Communion. Jean-Marie was instructed by them in company with some fifteen others. A retreat preceded the great day. All this time young Vianney seemed wholly absorbed in God. "Even then we looked upon him as a little saint," was the subsequent testimony of Fleury Véricel, of Dardilly. He was for ever at his prayers, and seemed to have no relish for anything else: "Look at little 'fatty' competing with his Guardian Angel," his comrades would say, giving him a nickname which in all probability was applicable to the family of Matthieu Vianney.

It was the year 1799, during the "second Terror," and the season of the hay harvest had come. The lull that followed upon the fall of Robespierre was of short duration. Catholics still suffered persecution, priests died in their hundreds, being either deported to Guiana or interned in the hulks of Rochefort, Ré or Oléron. The saintly pontiff, Pius VI, now eighty-two years of age, was a prisoner of the Revolution. The republican calendar remained in force, the Sunday being superseded by the *décadi*. Religious solemnities, so dear to the people's heart, were proscribed, and an endeavor was made to replace them by grotesque and ludicrous festivals.[1]

Perforce, divine worship had to take place in secret. There was at Ecully the house of Madame de Pingon, with its extensive grounds. MM. Groboz and Balley chose this spot as the scene of the greatest event in a child's life, a white and radiant solemnity in times of peace, but forgotten by the multitude in those troublous spring days. At an early hour the sixteen first communicants, in their ordinary clothes, were conducted one by one into a large room, the shutters of which had been carefully closed, for it had been decided that each child was to carry the wonted lighted taper, the flame of which must needs remain invisible from without. By a refinement of caution carts laden with hay were placed in front of the windows, and were actually unloaded whilst the sacred ceremony was in progress. The mother of each child brought, carefully hidden under her cape, the white veil or armlet which was to be worn by the first communicant.

Jean-Marie was a little over thirteen years of age. Where

1. Thus there was kept the Feast of the Theanthrophily instituted by Chemin-Dupontès, and subsequently that of the Theophilanthropy of Larevelliére-Lépaux.

the supernatural was concerned his mind was quick, and he was well able to appreciate the gift that was about to be bestowed upon him. He felt a keen longing for Our Lord, and the sadness of those days only intensified his eagerness; thus he received the Holy Eucharist with a heart full of faith, longing and love. "I was present . . ." Marguerite Vianney afterwards related, "my brother felt such happiness that he was unwilling to leave the room."

Already at that time he doubtless experienced something of those ardors which later on he expressed in such burning language: "When we receive Holy Communion, we experience something extraordinary—a joy—a fragrance—a well-being that thrills the whole body and causes it to exult. With St. John we feel compelled to exclaim: 'It is the Lord!' 'O my God! what joy is a Christian's who, as he rises from the holy table, carries all Heaven in his heart!'"[2]

In later years he could never speak of his first Communion without shedding tears of joy. After a lapse of fifty years he would still show to the children of Ars the plain rosary beads which he received on that occasion, exhorting them to preserve theirs also with jealous care.

On the same day, in company with his parents, Jean-Marie returned to Dardilly. The years of his childhood were at an end, and with them the time of study. Though his development had been slow, he was strong for his age. Work on the farm now claimed him. Even more than before the parental house was perfumed with the fragrance of his virtues, and his frankness and courtesy in dealing with the villagers speedily won for him the hearts of all.

---

2. Catechisms on Holy Communion (*Esprit du Curé d'Ars,* XII, XIII, *passim*).

Chapter 4

LABORER AND VINE-DRESSER (1799-1805)

THE BOLD stroke of 18 brumaire, year IV (November 9, 1799), which placed the fate of France in the hands of General Bonaparte, brought about the liberation of the Church from the yoke under which she had groaned for so long. This happy release was achieved practically without fresh legislation. Taking advantage of the toleration of the first Consul, the priests returned from exile, churches were reopened, and at Ecully in particular MM. Groboz and Balley began to say Mass publicly. The people of Dardilly flocked to Ecully, foremost among them being the Vianney family. Jean-Marie felt glad at sight of the flickering light which pointed to a beloved Presence upon the altar. When would Dardilly also have its priest? In the meantime everyone lived in hope. Henceforth field work would seem less arduous, for the laborer could take heart at the sight of the steeple of his beloved church. The time was now come when Jean-Marie was considered fit for heavy work, for the flocks could be tended by Gothon and François (Cadet), who had almost reached his ninth year, while Jean-Marie could assist his father, his eldest brother, and the farm laborer. According to the season, he tilled the ground, loosened the earth round the vine, gathered the nuts and apples, dug trenches, pruned trees, or made faggots in the coppice. The cattle must be attended to whilst in the stable. Then there was the haymaking and harvesting, the gathering of the grapes, and the labor of the wine-press—trifles in themselves, remaining small or rendered great according to the intention with which they were performed. For Jean-Marie all these were actions of importance, inasmuch as he was wont to offer them to God. Subsequently he gave away the secret of his inner life during those youthful years. In one of his catechisms he says: "Oh what a beautiful thing it is to do all things in union with the good God! Courage, my soul, if you work with God; you shall, indeed, do the work, but He will bless it; you shall walk and He will bless your steps. Everything shall be taken count of, the forgoing of a look, of some gratification—all shall be recorded. There are people who make capital out of everything, even the winter. If it is cold they offer their little sufferings to God. Oh! what a beautiful thing it is to offer oneself, each morning, as a victim to God!" In this manner Jean-Marie sanctified himself whilst at work in the field or in the house. The supernatural world was ever present to him, but for all that he was neither a slacker nor a dreamer, his being a healthy and active temperament.

Shortly after his first Communion he went one day with his brother François into the vineyard. Do what he could, he was unable to keep pace with the eighteen-year-old youth, and at the end of the day he felt utterly worn out. He confided to his mother that the exertion had exhausted him. Moved to pity, she said: "François, go more slowly, or help your brother; surely you see that he is not so strong as you." "Oh," François calmly replied, "he is not bound to do as much as I. But what would people say if the elder brother did no more than the younger?"

Now it so happened that the very next day a sister of the Antiquaille[1] of Lyons called at the farm. Marguerite Vianney gives the following details of this visit: "The Sister gave to each one of us a holy picture. She also had a small statue of the Blessed Virgin enclosed in a case. We all wanted that statue; however, she gave it to Jean-Marie. The day after this visit he again worked with

1. The Antiquaille is today one of the hospitals of Lyons. It was formerly a convent of the Visitation which had been constructed with stones taken from some ancient building, whence its name *"l'Antiquaille."* In the modern hospital the visitor is still shown the prison in which St. Pothinus was at one time confined.

François. Before beginning his task he devoutly kissed the feet of the image, and then threw it in front of him as far as he could. When he came up to it, he reverently picked it up and did as before. On his return, in the evening, he said to my mother: 'Always trust the Blessed Virgin. I earnestly called upon her today, and she has helped me much, for I was able to keep up with my brother without being tired out.'" For eight days François and Jean-Marie worked thus side by side. They went forward in silence, like two Trappists. Lest he should inconvenience his brother, the lad prayed silently. Whilst handling his mattock, he would say to himself: "I must see to it that I till the soil of my soul and pull out all weeds so that it may be ready to receive the good seed."

When, however, he found himself alone in the fields, he gave full vent to his transports, mingling his voice with the chirping of the birds and singing hymns. He remained true to the habit formed in childhood, of "blessing the hour," but to the "Hail Mary," which he was wont to say as the clock struck the hour, he now added the following prayers: "Blessed be God! Courage, my soul! Time passes, eternity approaches. Let me live as I hope to die! Blessed be the holy and immaculate Conception of the Blessed Virgin Mary, Mother of God!"

After the midday meal, when all lay down to rest, Jean-Marie stretched himself on the grass like the others, but, whilst pretending to sleep, he gave himself up to fervent prayer.

Jean-Marie's schooldays had been very short, so that his mental powers reached their development amid the labors of the field. But the rough toil prepared him for subsequent austerities, whilst at the same time it furnished his mind with mental pictures that stood him in good stead, when, after the example of Our Lord, he sought to illustrate the truths of religion by means of the homely scenes of country life. He watched white doves on the wing, and was reminded of the Holy Ghost. The grain of corn cast into the earth and needing rain and sunshine if it were to come to maturity was an image of the soul rendered fruitful by divine grace. When he observed fruit that showed signs of premature ripeness because it had been attacked by the worm, he saw in it a symbol of actions that appear indeed perfect, whereas in reality they spring from pride. The perfume of the flowering vine was found less fragrant than the sweet odor of a soul at peace with God. The juice flowing from the ripe grape was to him an image of the sweetness experienced in prayer. A field allowed to lie fallow reminded him of the disorderly state of the sinner's conscience. As he watched the smoke of the shepherds' fires eddying in the chilly air of a winter's day he bethought himself of our daily crosses which, if they are cast into the fire of love, are reduced to ashes like the thorns and brambles with which the shepherds fed the flame—the thorns are hard indeed, but the ashes are soft to the touch.[2]

At nightfall those workers who lived in the same quarter often returned home together forming merry groups. There was much talk, snatches of songs, and at times, much to the distress of Jean-Marie, rough jokes would be exchanged. At this hour of the day, when even nature seems to recollect herself, he felt the need of solitude and silence. Resolutely he would walk behind the others, absorbed in prayer and fingering his beads: "His lips moved constantly." Some of his fellow-laborers would turn round to contemplate so good and pious a lad; others, infected by the spirit of the times, made game of his piety.

"François," they jeered, "aren't you going to mumble prayers with Jean-Marie?" François resented the taunts of which his brother was the victim, but he only blushed and made no reply. However, Jean-Marie soon reduced the scoffers to silence. He was very observant; the defects of others did not escape him, and his repartees could be both swift and very much to the point. But he chose to keep silence and to go on with his Rosary: after a while the foolish young men felt uncomfortable and were glad to change the subject.

2. These comparisons, besides many others, are found in the well-known *Catechisms* of Ars, of which we shall speak hereafter.

No doubt it was these same companions who deemed it funny to hide Jean-Marie's tools. It would seem that this feeble joke was frequently repeated. The patience of the meekest would have been sorely tried, but Jean-Marie was apparently incapable of resentment. With a smile on his lips he would look in the hedge for his shovel or his hoe, and, having found it, he quietly proceeded with his task. One day, for a quite trivial motive, his elder brother took him somewhat rudely to task. Jean-Marie could easily have justified his conduct, but preferred to remain silent. Such examples were bound to bear fruit in time. The Dardilly critics must eventually have come to feel like the good old man who said to Mgr. Richard, Bishop of Belley: "Jean-Marie Vianney was a model. Some indeed found fault with him, but in the end it was he who was right; wisdom was on his side."[3]

In the meantime a new day was dawning for the Church of France. The first Consul was keen on establishing order in the country by the restoration of internal peace. He had the wisdom to understand that unless it were based on religion his work would not last. A concordat was negotiated with the Pope. This famous document was signed at Paris, July 16, 1801, ratified in Rome on August 15 and on April 5, 1802, it became law. Who could describe the emotion of the people of Paris when in the early dawn of April 18 the great bell of Notre-Dame, which had been dumb during ten long years, filled the sky with its song of victory, proclaiming at one and the same time the feast of Easter and the resurrection of the Catholic Church in France. The Vianneys, and Jean-Marie in particular, shed tears of joy on learning the glorious news.

Exile having robbed him of neither his lawful title of parish priest nor of the affection of his flock, M. Jacques Rey had returned to Dardilly a few months earlier. As early as the spring of 1802 the feasts of the Church, which were but a vague memory for Jean-Marie, began

3. Mgr. Odelin, *Le cardinal Richard,* Paris, de Gigord, 1922, p. 22.

to be observed once more with all the pomp that had characterized them prior to the storm. When the feast of Corpus Christi came round, Jean-Marie plucked the roses on the garden hedge and scattered their petals along the road, and helped his brothers and sisters to weave garlands of box and holly. His whole being exulted as the church doors opened wide and the monstrance shed its golden rays upon the praying multitude amid the strains of the *Pange lingua*.

Henceforth, whenever it was possible, Jean-Marie contrived to visit the church before going to work, for he needed courage—the day was so long! In the summer months, when it was day before the *Angelus,* advantage must be taken of the additional hour of light, hence the time of early Mass would find Jean-Marie already in the fields. The devout youth never shirked work under pretence of piety, his religion made him obedient, and he was wholly free from scrupulosity. So he united himself with the priest from afar by saying five *Paters* and five *Aves,* and his keen longing for the Body and Blood of Jesus Christ filled his heart with heavenly sweetness.

Times there were, however, when he experienced an irresistible attraction to the church; this happened especially on certain afternoons when the chiming of the bell announced that there would be Benediction. His father was a victim to rheumatism, so, in order to secure permission to run to church, Jean-Marie would say: "Father, let me off for half an hour and I'll pray that you may be freed from your pain."

Even during the years of persecution, when the *décadi* was the legal day of rest, the Vianneys had not ceased to sanctify the Lord's day. During the night of Saturday to Sunday they assisted at the Mass of some proscribed priest, the remainder of the day being spent in prayer, holy reading and in visiting friends and relations. The restoration of public worship entailed but little change in their mode of life, except, of course, that their piety benefited immensely by the general revival of religion, and the example of their own son must have proved a great incentive to perfection. On Sunday Jean-Marie was soon ready for church. He remained in the house of God for as long a time as possible, gazing intently upon the tabernacle, kneeling in adoration like one of the angels that worship there and proving a source of edification to all who beheld him.

As he advanced in piety, Jean-Marie's thirst for religious knowledge increased. Unfortunately, with the exception of Sunday, the only time he could give to study was a few moments at night. Above his bed in the stable was a small shelf, still to be seen, on which he kept his devotional books. In the unsteady light of a candle made of resin he would read from one of his books, selecting at one time the Gospels, at another the *Imitation.* François, his elder brother, who occupied the same bed, would have preferred to sleep. For some time he bore with his younger brother, but in the end he informed their mother, who wisely forbade Jean-Marie to prolong his reading and bade him to take the repose he needed. He obeyed without a murmur, but whilst François slept he lay awake for many an hour of the silent night, thinking of God and his own future career. What were his thoughts? Deep down in his soul he heard an echo of the voice which once on the shore of the lake of Galilee called Peter, Andrew, James, and John to follow Jesus. Jean-Marie wished to become a priest. This secret longing was the explanation of his holy life. But how is such an ambition to be realized? He is nearly seventeen years old, his elementary studies are quite inadequate, yet he must needs learn Latin. And what will his people say when he declares his secret? Where his mother is concerned, he feels easy enough—she will gladly give her favorite child to the Lord. But his father? He is indeed given to works of charity, but his piety is more pedestrian, for his mind is absorbed by the rough labor of the fields. Conscription is about to claim François unless he is bought out of the army, and Catherine is engaged to be married and must be provided with a dowry. Thus the outlook for Jean-Marie is none too bright.

Yet there are souls to be saved! So many parishes are without priests; so many children are deprived of all religious teaching and of the Sacraments. Is so rich a harvest to be lost for the lack of laborers? It is well worth his while to face every difficulty, to master every obstacle.

His mother and then his aunt received his earliest confidences. From the first he stated the true motive of his vocation: "If I were a priest I should gain many souls to God." In this quarter his intention was approved without discussion or argument; all he did was to throw himself into the arms of his mother who wept happy tears. The rugged father would prove more difficult. Jean-Marie appears to have hesitated before revealing his secret. Encouraged by his mother, he at last took heart and spoke to his father whilst they were both resting after their work. Jean-Marie's forebodings proved only too well-founded. Matthieu Vianney remained inflexible in his refusal. He had just paid the dowry of Catherine, recently married to M. Melin of Ecully, and had bought François out of the army—for François had drawn an unlucky number and a substitute had to be found—surely it would spell ruination if he were now asked to pay for the education of Jean-Marie! Was there anything so precarious as a priest's life? and who would undertake the education of a youth of eighteen? Was there a chance that he would succeed? Silence was the only answer of the disappointed youth. Matthieu Vianney related to his wife the confidences that had passed between him and his son and his own decision. The good woman pleaded in vain that the best and most hard working of their children was concerned: her very arguments served to defeat the object she had at heart. Jean-Marie was a reliable and experienced worker: it was an additional reason that he should stay at home. Besides, Matthieu was ageing; was he to engage yet another farm hand? Good man as he was, he could not see his way to surrender his treasure even to God.

The struggle was long and obstinate and lasted for

close on two years.[4] Jean-Marie kept silence, but his face betrayed his thoughts. His exemplary conduct might have convinced the obstinate father that here he was confronted with an irresistible vocation which would never capitulate, the more so that the young man had the approval of his confessor.

It is probable that Jean-Marie confided to M. Rey both his longing and his disappointment. Unfortunately during the years of exile that venerable priest had contracted several painful infirmities. At the beginning of 1803 the ecclesiastical authority had indeed confirmed his title as parish priest of Dardilly, but within a few months he sent in his resignation and retired to Lyons. The Abbé Jacques Tournier replaced him on July 7, but it took time before he became acquainted with the Vianney family. However, God was not unmindful of his lowly and generous servant. He was even then preparing the way by which he was to reach both the priesthood and the heights of sanctity.

Cardinal Fesch had entrusted to Mgr. de Mérinville the duty of reorganizing the diocese of Lyons. In this way it came about that, at the very time when M. Rey was appointed to Dardilly, another confessor of the faith, M. Charles Balley, was named parish priest of Ecully.

M. Balley, the youngest of a family of sixteen children, was born at Lyons, on September 30, 1751. His brother, Dom Etienne, was a Carthusian, whilst he himself and another brother, Jean-Alexandre, entered the Order of the Genovefans.[5] At the outbreak of the Revolution he was parish priest of Saint-Clément-de-Choue, in the diocese of Blois. When the Revolution drove him from his

4. "His mother and his aunt of Ecully were anxious for him to embrace this career, but his father opposed the plan for nearly two years." (Abbé Raymond, *Procès de l'Ordinaire,* p. 282).

5. Charles Balley, owing to a confusion with his elder brother, Dom Etienne, has been described as a Carthusian. The Genovefans, called Canons of St. Geneviève, or Canons Regular of the Congregation of France, were, previous to the Revolution, an Order of considerable importance. At the close of the eighteenth century they numbered 1,300 religious, living in 107 houses. They took charge of parishes—St. Etienne-du-Mont at Paris was of their number—hospitals, and seminaries. A white cassock with a black cloak formed their costume. The coat of arms of the Congregation displayed a hand holding a heart surrounded by flames, on a field of azure, the motto being *Superemineat caritas.* A fit motto for a priest like Charles Balley.

post, he took refuge at Lyons. There he lived, now in a small apartment, which he had inherited from his family, now in the houses of trustworthy persons, but chiefly with M. Loras. It was at Lyons that he had the sorrow of seeing his brother's apostasy.[6] His other brother, Dom Etienne, was guillotined in the "Place des Terreaux" on January 14, 1794: the Carthusian went to his martyrdom with a smile on his lips. Three months later the Abbé Charles enrolled himself in the band of missionaries who staked their lives a hundred times whilst they endeavored to keep up the faith in the village of Ecully and the surrounding district. When in 1803 he was definitely appointed to Ecully, his sister came to live with him. She had been a religious of the Annonciade-Céleste, and was eighteen years his senior.

On his appointment to Ecully, M. Balley's first care was to discover ecclesiastical vocations. His efforts were not in vain, and he was enabled to open a school at his presbytery. The husband of Catherine Vianney, himself an excellent Catholic, mentioned this fact to his youthful brother-in-law. M. Balley was no stranger to Jean-Marie, since he had assisted at his Mass during the Terror.

The task of the new pastor of Ecully was a well-nigh overwhelming one, for the parish, which was not far from Lyons, was of considerable importance, and had suffered a good deal from the ravages of the Revolution. M. Balley was barely fifty-two years of age, yet his health was impaired by the trials and perils to which he had been exposed during so many years of his wandering existence. But he was not to be daunted by difficulties. With a view to securing the continuation of his own ministry he scoured the district, calling on rich and poor alike, in the hope of discovering boys or young men who gave some indication of a supernatural vocation. For a time his roof sheltered a future Jesuit, Deschamps; also Mathias and

6. Jean Alexandre Balley, on taking the oath, was sent as parish priest to Pollionay by Lamourette, the constitutional bishop of the *département* of the Rhône. Later he was rehabilitated. His last post was the parish of Arnas, where he died after a sojourn of only two months (February 7-April 16, 1823).

Jacques Loras, who died on the scaffold, and the sons of the good man who had sheltered him in his house during the darkest days of the Revolution.

Jean-Marie's hopes quickened when he heard of the existence of the small presbytery school. Was not this a favorable occasion for a supreme effort to win over his father? His mother, who had never failed to encourage her son's vocation, once more undertook to plead on his behalf. She pointed out to her husband that there was no question of sending their boy to a distant seminary.[7] He would remain close at hand, at Ecully, where he had made his first Communion, and where he would lodge with the Humberts. The outlay would not be considerable; Jean-Marie would go to M. Balley for lessons only; he would have his board as well as his lodging with his Aunt Marguerite. After all, what else did their boy seek but to do the will of God? Matthieu Vianney's resistance was at an end. "Since the boy has set his heart on this thing," he said, "we cannot oppose him any longer."

On hearing the gladsome news, Jean-Marie urged his mother to call on M. Balley without further delay. Therefore Marie Vianney, accompanied by her sister Marguerite Humbert, presented herself at the presbytery of Ecully. Tall and slender, with features strikingly "Roman," M. Balley looked imposing, almost awe-inspiring. Taking their courage in both hands, the two women stated the purpose of their visit. No doubt they explained how the youth came to hear the divine call. They spoke of his ever increasing piety and his exemplary conduct. M. Balley listened but would not commit himself. The two women insisted. "No, I cannot, I cannot," the priest declared. The first interview had proved a failure.

The messengers communicated the sad news to Catherine's husband. At their request M. Melin undertook to plead once more with M. Balley, only to be met with

7. Even before the storm clouds had been swept from the sky seminaries were reestablished at Saint-Jodard, at Marboz—soon to be transferred to Meximieux—at Roche, from which was founded Saint-Galmier. Later on, at the instigation of Cardinal Fesch, who had this great work sincerely at heart, presbytery schools were opened all over the province of Lyons.

another refusal.

"But," said M. Melin, "you should at least consent to interview my brother-in-law. I am sure you will accept him as soon as you see him."

"Very well, let him come."

Thus it came about that, accompanied by his mother, the lowly field laborer presented himself before him who was destined to introduce him into the vineyard of the Lord. The austere M. Balley closely scrutinized the nineteen-year-old lad, who looked so pale and lean, but also so earnest and recollected. He made him talk, and found him well informed in religious subjects, and the frank and open countenance of the youth decided the priest to admit him among his pupils. Turning to Jean-Marie, he said in a very kindly voice: "Do not worry, my friend; if need be I will sacrifice myself for your sake."

Chapter 5

A LATE VOCATION (1805-1809)

FOR THE second time Jean-Marie bade farewell to the fields of Dardilly and to his father's house. Though he had grown since the day of his first Communion, the good people of Point-du-Jour soon discovered that the youth of twenty retained the simplicity and innocence which they had admired in the child.

This is not to say he was perfect, but he already gave indications of the lofty heights to which he would one day attain. At meals he nearly always contented himself with his portion of porridge, refusing to touch the other dishes, even when urged to do so.[1] Yet he was of an age when the desire for food is most clamorous. But he knew his own mind when he laid this penance on himself; in fact, he soon added to it. In order to draw down the blessing of God upon his studies he requested his aunt not to season his porridge with butter. Whether it was through forgetfulness, or through a wish to simplify her task, Marguerite Humbert often served him like the other members of her family. On those occasions her nephew, who as yet had not completely mastered his quick temperament, would make a wry face, as if each mouthful would choke him. The day was not yet when, completely transformed by grace, he would meet with a smile far more unpleasant circumstances.

Always a great lover of the poor, he sometimes took to the house of the Humberts for a night's lodging, all the beggars with whom he happened to fall in: more than once

1. At Point-du-Jour the visitor is still shown the fireplace where Jean-Marie himself occasionally warmed up his porridge.

he filled the house with such guests. On a certain day he walked over to Dardilly to see his parents. On the way he met a beggar to whom he gave the new shoes his father had bought for him. Doubtless he thought they were his personal property; had he not paid for them with his labor? Nonetheless he was sharply reprimanded on reaching home barefooted. However, he remained incorrigible, for soon after, happening to pass a poor woman and her small children, he was so moved to pity that he gave her seven francs, which was all the money he had with him.

He had now entered upon his ecclesiastical studies. Henceforth his mornings and evenings were spent at the presbytery. Mlle. Balley welcomed him on the threshold. Though garbed in lay attire, she still retained the gentle ways of Sister Marie Joseph Dorothée.[2] Her brother Charles had the reputation of being a good theologian. He repeatedly declined the chair of moral theology at the Grand Séminaire of Lyons. Notwithstanding a certain sternness in manner and speech, his eyes bespoke a kindly disposition, so that Jean-Marie soon felt quite at ease in the priest's house.

But the Latin grammar proved far more forbidding than the teacher. The young student was lively enough in conversation; his repartees were quick and neat. It was a pleasure to listen to him. But intellectual pursuits rather bewildered him, and he seemed to become helpless as soon as he felt a pen in his hand. Through no fault of his, his intellect had been too long permitted to lie fallow. The rudiments are always a matter of memory. Whilst his spade shone, thanks to constant handling, his memory had become rusty. He had forgotten the scanty notions of grammar which he had assimilated in the school of citizen Dumas, and it seemed a desperate undertaking to tackle Latin syntax when he was ignorant of the grammar of his native tongue.

---

2. Mlle. Balley was a wise, cultured, and deeply religious woman. At the outbreak of the Revolution her convent was closed. She died at the presbytery of Ecully, on August 3, 1808, at the age of seventy-five. In the archives of the archdiocese of Lyons is preserved a touching manuscript account of her martyred brother, Dom Etienne.

Young Deschamps and Loras, well-bred children though they were, laughed in their sleeves on hearing the big lad blundering through lessons which they had learned and retained with the utmost facility. M. Balley was not in a laughing mood. Would that youth, so sound in his judgement and so sincere in his piety, stumble at the very first difficulty? Here was a task more arduous than work in the vineyard. Evening after evening, by the light of a small lamp, this beginner of twenty would resolutely bend over his book. At the end of his task he besought the Holy Ghost to fix the words in his "poor head." Alas! on the morrow they were all gone. He tried his hand at childish translations from the *Selected Stories of the Old Testament,*[3] a book which at that time was the classic for beginners. Père Deschamps relates how he used to help his fellow-student to find the words in the dictionary and to make somehow tolerable translations. A like assistance was rendered by Mathias Loras, the most intelligent, perhaps, among the pupils of M. Balley. However, Mathias was of a nervous and excitable temperament. One day his patience was exhausted by the sheer incapacity of the big young man, and he boxed his ears before all the others. Jean-Marie was also excitable, but he knelt down before the boy of twelve who had treated him so outrageously and humbly asked his forgiveness. Mathias had a golden heart. Suddenly he felt smitten with grief and, his face bathed in tears, he threw himself into the arms of Jean-Marie who was still on his knees. This incident marked the beginning of an abiding friendship. Mathias Loras subsequently became a missionary in the United States, and eventually Bishop of Dubuque, but never could he forget the action of Jean-Marie and the accent with which he spoke on this occasion.[4]

---

3. *Selectae e Veteri Testamento Historiae.*
4. Mgr. Loras appears to have emulated on the episcopal throne the holiness of the Curé d'Ars, and there is question of introducing the cause of his canonization. Such is the reputation for sanctity that he has left in the Diocese of Dubuque that, at the time of their Confirmation, many candidates take his name, and so put themselves under his protection (Mgr. Convert, *Annales d'Ars*, 1925, p. 534).

During several months the progress made by Jean-Marie was practically nil. Yet his application was amazingly persistent and in addition he prayed and fasted. His outward appearance ended by betraying the fact that he was underfed and exhausted. Mme. Humbert felt rather helpless, so she spoke to M. Balley who, austere himself, was not aware of anything amiss. If his strength was to be maintained Jean-Marie needed a good deal of food, yet he observed a rigorous fast. Finally, M. Balley spoke to him: "See, my child, we must indeed pray much and do penance, but it is likewise a duty to take food and not to ruin one's health."

A spiritual crisis was now at hand, the issue whereof would be fraught with tremendous consequences. Was he not undertaking far more than he could hope to achieve? In this form did temptation swoop down upon his soul. He now experienced intense disgust for that which he had so eagerly desired. His mind wandered back to the fireside at Dardilly, the familiar fields and the labors in which his youthful vigor had achieved far easier success. "I want to return home," he sadly avowed to M. Balley who was not less grieved.

The keen eye of the old priest had detected the secret sorrow of his beloved pupil. Realizing the worth of the soul entrusted to his care he spoke thus: "What are you doing, my poor child? You seek to hide your trouble? Do you not know that your father is only too anxious to have you at home? When he sees you so depressed, he will keep you. That will be the end of your plans; it will be the end also of the priesthood and work for souls."

Not to labor for souls! Oh no, surely God would not permit that. The thought of the priesthood, the altar, the salvation of sinners, the plentiful harvest, and the scanty number of reapers—that was enough to bring to a head a very dangerous phase. Henceforth the evil spirit of discouragement could no longer exercise its fatal influence. For all that his memory was just as unretentive; on his own confession, he was unable "to lodge anything in his bad head."[5] Realizing that his vocation was at stake and anxious to obtain the speedy help of Heaven, he bethought himself of a heroic expedient. He made a vow to go on foot, begging his bread both on the outward and the homeward journey, to the sanctuary of La Louvesc where the shrine of St. Francis Régis, the apostle of the province of Velay and Vivarais, is venerated.

It was in the summer of 1806. The distance between Ecully and La Louvesc, a village situated in the Ardèche, is about a hundred kilometers. Notwithstanding his ascetic leanness Jean-Marie was yet strong and active. His keenness caused him to overlook the possibility that his healthy appearance would prove the occasion of many annoyances during his pilgrimage. One day, then, after Mass and Communion, he set out on his errand, a stick in one hand, a rosary in the other. He walked for a long time until hunger and thirst compelled him to give in, when he sat down on the threshold of a house by the roadside. What could be the design of this vagabond? Whilst affecting holiness was he not planning mischief? And what a cock-and-bull story he told! His studies, forsooth! and the shrine of St. Francis Régis! Who would be fool enough to believe such tales? In the guise of a pilgrim was he not in reality a deserter, a recruit fleeing from the colors and attempting even now to get across the frontier into Savoy or Piedmont? Small wonder that our pilgrim was driven from the farmers' houses and that the epithets of "glutton," "lazy fellow," were hurled after him; he was even threatened with the gendarmes.

Jean-Marie might have bought provisions, for, in order to meet every contingency, he carried some money; however he wished to refrain from purchasing anything so as to keep his vow. He proceeded on his journey, eating herbs and drinking from the wayside brook until he was almost faint with hunger and exhaustion. He knew he could hold out no longer, so he took courage and entered a house. He hoped the woman of the house would give

5. "Il ne pouvait rien loger dans sa mauvaise tête."

him something to eat. She was engaged in undoing a ball of thread, and bade him pull at one end of the thread. He, thinking it was a case of rendering a service, did as he was told, but, when he reached the threshold of the house, the woman shut the door in his face.

The following night he failed to secure a lodging, so that he had, perforce, to spend the night in the open. Fortunately he soon fell in with kindlier people who supplied him with odd pieces of bread. On this meagre fare he travelled over almost impossible roads. He felt exhausted but happy when he finally reached the celebrated sanctuary of La Louvesc amid the mountains of the Vivarais, at an altitude of 1,100 meters above sea level.

The only thought of our pilgrim, on entering the village, was to prostrate himself at the shrine and to tell the saint of the motive of his journey—namely, "the grace to learn enough Latin to enable him to do his theology." He obtained that grace even though it was doled out with parsimony and in a measure only just sufficient. God has His own plans for every soul, and He wished to try the faith of His servant so as to inure him against yet severer struggles. He visited the places sanctified by the presence of St. Régis. He studied the old, low-roofed church in which the apostle of the Vivarais, though consumed by a violent fever, gave a mission at the Christmas of 1640, his zeal burning the keener in that he realized that he suffered from a fatal disease. On December 26, in an agony of thirst, the saint heard Confessions and preached until two in the afternoon, when he said his Mass and again heard Confessions under a paneless window, until he collapsed in a dead swoon. They carried him into the presbytery and placed him near a big fire, but he no sooner came round than he resumed his Confessions. On December 31, about midnight, he succumbed to an attack of galloping pneumonia. What an example, what a stimulus was all this for Jean-Marie! As he visited the old church and presbytery he took note of the lessons taught by the saint's life, never dreaming for one moment that the day would come when pilgrims would flock to his own church and presbytery in order to learn a like lesson.

Jean-Marie went to Confession and Communion. He confided to the Jesuit who heard him what difficulties he had experienced on the way by reason of the vow to beg his food. Should he risk a repetition of these trials and affronts? The confessor was not of opinion that he should do so and commuted his vow, laying on him the duty of giving instead of receiving alms.

He made the return journey on foot, paying for his food and lodging. He bestowed alms on all who appealed to his charity. This proves that he did not himself bear the appearance of a beggar. This mode of traveling gave him such pleasure that later on he declared: "I have experienced the truth of the saying of Holy Scripture: 'It is more blessed to give than to receive.'" And he added: "I should never advise anyone to take a vow to beg." The vexations to which he was subjected gave him a first-hand knowledge of the wretched lot of the poor and the destitute and served to increase the compassion he felt towards beggars and tramps.

M. Balley had accompanied his pupil in spirit, and on his return he received him with open arms. "From this time onward his progress was such as at least to prevent a feeling of discouragement."[6] School books no longer filled him with dismay. For being less thankless, his toil became more fruitful. He felt that the path to the priesthood was being smoothed for him; M. Balley likewise was less fearful of the future. The dearest hope of the master was one day to assist his big pupil at the altar of God.

The latter, however, had now reached the age of conscription. The *classe* 1807—his *classe*—was being drawn upon before the time. In November, 1806, after the bloody campaign of Jéna, Napoleon, though victorious, felt

6. Frère Athanase, *Procès apostolique in genere,* p. 196. The good Brother appears to strike the right note. The Abbé Monnin, on the other hand, falls into exaggeration when he writes: "From that day difficulties vanished as if by enchantment" *(Le Curé d'Ars,* I, p. 69). All his life long the holy curé entertained a great devotion towards St. Francis Régis. At Ars the saint's image—a pen and ink drawing, still to be seen on the wall—adorned his room, and a statue was put up by him in the church.

constrained to call to the colors 80,000 of these young men. Jean-Marie had begun to study for the priesthood, and was destined for the diocese of Lyons; hence he was exempt from military service. Cardinal Fesch at that time enjoyed the favor of his nephew, and had secured a privilege in virtue of which all ecclesiastical students inscribed on the official lists of his archdiocese were exempt from military duties, as were clerics in Holy Orders. Accordingly the parish priest of Ecully requested the secretary of the Cardinal, who was no other than M. Groboz, his former fellow-laborer during the Revolution, to inscribe the name of Vianney among the aspirants to the priesthood.

In Lent, 1807, Jean-Marie received the sacrament of Confirmation at Ecully. He was about to complete his twenty-first year. Cardinal Fesch, notwithstanding his zeal in the discharge of his duties,[7] had until that time held only one visitation, that of 1803. It was no easy task to cope with so large a diocese, embracing no fewer than three *départements*—viz., those of the Rhône, the Ain, and the Loire. This second visitation was, therefore, an important event. A pastoral letter, dated January 22, 1807, announced it to the diocese. The winter of that year was a very severe one, but, says an account written at the time, "as soon as His Eminence had completed the visitation of the parishes of Lyons, he turned to those of the suburbs and the adjoining villages." In this way it happened that Ecully was one of the first parishes to be visited by the energetic prelate. "His Eminence the Cardinal Archbishop of Lyons," to quote once more from the abovementioned report, "proceeded with his pastoral visitation. At one place, where we were present, His Eminence was

7. Joseph Fesch, born January 3, 1763, a brother of Laetitia Bonaparte, and thus a maternal uncle of Napoleon I, had up till then a very checkered career. A priest and canon of Ajaccio before the Revolution, he became a *commissaire des guerres* in the Republican armies. In this capacity he accompanied his nephew, then General Bonaparte, on the famous campaign of Italy. He was converted by M. Emery, the Superior of St. Sulpice, under whose direction he made, at Paris, a strict retreat of thirty days. When the Concordat was signed, he was at once appointed Archbishop of Lyons. In 1803, Pius VII created him Cardinal of St. Maria in Victoria. He was then forty years of age (Lyonnet, *Le Cardinal Fesch,* passim).

still giving Holy Communion at half-past three in the afternoon. Subsequently he proceeded to confirm until five o'clock. The number of men who communicated equalled that of the women, and all did so in a spirit of great faith and recollection.

"It was very cold that day, and it was snowing heavily. The inhabitants of several parishes only reached the place where Confirmation was being administered after walking for three and even four hours, and the church being too small to admit them all, the greater number waited outside without a murmur, though they were exposed to the cold and the snow.

"Many people, especially the young men, went to meet His Eminence, walking a distance of as much as a league, and, at the first glimpse of the approaching carriages, threw themselves upon their knees in expectation of the blessing which His Eminence would bestow upon them as he drove past. The communicants generally numbered two thousand a day, and those who received Confirmation about three thousand."[8]

The manner in which the Cardinal administered both sacraments is curious but most practical and deserves to be recorded. He caused to be made an oblong vessel, a kind of silver-gilt basket capable of holding more than three thousand hosts. From this basket he refilled the ciborium with which he went round the church. The communicants and the candidates for Confirmation were lined up in two rows down the centre of the nave. Such was the concourse that frequently the lines of people stretched out into the porch and even into the square in front of the church.[9] At the conclusion of Mass the multitudes received Confirmation. It is reckoned that in 1807 some

8. *Mélanges de philosophie et de littérature; Nouvelles de Lyon,* t. VII, p. 287; (cité par Lyonnet, *Le Cardinal Fesch,* t. II, p. 76, 77).

9. In the church of Saint-Nizier, at Lyons, the Cardinal communicated, with his own hand, over 1,200 persons (Lyonnet, *op. cit.,* p. 67). It took him three days to administer Confirmation at Bourg and the adjacent district. At Bourg, on May 11, "there was such a concourse in the principal church, which is large enough to make a cathedral, that it could not hold all those who came, so they were ranged in the porch, in the adjacent streets, and even in the main square of the town. The town itself presented the appearance of a church as His Eminence walked down the lines and confirmed in the open air." *(ibid.,* p. 97).

30,000 persons were confirmed, among whom were many young people well on in their teens, and even grown-up men, former revolutionaries who had returned to the Faith of their fathers.

Jean-Marie Vianney was confirmed on the same day as his sister Marguerite, who was nearly twenty. Knowing as we do his tender piety, it is easy to imagine the recollectedness of the young man. Instead of setting out to meet the Cardinal, it is more likely that he and his fellow students remained with M. Balley, to help him in the preparations for the great day. He must have been among those who were the first to receive the Sacrament and within the precincts of the church. He would not be distracted by the sight of the purple robes of the Emperor's uncle, nor by the unaccustomed ceremonies and the singing of the crowd. The archbishop paused in front of him, read a name written on a ticket held by the candidate and anointing his forehead, he pronounced the sacramental words: "John Baptist, I sign thee with the Sign of the Cross and confirm thee with the chrism of salvation, in the name of the Father, and of the Son, and of the Holy Ghost."

Vianney chose the Precursor as his Confirmation patron saint. Henceforth he signed: *Jean-Marie-Baptiste,* or *Jean-Baptiste-Marie,* and throughout his life the Baptist remained one of his favorite saints. Surely the Holy Ghost, "who rested in this just soul, like a fair dove in its nest,"[10] fostered in it all manner of holy desires, thus disposing it for those marvels of grace which were one day to raise the pious youth on the altars of the Church. For the space of two whole years Jean-Marie-Baptiste was to enjoy the sweets of a wonderful interior peace, but at the close of that time a bolt from the blue suddenly changed this happy condition. In the autumn of 1809 a police officer came from Lyons to the farm at Dardilly to deliver a *feuille-de-route,* on which appeared the name of Jean-Marie Vianney.

---

10. An expression of the Curé d'Ars (*Spirit of the Curé d'Ars,* English trans., p. 52).

Chapter 6

THE DEFAULTER OF LES NOËS (1809-1811)

WE NOW come to an incident in the life of our saint about which there was, until quite recently, a good deal of obscurity. The whole episode is somewhat puzzling, but, thanks to unexceptionable documents, we hope to put it in the clearest light possible.

The parish priest of Ecully had secured the insertion of his pupil's name in the list of those who were to be exempted from military service. The law only excepted clerics in major Orders, hence the exception of the seminarists of Lyons was due to a special favor and was merely a temporary concession on the part of the Emperor.[1] In 1809 Napoleon seemed to be at bay. He was simultaneously attacked on both flanks: Austria and Spain, when threatened with disruption and annihilation, appealed to the sword. Spain would have none of the rule of Joseph Bonaparte; the marshals of France were despatched south to enforce that rule. The Emperor marched in person against those whom he held to be his most dangerous enemies. Once again his genius triumphed at Eckmuhl (April 22) and at Wagram (July 6).[2] The eagle, however,

1. When, in 1803, Mgr. Fesch, now a Cardinal, went to Paris to receive the biretta at the hands of his nephew, he paid repeated visits, in February and March, to the Ministry of the Interior, where he saw the counsellor of State Portalis. The purpose of these visits was "now the restoration to the Church of some confiscated sacred edifice, now the exemption from military service of young clerical students of his diocese" (Lyonnet, *op. cit.,* I, p. 225). This makes it quite clear that there was question only of a special and temporary privilege. But the Cardinal was not ignorant of the law of the Church. With a view to obtaining even such partial concessions, he doubtless pleaded the law of clerical immunity, on which the Church has always insisted. The new code, published by Benedict XV, in 1917, lays down that "all clerics are exempt—*immunes sunt*—from military service and all such public duties or offices as are incompatible with their state." *(Canon* 121).
2. In the meantime (July 6, 1809) the Emperor caused Pope Pius VII to be arrested

was showing signs of weariness; the Emperor's star was beginning to pale; he was about to meet with his first reverses. Spain refused to admit defeat and prolonged the struggle until 1814.

Fresh campaigns required fresh levies; but France was exhausted. Previous to 1809 the law was already hard enough, but in that year "it became monstrous, and yet it grew steadily worse until, in order to provide cannon fodder, immature youths were called up as well as men who had hitherto been exempt, or who had bought themselves out."[3] The indignant rationalist who penned these lines never knew of the law of compulsory service for all and died without seeing the far more terrible hecatombs of which we have been the witnesses. In 1809 two classes were called up before their time, and were drafted into the army together with those that had escaped conscription since 1806.

The privilege exempting ecclesiastical students of the diocese of Lyons from military service had not been revoked, hence the summons to the colors of Jean-Marie Vianney and three other seminarists came as a great surprise.

What had happened? Maybe M. Balley had judged it unnecessary that year to remind the authorities at Archbishop's house that young Vianney was pursuing his studies; perhaps the vicar-general forgot to register him among the students of the seminary; the fact remained that the recruiting agents enrolled this conscript of the *classe* 1807 with those of the classes 1810 and 1811. Vianney was informed that he was destined for the army in Spain and must join without delay the drafts then at the depot of Bayonne.

The document summoning him to the colors was forwarded from Dardilly to Ecully. M. Balley was staggered by the suddenness of the blow, and hastened to Lyons to

in the Quirinal and dragged from Rome to Grenoble and from Grenoble to Savona. Napoleon had been excommunicated by a brief of June 12.

3. H. Taine, *Les origines de la France contemporaine,* II, p. 130. To prove the above statement, we need only take the *département* of the Ain, which formed part of the archdiocese of Lyons until 1823, and in which the central figure in this book spent forty years of his life. In 1789 the Ain counted 323 men with the colors, but in 1806 there were as many as 6,764.

explain the situation. The recruiting authorities refused to consider as a seminarist this belated student who lodged with a farmer's family and took lessons at a village presbytery. Besides, his name did not figure on the official list submitted by the authorities of the diocese. The note written by M. Courbon, the Vicar-General, and presented by M. Balley when he made a supreme appeal on behalf of his pupil, came, unfortuntely, too late: nothing more could be done.

In fact, there was nothing else to do but to obey. But how disconcerting was this latest trial! Jean-Marie would soon be twenty-four, though in his studies he had reached no higher standard than that of a boy of fifteen. What prospect had he of ever becoming a priest? Surely this was the end of his hopes; at any rate, he might have been excused had he thought so.

According to the law, it was possible to secure exemption by providing a substitute. Jean-Marie besought his father to pay for such a substitute, this being the only means by which he might proceed with his studies. Matthieu Vianney, who had given but a grudging consent to his son's vocation, at first refused. Had he not already bought out his eldest son François? Impossible to do the same for Jean-Marie. But the farmer's heart was moved by his son's grief and the mother's tears. Putting together what ready money he possessed, he walked the eight kilometers which separated Dardilly from Lyons in order to look for a substitute. "A certain young man," says Marguerite Vianney, "agreed to the bargain for the sum of 3,000 francs, a gratuity of 200 francs, and part of his outfit. However, two or three days later the youth deposited on the doorstep of the Vianneys the sack and the 200 francs which he had received. So Jean-Marie was compelled to obey orders."[4]

On October 26 he entered one of the military depots of Lyons. Though he saw but little of life in barracks, he kept no pleasant memories of it, for he was much shocked

4. *Procès de l'Ordinaire,* p. 1020.

by the bad conduct and the blasphemies of his companions. His ceaseless application to study and his penances had undermined his health. So sudden a change in his mode of life could but increase the slow fever which had been sapping his strength. On October 28 he felt unable to rise. The physician attached to the depot judged his condition grave and had him transferred to the general hospital of the city, where the ward Saint-Roch was reserved for soldiers. "I have only eaten twice of the Government rations,"[5] he often repeated in afterlife in allusion to the two only days he had spent in barracks.[6]

During the fortnight he spent in the hospital of Lyons, M. Balley and his parents and relations of Dardilly and Ecully came to see him. "I was among them," says Marguerite Humbert, his cousin, then seventeen years old, "and I had the happiness of spending part of the evening with him and of sharing his small supper. He practically spoke of nothing but God and the necessity of doing His Holy Will."

On November 12 a draft destined for the army in Spain set out from Lyons for Roanne, where the recruits were to be given some further training. Jean-Marie Vianney, now convalescent, formed part of that draft. But he was too weak to keep in step with his companions, and followed in a conveyance. He had, as yet, received no equipment; the only military object so far issued to him was the regulation sack. The jolting of the car and the cold, which was already fairly sharp, upset him considerably. No wonder he had a relapse. It was a shivering young man that was finally committed to the care of the Sisters of St. Augustine who ran the hospital of Roanne, and there he was obliged to remain for six weeks. He got someone to write home. François, his elder brother, whose favorite he was, set out to visit the invalid, who was clamoring for a sight of him. The anxiety of his parents was so keen that they could not refrain from undertaking the long journey. In vain did Jean-Marie strive to comfort

5. "Je n'ai mangé au gouvernement qu'un pain de munition."
6. Frère Athanase, *Procès apostolique in genere,* p. 196.

them, in vain did he display the most tender affection when the time came for parting; they returned to Dardilly with a heavy heart and a feeling that their boy was lost to them forever.

His mother besought the Sisters to replace her by the bedside of her son. The request was superfluous; the Sisters had been struck from the first by the young recruit, whose courtesy, patience, and gentleness singled him out from among his fellows. When they saw with what devotion he said his beads, they could no longer resist their impulse to spoil him. In this matter we have his own avowal: "I shall never forget the little attentions of which I was the object on the part of all the Sisters at Roanne." "That youth will never make a soldier," the latter said among themselves, and, letting kindness outstrip discretion, they openly lamented the fact that he should have to leave so soon. "But, my good Sisters," he would say, "surely I must obey the law." "You would be more useful to France by your prayers than by going to the war." "I am grateful for what you say, my good Sisters; but I only ask you to remember me hereafter in your prayers."

On January 5, 1810, an orderly of Captain Blanchard informed Infantryman Vianney that he would be one of a detachment that was to set out on the morrow for the Spanish frontier. He was to present himself at the Captain's office at a given hour in the afternoon, there to receive his *feuille-de-route.* Full of anxiety and lost in thought, Jean-Marie set out from the hospital some time before the appointed hour. There was no need to hurry. His way took him past a church. Our seminarist soldier entered to pray; he had so much to confide to Our Lord. "There," he afterwards related, "all my sorrows melted away like snow under the sun." So absorbed was he in his prayers that he lost count of time. When he reached the office he found it closed.

The following day, January 6, the Feast of the Epiphany, Jean-Marie, notwithstanding his weakness, prepared for the journey. At an early hour of the morning he shouldered his sack and took leave of his devoted nurses. "They accompanied him to the outer gate of the hospital and bade him farewell with many tears."[7] Once more he called at the office. Some soldiers on duty informed him that the detachment had set out without waiting for him, and it may be taken for granted that they did not mince words as they explained the situation to him. When the office opened matters only grew worse. Captain Blanchard was very angry and casually mentioned chains and gendarmes. The recruit shook with fear, "for he was wont to lament the fate of the wretched young deserters who, cursing their hard lot, were dragged in chains along the highroads of France."[8] Fortunately a subaltern had the courage to intervene: "Did that poor boy seriously meditate flight? He has only just left hospital and now reports of his own accord." And Blanchard said no more. The *feuille-de-route* was delivered, and the soldier Vianney was told to join at least the rearguard.

He set out alone for Renaison. The pale convalescent had, assuredly, none of the air of an old campaigner. His sack weighed heavily on his shoulders, and his step was far from steady. What chance had he of overtaking the others at their first halt? A great distress stole over his soul. He cried out to God and began to finger his beads. "Never, perhaps, have I said the Rosary with so much confidence," he declared later to some people of Ars.[9]

On this same January 6 his sister Gothon, who had journeyed all alone from Ecully to Roanne, called at the hospital to see him. Grievous indeed was her disappointment on learning of the departure of her poor brother.

In the meantime Jean-Marie was drawing near to the mountains of Le Forez, the aspect of which, smiling and desolate in turn, is the delight of the traveler. However, he had no eyes for these things, for he could scarcely

7. We are able to reconstruct these events with great accuracy, thanks to the reminiscences of the Abbé Raymond, who, in 1843, drew a good deal of information from M. Vianney concerning this incident of his life. The good Abbé's account will be mentioned again later on.
8. Catherine Lassagne, *Petit mémoire,* 3me rédaction, p. 6.
9. "Jamais, peut-être, je ne l'ai récité de si bon courage" (Catherine Lassagne, *id.,* p. 7).

drag himself along from sheer exhaustion. Presently he perceived a coppice which would protect him from the wintry breeze. Stepping off from the main road he walked across the fields to a distance of about a hundred paces, and sat down to rest awhile on the edge of a narrow road leading up to the mountain. "Seated on his sack, and anxious to drive away his sombre thoughts, he began to say his Rosary. Our Lady had ever been his refuge. He now besought her to come to his assistance." "All of a sudden," so he himself related, "a stranger appeared, who asked me: 'What are you doing here? . . . Come with me.' He shouldered my heavy sack, and told me to follow him. We walked for a long time, in the dark, up the tree-clad side of the mountain. I was so tired I could hardly keep pace with him."

The mysterious stranger was none other than a certain Guy, of Saint-Priest-la-Prugne, a village situate in the mountains of the Bois-Noir. In order to avoid conscription, he, with numerous other defaulters, lay in hiding on the wooded heights of Le Forez.[10] Jean-Marie followed the stranger almost mechanically; the only thing he knew was that he was exhausted with fatigue and consumed by fever. He was in need of shelter for the night, and the detachment to which he belonged was by that time far on its way to the frontier.

The two men soon penetrated into broken country and tortuous gorges which formed the narrow bed of the river Crèches then swollen by the rains of winter. Thus they came to the village of Les Noës, which, however, they left on their right to enter the Forest of La Madeleine, on the confines of the Allier and the Loire. At the present time the trees have disappeared, except on the highest peaks of the mountains. At the period of which we write, Les Noës formed an island in a sea of verdure.

---

10. The mountains of Le Forez, La Madeleine, Bois-Noir, and Le Puy de Montoncel (1,292 mètres) were at that period covered with trees, hence all that western district of the *département* of the Loire served for a long time as a refuge for deserters. It was in those mountains that the hero of *Pernette,* the rustic epic of Victor Laprade, lay in hiding:

> "Nos forêts des hauts lieux sont encore insoumises,
> Un conscrit peut y fuir et sauver ses franchises . . ."

The two travelers conversed together. As yet Guy had not made himself known, but by shouldering the sack he won the confidence of Vianney, who hesitated no longer to declare his identity. "You have hardly the look of a soldier," the other remarked.

"Oh, that is true enough, but I must obey."

"If you follow me you can hide in our village, which is completely surrounded by forests."

"Oh no! My parents have been sufficiently worried as it is."

"Do not let that trouble you; there are already a good few in hiding in these parts."

What was he to do? He must stick to his friend, at least for this one night. The morrow would bring counsel; for the moment he would leave himself in the hands of Providence.

The village of Les Noës is situated at 660 meters above sea-level. Guy was familiar with every path and track. They climbed beyond the village until they came to the hut of a sabot-maker, who was known in the district by the nickname of Gustin.[11] The man's real name was Augustin Chambonnière. His young wife shared his lonely life. Guy knocked, whispered his name, and the door opened at once. Young Vianney was faint from hunger and fatigue, so Gustin gave him something to eat whilst his wife prepared the only bed the place could boast. The youth soon sank into a deep sleep. The other three lay down on a layer of straw.

The very next day—it being necessary that he should earn his bread—Guy took his new friend to the mountain hut of Claude Tornaire, for whom they sawed wood for two days. They would have wished to stay longer, but, though there was plenty of work at this season, Claude only consented to keep the stronger of the two. Guy continued to work for Claude, but Vianney was compelled to look elsewhere for employment. He went to a place called

11. Survey maps still show, under the term *Chez Gustin,* a small structure marking the spot where the Chambonnières used to live. The shelter was built with what remained of their house.

Pont, in the commune of Les Noës, where he volunteered to act as schoolmaster. He tendered his services to Antoinette Mivière, now the widow Préfolle, but she was reluctantly compelled to decline his offer, as she already had a teacher.

Things became more and more complicated. Lost in these mountains, the conscript Vianney, without premeditation on his part, was now a defaulter. He presented himself before M. Paul Fayot, the Mayor of the commune. The Mayor, himself a simple farmer, lived, not at Les Noës, but two kilometers higher up, in a hamlet called Les Robins, set on a spur of rock and surrounded by fields.

Paul Fayot is even now remembered at Les Noës as an excellent man. Most of his successors in office have been chosen from among his descendants or his kindred. In the execution of imperial laws, however, the good man had a way of his own. In January, 1810, at the very time Jean-Marie Vianney committed his fate into his hands, the Mayor was hiding two other deserters in one of the outhouses of his farm.[12] The arrival of yet another caused the worthy man but little pleasure. He had a large family to support. From time to time the police searched this wooded district, which teemed with fugitives who, it would almost appear, had given rendezvous to one another in this spot. And it was at his house, the house of the Mayor of Les Noës, that the gendarmes were wont to stop and clink their glasses!

But could he cast adrift this poor lad? As for giving him up to the authorities, the thought never entered his mind, for with respect to military service he shared the opinions of many of his contemporaries.[13] He reassured the youth, whose fate he thus decided. He told him it

12. When he hid a defaulter, the Mayor must have known what risks he ran. A deserter was an outlaw. In virtue of a decree of February 20, 1807, "whosoever knowingly harboured a deserter was liable to a fine of from 1,000 to 3,000 francs and one year's imprisonment. Two years' imprisonment was inflicted if the deserter carried arms and baggage" (Abbé Guilloux, Brandivy, *Revue historique de l'Ouest,* January 1893, p. 35).

13. We must not judge the mentality of Frenchmen of the year 1810 by our own standards. In many parts of the country, notably in Brittany, antipathy to the government of Napoleon showed itself by a refusal to serve in the army. In certain

was too late to think of rejoining his detachment; that he was already considered as a deserter; consequently the only thing to do was to try to escape from the vigilance of the gendarmes. In his determination to see this thing through, the Mayor assigned to him a lodging in a house facing his own—namely, that of his cousin, Claudine Fayot.[14] This good woman was a widow with four children, the eldest of whom was fourteen. She was known for her kindness and charity; nevertheless, the Mayor promised to help her to feed the new guest. Prying inquirers must, however, be put off the scent; hence it was agreed that Jean-Marie Vianney should for the future be known as Jérôme Vincent.

Claudine Bouffaron, the widow of Pierre Fayot, was a woman with a heart of gold: no one ever appealed in vain to her charity. She was thirty-eight years of age. A strenuous worker, she managed her own farm. On baking days one loaf was always set apart for the poor. She was perfectly willing to give shelter to the young man who came to be entrusted to her in so strange a manner.

Besides being very prudent herself, Claudine made sure of the discretion of her children. To this end she made them believe that the newcomer was a cousin who sought the hospitality of her farm. At first the defaulter lay in hiding during the daytime. He spent the first two months in the barn, or in the stable which adjoined the Mayor's house. The patrols, if any called, had no inkling of his presence. By a refinement of precaution, during the whole of eight long weeks Mère Fayot—for so everybody called her—took the fugitive his food in a wooden basket exactly resembling that in which she carried the food for the animals. Only at night did the poor young man dare to leave

---

outlying districts "desertion became the rule, obedience the exception . . . the deserts and woods were more densely populated than the villages" *(Revue historique de l'Ouest,* January 1893, p. 34). "From that date—viz., the year 1806, in fact from the outset, there was extreme repugnance to conscription, a repugnance that could only be overcome by extreme measures." Thus the *préfet* of the Ardèche *(Comptes rendus par les préfets,* 1806, Archives Nationales, F. 7, 3014). The situation did not improve in subsequent years.

14. The house, of very ancient construction, stands to this day. It is occupied by M. Jules Fayot, great-grandson of the widow who took in Jean-Marie Vianney.

his shelter for a breath of fresh air and to mingle with the people of the farm.[15] He would read them the Gospel or the *Lives* of the saints, or tell them some of the beautiful stories he had heard from the lips of M. Balley or those of his mother. All were won by his gentleness and edified by his piety. Jérôme Fayot, fifteen years his junior, still remembered in his extreme old age the gentle blows which "the cousin" dealt him with his hat when the mischievous boy did not behave himself during night prayers.

By means of a rough partition a room had been arranged near a window in a corner of the stable.[16] In this recess Jean-Marie shared a bed with Louis, the eldest of the boys, then thirteen years old. This arrangement, however, did not last; after three nights the lad complained to his mother of his inability to sleep. "'Cousin' does not let me sleep; he spends all his time saying prayers. I do not want to sleep in his bed." Thus Mère Fayot was compelled to make up a second bed in the stable.

Our involuntary defaulter[17] had no wish to be idle; winter had, however, put an end to work in the fields. In these mountains snow usually falls very heavily and covers the frozen ground for a long time. Jérôme Vincent reverted once more to a plan which he had already tried elsewhere: he assumed the role of schoolmaster. At Les Robins the illiterate formed the majority; they should at least learn to read the text of the Mass. So it came about that widow Fayot's children and others, some youths, and even a few adults, frequented the farmhouse to take lessons in reading, writing, and the Catechism. It would seem that no one suspected the real reason of the presence at Les Robins of one who appeared to be nothing more than a farmer.

15. These details—and many others—which have been handed down orally from one generation to another, were given us by M. Jules Fayot, on August 8, 1923, when we called on him accompanied by M. l'Abbé Villand, vicaire of Ars.

16. The stable—a large one—still stands, as well as the barn that then adjoined it. Nothing has been altered since 1810; the wooden partition alone has been removed, but it is easy to trace the low platform on which the bed stood. The wall of soft stone bears the marks of where the bed rubbed against it. Above the stable and the barn is the hayloft which also plays a role in this history.

17. "Réfractaire malgré lui" is the expression of M. l'Abbé Renoud, *Vie du Bienheureux Jean-Marie Vianney,* Lille, Desclée, 1909, p. 1229.

As for Guy, he remained hidden in the forest. Only the Mayor and his sister Claudine knew the stranger's real name. Jean-Marie, however, resolved to bide his time before he ventured to go down to Les Noës, where Mass was said each morning. But what pangs he felt on hearing the bell when he realized that he must not obey its summons! M. Jacquet, who had been in exile during the Revolution, was the parish priest. On weekdays he was in the habit of saying Mass at a very early hour, and Jean-Marie thought that he might take the risk of going to it in the dark, at least once a week. When he noticed that the church was almost empty, he also went to Confession and Holy Communion.

In these lonely mountain villages it is customary for someone to remain at home on Sunday mornings to guard the house; he who is selected for this duty is expected to unite himself in spirit with those more fortunate ones who are able to assist at Mass. The call of the bell, which sounds so sweet in these solitudes, informs the watchers of the part of the Mass at which the priest has arrived. Jean-Marie was for some time official watchman on Sunday mornings.

The road from Les Robins to Les Noës is exceedingly steep and rugged. For this reason Mère Fayot would not take with her her youngest child, Claudine, aged three. Jean-Marie, now twenty-four years of age, looked after that innocent little one with all the tenderness and delicacy that an elder brother might have brought to the task. He listened to her chatter and took part in her games. But during the hour of the parochial Mass he remained very recollected, and when the sacring bell rang he made the child kneel beside him while he explained to her what that bell meant. One day, on their return from Mass, the servant laughingly said to the child: "Claudine, give your cousin a kiss for having looked after you so well." Jean-Marie's extreme delicacy caused him to restrain the little arms that were about to embrace him. Mère Fayot rebuked the maid and bade her not to repeat the jest.

But what a struggle he had with himself whenever he thought of M. Balley, of his books, of the priesthood! When would this trial end? He dared not dwell on these things. All he could do was to throw himself more unreservedly than ever into the arms of divine Providence. God was his only hope, prayer his one refuge. But a secret sorrow was gnawing at the vitals of his soul. What had become of his dear ones at Dardilly? They imagined him to be in the army. Worse than that, by now Captain Blanchard had surely taken action. Probably at this very moment some grave threat was hanging over his father's head, and his mother was torn with grief![18]

At Les Noës also there was cause for anxiety. The good widow Fayot, who had become a second mother to Jean-Marie, and who treated him as one of her own children, was obviously in a decline. With a view to helping her, and in the hope of forgetting his own troubles, the young man threw himself whole-heartedly into the daily task. He had seemingly become just like one of the laborers of

---

18. "That which worried him (the defaulter) was the knowledge that the Government, unable to reach him, was doing all it could to injure his parents. From the depths of the forest his thoughts drifted towards the paternal roof under which, because of him, a bitter struggle was taking place. The various phases of the struggle are instructive and deserve to be described.

"The recruiting officer began by drawing up a list of all the men who had failed to answer the summons to the colors. This he sent to the *préfet.* On receipt of the list, and acting on the instructions of the *directeur général des revues,* dated December 31, 1806, the *préfet* declared the absentees to have defaulted.

"This declaration entailed terrible consequences for the families of the defaulters. The list of the men was put up in the place where they were domiciled, together with the names of their parents. They were given eight days in which to submit. If at the end of this respite they failed to present themselves at the *chef-lieu,* armed men set out for the commune and established themselves on the premises of the deserters, living there at the expense of their fathers, mothers, or guardians, who were held responsible for their conduct. . . .

"Sometimes only one man was despatched to begin with, in the hope that it would suffice to bring about a submission. If this measure failed, the garrison was increased.

"At times the garrison quartered itself in the village or on the neighboring farms. This did not free the families from the appointed indemnity, which had to be paid in advance. In case of non-payment within a given time, the *huissier* made what was called *itératif commandement.* If this second summons produced no effect, he at once proceeded to seize and sell the movables, until the requisite sum was realized." (Generally speaking the animals belonging to the farm were sold) *(Revue historique de l'Ouest,* art. cit., pp. 36-40).

"The 'garrison' withdrew when the defaulters were arrested or made their submission. They likewise departed if the family paid a fine equal to the price of a substitute" (Law of 8 fructidor, year XIII, a. 73).

Les Robins. Lack of food—for, notwithstanding the remonstrances of Mère Fayot, he ate but sparingly—caused him to contract a chill. The following night he was taken with a violent fever, and pneumonia ensued. The good people treated him as best they could, and his robust constitution saved him.

Though careful not to commit any rash act, he began to worry less and less about the possible visits of the gendarmes. He was no longer afraid to attend church on Sundays. Some among the villagers took notice of him and observed that "they had never seen so perfect a young man."

The house of the curé of Les Noës is hard by the church. A little lower down the mountainside, in the direction of the forests of La Madeleine, there stood a small cottage in which lived two sisters, the Demoiselles Dadolle. On coming out from early Mass, Jean-Marie loved to make a brief halt at the home of these devout ladies and to talk with them about holy things.

When the snow had melted and the roads were less impassible, the gendarmes made a reappearance. The men, however, took but little interest in this wooded corner of France. Sometimes the dreaded uniforms appeared suddenly at Les Robins, now by day, now in the nighttime. According to the traditions handed down in the Fayot family, whenever the gendarmes came up at night from La Pacaudière, Saint-Haon-le-Chatel, or Renaison, to inspect the stable of the widow Fayot at Les Robins, the defaulting conscript could not be found. On each of these occasions, as if warned by a mysterious instinct, Jean-Marie had invariably gone into the forest.

One day, however, he was all but caught. It was on a summer's afternoon in 1810, when, without any warning, the gendarmes suddenly appeared on the scene. Jérôme Vincent, who was at work in the neighborhood of the farm, was given the signal agreed upon, for the elder Fayot children and the Mayor's sons had been in the secret for some time. Emergencies like the present one were always to be expected. With this eventuality in view a hole large enough to permit of the passage of a man had been made in the floor of the hayloft, just above the rack from which the cattle fed.[19] The nimble youth had only time to rush into the stable, where he gripped the rack and swung himself into his hiding-place. Here he crouched under a heap of hay, allaying his anxiety by fervent prayer.

Had he been seen by the gendarmes? It was just possible. Anyhow, they submitted the hayloft to a meticulous search, which must have made those who witnessed it tremble. Jean-Marie scarcely dared to breathe, yet he was almost overcome by the fumes of the hay in fermentation, for it was heated by the effluvia of the stable below and by the rays of the sun which beat on the roof above. In addition to all this, whilst in the act of exploring the bundle of hay beneath which he was undergoing such agonies, one of the gendarmes pricked him with the point of his sword. Jean-Marie did not betray himself, though he felt acute pain. When he subsequently related his experiences at Les Noës he avowed that at no time of his life had he suffered so much. In that moment he made a promise to God never to complain. "I have kept my word," he added in all simplicity. Nevertheless, had his martyrdom been prolonged for a few moments, he must have died from asphyxiation. Luckily the gendarmes, who deemed that they had done their duty, went to seek refreshment in the Mayor's parlor, barely a couple of yards away.

About the same period another irruption of the police gave rise to an incident which we only know through the testimony of a most unexpected witness, one always suspect, but who that day spoke the truth. About the year 1850 a poor woman who showed signs of diabolical possession was brought to the village of Ars. She leaped and danced and talked extravagantly. A crowd soon collected around her, when she began to relate the life of every

19. This can still be seen in the stable of Les Robins.

person present. Whilst this was going on, M. Vianney also appeared on the scene. On seeing him, the woman, who was but the mouthpiece of the evil spirit, cried out: "As for you, I have nothing with which to reproach you," adding, however, as if by an afterthought: "Yes; once you took a grape."

"That is true," said M. Vianney, "but by way of payment I placed one sou in the wall at the foot of the vine."

"But the owner of the vine never got it." M. Vianney, in fact, related to us that once he had helped himself to a grape when he was dying of thirst on one of the occasions when he was compelled to hide from the gendarmes.[20]

Towards the middle of 1810 Jean-Marie received news of his family. The physician had ordered Mère Fayot to take the waters at Charbonnières-les-Bains, a watering-place situated some nine kilometers west of Lyons and, consequently, quite close to Dardilly. The good woman was slow in making up her mind, for she liked neither the bother nor the expense of the journey. Jean-Marie insisted on her obeying the doctor's orders. She would thus recover her strength and, incidentally, bring him news of home. Why worry about traveling expenses? He owed her his life; he would lend her money, and she would lodge with his parents. The poor exile wrote a letter home "full of sorrow and repentance,"[21] but without betraying his hiding-place. Claudine Fayot borrowed one hundred francs from him and set out for Charbonnières.[22]

According to the statement of her son Jérôme, "she called at the Vianney's house. When difficulties were made about giving her a lodging she showed Jean-Marie's letter, of which she was the bearer. Mme. Vianney was so

20. Related by Jean Picard, farrier of Ars (*Procès de l'Ordinaire,* p. 1312).

21. "Une lettre de douleur et de repentir" (Abbé Monnin, *Procès apostolique ne pereant,* p. 949).

22. Jean-Marie consistently refused to accept the one hundred francs when Mère Fayot wished to refund them. "My good mother," he wrote to her on November 7, 1823, when he was already Curé d'Ars, "as regards the money you owe me, I make you a present of it with all my heart. I would only ask you, if the good P____ is still alive, to give something to her, asking her to think of me in her prayers; also to the good D____who may be in great want."

overcome at getting news of her son that she wept for joy and embraced my mother. 'You must stay with us,' she exclaimed, 'and we shall take good care of you.' Thereupon she related how one day, feeling very sad, she called upon M. Balley, the parish priest of Ecully, who said to her: 'Do not worry about your son, mother. He is neither dead nor sick. He will never be a soldier, for he is destined to be a priest.'"

Matthieu Vianney was by no means so charmed with the visit. What were these two women talking about? Nor did the perusal of the letter smooth his ruffled feelings. Several fines had already been inflicted on him, and he now expected to have the gendarmes quartered on him. "I shall wrest the last sou from you," Captain Blanchard had threatened when he came to Dardilly to inquire into the fact of the disappearance of the conscript Vianney. "Why should Jean-Marie not march as the others did? Had he done so there would have been none of this bother." "It seemingly gives you no joy," Claudine remarked, "to know that your son is staying at my house."

"Where do you live, that I may go and fetch him?" "If you were to discover the place where I live, I should hide him yet more carefully, for he is worth more than all your possessions," was her reply.

At the end of eighteen days Mère Fayot returned to Les Noës, Jean-Marie's father escorting her as far as Tarare. Great was the youth's joy on hearing from his dear ones, yet this sentiment soon gave place to a fresh fit of depression when he came to think of his father's displeasure, of which he was the cause. He had not foreseen or intended all this. Was he not, in fact, the victim of circumstances? So he began to think how he might extricate himself from this impasse. His keenness to become a priest had not abated. About the middle of September he decided to have his books sent up to his hiding-place. "I am getting behind in my studies," he explained to his "good mother" of Les Noës; "with your permission, I shall study in my room and pay you for my keep." He also asked to be excused from the heavy autumn work.

A letter reached Ecully safely, and the widow Bibost, a trustworthy person who lived close to the presbytery and who had seen Claudine Fayot on the occasion of the latter's stay at the Vianneys', carried over to Les Robins the bundle of books which Jean-Marie had left at the house of M. Melin, his brother-in-law.

He was twenty-four years old when he thus reopened his Latin grammar. However, he was not destined to do much work in his cell of more than monastic austerity. Towards the end of October the same messenger brought him news that sent a thrill through his whole being: he was a free man! He need fear no persecution; Ecully, Dardilly, awaited his return!

Better days had now dawned for France. For once peace reigned throughout the whole of Europe. After crushing Austria, Napoleon had just married the Archduchess Marie-Louise (April 2). A general amnesty signalized the occasion.[23] Captain Blanchard, now less formidable, informed the Vianneys that their son might benefit by the amnesty and even escape conscription altogether if he would furnish a substitute. Thus the very man who only a year ago had threatened to have Jean-Marie taken in chains to the depot of Bayonne was now doing his best to extricate him from his awkward predicament.

The youngest of Vianney's sons, François, called "Cadet," was now in his twentieth year, having been born on October 20, 1790. He had drawn a high number in the military lottery, and his enrollment had been deferred in consequence. Captain Blanchard urged him to come up before the date on which his *classe* would be called; by so doing he would act as the substitute required by the law. Vianney approved of a scheme that would rid him of the plague of the *garnisaires,* who had been his unwelcome guests during the whole period of Jean-Marie's desertion.

The Cadet yielded to persuasion. A deed was drawn

23. An imperial decree of March 25, 1810, extended an amnesty to all defaulters of the classes 1806, 1807, 1808, 1809, and 1810.

up by which he undertook to enlist in place of his brother, and for this service he was to receive three thousand francs, to be paid by Jean-Marie out of his share of the paternal inheritance. The Cadet was assigned to the sixth regiment of the line, then on its way to Phalsbourg, which it reached on August 20. The last that was heard of François—then a corporal—was from Frankfurt-on-the-Main, at the opening of the campaign of 1813. His parents never saw him again, though he apparently did not fall in battle.

There were many tears shed under widow Fayot's roof when the family were informed of the impending departure of Jérôme Vincent. Little Claudine, who loved him tenderly, wept more than the rest. "We shall have no more cousin," she kept saying to her mother. "All those whom he had had the happiness of knowing at Les Noës"[24] learned with regret that they would no longer have before them the example of that perfect young man to urge them on in the practice of virtue. Everybody strove to outdo everybody else in their demonstrations of attachment to his person. Most assuredly M. Jérôme would some day be a priest. Was it premature even now to provide the outfit he would require once he was a parish priest? Mère Fayot forced him to accept the table napkins which had been a wedding present to herself. The Demoiselles Dadolle, who lived next door to the presbytery, made a collection through the parish. A tailor was summoned from Renaison to make a cassock for the future Abbé Vianney, and he was made to wear it for an hour or two, so that his friends of Les Robins might see what he would look like in days to come. "You must come back to us as our parish priest," they told him between their tears and smiles. A kindly old woman brought him thirty francs.

"My good woman," Jean-Marie asked, "have you not run into debt for the purpose of making me so handsome an offering?"

---

24. *Letter* of November 7, 1823, written by the Abbé Vianney, Curé d'Ars, to Mme. Claudine Fayot.

"Oh no! It is the price of my pig. I still have the goat, and that is enough. Please take the money and think of me when you are a priest."

One of the pupils of the former M. Jérôme—maybe one of the Mayor's sons—was anxious to defray the expenses of his journey home.

And so it came about that one winter's morning—probably at the beginning of January, 1811—Jean-Marie took a final and tearful leave of Les Robins. His exile, "the time of his sorrow and banishment,"[25] was at an end. His "good mother," his "beloved benefactress,"[26] would have dearly loved personally to restore to his mother this child of her adoption. But she was too weak for such a journey, so her eldest son Louis, aged fourteen, accompanied his friend to the house at Dardilly.

With transports of joy Marie Vianney clasped to her breast this boy of hers who had endured so much. Her face, too, bore traces of prolonged sorrow. She had wept much in secret. Her heart had been rent by so many hidden emotions. However, her dear priest—for as such she already beheld him—was at long last restored to her affections. How long would the present happiness last?

Jean-Marie had been at home barely a couple of weeks when, on February 8, the saintly woman died at the age of fifty-eight. To the end of his life the memory of his mother remained fresh in the mind of Jean-Marie. He could never speak of her without tears, and he confessed that after he had lost her he felt no longer any attachment to whatever the world might hold.[27]

Jean-Marie never forgot the time he spent at Les Robins. Notwithstanding his promise and his own wishes, he never revisited the village, though until the end of his life he received an occasional visit from some one or other of

25. *Letter* of November 7, 1823.
26. *Ibid.*
27. "Eight years later his father died, July 8, 1819. All his life he occasionally celebrated Mass for the souls of his parents." (Abbé Raymond, *Procès apostolique ne pereant,* p. 533).

those who had been his friends during the time of his banishment. After his death many a pilgrim came from Les Noës to pray at his tomb. In May, 1864, the Abbé Dubois, curé of Fareins, made the following declaration: "A person of Les Noës whom I met last year assured me that the memory of his piety is still fresh in the mind of the inhabitants."[28] Not one of those good people ever raised his voice to accuse Jean-Marie of having deliberately absconded from military service. He himself never thought that he had done anything wrong. In this matter his good faith was absolute, and he believed in a divine intervention on his behalf. Such is the testimony of the Abbé Toccanier, one of his intimates: "I have never heard him say a word either in excuse or justification of his conduct. But I have heard him quoting his own experience as an illustration of some point in his catechetical instructions." "When I was a defaulter I was for ever afraid of the gendarmes. In like manner the sinner, because of the reproaches of his conscience, fears at every moment lest he be overtaken by divine justice."[29] "There never was a note of regret in his words," says the Comtesse Prosper des Garets.[30]

In point of fact, the incident, which happened in 1810, must not be judged according to our standards, but according to those of his contemporaries. The Mayor of Ars, Comte des Garets, puts the occurrence in its true perspective when he says: "Unpremeditated circumstances brought it about that M. Vianney found himself a defaulter."[31] Had Captain Blanchard provided the youthful convalescent with the means of joining his companions, instead of sending him all by himself on the road to Renaison, and if the Mayor of Les Noës, to whom he exposed the plight he was in, had helped him to right his awkward position, there is no doubt that the young

28. *Procès de l'Ordinaire,* p. 1227.
29. *Procès apostolique in genere,* p. 145.
30. *Procès de l'Ordinaire,* p. 895.
31. "As regards the incident of Les Noës, I believe his disobedience to have been apparent rather than real. If he did not join his regiment, it was the result of circumstances rather than of a concerted plan." (Jeanne-Marie Chanay, directress of the Providence of Ars, *Procès de l'Ordinaire,* p. 699).

recruit would have taken part in the Spanish campaign. "He was prevented from doing so by circumstances that appear providential."[32]

32. Baronne de Belvey, *Procès de l'Ordinaire,* p. 130. Mlle. Alix Henriette de Belvey, whose interesting testimony we shall often have occasion to quote, was born at Bourg-en-Bresse, April 22, 1808. "My family," she relates, "owned property at Chaneins, a parish in the neighborhood of Ars. The servants told us wonderful tales about the new curé." The baronne spent the greater part of the year in her château of Montplaisant, in the commune of Montagnat, near Bourg. From the very beginning of the pilgrimage—that is about 1830—her visits to Ars were frequent. M. Vianney was her chief director, and she remained faithful to him until the end.

Chapter 7

THE YEAR OF PHILOSOPHY AT VERRIÈRES (1812-1813)

JEAN-MARIE lost his "poor mother" at a time when he stood in extreme need of her. Who would comfort him now amid the fresh trials that awaited him? He had lost her to whom he had made his first confidences concerning his vocation; the gentle advocate who knew how to soothe the ruffled spirit of his father. However, Matthieu Vianney, thanks, perhaps, to the last wishes of his dying wife, was now no longer opposed to the return of his son to the house of M. Balley.

Though the hour was a sorrowful one, there was much joy at the presbytery of Ecully on Jean-Marie's return. M. Balley had never given up hope. Night after night during the last sixteen months he had prayed for his beloved pupil. A woman of the parish who was all for brevity where prayers were concerned is said to have exclaimed at the sight of Vianney: "At last! Henceforth there will be one *Pater* and one *Ave* less each day."

From now onwards our seminarist resided no longer at his aunt's house, but stayed at the presbytery. The two brothers, Loras and young Deschamps, had returned to the Petit Séminaire. M. Balley was anxious to have Vianney near at hand so as to superintend more closely the young man's studies, which up till then had been somewhat superficial and subject to many interruptions. Vianney, on his part, was able to render a good many services to his old master, for his stay at the presbytery was rather in the nature of a domestic servant. His recreations were spent in working in the garden. He combined the double role of sacristan and altar boy, and accompanied his teacher on the latter's rounds of the parish. Nor were those wasted hours. He was now twenty-four years of age. Time was pressing, and M. Balley was in a hurry to see his pupil ordained. He had him placed on the same footing as the students of rhetoric in the Petit Séminaire. In this way he was in a position to present him for the Tonsure, on May 28, 1811.[1] On that date Jean-Marie took the first step in his ecclesiastical career; he was on the road the end of which was the priesthood. He was still mourning the loss of his mother, yet the day was one of great joy at the presbytery of Ecully.

In M. Balley, Jean-Marie had found an excellent but austere teacher. An old parishioner thus described his curé: "He was a tall man, made, apparently, of nothing but skin and bones. One might have thought that he never ate a square meal." The pupil set himself to copy the penitential life of his master. His daily association with the saintly man was a constant source of edification. If M. Balley was an austere man, his piety was exceedingly simple and tender. Whilst saying Mass he was wont to shed copious tears. Attired in his snow-white surplice, the pupil ministered at the altar and thus learned the manner in which the Sacred Mysteries should be performed.

Whenever he could snatch a few moments from his work in the garden or the church, the Abbé Vianney loved to visit good Mère Bibost, who, for the love of God, attended to his wardrobe, and who, moreover, had a son at the seminary. During the holidays the two youths would meet and converse about that mysterious future which for Vianney had but one luminous summit—the altar.

His obedience was perfect. "At M. Balley's," he used to say: "I never did my own will." His favorite reading was the *Lives* of the saints. A letter of his is still extant, addressed to Jacques Loras, his former fellow-student at Ecully, asking him to oblige him by "fetching from

1. Cf. *Le vénérable Colin,* Lyon, Vitte, 1900, p. 21. In the diocese of Lyons the Tonsure was given to the students of the Petit Séminaire during the year of rhetoric.

M. Ruzand's, the bookseller's, an old volume in folio entitled *'History of the Fathers of the Desert.'*"[2]

During the last term of 1812, M. Balley judged that the moment had arrived when this big student of twenty-six should be subjected to the regular routine of clerical education. At that time candidates for the priesthood were required to do one year of philosophy and at least two years of theology. The unhappy conditions of the times inclined the authorities to leniency.[3]

Jean-Marie was therefore sent to the Petit Séminaire of Verrières, near Montbrison. The house of studies, founded in 1803, was originally nothing more than a presbytery school like that of M. Balley at Ecully. The curé of the place, M. Perier, turned his old house and barn into an improvised school for the training of country lads who showed some signs of a vocation to the priesthood. The undertaking was visibly blessed by God. Very soon the school numbered fifty pupils. A dilapidated house close by was joined on to the presbytery to accommodate the boarders. The boys paid ten francs a month; their board and lodging was in accordance with that modest fee. The dormitory was an attic which was reached by means of a trap ladder. At mealtimes the students filed into the kitchen, where each one was served with a ration of meat and potatoes. Recreation was spent in gathering firewood or repairing the crumbling masonry of the college building. At the time of its erection into a Petit Séminaire, Cardinal Fesch procured somewhat less uncomfortable premises for the students of M. Périer. As

2. *Letter* of February 12, 1810, to "M. Jacques Loras, rue Lainerie, Lyon."

3. The pressing and varied needs of his diocese did not admit of the Cardinal waiting for the time when the young aspirants to the priesthood would have completed their studies. At the end of barely two or three years' theological studies, he ordained them and employed them in the sacred ministry. There was one point only on which he was inflexible—piety. As for knowledge, he was satisfied if their instruction was sufficient—that is, if they could resolve ordinary cases and take counsel when faced with unusual ones.

The Cardinal, however, hoped for better times. "A day will come," so he wrote to M. Courbon, his Vicar-General, "when we shall insist on a four years' course at the Grand Séminaire, for the study of the Sacred Scriptures, theology, liturgy, and canon law. In the meantime we must needs go to the rescue of so many parishes left entirely without priests." (Lyonnet, *Le Cardinal Fesch,* op. cit., II, pp. 394, 395).

early as 1807 one hundred and fifty seminarists were gathered within the new establishment; in 1809 they numbered as many as three hundred and thirteen. That year the devoted curé of Verrières, now utterly worn out, felt compelled to surrender his task to other hands. His place was taken by the Abbé Baron, till then professor of philosophy at the Petit Séminaire of l'Argentière.

In 1811 utter ruin threatened the enterprise; Napoleon took it upon himself to name bishops without the intervention of the Pope. On June 17, in order to insure the concurrence of the French hierarchy, the Emperor convened a national council at the residence of the Archbishop of Paris. The bishops, however, declared that papal bulls were indispensable. Their decision was at variance with the imperial wishes, and punishment was not long delayed. On July 10 a decree dissolved the assembly. At three o'clock on the morning of the twelfth the Bishops of Tournai, Ghent, and Troyes were arrested in their beds and taken to Vincennes. The seminarists of their respective dioceses were summoned to the colors. M. Emery had boldly braved the wrath of the monarch. To punish him a decree of October 20 suppressed the Society of Saint-Sulpice.[4] A decree of November 15 ordered the closure of all Petit Séminaires; their pupils, were they so minded, might attend the classes of the municipal schools.

Although his influence was already on the wane, the Cardinal of Lyons obtained from his nephew a respite for a few months.[5] However, at the end of the scholastic year of 1812 all the Petits Séminaires of the diocese—

4. M. Emery, who died not long afterwards, did not hesitate to say to the Emperor, who, in order to dominate the Pope, claimed to be the sole master of Europe: "That which exists today may not exist always." M. Emery was born at Gex, and is one of the glories of the Diocese of Belley.

5. The Cardinal had incurred the displeasure of Napoleon by definitely taking the part of the Holy See, as he was in duty bound. When he informed the Emperor of the decisions of the Synod, the latter exclaimed: "I will not be beaten." "If you wish to make martyrs," his uncle replied, "begin with your own family. I am ready to seal my faith with my blood, but you must know that so long as the Pope refuses to approve this measure—the appointment of bishops by the metropolitan alone—I, in my capacity as metropolitan, shall never appoint any of my suffragans. I will even go further and say that, were one of my suffragans to attempt to institute a bishop in my province, I should instantly excommunicate him" (Lyonnet, *op. cit.*, II, p. 336).

Verrières, la Roche, Saint-Jodard, l'Argentière, Alix, Meximieux—were compelled to close their doors. Twelve hundred students were thus cast adrift. The indefatigable M. Courbon, whose special task it was to watch over educational establishments, succeeded in organizing day-schools in those towns which already possessed public colleges, such as Bourg, Belley, Villefranche, Roanne and Saint-Chamond. At one moment the suggestion was made to the archiepiscopal council that the youths should be sent to the State schools. "No, no!" exclaimed the Cardinal. "I do not wish to incur damnation. Nothing on earth will ever induce me to subject my children to the rule of the University. The University is just a big barracks: there they drill soldiers; what I want is priests."[6]

Impelled by sentiments such as these, the Cardinal took a bold step: he reopened Verrières. The event, however, was kept as quiet as possible. This was comparatively easy, for the place was isolated and far removed from the main roads. Even should the police make inquiries, it could always truthfully be said that the house at Verrières was an annexe of the Grand Séminaire of Saint-Irénée, which that year could not accommodate all the candidates for Holy Orders belonging to the diocese of Lyons. So it came about that in the course of October and November, 1812, all those students who had finished their classical studies were sent to Verrières. Their number was about two hundred. They were sent to Verrières for the year of philosophy, prior to their admission to Saint Irénée. Notwithstanding his scanty literary equipment, Jean-Marie was permitted to attend this obligatory course.

M. Baron divided his philosophers into two sections, one of which was entrusted to the Abbé Grange, and the other to the Abbé Chazelles. Four masters at least were really required, but they were not to be procured. Jean-Marie was assigned to M. Chazelles' class, in which he was senior to all, even his professor being his junior. But

---

6. Lyonnet, *op. cit.*, II, p. 436.

this circumstance did not disturb Vianney, for, if he had not made much progress in human learning, he had made great strides in the virtue of humility, which is the science of the saints.

The very first time he was questioned in class he was unable to grasp the purport of the master's query, and had perforce to remain silent. There was a burst of laughter from the whole class; boys at that age are ever merciless. According to the practice which obtains at seminaries, the professor put his question in Latin. Now our poor philosopher experienced immense difficulty in translating his lesson, line by line, from the pages of his textbook. True, not a few of his fellow-students were scarcely more advanced than he. In the end it was deemed best to detach from M. Chazelles' class a group of seven pupils, who were taught in French.[7]

With the best of wills, the saintly youth understood but little of dialectics; but *majors* and *minors* were not indispensable in order to train in logic a mind which was blessed with abundant practical common sense and sound judgement. On June 13, 1813, at the end of seven or eight months at Verrières, he wrote to his "most dear father," "As regards my studies, things are slightly better than I had expected," for at first he had greatly feared lest he should be wholly incapable of understanding anything at all. For all that, he remained "an exceedingly poor student—un *élève d'une faiblesse extrême.*"[8]

God willed that he should be like St. Paul—"ignorant of the artifices of human eloquence." Had his profound humility not silenced him, he might have said to the more successful students of his class what was said by another saint, the Italian poet Jacopone da Todi: "I abandon to you your syllogisms, the tricks and subtleties of speech. I abandon to you the art of which Aristotle holds the secret. A simple and pure mind needs not the help of

7. Abbé J. B. Tournier, curé of Grand-Corent (Ain), a former fellow-student of M. Vianney at Verrières. To him we owe most of the details concerning this period of the saint's life.
8. *Ibid.*

philosophy; it finds itself in the presence of God without such means."[9]

Little understood of men, Jean-Marie turned to the unfailing Friend who hears our silence and listens to the innermost yearnings of our hearts. In the chapel, at least, he was free to pour out his soul in sighs and tears. Though his beloved mother reposed in the little cemetery on the hillside above Dardilly, he yet felt that she was closer to his soul now than when she was alive, so that he could make her the confidant of all his anxieties. Some of his companions laughed at him; his teachers were not lavish with their encouragements. "At Verrières," he confessed later on, "I had somewhat to suffer." How much charitable reticence there must have been in that "somewhat" as uttered by him! Long visits to the oratory revived his spirits. Since, alas! he was now deprived of that which nothing on earth can replace—a mother's love—his devotion to Mary became the more tender and filial. This devotion prompted him to consecrate himself to Mary as her slave, so that he might wholly belong to his great Queen.[10]

It would be untrue to say that at Verrières Jean-Marie was subjected to persecution or was a prey to loneliness. "The more serious and fervent among the students took him as a model," says one of his former companions; "they enjoyed being in his company because he habitually conversed with them about God and the Blessed Virgin."[11] In this way he won the friendship of Marcellin Champagnat, the future founder of the Little Brothers of Mary. Nor was Marcellin considered a genius. He was seventeen years old when he began the study of Latin. After a year's effort he was dismissed as being quite incapable, when, like Jean-Marie, he made a vow to go on pilgrimage to the sanctuary of La Louvesc. A second time he was admitted at Verrières. After five years of relentless toil he began his course of rhetoric, which he was made

9. *Spiritual Poems,* I, sat. 1.
10. *"L'esclavage de Marie,"* is a devout invention of Bl. Louis Marie Grignon de Montfort.
11. Abbé Etienne Dubouis, curé of Fareins *(Procès apostolique ne pereant,* p. 880).

to do twice over. At the beginning of the school year 1812 he found himself in the philosophy class by the side of the pupil of M. Balley. Marcellin was twenty-three, Jean-Marie twenty-six and a half. Their age, the similarity of their trials, a like desire of holiness, all combined to make them fast friends.[12]

At Verrières opportunities were not wanting for the practice of heroic virtue. Even though the accommodation had become less inadequate, life was still hard, the meals were most frugal, and discipline was very stringent. Not only did he not complain, but, on the contrary, Jean-Marie was perfectly happy. He was never known to fail in the discharge of his duties. However, no one took any special notice of him; he was too fond of obscurity and self-effacement for that. Nothing leads us to believe that he was ever singled out as a model. Failure in his studies led to his being underestimated. We gather this from the marks that were given him at the close of the year:

Application ....Good
General knowledge ....Very weak
Conduct ....Good
Character ....Good

Good educationalist as he was, M. Baron was not necessarily a prophet. He could only judge by outward appearances; thus he was unable to appreciate the exquisite treasure that Providence had momentarily entrusted to his keeping.

12. *Cf.* Mgr. Laveille, *Un condisciple et émule du Curé d'Ars, Marcellin Champagnat,* Paris, Téqui, pp. 34-36.

Chapter 8

AT THE GRAND SÉMINAIRE OF LYONS (1813-1814)

JEAN-MARIE was none too happy at Verrières. The philosophy of Descartes was taught there, after the fashion of the old Sorbonne. It appeared to him cold and insipid and remained all but unintelligible as far as he was concerned. He was glad, therefore, in July, 1813, to return to Ecully, where he found his old master, who also was happy to see him again. They spoke of the hope they both cherished. The ascent to the priesthood might be laborious, but already the summit appeared less remote. Once a priest he would breathe more freely. The sacred ministry would be so different from his arid class-books. Without loss of time, M. Balley set himself to prepare his pupil for the Grand Séminaire. Doubtless the vacation of 1813 was the pleasantest, even as it was the last, holiday the Abbé Vianney enjoyed in all his life.

The Grand Séminaire Saint-Irénée stood in the Place Croix-Paquet, at the foot of the Croix-Rousse. During the Revolution it was in turn used as an armory and as a military hospital, but on November 2, 1805, it was restored to its original purpose. The building was an immense, three-storied structure. The garden was intersected by a beautiful avenue of lime trees. The Sulpicians had been withdrawn from the direction of the establishment two years earlier, having been expelled from Lyons by the decree of December 26, 1811, which took from the sons of M. Olier the government of all French seminaries. The protests and supplications of Cardinal Fesch were of no avail, Napoleon maintaining the same inflexible attitude towards him as he did towards the other bishops.

The Sulpicians were replaced by some young priests, natives of the diocese, but the hearts of the seminarists remained attached to their former teachers. Complaints were not wanting: the new masters lacked experience; their school days were too well remembered. They were, for all that, excellent men.

M. Gardette was the new superior. Ordained during the Terror, he had been a prisoner in the dreaded hulks of Rochefort. His piety was profound, but, possibly by reason of his past sufferings, his manner was dour. He was a great stickler for an exact observance of the rule. The director of the seminary was the gentle, learned and distinguished M. de la Croix d'Azolette, who was to become Archbishop of Auch. M. Menaide, the most unassuming of men, was the procurator. The professor of Holy Scripture and Liturgy was M. Mioland, a young priest of twenty-five, gentle and courteous in manner, and destined to become Archbishop of Toulouse. M. Cholleton and M. Cattet, who had only just left Saint-Sulpice, respectively taught dogmatic and moral theology. All these professors were solidly learned, and even brilliant. With a view to forming the seminarists of Lyons in piety no less than in learning, they endeavoured to keep alive the Sulpician method.

The Abbé Vianney entered the seminary in October. Among his companions he found Marcellin Champagnat, Jean-Claude Colin, the future founder of the Society of Mary, and Ferdinand Donnet, who was to live to the age of eighty-seven, and die as Cardinal Archbishop of Bordeaux.

Some of the ordinances of the rule must have proved embarrassing to the new grand-séminariste, and no one has told us how he acquitted himself. "Whenever His Eminence visited the seminary he never failed to urge the importance of ecclesiastical deportment. He wished his priests to cultivate at all times a neat and becoming outward appearance. To this end he prescribed the use of powder for the hair and the wearing of buckled shoes.

He would also have liked to see long cloaks for outdoor wear, such as those worn by the seminarists in Paris."[1]

The scholastic year 1813-1814 opened on or about All Saints' Day, and was preceded by the customary retreat. A future canon theologian of Belley, the Abbé Jean-Augustin Pansut, who was finishing his theological course that year, still cherished in his extreme old age a remembrance of the newcomer whose appearance struck him at once. Jean-Marie may have loved silence and retirement, but he could not long remain unnoticed. He was now twenty-seven years of age: his whole person spoke of asceticism, penance, modesty, and recollection. Had the two hundred and fifty seminarists who were his schoolfellows been so many Vianneys, the seminary of Saint-Irénée, at the time of recreations and walks, would have been a faithful replica of a Trappist monastery.[2]

There were witnesses who were afforded a yet closer observation of so edifying an existence. Only with difficulty could Saint-Irénée accommodate its numerous pupils. The larger rooms had perforce to be shared by several students. Thus it came about that M. Vianney shared his with the Abbé Bezacier, whom he had not met before, and with the Abbés Declas and Duplay, whom he had known at Verrières. "His regularity was absolute," M. Bezacier stated later on. "Only a few steps away from our room was a window from which we might watch the march-past of a regiment of Swiss soldiers in the pay of France, and listen to their splendid band. Several seminarists yielded to the temptation to see and hear; as for the Abbé Vianney, I cannot recollect that he ever made a movement."

M. Declas, then a Marist, said of him to his nephew, the Abbé Etienne Dubouis: "I used to know him well; he is a saint."

It might be thought that there was a certain amount of singularity about Vianney. Far from this being so, there is a unanimous verdict that "there was nothing extraor-

1. Lyonnet, *Le Cardinal Fesch,* II, p. 397.
2. *Procès de l'Ordinaire,* p. 1272.

dinary about his conduct; he was perfectly simple."

Unfortunately, on the authority of M. Bezacier, "the result of his studies was nil, the cause being his inadequate knowledge of Latin. More than once I explained things to him, but he did not seem able to grasp them; his application, nevertheless, was unfailing."[3]

"We all knew," says M. Pansut, "that the Abbé Vianney had followed no regular course of studies, so no one was surprised at his ill-success. If, subsequently, he wrought real miracles in the cure of souls, it was owing to his persevering toil and, above all, to the graces with which God visibly favored him.[4]

M. Gardette, the superior, must surely have taken special interest in this old seminarist, with whose piety and heroic application to work he was not unacquainted. He assigned to Jean-Marie a tutor, in the person of Jean Duplay, one of the best students at the seminary. Vianney was less overawed by a fellow-student, who questioned him in French, thus enabling him to return in the same tongue answers which, besides being accurate, bore the hallmark of good sense.

M. Mioland, one of the professors, seeing his backwardness, was kind enough to give him a few private lessons. He based his explanations on a very clear and well written French textbook, *Le Rituel de Toulon.*[5] This teaching was more within the grasp of M. Vianney—by its help he might have acquired sufficient professional knowledge at the seminary itself. However, Latin was the official language of the classroom as well as of the examination hall, so the public lectures were wasted on him,[6] and after a certain number of experiments the masters refrained from questioning him.

How keenly he must have suffered when he realized the futility of his efforts. There was no one within the

---

3. *Procès de l'Ordinaire,* p. 1273. The manual then in use at Saint-Irénée was that of Bailly: *Theologia dogmatica et moralis ad usum seminariorum,* auctore L. Bailly.
4. *Procès de l'Ordinaire,* p. 1620.
5. This manual is the work of Mgr. Joly, who became Bishop of Toulon in 1738.
6. "He understood Latin insufficiently and spoke it with yet greater difficulty " (Abbé Dubouis, *Procès apostolique ne pereant,* on the authority of P. Declas, his uncle).

walls of Saint-Irénée who longed for the priesthood as he did, yet no one seemed so far removed from the desired goal. But who could describe his anguish when, after the lapse of some five or six months, the authorities came to the conclusion that there was no hope of his succeeding, and, in consequence, asked him to leave the seminary?[7]

He was dismissed! he whose relics were one day to be solemnly censed by the Supreme Pontiff under the dome of St. Peter's in Rome! This was the bitterest trial of his whole life. Later on he loved to speak of his sufferings and trials; but never, it would seem, did he allude to this dismissal.

"Many among his companions were grieved at his departure from the Grand Séminaire." As for himself, he sub-

---

7. Following a statement of M. Monnin *(Le Curé d'Ars)* it is commonly asserted that Jean-Marie Vianney was rejected after the preliminary examination which preceded admission, so that he was compelled to return at once to the presbytery of Ecully. Now, apart from the assertion of M. Monnin, all our information goes to prove definitely that the examination at which the saint failed took place in the course of the scholastic year 1813-1814. The result was that he left the Grand Séminaire at the end of the first term.

1. "At the end of five or six months," says M. Bezacier, then curé of Lescheroux, in the Diocese of Belley, "the directors, thinking he would fail, asked him to leave. He returned to M. Balley, curé of Ecully" (*Procès de l'Ordinaire,* p. 1273).

2. "My uncle and many seminarists were very much grieved to see him leave the seminary, and very happy to see him come back to be ordained priest with them," says the Abbé Dubouis, nephew of Père Declas (*Procès apostolique ne pereant,* p. 881).

3. The Abbé Raymond is even more explicit: "In the holidays which followed the year of philosophy, M. Balley gave him some first notions of theology. About All Saints' Day, 1813, he entered the Grand Séminaire of Lyons with the others. The first examination took place at Easter, when he failed; so he returned to M. Balley in order to complete his theological studies in French" (*Procès de l'Ordinaire,* p. 275).

What is it that led M. Monnin astray? The mistake, which mixes up the chronology of at least two years, arises from an alteration made in the fragmentary manuscript *Life* left by the Abbé Raymond (p. 60). M. Raymond writes: "After *two or three months* of careful teaching on the part of the master, and persevering efforts on the part of the pupil," M. Balley caused Jean-Marie Vianney to return to Saint-Irénée. M. Monnin transcribed the passage thus: "*After one or two years* of careful teaching . . .," etc. Then the Abbé Raymond goes on to say that when Vianney felt he could not understand the Latin lectures, the Abbé Mioland became his tutor, explaining theology in French. However, "when the time came for his first examination, he was unable to give satisfactory answers." M. Monnin, having retarded Vianney's entrance at Saint Irénée by as much as a year, or even two years, could no longer get his dates right, since the dismissed seminarian had come back for his ordination to the subdiaconate in July, 1814. Hence he supposes a first examination—which proved a failure—at the moment of Vianney's admission into the Grand Séminaire, and another at the presbytery of Ecully, by which he was enabled to return to Saint-Irénée until the time of his ordination to the priesthood. We shall see that the course of events was quite different.

mitted to the decision without a murmur. Fifty years later Cardinal Donnet, one of his confidants of those early days, declared that "the remembrance of his humility and the sound common sense of the words I had the good fortune to exchange with him on that occasion have remained deeply stamped upon my mind."

What was to become of him? The door of the sanctuary seemed definitely closed to him. Should he return to the world when he had but one desire—to give himself to God? In his distress Jean-Marie bethought himself of a companion of his childish years, one Jean Dumond, who, on November 27 of the preceding year, had taken the habit of the Brothers at the Petit Collège, their noviciate house at Lyons. A new vision took shape in the mind of the dismissed seminarian—he would exchange cassock for cassock; in place of the one he now wore he would don that of a Brother. Without so much as consulting M. Balley, he left Saint-Irénée to knock at the door of the Petit Collège, hard by the cathedral church of St. John. "I do not know enough Latin to become a priest," he confided to his friend, Jean Dumond, now Brother Gérard: "I shall come here to become a Brother." With this resolution in his heart he returned, for a few days as he thought, to the presbytery at Ecully.

M. Balley received him with open arms, let him weep on his breast, and listened to his tale of woe. Then he spoke in his turn, declaring once more that God had singled him out for the service of the altar. "Write to your friend at Lyons," he added, "not to breathe a word of what you told him, and say that I want you to go on with your studies." In this way it was decided to make yet another trial.

Master and pupil first had recourse to prayer, and then took up the textbook. The study of the *Rituel de Toulon* was resumed. M. Balley varied French with Latin, for he deemed it necessary that Jean-Marie should be capable of translating at least the most elementary notions into the language of the Church. As for the rest, the Holy Ghost, who dwelt in this chosen soul, would assuredly supply whatever might be wanting. Still, how was all this to be realized? The person most concerned knew not, consequently he experienced frequent periods of acute distress. His deep piety, however, sustained him, and divine help was given him. "When I was still at my studies," he confessed later on, "I was almost in despair; I knew not which way to turn. I can still see a certain spot at Ecully, near the house of La Bibost, where I heard the voice as of one speaking into my ear: 'Do not fret, you will one day be a priest.'"

In the meantime the date of the ordination was approaching. The examinations prescribed by the canons began towards the end of May. M. Balley decided to present his pupil. The need of priests had not grown less; the candidate had entered upon his twenty-ninth year; three years previously he had received the Tonsure. If his case were not quite hopeless it was high time that he should receive at least the minor Orders. All these reasons appeared conclusive to M. Balley.

Three months had hardly elapsed since his departure from the Grand Séminaire, when the Abbé Vianney reappeared among his former companions, who rejoiced to see him. He took the last place and awaited his turn. On entering the examination room he found himself confronted by a venerable jury, presided over by Canon Bochard, the Vicar-General, and composed of the most learned and most distinguished among the priests of the diocese of Lyons. Jean-Marie was overawed from the very first, but he lost his nerve completely when he heard his name called. He could not grasp the meaning of the Latin questions, and was confused in his answers, which were found unsatisfactory.

The examiners were themselves nonplussed. They were fully conscious of the wisdom and prudence of M. Balley, nor were they ignorant of the encomiums he had bestowed upon the keenness and piety of his pupil. Should they definitely reject this poor seminarist, so full of good will, or should they simply keep him waiting? In the end they came to the conclusion that it was best to decline all responsibility in so perplexing a situation. If the Abbé Vianney should succeed in finding a bishop willing to accept him, he was to be at liberty to seek admission in another diocese.

That same evening Jean-Marie returned to the presbytery of Ecully. M. Balley realized the peril. The very next morning he hastened to Lyons. He began by taking counsel with the priest who had heard Jean-Marie's first Confession and given him his first Communion. M. Groboz, now Secretary-General at the archiepiscopal curia, accompanied M. Balley to the office of the Vicar-General, who had been one of the examiners of the preceding day. The parish priest once more spoke of his high esteem for his pupil, the least learned, maybe, but assuredly the most devout of all the seminarists of Lyons. M. Groboz added his own impressions and reminiscences. M. Bochard allowed himself to be persuaded, and promised to reconsider the matter. Better still, at the earnest request of M. Balley, he promised to visit the presbytery of Ecully on the following day, and to bring with him the Superior of the Grand Séminaire. Thus they both would see the unhappy aspirant to Orders in his familiar surroundings.

This arrangement, which could only have been inspired by their kindness, greatly reassured Jean-Marie, so that "he gave very good and satisfactory answers to all the questions put to him." Such is the testimony of M. Bétemps, Canon of Saint-Jean of Lyons, and an old friend of M. Balley. After the death of M. Balley, Canon Bétemps acted, for a few weeks, as confessor to our saint. M. Bochard carried away from the presbytery of Ecully a very favorable impression of Jean-Marie; however, it was not for him to take a final decision.

After the sanguinary battle of Leipzig (October 20, 1813), France was invaded by the allied armies of Russia, Austria, Germany, Sweden, England, and Spain. On April 11 of the following year Napoleon signed his abdication. The fallen Emperor's mother and uncle, Cardinal Fesch, found a refuge near the saintly Pontiff, Pius VII. In the absence of His Eminence, the first Vicar-General,

M. Courbon, governed the Diocese of Lyons. It was he who decided the fate of M. Vianney. There were not wanting those who pointed to the fact that the pupil of M. Balley only knew his native tongue, and that there was little hope that he would ever acquire a knowledge of Latin. The Vicar-General inclined towards leniency. Could the Archbishop himself be considered hard when, barely two years before, at Christmas, 1812, in order to guard them from the danger of conscription, His Eminence called to Holy Orders all those who were in their first year of theology—and they were many—and likewise those who were more advanced in their studies but had not yet received the subdiaconate?[8] M. Courbon, a simple and unsophisticated man, was content to ask: "Is the Abbé Vianney pious? Has he a devotion to Our Lady? Does he know how to say his Rosary?"

"Oh yes! he is a model of piety."

"A model of piety! Very well, I summon him to come up for ordination. The grace of God will do the rest."[9]

Never in all his life was M. Courbon better inspired.

---

8. "These students, therefore, were not submitted to the counsel of the directors, nor did they undergo any preliminary examination. The Cardinal declared that if a student had reached his twenty-first year but refused to present himself for the subdiaconate, he would by that simple fact be dismissed from the seminary. This meant that he would have to serve with the colors" *(La vérité sur le Cardinal Fesch, ou réflexions d'un ancien Vicaire-General de Lyon,* Lyon, Lesne, 1842, p. 164). This wholesale call to Holy Orders provoked a spirited protest on the part of the Superior of Saint-Irénée, M. Gardette, but his objections were overridden. Napoleon was away in Russia, and "His Eminence had every reason to fear lest a lost battle should be made the pretext for summoning to the colors all the young men not yet ordained." *(Ibid.,* p. 166).
9. Abbé Toccanier, *Procès de l'Ordinaire,* p. 115.

Chapter 9

SUBDIACONATE, DIACONATE, PRIESTHOOD (1814-1815)

BY MEANS of humiliations and sufferings, the divine Artist had now sufficiently molded and embellished the soul of Jean-Marie Vianney. The hour of its final consecration had struck. It was with unutterable thankfulness that the Abbé Vianney learned that on July 2, the feast of the Visitation of Our Lady, he was to receive minor Orders and the subdiaconate. The authorities of the diocese had granted a dispensation from the canonical interstices. At this glorious news the presbytery rang with a joyful *Te Deum.*

A month before the date of his ordination, Jean-Marie returned to the seminary, to take part in the preliminary retreat and to receive the necessary instructions regarding the ceremonies of the day and the mysterious powers with which he was to be invested.

At last the morning of July 2 dawned upon the world. Clothed in his snow-white alb, the candidate took that symbolic step which severed him for ever from the pursuits of a purely secular life. The ceremony took place in the cathedral of Saint-Jean. Marcellin Champagnat, the beloved fellow-student of Verrières, had received the subdiaconate at Grenoble, at the hands of Mgr. Simon, on the preceding January 6. Jean-Claude Colin had been kept back on that earlier date by his scruples. He was now by the side of M. Vianney. Mgr. Simon came over from Grenoble to hold the ordination.

"I had the happiness of being close to M. Vianney on that morning," says the Abbé Pierre Millon, curé of Bény.

"It was the custom to return in procession from the cathedral to the seminary. I was struck by the enthusiasm with which he sang the *Benedictus,* our processional hymn. His face was radiant. Moved by a presentiment, I applied to him the verse: *Et tu puer propheta Altissimi vocaberis!* saying to myself: 'He is less learned than many of his companions, but he will do far more than they in the sacred ministry.'"[1]

M. Balley had made himself responsible for his protégé; consequently Jean-Marie was entrusted to his care during the whole of the scholastic year 1814-1815. Master and pupil had reason to rejoice at this arrangement, for the year was a disastrous one for the seminary. Recollection was rendered all but utterly impossible, yet without it there can be neither application to study nor formation of character.

If we may believe a contemporary, the news of the Emperor's abdication was received at Lyons "with delirious joy. People thought that at last the iron age would be succeeded by that golden era so enthusiastically sung by the poets."[2]

Whilst Napoleon set out for his place of banishment at Elba the unfortunate Cardinal Fesch who, assuredly, deserved a kindlier fate, wandered from Nimes to Montpellier, from Montpellier to Blois, and from Blois to Bourges. He even returned to Lyons for a few days, but left again on April 27. His wanderings only ended when he reached Rome, where the Pope received him with infinite kindness.

On April 14, hearing that Louis XVIII had been proclaimed King of France and Navarre, the Chapter of Lyons, in the absence and without the knowledge of the archbishop, commanded that the *Te Deum* be sung in the cathedral and in every church of the diocese. M. Groboz, first secretary at archbishop's house and a great friend of M. Balley "allowed himself to be carried away by his

1. *Procès de l'Ordinaire,* p. 1281.
2. Lyonnet, *Le Cardinal Fesch,* II, pp. 513, 517.

old monarchical ideas and his memories of the *émigration.*" In consequence, his exaltation exceeded that of all others. The seminarists followed his example. All those youthful heads were in an indescribable state of ferment. Under the limes of Saint-Irénée there was more talk of politics than of theology. Officially, the Cardinal was still supposed to rule his diocese from Rome, where he now resided. But his possessions had been sequestrated and his authority was held to be at an end. However, an unforeseen event happened. In the first days of March, 1815, it was rumored that the dethroned Emperor had landed on the soil of France. His progress was as rapid as the lightning. On the tenth he entered Lyons in triumph. Several priests were thrown into prison for their legitimist sentiments. On May 26, amid the ringing of all the bells, Cardinal Fesch re-entered his "good city" of Lyons. His stay was of but three days. On the twenty-ninth he left the town never to return.

On the eve of his departure he paid a visit to the seminary. We have an account of the incident, written by a contemporary, in the affected style of the period: "Numerous complaints had reached His Eminence of the ultra-royalist spirit prevalent in the house. The police knew it, and had a mind to take proceedings. Documents were in their possession that jeopardized the very existence of the establishment. Carried away by their fevered imaginations and with an utter disregard of consequences, several young hotheads gave their names to a legitimist federation which was being organized in the mountains of Le Forez. They also refused to sing the *Domine salvum fac imperatorem Napoleonem,* as had been prescribed.

His Eminence was not prepared, for the sake of a handful of foolish persons, to sacrifice an establishment on which he had lavished so much care and of which there was imperative need. What would become of the diocese if the source of the priesthood were to be choked? Accompanied by M. Courbon and M. Bochard, His Eminence went to address a few words of peace and counsels of moderation to the young theologians who had suffered from influences that were gravely detrimental to their vocation. When the young men espied from a distance the scarlet cassock of the prelate they at once guessed the purpose of his visit. Some, full of alarm, fled to their rooms, others kept apart, and some muttered in a low voice. Not without difficulty did the Vicar-General at last succeed in collecting and calming a certain number of the students. The prelate saw at once that it was useless to reason with these hotheads, so, after briefly exhorting them to be wise and prudent, he withdrew, more than ever despairing of his nephew's cause.

Whilst the archbishop was entering his carriage (it was a miserable hackney coach, well in keeping with his present distress), one of the cassocked royalists chalked upon a panel of the conveyance the slogan of 1814: *Vive le roi!* The Cardinal crossed the whole city with this singular inscription upon his carriage door—an inscription that can only be described as seditious for a prince of the imperial family, who recognized no emblem save that of the eagle and the trophies.[3]

As he set out for Paris, on May 29, little did the Cardinal suspect that everything hung in the balance. On the evening of Waterloo, June 18, the eagle fell wounded unto death. The news of the disaster reached Mgr. Fesch at Paris. He fled at once to Rome, where twenty-five years later, May 13, 1839, he died a holy death.

There is no cloud so dark as not to have a silver lining. Gentle Vianney was never mixed up in the excitement that swayed his fellow-seminarians. Wise M. Balley, who knew of the events that took place at the Séminaire, must indeed have praised divine Providence for that wretched examination, which the year before sent back to his presbytery the last and yet the most deserving of all the inmates of Saint-Irénée.

Vianney returned to the seminary towards the end of May, 1815, to prepare for the diaconate. He kept aloof from all discussions, and created a solitude within his

3. Lyonnet, *Le Cardinal Fesch,* II, pp. 578-580.

own soul, which he would not suffer to be disturbed. On June 23, the eve of the feast of his patron saint, Mgr. Simon, Bishop of Grenoble, raised him to the diaconate in the cathedral of Saint-Jean of Lyons. The spirit of strength descending upon him as the eagle swoops down upon its prey, filled every recess of his soul already so full of courage and generosity.

No sooner had he received the diaconate than there was question of raising him to the priesthood. This unlooked for favor was due, no doubt, to the efforts of his devoted teacher and to the renown of his own virtues.

So he underwent yet another canonical examination at the presbytery of Ecully, in the presence of M. Bochard, the Vicar-General. The examiner noted with satisfaction that since the previous year "our theologian" had made real progress. For more than an hour the learned examiner questioned M. Vianney on the most thorny cases of moral theology. He was satisfied with his replies, nay, he expressed surprise at their clearness and precision. So it was decided that after a few days' retreat the new deacon should go to Grenoble to be ordained priest. His classmates, the Abbés Pansut, Bezacier, Colin, and Champagnat were to be raised to the priesthood only on July 22 of the following year.[4]

On Wednesday, July 9, the Abbé Vianney presented himself at the office of M. Courbon, who delivered to him his letters testimonial. These letters were to the effect that the Bishop of Grenoble was empowered to ordain him for the diocese of Lyons. One reservation only was made: that the young priest would not receive his faculties for hearing Confessions until later, and then at the discretion of his ordinary. Verily, the thoughts of men are not the thoughts of God, (*Is.* 55:8) for the timid deacon who that day set out for Grenoble was destined to spend

---

4. The author of the *Vie du Vénérable Colin* (Lyon, Vitte) after stating (p. 24) that Jean-Claude Colin was ordained deacon by Mgr. Simon, errs when he adds: "He had by his side two young abbés, who also received the priesthood with him, namely, MM. Jean-Marie Vianney and Marcellin Champagnat."

three-fourths of his life in the confessional. "The Church," M. Courbon remarked as he put his name to the document, "is in need not only of learned priests, she wants, above all, holy priests."

Under the blazing August sun the Abbé Vianney journeyed on foot, all alone, carrying a small parcel which held some provisions, and an alb for his first Mass.[5] A hundred kilometers separated Lyons from Grenoble. But the candidate felt as if he were endowed with wings—was not his greatest desire to be fulfilled at last? He set out full of joy, though the journey was not without its risks. For a second time France had been invaded, and the roads of the Dauphiné were covered with armed enemies. What could be the business of this lean abbé with his slender baggage? Was he a spy in the service of France? The Austrians of Bubna's corps, whose speech sounded so strange in his ears, stopped him, and threatened him with their bayonets.

At length, on the evening of Saturday, August 12, our candidate found himself within the walls of the Grand Séminaire of Grenoble. On the morrow, which was the thirteenth Sunday after Pentecost, he was led, at an early hour, to the chapel, which, prior to the Revolution, had been the church of the Minims.

Mgr. Simon arrived in a very humble conveyance. He was a prelate of deep piety, and his manner was gentle and affable. Excuses were offered to the Bishop for his having been put to so much trouble for so little—only one candidate, and he a stranger! The venerable prelate contemplated for a moment the ascetic-looking deacon, who was unaccompanied by relatives or friends: "It is not too much trouble to ordain a good priest," he replied with a grave smile.[6]

No doubt because he felt them to be ineffable, M. Vianney made no attempt to reveal the emotions of that heavenly morning. Later on, in his catechetical instructions,

5. This modest alb is carefully preserved in the old presbytery at Ars.
6. "The servant of God overheard this remark and he himself related it to me." (Abbé Raymond, *Procès de l'Ordinaire,* p. 283).

when he spoke of the sublime dignity of the priesthood—and he often did so—he must have lived all over again the unforgettable hours of that day in August, 1815. "Oh! how great is the priest. The priest will only be understood in Heaven. Were he understood on earth, people would die, not of fear, but of love."[7]

Thus at the age of twenty-nine years and three months, after so many uncertainties, failures and tears, Jean-Marie was at last a priest, and about to draw nigh unto the altar of God. From the moment of his ordination he looked upon himself—soul and body—as a sacred vessel destined exclusively for the service of God. In the days of his youth, when his saintly mother was still with him, he used to sigh: "If I were a priest I should wish to win many souls to God." Souls were even now waiting for him.

---

7. *Esprit du Curé d'Ars,* p. 113.

Chapter 10

VICAIRE AT ECULLY (1815-1818)

ON MONDAY, August 14, the eve of the Assumption, M. Vianney celebrated his first Mass, in the chapel of the seminary in which he had received the unction of the priesthood. Two chaplains of the Austrian army were saying their Masses at the same time at two altars close by. It is probable that he did not at once return to Ecully, but that he remained at Grenoble for the solemnity of the morrow. His delicate conscience, his tender love for Our Lady, would not have allowed of his traveling on such a day. Everything points to his having left the seminary on the sixteenth, when he had celebrated the Holy Sacrifice within the walls of its chapel.[1]

On the return journey he met with the same trials which he had encountered on the road to Grenoble, but at length he reached Ecully, where his old master impatiently awaited his return. A pleasing surprise was in store for the new priest. After he had fallen on his knees and received his blessing, M. Balley imparted to him the welcome news that the Vicar-General had granted a vicaire to the parish of Ecully, and the priest appointed to the post was none other than M. Vianney. In this way the adopted child would remain with his father, assist him in his work, and eventually close his eyes.

There was likewise great joy in the old house at Dardilly. An entire past, with its countless anxieties, was blot-

1. "We do not know," writes the Abbé Monnin, "where the new priest said his first Mass, nor the circumstances that accompanied this great and solemn act. It seems to us that it must haye been at Ecully, when he was assuredly assisted by M. Balley." M. Monnin did not know that the saint said his first Mass at Grenoble, the very next day after his ordination.

ted out when the new priest stood in the midst of his own. If only his mother were there! He prayed long over her beloved tomb.

A letter informed Les Noës and Les Robins of the ordination of Jérôme Vincent. The year before, immediately after his ordination as a subdeacon, the Abbé Vianney had written to the venerable M. Jacquet offering his services as vicaire once he was ordained priest. All he asked was his keep. He confessed that he loved Les Noës so much that he never ceased from thinking of that picturesque village. Who could describe the happiness of Mère Fayot now that her "big son" had at last reached the object of his aspirations? True, he would have to remain at Ecully for a time, but the day would come when he would be made a curé. And then, who could tell what might happen? So the good people of Les Robins agreed that they would call at the presbytery of M. Balley as soon as possible, in order to see his saintly and kind vicaire.

The parishioners of Ecully shared the satisfaction of their pastor. "M. Vianney," they said amongst themselves, "has edified us all during the time he studied here; what will he not do now that he is a priest?" As a matter of fact he speedily won the confidence of everybody, though at first they had to be content with asking his advice outside the confessional, because M. Vianney only received his faculties to hear Confessions several months after his appointment as vicaire. So it had been decided by M. Courbon. The very first penitent to throw himself at the feet of M. Vianney was his own confessor, M. Balley. The austere and learned pastor of Ecully had been looking for a new director. He came to the conclusion that none was more suitable to be the guide of his soul than this former shepherd-boy of whose abilities people had too long doubted. The grand old man had watched the steady work of divine grace in that chosen soul; so he represented to M. Courbon that the time had come "to give full play to the powers" of his young vicaire. The Vicar-General at once granted a request that was so eminently reasonable.

The first pastoral act performed by M. Vianney was a

Baptism, registered August 27, 1815. It no sooner became known that he was "approved" for Confessions than his confessional was besieged, and the sick sent almost exclusively for him. In this way much of his time was taken up, and he began to neglect his meals. A little later, what had been at first a casual neglect became a habit. But his labor yielded both fruit and consolation, for many, who until then could scarcely be said to have edified the parish, altered their conduct as soon as they had been to him.

He prepared and explained most carefully his Catechism lessons, adapting them to the understanding of the little ones, the more backward amongst whom he took to his own room, where he taught them with indefatigable patience, remembering all the time what had been done for himself during the Revolution.

In the pulpit he was short but to the point.[2] Thus did he enter, at Ecully, upon a ministry that cost him much toil, but which was destined to yield truly marvellous results. "To my thinking, he did not preach well as yet," said his sister Marguerite when she came from Dardilly to hear him, "but when it was his turn to speak, people flocked to the church." Yet he was not afraid to utter stern truths and to castigate certain vices. Ecully was not an oasis peopled by perfect souls; the Revolution had left its mark, and the proximity of the great city of Lyons was calculated to foster evil. The villagers were fond of pleasure; dances were arranged on the smallest pretext. "In the place where I was vicaire," M. Vianney subsequently said in one of his Catechism instructions, "a young man who was to stand godfather, and who for this reason had engaged a fiddler for the dancing, was crushed by the fall of a beam the very next day. He had not so much as an instant to enter into himself. The musician came in due time, but even as he arrived the bells were

---

2. Catherine Lassagne, *Procès apostolique in genere,* p. 104. Mlle. Lassagne must have had this detail from one of the parishioners at Ecully. It is peculiar to this period of the life of M. Vianney, for when he became Curé d'Ars, he began to preach very long sermons.

tolling the knell of that unhappy youth."

When he exhorted the people to lead a moral life and even to aspire after perfection, M. Vianney only preached what he practiced in his own person. His reserve, simplicity, and kindness were admirable. For all that, no one could take liberties with him. He possessed that gift peculiar to the saints which, according to gentle St. Francis de Sales, consists in "seeing everyone without looking at anyone."[3] He had made a covenant with his eyes because he felt himself to be as frail as any other human being. He prayed and mortified himself so as to subdue the flesh, for his lower nature was not as yet insensible to the fatal fascination of evil.

"On October 3, 1839," relates M. l'Abbé Tailhades, of Montpellier, "M. Vianney made an important admission to me. I asked him what he had done in order to free himself from sensual temptations. After a while he confessed that twenty-three years earlier, at the time when he was vicaire at Ecully, he made a vow to say daily the *Regina coeli* and six times the ejaculation: 'Blessed be for ever the most holy and immaculate Conception of the Blessed Virgin Mary, Mother of God! Amen.'"[4]

M. Balley was far from being rich and to keep a vicaire might easily have proved an excessive burden. Some of the parishioners understood this, so they provided gratuitously, or at half-price, all that was required for the priests' household. The good people deemed it a duty and a privilege to do so. As regards the personal possessions of M. Vianney, they found their way into the hands of the poor; he gave away even his clothes. "One winter's day," Marguerite relates, "M. Balley said to my brother: 'You are going to see Mme. So-and-So, at Lyons. You must put on the trousers that have just been given to you.' When he came home at night he was wearing a very threadbare pair of breeches. When asked what had become of the others, he confessed that he had fallen in with a poor fellow who was half dead with cold. He took pity on

3. "Voir tout le monde sans regarder personne."
4. Abbé Tailhades, *Procès de l'Ordinaire,* p. 1517.

him and exchanged his new trousers for the beggar's old ones."

"How is Jean-Marie?" M. Balley was sometimes asked by André Provin, a former comrade of Vianney's at Dardilly. "M. Vianney is always the same," the answer would be; "he gives away all he possesses."

When M. Courbon appointed the Abbé Vianney to be vicaire at Ecully, M. Balley stipulated that he should live at the presbytery, so that he might help him in the continuation of his theological studies. This was done. In their free time the *Rituel de Toulon* was once more taken down from the shelf, and the teacher gave some further practical explanation of dogma, morals, and liturgy. When they went out together the parish priest would propose a case of conscience which the assistant had to solve, stating at the same time the principles on which he based his decision.

God sent the Abbé Vianney to Ecully, not merely in order that he might be initiated into the sacred ministry; the presbytery was likewise a school of holiness.

We have already stated that M. Balley was much addicted to the practice of penance. Between him and his assistant there soon arose a rather terrifying emulation in austerity. In the opinion of Canon Pelletier, arch-priest of Treffort, it was the case of a holy rivalry between two saints. Later on M. Vianney himself made the following avowal: "I should have ended by acquiring a small measure of goodness, had I had the happiness of living always with M. Balley.[5] No one has shown me more plainly to what extent the soul may rise above the senses and become akin to the Angels. To make one wish to love God it was enough to hear him say: 'My God, I love Thee with my whole heart.'"[6]

M. Balley wore a hair-shirt. M. Vianney secretly requested Claudine Bibost and her daughter Colombe to

5. "J'aurais fini par être un peu sage, si j'avais eu le bonheur d'être toujours avec M. Balley."
6. Abbé Monnin, *Le Curé d'Ars,* I, pp. 144, 145

make one for him also, and he began to wear it next to the skin. If there were no visitors to interfere with the little habits of curé and vicaire, meals were liable to be very haphazard affairs—*attrape-qu'attrape,* as M. Vianney was wont to say. There was no wine with the few potatoes and the brown bread. By reason of its repeated appearance on the table, the piece of boiled beef ended by becoming perfectly black. Things came to such a pass that some of the parishioners deemed it their duty to inform M. Courbon. "You people of Ecully are fortunate to have such priests to do penance for you," was the Vicar-General's reply. Better still, the curé denounced his vicaire to the authorities for "exceeding all bounds," whilst the latter reported that the rector practiced excessive mortifications. M. Courbon laughingly sent both of them back to their presbytery.[7] All this austerity, however, was not without an occasional respite, and there were times when the curé's table presented a less forbidding aspect. On days when guests were expected—the Vicar-General and M. Groboz were sometimes of their number—the menu was a little more varied.

It was on some such festive occasion, one fine afternoon in October 1815, that there suddenly appeared at the door of the presbytery of Ecully a peasant woman dressed in the fashion of Le Forez. She asked to see M. Jean-Marie Vianney. The servant explained that the gentlemen were at table and that there were many guests in the dining-room. Mère Fayot—for it was none other—absorbed as she was by a single thought, was not afraid to disturb the feast. Breaking into the dining-room, she scanned the faces of the diners, among whom were M. Courbon and M. Bochard. She quickly recognized her "dear child." Flushed with joy, the Abbé Vianney had risen from table to go to his "good mother," who took him into her arms and pressed a resounding kiss upon both his cheeks.

Notwithstanding his personal austerity, M. Balley was not a misanthrope. He kept up a friendly intercourse with

7. Comtesse des Garets, *Procès de l'Ordinaire,* p. 766.

several persons of Lyons. Thus he continued to visit the Loras family, and he was intimate with M. Antoine Jaricot. This last named was a big industrialist who had bought Tassin, a country house near Ecully, but which he soon made over to his eldest daughter, who, on her marriage, became Mme. Perrin. Mme. Perrin's charming sister, Pauline Jaricot, who attained her seventeenth year in 1817, used to spend the summer at Tassin. For a time she had given herself up to a worldliness of which she did not suspect the dangers, but touched by grace she resolutely abandoned all her finery and became a model of piety. The old house often saw gathered within its walls, besides the Jaricot family and the clergy of Ecully, distinguished ecclesiastics, such as the future Cardinal Villecourt, the Abbé Wurtz, then vicaire at Saint-Nizier of Lyons and Pauline's confessor, and many others.

It was at these gatherings that the Abbé Vianney, humbly seated, like Pauline, at the end of the table, heard for the first time the name of the virgin martyr, St. Philomena, whose body had been recently found in the catacombs of Rome, and to whom a number of miracles were attributed. Little did he then realize what a place this martyr of the early years of the Church was destined to occupy in his heart and in his life.

In pursuance of the statutes of the diocese of Lyons, the two priests lived in common, their days being days of unclouded peace. Together they performed their exercises of piety; together they made an occasional pilgrimage to our Lady of Fourvière. But so poor were they that on these journeys the one and only umbrella of the presbytery had to shelter the two of them.[8] Together they wrote out prayers to Our Lady for distribution in the parish. Between them they composed the chaplet of the Immaculate Conception which is recited to this day in the church of Ars, before the usual night prayers.

---

8. Abbé Claude Rougement: *Procès apostolique continuatif*, p. 742. All his life M. Vianney jealously kept this umbrella as a precious relic. It is still to be seen among the collection of souvenirs which is preserved at the old presbytery of Ars.

In this way the year 1816 went by, as well as the first few weeks of 1817. M. Balley was only sixty-five years of age, but he had been proscribed during the Terror, and every year of persecution counts for two. Old before his time, he was about to enter on the last stage of the journey into the next world. In February an ulcer in the leg nailed him to his bed, which he afterwards hardly ever left. From that time he who had always been so active seems to have taken but very little part in the work of the parish. Only one act in the register of 1817 bears his name—namely, a funeral, under the date of June 5. During this period of ever-increasing suffering he was almost entirely replaced by his devoted assistant. As for himself, he suffered without a murmur. Finally the ulcer became gangrenous; the physicians pronounced his condition hopeless.

On December 17, after making his Confession to his beloved pupil, the son of his predilection, and receiving Holy Viaticum and Extreme Unction at his hands, the venerable pastor of Ecully, full of merits, fell asleep in the Lord.

It is said that after witnessing the administration of the last rites the parishioners departed, leaving the two priests alone. The dying man gave his "beloved Vianney" his supreme counsels and commended himself to his prayers. After that, taking his instruments of penance from under his pillow: "Look, my poor child," he whispered into his ear, "hide these things; if they were found after my death people would imagine that I have sufficiently expiated my sins, and so they would leave me in Purgatory until the end of the world." But the discipline and hair-shirt of M. Balley had not as yet completed their task.

The Abbé Vianney wept for M. Balley as for a father. Did he not owe him everything? He cherished a memory of the saintly man that nothing could efface. "I have seen beautiful souls," he exclaimed, "but none so beautiful." The features of his old master were so deeply engraved upon his mind that he could say, even in his extreme old age: "If I were an artist, I could still paint his portrait." He often spoke of him, his eyes streaming with tears. Each morning he mentioned his name at the *Memento*. Until the day of his own death, he who was detached from all things insisted on keeping on his mantelpiece M. Balley's small looking-glass, "because it had reflected his face." In the whole district of Ecully the memory of the saintly priest long remained an object of veneration.[9]

Shortly after M. Balley's death several parishioners of Ecully approached the archbishop with a request that gave ample proof of their regard for M. Vianney. They petitioned that he should be appointed to be their parish priest. The authorities refused to accede to their demand. It is probable that M. Vianney would have declined the post. " I would not have liked to be parish priest of Ecully," he declared later on; "it was too big a parish." Be this as it may, M. Tripier succeeded M. Balley, Jean-Marie Vianney retaining the post of vicaire.

M. Tripier did not feel bound to walk in the footsteps of his predecessor. He had no intention whatever to make of his presbytery a Trappist or Carthusian monastery. Very soon he came to the conclusion that his vicaire's conduct was far too rigid. Did he not refuse to accompany him on his visits to clerical colleagues or to well-to-do parishioners, under the specious pretext that he possessed but one cassock, which was no longer presentable in respectable company? Did M. Tripier petition for another vicaire? It may be so. In any case, shortly after M. Tripier's appointment the diocesan authorities reconsidered the position of M. Vianney.

Since January 21—we are now in the year 1818—a small chaplaincy in the *département* of the Ain had remained vacant. Its chaplain, M. Antoine Déplace, a young priest of twenty-seven, had died of consumption after a

9. The body of M. Balley was laid to rest in the old church of Ecully. When that edifice was reconstructed, the body was exhumed and reburied in the chancel of the church. At the exhumation survivors among his former parishioners expressed a desire to view the body, feeling convinced that it would be found to be incorrupt. The work was carried out at night, but only bones were found. The belief of the people, however, is eloquent proof of his reputation for sanctity. M. Balley's tombstone, the inscription of which has worn away, forms the base of the baptismal font.

ministry of only twenty-three days. Ars was vacant. It was a very small and impoverished village, with a population of barely 230 souls. Was it even worthwhile to send a priest there? True, Mizérieux, the central parish, lay at a distance of three kilometers. M. Durand, curé of Savigneux, was asked to supply, pending the appointment of another chaplain. For several weeks it seemed as if Ars had been forgotten. The personal intervention of the lady of the manor, Mlle. Anne des Garets, who insisted that her village should be treated as a real parish, hastened the decision of the authorities.

At the beginning of February the Abbé Jean-Marie Baptiste Vianney, until now vicaire at Ecully, was informed that the chapel and village of Ars-en-Dombes were to be entrusted to his pastoral zeal. Not for a moment did he stop to consider whether there was any truth in the statement often made that M. Courbon was in the habit of sending to the parishes of the *département* of the Ain, "which was held to be a kind of Siberia for the clergy of Lyons, those subjects that appeared the least promising."[10] In utter single-mindedness he called on the Vicar-General, who, after signing the document that appointed him, remarked: "There is not much love for God in that parish; you will bring some into it." The Abbé Vianney protested that he had no other desire. M. Courbon thought it incumbent on him to encourage the new parish priest. Assuredly the portion of the vineyard allotted to him was lowly among the lowliest. There were scarcely any temporal resources; just the pay of a vicaire—that is five hundred francs provided by the commune.[11] Providence, however, would not forsake him in his remote hamlet.

---

10. "Without doubt the most forsaken section of the diocese of Lyons was the *département* of the Ain. Far removed from the city, destitute of every sort of help, it sent but a few pupils to the seminary. M. Courbon, by far the most influential member of the governing body of the diocese, deemed it his duty to restore to the *départements* of the Rhône and the Loire the subjects they had furnished. In this way many parishes of the Ain were left without a priest, whilst others only received the less promising among the younger clergy. Thus it came about that the Ain was considered a kind of Siberia, so much so that for a man to be sent into Bugey, or La Dombes, was held by his brother priests to be equivalent to disgrace" (Abbé J. Cognat, *Vie de Mgr. Devie, évêque de Belley,* Lyon, Pelagaud, 1865, Vol. I, pp. 182-183).
11. Whilst ceasing to be a parish Ars had remained a commune.

Ars had the good fortune of boasting a château; "the lady of the manor was an excellent person who would assist her parish priest both financially and by the weight of her personal influence." This was all the comfort the new parish priest received at the hands of his ecclesiastical superior.

On February 3, 1818, M. Vianney performed his last official function at Ecully. On the morning of February 9 he set out for Ars.

PART II

PASTORATE OF ARS
(1818-1859)

Chapter 1

ARRIVAL AT ARS AND FIRST CONTACT WITH HIS PARISH

ARS, called successively *Artis villa, Artz,* then *Arz,* and finally *Ars,* apparently dates from a remote antiquity.[1] Until quite recently a druidical stone was still to be seen at no great distance from the village. From this we are led to infer that the whole district was already inhabited at an early period. Nonetheless, the name of Ars is not met with in any document previous to the tenth century. A charter of 980 seems to imply that there existed by then both a church and an organized parish. However, the place was never more than a small village.

Ars is situate some thirty-five kilometers from Lyons, in the *canton* and *arrondissement* of Trévoux, on the plateau of La Dombes. Whereas other parts of the Ain are hilly and wooded, La Dombes is a plain of clayey soil and stagnant waters. There are no forests, but only copses of birches and oaks; the edges of the roads and fields are marked by slender elms; alders, hazels, and willows line the river banks.

Towards the west the horizon is limited by the tranquil hills of the Beaujolais. The village itself stands in an undulating plain from whence rises an occasional cluster of trees. Here we have no longer the flat, monotonous plain with its innumerable pools of water, nor have we as yet the fertile hills that slope down towards the Saône.

Ars is built on either side of a valley through which flows the Fontblin, a small stream in winter, but in summer no more than a narrow rivulet winding its way

1. One also meets with *Arsa*—the burnt village.

through the shingle. In this year of grace, 1818, the village wore a sad and wretched aspect. All there was to be seen were some forty low houses, built of clay and scattered amid the orchards; halfway up one side of the valley stood a church, if one could grace with such a name a yellowish structure pierced by quite common windows and surmounted by five beams, four upright and one cross beam, which supported the sadly cracked bell. In accordance with ancient custom, the dead were buried by the side of the sacred edifice. Behind the apse was a small square planted with twenty-two splendid walnut-trees. Hard by the church stood the presbytery, which was no better than a peasant's house. In front of it lay a small yard a few square feet in size.

At the bottom of the valley and wellnigh lost among the tall trees that surrounded it stood the château of Les Garets d'Ars. The house dated from the eleventh century. At one time it had been a feudal manor, flanked by a tower, surrounded by a moat and crowned with battlements. These warlike features were now things of the past. The château was nothing more than a spacious country house, peaceful and melancholy, with barely a memory of the hunting expeditions and other merry diversions of the days of old.

As a result of bad roads, Ars seemed, as it were, lost in an inaccessible wilderness. In the fullest sense of the word, it was but a hole. Its inhabitants hardly ever left it, Nature having made them stay-at-homes.

The distance from Ecully to Ars is thirty kilometers. M. Vianney journeyed on foot and with very few *impedimenta.* Mère Bibost, who, in his student days, had looked after his wardrobe, accompanied him on the present journey. A few clothes, a wooden bedstead, and the books left to him by M. Balley, followed in a cart. The name of the driver has not been recorded.

The new curé experienced some difficulty in finding his parish. A mist had obliterated the landscape, so that it was impossible to make out distant objects. After passing the village of Toussieux, where no one seemed able to offer further guidance, the travellers lost their way completely. Eventually they espied through the haze some children tending their flocks. M. Vianney approached them, but as the little shepherds only spoke the local *patois,* they were unable to understand him. He asked them to show him the way to the château of Ars, under an impression that it was situate within the village itself. He repeated his question and at last the most intelligent of the children, a boy of the name of Antoine Givre, put the stranger on the right road. "My young friend," said the priest, by way of thanking the lad, "you have shown me the way to Ars; I shall show you the way to Heaven."[2] The young shepherd added that the spot where they stood marked the boundary of the parish. On hearing this the new curé knelt down to pray.

Soon, the humble group of travellers descended the declivity which leads to the Fontblin. From thence M. Vianney could descry a few scattered huts in the midst of which stood a very small and poor church. On beholding those low, thatched cottages, which looked very depressing in the gathering gloom, he said to himself: "How small it all is"; but, moved by a divine instinct, he added: "Yet this parish will not be able to contain the multitude of those who shall journey hither."[3]

Ars had indeed received a good priest, in the fullest sense of that great word—that is, a holy priest, but of whom no one could as yet prophesy that one day he would be canonized. True, up till then the world knew nothing of his eminent virtue. But even lofty virtue is not yet sanctity. Notwithstanding his great spirit of mortification and renouncement, M. Vianney had not as yet attained to the ineffable meekness, the marvellous penance and self-sacrifice which, in 1925, would cause

---

2. Catherine Lassagne, *Procès apostolique ne pereant,* p. 104. The simple soul of Antoine Givre probably thought but little of this prophecy. But he was the first among the inhabitants of Ars to follow M. Vianney in death.
3. Frère Athanase, *Procès de l'Ordinaire,* p. 667. "I asked him," says Frère Athanase elsewhere, "how he came to conceive this idea. The servant of God eluded the question, as was his habit whenever his humility was at stake. 'Bast,' he replied with a smile, 'so many strange ideas cross my mind: *il me passe tant d'idées baroques par la tête.*'"

him to be ranked among the greatest and most popular of those heroes whom we call the saints.

On the morning of February 10, the bell rang for Mass: in this way did Ars learn that it had a new pastor. A few devout souls rejoiced; the bulk of the population remained indifferent. "There was some surprise when the bell was heard," Mme. des Garets notes, "and people remarked: 'Ah! there is a new parish priest.'"

In the eighteenth century Ars was a truly Christian parish, and the reader should not allow exaggerated tales to lead him to the conclusion that in 1818 M. Vianney entered upon a missionary district inhabited by a people bereft of both faith and morals. In 1724 the parish priest of Ars was a young licentiate in theology and canon law, learned, energetic and burning with apostolic zeal. This priest, Messire François Hescalle, has left us in the archives of the parish a picture of the religious condition of his flock. The faithful, he writes, at first requested him and ended by compelling him to establish in their church the confraternities of the Blessed Sacrament, the Rosary, and the Scapular. On the first Sunday of the month the good people came together to make a meditation on death. The feast of the Sacred Heart, recently established in the diocese of Lyons, was kept with great devotion.[4]

On June 24, 1734, the entire parish, with its priest at its head, journeyed to Lyons in order to gain the Indulgence of the Jubilee of St. John.[5] In fact, in this part of La Dombes, processions and pilgrimages were very popular. The people visited the church of the Minims at Montmerle, on St. Mark's day; that of St. Euphemia on St. George's day, and that of Rance on

4. Mgr. de Neuville, by an ordinance of December 3, 1718, established a feast of the Sacred Heart as a day of obligation for the whole diocese of Lyons. On October 27, 1722, the Bishop ordained that in country districts the feast should be kept on the Sunday after Corpus Christi. M. Hescalle notes in his register: "I witness great keenness on the part of my people to perform their devotions on that day."

5. By a special privilege—it is a rare occurrence—whenever the feast of Corpus Christi coincides with that of St. John the Baptist, there is a jubilee at Lyons. This has happened only once since 1734—namely, in 1886.

the Tuesday after Easter. However, some at least among the parish priests were not without anxiety about the effect of these incursions upon their neighbors' parishes; they even made their misgivings known to the archbishop. These religious festivals tended to become profane—there was much feasting, games, and dancing. M. Hescalle noted, not without satisfaction: "I do not say that my parishioners have been guilty of like excesses."

M. Hescalle's successor was M. Claude Garnier (1740-1775). Between 1762 and 1763 "the church tower was built up in stone from the plinth, to replace a sort of wooden cage which was all that existed up till then." In 1794 this tower was levelled to the ground by order of the *sans-culotte* Albitte, so that there was no trace of it left when M. Vianney took possession.

M. Garnier was succeeded by M. Symphorien Eymard (1775-1788). There remain but a few faint indications of his passage. He registered Baptisms, marriages, and burials—that is all we know of him, except that at the end of the register of 1780 he notes that five of his parishioners have each planted a vineyard. He evidently had at heart the material as well as the spiritual well-being of his people, hence he jotted down this item in order to put on record that the clearance of the land was beginning to yield appreciable results.

On January 31, 1788, Messire Etienne Saunier was named curé of Ars. He was twenty-eight years old, came from Lyons, and was a bachelor of the Sorbonne. He himself set down these personal details in the parochial register. In 1791 he took the oath prescribed by the Constituent Assembly, so he must have officiated in the parish at least until the beginning of 1793.[6]

In March of the following year the church was looted by a band of hooligans from Trévoux. Though he had taken the *civil* oath, citizen Saunier was arrested, but

6. In 1791 M. Saunier registered one marriage, five Baptisms, and nine burials. That same year he records how he gave a "patriotic banquet" to the children who made their first Communion. This is the very last item set down by him. On November 13, 1792, in compliance with the law of September 20, he surrendered the parish registers to the municipality.

promptly set at liberty: to save his life the unhappy man gave up the priesthood. In October, 1793, the apostate reappeared in the capacity of a merchant in the village where he had held the office of parish priest. The humble sanctuary in which he had been wont to say Mass had now become a club where the free-thinkers of the district held their wordy meetings. The assemblies of the *décadi* likewise took place within its walls. According to a local tradition, still lingering in the district, a former usher of Trévoux, the citizen Ruf, constituted himself the apostle of the ridiculous worship of the *goddess Reason* for that part of La Dombes.

In the meantime, under various disguises, a few faithful priests remained in the district. An abstract of the list of Baptisms, based on the testimony of godfathers and godmothers, mentions the passage through Ars of M. Chauas, curé of Trévoux (1793); of Fr. Jean-Baptiste, a Capuchin (1794), and of M. Blanc and M. Condamin (1795). There is every likelihood that all these priests celebrated Mass and administered the Sacraments in the two places pointed out by a constant tradition—namely, at a farm called *l'Epoux,* belonging to a family of the name of Dutang, and at the château des Garets. Unfortunately these confessors of the faith could only pay flying visits to Ars, at prearranged times and for the benefit of but small groups. The bulk of the population knew nothing of their comings and goings. When in 1801 the Church of France entered upon the task of restoration, the parish of Ars, as regards faith and morals, was in a state of total disintegration.

But this spiritual lethargy was not destined to last forever. In March, 1802, a priest named Jean Lecourt, who styled himself "a missionary delegated by the Council," came to preach a mission to these poor, long-neglected populations. The registers show that he baptized a number of children who had already reached a certain age, and legitimized many marriages. The mission ended, M. Lecourt departed from Ars in order to confer a like benefit upon other villages. On May 30, 1803, the municipal council—Ars was no longer a parish, though it remained a commune—voted a sum of 1,800 livres for the restoration of the church, the rent of the presbytery, the stipend of a curate and the purchase of vestments and a bell.

The diocesan authorities could not overlook so much good will. At the beginning of 1804 the Abbé Lecourt returned to Ars with the title of *prêtre desservant.* Like a true missionary, he went forth in search of the stray sheep. Alas! his stay was all too short. At the end of one year he was transferred to Jassans, so that until March 1806, the village of Ars, now directly attached to Mizérieux, knew no priest other than M. Aimé Verrier, who was simultaneously parish priest of Mizérieux, Ars, Toussieux, Sainte-Euphémie, and Saint-Didier-de-Formans.

At length M. Berger was sent to Mizérieux as assistant priest. He administered the chaplaincy of Ars, having been given the title of vicaire. When Cardinal Fesch gave confirmation at Trévoux on April 22, 1807, M. Berger took thither ninety-five persons of Ars—that is, a good third of the entire population. He was greatly esteemed by the châtelaine, Mlle. des Garets, and she would have wished to keep him. But the priest asked for a change, and in consequence of his request, in October, 1817, he was sent, in the capacity of vicaire, to Sury-le-Comtal.[7]

He was succeeded, in December, by M. Déplace, a young priest of twenty-six, who came to Ars only to die. It was in the depth of winter. When the people saw the state of exhaustion in which he was, they were moved to compassion, and vied with one another to bring him faggots, some four, others fifteen, others fifty; "all this shows," writes the châtelaine, "the esteem they felt for their parish priest, and their desire for his comfort whilst he was amongst them."[8]

7. "You must forgive me if I feel unable to understand this instability from which you should not have had to suffer. So at least it seems to me, seeing the kindly, and I may say, the delicate way in which you have always acted towards M. Berger. "(Extract from a letter addressed to Mlle. d'Ars on December 17, 1817, by Canon Mayet, one of the secretaries of the archbishop).

8. Extract from an unpublished note of Mlle. d'Ars. The châtelaine set down on loose sheets numerous facts dealing with the history of the parish. We still possess her ledger—*livre de raison*—which throws light on many points of this story.

We must admit, however, that during the last twenty-five years, the religious condition of Ars had not been brilliant. Many of the inhabitants were pagans in practice, and if all faith had not vanished, very little was left. "There was a good deal of *laisser-aller* in the parish," says a well-informed witness, "and even a measure of carelessness and indifference. But I do not think there were disorders of an outstanding nature at Ars. The most deplorable aspect of the situation was simply the forgetfulness of religious practices."[9]

People felt no scruple in missing Mass from the most trivial motives. Unnecessary work was done on Sunday, especially during harvest time. Adults, youths, and even children had contracted the execrable habit of blaspheming. "Ars possessed four taverns where the heads of families squandered their substance." On Sunday and Monday nights especially the peace of the village was disturbed by the rowdyism of drunken men. The young women were passionately addicted to dancing. Social gatherings, protracted far into the night, gave occasion to manifold and grievous evils. As if this were not enough, the people were exceedingly ignorant in all that concerned religion. The children stayed away from the Catechism instructions; only a minority could read; there was no regular teaching; at an early age they were forced to work in the fields and in the summer every day was spent in this way. With the return of winter some chance teacher would open a school for boys and girls, but the very young children never went to school at all.

This is not a pretty picture. But, after all, Ars was neither better nor worse than the neighboring villages. The priest was not hated; a remnant of religion had weathered the storm, but there was no real piety. To get an idea of the condition of Ars at that time we need but to read the sermons of its Curé; most of those which we still possess date from the early years of his ministry. In them we see a picture of the mentality of those country

9. Comte Prosper des Garets, Mayor of Ars. *Procès de l'Ordinaire*, p. 942.

folk in whose estimation the things of this world held the foremost place.[10]

The divine householder's field did not exclusively yield cockle. The confraternity of the Blessed Sacrament instituted by M. Hescalle was not quite defunct. A few truly Christian families were yet to be found at Ars. Thus Antoine Mandy, the Mayor, and Michel Cinier, municipal councillor, made it a point to second the efforts of M. Vianney in his attempt at the moral regeneration of the village. Their families, as well as those of Lassagne, Chaffangeon, and Verchère, attended church regularly on Sunday. The Abbé Renard, a native of Ars, was studying for the priesthood at the Seminary of Saint-Irénée of Lyons.[11] On the other hand the châtelaine, Mlle. Marie-Anne-Colombe Garnier des Garets, better known as Mlle. d'Ars, divided her time between the care of her household, visits to the sick, and the exercises of a somewhat meticulous piety. Faithful to a practice inherited from her mother, she daily recited the divine Office with a devoted old servant, whom the villagers respectfully called "Monsieur Saint-Phal."

At the time of M. Vianney's appointment Mlle. d'Ars was sixty-four years of age. Though short of stature, her appearance was extremely distinguished. She had been educated at Saint-Cyr and had retained the manner of the *ancien régime,* so characteristically French, and which lent so much charm to social intercourse. The family must have enjoyed a real popularity in the district, else it would not be easy to account for the fact that the Revolution failed to deprive Mlle. d'Ars of her estate. She, together with her aged mother, had remained in residence throughout that stormy period. At times Mass was secretly said in the chapel of the château. It does not seem that the châtelaine was ever molested because of her anti-revolutionary conduct. The poor loved her; she

10. *Sermons du vénérable serviteur de Dieu J. B. M. Vianney, Curé d'Ars,* publiés par les soins des abbés Delaroche, 4 vols. in 12, Lyon, Vitte, 1883. Some of the sermons have been published in English by Joseph F. Wagner, New York.

11. He was ordained priest in 1820.

paid their rent and provided them with food and clothing. Her account books show how carefully she noted even the smallest item of expenditure. Yet, notwithstanding her charity, her influence upon the bulk of the population, previous to M. Vianney's arrival, would seem to have been inconsiderable. Life in her brick-built manor was apt to be lonely, except for the visits of the gentry of the district. Her brother, Vicomte François, who was three years her junior, lived in Paris, in the Boulevard Saint-Germain, and only paid an occasional visit to the château. He had held the rank of a captain of dragoons, in the regiment of Penthièvre, was a knight of Saint-Louis, and had married a demoiselle de Bondy. Their union, however, remained childless.

The field entrusted to M. Vianney was a barren one, and though he was not slow in discovering the wheat, it seemed so choked by the cockle that he took alarm. Also, he viewed his parish in the light of his own most sensitive conscience, which caused him to shrink ineffably from sin. He saw miseries which other eyes might have failed to detect. However, instead of wasting time in idle regrets, he set to work. He did not pretend to convert the world; the field he meant to till was the tiny village that God had entrusted to him. It is from this point of view that we must judge both the preaching and the line of conduct adopted by M. Vianney during these opening years of his pastoral office. He spoke for the benefit of Ars; he thundered against the abuses that were rampant at Ars. Had his surroundings been other than they were, his zeal, no doubt, would have taken a different form. He knew that though abuses and vices assume ever-varying shapes, they remain essentially the same. Hence he was not on the lookout for new remedies, but contented himself with adopting those that have been tested and proved by preceding ages.

His programme—which he had pondered before the tabernacle—was that of every pastor who has at heart the welfare of souls. He resolved to get into touch with the people as early as possible; to make sure of the concurrence of those families who enjoyed general respect; to make the good yet more perfect; to bring back the indifferent; to convert open and public evil-doers; above all, to persevere in prayer to God from whom all blessings flow; to sanctify himself so as to be able to sanctify others, and to offer expiation for the sins of those who refused to do penance for themselves. How weak and helpless he felt when he considered the magnitude of his task! But his soul was filled with a divine energy, and God makes choice of the helplessness of the lowly ones to crush the power of human pride. A holy priest is able to achieve great results with means that would seem wholly inadequate.

Although the Abbé Vianney was only vicaire-chapelain of Ars, his flock gave him the title of curé as they had done to his predecessors. In this capacity he was duly installed on Sunday, February 13. Practically the entire parish was present on the occasion. The spectators were visibly impressed by the simple yet striking ceremony. M. Ducreux, the aged curé of Mizérieux, to whom the new chaplain was no stranger, accompanied by the municipal council, met him at the presbytery.[12] At the church door he placed round his neck the stole, symbol of his mission and authority, He was then conducted to the altar, where he opened the tabernacle; from thence they went to the confessional, the pulpit, and the baptismal font. In an address, M. Vianney assured the people of his affection and good will; finally he celebrated Mass for his parishioners. No doubt the chants that resounded through the humble sanctuary must have been poor enough—for all that, this first Sunday was a red-letter day for the whole population.

As the ceremony proceeded, the congregation watched their new priest with close attention. A few had already

12. In 1808, M. Julien-Marie Ducreux, at one time Superior of the Petit Séminaire of Saint-Jean, Lyons, succeeded M. Verrier as curé of Mizérieux. During the time of his studies at Ecully, M. Balley must have presented Jean-Marie Vianney to the Superior of Saint-Jean.

seen him on his way to the church or in the cemetery. He appeared of medium height and somewhat awkward in manner. His cassock was made of coarse material, and his shoes were such as were worn by the peasantry. The people were filled with veneration for their priest, and a murmur of admiration might have been heard along the pews, as they beheld M. Vianney at the altar, radiant and, as it were, transfigured, saying Mass with a solemnity they had not witnessed before. The Mayor, as natural spokesman of the population and a man of much good sense who had administered the commune during the past twenty years, thus expressed his feelings: "We have a poor church but a holy parish priest."[13]

M. Vianney took no interest whatever in the furnishing of his presbytery: in this matter he left himself unreservedly in the hands of the widow Bibost, who was supposed to understand these domestic details far better than himself. "He had brought her with him in the capacity of housekeeper, but her position was a precarious one, because M. le Curé was only too ready to dispense with the services of a cook."[14]

The presbytery contained five rooms, each with one window. On the ground floor were the dining room and kitchen. The first storey, which was reached by a stone staircase, was divided into three rooms, one for the curé, the others for the accommodation of visitors. M. Vianney deemed the furniture adequate. Inventories of the period mention, among other items, "six high-backed velvet pile chairs and one armchair to match; another armchair covered with green and red Siam cotton; a dinner table with four leaves; two tester beds, with blue and white hangings and counterpanes of the same colors; a quilted coverlet of white and gold taffeta; two flock mattresses covered with new check ticking," besides a great many other more or less valuable objects, the whole being a gratuitous loan from the châtelaine of Ars.

The Abbé Vianney, already rich in the possession of

13. Abbé Raymond, *Procès de l'Ordinaire,* p. 284.
14. Catherine Lassagne, *Procès de l'Ordinaire,* p. 512.

the old bedstead bequeathed to him by M. Balley, was anxious to retain nothing except what was indispensable. Was he not now his own master? On the occasion of a visit to the château, he asked Mlle. d'Ars to remove the beautiful things for which he had no use whatever. What would he do with a "roasting jack" and other kitchen utensils? His way of living would be so very plain! All he wished to retain, with her consent, was an ordinary bed, two old tables, a bookcase, a few cupboards, some strawbottomed chairs, a cast-iron saucepan, a frying-pan, and a few odds and ends which might prove useful.

So much simplicity impressed the humbler section of the population. Those in easier circumstances, landowners and prosperous farmers, who deemed it an extortion when they were asked to give a small alms, were amazed on learning that their curé kept nothing whatever for himself. By this they knew him to be a man of God indeed. Beggars who had received bountiful alms at his hands began to spread his fame. "M. Vianney had brought from Ecully a fairly well-lined purse: it did not long remain in that prosperous condition."[15]

The Curé d'Ars was not so naive as to imagine that his mere presence would effectively suppress the disorders rampant in the parish. His zeal for the salvation of souls was impatient of delay. He was no sooner canonically installed than he entered upon his arduous task. He was anxious to secure an immediate ascendency over those rough villagers in whose hearts there was less malice than ignorance.

Sixty households to visit does not appear a heavy task; but the manner of performing it may render it laborious. About midday, with his broad, three-cornered hat under his arm—he hardly ever carried it any other way—the Abbé Vianney could be seen leaving the church or the presbytery. At that hour he was sure to find everybody in. At first his visits were not uniformly welcomed. But, according to the testimony of Guillaume Villiers,

15. This detail was confided to Frère Athanase by the saint himself.

a peasant of Ars then nineteen years old, "the majority judged him to be full of kindness, cheerfulness, and affability, though we never realized his great holiness." On these preliminary visits, by which he strove to get a knowledge of the people, he confined the conversation almost exclusively to ordinary topics: the work in hand, the prospects of the crops, and so forth. He was anxious to know the position of every family, the number and ages of the children, and the relations and connections between the various families. Before leaving he would make some remark about religion. The manner in which his words were taken enabled him to gauge the faith or lack of faith of the members of the household.

In this respect, alas! he made some sad discoveries. A number of his parishioners were ignorant of the most elementary notions of the catechism. This was especially true of those who had grown up during the Revolution—that is, the young men and women between the ages of twenty-five and thirty-five. It was they who were the chief causes of scandal. Some of them went so far as to boast of their conduct, openly asserting that they saw no harm in their dances, their profanation of the Sunday and other disorders. How were these wandering sheep to be brought back to the fold? The new pastor was painfully aware of his helplessness; he did not lose heart, however—God and time would work for him.

Chapter 2

THE CONVERSION OF ARS
I. Prayer and Penance

TO HIS love for God and for souls, the Curé d'Ars united what has been aptly called "the instinct of conquest."[1] Full of energy and enterprise, he had always cherished visions of a busy and useful existence. We are now about to see him at work in this diminutive corner of the vineyard assigned to him by God. Where others might have had too much leisure, he spent, from the very outset, well filled and laborious days.

Long before the first rays of dawn appeared on the horizon, whilst Ars was as yet plunged in deep sleep, a flickering light might have been seen in the cemetery that surrounded the church. At that hour M. Vianney, lantern in hand, passed from his house into the church. The good soldier of Jesus Christ was going to his post of intercessor for the people. He went straight up to the chancel, where he prostrated himself on the ground. There he poured out his heart, full of ardent desires, heavy already with many sorrows. During these silent hours of the night he prayed aloud that the Lord would show pity to pastor and flock alike. "My God," he pleaded, "grant me the conversion of my parish; I am willing to suffer all my life whatsoever it may please Thee to lay upon me; yes, even for a hundred years am I prepared to endure the sharpest pains, only let my people be converted." And he bathed the pavement with his tears. At

1. "Pastoral devotedness seems to consist of three qualities—the love of God, the love of souls, and what I may call the instinct of conquest." (Bishop Hedley, *Lex. Levitarum,* p. 23).

break of day he was still at his post. "This could be seen by the light which shone through the windows."[2]

The hours of the morning were spent in like manner, unless duty summoned him elsewhere. For a sick-call there was no need to go to the presbytery—people knew where to find him. There were days when he only left the church after the evening *Angelus.* In the afternoon, whether there were visits to pay or not, he would go out into the open air for exercise. He took advantage of these walks to pray even more, or to read his breviary. Occasionally he would stop to exchange a few words with the laborers, or, rosary in hand, he would wander along the sunken roads or seek seclusion in the underwood. His was the soul of a mystic, thirsting for solitude and peace. He loved the fresh breezes of the open country and its rural charms gladdened his spirit. It was well he should enjoy the beauty of nature, for the time was drawing near when there would be no more peace for him, when he would have to live like a prisoner, deprived of light and the open air. It has been said of this new Francis of Assisi that "his happiness was to pray in the woods. There, alone with God, he contemplated the divine greatness, making use of anything and everything, even of the song of the birds, to raise his soul to his Creator."

His happiness, however, was tempered by many a bitter thought. One day Père Mandy was going through the forest of La Papesse when he came upon M. Vianney, who was praying on bended knees. The priest had not noticed the good man. He was weeping bitterly, repeating again and again: "My God, convert my parish." The farmer withdrew very quietly, not daring to disturb so moving a prayer.

The saintly curé had a predilection for the beautiful woods which surrounded the château of Cibeins. By following the course of the Fontblin, he reached the shel-

2. Mlle. Marthe des Garets, *Procès apostolique in genere,* p. 289. "A man who lived near the church, seeing him with his candle, felt curious to know what he did in church at that early hour. Having found him engaged in prayer, the man walked away, saying: 'He is not like other men.'" (Catherine Lassagne, *Petit mémoire,* 3me rédaction, p. 469).

ter of the stately oaks. There, deeming himself unobserved, he would often throw himself upon the ground, probably whenever he came to the *Gloria Patri* in the divine Office. If he were saying his Office whilst walking in the fields, he invariably knelt down at the beginning and the end, with complete disregard of the weather.

To prayer the Curé d'Ars joined penance. The desire he had to spend his life alone in his presbytery was doubtless to the end that his terrifying austerities might remain his own secret. Surely God would forgive sinners more readily if someone paid the ransom of their sins! To save souls the price must be paid.[3]

Shortly after his arrival at Ars, M. Vianney gave his own mattress to some destitute person. Two others, which he had not as yet given away, remained on the chairs in the spare room. What need was there even of a bed? For several weeks he was content to stretch himself upon a few faggots on the floor of one of the lower rooms. Both the pavement and the walls were damp. He very soon contracted that facial neuralgia which was to be his torment for fifteen years. But instead of returning to his bedroom he went to sleep in the attic. One of the villagers who came to fetch him in the middle of the night to the bedside of a dying man heard him come down from this uncomfortable loft. As long as he slept in the attic he lay down on the bare boards, a log of wood doing duty as a pillow. The widow Renard and her daughter who lived hard by the presbytery heard him move this strange pillow when he had occasion to leave the house by night.

More often than not, before retiring to this rude resting-place, he subjected his body to a yet more severe punishment. Armed with a discipline, the effectiveness of which had been increased by sharp iron points, he mercilessly struck his *"corpse," "this old Adam,"* as he used to call his poor body. On certain nights a woman of Lyons, who lodged

3. "Il faut qu'il en coute pour sauver les âmes." Letter of Bossuet to the Maréchal de Bellefonds, August 5, 1674.

with Mère Renard, heard him thus punishing himself for the space of an hour or more; now and again he would pause for a moment, only to resume with renewed energy. "When is he going to stop?" the compassionate neighbors would say. He made his own instruments of penance, or, at least, he repaired and *improved* them. The person who did his room in the morning used to find under the furniture fragments of chains, small keys, and bits of iron or lead which had come off his disciplines. A discipline lasted him only fifteen days. "It was pitiful to see the left sleeve of his shirt all cut up and dyed with blood," says Catherine Lassagne.

He apparently fainted more than once, when he would lie, covered with blood, against the wall. In a corner of his room, hidden by the curtain that hangs from the tester of the bed, the yellow plastering is bespattered with drops of blood which are still discernible. Three large stains give fairly distinct impressions of a shoulder, and from these dark patches thin streaks have trickled down to the pavement. Other stains show impressions of fingers and the palm of a hand. The saint left these marks upon the wall when leaning against it for support, or in an endeavor to rise from the floor when he had swooned.

The beginning of the pastoral ministry of M. Vianney coincided with the holy season of Lent. What a splendid opportunity to inaugurate that rigorous fast which was to end only with his life! Already he was freed from at least one source of worry, for he dispensed with a servant. He now reduced his material wants to a minimum. "His meals were never at regular intervals."[4] During the first years of his ministry, however, his penances exceeded all bounds. Later on he called these excesses his "youthful follies." Happy they who need repent of none other! He went so far as to agree, rather vaguely, that then he overstepped the limits of prudence: "When one is young," he said to a priest, "one is apt to be indiscreet."[5]

4. Jeanne-Marie Chanay, *Procès de l'Ordinaire,* p. 765.
5. Abbé Toccanier, *Procès apostolique in genere,* p. 166.

About a fortnight after his installation his sister Marguerite came from Dardilly to see him, accompanied by the widow Bibost, the purely "honorary" cook at the presbytery of Ars. Their reception by M. Vianney was extremely cordial, but it stopped at that. "O my children," he said to the visitors, "what can I offer you? There is nothing in the house!" After a few moments' reflection he bethought himself of some potatoes, already musty, which he had boiled for his personal use. "We had not the courage to touch them," Marguerite related. As for himself, he ate two or three in our presence, remarking: "They are not a bit spoilt; I find them still quite good." Then he added: "I am expected in the church, I must go; try to manage for yourselves as well as you can."

Luckily for them, on their way through Trévoux, Gothon and Mère Bibost had taken the precaution of buying a loaf of bread. They ended by discovering a small quantity of flour, a few eggs, and a little butter, which a kindly soul had presented to M. Vianney, and which he had quite forgotten. With these materials they made a few *matefaims,* "because they knew he liked them."[6] Better still, they caught and killed two young pigeons which were marauding in the small yard of the house, and roasted them on the spit. "Oh! the poor creatures," he exclaimed as he beheld the unexpected dish, "so you have killed them! I did indeed wish to get rid of them because they annoy the neighbors, but you should not have cooked them." He refused to touch the meat, and would only eat a pancake.

François, his eldest brother, likewise paid him a visit. Less provident than his sister, he brought no provisions, so he was obliged himself to dig up some potatoes in the garden and to boil them in the one saucepan of the presbytery kitchen. We shall see later on that a time would come when the Abbé Vianney would make a real effort

6. A *matefaim* is a kind of pancake which at one time was very popular among the inhabitants of both banks of the Saône. It is a very thin cake made of wheaten flour, or buckwheat, diluted in water and baked in a pan. It served as a substitute for bread in the farms of La Dombes.

to entertain his visitors.

This first period of his work at Ars was assuredly the most austere of his whole life. At that time he lived practically alone,[7] and he took full advantage of his independence. Sometimes he would let two, or even three, days go by without touching any food. One Holy Week—possibly that of 1818—he only ate twice.[8] After a time he ceased to take in provisions, and he never thought of the morrow.[9]

Before her return to Ecully the widow Bibost secured the services of a substitute in the person of the widow Renard. At first this woman took her rôle seriously and ordered fresh bread for the presbytery. She soon discovered that, without so much as tasting it, M. Vianney distributed it to the poor. In exchange he accepted at their hands, or even bought from them, the crusts they carried in the recesses of their wallets.

Mère Renard made a few *matefaims* and boiled some potatoes. These he would eat when he could find time. More than once, with tears in her eyes, the good woman was compelled to take away the dish that had remained untouched. When she noticed that M. le Curé had come in from church, she would knock at his door. For a while there would be no reply. On her insisting, he would say, without opening the door: "I am not in need of anything; I wish for nothing." Frequently he would say to his housekeeper: "Do not come until such a day"—which meant several days—and if she disregarded her instructions he, on his part, remained inflexible. Several other persons had a like experience. One of them said with a sigh: "Oh! it is very hard to serve a saint!"[10]

At other times M. Vianney himself cooked, in his famous saucepan, enough potatoes to last him a whole week. When they were boiled he put them in a kind of iron basket, which he suspended from the wall. When

---

7. Guillaume Villier, *Procès de l'Ordinaire,* p. 646.
8. Comtesse Des Garets, *id.,* p. 911.
9. Guillaume Villier, *Procès de l'Ordinaire,* p. 650.
10. Catherine Lassagne, *Procès apostoliqne in genere,* p. 456.

he felt the pangs of hunger he took out one or two—to eat three would have been, according to him, "solely for the pleasure of eating." He ate them cold, even when, towards the end of the week, they were covered with a musty down. At other times he cooked an egg on the hot cinders, or baked a few indigestible *matefaims* made of flour mixed with salt and water. He lived on this diet until 1827, that is, until the *Providence* of Ars came to be established, when he went there to take his meals. "How happy I was," he jokingly remarked, "when I lived all by myself. If I needed food, I baked three *matefaims*. Whilst eating the first, I made the second, which I ate whilst preparing the third. The last was eaten whilst I saw to my frying pan and the fire. I concluded with a glass of water, and a meal like this served me for several days.'"[11]

On Sundays he neglected himself altogether. His breakfast consisted of a small piece of *pain bénit,* and only at night would he consent to take something more substantial. One day, when the pangs of hunger had become too agonizing, he went to his potato basket only to find it empty. In his sublime improvidence he had forgotten to lay in provisions. He was compelled to knock at a neighbor's door. His haggard features spoke more eloquently than words. "What is the matter, M. le Curé?" the neighbor asked in his alarm. "Oh! my friend, I have had no food for three days." The man promptly gave him half a loaf.

Another day he was on a visit to the house of Jean Cinier. It was the dinner hour, and freshly cooked potatoes lay steaming on the table. "They look fine," remarked M. Vianney, taking up a potato. He looked at it for a moment and put it back in the dish. "It was a penance that he imposed upon himself," says Antoine Cinier, one

11. A legend has sprung up according to which the Curé, during the whole of his forty-one years at Ars, lived exclusively on potatoes boiled by himself. This is quite incorrect. All the witnesses to his life agree in stating that he occasionally had them cooked for him. Moreover, this régime did not last beyond 1827, that is, a little under six years. From the day when M. Vianney took his meals at the *Providence* he had perforce to lay aside his potato pot and to eat what was put before him. We shall see that even then his penances were terrifying.

of Jean's children and a witness of the scene.

A woman of the village had obtained leave to take her cow to graze in the presbytery garden which was running wild. One day she surprised the Curé in the act of gathering sorrel. "So you feed on grass," the woman said. "Yes, my poor Mère Renard," he replied somewhat annoyed at having been caught, "I have tried to eat nothing else, but I could not go on with it."

The good woman, no doubt, talked in the village, but even had she remained silent, the emaciated form of the Curé would have been sufficient evidence of the austerities to which he subjected himself on behalf of the people of Ars. His instinct warned him that the evil spirits wield a tyrannical power over impure souls, and his keenest anxiety was to set souls free from so dreadful a bondage. "This kind is not cast out but by prayer and fasting," says the Gospel. (*Matt.* 17:20). That saying of the Master became the watchword of the Curé d'Ars. Twenty years later, on October 14, 1839, he betrayed the secret of his first conquests in a confidential conversation with the Abbé Tailhades, then a young priest of Montpellier, who was spending a few weeks with him in order to complete his training for an apostolic career: "My friend, the devil is not greatly afraid of the discipline and other instruments of penance. That which beats him is the curtailment of one's food, drink and sleep. There is nothing the devil fears more, consequently, nothing is more pleasing to God. Oh! how often have I experienced it! Whilst I was alone—and I was alone during eight or nine years, and therefore quite free to yield to my attraction—it happened at times that I refrained from food for entire days. On those occasions I obtained, both for myself and for others, whatsoever I asked of Almighty God."

Tears were streaming down his cheeks as he spoke. After a while he continued:

"Now things are not quite the same. I cannot do without food for so long a time—if I attempt it, I lose the power even of speech. But how happy I was whilst I lived alone! I bought from the poor the morsels of bread that were given them; I spent a good part of the night in the church; there were not so many people to confess, and the good God granted me extraordinary graces."[12]

In this way the period of his most severe penances was for M. Vianney also the time of his greatest consolations.

12. *Procès de l'Ordinaire,* p. 1516.

Chapter 3

THE CONVERSION OF ARS *(continued)*

II. War against Religious Ignorance

M. VIANNEY was well aware that the most formidable obstacle that lay in his way was the inertness of a population that did not wish to be disturbed in its habits of life. He had been received in every house. Those who were faithful in attending Sunday Mass would go on doing so, but he must not ask for more.

He, however, would not leave them undisturbed in their sluggish tranquillity. Conscious of his responsibility towards his flock, he was fully resolved to give them no peace until the day when abuses should have vanished from the parish. He would indeed pray and do penance, but he would likewise speak and act.

His first objective was the sanctification of the Lord's day, since there can be no Christian life without it. The house of God was deserted; the faithful must be brought back to it, and to this end it must be rendered more attractive. At the time of his appointment the parish church of Ars, which was dedicated to St. Sixtus, was poor within and without. The building consisted of a plain nave—eleven meters by five—terminating in a small apse, just large enough to receive the church's one altar. The decoration was of the plainest. Up to about six feet from the floor the whitewashed walls were covered with panelling then wholly discolored. The plainness of the wooden high altar was unrelieved by either carving or sculpture. The nave was not vaulted, and its flat ceiling, barely seven meters from the ground, was seamed with countless cracks. The vestments were poor and threadbare and few in number, so that they could add no lustre to the sacred ceremonies. "Such poverty aroused the compassion of passing priests, who occasionally stopped at Ars to say Mass."[1]

From the moment he saw it, M. Vianney loved the old church as he had loved the paternal home. When he undertook its restoration he began with what holds the foremost place, the altar, which is the centre and *raison d'être* of the sanctuary. Out of reverence for the Holy Eucharist, he wished to secure as beautiful an altar as possible. His first purchase was made with his own money, and he refused to appeal to the charitable châtelaine. It gave him boundless joy to help the workmen in the setting up of the new altar. In order to get some additional ornaments he journeyed on foot to Lyons. He came back from his pilgrimage, also on foot, with two small heads of angels, which he placed on either side of the tabernacle. Finally, in order that the frame might harmonize with the picture, he himself painted afresh all the faded woodwork.

After these improvements he undertook the task, to use his own picturesque and touching phrase, of adding to the household possessions of the good God—*le ménage du bon Dieu.* He went to Lyons to visit the workshops of embroiderers and goldsmiths. Whatever was most precious he purchased, so that the purveyors of church furniture would say with astonishment: "In this district there lives a little curé, lean, badly dressed, looking as if he had not a sou in his pocket, yet only the very best things are good enough for his church." One day, in 1825, Mlle. d'Ars took him into the city for the purpose of buying a vestment for Mass. Vestment after vestment was exhibited, but he kept repeating: "Not good enough! I must have something better than that."

These material improvements were not without bear-

1. Vestments and church linen "were in a deplorable state. Yet how could they be kept in good condition? The yearly income of the parish council amounted to barely fifty francs". (Catherine Lassagne, *Petit mémoire,* 3me rédaction, pp. 10 and 91).

ing fruit. They testified to the zeal of the pastor, gladdened the hearts of the devout, and in the end new faces came to be seen in church on Sunday, though they may have been those of people attracted rather by curiosity than by devotion.[2]

The great misfortune of those poor people was their ignorance of religion and the indifference that resulted therefrom. They were by no means unbelievers, for they had preserved a remnant of faith. Their parish priest, severe but clear-sighted, saw in their ignorance more than a mere deficiency—he thought it a sin. "We are convinced," he declared from the pulpit, "that this sin alone causes the loss of more souls than all the other sins together, because he who is ignorant does not realize the harm he does by his sin, nor the great good he thus forfeits." Hence the holy passion with which he instructed them. In days gone by he had tilled the soil in the sweat of his brow, but that heavy manual labor was a recreation in comparison with the unheard of task that he now set himself.

His first care was the instruction of the youth of the village. The children of Ars were employed in the fields from an early age. They no sooner reached the age of six or seven than they were made to tend the sheep and cattle. At the age of twelve a boy had to help his father at seed and harvest time. Agricultural laborers were scarce in La Dombes. Very few children could read. They attended catechism lessons only during the winter months, nor did they take much interest in them since they had not been able to learn the text. Not infrequently they missed Mass on Sunday. If on that day they were not sent into the fields—this did occur!—there was work to be done about the house. At an early age evil associations and ignorance of religion caused them to contract bad habits. Thus, degraded and unable to lift their heads towards Heaven, a great many of these poor children lived and grew up as if they had no immortal soul. Their first Com-

2. These details, concerning the first transformation of the church of Ars, under M. Vianney, are supplied by Mme. des Garets, *Procès de l'Ordinaire,* p. 772.

munion was nothing more than an ephemeral incident in their lives.

The Curé d'Ars undertook the task of gathering together these unhappy children as early as six o'clock every weekday morning, from the feast of All Saints until the date fixed for their first Communion. On Sunday there was a catechism class before Vespers, at about one o'clock in the afternoon. In order to draw the little people to church, M. Vianney had recourse to all manner of pious expedients. François Pertinand, innkeeper and carrier at Ars, relates this detail: "I remember that when I was a child he used to tell us: 'He who arrives first in church shall have a picture.' In order to secure this prize, some children arrived before four o'clock in the morning."[3] Obviously this must have been during the summer months.

M. Vianney only ceased catechizing in person on the day an assistant was given to him—that is, in 1845. During the space of twenty-seven years he carried out singlehanded all the obligations of the sacred ministry. "He himself rang the bell for his catechism to the children," the Abbé Tailhades relates, "and he invariably recited the preliminary prayers upon his knees, without ever supporting himself in any way. In order to rouse the attention of the little ones, he would begin with some impressive reflections which were so touching that the listeners were usually moved to tears. After the lesson had been recited he gave a short explanation, one that was easy to understand and full of unction." He required strict attention, kept the children well in hand, and at times inflicted slight punishments. But his chief object was to encourage them, and by his gentleness to inspire them with that filial affection which includes perfect reverence. He wanted them to carry a rosary on their persons, and he always had several in his pockets for the benefit of those who had lost theirs. Seventy years later some good old folk delighted in relating the experiences of those far-off days.

---

3. *Procès apostolique ne pereant,* p. 814.

This is what *Père* Drémieux related to Mgr. Convert in March, 1895: "At catechism time, whilst waiting for all to be there, he used to pray in the benches of the old chancel under the bells.[4] Oh! how he prayed! From time to time he raised his eyes to Heaven and smiled . . . I am sure that man saw something."

Questioned in her turn how the holy Curé taught the children, *Mère* Drémieux described him as going to and fro among them, frequently giving little slaps—"Oh! not hard ones, he was so gentle!"—to the little ones who would not keep quiet. On Sunday everybody was admitted to these lessons, *Mère* Verchére used to feel rather sleepy after her Sunday dinner; she was often called to order in exactly the same way as the children. M. le Curé, passing near her, would rouse her by means of a gentle slap. The good woman quite enjoyed these attentions and seemed proud of them.

The man of God never wearied of repeating the same thing again and again. Thanks to his heroic zeal, the children of Ars came to know their catechism better than any others in the district. Mgr. Devie publicly proclaimed this fact one Confirmation day. Later on, those who succeeded M. Vianney as parish priests of Ars were frequently astonished and edified at the knowledge of their religion displayed by quite simple people to whom they were giving the last Sacraments. The fact was that from their childhood upwards these good people had had the privilege of being taught by a saint.

It must be owned, nevertheless, that all did not equally benefit by these lessons. The holy Curé exacted a faithful word for word recitation of the text. This was too much for some rebellious memories. Yielding to scruples which may possibly be excused by the excessive rigorisms of certain moralists—his predecessors as well as his contemporaries—M. Vianney imposed on some young people several years of supplementary catechism lessons, thus

4. Until 1845, when the chancel of the old church of Ars was considerably enlarged, the altar stood in what is now the nave, between the first two pillars of the belfry, so that the chancel of the Curé's time was actually "under the bells."

putting off their first Communion in a way that seems almost incredible.[5]

On this subject we have the confidences of *Père* Drémieux: "Pierre Cinier, Etienne Perroud, Cinier des Gardes, made their first Communion when they were over sixteen years of age. Cinier des Gardes made his at Ambérieux, and as for me, they had to send me to Mizérieux. It really was annoying to have to go to catechism at such an age."[6]

M. Vianney burned with an even more fiery zeal for the instruction of the adult population of his parish.

He installed himself in the sacristy. Opening as it did on the Sanctuary, he would be laboring under the very eye of the divine Master. The vestment press became his writing table. He made a study of the *Lives of the Saints,* the *Catechism of the Council of Trent,* the *Dictionnaire de théologie* of Bergier, the spiritual treatises of Rodriguez, and the sermon books of Le Jeune, Joly, and Bonnardel. The only respite from these feverish labors was an occasional glance at the tabernacle. He sought inspiration at the foot of the altar. Kneeling on its step, he pondered what he had read, visualizing at the same time the poor people whom he had to evangelize. Before the Master, who knew how to utter the most sublime truths in such wise that fishermen, field laborers, and shepherds were able to grasp them, he pleaded with tears that He would suggest also to him the thoughts and accents that would convert his parish.

Returning once more to the sacristy, he began to write,

---

5. "When the time came to make a final selection of those who were to be permitted to make their first Communion, if he found any that were unprepared, he proved inflexible and kept them back for another year, whatever might be their age. It is true the biggest children formed a section apart in his Catechism class." (Magdeleine Mandy-Scipiot, *Procès apostolique in genere,* p. 263).

6. M. Vianney's line of action cannot in any way affect the teaching of the Church, whose principles have never varied. Every Christian is fit to approach the altar if he knows the great truths of religion, is free from grave sin, and is sincerely desirous of benefiting by the reception of the Holy Eucharist. At the period when our saint entered upon his ministry, Jansenism was not quite dead—it was an age of *practical,* if not *theoretical* rigorism. The priests of the neighboring villages acted just as M. Vianney did. As he grew older the saint grew also more lenient. Were he alive today, there would be none so keen as he to carry out the directions of the Pope in respect to the first Communion of children.

in a standing position, as became one who was prepared to do battle for the truth of which he wished to be the champion. His pen ran rapidly over the paper, so that at times he covered as many as ten large sheets with his fine, sloping handwriting. Occasionally he worked for seven hours on end and far into the night. His manuscripts show hardly any erasures. Unfinished sentences bear witness to his haste and to the ardor of his zeal. Time was precious—he felt he must get on at all costs.

But the hour came when the manuscript had to be committed to memory. This proved the hardest part of his task. His memory was never retentive, and yet it was necessary that he should assimilate some thirty to forty pages written at one sitting, and showing no apparent division into paragraphs. The night of Saturday to Sunday was spent in reciting his discourse aloud. From the road that skirts the cemetery belated passers-by could hear him reciting his sermon of the following morning. When sleep could be denied no longer, he sat down on the bare floor and, leaning his shoulders against the oaken credence table, he would doze for a few minutes. Surely those terrible hours were among the most meritorious and most heart-stirring of his whole life!

When morning came there was the audience to face. With the exception of the pew reserved for the people of the château, which was occupied by Mlle. d'Ars, the congregation was made up of peasants. These watched him with the eyes of a lynx, prepared to scoff on the slightest pretext. Many of them, especially among the young people, would have preferred to be elsewhere.

M. Vianney's only thought was of the salvation of these poor souls. He knew that in the pulpit a priest fulfills one of the most important duties of his sacred office. This conviction fired his zeal and gave him courage. Alas! the poor Curé's head ached sorely from the exertions of the previous night. Eleven o'clock was about to strike; he was still fasting, and he had eaten nothing since Saturday midday. On Sunday he sang Mass and preached, and, to fill up the measure, every one of his sermons lasted an hour.

His exhortations were delivered in a guttural voice, though the high-pitched note predominated; but both voice and gesture remained natural. Mlle. d'Ars, seeing his exertion in the pulpit, was greatly concerned about him. In her anxiety she said one day: "Why do you speak so loudly when you preach? Do take some care of yourself." "Monsieur le Curé," another asked, "why is it that you speak so softly when you pray and so loudly when you preach?" "Oh," was his good-natured reply, "the reason is that when I preach I speak to people who are either deaf or asleep, but when I pray, I speak to the good God who is not deaf."

Is it to be wondered at that his memory, thus overtaxed, should at times have failed him altogether? "In the pulpit," says Jean Pertinand, the village schoolmaster, "he sometimes got so lost that he had to come down without finishing his discourse." A humiliation like this before a congregation that had just been severely rebuked by him, far from disconcerting him, only added fuel to his zeal. When Sunday came round once more he went up into the pulpit as if nothing had happened. All the same, he fully realized that such failures tended to undermine his prestige as parish priest. So he prayed, and got others to pray. In the end his memory became less refractory, and he even felt that he could, on occasion, extemporize a few words.

What formed the subject matter of the sermons of this holy man who knew none of the arts of human eloquence? He spoke for the benefit of his flock alone, and he did so with great clearness, directness, and without a shadow of flattery. Some of his sayings strike us as very harsh indeed, but in those first years he struck hard to the end that the shaft might penetrate. At times his manner was calm, gentle, appealing, for he was not only an apostle out to convert, he was likewise a shepherd and a father. Among the audience there were necessarily hearts that sought comfort, wills that needed encouragement.

At the time of M. Vianney's arrival Guillaume Villier was a lad of nineteen. This is what he relates: "M. Vianney often spoke to us after this fashion: 'O my dear parishioners, let us endeavor to get to Heaven! There we shall see God. How happy we shall feel! If the parish is converted we shall go there in procession with the parish priest at the head.' At another time he would say: 'We must get to Heaven! What a pity it would be if some of you were to find yourselves on the other side!' And he loved to repeat that salvation is easy for country folk; it is so easy for them to pray whilst they are at work. With much discretion and tact he likewise congratulated those youths and maidens of Ars who gave up evil ways and resolutely set out on the road of virtue.

"His first endeavor was to obtain from those who were present in church—the absentees would have their turn!—a behavior worthy of Christians who were assisting at the most sacred of mysteries. Alas! the greater part of the congregation affected a *nonchalance* that clearly betrayed their lack of interest; there was much whispering and much coarse and noisy yawning. Latecomers banged the door; people in a hurry left in the middle of Mass; the young people looked about in every direction, to see how this person or that was dressed. The children were no better: 'Look at them laughing! Look how these wicked and ignorant little people nudge each other!'"[7]

The souls of this people were truly of the hardness of the rock. Such a soil could only be broken up by hard blows. Hence when he reproached them with their lack of faith, M. Vianney spoke their own language and used the expressions current among them. His language was at times so forcible that only the ardor of his zeal can explain or excuse it. At the risk of publicly inflicting mortification on some of the inhabitants of Ars, he was "unsparing in his invectives, which were often expressed in realistic and even crude phraseology." "His remonstrances were sharp, direct, and personal."[8] *"Rebuke them sharply that they may be sound in the faith,"* was St. Paul's injunction to Titus. (*Titus* 1:13).

---

7. "Voyez ces rires, voyez ces signes que se font tous ces petits impies, tous ces petits ignorants." *Sermons du Curé d'Ars,* t. I, pp. 199, 200.
8. Mgr. Convert, *Notes MSS.,* Cahier I, No. 39.

At the beginning of his ministry M. Vianney took this counsel literally. It must be owned that, though he strove to repress it, his caustic, mocking temperament showed itself occasionally: he had not as yet acquired perfect meekness. Nor was he as yet matured by experience. Strict with himself to a heroic degree, he was liable to be exacting with others also. He did not wholly escape from the spirit of the period. The evil tree of Jansenism lay indeed prostrate on the ground, but the soil still hid many a dangerous root. The pulpits of the neighboring churches resounded with like accents, though they were not occupied by great saints.[9]

In the work of spiritual husbandry it is not enough to root up—above all else it is necessary to plant. In conformity with the decrees of the Council of Trent, which lay on pastors the duty of frequently explaining the solemn rites of the Mass, the Curé d'Ars strove to instill into the minds of those of his parishioners who practiced their religion, a real love and understanding of the sacred ceremonies. He explained in turn the nature, the necessity, the value, and the fruits of the Eucharistic Sacrifice. The leading idea of his whole priestly career was to detach souls from earthly preoccupations and to draw them to the altar of God.

But there were those in the parish who, instead of going to Mass, "go to the house of a neighbor to drink a bottle"; those "who do not scruple, should they chance to meet a friend on the road, to ask him into their house and to put off Mass until another day"; those "who spend the hour of divine service at play, at the tavern, or in working, travelling, or dancing, people who live as if they were certain they had no soul to save."[10]

All these the Curé threatened with punishment in another world: "You poor people, how wretched you are!

9. M. l'Abbé Martin, some time vicaire at Grand-Corent (Ain) to the Abbé Tournier, an old uncle of his who had been a fellow-student of M. Vianney at Saint-Irénée of Lyons, told Mgr. Convert that that venerable priest also was most severe in the pulpit and in the confessional. M. Martin compared the sermons of his uncle with those of M. Vianney and found little difference between them, both as regards the matter and the manner.

10. *Sermons,* t. II, p. 160; III, p. 128.

Pursue your wonted way! go on! but all you may expect is Hell." He sought to touch them in a weak spot—their own interest: "From the first it is clear that they (the sinners) nearly always perish miserably. Faith dies in their hearts, and their worldly substance decays, so that they are doubly miserable."[11]

Unfortunately the preacher, who was well aware of it, spoke for the benefit of people who were absent, and "only addressed the walls." Notwithstanding so much indifference, on certain great feasts the whole village still went to church. This was the result of a custom that had come down from a more religious age. The new parish priest took the fullest advantage of those occasions to inveigh against vices that were playing havoc with souls. Thus on the feast of the Ascension he attacked all the vices together. His sermon on the feast of Corpus Christi opens with a frontal attack against sinners "who drag about with them wherever they go their fetters and their Hell." Then there is an abrupt pause: "No, my brethren, let us go no further; the thought would fill us with despair, and such language ill becomes a day like this. Let us leave those wretches in their gloom, since they love darkness; and since they do not wish to be saved, we must leave them to incur damnation." Having said this much, he turned at once towards the more fervent section of his flock: "Come, my children. . .!"[12] On the feast of the patron saint of the church, even those would not dare to miss Mass, who were about to spend the day and the ensuing night in dancing and drinking—M. Vianney has them in his grasp; they will not escape before they have been subjected to a wholesome castigation. He makes a virulent attack upon those who are preparing to go to the dance: "You will say," he exclaims, "that it is waste of time to speak about dances and the evils they lead to." Nothing will stop him: "In acting as I do I fulfill my duty." Then he rebukes in turn "the boys and girls who drink from the source of all crimes," as well as those "purblind and

11. *Ibid.*, t. II, pp. 158, 159.
12. *Sermons,* t. II, p. 120.

criminal parents who have set them the example."[13]

The battle was launched. The Curé d'Ars was determined, if God granted him life, not to lay down his arms until he had won a complete victory.

---

13. *Ibid.,* t. IV, pp. 201 SS.

Chapter 4

THE CONVERSION OF ARS *(continued)*

III. Fight against the Profanation of the Sunday, against Taverns and Blasphemies

DURING the first weeks of M. Vianney's ministry at Ars, in 1818, the tiny village church may have appeared tolerably full on Sunday, and it may be that the new parish priest entertained, for a time at least, a pleasing delusion as to the real state of religion among his people. But with the return of warmer weather he was sadly disillusioned. Easter brought him but little consolation. Most of the men refused to perform their duties; a number of them had not fulfilled this essential obligation for ten, fifteen, or even twenty years.

By midsummer M. Vianney made the painful *constatation* that the humble nave of his church remained almost empty. Scarcely any men or youths were now to be seen, and the number even of women worshippers was greatly diminished, Where were the absentees? At daybreak they had gone into the fields, in their workaday clothes, with fork or scythe upon their shoulders. It must have been heartbreaking, on those peaceful Sunday mornings, to hear the rumbling of carts on their way to the fields, or to listen to the anvil resounding under the blows of the hammer, for the smith could not keep the holy day, since there was no rest for the implements made by him. What a cynical response was this to the summons issuing from the lowly belfry of the village church!

This desecration of the Lord's day went on for many hours; in fact, the men worked as long as they had a mind to do so; but on their return the greater number donned their Sunday best. Some would sit down at the table of one of the taverns, for this village of two hundred inhabitants boasted no fewer than four inns. After discussing business, sales and markets, they would indulge in drink until complete intoxication was reached. Others again—that is, youths and maidens who could think of nothing but of pleasure and amusement, grown-up men and women, nay, even "old bespectacled villains"[1]—would group themselves under the walnut trees of the village green. There, in close proximity to the cemetery, the low enclosure wall of which did not even hide the graves and crosses, they danced to the shrill accompaniment of a fiddle. Far into the night the air was filled with snatches of songs and coarse jokes interspersed with loud guffaws and blasphemies.[2]

These things could be seen and heard by M. Vianney, since at that time a quickset hedge formed the only enclosure of his garden. He shed bitter tears, but his grief reached its climax when he learned that these disorders would be renewed week after week until the autumn, and that they would become even graver about the feast of St. Sixtus, the patron saint of Ars, when the annual fair *(vogue)* would be held, with booths, mountebanks, and rustic bands of music. Worse still: Ars was famous for its gaiety, hence dancers of both sexes flocked to it from all the neighboring villages.[3]

Whence came this universal and feverish love of pleasure? Ars lies almost exactly midway between the River Saône and the marshes of La Dombes. The climate of all that country is most enervating. Even M. Vianney felt afraid of losing his soul in such surroundings! The speech of the people has a musical softness, but its languidness betrays a flabby character. They eagerly seek comfort and

1. "Des vieux *mal embouchés* et portant lunettes. . . ." *(Sermons,* I, p. 248).
2. In a pastoral letter of January 22, 1807, Cardinal Fesch, to whose diocese Ars belonged, spoke very strongly in condemnation of the disorders of the time: "Ungrateful children, alas! stay away from the house of their heavenly Father, and the sacred solemnities of religion are turned into days of worldly business and criminal dissipation."
3. Frère Athanase, *Procès apostolique ne pereant,* p. 1010.

are keen in the pursuit of pleasure. Only a lively faith can save them from a headlong rush into sensual enjoyment.[4]

We know what little faith there was in that country about the year 1818. Nor were the gentry without reproach. Their amusements, though more refined, still reacted unfavorably upon the peasantry. Mlle. d'Ars, a discreet person if ever there was one, saw no harm in people dancing at her house, when, besides her own family, she entertained the de Cibeins, the Gillet de Valbreuse, and others.

Poor M. Vianney! Here, under his very eyes, were a thousand occasions of sin. Could he tolerate such a state of things? It was his duty to save these souls, to avenge the honor of God. Blasphemies, profanation of the Sunday, dances and gatherings at taverns, excursions and meetings in private houses at night, immodest songs and conversations—all these evils must be lumped together in a common reprobation. He would fight all these enemies in a sustained frontal attack. During long years, acting on the counsels of St. Paul, (*2 Tim.* 4:2) he was "instant in season, out of season," he "reproved, entreated, rebuked," in the pulpit, in the confessional, when visiting the people on the occasion of chance meetings, "in season and out of season." Nothing stopped him.

What likelihood was there that the Lord's day should be kept holy so long as the tavern competed with the house of God? The Curé d'Ars felt that if he succeeded in emptying the one he would fill the other. In the eighteenth century a tavern was deemed "an evil resort."[5] This was likewise M. Vianney's opinion. Was it not in those houses that dancers congregated and men forgot their duty? He tackled this enemy from the outset, nor did a holy indignation allow him to mince his words. He made his own the phraseology of St. John Climacus, in order to strike the harder: "The tavern," he exclaimed, "is the

4. Mgr. Convert, *A l'école du Bienheureux Curé d'Ars,* p. 195.
5. "Among evil resorts must be numbered, in a special manner, all taverns, for they are a source of great danger to country people" (Joseph Lambert, *La manière de bien instruire les pauvres et en particulier les gens de la campagne,* Paris, Morin, 1739, p. 133).

devil's own shop, the school where Hell retails its dogmas, the market where souls are bartered, the place where families are broken up, where health is undermined, where quarrels are started and murders committed."[6]

Drunkards, it may be imagined, were not spared. Trembling with a holy indignation, and in terms truly eloquent in their realism, the saintly Curé reproached them for "degrading themselves below the lowest of the beasts."[7]

If the patrons of the tavern received such treatment, how did the hosts fare? Two bars had been opened in the very centre of the village. These were the object of a particularly violent attack on the part of M. Vianney. Little did he care whether or not the tenants of these booths enjoyed much prestige among the villagers; he fought them fearlessly and unsparingly.

"The innkeepers," he used to say, "steal the bread of a poor woman and her children by selling wine to drunkards who spend on Sunday what they have earned during the week. If he wishes to escape eternal damnation a priest may not and cannot absolve innkeepers who, either at night or during church hours, serve those drunkards with wine. Ah! the innkeepers! The devil does not trouble them much; on the contrary, he despises them and spits upon them."[8]

No doubt such strong language made a deeper impression on the faithful who heard it than upon the innkeepers themselves, for, doubtless, these were not often seen in church. All the same, the preacher won his point, for the number of those who patronized the local inns became increasingly smaller. One innkeeper complained to the Curé that this meant his ruin. M. Vianney gave the man money and prevailed on him to close his establishment. Eventually the man became a most excellent Christian. For a time his partner continued to brave the anathemas of the parish priest, but in the end he, too, yielded, closed the tavern, and took up another occupation. In this way

6. *Sermons,* t. III, pp. 337, 334, 335.
7. *Ibid.*
8. "Il les méprise et leur crache dessus." *(Sermons,* I, p. 310).

did M. Vianney bring about the removal of both taverns from the neighborhood of the church.[9]

Two others, which stood in remoter parts of the village, were eventually compelled to close their doors also. The good curé of Fareins, M. Dubouis, was wont to say that this constituted one of the most signal victories of M. Vianney. But when money is at stake men are obstinate. Seven taverns were opened in succession; their owners were obliged, one after another, to retire from the business. A saint's curse lay upon them. "You shall see," he had prophesied, "you shall see; those who open an inn in this parish shall be ruined."[10]

This ruthless struggle yielded some unexpected results. The plague of pauperism abated. "There were very few destitute persons at Ars itself," says M. Pertinand, the schoolmaster; "by suppressing the taverns M. le Curé had eliminated the main cause of poverty."[11]

Later on, when strangers began to flock to Ars, modest hostelries were opened—there were five of them in 1858—and M. Vianney was in no way opposed to their erection. François Pertinand, a younger brother of the village schoolmaster, was at work with a confectioner of Mâcon. On learning that his employer compelled the young man to work on Sundays, M. Vianney brought about his return to Ars, where he managed a hostelry which became well known to pilgrims.

Had the taverns been nothing more than places where people met for innocent amusement, M. Vianney would have left them in peace. But God was blasphemed there! For a soul penetrated with such profound reverence for the holy Name the mere thought of such a thing was unbearable. And yet he experienced the sorrow "of hearing blasphemies issuing from the mouths of the village children who scarcely knew the Lord's Prayer."[12] He never alluded to this painful subject without shedding copious

9. Frère Athanase, *Procès apostolique ne pereant,* p. 832.
10. Frère Athanase, *Procès de l'Ordinaire,* p. 832.
11. *Procès apostolique ne pereant,* p. 858.
12. *Sermons,* t. II, p. 217.

tears, and in his sermons and catechisms he returned to it again and again. Blasphemers were threatened with heavy punishment, both in this world and in the world to come. "Is it not an astounding miracle that the house of a blasphemer is not struck by lightning or by some other misfortune? If the sin of blasphemy is rampant in your home, it will surely perish."[13]

For this cause he sought to repress the sin with boldness and severity, leaving no means untried by which he might instill a horror of it into the minds of youths and children.

"We recollect," Mgr. Convert writes, "a venerable priest who related to us how, as a young priest, he went to Ars, accompanied by a child of twelve or fourteen years. Both priest and child made their Confession to M. Vianney.

"'You will go to Holy Communion at my Mass,' the priest said to the child.

"'No, I cannot.'

"'Why not?'

"'M. le Curé has refused to give me absolution for this once, because I have blasphemed the holy Name of God.'"[14]

So successful was M. Vianney's campaign against cursing and swearing that even expressions that were merely coarse—he did not shrink from mentioning them in the pulpit—gradually vanished from the vocabulary of the people of Ars. In their place they would recite the Lord's Prayer, the "Hail Mary," or formulas such as "How good God is! Blessed be God!"

The struggle against the profanation of the Sunday exacted eight years of ceaseless efforts, and even so the Curé's success was not complete.[15] It is said that the first time he spoke of this subject in the pulpit he did it with so many tears, such an accent of indignation and a shaking of his whole being, that after the lapse of half a cen-

13. *Ibid.*
14. *A l'école du Bienheureux Curé d'Ars,* p. 268.
15. "'Il parvint à faire cesser, presque complètement, le travail du dimanche." (J. B. Mandy, *Procès de l'Ordinaire,* p. 597).

tury old men still spoke of it with emotion. In fact, all through life he ever spoke with a holy indignation whenever he mentioned the subject of the profanation of the Lord's day. "You labor, but what you earn proves the ruin of your soul and your body. If we ask those who work on Sunday, 'What have you been doing?' they might answer: 'I have been selling my soul to the devil and crucifying our Lord. . . . I am doomed to Hell. . . .' When I behold people driving carts on Sunday, it seems to me I see them carting their souls to Hell.

"Sunday is the property of the good God; it is His own day, the Lord's day. He made all the days of the week; He might have kept them all; He has given you six and has reserved only the seventh for Himself. What right have you to meddle with what does not belong to you? You know very well that stolen goods never yield any profit. Neither will the day that you steal from the Lord procure for you any advantage. I know two infallible ways to become poor, and they are: Sunday work and taking other people's property."[16]

His objurgations, his maledictions, were the talk of every household, and were duly related to the transgressors of the divine law. M. Vianney himself took good care to refresh their memories. On certain Sundays, contrary to his usual practice, he could be seen to leave the church and to take one of the roads close by. In this way, one Sunday in July, he suddenly came upon a man who was taking in his crop. Ashamed at being caught, the peasant tried to hide himself behind his cart. With an accent of intense grief the curé said to the man, whom he had recognized: "Oh my friend, you seem very much surprised to find me here . . . but the good God sees you at all times; He it is whom you must fear." That evening, instead of the usual homily, he forcibly inveighed against Sunday work. "Go," he cried with biting sarcasm, "go through the fields of those who work today; they always have land to sell!" He often spoke in this strain and with

16. *Esprit du Curé d'Ars* (English translation by Fr. Bowden. Burns and Oates, pp. 58, 59.)

such vehemence that "he lost his voice."[17]

It was useless, after that, to come to him for a dispensation from the law of the Church. On this point he obstinately refused to yield. He feared lest dispensations should pave the way for abuses, even by the best among his people. And then he felt such confidence in Him from whom all good things do proceed! Surely God would protect those who kept His law! In all such emergencies he ever spoke in the tone and with the authority of a prophet.

One Sunday in July the recently cut corn still lay on the ground. At the hour of Mass a strong wind arose, driving before it dark and threatening clouds. Should they not rush to save the crops? M. le Curé would not give an immediate decision; however, at the hour of the sermon he promised the good people who had come to listen to him that the weather would remain fine all the time—and even longer than they would need to save the harvest. In fact, the storm did pass over Ars without breaking, and that Sunday was followed by two weeks of sunshine and clear skies.[18]

There occurred, however, cases of real necessity, when M. Vianney yielded. Thus, for instance, he made no objection when he learned that the sinking of a well was being proceeded with on a Sunday, nor did he forbid the breaking of the Sunday rest when the crops were threatened with destruction owing to persistent bad weather. But neither publicly nor privately did he ever give such authorization. "Do as you like," he would say to those who made a private request to him; "it is your affair." At other times he would say: "Yes, elsewhere priests may grant permission to work on Sunday; I, at Ars, cannot do so."

He knew what he was doing in taking so strong a line of action. We shall soon have occasion to show how, for the overwhelming majority of the people of Ars, the Sunday became indeed the Lord's day.

---

17. *Procès apostolique ne pereant,* p. 917.
18. Baronne de Belvey, an eyewitness of the occurrence. *Procès de l'Ordinaire, p.* 202.

Chapter 5

THE CONVERSION OF ARS *(continued)*

IV. Campaign against Dancing

THE MEANS by which M. Vianney brought about the suppression of dances in his parish have become famous. His victory, in this matter, was decisive, but the struggle was long and obstinate. So inveterate was the passion for dancing that it cost the holy priest twenty-five years' efforts before he succeeded in extirpating it. It has been said that with some people dancing had become a kind of mania or intoxication. Like heathens who are unable to realize their wretched condition, the patrons of the dance were loud in asserting the innocence, and consequently the lawfulness, of this form of recreation. M. Vianney felt it incumbent on him to enlighten their consciences.

A girl who loves dancing until it becomes a passion is unable to relish pure and simple pleasures; she has no true Christian spirit. If her parents approve of her conduct, their household cannot be one in which the practices of a devout life are held in honor. Before they can become truly religious, such persons must begin by renouncing their worldly ideas and habits of life. They who wish to avoid sin must flee from the occasion of sin.

These were the principles from which the Curé d'Ars started when he entered upon his campaign, and he never swerved from the road on which he had thus set out. Though he condemned balls because of the dances that accompany them, gentle St. Francis de Sales had put on gloves when handling the subject. St. Jean-Marie Vianney, who in the end rivalled the Bishop of Geneva in meekness, refused to put on gloves because he deemed the precaution unnecessary. He was pitiless; sin and the occasion of sin were joined together in a common reprobation. But then, he was so farseeing! Together with the dance, he fought the impure passions which it fosters. Hence also his anathemas against the *veilles*[1] as they were practiced at the time, and the rejoicings in which the young people indulged on the occasions of betrothals. The peasants of Ars were wont to spend together the long winter evenings. None of the houses possessed rooms large enough to hold all those who attended, so the company adjourned to the stable, where the temperature was moderate. There, "under the eyes of parents who were either dumb or accomplices, things were done reminiscent of pagan times."[2] Ignorance and thoughtlessness may have excused these poor people, at least in some small measure. Be this as it may, these shameful disorders came to an end after M. Vianney had branded and condemned them from the pulpit.

As regards dances, resistance was obstinate, and victory was slow in coming. Again and again, during ten long years, M. Vianney had to return to the charge. "There is not a commandment of God," he explained, "which dancing does not cause men to break. . . . Mothers may indeed say: 'Oh, I keep an eye on my daughters.' You keep an eye on their dress; you cannot keep guard over their heart. Go, you wicked parents, go down to Hell where the wrath of God awaits you, because of your conduct when you gave free scope to your children; go! It will not be long before they join you, seeing that you have shown them the way so well. . . . Then you will see whether your pastor was right in forbidding those hellish amusements.

"My God, is it possible, is it possible to be purblind to the extent of believing that there is no harm in the dance, whereas it is the rope by which the devil drags the greatest number of souls into the abyss of Hell?"[3]

Here again the Curé d'Ars was not content with words:

---

1. Familiar gatherings at nighttime.
2. *Sermon sur la sanctification du chrétien,* t. I, pp. 136-139.
3. *Sermons,* t. III, p. 206.

he took direct action. One day he set out to meet the fiddler who was to play for the dancing. He who does away with the fiddle, he thought, will perhaps do away with the dance as well. The man was just entering the village, carrying his instrument under his arm. "How much do you get for playing at a dance?" M. Vianney asked. "I do not remember," says Frère Athanase, who relates the story, "whether the fiddler said five francs or ten. Anyhow, M. Vianney gave him double the sum asked, so that the man went away satisfied, and the dance did not take place."[4]

He dealt in like manner with an innkeeper of the name of Bachelard, on the occasion of a *vogue,* or village fair.

"How much money do you expect to make today?"

"So much, M. le Curé."

"Well, here is the money, but do not transact any business."

The man agreed and acted accordingly.[5]

One Sunday a ball was about to open in the village square. More than that, a rustic pageant was being organized, which was ever popular in that district. It was called "Mener l'âne," and took place when a wife had beaten her husband.[6] Suddenly M. Vianney was seen leaving his house. He had scarcely crossed the space separating the presbytery from the church when fear seized the people and scattered them in every direction. "They fled like a flock of pigeons," M. Vianney used to say laughingly whenever he related the incident. It was the end of that feast.[7]

All the women of Ars were not dancing-mad, for there were those who had been carefully brought up and whose good character had preserved them from the contagion.

---

4. *Procès apostolique in genere,* p. 202.
5. Jean Picard, blacksmith of Ars, *Procès de l'Ordinaire,* p. 1311.
6. In certain districts of the Rhône and the Ain, whenever a married man had been publicly beaten by his wife, a grotesque procession was organized. The central figure of the pageant was a lay figure representing the husband riding on a donkey. The wife walked behind belaboring the dummy with a broomstick. Appropriate songs accompanied the proceedings. Such a custom was hardly calculated to restore harmony in a household. It has now completely disappeared.
7. Frère Athanase, *Procès apostolique in genere,* p. 202.

M. Vianney was intensely keen to preserve this choice section of his flock. Others who had already taken the first step on the downward path experienced a feeling of shame. The grace of God, the fruit of the prayers and penances of the saint, was silently doing its work. Above all, the life of the parish priest was the most persuasive of all sermons; in it men could see the Gospel in action. When families were gathered round the hearth of an evening they used to say to one another: "Whatever our parish priest recommends, he first does himself. He practices what he teaches; we have never seen him take part in any amusement; his only pleasure is, apparently, to pray to the good God. Surely there must be some satisfaction in prayer, since he does nothing else. Let us follow his advice; he only seeks our good."[8]

Whilst boldly attacking every kind of disorder, M. Vianney fully realized that the training of an élite would greatly hasten his ultimate triumph. Sunday Vespers, which at one time had been almost completely neglected, began to be better attended. Every Sunday a few women and girls remained behind for private prayer. On weekdays, at about eight o'clock, M. Vianney recited night prayers with the few people who, at that hour, came to pay a visit to the Blessed Sacrament; very soon others joined this devout group.

It so happened that one Sunday afternoon, at the end of Vespers, a small band of young women stayed in church to go to Confession. They were good souls, no doubt, but they did not as yet realize that they were members of one family. M. Vianney felt inspired to address them all together in order to unite them in a common act of worship. "My children," he suggested, "if you will agree to it, we might say the Rosary together to the end that the Blessed Virgin may obtain for you the grace to perform well that which you are about to do." Among the girls there was one who was more mischievous than frivolous. "She was proud of the fact that she could answer the

8. Abbé Renard, *Notes MSS.*, p. 5.

Rosary." Before M. Vianney's time the Rosary was publicly recited in church once a year only, on the feast of the Annunciation.[9] The words of the priest made a deep impression upon the pure soul of this girl. "I really believe," she admitted later on, "that was the day on which M. le Curé changed my heart." She who would have been passionately addicted to pleasure now became a pattern of every virtue. The apostle had discovered the good leaven which would cause the whole paste to ferment. "This took place during his first years at Ars," says Catherine Lassagne, herself one of the souls he delighted in training. "One Sunday, during a *vogue,* he invited the young maidens to come into his garden to eat the fruit that grew there. He himself did not enter it. I plucked up courage and went with them, though I was still very young [Catherine was only twelve years old]. M. le Curé joined us for a few moments. I remember his saying to us: 'Do you not feel happier than those who are now dancing on the village green?' Later on he made us go into the kitchen of the presbytery, where he read to us the *Life* of my patron saint and spoke to us of the things of God."[10] These girls, with others who were, in turn, drawn by their example, were the nucleus of the first pious association established in the parish under the title of "The Guild of the Holy Rosary."

Towards those who proved rebellious to his warnings and exhortations M. Vianney adopted a line of conduct of exceeding severity. Starting from the principle that those who deliberately live in the occasion of sin may not be absolved unless they first give up that which is to them a cause of spiritual ruin, he persistently refused to absolve recidivists, even if there had been no more than an isolated relapse. He found excellent reasons to justify his conduct. In this way it came about that some of his parishioners, even though their lives were not scandalous, were compelled to wait for months and even years before they were admitted to the Sacraments. This is proved by the

9. Guillaume Villier, *Procès de l'Ordinaire,* p. 620.
10. These details are borrowed from the *Petit mémoire* of Catherine Lassagne.

admission made to Mgr. Convert in March, 1895, by a venerable old lady, whose statements were confirmed by her husband, who was present at the interview: "I have spent six years without making my Easter duties."

"Six years!"

"Yes, from the age of sixteen to twenty-two. Every year I used to visit my parents at Mizérieux, at the time of the annual *vogue,* when I danced for a while. The whole year round I never went anywhere, except on that one day. At Ars dances had been abolished long ago—for this happened between the years 1835 and 1841—but this little escapade, which occurred just once in the course of a whole year, was the cause of my being refused absolution."

"Did you go to Confession all the same?"

"Yes, before all the great feasts,[11] but M. le Curé only gave me his blessing."

"And what did he tell you?"

"'If you do not amend and stay away from the dance, you will be damned!' He did not mince words."

"But surely you must have danced on other occasions as well?"

"Never!"

"Why, then, did you go to Confession?"

"I said to myself: 'If the good God takes me before I have been given absolution, I trust that He will accept my desire to receive it.' My mother once asked M. le Curé whether I might go to Confession elsewhere. 'As you like,' he replied, 'but I would rather she should not make her Easter duties than that she should go to another confessor.'"[12]

Mlle. Claudine Trève also related how she once danced on the occasion of a wedding which took place in about the month of February. M. Vianney put off giving her absolution until the Feast of the Ascension.

11. "Pour toutes les bonnes fêtes."

12. Mgr. Convert, *Notes MSS.,* Cahier I, No. 21. In connection with cases like the above, M. Vianney used to say in the pulpit: "What anguish of conscience! If only their parish priest were less scrupulous! What are they to do? They look for a more tractable confessor who will absolve them on condition that they promise to be very good. . . . After that they go and crucify our Lord by an unworthy Communion." (*Sermon sur la tiédeur,* t. III, *passim).*

The father of a family, as yet not fully acquainted with the principles of his pastor, put to him a simple case of conscience: "May I take my daughter to the dance?"

"No, my friend."

"But I shall not let her dance."

"Oh, if her body does not dance, her heart will," was M. le Curé's last word; and surely it was indicative of a thorough knowledge of human nature.

On certain points M. Vianney may have been less exacting with strangers than with his own people, but as regards dancing he was ever absolutely unyielding. Men and women of the world, when kneeling at his feet, protested in vain that they were sure of themselves and that they felt immune from evil. He never wavered. He would not allow anyone to take part in society dances, even in the role of a simple spectator. Shortly after his arrival in the parish a few private dances were arranged at the château. But the family soon refrained from such diversions, "out of respect for his prohibition."[13]

All his life M. Vianney remained steadfast in his attitude towards dancing. He spared no effort in order to implant in the minds of parents sound ideas on a subject that he deemed of the utmost gravity. He strove to make them realize what were their duties to their children—namely, tender love mixed with firmness, good example, watchfulness, and correction. The escapades of sons and daughters were imputed to their parents. "You must answer for their souls as you will answer for your own. I wonder whether you are doing all that lies in your power . . . but what I do know is that if your children lose their souls whilst they are as yet under your care, it is to be feared that your lack of watchfulness may be the cause of your own damnation. . . . I know you will not take another step in order to do your duty by your children; these things do not greatly trouble you, and I should almost say you are right, for you will have plenty of time

13. Mlle. Marthe des Garets, *Procès apostolique in genere,* p. 290.

to worry during an endless eternity."[14]

It would seem that this biting sarcasm was the right treatment for the people of Ars. Parents began to interpret the admonitions of their pastor in their literal meaning. One Sunday afternoon, at the conclusion of Vespers, two sisters went to look at the dancing during the *vogue* of Savigneux, a village situate at about two kilometers from Ars. The girls fancied that their father was ignorant of their movements. They took no part in the dance, for they were in a hurry to get home. However, their absence had been noticed. When they reached home their father seized a stick and administered a severe correction to both.

One of the sons of Cinier—Antoine, aged twenty—had gone to a dance in a neighboring village. He returned home late at night and twice greeted his mother, without, however, eliciting a reply. Such unwonted coldness on her part seemed already punishment enough, but the indignant mother deemed it inadequate, for, seizing a stick, she administered a thrashing to that big lad of hers.

By the year 1830 dances had been completely suppressed as regards the center of the village. By order of the Mayor, Antoine Mandy, public balls were tolerated only in the upper part of the village. It came as a great humiliation to the organizers of the local fête when they were refused permission to hold a dance in the square in front of the church. It so happened that the feast of St. Sixtus was at hand. Those young men who were still hostile to their parish priest remonstrated with M. Mandy, and requested him to re-establish the yearly fête in its traditional setting. The aged Mayor replied that, having pledged his word to M. Vianney, he was unable to go back on it. The matter was taken a step further, for the thoughtless youths appealed to the Sous-Préfet of Trévoux. The latter revoked the ordinance of the Mayor of Ars, who could but bow to higher authority.

In due time came the solemnity of St. Sixtus, and with

---

14. *Sermons,* t. III, p. 316.

it the annual *vogue*. In the course of the Sunday afternoon the dancers arrived, gaily beribboned, preceded by a fiddler, and the air resounded with songs and shouts. What merry jests were bandied to and fro, of which the Curé and the Mayor were the butt! Suddenly the songs were hushed, faces became clouded. Where were the women dancers? Two or three servants from some of the farmsteads of Ars and a few strangers; these were the only partners to be secured that afternoon, for the girls of Ars were in church for Vespers and Benediction. That ball was a very dull affair.

When the bell rang for night prayers, the Mayor, who expected trouble, and for that reason had put on his insignia of office, saw there was no need for him to intervene, for the merrymakers quickly disbanded. But the church was full when M. Vianney delivered his usual homily. He wept, and his people wept with him. Not a few among the giddy youths realized their foolishness when they beheld the eyes of their mothers and sisters red from the tears they had shed during night prayers. So they, too, had themselves enrolled in one or other of the parochial guilds and renounced the dance.[15] Henceforth peace reigned on Sunday afternoons. The only people to be seen in the square were the faithful on their way to Vespers or to the cemetery, or, at the conclusion of the service, some harmless players at ball or skittles. If any young men still harbored a passion for the dance, they could find no partners among the girls of Ars.

"Go and look for such-and-such a girl," was M. Vianney's triumphant challenge, "at that entertainment, at those dances and other suchlike gatherings! And what will you be told? 'It is some time since we have noticed her here; I believe that, if you wish to see her, you must look in the church, where you will find her giving thanks to God for having wrought so great a change in her: you will observe modesty depicted on her brow.'"[16]

Enraged at seeing the girls of Ars forsaking the ball

15. Mgr. Convert, *A l'école du Bienheureux Curé d'Ars,* pp. 219-221.
16. *Sermons sur la contrition,* t. I, pp. 416, 417.

for the church, the libertines of Ars and the surrounding villages sought to revenge themselves in a way which we shall presently describe. In the meantime, what were they to do, with no dancing partners? Secret gatherings were arranged in remote hamlets. When the saint heard of it he thundered in the pulpit so vehemently and so successfully that after 1832 no dances took place within the bounds of his parish.

Incredible as it may appear, M. Vianney's victory was not as yet complete. If there was a *vogue* or ball in a commune of the neighborhood, excursions would be arranged. Thus, deeming themselves free at last, many imagined that they could indulge to the full in their favorite pastime. A few girls of Ars allowed themselves to be inveigled. M. Vianney experienced no difficulty in finding out who they were. Determined not to lay aside the axe so long as even one root of the evil tree remained, he gave no quarter. God often prompts his saints to do seemingly strange things. It was necessary to speak yet louder if he wanted to be understood. Hence M. Vianney resolved to refuse absolution even to those who had danced, were it only once, until he had secured a firm promise of amendment. Complete and final victory only crowned his efforts at the close of a mission which was given at Ars in the year 1847.

Hereafter all attempts to revive the *vogue* of St. Sixtus proved abortive. When Comte Claude des Garets became Mayor of Ars in 1839 he took the matter in hand and settled it once for all. At a subsequent period, about 1855, some people began once again to frequent fairs more than was necessary. A young priest was then able to judge for himself of the vigor of M. Vianney's language when disorder threatened to raise its head. "I heard him one night," says the Abbé Pelletier, "inveighing against the fair of Villefranche, to which people formerly flocked in crowds because of the amusements connected with it. The congregation seemed utterly crushed."[17]

A last and severe warning seemed necessary in con-

17. *Procès apostolique in genere,* p. 290.

nection with certain amusements, which may have appeared harmless enough, but which the saint deemed unworthy of his good people. On February 9, 1858—exactly forty years after M. Vianney's arrival at Ars—Jean-Baptiste Mandy married his cousin, Claudine Trève. A few weeks previous to the event some men—not all of them young ones—forgetting the endless quarrels to which the custom was wont to lead, endeavored to revive an observance that had been rightly abolished. It consisted in a visit to the poultry yards of the Mandy and Trève families, where they helped themselves to the best of the birds. In this way—in accordance with ancient use—a sumptuous banquet was provided for, in honor of the engaged couple, one fine Saturday evening. The feast lasted far into the night. M. Vianney was now an old man of seventy-two years of age, and utterly worn out by his fasts and labors. That Sunday morning, however, he found the accents of former days, the days of his first struggles. He told his people—and especially the guilty ones, who already felt sorry for their folly—what pain their childish behavior had caused him. "In the near future another wedding is to take place in this parish," exclaimed the preacher, "but if you do it again you will see that I shall go away." They did not do it again.

Scandalous dress goes with corrupting pleasures. To judge by certain of his sermons, it would seem that at the time of M. Vianney's arrival at Ars there were women who outraged the most elementary rules of modesty. Their conduct roused him to indignation. His anger included parents who idolized their children and fostered their vanity. Let us listen to him castigating "that mother who can think of nothing but her daughter. She is far more concerned whether her bonnet is put on properly than whether the child has given her heart to God. She beseeches her daughter not to be unsociable—to be gracious to everybody so as to form acquaintances and eventually to 'get off.' Soon the girl's one aim will be to attract. Her extravagant and indecent dress proclaims her to be a tool by means of which Hell seeks the ruin of souls. Only at the judgement-seat of God will such a one know the number of crimes of which she has been the cause."[18]

Generally speaking, mothers quickly realized what was their duty. The parish priest came to their assistance either by refusing absolution to those who offended in this matter, or by himself laying down the law in connection with the fashions. It was a matter requiring careful handling, but the saint looked ahead. He wanted the women and girls of his parish to attain to the high degree of perfection of which he knew them to be capable. For this cause he came down to details that at first sight seem almost childish.

"The women and girls had adopted a head-dress which was very becoming," and showed their hair to advantage. M. Vianney forced them to give it up in favor of bonnets that successfully hid the hair.[19] Marthe Miard, who kept a shop not far from the church, was bidden to rearrange her bonnet because he did not think it was plain enough. "We looked like little old women," said Claudine Trève, who yet never had a taste for vanity. Here is another incident related by Marthe Miard: "One day M. le Curé met me when I was somewhat better dressed than usual" (she was wearing a muslin dress of a bright color). "Instead of greeting me with his usual 'Good-day, my child!' he made me a deep bow and said: 'Good-day, mademoiselle!' I felt very much humiliated."

Little Jeanne Lardet was proudly showing off a pretty new collar. "Will you sell me your collar?" M. Vianney laughingly asked. "I will give you five sous for it."

"What for, M. le Curé?"

"For my cat."

Low necks and bare arms, to be sure, would never have been tolerated in his church. He allowed them neither to the little ones nor to the great ones of this world. One day, whilst calling at the château, he noticed for the first time the portrait of a lady in evening dress. "One might

18. *Sermons,* t. III, p. 232.
19. Mme. Christine de Cibeins, *Procès apostolique continuatif,* p. 138.

think she was going to be guillotined," he observed, pointing his finger at the portrait. Mlle. d'Ars took the hint and removed the picture.

Towards the end of his life he poked fun at the crinoline—even in his catechisms: "The Emperor has done many fine things, but there is something that he has overlooked; he should have had the doors widened to permit of the passage of crinolines." Notwithstanding his satire, a few women of Ars began to wear that cumbersome garment. M. Vianney did not insist, for he deemed the fashion nothing worse than ridiculous. Besides, these few women of his parish were wholly submerged, on Sundays and holidays, under the mass of strangers who freely conformed to the decrees of the fashion of those days. The fact remains that during thirty years, whether they were met with in church, in the street, or on some country road, such was the modesty and reserve of the women and girls of Ars that they became the rivals of religious Sisters and the edification of the pilgrims who flocked to that favored village.

Chapter 6

RESTORATION OF THE OLD CHURCH OF ARS

THE love of God and the love of souls were the motive power of the Curé d'Ars. His very temperament spurred him to action. Enforced leisure would have proved unbearably irksome to him. Though weakened at an early age by superhuman penances and tortured by an intermittent fever which was supposed to have been due to the unhealthy climate of La Dombes, M. Vianney would not take as much as an hour's rest.

His parochial duties were far from absorbing,[1] but his ingenuity found work that satisfied both his zeal and his need of activity. On the one hand, he allowed his garden to run waste, after having had the trees cut down, because thieves were in the habit of breaking through the hedge to steal the apples, so that "the good God was offended." On the other hand, his presbytery was being gradually stripped of all its furniture, which he gave to the poor. His house only saw him when he came in at night for the brief rest that he allowed himself. The time not taken up with study and prayer was spent in transforming the lowly village church. We have already seen him restoring the high altar and repainting the panelling of the walls. He was meditating an even more

1. The following extract from the parish registers proves our assertion:

	Baptisms	*Marriages*	*Burials*
1818	10	2	3
1819	12	0	5
1820	13	4	0
1821	12	1	2
1822	14	2	11
1823	15	2	6
1824	11	8	6
1825	11	8	7

ambitious scheme when an unforeseen event threatened to stop everything.

At the beginning of April, 1820, M. Vianney received a communication from the ecclesiastical authorities at Lyons—Ars belonged to the archdiocese of Lyons—that he had been appointed to the parish of Salles en Beaujolais, in the deanery of Villefranche-sur-Saône.[2] He was to exchange the *département* of the Ain for that of the Rhône.

By some means or other his ecclesiastical superiors had come to know of the precarious state of M. Vianney's health; hence their decision to send him to Salles, a pretty village nestling on the slope of verdant hills. There he would breathe a purer air. The population amounted to about three hundred souls; they enjoyed a reputation for courtesy and a certain amount of religion.

M. Vianney was greatly attached to his lowly village of Ars. However, it never occurred to him to remonstrate; he just made ready to leave for his new post. His books and furniture were soon packed and put on a cart. When the news of his departure became known there was no small stir among the more fervent section of the population. The mothers of families seem to have had a presentiment of the event. "How happy we should be," they said, "if our children made their first Communion under the guidance of this priest! He is a saint. . . . But there, they will not let him stay with us." Great was the emotion of Mlle. d'Ars, nor could the authorities wholly override her opinion. In a letter to an intimate friend, in which the venerable châtelaine gave full vent to her mood,

---

2. The archives of Lyons show not a trace of the projected transfer of M. Vianney to Salles. We are able to give the approximate date of the occurrence by means of a letter which the person most interested, who, to be sure, was no great letter writer, addressed to his eldest brother.

"ARS,
"*April* 8, 1820.

"MY DEAR BROTHER,

"I leave La Bresse for Le Beaujolais. I am to set out next week. They are sending me into a parish not far from Villefranche. I hope to see you soon."

Salles is noteworthy for its abbey, built in the purest romanesque style. It was occupied in turn by Benedictine monks and Benedictine nuns. The latter constituted themselves into a "noble chapter"—*chapitre noble de chanoinesses-comtesses.* The convent was ravaged in 1793. There only remains part of the cloister with its graceful columns.

she spoke of nothing less than strangling the Vicar-General.[3] No doubt this was only a pleasant way of relieving her feelings. However, M. Vianney allowed himself to be impressed by "the deep regrets" of a number of his people. With his full knowledge, a deputation, with the Mayor at its head, set out for Lyons. "Ars wanted to keep its parish priest."[4] "If that be so," M. Courbon declared, "let him remain as long as he likes," at the same time handing to the delighted deputation an official document cancelling the appointment to Salles. So M. Vianney remained at his post.

Moreover, God Himself, it would seem, had made known His Will. On the appointed day M. Vianney had duly set out with all his belongings. He had perforce to cross the Saône, but on reaching the bank he found the river in flood and so wildly agitated that the ferryman was unable to take him across. In those days the beautiful suspension bridge of Jassans did not as yet exist. After two unsuccessful attempts had been made, both library and furniture had to be taken back to Ars.

M. Vianney's position was, nevertheless, exceedingly precarious. In his capacity as a simple chaplain his stay at Ars seemed likely to be but a passing one. Barely two years after his arrival, just as people were beginning to value him, he very nearly left for another sphere of work. In fact, during those hours of alarm the good people of Ars asked themselves with justifiable anxiety whether the authorities at Lyons would even send a priest to take his place.

The châtelaine of Ars had long ago taken steps to secure once more for the village its ecclesiastical independence and the title of a parish. During the Revolution François Cinier had become the owner of the presbytery, the garden and the orchard of which the priest had, until then,

3. The Abbé Monnin *(Le Curé d'Ars)* speaks of "a holy anger." On the other hand, Mlle. d'Ars wrote a letter to M. Courbon, for whom she entertained a high esteem. The latter replied: "I am leaving nothing undone to induce M. Vianney to alter his manner of life; but I make no impression on him. His friends are not more successful. He listens and then goes on as before. Let him go to Salles. I want him to enjoy better health, though I dare not hope for an improvement in this respect." (*Letter* of April 17, 1820).

4. J. B. Mandy, *Procès apostolique in genere,* p. 242.

enjoyed the use. As early as 1806 the Dowager Comtesse des Garets had rented the whole of this property, in the hope of one day restoring it to its original purpose. Less than two years later, as we learn from a letter of the Vicomte to his mother (March 18, 1808), the Comtesse bought the presbytery with all its dependencies. In her eyes the transaction would secure for Ars its privileges as a *succursale* (chapel-of-ease). Finally, on June 19, 1821, during the pastorate of M. Vianney, the Vicomte surrendered to the *fabrique* (vestry board) of the church the whole of the property of which the death of his mother had made him the owner. Thanks to his generosity, the erection of the chaplaincy into a parish had entered into the realm of possibilities.[5]

The people of Ars, on their part, addressed to Louis XVIII a petition in which they stated their legitimate grievances—viz., the excessive distance of Mizérieux, the impossibility for the children to attend the catechism instructions during the winter months owing to the swollen rivers and the bad state of the roads; above all, they insisted on their fear lest, because of their having no resident priest, their chaplaincy should be suppressed altogether. Hence they begged to be given the status of a parish. The conclusion ran thus: "The inhabitants of Ars, true to their faith and zealous for the practice of religion and virtue, wish to keep a priest at their own expense. The priest in question is a man of eminent virtue, who does an immense amount of good, not only in his

5. On the day following this memorable transaction the Vicomte wrote to his sister: "Today, the Council of State is to present to the King the Minister's report, in which it is stated that I bestow the gift on the *express condition* (he underlined it himself) *that Ars shall be set up as a chapel-of-ease.* I make the further stipulation that we shall reserve our pew and the tribune in the church for ourselves and our descendants. . . . I shall always continue to allow M. le Curé the use of the hemp-field adjoining the rectory." (*Letter* of June 20, 1821). It is but fair to add that the Municipality of Ars did not show itself indifferent to the religious position of those subject to its jurisdiction, as is testified by the deliberative assembly of the Municipal Council of November 5, 1808, where the Commune of Ars itself offers to pay the future chaplain: "We settle the sum of five hundred francs, as stipend, on the priest who serves the annex"; and again, as evidenced from the deliberations of June 18, 1809, where the Municipality undertakes to "maintain the church and cemetery, to provide a presbytery and a garden for the vicaire *(sic)*, as well as the sacred vessels, ornaments, and all furniture in general, as required for the ministrations of religion." (Archives of the Mairie of Ars).

Basilica and Old Church of Ars

Interior of the Curé d'Ars' Room
(showing his deathbed)

THE CHURCH OF ARS
(1818-1859)

THE PRESBYTERY AT ARS
(1818-1859)

own parish, but likewise in the district around Ars. Unhappily all the good that is being done may come to an abrupt end if the pastor is withdrawn from us."[6]

The Vicomte was in Paris at the time. He gave his support to the demand of his countrymen. In this way it came about that, though the village did not muster the five hundred souls required by the decree of August 25, 1819, for the erection of a *succursale,* a decree of June 20, 1821, raised Ars to the rank of a parish, and Mizérieux was deprived of its brightest jewel, though it could not then gauge the magnitude of its loss. Nor could M. Courbon, the Vicar-General who cancelled M. Vianney's appointment to Salles, foresee that the parish where he was happy to allow him to remain would itself ere long be severed from the archdiocese of Lyons.

The incidents that we have just recorded—of diminutive importance in the history of the world or that of the Church, but fraught with weighty consequences for the lowly village of Ars—took place at a moment when M. Vianney was actively engaged in beautifying his church. By 1820 the construction of a bell-tower, however simple it might have to be, had become imperative. The wooden structure, which carried a bell that was too heavy for it, threatened to collapse at any moment. Though the bell was no longer swung, but merely chimed, people trembled lest tower and bell should come crashing down upon the graves in the cemetery. In August, at the request of M. le Curé, the Mayor gave orders for the work to start. M. Vianney rejoiced as he watched rising in the sky of Ars a solid brick tower, square and squat in appearance, and pierced by double windows that formed a frame for some graceful romanesque columns.[7] No sooner was the

6. Petition of February 22, 1821 (Archives of the Mairie of Ars).

7. These columns were taken from the cloister of Salles en Beaujolais. They were "old materials" previously acquired by the builder. In the accounts of the masons, who constructed the tower, we read: "6 pillars of free stone, 36 francs." This was cheap, even for those days.

The bell tower cost 1,106 francs in all. A collection taken in the parish yielded 265 francs. The list of subscribers consists of forty-four names. M. le Curé is down for 4 francs; Antoine Mandy the mayor, Jean Cinier the *adjoint,* the elder Dupont, are down for 30 francs each. Mlle. d'Ars, whose name does not figure on the list, paid directly for much of the building material.

tower completed than the second bell was installed in it. M. Vianney bought it himself, and called it "the bell of the Holy Rosary."[8]

Whilst scaffoldings rose higher and higher above the roof, much work was done within the sacred edifice. As yet the thought of dismantling the church had not presented itself to M. Vianney's mind; it is so easy to pray within the walls of an old church! Moreover, the erection of a new church would have proved too heavy an outlay.[9]

Close to the altar rails, which at that period marked off the entrance into the sacristy and the part of the church under the bells, there stood an altar and a statue of the Blessed Virgin. But the worm-eaten shrine, with its four candlesticks, from which every trace of gilding had vanished, presented a sorry appearance. M. Vianney wished to honor Our Lady in proportion to his love for her. In pursuance of this thought, he conceived the plan of opening a side chapel which should be dedicated to the Blessed Virgin. The work proceeded apace: begun in January, 1820, it was completed by August 6, the patronal feast of Ars. The new chapel with its flat ceiling, its mouldings and gildings and gaily painted statue—the work of a plasterer and painter of Villefranche—were in keeping with the taste of the period. M. Vianney conceived a special love for this quiet, half-secluded corner of his church. Every Saturday, for forty years, he said his Mass in the new chapel.[10]

---

8. The two bells hung in the new tower by M. Vianney are still there. The first bears the following inscription: "J'ai été bénite par Messire J.-M. Vianney, curé; nommée Colombe par F. Garnier, vicomte d'Ars, ancien capitaine de dragons, chevalier de l'ordre royal et militaire de Saint-Louis, et par Mlle. Colombe Garnier, Ars, l'an 1819."

   The other bell, that of the Holy Rosary, is thus inscribed: "J'ai été donnée par Messire Jean-Marie Vianney. J'ai été baptisée par Messire Pasquier, curé de Trevoux, et nommée Jeanne-Marie-Félicité par Denis-Félicité Garnier, comte des Garets, chevalier de l'ordre royal de la Légion d'honneur, et par Marie-Jeanne Dareste son épouse. 1820. VOX DILECTI MEI PULSANTIS.

9. It is quite true that "the sums spent in the erection and decoration of one chapel after another would have been sufficient for the reconstruction of the sacred edifice. But funds came in intermittently, and as soon as M. Vianney had enough money in hand he made haste to spend it in the service of God." (Frère Athanase, *Procès apostolique in genere,* p. 217).

10. "M. Vianney had likewise planned the erection of a chapel in honor of St. Joseph." (Catherine Lassagne, *Petit mémoire,* premiere rédaction, p. 17).

In 1822 the ceiling of the nave threatened to collapse. Its restoration was undertaken at the expense of the commune and paid for by an extraordinary levy. The cost amounted to 459 francs.

In the course of the year 1823, with a view to rendering public homage to the great saint whom he had chosen for his patron at Confirmation, M. Vianney, at his own expense, erected yet another chapel and dedicated it to St. John the Baptist. It was blessed and inaugurated on the feast of the saint, June 24, by the Abbé Mathias Loras, a fellow-student of M. Vianney at Ecully, and at that time Superior of the Petit Séminaire of Meximieux. The occasion was devoutly and joyfully celebrated by the bulk of the population, for already those who practiced their religion formed the majority. However, the lovers of worldly amusements, who on that day mixed with the congregation, could not read without a feeling of resentment an inscription which, for their special benefit, the parish priest had caused to be painted over the arch of the new chapel: *Sa tête fut le prix d'une danse* ("His head was the price of a dance").

It was subsequently rumored that on the occasion of the blessing of the chapel M. Vianney had been favored with a vision of the future. Catharine Lassagne thus refers to the report: "Did the good God that day reveal to him what was to take place hereafter—that is, the conversion of so many souls? I could not say. But this is what he told us in a sermon one Sunday: 'My brethren, if you knew what had happened in that chapel, you would be afraid to go into it. . . . I will say no more. . . .' This he repeated several times, as if his mind were full of it."[11]

People thought that the Precursor had appeared to him, showing him in a prophetic vision the famous confessional which stood in that chapel, and the crowd of kneeling penitents.

Whilst the erection of the altar of St. John the Baptist gladdened the heart of the Curé d'Ars, it caused him also

11. Catherine Lassagne, *Petit mémoire,* troisième rédaction, p. 100.

grave anxiety. He had made himself responsible for the full cost, and he owed 500 francs to the carpenter when he was without a sou. His slender income as *succursaliste,* as well as the annuity paid to him by his brother François as his share of the paternal inheritance—all had gone into the hands of the master mason. The carpenter, on his part, pressed for payment. One day, "feeling very worried, poor M. Vianney left his house in order to get some relief from his anxiety. Whilst he was thus walking along one of the roads near the church, he met a woman, unknown to him, who asked him: 'Are you M. le Curé d'Ars?' On his replying in the affirmative, the woman handed him 600 francs for his charities."[12]

Though he deemed the incident an extraordinary intervention on the part of God, he did not dare to draw the conclusion that henceforth divine Providence would be his banker. On the contrary, cautious both by nature and grace, he declared that he had had a lesson and that he would never again incur such risks. He made it a rule to pay in advance, except in extraordinary circumstances.

At a much later date the church was still further enlarged. Three chapels were destined to rise in turn—viz., in 1837 that of St. Philomena, and, at dates that have not been recorded, a chapel called "Ecce Homo," and another, the fifth and last, dedicated to the holy angels.

In 1845 the small apsidal chancel, just large enough to hold the altar, made room for a lengthened sanctuary, which was almost as long as the nave. A second sacristy opened from this new chancel, and behind the altar the saint put up a confessional, which was specially reserved for priests.

To satisfy his own devotion, and because experience had taught him that good and simple souls are much moved by the sight of pictures, M. Vianney decorated his church with a number of statues and images. The effigies of St. Joseph and St. Peter adorned the chancel, whilst those of St. Sixtus, the patron of the parish, and

---

12. *Procès de l'Ordinaire,* p. 345.

of St. Blaise, stood at the entrance to the chancel. A recumbent statue of Christ in the tomb, and a similar one of St. Philomena, adorned respective chapels. In recesses, or simply fixed on the wall, were to be seen Our Lady of the miraculous medal, a Madonna with the divine Child, St. John the Baptist, St. Lawrence, St. Francis of Assisi, St. Catherine of Siena, St. Benedict Labre, the archangel St. Michael, the Annunciation, the archangel Raphael with Tobias. In the chapel of the Ecce Homo, in addition to the chief figure—viz., that of Christ crowned with thorns—there were reliefs of the holy Face and the instruments of the Passion. Everything in the tiny chapel spoke to the heart of the Christian. "Sometimes the mere sight of a picture is enough to move and convert us," M. Vianney was wont to say; "at times pictures make almost as deep an impression as the objects they represent."[13]

"The big statues threw him into raptures," says the Comtesse des Garets. "Ah! if we had faith!" he exclaimed with tears as he gazed at an *Ecce Homo.*[14]

In this work of material restoration and beautifying, M. Vianney had the advantage of the powerful help of a gentleman to whom Ars owes a debt of undying gratitude—namely, the Vicomte Françoise, brother of Mlle. Anne-Marie Garnier des Garets. It was this sister who informed the Vicomte, who lived in Paris, of the arrival in the parish of a former vicaire of Ecully of the name of Vianney. In the spring of 1819 the Vicomte came to the ancestral home for a few weeks' rest. In this way he became acquainted with the new parish priest, who, though not yet thirty-three years old, seemed already worn out by his night watches, his fasts, and his apostolic labors. From the first the Vicomte fell under the spell of M. Vianney. His trust in him was unconditional, and he never wrote to his sister without mentioning her "devoted and respected parish priest."

Mlle. d'Ars kept her brother fully informed of M. Vian-

13. *Sermon,* t. IV, p. 155.
14. *Procès de l'Ordinaire,* p. 772.

ney's undertakings. She cannot have failed to explain that the work had indeed been well begun, but that for lack of funds it would have to come to an abrupt end. What a disappointment for the saintly priest! So eloquently and so successfully did the old châtelaine plead the cause of her beloved little parish that the Vicomte decided to go on with the work begun by the curé. "The village sanctuary will never appear so splendid and magnificent as I wish to see it," he wrote to his sister.

Commissions were at once given to the most skillful workers in Paris. On May 5, 1823, he was happy to announce the arrival of a first parcel containing three banners embroidered in silver thread, the subjects being the Blessed Sacrament, the Blessed Virgin Mary, and St. Sixtus. He wrote to M. Vianney: "What your goodness prompts you to undertake in behalf of the church of Ars is an incentive to me to do something on my part. Your parishioners have informed me that your solid instructions and your good example are a source of edification to them and draw their souls to God." Later on there came Mass vestments of silk or cloth of gold and one vestment of black velvet with red fringes for the office of Good Friday.

A canopy was promised for May, 1824. M. le Curé was asked to choose the material himself. "Since the best material is made at Lyons, and *in order that your own taste may be suited,* I ask you, my excellent friend and most respected parish priest, to make the purchase yourself." In due time the canopy arrived. Alas! it was too big for the small door of the church; it could not be got through until the year 1826, when the Vicomte enlarged the sacred edifice by eight feet and added a new porch, which, at a later date, was crowned with a statue of Mary Immaculate.

If there was a man who exulted on the arrival of the successive gifts of the generous Vicomte, M. Vianney was that man. It seems that it was a joy merely to see him and hear his comments when the heavy cases were opened on their arrival from Lyons, whence they had been fetched by some men of good will. Like a child he laughed and wept all at once. "*Mère,* come!" he said to a good old woman who was going by, "come and see a beautiful thing before you die!" Soon a whole band of admiring persons would be gathered round the treasures. "Ah!" he exclaimed, "in Heaven everything will be even more beautiful."[15]

The generosity of the Vicomte made it possible to widen the entrance to the church, but the access to it remained difficult. The church was approached by a winding staircase, which was in a ruinous condition. It was decided to replace it by a flight of steps flanked by a graceful balustrade. The Vicomte was anxious to achieve something out of the common. "I want the entrance to the church to be very beautiful," he wrote to Mandy, the Mayor. "This is imperative, for if the beauty of the palaces of kings is enhanced by the magnificent approaches that lead up to them, how much more sumptuous should be the approach to a church? There must be no stinting in this matter."

In the year 1826 the flight of steps and the balustrade which we see today were erected. All the inhabitants lent their aid by carrying the building materials to the site.

Whilst this work was in progress the Vicomte did not remain idle. On May 15, 1827, the Mayor received a letter from him, begging him to inform M. le Curé and the vestrymen that he gave to the parish church 1) a silver-gilt monstrance;[16] 2) a throne for Exposition, covered with velvet, the roof, columns, base, and top being of gilt brass; 3) a tabernacle of gilt brass, in keeping with the throne, etc."

M. Vianney likewise received from his "beloved bene-

---

15. All the ornaments acquired or received at that period by M. Vianney were really valuable, but none of them have any truly artistic merit. The canopy, which was of very rich material, was the only article the embroidery of which was in good taste.

16. This monstrance, surmounted by a large cross adorned with paste jewels, was stolen from the sacristy. M. Vianney grieved more because of the crime than by reason of the loss. "It is a temporal loss and can be made good." He appealed to the generosity of his people, who bought him another monstrance. According to the Comte des Garets, "M. Vianney needed but to ask when he would immediately obtain all that he required for his church." (Comtesse des Garets, *Procès de l'Ordinaire,* pp. 773 and 951).

factor" large reliquaries for the adornment of the chapels of the Blessed Virgin and St. John the Baptist.[17]

The Vicomte's first reward was the approval of his "fond sister," as he styles her in some of his letters, and the pleasure he gave to the holy Curé d'Ars. This is how he writes to his sister: "You mention our respected M. l'Abbé Vianney. From this I gather *that you are satisfied with all that I do and shall yet do for Ars, if God grants me life,* but that it is likewise your intention to leave me to do almost everything myself, since you appear to be attracted to other good works. . . . I ask you as a favor to tell me frankly what our Curé thinks of the things I send him, because if he is really satisfied my happiness will be complete."[18]

Barely three years had elapsed since our saint's arrival at Ars, and already the old church had undergone those external and internal alterations which made it, at least in part, the building that the visitor beholds today. The lowly Abbé Vianney had done good work. All was now ready for the famous *pilgrimage* to Ars, for that endless procession of strangers of every nation, of saints and sinners, who came to seek health, light, and change of heart from one whom long before the infallible decrees of the Apostolic See, they delighted in calling *the saint.*

---

17. *Procès de l'Ordinaire,* p. 772.
18. *Letters* of May 21, 1827, and March 25, 1828.

Chapter 7

GREAT TRIALS OF THE FIRST YEARS: CALUMNIES AND TEMPTATIONS

NO GOOD work ever succeeds unless it be accompanied by suffering. "Without shedding of blood there is no remission." (*Heb.* 9:22). Sacrifice is the groundwork of every achievement of God's saints. The pastor of Ars knew this secret of the saints, hence the cruel scourgings and severe fasts which he undertook in order to obtain the conversion of his beloved flock. God was now about to permit sufferings that were to cut even deeper into the quick of his soul, wounds that were to be inflicted by the malice, more or less conscious, of men.

When a man attacks inveterate disorders and popular vices, he challenges opposition. M. Vianney was not unprepared—he knew the enemy would raise his head. "If a priest is determined not to lose his soul," he exclaimed, "so soon as any disorder arises in the parish he must trample underfoot all human considerations as well as the fear of the contempt and hatred of his people. He must not allow anything to bar his way in the discharge of duty, even were he certain of being murdered on coming down from the pulpit. A pastor who wants to do his duty must keep his sword in hand at all times."[1]

Did not St. Paul himself write to the faithful of Corinth: "I most gladly will spend and be spent myself for your souls, although loving you more, I be loved less." (*2 Cor.* 12:15).

M. Vianney had no wish to be the cause of his own damnation. At an early date his people saw proofs of this

1. *Sermons,* Sur la colère, t. III, p. 352.

determination. During several months those of their number who attended church had poured over them from the pulpit an almost uninterrupted stream of reproaches, adjurations, and threats. It was in vain that the preacher, seeing their weariness and their yawns, kept repeating: "When I am with you I do not feel weary"; they only called him "*ingrat,*" a word which in their language meant a disagreeable and tiresome person.[2]

"Did M. le Curé preach long sermons?" Mgr. Convert one day asked *Père* Drémieux. "Yes, long ones, and always on Hell. . . . He would strike his hands together, saying: 'My children, you are lost!' Or he struck his breast. What a constitution he had! . . . There are people who say there is no Hell. Ah, well! he believed in it."

At a later period, when a marked improvement had taken place in the parish, he chose rather to show the beauty of virtue than the heinousness of sin. At the time of which we are writing, his descriptions of his flock are far from flattering. At first, all unconsciously no doubt, he allowed himself to be carried away by his nervous, sensitive, and impetuous temperament. "I want you to understand," he explained, "that there is such a thing as a holy anger that springs from the zeal that we have for the interests of God." He had no use for half-measures. But he was less dominated by temperament than by a sense of duty. If he was never harsh when a meek and conciliatory spirit was required, he never hesitated when strong measures were needed. Behind the sinner whom he surrounded with the most tender compassion he beheld sin towards which he was pitiless.

His methods, to be sure, were not quite those of his

---

2. "The first historian of the Curé d'Ars (M. Monnin) makes him say that he has never addressed reproaches to his people. Such a statement can only be described as a naïvety against which protest all the pages of the sermons of the servant of God. The saint's contemporaries were astonished at so erroneous an affirmation, and they themselves pointed it out with a laugh . . . What a fine thing it would have been, to be sure, if the disorders that were rampant at Ars had collapsed of their own accord, like the walls of Jericho! The truth is that nothing of the kind happened, but the Curé d'Ars grappled with abuses 'with a face like an adamant and like flint' (*Ezechiel* 3:9), with the 'generous boldness' spoken of by Tertullian, 'that unmasks everything and is afraid of no one'"(Mgr. Convert, *Le Curé d'Ars et les dons du Saint-Esprit,* p. 329).

predecessors: murmurs arose in many a household. M. le Curé was too strict. When a child had been judged unworthy of absolution, and consequently its first Communion was put off for a whole year, if not longer, its mother, wounded in her self-love, would groan: "It is because it is *my* child." Moreover, was not the new parish priest far too hard on those who profaned the Sunday, on the patrons of the tavern, on those who haunted the dance hall? It goes without saying that the fearless reformer had the innkeepers arrayed against him. If the priest chose to live unlike other people, well, it was his own lookout, but let him leave others alone! Such were, between their potations, the mutterings of the village philosophers.

Will it be believed that there were a few persons of solid piety who did not readily "take to" M. Vianney? For nearly ten years—ten years of distress—the excellent Catherine Lassagne, who ended by becoming one of his most ardent admirers, experienced towards his person feelings in which fear had as large a share as reverence. She went even so far as to beseech God to remove from Ars a priest whose direction she deemed utterly unbearable. The fact was that M. Vianney wanted her to become perfect; for that reason he would not condone the slightest fault in her conduct. He followed the same line of action in regard to all those who were his most fervent disciples. "He led over exceedingly rough roads that devoted demoiselle Pignault, who, having until then lived in ease and comfort, gave up her rooms at Lyons in order to live with poor *Mère* Renard. "He let slip no opportunity to mortify her and to exercise her in the practice of renouncement. In this respect he went so far as to forbid her to assist at his catechism classes."[3] He did not reject the devotion of those women who sought to help him in his various undertakings, but he wished their devotion to be disinterested and supernatural.

The complaints, the mutterings of people whom he had rebuked, and of penitents from whom he had withheld

3. M. Monnin, *Le Curé d'Ars*.

absolution, duly came to the ears of the austere confessor. He made no secret of his knowledge. After some violent invectives against parents who set their children a bad example, he said: "If a villager has a misunderstanding with his pastor because, for the good of his soul, the latter has admonished him, the man at once conceives a hatred for the priest: he speaks ill of him; he loves to hear him criticized; he will distort everything that is said to him. Here is another who, in the priest's opinion, is not fit to approach the Holy Table: he will answer you rudely and foster resentment against you, as if you were the cause of his evil conduct. Another time it is a woman to whom you have refused absolution: at once she rebels against her confessor; in her eyes he is worse than the devil himself."[4]

The resentment of a few families was obstinate. M. Vianney became painfully aware of the fact on the occasion of the Revolution of 1830. It is indeed surprising that the *journées de juillet* should have had their repercussion in so tiny a village; but they did. "Seven of his parishioners, who deemed his strictures excessive, summoned him to quit the village.[5] Those men, it is true, were not the most edifying. Although he nursed no resentment and never spoke of it except with the utmost gentleness and only among his intimates, it is certain that the incident caused M. Vianney much pain."[6]

But a blow of a different kind had already struck him to the heart. We have already seen how the young women of Ars, yielding to his remonstrances, had ended by rang-

4. *Sermons,* t. IV, p. 56; t. II, p. 275.
5. The experience of M. Vianney in July, 1830, was not unique. "The looting of the house of the Archbishop of Paris spurred the hooligans of the *départements* to emulation. The free-thinkers of the villages eagerly snatched at the chance of avenging themselves for the sermons of their curés by driving them from their presbyteries. The clergy of the Diocese of Belley did not escape these outrages and persecutions. A number of priests became the butt of insults, they were ill-treated, and some were forcibly ejected from their presbyteries. The most odious and absurd calumnies were circulated among the populace. Thus a rumor was spread that the Government had issued an order for the pulling down of all crucifixes. This false intelligence led to a few sacrileges." (J. Cognat, *Mgr. Devie,* t. II, pp. 2-3).
6. *Sermons,* t. II, p. 275.

ing themselves under the staff of their pastor. But a few evil-living strangers and those youths of the village who were now unable to find accomplices in their wickedness, sought to besmirch him with their own vileness. They were shameless enough to attribute his pallor and emaciation not to his terrible macerations, but to a life of secret debauchery. The name of M. Vianney got into their low songs; anonymous letters, full of the basest insinuations, were sent to him; broadsheets of a like nature were placarded on the door of the presbytery, and at night a wild hubbub took place under his windows.

Worse was to follow. At times God allows the purest souls to become the victims of the vilest calumnies, nor are the ministers of the altar immune from such trials. "On the occasion of a village scandal—a wretched girl, having lost her honor, had become a mother in a house close to the presbytery—some criminals sought to tarnish the reputation of the servant of God. It was but a rumor, utterly baseless, for it was not possible to detect in his conduct anything that could have risen to the veriest shadow of a suspicion."[7] Nevertheless, his front door was splashed with dirt, and for the space of eighteen months a miserable creature stood, night after night, under his windows, insulting and reproaching him as if he had been guilty of leading a disorderly life.

Apparently he was to be spared no humiliation, no anguish of mind. In 1823 the diocese of Belley was re-established, and Ars ceased to form part of the archdiocese of Lyons. M. Vianney was a stranger to Mgr. Devie, his new Bishop. Anonymous letters full of venom having reached the prelate, he deemed it his duty to send the curé of Trévoux, M. Vianney's dean, to make investigations. We do not know how this inquiry was conducted, but it is certain that it silenced the slanderers.

Was our saint thinking of those most bitter trials when, towards the end of his life, he one day remarked: "If on my arrival at Ars I had foreseen all that I was to suffer

---

7. Catherine Lassagne, *Procès de l'Ordinaire,* p. 521.

there, I should have died on the spot"? Those were indeed hours of agony. We are informed by a contemporary that at one moment "he felt so depressed by reason of the wicked gossip that was circulated about him that he decided to quit the parish. This plan he would assuredly have carried into effect if one of his intimate friends had not succeeded in convincing him that by so doing he would give a measure of plausibility to those infamous rumors."

So he abandoned himself yet more completely into the hands of God, and whilst his heart sickened at the ignominy—for his honor as a priest was at stake—he forgave the guilty ones; nay, he went so far as to bestow on them marks of friendship. Had he been in a position to shower benefits upon them he would have done so. Thus, for instance, he relieved a certain family that had grievously wronged him, when misfortune befell them. One member of that household died in a mental hospital. Though he knew the persons concerned, he never uttered their names; on the contrary, he seized every opportunity of doing them a good turn. "We must pray for them," he kept repeating to Mayor Mandy, who was full of indignation at the conduct of those wretches. To a priest who complained of being the butt of evil tongues he gave the following advice: "Do as I did; I let them say all they wished, and in this way they ended by holding their tongues."[8] A holy soul "turns all bitterness into sweetness," says St. Thérèse of Lisieux. Here is the testimony of an eyewitness: "I know that M. Vianney not only endured these indignities with patience, but that his heart felt a wholly supernatural joy in the midst of his sufferings. Later on he called this period the happiest time of his life. He would have wished that the Bishop, believing him guilty, would remove him from his parish, so that he might have time to weep over his "poor life" in quiet retirement.[9]

In February, 1843, he made the following amazing statement in the hearing of several persons: "I thought a time would come when people would rout me out of Ars with

8. *Procès apostolique in genere,* p. 432.
9. Frère Athanase, *Procès de l'Ordinaire,* p. 662.

sticks, when the Bishop would suspend me, and I should end my days in prison. I see, however, that I am not worthy of such a grace."[10]

When, after the inquiry by the curé of Trévoux, he saw that Mgr. Devie, far from removing him, was only too happy to leave him in his parish, he gave utterance to his lamentations: "They leave me here like a little dog on the leash . . . and yet they ought to know me well enough!"[11]

Such words betray the saint. The Curé d'Ars had reached the highest degree of heroic humility. He was not merely detached from worldly honors, he despised honor and reputation. So far from crushing his spirit, moral suffering only proved an incentive, and in this way God molded his soul even as the sculptor carves a statue by means of chisel and mallet.

Assuredly M. Vianney might have defended himself, and that publicly, since he was publicly attacked. More than once he was advised to do so—he preferred to weep in silence under the eye of God. His admirable life bore eloquent witness to his virtues and the overwhelming number of his parishioners held him in the highest esteem. As a tender child, an excess of delicacy had caused him to shrink even from the embraces of his "poor mother." At this period of his life his reserve and modesty were such that he would not touch even a child. When the small boys and girls of the château trooped around him, all smiles, he occasionally caressed the former, the latter never. "He was so scrupulous in this matter that he rebuked some little girls who had presumed to touch the hand of a passing ecclesiastic."[12] In all his illnesses he would only be nursed by men. As regards the women whom he permitted to render him some services, he found means, as we have seen, to make them do purely for God what they did unto him. "I scarcely dared look at him or speak to him," says Catherine Lassagne. "I have served him, I think,

10. Catherine Lassagne, *Petit mémoire,* première rédaction, p. 16.
11. *Procès de l'Ordinaire,* p. 174.
12. Comte Félix des Garets, *Procès apostolique in genere,* p. 415.

solely for the love of God and without any natural affection. Whenever I brought him anything I was always prepared to be sent away." Now we know why he never kept a servant.[13] The devout woman who on occasion looked after the interior arrangements of the presbytery had strict orders never to be there except when he was away. Moreover, these women enjoyed an irreproachable reputation. As for his treatment of ladies who called on him, when we consider the fewness of his words, the strict custody of his eyes, the gravity of his demeanor—he never sat down in their presence—he might have been taken for an angel in human form. One of his most assiduous penitents could say of him: "His first glance seemed to reach the very depths of your soul, but after that he never again looked at you. He did not heed the individual; his one care was to lead a soul to God."[14] But for all his reserve M. Vianney was absolutely free from affectation or prudishness. In a word, he himself confessed that but for the fact of his being a priest and a confessor, he would have been unacquainted with evil—he only knew it through the confessional.

In the light of these facts we need not wonder that the gossip of evil-minded persons gained no credence whatever among the healthy section of the population. Even though they misjudged him at times, his brother priests, at any rate, never lent a complacent ear to those vile rumors. Already in 1822 the clergy looked upon him as a saint. His good people, also, never let slip an occasion to defend him: "Sometimes wicked men told me: 'Oh! that parish priest of yours—he is very much like other people,'" says Antoine Mandy, the Mayor's son. "I used to reply: 'You are very much mistaken; I have watched him for a long time; our parish priest is a saint.'"[15] Better still, this cruelly calumniated priest found his champions

13. In the minutes of the episcopal visitation of October 10, 1829, only two questions remain unanswered: *Quomodo vocatur Ancilla Pastoris?* (What is the name of the priest's housekeeper?) *Quo loco, quo anno et qua die nata est?* (Where and when was she born?)
14. Mme. Christine de Cibeins, *Procès apostolique continuatif,* p. 156.
15. *Procès de l'Ordinaire,* p. 1358.

even among unbelievers. A physician of Trévoux, Dr. Thiébaut, who was eventually converted, had seen M. Vianney and knew perfectly well the cause of his physical exhaustion. He was chivalrous enough to defend him publicly in a café of Trévoux against the gibes of some free-thinkers who sought to cast doubts upon the holiness of the curé's life.

The storm passed, never again to return. For his own person the Curé d'Ars may have wished for naught but abjection—it was his own affair. But God who exalts the lowly would not allow calumny to besmirch too long the name of a priest who was called above all others to spread among men the sweet odor of Jesus Christ. Once the flow of pilgrims had begun, no one ever dared to cast even the shadow of a doubt upon his perfect integrity of life. To convince himself of it, the visitor had but to contemplate the limpid candor of his blue eyes, nor were there wanting most significant facts which drew the attention even of the crowds.

The incident that follows has been told us by a priest. One day in the year 1853 this priest's mother, Mme. Gauthey-Degueurce, of Montchanin, Saône-et-Loire, was engaged in prayer near the confessional of the saint. There she beheld, not without emotion, a certain woman who had already spent a considerable time in the village, but who, notwithstanding all her efforts, could not get near M. Vianney. The woman, it was said, was a person of evil life. She wept and screamed, but was unable to walk up to the confessional.[16]

Twenty-five years earlier another significant incident had taken place which likewise bore supernatural characteristics. Every year, on the occasion of the feast of St. John the Baptist, Mlle. des Garets was wont to offer M. le Curé a bouquet of lilies, just plain lilies. One year she was prevented from making this presentation on the eve of the feast, so she made it on the day itself, in the sacristy. M. Vianney accepted the flowers, admired the fresh-

16. Mémoire of M. l'Abbé Gauthey, a priest living in retirement at Chauffailles (Saône-et-Loire), December 20, 1901, p. 7.

ness and arrangement of the bouquet and finally laid it on the sill of a window facing due south. Here the burning sun of June should have caused them to wither within the space of a few hours, but after the lapse of eight days the flowers still retained all their beauty and fragrance.

These lilies, which, under the rays of a summer sun, kept their whiteness and freshness for so long a time, are a symbol of M. Vianney's spotless honor that could not be tarnished by the wickedness of evil men.

The injuries inflicted by men were not the only trials of M. Vianney during those opening years of his ministry. Whilst he suffered externally from the ill-will of men, he underwent within his soul a torture of a very different kind.

However great may have been his trust in God, the sight of what he called his profound wretchedness and the duties of his ministry, filled him with an exceeding fear of the judgements of God. He experienced something that was closely akin to despair. "My God," he groaned, "make me suffer whatsoever you wish to inflict on me, but grant that I may not fall into Hell." From fear he passed to hope, and from hope he relapsed into fear.[17]

He had to go through those awful crises, when the soul receives no comfort from the world to which it no longer belongs, nor from Heaven from which it is as yet banished; those hours of searching torture when it deems itself forsaken by God wholly and for all time. It was at times such as these that he longed to hide himself in some lonely corner there to weep over his "poor life."

Truly the cross that weighed on him was proportioned to his destiny. But when once he began to love it, how much lighter it felt! "To suffer lovingly," he exclaimed, "is to suffer no longer. To flee from the cross is to be crushed beneath its weight. We should pray for a love of the cross—then it will become sweet. I experienced it myself during four or five years. I was grievously calumniated and con-

17. Catherine Lassagne, *Procès de l'Ordinaire,* p. 486; J. Pertinand, *ibid.,* p. 361.

tradicted. Oh! I did have crosses, almost more than I could bear. Then I started praying for a love of crosses and I felt happy. I said to myself: 'Verily, there is no happiness but in the cross.'"[18]

Thus though the tempest raged round his soul, it did not disturb that highest point where hope and peace reside. "One day," writes the Abbé Monnin, then a young missionary, "I asked him whether his trials had caused him at any time to lose his interior peace." "What?" he exclaimed, with a heavenly expression on his countenance, "the cross make us lose our inward peace? Surely it is the cross that bestows it on our hearts. All our miseries come from our not loving it."[19]

To this unshakable faith the Curé d'Ars owes it that he not only never yielded to discouragement, but carried out works that others more talented but less supernatural would have failed to execute. His life demonstrates what moral greatness and what merit may be won from the humiliations of this life. Expecting neither recognition nor reward from men, he went on working solely for the glory of God. "Far more is done for God," he said, "when we do things without pleasure or relish. It may happen that I shall be driven from my parish—in the meantime I act as if I were to remain for ever."[20]

However, his was an instance when the sword wears out the scabbard. His patience might win splendid victories, but his strength was being undermined by the struggle. In the summer of 1827 he consented to call at the château that he might see a physician. Dr. Timécourt took a serious view of his condition. He prescribed "a more substantial diet so as to forestall the nervous affections to which he was subject and which threatened to become chronic. . . ."

The good doctor's prescription is quaint in its meticulousness: "Apart from the remedies that I have prescribed, it is necessary that M. le Curé should take meat or milk

18. Baronne de Belvey, *Procès de l'Ordinaire,* p. 206; Abbé Monnin, *ibid.,* p. 1098.
19. *Procès de l'Ordinaire,* p. 1124.
20. Catherine Lassagne, *Procès de l'Ordinaire,* p. 502.

soups, chicken, veal, beer, raw or stewed fruit, together with fresh bread, toast with fresh butter and honey, tea with milk and sugar, and plenty of very ripe grapes."

None of M. Vianney's familiars have been able to tell us to what extent he carried out these prescriptions of the medical faculty. It is not likely that he made much account of them. The only thing to which he consented, after the gratuitous consultation, was to accept a packet of tea at the hands of Mlle. d'Ars.[21]

M. Vianney had only reached his fortieth year, yet he felt utterly exhausted. The fever never left him. Whether the step was prompted by physical fatigue or weariness of mind, the fact is that about this time he himself asked for a change. The châtelains were very much perturbed by this intelligence. They wished to keep their Curé, and to this end they intervened with Mgr. Devie. The Bishop's reply was slow in coming. On April 1, 1828, M. Gillet de Valbreuse wrote as follows to his cousin, des Garets: "I do not think that the bishop will accede to M. Vianney's petition without previously ascertaining the motive of his demand. What would become of the school if he were to leave?"

The school in question was "the house of Providence," a big undertaking which M. Vianney had greatly at heart. The châtelains were likewise interested in the work. The departure of the founder jeopardized its very existence.

Mgr. Devie did not reject M. Vianney's request, and offered him the parish of Fareins. The appointment spelled promotion and was an apt answer to the whilom revilers of the Curé. In the new parish, which was not far from Ars but five times its size, the saint would have a far wider scope for his zeal, and he might found another *Providence* which would house many more children than the one at Ars. M. Vianney hesitated for a moment, then decided to accept the offer, and finally, on considering "his poor life," he once more abruptly changed his mind. "Unhappy man that I am!" he said in confidence to the

21. Dr. Timécourt's prescription bears the date of July 28, 1827. Mlle. d'Ars added to it a paragraph in which mention is made of tea.

directresses of the school, "here am I prepared to take charge of a large parish when I am hard put to it not to give way to despair in a small one." So he wrote to inform the bishop of his decision.[22]

The Bishop of Belley, who now knew the zeal of M. Vianney, had had his own reasons when he offered him the parish of Fareins. In the eighteenth century this important village of the Ain had undergone uncommon trials, and the faith of the population, who up till then had remained good Catholics, was seriously shaken. Shortly before the Revolution a strange sect was founded at Fareins under two successive Jansenistic parish priests, the brothers Claude and François Bonjour. Their followers were called Fareinists. These fanatics, the women in particular, surpassed in their excesses even the Flagellants of old. They delighted in getting themselves scourged to the blood. Yielding to fanatical suggestions, a young woman of the name of Etiennette Thomasson went so far as to allow herself to be crucified within the walls of the church.[23] It is easy to see that follies such as these were bound to pave the way for immorality and skepticism.

In 1828 one half of the village still clung to the doctrines of the brothers Bonjour. Mgr. Devie had thought of M. Vianney as the man who would best succeed in bringing back those erring sheep who had too long strayed from the fold. He was to be assisted by a vicaire, so that his duties would not have been so heavy. But he would assuredly have indulged in his wonted fasts and penances so that the change to Fareins would have failed to restore him to health.

Why did M. Vianney feel compelled, at the last moment, to refuse the post thus offered to him? It was his fear

---

22. Catherine Lassagne, *Petit mémoire,* troisième rédaction, p. 80.

23. It is a fact that on October 12, 1787, at 3 o'clock in the afternoon, Etiennette Thomasson, clad in her ordinary dress, was nailed to a cross against the wall of the Lady Chapel. Several people witnessed the monstrous scene. According to François Bonjour and the witnesses who put their names to the minutes of the inquiry held by Messire Joly Clerc, Vicar-General of Lyons—for the ecclesiastical authorities proceeded against the perpetrators of the deed—the girl was taken off the cross and her wounds healed. The civil power likewise intervened and punished the culprits with banishment.

lest he should prove unequal to the task. The Fareinists were supposed to be incapable of conversion. Quite wrongly, yet in all good faith, M. Vianney thought that any other priest would be far more likely to overcome the obstinacy of those misguided people. In 1834 M. Dubouis was appointed to Fareins, and he held the post for the space of forty-eight years. One day M. Vianney told him: "Mgr. Devie thought at one time of sending me where you are, but I was afraid of the sect. Pagans are more quickly converted than Jansenists. One day four of your people came to ask me whether they could save their souls if they stayed away from church but prayed at home. 'My friends,' I replied, 'what would you think of a child if it were to say: "I love my father dearly, but as for my mother, I have no wish ever to see her again?"'"

Mgr. Devie did not insist, nor did he make any other proposal to M. Vianney, but left him in his little village.

Chapter 8

THE TRIUMPH OF GOODNESS: APOSTOLIC LABORS

THE AFFRONTS which M. Vianney had to endure in the first few years of his ministry were the work of a handful of ignorant, blind, and misguided persons. We already have seen that the field entrusted to him by Providence, besides brambles, yielded likewise flowers of innocence and piety which lacked neither beauty nor fragrance. These he strove to tend and multiply.

His plan was to form an élite which, together with the priest, should be the heart, so to speak, of the parish and should help him in his task of reaching and winning souls. This humble country parish priest, even though he did not wholly escape the influences of the period, was yet far ahead of his contemporaries, for he was far-sighted enough to realize that devotion to the Eucharist is, and always will be, the most powerful means towards the regeneration of a people.

Mlle. d'Ars, to be sure, was a truly valiant and most kindly woman, but it could not be said as yet that she was sufficiently fervent. Her piety was austere, narrow; until then she had lacked a skilled and clear-sighted guide. If we may believe her cousin, Jean-Félix des Garets, she was one of those whose souls had shrivelled up and hardened under the rigoristic influences of Jansenism of the preceding century. Hers was a regular life, but one lived apart from the Sacraments. By degrees M. Vianney led her to the practice of frequent Communions and the exercises of a most tender piety.[1] Henceforth she was to be seen at Mass

1. *Procès apostolique in genere,* p. 413. We possess all the letters written to Mlle. d'Ars by her mistresses of Saint-Cyr. They consist of formal and complimentary expressions without a trace of true tenderness for the soul of a child that, no doubt, would

every day. She always went on foot, even when snow lay on the ground, for she preferred to spend on the relief of the poor the money she would have expended on a carriage and horses. In the evening the village saw her once more on her way to visit the Blessed Sacrament.

The example of Mlle. d'Ars was soon followed by others of humbler condition, who thus became the workers of the first hour. Among them we must count the widow Claudine Renard, the mother of a priest; Mlle. Lacand, a discreet woman of sixty years of age, "who was thought to be a Sister," says Catherine Lassagne in her naive way, "because she always wore black, or because she may have at one time lived in community";[2] Mlle. Antoinette Pignaut who, drawn by the reputation for sanctity of the former vicaire of Ecully, had come to live at Ars in order to be a daily witness of the admirable virtues of its parish priest. These fervent souls won others. They were also joined by the girls whom M. Vianney had grouped together in the Confraternity of the Rosary, and finally by the directresses of the *Providence,* whom we shall presently see at work. In this way, as early as 1825, "even before the great rush of pilgrims, besides M. le Curé, who spent all his time before the Blessed Sacrament, there were always people engaged in prayer in the church. . . . I cannot recollect a single occasion," says Pertinand, the schoolmaster, "when, on entering the church, I did not find someone or other in adoration."[3] Several among these excellent women whom M. Vianney, according to the expression of Mlle. Marthe des Garets, "had enkindled with the fire of his own charity, eventually died like saints."[4]

Without their being aware of it, these good souls were true mystics. In their prolonged visits to Our Lord they spoke but little, but how happy they felt to be there! Borrowing the words of the Curé, they would say: "Come, my

---

have expanded under such influences. Her mother's letters were in the same strain.

2. *Petit mémoire* première rédaction, p. 12. Mlle. Lacand, a native of Auvergne, kept a repository of pious objects at Ars.
3. Jean Pertinand, *Procès apostolique ne pereant,* p. 846; François Pertinand, *ibid.,* p. 812.
4. *Procès apostolique in genere,* p. 298.

soul, let us redouble our fervor. You are alone to worship God; his eyes rest upon you alone."[5]

Now it came to pass that, unobserved by M. Vianney, a good husbandman of Ars had followed the example of those women. *Père* Louis Chaffangeon belonged to the ancient Guild of the Blessed Sacrament, but apparently until then he had been just one of the crowd, "content to carry a candle" on days of Benediction or processions.[6] A man of solid faith, and, like Job or Tobias, somewhat lost amid the Gentiles, he was won over by the fiery exhortations of his pastor. But let the Curé d'Ars himself tell the touching story: "A few years ago there died a man of this parish, who, entering the church in the morning to pray before setting out for the fields, left his hoe at the door and then became wholly lost in God. A neighbor who worked not far from him, and thus used to see him in the fields, wondered at his absence. On his way home he bethought himself of looking into the church, thinking that the man might be there. As a matter of fact, he did find him in the church. 'What are you doing here all this time?' he asked. And the other made reply: 'I look at the good God, and He looks at me.' *(J'avise le bon Dieu et le bon Dieu m'avise).*"

Whenever he told this anecdote—and he did so frequently and never without tears—the Curé used to add: "He looked at the good God, and the good God looked at him. Everything is in that, my children."[7]

M. Vianney was rightly convinced that his people would not take up seriously the practice of religion until the day when he should have won over the youths and the men of the village. With a view to fostering among them a devotion to the holy Eucharist, he made no innovation, but contented himself with breathing fresh life into the existing Guild of the Blessed Sacrament, which was moribund. "The men," he was wont to say, "have a soul to save as

5. *Spirit of the Curé of Ars.*
6. *Sermon sur la Fête-Dieu,* t. II, p. 130.
7. *Instructions de onze heures,* MSS. of M. de la Bastie, p. 58.

well as the women. They are everywhere first: why should they not be first in the service of God and in doing homage to Jesus Christ in the Sacrament of His love? A devotion gains in general esteem when they take it up. And make no mistake," he added, addressing himself to the members of the Guild of the Blessed Sacrament, "you are bound to lead a more perfect life than ordinary Christians."[8]

We have to own that with the youths and men of Ars M. Vianney's success did not come up to his hopes. Perhaps his burning zeal rendered him too exacting. That he should have failed to get them to make a daily visit to the Blessed Sacrament, as prescribed by the statutes of the guild, we can understand readily enough: their work kept them in the fields all day long. As far as we know, *Père* Chaffangeon found no strict imitators. Nevertheless, the purpose of the guild seemed sufficiently realized when all the men appeared regularly at the Sunday services in that irreproachable attitude which was the admiration of visitors. Moreover, at the conclusion of Vespers there were always some who remained behind to spend an hour before the Blessed Sacrament exposed.

No special feature characterized the feast of Corpus Christi of the year 1818, but the following year M. Vianney displayed the greatest possible pomp and solemnity. He went to considerable expense that all the children of the parish might be dressed in white, and as he himself helped them to don their tunics he said: "Come, you must think that you are before the good God and hold the place of the angels."[9] The little ones, no doubt, were delighted to play such a role, their elders seemed less pleased to be called upon to represent the Church Militant. Slaves as yet to human respect, a number of them refused to carry lighted tapers behind the canopy. The parish registers of the years between 1824 and 1839 show that only about a fifth of the members of the guild were faithful to their engagements. True, the Curé did not make these prescriptions binding in conscience. But the upshot of it

8. *Sermons,* t. II, p. 130.
9. Abbé Monnin, *Procès de l'Ordinaire,* p. 1082.

was that the guild, meant to be a men's guild, had to be enlarged so as to admit women and girls, who gave proof of much greater keenness. On the other hand, curiously enough, men and youths obtained the privilege of enrollment in the Confraternity of the Rosary, which had at first been reserved exclusively for women. The duties it imposed were less exacting than those of the men's guild. In like manner, when, on December 17, 1845, M. Vianney affiliated his parish to the archconfraternity of Notre Dame des Victories, founded in Paris for the purpose of praying for the conversion of sinners, sixty men and youths gave in their names, The only obligation of the new guild was the recitation of a "Hail Mary" every day, and it should be noted that the new devotion was specially dear to their parish priest, whose authority and renown had now become extraordinary.

M. Vianney did not fail to realize that purely parochial undertakings would only appeal to an élite; if he wished to extend his influence for good he must needs look for other means. The great longing of his heart was to see every family animated by a truly Christian spirit. Obviously those peasants who were bound to work all day for their daily bread could not be expected to be present at Mass on weekdays. But was it not possible for them to say their morning and night prayers, and even to spend a few moments in church before retiring for the night? Alas! about the year 1818 there was but little prayer at Ars. The lamentations of the newly appointed Curé sufficiently establish the truth of the sad fact. The touching custom of family prayers having died out, M. Vianney did all that was in his power to reintroduce it. By a spontaneous transition he sought to transform this private prayer into a public exercise. The hour would come when, every evening throughout the whole year, the church bell would ring out a last summons to prayer, and the entire parish, which is but a large family, would be seen wending its way to the house of God for a common recitation of the Rosary and night prayers.

M. Vianney dared to attempt still more. He induced

those humble laborers to take up some of the more uncommon practices of devotion that give a certain finish to piety. Thus he advised a daily examination of conscience, and at bedtime, at least in the winter months, a short spiritual reading, so that the salutary truths of religion might become more deeply engraved upon their hearts. M. Vianney was not one to think that people were incapable of a deeply spiritual life because they were bound to the soil or to the pursuit of a mechanical craft. He taught the secret art of prayer and meditation to those simple peasants who were forever reading the book of Nature, the writer whereof is God Himself.

"My brethren," he said, "the good God looks neither at long nor at beautiful prayers, but at those that come from the bottom of the heart. . . . There is nothing easier than to pray to the good God and nothing is more comforting."

To finer souls whom he discerned in the crowd—the saints are full of a holy daring—he pointed out unsuspected heights. There are not two conceptions of the supernatural life—to be applied, one to ourselves, the other to our neighbors. The Curé d'Ars simply poured out upon some privileged souls the superabundance of his own heart:

"If we love someone very much, is it necessary that we should see him in order to think of him? Of course not. In like manner, if we love the good God we shall pray as naturally as we take our breath. Oh, how I love those words said the first thing in the morning: 'I will do and suffer everything today for the glory of God . . . nothing for the world or personal interest; all to please my Saviour'! In this way the soul unites itself to God and works for God alone. Let us often say, 'My God, have mercy on me!' just as a child says to its mother: 'Give me your hand; give me some bread.' If we have a burden to carry, let us promptly remember that we are following Jesus Christ carrying His Cross; let us unite our sufferings to those of our divine Saviour."[10]

Not a few of the villagers carried out these exhorta-

10. *Sermons,* t. II, p. 63; t. III, p. 32.

tions to the letter, so that the pilgrims to Ars, whilst admiring the serene countenances of its inhabitants, were able to realize the profound peace enjoyed by souls that are united to God.

Several of the surrounding parishes benefited by M. Vianney's teaching. If duty and charity kept him in his own church, one or other of these virtues caused him to forsake it from time to time. In 1820 the moral havoc wrought by the Revolution was far from having been made good. Everywhere there was a vast amount of ignorance, prejudice, and corruption. That part of the *département* of the Ain which belonged to the archdiocese of Lyons seems to have been particularly neglected. Sad symbols of forsaken souls, of the church towers levelled to the ground by citizen Albitte, hardly any had been re-erected. All this territory had formerly belonged to the diocese of Belley; only once in thirty years—in 1813—had it been visited by the Archbishop of Lyons, its spiritual head. Owing to the scarcity of priests, many small parishes were without a shepherd. In all probability—but for the influence of the family des Garets—the tiny village of Ars would have shared a like fate.

The best—in fact, the only—means of rousing these too-long-neglected populations was the preaching of missions. To this end the priests of a district joined forces, for the missionaries of the Carthusians of Lyons were unable to cope with all the demands for their ministrations. Thus it came about that the Curé d'Ars was called upon to exercise, in various parishes of the neighborhood, the functions of preacher and confessor. He took part in the missions or jubilees that were given at Trévoux, Saint-Trivier-sur-Moignans, Montmerle, Chaneins, Limas and Saint-Bernard. We do not know whether he merely accepted an invitation from his colleagues or obeyed an order of his bishop. The fact is that M. Vianney eagerly threw himself into the work. At the beginning the priests who watched him at work may have had some misgivings as to his competency; it was not long before hesitation yielded to esteem. The austerity of his life, his deep piety, and—who would believe it?—even his unadorned eloquence won for him the confidence, if not the admiration, of all.

During the great mission at Trévoux, which opened at the beginning of 1823, he achieved a notable success. The chapel in which he confessed was never empty. He lodged with a former fellow-student of Verrières, M. Morel, who now kept a boarding-house. At night that worthy used to wait in vain for M. Vianney's return for dinner. On successive occasions he went to look for him in the church—often after midnight—where he found him still in the confessional. On the night preceding the conclusion of the mission there was such a crush round the Curé d'Ars that the surging crowd very nearly pushed over both confessor and confessional. This was the only incident of the mission that M. Vianney delighted in relating subsequently, and he always laughed heartily when telling it. He deliberately sought to throw a veil over the fact of the enormous affluence of people who sought his direction and the conversions wrought by his zeal. "The gentlemen of the *sous-préfecture* and of the law courts came to him" about matters of conscience.[11] He did his duty without respect of persons and with truly apostolic freedom. "Ever afterwards the *sous-préfet* spoke of him in terms of admiration. But though he prized his wisdom and the gentle firmness of his direction, he realized with a feeling of resignation and submission that the Curé d'Ars had been relentless where the *soirées* and balls of the *sous-préfecture* were concerned." But what happy times those were when the *sous-préfets* took counsel with a saint![12]

At that period the close of a mission was wont to be marked by a ceremony which consisted in the renewal by the priests of the vows made at their ordination. The ceremony took place in the presence of all the faithful. At Trévoux it was M. Vianney who presented the book of the Gospels to each of his colleagues, whilst pronouncing the

11. Frère Athanase, *Procès apostolique in genere,* p. 203.
12. Abbé Monnin, *Procès de l'Ordinaire,* p. 1082.

usual formula: "Do you believe in the holy Gospel of our Lord Jesus Christ?" This he did with such devotion that his manner and the tone of his voice deeply stirred the hearts of all the priests.

During the mission at Saint-Trivier, M. Vianney absented himself for a fortnight. Suddenly a dreadful piece of intelligence alarmed his people of Ars. It was said that their parish priest had died of exhaustion in his confessional. The rumor, which was not wholly groundless, was promptly contradicted. It had originated in the fact that the holy man, having set out, fasting, for Saint-Trivier, lost his way in the snow and was picked up unconscious.

People came from the neighboring parishes in order to go to Confession to him. He sat in the confessional from an early hour until noon. The atmosphere of the church was icy. When they brought him a foot-warmer, he accepted it so as not to give offense, but pushed it out of his way as being of no use to him.[13]

During the jubilee at Montmerle in 1826, there being no room for him at the presbytery, M. Vianney lodged with a Mlle. Mondésert, in close proximity to the church. He had hardly installed himself in the house of the venerable sexagenarian, who was also the honorary sacristan of the church, than he secretly asked the servant to boil a saucepan of potatoes for him and to put them in his room. At the conclusion of the jubilee the parish priest went to thank the obliging old lady and to compensate her for the expenses she must have incurred in entertaining her guest. "Oh, M. le Curé," she said, "it is not worth while troubling about a pair of sheets." "But you gave him his meals. We never saw him at the presbytery at mealtime." "Neither did he have anything here," said Mlle. Mondésert; "he used to come into the house for five minutes, at about noon." Whilst this conversation was in progress the servant appeared on the scene and told the story of the saucepan of potatoes. So they all went upstairs together. There was the saucepan, sure enough, hidden

13. Denise Lanvis, housekeeper, at the time, to the cure of Saint-Trivier, *Procès de l'Ordinaire,* p. 1361.

behind the mantelpiece and quite empty. During the six days that he spent at Montmerle when he, so to speak, never left the church, M. Vianney had had no food except those potatoes. The curé of Montmerle made further inquiries in the village: his holy collaborator had never eaten at the house of any of the parishioners.[14]

At the jubilee of Saint-Bernard none but M. Vianney came forward to help the pastor of that parish. Everybody wished to go to Confession to the Curé d'Ars. The other did not mind being forsaken; to some colleagues who came to see him he laughingly declared: "I have a splendid missioner; he works well and eats nothing." The whole population flocked to M. Vianney's sermons. The vine-dressers and farm laborers left their work and ran to the church, fearful lest they should miss even one word that fell from his lips. "If we must pay for lost time," they declared to their astonished employers, "we will pay, but we, too, want to hear the Curé d'Ars." Much and lasting good was wrought by him at Saint-Bernard.

About the same time he was invited by the curé of Limas to preach on the occasion of the forty hours' prayer. "They played me a trick there,"[15] he used to say afterwards. "I at first excused myself, because I did not deem myself capable of speaking before so distinguished an audience. M. le Curé stated that there was only question of a country parish. . . . So I went. On entering the church, I beheld the chancel full of clergy and the body of the church packed with people of every condition. At first I felt unnerved by the spectacle. However I began to speak of the love of God, and apparently everything went well: everybody wept."[16]

Before setting out on these apostolic expeditions M. Vianney took care to provide for his own parish by asking a confrère to replace him were the necessity to arise.

---

14. These details were related to Mgr. Convert on July 1, 1910, by Mme. Serve, of Lyons, a great-grand-niece of Mlle. Mondésert. The heirs of the latter (she died in 1846, aged 86) still possess the bed in which M. Vianney slept during the jubilee of 1826.
15. "On me fit une farce."
16. Frère Athanase, *Procès apostolique in genere,* p. 204.

The curé of Savigneux, a village only two kilometers distant, was most frequently asked by him. Moreover, every week he revisited his own people and always spent the Sunday in their midst. During the mission at Trévoux, in the middle of January, the heroic priest, the Confessions once over, would go on foot, in the darkness of night and over appalling roads, the two long leagues that separated him from his parish. Anxious about his holy Curé, Mayor Mandy sent his son Antoine to accompany him on many a Saturday night when he was returning to Ars. "Even amid the snows and cold of winter," Antoine Mandy afterwards related, "we rarely took the shortest and best road. M. le Curé had invariably to visit some sick person. Yet the tramp never seemed really long, for the servant of God well knew how to shorten it by relating most interesting episodes from the *Lives* of the saints. If I happened to make some remark about the sharpness of the cold or the ruggedness of the roads, he was always ready with an answer. 'My friend, the saints have suffered far more; let us offer it all to the good God.' When he ceased from speaking of holy things we began the Rosary. Even today I still cherish the memory of those holy conversations."[17]

During the whole of his life as a priest M. Vianney never travelled for pleasure, but he frequently did so—even in his last years—in order to oblige a colleague. Since his readiness, which was wholly supernatural, was so manifest, he was deemed useful in every imaginable emergency; in fact, he allowed himself to be exploited. But, according to the remark of St. Thérèse of Lisieux, people feel no scruple in asking for the help of those who are for ever ready to render service.

When some parish happened to become vacant—as, for instance, in the case of Rancé and Saint-Jean-de-Thurigneux—the Abbé Vianney was requested to supply in the meantime. If a poor parish priest, such as those

17. *Procès de l'Ordinaire,* p. 1368. Antoine Mandy, born May 14, 1799, related this incident during the process of canonization in 1864.

of Villeneuve and of Mizérieux, was too old to look after his flock, his colleague of Ars volunteered to help, declaring himself ready to answer the very first summons, both by day and by night. "He visited the sick at night, not only at Rancé and at Saint-Jean-de-Thurigneux, but likewise at Savigneux and at Ambérieux-en-Dombes. If he was sent for on a Sunday he would set out as soon as ever Mass was over, without entering the presbytery at all, and he would return, still fasting, in time for Vespers.

M. Julien Ducreux, at one time Superior of the Petit Séminaire Saint-Jean at Lyons, and from 1808 parish priest of Mizérieux, Toussieux, Sainte-Euphémie, and Saint-Didier-de-Formans, had worn himself out in the work of the sacred ministry.[18] M. Vianney seems to have been particularly intimate with this venerable neighbor of his. It may be that M. Ducreux had been a friend of the much-loved and ever-regretted M. Balley. Be this as it may, the registers of Mizérieux, between April, 1820, and May, 1821, show that the Curé d'Ars frequently walked the three kilometers that separate the two small villages, in order to perform a Baptism, a marriage, or a funeral in M. Ducreux's parish. One intensely cold day he set out on foot to take a burial. On his return his face was almost frozen. Another day, after officiating on a like occasion, he walked home at night over roads covered in slush and mud. He was in a pitiable condition when he at last reached his presbytery, but, far from complaining, he looked the picture of content.

Another day, when he was himself very unwell, he walked to Savigneux for the purpose of hearing a sick man's Confession. So exhausted was he that he had to be brought back in a carriage. The same thing happened when, one wet October day, a family of Rancé asked for his ministrations. He reached the house wet to the skin and shaken by fever, so that he was compelled to lie down by the bedside of the invalid, and it was in this attitude

18. M. Ducreux remained at Mizérieux until 1828, when he retired and settled at Lyons. He died within a short time of his resignation, aged more than eighty years.

that he heard his Confession. "I was more ill than the sick man," he confessed on his return.

The registers of Savigneux reveal yet another incident. On July 15, 1823, M. Vianney went thither to baptize a child of Pierre Lassagne and Françoise Thomas, of the hamlet of Juys. By doing this he no doubt wanted to do honor to a family that was related to some excellent people of his own parish. The godmother was none other than Catherine Lassagne, then seventeen years of age, who was preparing herself for the duties of schoolmistress in her native village.

He never refused except when a thing was obviously impossible; all his life he spent himself for others, without ever counting the cost. A woman of Fareins, who was stricken with cancer, wished for one supreme consolation before her death—namely, to behold once more the Curé d'Ars, of whom people told such wonderful things. The Abbé Dubouis wrote a few lines to M. Vianney, informing him of the wish of the sick woman. It was the Maundy Thursday of 1837 and the servant of God was preparing to spend the whole of the ensuing night in the church (this was his invariable custom on that day). He set out at once, however, but lost his way, so that when he eventually reached Fareins he was covered with mud and worn out with fatigue. He would not consent to take anything, not even a glass of water. Already at that time his reputation for sanctity was such that the whole village turned out to see him. After blessing and comforting the poor dying woman, the lowly priest made haste to return to his parish. He refused the carriage that was offered him.[19] M. Beau, curé of Jassans and for thirteen years the ordinary confessor of the saint, writes as follows: "In 1852 I fell seriously ill. My colleague of Ars came to see me; it was the afternoon of Corpus Christi, June 11. He had made the whole of the journey on foot, the day being exceedingly hot, and he had already officiated at the procession of the Blessed Sacrament."[20]

---

19. Abbé Dubouis, curé of Fareins, *Procès de l'Ordinaire,* p. 1242.
20. *Procès de l'Ordinaire,* p. 1204.

How many other facts of a like nature have remained unrecorded! Such deeds exceed the normal strength of man and presuppose extraordinary heroism in him who performed them. "It was thus," says Catherine Lassagne, "that our holy Curé sacrificed himself for souls."

Chapter 9

THE "PROVIDENCE" OF ARS

ARS possessed no school worthy of the name. There were neither masters nor mistresses. In the winter months some stranger would be summoned to the village, when the boys and girls would go to school all together—very much to M. Vianney's displeasure. He was not slow in coming to a decision. He would begin by establishing a girls' school, and whilst waiting for better times the boys would have to attend by themselves the more or less regular classes of the schoolmaster.[1]

Between 1820 and 1823 M. Vianney studied his plan and collected funds. For the choice of mistresses he refused to look beyond the parish itself and selected for the delicate post two simple and pious girls, Catherine Lassagne and Benoîte Lardet. Until then the two maidens had worked in the fields and were devoid of both knowledge and experience, but they possessed intelligence and good sense and a character in which strength blended with gentleness. In the beginning of 1823 M. Vianney sent them to the convent of the Sisters of St. Joseph at Fareins. He made himself entirely responsible for their board. There the girls resumed their interrupted studies and prepared themselves for their future task by teaching the youngest of the Sisters' pupils.

In March of that same year M. le Curé acquired a newly erected house, standing at the east end of the church and styled "maison Givre" in the legal documents. To raise the purchase money he appealed to charity, besides mak-

1. A teacher came to settle in the village, but during the summer months he seems to have been engaged in agricultural labors, for we are told that at that time the school of Ars opened its doors only in winter. In the parish registers of 1827 we find, under date of July 4, among the witnesses to a marriage, one Gaillard, schoolmaster at Ars.

ing the sacrifice of all his personal property.[2] His intention was to run it as a college, so we are informed by an item in the registers of the commune entered by the excellent mayor, Antoine Mandy.[3] The house was neither luxurious nor spacious. On the ground-floor there was one large room, destined to be a classroom, and two small rooms formed the first storey. It was, however, thought adequate to receive twenty pupils and to lodge their teachers. The school buildings of the surrounding villages were hardly more commodious. M. Vianney liked the house because it stood in the middle of Ars and near the church. But in purchasing it he completely drained his resources so that he had no money left to pay the notary who drew up the deeds.

The free school for girls was inaugurated in November, 1824, under the direction of Catherine and Benoîte. A young woman of twenty-six, Jeanne-Marie Chanay by name, whom the advice of M. Vianney had cured of a suspicion of worldliness, came over from Jassans at the very start in order to assist the youthful mistresses. Less well-bred, less refined than her companions, she was well fitted for manual tasks. M. le Curé had her taught sewing. Jeanne-Marie was in turn monitress in the school, and cook, baker, and laundress of the little convent. M. Vianney gave to his teachers no distinctive dress, no written rule; he imposed no vows; however, without turning them into nuns, he wanted them to live their holy life. Catherine Lassagne was destined to preside over the institution for the space of twenty-two years. She never proved unworthy of the absolute confidence that M. Vianney placed in her. From him her simple and trustful soul learned how to bear without a murmur privations, anxieties and arduous toil. Though most devoted, the difficult character of Jeanne-Marie Chanay was destined to subject the patience of Catherine to a fresh trial with each succeeding day. In

---

2. Matthieu Vianney, his father, who died at Dardilly on July 8, 1819, at the age of sixty-five, had left the Curé d'Ars a small legacy.
3. "M. Vianney a acheté une maison au mois de mars 1824 pour tenir un college. Elle lui a couté 2,400 francs." *(Registre* de la commune d'Ars).

1830 Catherine suffered a grievous loss through the death of her pious and gentle friend, Benoîte Lardet. Her place was taken by Marie Filliat of Mizérieux, a seamstress by occupation. She, too, all unconsciously, proved a very heavy cross for Catherine Lassagne, by reason of her imperious and difficult character. We must see the permission of God in all this, for it was only after prayer that M. Vianney had made the selection.[4] It was necessary for Catherine to add lustre to her crown; it was good that by the side of the gentle mystic there should stand stern co-operators who had more head than heart.

Be it said to the praise of the various persons secured by M. Vianney for the execution of his great work that their disinterestedness was absolute, for it was agreed at the outset that they would be paid no salary, and that, apart from board and lodging, their only earthly reward would be the knowledge that they were doing good.

Thus it came about that at Martinmas, 1824, Catherine and Benoîte, having got together a few indispensable pieces of furniture, installed themselves in their school. Extreme poverty prevailed in the house. M. Vianney had guaranteed to feed and lodge them, but when the hour struck for the first meal there was nothing to eat. After cleaning the premises they bethought themselves of returning to their respective homes in order to get something to eat. "Well, no, let us stay on!" they said, "some dinner will surely be sent to us." Whilst they were yet speaking, the mothers of both girls arrived with provisions. Thus the house deserved from the first hour of its existence the beautiful name under which it was destined to become famous: *La Providence.*

The following morning the little girls of the village came to school. However, as Catherine writes, "the other villagers sought to take advantage of the fact that the teaching was gratuitous. Children came from Mizérieux, Savigneux, Villeneuve and other places. The attic had to be turned into a dormitory. In the very first year (1825-

4. Catherine Lassagne and Marie Filliat lived together until 1882—that is, more than half a century.

1826) we had sixteen boarders." In this way a small boarding school had been improvised. No fees were charged—M. le Curé would not hear of such a thing. Parents provided beds and sheets and got into the habit of sending in provisions. At all events everything was arranged after a fashion.

As soon as M. Vianney saw his school filled he conceived a new idea. On his pastoral rounds he had often discovered both in the village and in the surrounding country places, little homeless orphans, the offspring of unnatural or destitute parents. These poor little creatures were sent out to beg or were placed at that early age as domestic servants with employers wholly bereft of religion. Of God they knew nothing; vice was frequently the only thing that they were taught. Such a state of things was more than the compassionate heart of the Curé d'Ars could bear. He decided to establish, under the same roof as the school, a shelter or home that should bear the significant name of *Providence.* The house was to have no endowment other than the goodness of our Father in Heaven. And yet he was afraid to tempt God by a rash undertaking. One Sunday in January, 1827, he besought his beloved people to join him in a novena to the Blessed Virgin in order that he might know what was the will of God. His determination gained in strength and he set about its execution.

To begin with, the house had to be enlarged and to that end M. Vianney bought some land. He himself drew up the plan of the building. He made himself all things to all men, for, with a view to encouraging the workmen and hastening the completion of the building, he helped the masons and the carpenters, and assisted in preparing stones, mixing mortar and carrying building materials.

On the completion of the work he made it a condition that the establishment was to accept as boarders none but destitute children. Henceforth the girls of Ars would be received only as day scholars. From 1827 the well-to-do children of the neighborhood were no longer admitted. "We began by picking up two or three wretched little children," says Catherine Lassagne; "but by degrees their numbers increased to such an extent that the house could not hold them all. The orphans—the word was used to designate all the boarders at the *Providence* without discrimination—were not, as a rule, admitted before they had reached their eighth year and were only discharged after their first Communion. When some poor girls of fifteen, eighteen and even twenty, sought admission, M. le Curé received them readily. More than any others, perhaps, these Magdalens needed a home and a mother. "They often came only half clad and covered with vermin," says Jeanne-Marie Chanay. "Nothing could equal the tender compassion of our holy Curé towards those poor, forsaken creatures."

Some of them had been picked up on the road by M. Vianney. There were also a few utterly destitute creatures who had repulsive sores on their heads. So long as there was a vacant corner no one was ever turned away.

One day the saint brought in a girl whom he had found wandering about.

"Receive this child whom the good God sends to you," he said to Catherine Lassagne.

"But, M. le Curé, there is no vacant bed!"

"There is always yours."

The young directress had only momentarily doubted Providence. With touching contrition she opened her arms and pressed the poor girl to her heart.

The compassion of M. Vianney towards destitute children was not barren and content with lamentations; it was active and fruitful in results.

"Once I happened to find at the church door a newborn child," Jeanne-Marie Chanay relates. "M. le Curé ordered us to take it in and to find it a nurse after we had got together a little trousseau for the poor waif. Another time, on hearing that a very unfortunate woman was dying in an adjoining parish, he sent me to her with one of my companions to fetch her baby whom we brought up."[5]

5. *Procès de l'Ordinaire,* pp. 692-693.

M. Vianney would never claim a sou from the children educated in his institution. A few young girls had been employed on the farms and might have earned a little money; others had relations whom he could have asked to contribute towards their keep. Mgr. Mermod, who at the time of his death was parish priest of Gex, one day drew his attention to this aspect of the matter: "You receive gratuitously in your *Providence* girls who are able to pay."

"Oh!" he replied, "I do not trouble about that; my only ambition is to give them a sound training so as to make good Christians of them."

The orphanage cost its founder manifold anxieties. To begin with it swallowed up all his personal property. At the time that François brought him from Dardilly the money he had inherited from his father, the mayor of Ars happened to be in the presbytery. "Count the money with *Père* Mandy," he said to his brother, and then and there he disposed of the entire sum in favor of the *Providence*.

He had hoped that his parishioners would help him with gifts in kind; to that end he made a collection through the village, the net result of which was just one sack of potatoes. He made up his mind not to renew the attempt, and ever after he appealed only to the charity of the well-to-do. He used to say laughingly that "he was a traveller in behalf of the *Providence*." When the cash-box was empty he set out on a begging tour. Arming himself with courage, he knocked at the gates of the various châteaux; he also went on foot to Lyons, where he knew the families Laporte and Jaricot. Several times also he appealed to the charity of some of his men and women penitents whose generosity he knew. Thus, for instance, he wrote to the baronne Alix de Belvey: "My good demoiselle, I come to beg you to let me have a share in your charities, for my children, since I know what a kind heart you have towards the poor. I thank you in advance and offer you my most humble respects, and at the same time I earnestly recommend myself to your holy prayers."

On the wall of the church, close to the sacristy, he had hung a framed canvas bearing this text of the Gospel: "*Give and it shall be given unto you.*" (*Luke* 6:38).

For a while he toyed with the idea of becoming a landowner. He began by saving up, and when he had put together a fairly round sum, he bought land and some woods, which were to form an endowment for the *Providence.* However, he soon wearied of the responsibility and yielded the property to the comte de Cibeins for a yearly rent. The rent—"annual and perpetual"—amounted to five hundred francs. In addition, M. de Cibeins stipulated that he would furnish the orphanage with a provision of wood—viz., 500 faggots, valued at 100 francs. Every year, without fail, M. Vianney used to send Catherine Lassagne to collect the small rent, and to remind the châtelains of "the good custom they had of providing fuel for the *Providence* of Ars."[6]

It was only after this sale that M. Vianney, deeming himself somewhat wealthier, began to receive as many children as possible. From 1830, that is, during well nigh twenty years, the house was always full. At times it sheltered as many as sixty children and more. As a matter of fact, the directresses did not trouble to establish statistics, imitating in this the mother-hen that does not amuse herself by counting her chickens. One day a person worthy of respect and one who was well disposed towards the work, asked them how many children they had under their charge. In all simplicity and innocence the mistresses admitted that they did not know.

"What! You do not know?"

"No, we do not—God knows, and that is enough for us."

"But if one of them were to run away?"

"Oh! As for that, we know them too well, and we are always busy with them, so that if such a thing were to happen we should notice it at once."

If the *Providence* was to live and grow, notwithstanding such slender resources, prodigies of economy, ingenuity

6. Mme. Christine de Cibeins, *Procès apostolique continuatif,* p. 153.

and faith had to be performed. M. Vianney, having assumed full and sole responsibility, was thus under obligation to feed and clothe sixty children whose work was practically unproductive. All those little mouths were hungry. Those fledglings, fallen or thrown from the nest, must be sure of at least a piece of black bread each day. To this end 100 bushels of wheat were required each month. The father by adoption of so many poor orphans, would have spent his days amid endless anxieties had he not put his trust in the goodness of God, with all "the sublime improvidence of the saints, which has never been disappointed."[7]

Critical moments there were, however. Though the holy Curé begged at the doors of the charitably disposed, though he sold the few articles of furniture that he possessed,[8] on more than one occasion the orphans were in actual want. At such times the directresses, who did not feel his trust in God, underwent cruel anxieties. The servant of God rebuked them severely for their want of faith.

"One day," Catherine Lassagne relates with her wonted simplicity, "we felt some dissatisfaction at his having burdened us with so many children; we deemed the task beyond our strength, and for the first time a few murmurs escaped our lips. At that very moment Jeanne-Marie Chanay was on her way to the presbytery to take something to M. le Curé. He looked annoyed. He told Jeanne-Marie that we were no longer in the same dispositions as at the beginning; we were not sufficiently submissive to the will of God. Jeanne-Marie replied: 'As for me, M. le Curé, that is true enough, but the others do not murmur.'

"'You are all alike, the three of you,' said M. le Curé. On her return Jeanne-Marie related to us this conversation. Now it was precisely during her absence that Benoîte

7. Emmanuel de Broglie, *Saint Vincent de Paul,* p. 107.
8. "J'ai fait tous les commerces imaginables" ("I had recourse to every imaginable transaction.") M. Vianney said later on to Frère Athanase *(Procès de l'Ordinaire,* p. 831).

and myself had indulged in a grumble or two. We resolved never again to complain."[9]

But surely, notwithstanding his silent resignation, he himself must have shared their anxiety? He prayed unceasingly wherever he happened to be, in the church, in the solitude of his presbytery, in the street, and when the answer was slow in coming, according to his picturesque expression, "he just went on wearying the good saints."[10]

It was in extremities such as these that God intervened directly and miraculously. Here we have the testimony of eyewitnesses, whose trustworthiness is beyond cavil.

It must have been in the course of 1829 that the supply of corn, which at that period was stored in the attic of the presbytery, was reduced to a few handfuls of grain lying scattered about the floor. It was useless to hope for anything from the villagers; in all likelihood the harvest had been a bad one. True, there remained the kindly châtelaine, but her revenues were affected by the universal distress. And he had so often begged from Mlle. d'Ars! In short, he thought of sending away a certain number of orphans. But how heartbreaking a resolution for one who dearly loved those children! Poor mites! they would be compelled to go back to their former wretchedness, and their souls and their bodies would be exposed to countless perils. Having nothing to expect from men, he would make a supreme effort with God: he would ask for a real miracle through the intercession of "the good saint," who had helped him of yore, in his student days. Sweeping together into one heap all the grains that littered the floor of the attic, he hid in it a small relic of St. Francis Régis, the wonder-worker of La Louvesc. Then, after asking the orphans to unite with him in fervent prayer for their daily bread, he, too, set himself to pray, and, with a mind already at ease, he waited for a while. Presently Jeanne-Marie Chanay appeared on the scene.

9. *Petit mémoire,* troisième rédaction, pp. 101-102.
10. It is impossible to render the original French: "Il cassait la tête à ses bons saints." (Comtesse des Garets, *Procès de l'Ordinaire,* p. 916).

"Go and gather what corn there may be in the attic," he told her. Jeanne-Marie was the baker of the *Providence* and had probably come to tell him that the pantry was empty. What a surprise now awaited her! She experienced the greatest difficulty in opening the door of the attic, and as soon as she forced it ajar a stream of wheat escaped through the narrow opening. She ran downstairs in all haste: "You wanted to test my faith," she exclaimed, "your attic is full."

"What, the attic is full?"

"Yes, it is overflowing; come and see for yourself."

So they went up together—and they noticed that the color of the new corn differed from that of the old.[11]

Never before had the attic been so full. People were amazed that the main beam, which was somewhat worm-eaten, and the whole floor had not given way under so great a weight.[12] The corn heap was of pyramidal shape, and completely covered the floor of the attic. When Mgr. Devie asked him point-blank: "The corn reached up to here, did it not?" pointing with his finger to a fairly high mark on the wall, "No, my Lord, higher still—up to that spot,"[13] was the reply.

A little later on another prodigy took place which rendered famous the kneading trough of the Providence. A drought was spreading consternation over the entire countryside. Flour was scarce and dear: there only remained enough to bake three loaves. "We felt very anxious," says Jeanne-Marie Chanay, "because of our children. Catherine and I thought that if M. le Curé would pray to the good God, he could obtain that the handful

11. Abbé Raymond, *Procès de l'Ordinaire,* p. 335.
12. M. Vianney's attic was divided into three sections. The corn was stored in the part that was farthest from his room, above an unfurnished and unused room. Long after the saint's death it was still possible to find grains of corn on that spot in the crevices of the floor.
13. Baronne de Belvey, *Procès de l'Ordinaire,* p. 254. The following is the account of the miracle given by M. Vianney to M. Toccanier: "I had many orphans to feed, and there was but a handful of corn left in the attic. I thought that St. Francis Régis, who during his life miraculously fed the destitute, would do likewise after his death. I had a relic of the saint; I put it in the handful of grains that remained; the little ones prayed, and the attic was found to be full." *(Procès apostolique ne pereant,* p. 291).

of flour that was left should yield an ovenful of loaves. We went to inform him of our predicament. "You must make the dough," he said. So I set to work, not without a certain apprehension. I began by putting a very small quantity of water and flour in the kneading trough, but I saw that the flour remained too thick. I added some water and more flour, without my small stock being exhausted.

The trough was full of dough, as on a day when a whole sack of flour was emptied into it. We baked ten big loaves, each weighing from twenty to twenty-two pounds, and the oven was filled as usual, to the great astonishment of all present.

We told M. le Curé what had happened; his reply was: "The good God is very good! He takes care of his poor."

The foundation of the *Providence* of Ars proved of immense value. "I have frequently heard M. le Curé say," Catherine writes, "that only on the day of judgement will men see how much good has been accomplished in that institution." As a matter of fact the saint's undertaking was the means of preserving the virtue of hundreds of children who, in that sheltered retreat, were taught how to earn an honest livelihood. If a few did not persevere, "a great number derived most wonderful benefit from the guidance of M. Vianney. They eventually became mothers of families or excellent domestic servants—a few of them even embraced the religious life."[14] Their conscientiousness became proverbial. A certain Lacôte, well known in the village for his avarice, owned a vineyard. This man invariably chose the Ember days of September for the vintage, when he asked for the help of the orphans. The reason for his choice was the certainty that the children would not eat a single grape!

The children whom M. Vianney had snatched from the world were made to share his anxieties and penances on behalf of sinners. "When M. le Curé," says Catherine Lassagne, "learned that God had been offended at a fête or

14. Catherine Lassagne, *Procès de l'Ordinaire,* p. 1469.

dance, the big girls would ask for permission to spend the night in prayer that they might plead for the guilty ones. They themselves made all the arrangements and called each other in turn during the hours of the night. Everything was done so noiselessly that those who were not watching remained unaware of anything unusual having taken place. When they were out for walks they sometimes gathered nettles and struck their faces with them. M. le Curé had told them that we should suffer for sinners.[15]

The Saint's prestige in the orphanage was amazing, and he could obtain from the children whatever he wanted. The following pretty incident will suffice to prove our assertion. One of the little ones simply adored her ugly and badly made doll; so tenaciously did the child cling to her toy that she took it about with her wherever she went, even to church. One day M. Vianney asked her to give it up, nay, to throw it into the fire. (The incident took place in the kitchen of the *Providence.*) At first the child seemed greatly disconcerted, when all of a sudden her decision was made, and she consigned the beloved idol to the flames. Surely the act was simply heroic.

Several of the girls died amid circumstances so wonderful that they might be fitly recounted in some new Golden Legend. Some expressed their joy in dying because they were going to Heaven; others sang or asked their companions to intone a hymn of thanksgiving. One who had always felt a great fear of death, exclaimed shortly before she expired: "Oh! how happy I am! What happiness one finds in religion!" And she strove to the utmost to unite her voice with the voices of her companions who were singing a favorite hymn of hers.

Benoîte Lardet—one of the mistresses, buried on October 5, 1850—also died a most edifying death. To her sister, who shed tears at seeing her in pain, she said: "How kind of you to weep like this! but would you, then, keep me on this earth? It has never satisfied me." "What hap-

15. Nettle leaves have been found between the pages of books that belonged to M. Vianney. May we not infer from this fact that, long before his orphans, he himself had made use of this singular instrument of penance?

piness!" she exclaimed, on the physician informing her that her illness was mortal, "what joy! I am going to behold the good God!"

When the Curé d'Ars beheld his children of the *Providence* reaching such heights of virtue, he may well have believed that his purpose had been realized to the full. It had never been his aim to turn those poor waifs into blue-stockings. Moreover, he could be under no delusion as to the capabilities of his teachers. He was not at all shocked at the rather erratic spelling of the excellent Catherine. Nor did questions of hygiene greatly trouble the austere man who lived on that which would have been another man's death, and whose totally neglected presbytery was fit rather to be the abode of a spirit than of a being of flesh and blood. His excessive kindness caused him to pack together sixty children in a space where thirty would have felt uncomfortable. In like manner the confined space at his disposal made it necessary to put all the scholars—the orphans as well as the village girls—in one common classroom. In this way, whilst the little ones were spelling aloud the characters of the alphabet, the elder girls recited their lessons, and others again would listen to some explanation given by their teacher. Obviously the din and noise must have been considerable.[16] To this must be added that lessons went on all the year round, with no other holidays than the Thursday of each week. Catherine and her companions had undertaken a superhuman task: how could they find time to give overmuch attention to matters of order and cleanliness?

Strangers who visited the *Providence* left with the impression that it was unlike any other house. A lawyer of Lyons, who in the year 1841 saw the institution at close quarters, writes as follows: "The very existence of the orphanage founded by M. Vianney seemed to us a wonderful thing. The institution sheltered some fifty or

16. The largest room, in which at first everything had to be done, and which still retains its old features, measures about eleven meters in length, six in breadth, and two and a half in height.

sixty girls between the ages of twelve and eighteen years. They came from all parts, were admitted without payment, stayed for an unlimited period, and were finally placed in the farms of the surrounding district. During their stay at the home they were taught above all things how to know, love and serve God. They formed, as it were, a large family in which the older members taught the younger both by example and by counsel. The teaching imparted to the children was not extensive, but an admirable spirit of faith, piety, and docility seemed to pervade the house. This was no ordinary institution—it was truly the product of the holiness of its founder. The temporal resources, the life, spirit, and guidance of the home came from him: the work bore the hallmark of the supernatural. It could only live through the immediate influence of the noble spirit that had conceived it."[17]

In the estimation of the Curé d'Ars *education* always held a higher place than *instruction.* Nevertheless, contemporary witnesses assure us that the children of the *Providence* received an adequate elementary education. They were likewise trained in manual work, such as knitting, sewing, washing, and ironing. What more was required from children destined to spend their days in a country village? Above all, amid those exceptional conditions, they acquired that solid virtue and piety which would enable them to face the moral dangers and every other difficulty that awaited them. Pope Pius X, of holy memory, judged the *Providence* from this standpoint when he described it as a "model of popular education."[18]

Without any doubt, the *Providence* was M. Vianney's favorite work. "He loved the house," says the baronne de Belvey, one of its benefactresses, "because it was set apart for poor children. "So soon as the directresses were sufficiently acquainted with their duties—that is, about 1827—M. Vianney felt that he could free himself from a burden that weighed heavily on his shoulders—namely, the preparation of his meals. He, the foster-father of so large a

17. Paul Brac de la Perrière, *Souvenirs de deux pèlerinages,* p. 6.
18. Decree of February 21, 1904.

family, daily for twenty years begged from his children the alms of a cup of milk. There was no need to wait on him; he went himself to fetch from a corner of the kitchen the small glazed earthenware vessel that contained his daily pittance. Five minutes was ample time in which to despatch this summary lunch. More than once it happened that, being in a hurry and unable to wait, he took the jug with him and drank the contents on his way from the *Providence* to the church.

At the end of his meal, however, he loved to go for a few moments into the yard, where his adopted daughters were at play. Their bright eyes reflected the purity of their souls, and the sight of those innocent children was a respite from the spectacle of the heinousness of sin and the wickedness of men. He knew each one and took an interest in all of them. He asked them questions and put them at their ease by the charm of his smile. He himself gave them lessons in deportment, even going so far as to teach them how to behave at table. Whenever he sought to obtain a special favor from Heaven, he made them pray. He was wont to say that when they prayed he always obtained what he wanted. In fact he knew by personal experience the truth of his own assertion that "the prayers of children go up to Heaven laden with the fragrance of their innocence."[19]

For the benefit of his dear adopted children, he caused to be put up in the garden a pergola formed by the vines, which the erection of a statue of Our Lady soon turned into a rustic oratory. The girls decorated the shrine with flowers, and, when the evenings were fine, everybody gathered there in order to recite the Litany of the Blessed Virgin Mary, and to sing a hymn in her honor.

The greater number of the orphans only left the home for good at the age of nineteen or twenty. A few, it is true, went into service at an earlier age, but they did so only in the winter months. After their departure M. Vianney kept in touch with them. He found them good situations,

19. Comtesse des Garets, *Procès de l'Ordinaire,* p. 780.

and when the time came for them to be settled in life, he gave them advice and money for their trousseau. Most especially did he accompany with his counsels and his prayers those of his children who entered religion. Surely there never was a better father nor one better loved.

The schoolroom of the *Providence* witnessed the inauguration of the famous catechisms of Ars. They began very humbly; in fact, M. Vianney's action was no innovation. Every conscientious pastor knows that it is his duty to feed with the milk of doctrine the little ones of his flock.

We have already seen that from All Saints' Day until the time of their First Communion, the holy Curé catechised, as early as six o'clock in the morning, the little boys who had gathered in the church. The pupils of the *Providence* might have assisted at this lesson, but he preferred to teach them separately and at greater length, every day of the year. In this way he hoped to steep them more deeply in the principles of a Christian life.

The morning school always ended with the recitation of the litany of the *Providence.* During those minutes of recollection the door opened softly and M. le Curé came in. At first the catechism lesson was only attended by the directresses and the children. As yet M. Vianney's movements remained unnoticed. But when the number of pilgrims grew, they simply went down to the orphanage if they wanted him at that hour. At first people only ventured to remain outside, near the window. By degrees they became more enterprising, but stopped on the threshold, until one fine day, when there was a little more space, the classroom itself was invaded. This went on until 1845; moreover, the whole thing was transacted in a quite homely way.

Chanoine Champenois, of Bourg, was an eyewitness of these scenes between 1842 and 1843. He gives the following account: "There were present the children of the institution, some good women who went on spinning—the mistresses themselves spent their scanty moments of leisure in this way—and, if I am not mistaken, a few hens were roosting on a table. M. le Curé came in wearing a surplice, took a catechism, and, leaning against the kneading-trough, began after this fashion: 'My children, yesterday we stopped at the lesson on matrimony.' After this preamble he read the question: 'What is the most common cause of unhappy marriages?' and the answer which he set himself to explain: 'Ah! my children, when two people have just been married, they never weary of looking at each other; they deem themselves so lovable, so well endowed; they admire each other, and they pay each other a thousand compliments. But the honeymoon does not last forever, no, not forever. A moment comes when they forget the wonderful qualities they had discovered in each other, and defects show themselves which they had not hitherto suspected. That is the time when some people can no longer bear each other's company, and the husband calls his wife names, such as lazy, peevish woman, good-for-nothing, and so forth.'"

M. Champenois adds: "I was amazed at such familiarity, such freedom *(ce quasi sans-gêne),* and I glanced at the audience. Everybody had listened in a religious silence—there was not so much as a smile."[20]

From 1845 onwards the growing affluence of pilgrims, who were eager to assist at the catechisms, obliged M. Vianney to hold his classes in church. "A lady of Bourg," the Abbé Dufour relates, "who had attended the catechisms from the time they were held at the *Providence,* spoke of them with enthusiasm. Nevertheless, she regretted their transfer to the Church because in the schoolroom one could get a closer and better view of the servant of God." These regrets are intelligible enough, but the change of venue yielded most happy results. In this way a greater number of pilgrims were able to listen to M. Vianney, and he himself, without giving up his familiar manner, gave freer vent to his zeal and the ardent love that burned within his heart, for now he spoke in close proximity to the tabernacle.

---

20. Mgr. Convert, *Notes MSS.,* Cahier I, n. 46.

At an early stage of the undertaking and with the sanction of Mgr. Devie, the Curé d'Ars decided to add a chapel to the orphanage.[21] Some people might have questioned the usefulness of an oratory situated barely a few meters from the church, but the saint knew his own mind. Fortunately all his plans in connection with it were not carried out, for such was his longing for solitude that he wished to give up the cure of souls. Already he saw himself living in retirement at the *Providence* when, if such were God's good pleasure, he would establish there the "perpetual adoration."

The commune gave the requisite site and the chapel of his dreams was erected, but then also the Will of God was made manifest. The building was not yet completed when the *Providence* ceased to exist in the form which its founder had given to it. So he stayed at his presbytery, and to the end remained the Curé d'Ars.

21. It was in fact on the advice of his bishop that M. Vianney erected the humble sanctuary: "M. le Curé," Mme. des Garets wrote on September 20, 1843, "is very busy with an idea suggested to him by the bishop—namely, to erect a chapel at the *Providence,* where he intends to retire some day."

Chapter 10

ARS TRANSFORMED

ON May 7, 1820, one month after the appointment of M. Vianney to the parish of Salles en Beaujolais, the Abbé Renard, then a deacon and studying theology at Lyons, being as yet ignorant of the fact that the appointment had been cancelled, wrote as follows to his benefactress, the châtelaine of Ars: "My sorrow was as great as my surprise when I heard that you have lost your holy curé. Providence sent him to the parish that he might cause piety to flourish there. With all my heart I pray that his place may be taken by a priest capable of keeping up the fervor which at the present moment reigns at Ars."

This testimony is valuable. Ars could already be styled fervent, and only two years had elapsed since M. Vianney came into the parish. Three and a half years later—November 1, 1823—in a letter to Mme. Fayot of Les Noës, M. Vianney himself sounds a first note of triumph: "I am in a small parish which is very good and which serves God with its whole heart."

When he wrote in this strain to his "good mother" he could have had no intention of giving an accurate description of the parish, because, side by side with eminent virtue, there still existed divers evils. Most of all, he would not have risked from the pulpit so optimistic an estimate of the position. The statement, however, is a proof of progress. A change had certainly come over Ars. Speaking broadly, it might be said that the bulk of the population had passed either from vice to virtue, or from ordinary piety to genuine fervor.

A recent pilgrimage to Fourvière must have materially helped towards so desirable a change. Our forefathers were fond of these pious expeditions to various shrines. Previous to the Revolution the people of Ars were in the habit of making a yearly pilgrimage to Lyons for the purpose of praying in Our Lady's venerable sanctuary. M. Vianney resolved to revive the custom. The following account of the event is supplied by Guillaume Villier, a farm laborer twenty-four years of age at the time:

"On August 6, 1836, the feast of the patron saint of Ars, our good Curé led us in procession to Notre-Dame-de-Fourvière. I can speak of that pilgrimage because I took part in it. By this solemn act M. Vianney wished to express the gratitude of us all to Our Lady for the beautiful vestments given by M. le vicomte d'Ars.

"Two curés of the neighborhood journeyed with us—viz., M. Martin, curé of Savigneux, and M. Robert, curé of Sainte-Euphémie. The latter was close on eighty years of age.

"We started from home shortly after midnight. I think about two-thirds of the population took part in the pilgrimage. We marched processionally as far as Trévoux, preceded by our three fine banners, singing hymns and saying the Rosary. It was daylight when we reached Trévoux. Here we embarked in two spacious barges tugged by horses.

"We disembarked at Lyons, some distance beyond Vaise, and from there we walked in procession to Fourvière. M. le Curé celebrated Mass, at which we assisted with devotion; several of our number received Holy Communion at his hands.

"We came down the hill in the order in which we had gone up. People thronged the roads as we went by and gave expression to their astonishment.

"When we reached the barges once more, M. Vianney was among the first to embark with some of his people, but as the others were slow in coming, the boatmen began to swear, for they were rude and coarse men. M. Vianney disembarked at once, and his example was followed by others. He proceeded on foot as far as Neuville where, a few hours later, we rejoined him, having followed him in the boat. From Neuville we returned processionally to Ars. Whenever we passed near a church the bells were rung. It was quite dark by the time we reached home."[1]

This charming incident must not make us rush to the conclusion that all the people of Ars were by now model Christians. The fact was that some were irregular in the practice of religion. For several years to come they would feel no scruple, during the harvest season, in turning the hay or gathering in the crops after the Sunday Vespers. The young people especially seemed to be inoculated with a perfect frenzy for dancing. However, the jubilee of 1826 stirred a good many, and a mission given in 1827 proved a particularly happy date in the history of the parish.

Catherine Lassagne writes: "It will never be known what graces of conversion M. le Curé obtained by his prayers, and especially by the celebration of the holy Sacrifice. A real change has been wrought in the hearts of the people. Grace has proved so strong that not many were able to resist it. Nearly everybody did his best to free himself from sin. Human respect was completely reversed: people were ashamed not to do good or not to practice their religion. The men looked earnest and thoughtful; some who had stayed away for years from Confession were heard to mutter to themselves as they walked along the roads: 'I mean to go to Confession!' All were excellently disposed. In one of his instructions M. le Curé spoke these words: 'My brethren, Ars is Ars no longer! I have heard Confessions and preached at jubilees and missions, but never have I found anything to compare with what I witness here.' This was in 1827."[2]

The evil spirit, however, was not yet banished from every household; witness the seven parishioners who in 1830 brutally informed the holy Curé that the only thing for him to do was to quit the parish. True, their challenge found no echo, and it is plain that the rest of the village refused to countenance so ridiculous a step. Ars would never have consented to be left without a priest,

1. *Procès de l'Ordinaire,* p. 644.
2. *Procès de l'Ordinaire,* p. 1311.

and anxiously desired to keep M. Vianney.

When, in 1832, Jean Picard began business at Ars as a farrier, he found the village greatly altered. He had known it at an earlier period, when it was very much like the other villages in the vicinity. Now, thanks to its parish priest, whom all held to be a saint, "Ars was unrecognizable." "This parish incomparably surpassed all the others," declared the Abbé Pelletier; it formed, as it were, an island of holiness where countless souls were about to seek spiritual regeneration or the secret of a higher life.

Let us look at the life of Ars. On weekdays we might have seen young men fingering their rosaries whilst walking beside their carts. In the evening the bell summoned all to prayer, when those who were free to do so flocked to church. Those whom duty claimed at home would kneel down to pray before some holy picture; at that hour every house in the village which was not quite empty was turned into a house of prayer.

Little crosses formed of intertwined branches marked the boundaries of the fields, or crowned the corn-ricks at harvest-time. Naive songs and hymns cheered the hours of toil; never was a vulgar, unseemly, or blasphemous word heard. "I have walked through the fields at harvest-time," Mlle. Alix de Belvey used to relate, "but I never heard a coarse word. I expressed my admiration to a peasant who replied: 'Oh, we are no better than the others, but surely it would be too shameful a thing to commit such sins when we live close to a saint.'"[3]

"The first evening that we spent at the village," says a traveller from Lyons, "we witnessed a scene that gave us a high idea of the influence exercised by the Curé d'Ars. A pair of horses, harnessed to the trunk of a tree, were being driven by three men. They came to a small brook (the Fontblin) at the same moment as ourselves. When they tried to make the horses cross it, one of them

3. *Procès de l'Ordinaire,* p. 266.

reared and hurt itself as it fell. The men rushed to the rescue of the animal. But the thing that amazed us was the fact that those peasants apparently felt not the slightest inclination to anger; there was no recrimination among themselves, no cursing or beating of their poor beasts. We had never witnessed such self-control in peasants threatened in their material interests."[4]

M. Vianney had repeatedly implored his people to say their grace before and after meals—very few omitted to do so—and to recite the Angelus three times a day, without human respect and wherever they might happen to be at the time the bell rang. Hence, so soon as the first three strokes of the bell resounded through the valley and their echo floated upwards towards the low hills, all work came to a standstill, the men bared their heads, the women folded their hands, and all recited the prescribed prayers. Like scenes could be witnessed in the fields and in the streets of the village. More than that, M. Vianney had had put up in the church tower a clock with a very large dial. When it struck, many of the villagers, following the example of their pastor, *blessed the hour*—that is, they interrupted their work and said a "Hail Mary."

It was customary, in the springtime, to plant blessed crosses in the fields in order to obtain through the merits of Jesus Christ the preservation of the crops. Later in the year, when the corn fell under the scythe of the reapers, the laborers knelt down whenever they discovered one of these crosses and recited a *Pater* and *Ave,* or intoned the strophe, *O crux, ave.*

It has to be admitted that their behavior drew down on their heads the jeers of the neighboring villages. "If you listen to your Cure," they sneered, "he will turn you all into Capuchins." Banter of this kind made no impression, and the good people of Ars merely said: "Our Curé is a saint; we must obey him."

Thus even the outward appearance of Ars was altered. "That which struck us at the outset"—to quote once more

4. Paul Brac de la Perrière, *Souvenirs de deux pélerinages à Ars,* p. 3.

from the account of the above-mentioned pilgrims of Lyons—"was the tranquillity and peace of the place. Here more than elsewhere one seemed to breathe a genial atmosphere. The inhabitants gave us a kindly greeting, and when we asked to be directed, advice was eagerly tendered. Everyone seemed to be imbued with good will towards everybody else. We also noticed that the houses were adorned with statues of the Blessed Virgin or images of the saints."[5]

All these houses were still visited at stated times by M. Vianney, in order to foster by this means the religious customs and practices he had introduced. He was now on easy terms with everybody, so he called quite unexpectedly, very often at the hour of meals. Even before entering a house he would summon the head of the household, calling him by his Christian name. All honored him as a living saint and received him with joy and eagerness. He remained standing, but supported himself by leaning against a wall or a piece of furniture. In this attitude he spoke, now to one member of the family, now to another. He inquired after the health of parents and children, the work in hand, the state of the crops. Very soon, however, and without changing his familiar tone, he managed to slip in a few of those pious words that give wings to our poor earthly conversations and lift them to a higher plane. In this way he discreetly examined the consciences of all the members of the family. "Were they faithful to prayer, to Mass, the Sunday repose? Did the children obey their parents? Did they learn their catechism?" He took a particular interest in the young domestics, timid youths from neighboring villages whom he wished to see treated as members of the family. They, too, were to be taught their religion and sent to Mass and Vespers on Sunday.

"In our house," says Catherine Lassagne, "everybody rejoiced at his visits." "He sometimes took food in my father's house," says Antoine Mandy, the son of the aged mayor, "but never by invitation. He used to come in dur-

5. *Op. cit.*, p. 2.

ing meals and cheerfully share them with us. He accepted a potato, and did not even refuse to taste a little wine for the sake of drinking the health of the family."

Visits made in such a manner were bound to be most beneficial. In the pulpit the Curé d'Ars spoke for the benefit of all; in those private visits he was able to apportion to each family its own meed of advice and, at times, of blame.

When the cure of souls finally took up all M. Vianney's time, these house-to-house visits became less and less frequent, until they ceased altogether. It was a source of deep regret in every household of Ars.

Mgr. Convert, who became parish priest of Ars in 1889, has enjoyed the privilege of an intimate acquaintance with the last survivors of the families who had the honor of receiving the saint's visits. "Their countenances," he writes, "bore an impression of holiness that we have not often met with in the same degree; a calm serenity and a kind of radiant happiness distinguished them from among thousands."[6] But then, a saint had made their parents a pattern of every domestic virtue. Those peasants—most of them quite prosperous, for they worked hard and were parsimonious, though always kind to the poor—were the objects of the pilgrims' admiration. Their speech was characterized by good sense. Faith had ennobled their hearts, and thus they had a courtesy all their own—simple, naïve, yet stamped with the hallmark of uncommon distinction and refinement, as were the manners of the patriarchs of old. In a word, religion had refined and educated them.

At the age of eighty Catherine Lassagne was fond of relating reminiscences of her childhood. Two figures, dear above all others, dominated the scene—namely, those of the holy Curé and of her own mother. Claudine Lassagne was fairly devout when, in March, 1818, she put herself under the direction of M. Vianney. Her eldest daughter, who, though she tended the flocks in the fields more often

6. *A l'école du Bienheureux Curé d'Ars,* p. 301.

than she sought learning in the village school, was by no means a fool, soon became aware of a rapid change in her mother. "At first," Catherine relates, "she was forever dressing me up and doing my hair. She took infinite trouble with my toilette. But M. Vianney had been at Ars only a few weeks when all was changed. I was now ready in a moment, and off we went to church." Once there, Claudine, according to the expression of the Curé d'Ars, "lost herself in prayer as a fish in water," and time seemed to have come to a standstill. "Come, mother, let us go," Marie, the youngest of us, would sigh, whilst tugging at her mother's skirts. However, she did not move; it looked as if she had become deaf. During the whole of Lent she never allowed her children to touch food between meals. When an indult from Rome granted the use of flesh-meat on Saturday, Claudine Lassagne continued to make her family practice abstinence on that day. "But it is lawful now to eat meat on Saturday," one of her children once remarked. "Is it a command?" she asked. "No, mother." "Very well, then; go on doing penance." In the evening this admirable woman, who had never stopped praying whilst performing her daily round of duties, assembled her whole family for prayer in common. Before going to bed—the last of all—she would bend over Catherine's bed and ask: "Have you said your 'Visit, O Lord'?" "Visit, O Lord" is the beginning of the collect of Compline, the liturgical night prayers.

The native honesty of the people of Ars had now become proverbial; it influenced all their dealings with others. In former days—the forcible sermons of M. Vianney prove it—questions of equity troubled them none too much. They did as others did, they were wont to say. When selling they would cleverly disguise the defects of their cattle, and they sold as fresh rancid butter or addled eggs.[7] The weaver kept the good thread and used some of inferior quality; the spinner "placed the hemp in a damp place, to increase its weight."[8] People returned from the fields

7. *Sermon sur la restitution,* t. III, pp. 379, 380, 382.
8. *Ibid.*

with their aprons filled with stolen vegetables or roots. Parents merely laughed when their children came home with their hands full of pilfered goods. "Surely it is no great odds," they would say. Regenerated Ars shrank from the most trifling of petty thefts. Young Benoît Trève, who in his old age told the tale to Mgr. Convert, once took a pear from the stall of a saleswoman, and without any more ado went home to enjoy it. He had no time for this, however, for his mother wished to know where he had got the fruit. When the lad acknowledged his fault, she tied his hands behind his back and drove him to the door of the merchant, whipping him all the while. Then only did she untie the child's hands and make him apologize and restore the purloined pear.

Although M. Vianney received his visitors with equal kindness, he yet cherished a special affection for his own people. When Confessions kept him in church all day, he could no longer see "his dear children," as in former days. But whereas pilgrims were forced at times to wait whole days before he could grant them a few moments' interview, every Saturday a few hours were specially reserved for the people of Ars. On other days he used to send for them as soon as he noticed them, so that those who were anxious to make a lengthy preparation were obliged to hide themselves.

To the very end he gave his people proofs of his devotion to their interests. Even when the rush of strangers was greatest, he would leave everything in order to visit the sick of the village. On one occasion, at about eleven o'clock at night, Madeleine Scipiot came to summon him to the bedside of her mother, who was seriously ill. She called his name two or three times from without. At last he woke up and opened his window. "Yes, little one, I will be there in a moment," was his answer. When he reached the house Mme. Scipiot apologized for troubling him. "Oh no, it is nothing," he said; "I have not yet given my blood for you!" During the jubilee of Trévoux, in the winter of 1823, the cold and the snow did not deter him from returning to his parish one night for the purpose of visiting a sick woman. He arrived worn out with fatigue, white with hoar-frost, and frozen through and through. Nothing could stop him when his own people needed him. Great, also, was his joy at sight of their docility and good dispositions. At Ars he was loved as a father and obeyed like a king. Everybody and everything felt the spell of his influence.

Both in the pulpit and in the confessional he had never ceased from proclaiming the strictness and the sweetness of the laws of Christian marriage. He had been heard and understood. God's blessing rested upon the homesteads of the village. To use the imagery of the Bible, "the wife was as a fruitful vine, on the sides of the house," and "the children as olive plants, round about the table of their fathers." (*Ps.* 127:3).

Facing the church stood the house of the Ciniers with their ten children; *Père* Mandy was the father of twelve; twelve children formed a crown of honor for the châtelains, comte and comtesse des Garets; the families of Pertinand and Fleury Trève had fifteen children each. During the pastorate of M. Vianney the population of Ars was more than doubled. Between 1818 and 1824 there were ninety-eight baptisms as against forty burials.

Parents claimed a good deal of authority even over their grown-up children, and they would not suffer it to be whittled away. Neither boys nor girls were permitted to walk aimlessly about the streets or to remain idle at home. "When the girls came back from school," says Annette Scipiot, herself brought up under this severe régime, "instead of being allowed to play, they were made either to knit or to help in the housework. If they had to go out they were asked, on their return, how they had behaved and whom they had met. On Sunday the girls went out only with their mothers. Jeanne Cinier, who felt no call to a cloistered life, would groan at times: "Let us go for a walk today after Vespers; I am weary of being shut up at home!" So her mother would take her out into the fields. Once, however, Jeanne eluded her mother's watchfulness. Together with the Demoiselles Scipiot, she allowed herself to be persuaded by some young woman to go as far as the woods of La Papesse. They strolled about and gathered nuts. Suddenly shouts came from both ends of the wood: they proceeded from the youths of Mizérieux, who came to meet those of Ars, and were exchanging the signal agreed upon. The would-be nut-gatherers fled as fast as their legs would carry them, "as if all the snakes of the wood were after them," to quote Jeanne's own words. Never again did they feel tempted to repeat their disobedience.

This intensive cultivation of souls does not appear to have yielded an extraordinary crop of vocations either for the religious life or for the priesthood. M. Vianney would not push anyone, either towards the cloister or the altar, unless he saw unmistakable signs of a vocation. One day in 1824 he met, in the square, a youth of the village whose piety he evidently deemed to be above the average. "Would you like to go to the seminary, my child?" he asked. "Oh, M. le Curé, it is absolutely necessary that I should help my father; I cannot leave him." The answer settled M. Vianney's opinion about the youth whose future he would have wished to be brighter. "If that be so, you do well," he said.[9] Others, on the contrary, who could not make up their minds, he urged to enter at once either a convent or the seminary, as the case may have been.

Many persons planned their pilgrimage so as to spend a Sunday at Ars. "Thanks to M. Vianney's zeal," says the Baronne de Belvey, "the day that had been so much profaned previous to his arrival was now indeed the Lord's own day. There were many Communions. The church was never emptied. Services were numerous: there were but short intervals between them, yet all were well attended. M. le Curé gave catechism at one o'clock in the afternoon; the attendance at it was hardly less than at Mass. Vespers were followed by Compline. Then there came the

9. The youth was Jean Tête who, in his old age, gave evidence in the course of the process of canonization (*Procès apostolique continuatif,* p. 77). He remained a farmer, married, and had ten children.

recitation of the Rosary, in which everybody joined. At nightfall the bell rang out a third summons to church, and a third time the parish answered its call. At that hour M. Vianney left his confessional, recited night prayers and concluded the exercises of day with one of those touching homilies to which I used to listen with so much pleasure. I was much impressed by the behavior of all those good people, especially by that which the mothers exacted from their children."[10]

"Our stay at Ars," writes Paul Brac de la Perrière, "was prolonged until the Sunday. On that day the service began at eight o'clock and lasted until eleven. There was a procession before Mass and a sermon after the gospel. The church was quite full. An extraordinary spirit of recollection prevailed."[11]

Surely scenes like these were reminiscent of the first centuries of the Church; such were the gatherings of the early Christians.

The only fault with which M. Vianney had to reproach a few of his good parishioners was that too often they were late for church. Slackness formed an inveterate defect in those peasants of La Dombes. Even as late as 1850 the saint's success was not yet complete. "He commissioned Frère Jérôme, his sacristan, to walk round the exterior of the church before the *Asperges* that precedes the Mass, and with all gentleness to act on the principle of the *compelle intrare* of the Gospel. Frère Jérôme, in consequence, went out into the square, praying those who lingered there to enter at once. At first he met with some opposition, but they soon contracted the good habit, and at last the Curé d'Ars had the satisfaction of seeing all his beloved people gathered round his person from the very beginning of the service."[12]

Whilst men were thus engaged in the worship of God all work was at a standstill in field and garden. If there were some who, at harvest-time, violated the sacred

10. *Procès de l'Ordinaire,* p. 265.
11. *Souvenirs de deux pélerinages,* p. 8.
12. Mgr. Convert, *A l'école du Bienheureux Curé d'Ars,* pp. 44-45.

repose, they were few in number and worked furtively and for as short a time as possible. "With us," a good man remarked, "human respect is reversed."

Best of all, no trading whatever was now done in the village upon the Lord's day. M. Vianney would not tolerate that shops should open, and he always refused to bless objects that had been fraudulently purchased that day. Except for some grave reason, such as a death, or a visit to someone seriously ill, the people of Ars refrained from travelling on Sunday. Not a jarring note, not even the rumbling of a cart, troubled the peace of the day. We quote here the testimony of François Pertinand, the hotel keeper and carrier of Ars: "Our holy Curé would never allow me to do business on Sundays and feast days, nor did the other carters harness their horses on those days. When the railway was opened, the company, whose agent I was, demanded an uninterrupted service. M. Vianney, however, would not have the carts enter the village or leave it on the days I have mentioned. Nevertheless, without giving me formal leave, he allowed me to pick up passengers at a point beyond the first houses of the village or to take them as far as that same place."[13]

An unusual occurrence, and one that caused a great sensation at the time, was looked upon as a sanction by Heaven itself of the injunctions of the holy Curé. "We recollect," the Abbé Monnin writes, "that in 1856, on the Sunday within the octave of Corpus Christi, an omnibus had come as far as the front of the church, through the open door of which could be seen the Blessed Sacrament exposed on the altar. The horses, which were in full trot, brought up short, and, notwithstanding the driver's vigorous application of the whip, stood firm as Balaam's ass under her master's staff. There was no help for it; the equipage had to turn round and take the road back to the hotel."[14]

Thus, Sunday after Sunday, the village of Ars presented the picture of a monastery, where only the sound of the bell breaks in upon the recollection and silence of the

13. *Procès apostolique ne pereant,* p. 813.
14. Monnin, *The Cure of Ars,* English trans., p. 100.

inmates.[15] Uproarious fairs and the spectacle of drunken men shouting and reeling were things of the past. A gentleman who detested the breed used to say: "I am very happy at Ars: there I meet with no drunkards."[16]

The few hours of leisure between the church services were spent in friendly visits and conversations full of cordiality. The men played at skittles or bowls, old men might be seen taking their ease on the threshold of their homes, silently contemplating the familiar landscape. One such was Fleury Trève, the father of fifteen children. Every Sunday, after Vespers, he sat on his doorstep and recited the Rosary.

M. Vianney introduced the custom of keeping, in the same manner as the Sunday, certain *feasts of devotion,* such as the Mondays after Easter and Pentecost, the Thursday of Corpus Christi, SS Peter and Paul, St. John the Baptist, St. Sixtus, and the feast of his "beloved little St. Philomena."[17] On those days the people of Ars filled the church at Mass, at Vespers and at the time of the evening sermon. Nobody was the poorer for it. However, the Curé took good care not to proclaim those services as binding in conscience. Those who had to work did so without incurring any blame; but the custom was not to work. "I love those feasts very much," M. Vianney used to say, "because people come to church without compulsion, urged solely by the fervor of a more perfect love."

Even on weekdays some fifty women and about a dozen men were to be seen at early Mass. In some households the days were so mapped out that throughout the year at least one member of the family assisted at daily Mass. The members of the Guild of the Blessed Sacrament faithfully complied with the statute that enjoins them to carry tapers at Benediction and at processions of the Blessed Sacrament. Every Sunday they performed their hour of adoration. More than one of their number, after the exam-

15. "The parish had become like a monastery. I never saw anything like it. (Baronne de Belvey, *Procès de l'Ordinaire,* p. 194).
16. Baronne de Belvey, *ibid.,* p. 195.
17. Corpus Christi and SS Peter and Paul are not days of obligation in France as they are with us.

ple of *Père* Chaffangeon of holy memory, took delight in visiting Our Lord, either before or after his work. It was a touching sight to behold a row of dusty or muddy tools leaning against the wall of the old church whilst their owners were praying within.

M. Vianney was less successful when, after a fairly prolonged period of strictness—perhaps twenty years—he endeavored to accustom his people to a more frequent reception of the Sacraments. His desire was to see them at the holy table every Sunday, or at least once a month, but, seeing that he could not have his way, he thought that even a restricted number of good Communions would enable the men and youths not only to persevere in a Christian life, but even to go forward in the practice of virtue. "I have done all I could," he used to say towards the end of his life, "to induce the men to communicate four times a year; had they listened to me they would all be saints."[18] In order to achieve such a result, he both prayed and preached; his zeal made him inventive; to the better disposed he suggested that they should receive Holy Communion to celebrate the great anniversaries of their lives, such as the days of their Baptism, First Communion, marriage, and so forth. He desired those who were to stand godfather or godmother first to go to Holy Communion. Throughout his priestly life it was his most intense happiness to distribute Holy Communion. He would have loved to spend all his time in this consoling function, and when he fulfilled it his face was generally bathed in tears.

To draw his people more effectually to the Holy Eucharist, the Curé d'Ars had endeavored to communi-

18. With rare exceptions—according to M. Dufour, missionary in 1855 there were only seven or eight men who had not made their Easter duties —all the men and youths were regular in the fulfillment of the Easter precept; on All Saints' Day the number of men communicants was reduced to twenty-three or twenty-five, but almost all communicated at Christmas. In the end, M. Vianney had to be satisfied with this result, though it was very inadequate by comparison with his wishes. As for the women, most of them received Holy Communion at least once a month; those who only communicated on the great feasts were very few indeed. A goodly number communicated frequently and even daily. These facts were supplied by Mme. Butillon of Ars, and Mme. Colombier, her daughter, and collected by Mgr. Convert, *op. cit.*, No. 38.

cate to them a taste for all holy things, and his efforts were not in vain. Sunday after Sunday these good people feasted their eyes on beautiful banners and vestments.[19] For a long time the saint himself trained the altar boys, and he achieved wonderful results. He carried out with gravity, dignity, and the utmost care all the ceremonies of the rite of Lyons, which at that time was likewise in use in the diocese of Belley. Nor was the behavior of the altar servers less admirable when, in 1849, Frère Athanase undertook the functions of master of ceremonies.

He had so fine a liturgical spirit, and he drilled the children with so much precision and good taste, that Mgr. de Langalerie, during a clergy retreat, held him up as a pattern to the clergy of the diocese. "Do you wish to see a church where all the ceremonies are carried out to the letter? Go to Ars; Frère Athanase is a living and unerring ceremonial. His example will show you what you can achieve yourselves if you will only take the means."[20]

There were days when the people of Ars gave special edification to the pilgrims. On Maundy Thursday, in order to commemorate the institution of the Holy Eucharist, M. Vianney insisted on providing a splendid altar of repose, and his heart rejoiced at sight of the decorations which enhanced the majesty of the tabernacle. The whole of the chancel, which had been considerably enlarged in 1845, was draped with banners. Numerous and tastefully arranged lights transfigured the scene. However, he took every precaution lest these decorations should be a hindrance instead of a help to the interior recollection of the people. The day was spent in adoration by the whole parish. In the evening he held the exercise of "the Holy Hour." The whole night from Maundy Thursday to Good Friday was spent by him on his knees, for he refused to

19. In the minutes of the pastoral visitation held at Ars by the Bishop of Belley, on Monday, June 11, 1838, we read as follows: "After saying Mass and giving Confirmation, His Lordship contented himself with giving Benediction of the Blessed Sacrament and reciting the prayers for the departed. He deemed it unnecessary to examine the interior of the church, the chapels, vestments and sacred vessels, because everything is so beautiful and so rich that the beholder is filled with admiration."

20. Mgr. Convert. *Le Frére Athanase,* p. 4.

sit down for a single moment.

Corpus Christi was for Ars the feast of feasts, and a truly unique spectacle it always was. Elsewhere greater splendor may have been displayed; nowhere would there be manifestations of greater faith and love. The solemnity thrilled the Curé d'Ars, and caused him to expand with the naive gladness of a child. "The very manner in which he announced the feast was a revelation of how dear it was to his heart."[21] It would seem that it was a delight to behold him on that day. For once the confessional was deserted for a few hours. He breathed more freely, he expanded, he gave himself a holiday!

He went into his presbytery, where the altar boys vested. He always found there were not enough of them. *Père* Lardet relates the following incident: "On one occasion (I was then about twelve or thirteen years of age) I was waiting in the presbytery yard with the rest of the altar boys when M. le Curé came on the scene. 'Oh, my children,' he said, as he moved to and fro amongst us, 'if only your souls were as white as your surplices!' And he was all smiles." "He likewise wished the girls to wear white dresses," says Catherine Lassagne, "and those of his *Providence* were not the last to carry out this desire of his."

He wanted the villagers to erect as many altars of repose as possible, so as to multiply Benedictions in the parish. His heart overflowed with joy as he walked through the streets of the village; he even went as far as the château. Wherever he passed he spoke a cheerful word to the workers, often himself lending a hand; but before the procession he still found time to go to the church to hear a few Confessions, for there were always people waiting there for him.

The function was carried out in the midst of an enormous concourse of people, because at Ars the feast was kept on the day assigned to it by the Liturgy—viz., the Thursday after Trinity Sunday. Thus the people of the surrounding villages were able to flock to Ars, and they

21. Pierre Oriol, *Procès de l'Ordinaire,* p. 726.

never failed to take part in the procession. M. Vianney would not tolerate that the curious and the would-be lookers on should merely line the route of the procession; everybody had to walk in it.

When he was in the company of other priests he usually sought the last place, but on this day he would not yield to another the honor of carrying the Blessed Sacrament. Walking under the canopy given by the Vicomte d'Ars, and clad in sumptuous vestments, he advanced with a majesty that impressed the beholders. With his eyes steadily fixed on the Host, he prayed and wept. A religious awe swayed the crowd and prevented any attempt at conversation. Behind the canopy followed the mighty throng of humanity, from which arose no other sound than that of songs and prayers. It was truly the festival of God—*Fête-Dieu.*

A witness of this splendid manifestation of popular devotion has described it for us, but in the bombastic and affected style which the "*Génie du Christianisme*" at one time rendered fashionable. "It was, I remember well, on a fine afternoon in June of the year 1841. The sun was about to sink behind a cloud of purple and gold; the soft air was charged with an intoxicating fragrance. I had walked across the fields, sombre, weary, eager to be alone, but all unawares I had come upon the valley of Ars. I sat on a grassy bank skirting the meadows which spread out at my feet like an ocean of verdure. With my head between my hands, I remained lost in a deep reverie. Suddenly, from the northern part of the valley is heard the crash of artillery, fired in honor of a festival, and a threefold discharge answers the first report.[22] At the signal all the bells of the village ring out. Their harmony draws my eyes towards Ars, where, in the distance, they espy a considerable crowd surging round a church far too small to hold them all. The roads nearest to it are encumbered with conveyances hurrying to the feast. I also discover what looks like flags floating from the roof of the château

22. M. le Comte des Garets, then Mayor of Ars, arranged for the firing of explosives—*boîtes de poudre*—during the progress of the procession.

close by and from the church.

"At last it dawned on me that it was the Feast of Corpus Christi, a solemnity that has been famous in these parts for the last twenty years.[23] I went down into the valley, guided by the sound of many voices blending in one mighty chorus. What splendor now burst upon my astonished gaze! I beheld an immense procession formed of pilgrims from all parts advancing into the fields in the wake of divers banners. Every minute there was an explosion of artillery, which was answered by a detonation from the direction of the château on the opposite side of the valley. The procession advances—the canopy of cloth of gold, the silver-gilt monstrance, the copes of brocade reflect the rays of the sun that dart between the branches of the big trees. An aged priest, the venerable curé of the place, advances, carrying the God of all.

"On the borders that separate the territory of the commune from the property of the château a graceful altar of repose has been dressed. Clouds of smoke curl up from the censers. The canopy halts. Two thousand people fall on their knees and bow their heads to the earth whilst, with a trembling hand, the priest slowly lifts the monstrance.

"The crowd has risen. Fresh detonations have answered to the renewed *Alleluia*. The scene changes: we are now on land belonging to the château. Suddenly the bell rings out a sharp peal. It announces, as it were, the outbreak of the fire of joy. Ten explosions of saltpetre follow, and the procession advances into the meadows.

"The spectacle is reminiscent of the Middle Ages. There is a bridge to cross; it is decorated with banners and festoons of flaming hues. The triangular pennons of the house of Ars flap in the breeze; each tree has the appearance of a bouquet of flowers. At last we reach the iron gates of the château. They are intertwined with natural lilies. There are fewer grains in the sanded paths than there

---

23. The fame of the solemnity as kept at Ars spread rapidly. In 1819, only a year after his arrival, M. Vianney already displayed on that day all the splendor possible. (Abbé Monnin, *Procès de l'Ordinaire,* p. 1087).

are rose-petals strewn by pious hands. Antique tapestries adorn the base of the old donjon keep. The procession advances between hedges formed of lemon trees, spreads itself in the park, and finally retraces its steps until it reaches the entrance to the chapel of the château.

"A powerful, sonorous refrain sung by robust and trained voices rises in a tremendous crescendo. At the tinkling of a little silver bell it promptly subsides, the while the Curé d'Ars, with a shaking voice, pronounces from afar a blessing upon his flock. The last syllables have scarcely fallen from the lips of the priest when a sudden *Hosanna* once more shakes the walls of the oratory. Like an electric spark it runs through the crowd kneeling out in the park, and, mingling with a simultaneous explosion of the artillery of peace, its echoes roll down along the windings of the valley."[24]

On perusing this pompous description, we might almost imagine that at Ars the Feast of Corpus Christi was of a somewhat warlike character. But how happy were those excellent peasants, particularly the older ones, who had known the jejune festivals of former times. Even more than they, their Curé rejoiced on hearing "the powerful refrain" of the crowd and the "simultaneous explosion of the artillery of peace."

On the Feast of Corpus Christi of the year 1859—the last the Curé ever witnessed, for it was only forty days before his death—the Comte des Garets, without his knowledge, placed in the ranks of the procession the band of the College of Montgré. At the sudden crash of the music M. Vianney "trembled with joy."[25] When the procession was over he could not find words with which to thank the Jesuit Fathers who had given him this exquisite surprise.

That year he was exceedingly fatigued, so that, to his great regret, he could only carry the Blessed Sacrament as it reached the altars of repose. The preceding year he had carried the heavy monstrance for two hours, though

24. Extract from the *Album du pélerinage d'Ars,* etc., Lyon, Brunet, 1852.
25. Comte des Garets, *Procès de l'Ordinaire,* p. 789.

he was then seventy-two years of age. As he ascended the steps of those rustic altars he seemed to be possessed of the agility of a young man.[26] True, there were moments when he appeared unsteady and people trembled lest he should fall. But only strangers could nurse such fears; his own people felt no misgivings, for they were accustomed to seeing him holding his own in the midst of the most crushing labors.

As for himself, he was so lost in God that he knew no anxiety. Frère Athanase relates: "One Corpus Christi day, as he returned to the sacristy bathed in perspiration, we asked him: 'You must be very tired, M. le Curé?' 'Oh, why should I be tired? He whom I carried likewise carried me.'"[27]

Ars had now truly become a focus from which radiated holiness. In order to be always under its immediate influence, some fervent souls had either settled in the village or made prolonged stays in it. Among them were Mlles. Pignaut, Lacand, Berger, de Belvey, the sisters Ricotier, Marthe Miard, MM. Faure de la Bastie and Pierre Oriol, Hippolyte Pagès (of Beaucaire), Jean-Claude Viret (of Cousance, in the Jura), Sionnet (of Nantes), Sanchez Rémon, a Carlist officer banished from Spain. Some of these had sought the retirement of the village in the hope that their last moments would be cheered by the presence of its holy Curé. And, indeed, if it was sweet to live in so privileged a parish, it was even sweeter, so it would seem, to die there.

During the pastorate of M. Vianney there were some particularly serene and edifying deaths—deaths transfigured by a wholly supernatural joy.

On the last day of October, 1825, *Père* Louis Chaffangeon expired at the age of seventy-five. It was he who was the silent contemplative before the altar. In his agony his face appeared radiant, and, buoyed up by the hope that lay in his heart, he sang: *Je la verrai, cette Mère chérie!*

At Christmas, 1832, Mlle. Anne-Colombe des Garets

26. Abbé Monnin, *Procès de l'Ordinaire,* p. 1082.
27. *Procès apostolique in genere,* p. 277.

died the death of the predestined. She was seventy-eight years of age.

We have already seen how they died at the *Providence.* Assisted by their beloved pastor, his good people departed this life in a way that caused those who stood round the bed of death to say to themselves: "May the manner of my going hence be such as this!" Thus it came about that people in the neighborhood of Ars begged to receive the last Sacraments at the hands of M. Vianney. One person had herself carried as far as Ars in order to secure this privilege. Of the new cemetery which he had laid out in 1855, some three hundred feet from the church, and which he had himself blessed, the Cure d'Ars loved to say: "It is a reliquary!" He had stood by the deathbed of all those who reposed there, even of certain sinners of whom, according to the old folk of the village, none escaped him before they set out on the dreadful passage from hence. The saint believed that all were saved.

Even the devil, in his own characteristic fashion, bore witness to the change. The supernatural fragrance that emanated from the village drove him to fury. "What a filthy place this is!" he exclaimed one day, in the square, through the mouth of a possessed woman whom he ill-treated most horribly. "How ill the place smells! At Ars everybody smells bad. . . . Ah! talk to me of the Rotonde (a pleasure resort of evil repute at Lyons); it is the Rotonde that smells nice!"

Even in the purely material order Ars appeared to be under a special protection. "I have heard my mother say," Madeleine Mandy-Scipiot relates, "that since 1825, the year she came to live in the parish, until the death of M. Vianney, there never was a hailstorm. She ascribed this protection to the merits of the servant of God, the more so as he himself was in the habit of asking for prayers that we might be spared the scourge."[28]

"It has been remarked," Mlle. Marthe des Garets adds, "that during the whole time of his ministry at Ars no

28. *Procès apostolique in genere,* p. 277.

damage was ever done by storms. My mother once wrote to me the day after a storm: 'For us the thunder has only been like a voice that dies away.' M. le Curé had spent the night in prayer."[29]

It is not to be wondered at, therefore, that so many strangers who could only make an all too brief stay at Ars became attached to that blessed village. Those especially who best understood its spirit and most deeply relished its peace, even though they returned to their own homes, ever after felt as if they lived in exile.

"It was not without sadness that we came away," one of these pilgrims recounts. "How was it that we became so quickly attached to it? It was that on this poor, joyless earth we had found a mysterious interior happiness which turns into home any place where it may be tasted. When we found ourselves once more amid the noise and bustle of the city, we could not rid ourselves of a strange feeling of uneasiness and depression. Men appeared to us coarse and hostile; their speech, their shouts, even the sight of them at work, seemed like a discordant note or a betrayal of pain. The atmosphere of Christian peace and harmony which we had only just left increased our sensitiveness in respect to human miseries. Henceforth we shall ever feel compelled to fly to our memories of Ars as unto a sanctuary, and to conjure up before the eyes of our soul the saintly figure of M. Vianney. Only thus shall we find anew both encouragement and comfort."[30]

To the Abbé Toccanier, who enjoyed the wonderful privilege of being the saint's auxiliary, a person of very eminent piety wrote the following tear-stained lines:

"O Ars! Could I but transport thither my person even as my thoughts, you would see me every day. It is a fact that no sooner have I left than my soul wants to return. . . . I dream of the happiness of days that are no longer, those days I spent in your blessed country. . . . How happy you are!"[31]

29. *Ibid.*, p. 327.
30. Brac de la Perrière, *op. cit.*, p. 10.
31. Baronne de Belvey, *Letters* of December 17, 1855, and of November 19. 1856.

Chapter 11

THE CURÉ D'ARS AND THE DEVIL

THAT Hell exists and that there are fallen angels condemned to Hell, is a dogma of the Catholic Faith. The devil is a personal, living being, not a figment of the imagination. True, his activity in the world remains for the most part hidden; nonetheless, by divine permission, at times the evil one comes out into the open. The reason is, no doubt, that he has felt that on some spot or other of the earth his influence is in jeopardy, and since he cannot come to grips immediately with God, he endeavors, evildoer that he is, to render fruitless the labors of His servants. For the space of some thirty-five years—from 1824 to 1858—the Curé d'Ars was subjected, even outwardly, to the molestations of the evil one. What if, by preventing him from taking both food and sleep, Satan had succeeded in inspiring him with a distaste for prayer, penance, and the exertions of the apostolic life, and in obliging him to give up the cure of souls! But the enemy of our salvation was disappointed and defeated. "The struggles of M. Vianney with the devil," says Catherine Lassagne, "helped to render his charity more ardent and more disinterested." The evil one had not bargained for such a result.

The vexations of Hell "began at the time when the holy curé was planning his *Providence,* for which he had just bought a house"—that is, during the winter of 1824 to 1825.[1] As a matter of fact, they were but the sequel of previous internal temptations of great violence. In the course of a grave illness, due, perhaps, to what he called his "youthful follies," he was attacked by despairing

1. Catherine Lassagne, *Procès apostolique ne pereant,* p. 424.

thoughts at the very moment when he felt death near. It seemed to him that he heard a voice within himself saying: "Now is the time when you shall go down to Hell." However, he recovered his interior peace by protesting his trust in God.

Once resolved upon upsetting M. Vianney's outward tranquillity, the devil began with some rather trivial vexations. Every night the poor Curé heard the curtains of his bedstead being rent. In the beginning he imagined that he had to do only with common rodents. He placed a pitchfork near the head of his bed. Useless precaution: the more he shook the curtains in order to frighten off the rats, the louder became the sounds of rending, and in the morning, when he expected to find them in shreds, the curtains were undamaged. This game lasted for quite a while.[2]

It is evident that at first the Curé d'Ars did not realize that he had to deal with the spirit of darkness. He was not credulous, and it was with difficulty that he gave credence to extraordinary occurrences,[3] so much so that when divers cases of diabolical possession were submit-

---

2. Catherine Lassagne, *Procès de l'Ordinaire,* p. 481. In order that the reader may be able to appraise these strange phenomena, we subjoin the following theological principles: we must range under the heading of *extraordinary preternatural* facts the prolonged vexations of which, by God's permission, the Curé d'Ars was for so long a victim. M. Saudreau, who is an authority on this matter, writes as follows: "There are two kinds of diabolical operations: those that are *ordinary* and others of an *extraordinary* nature.

"The devil acts on all men by tempting them; no one can escape those attacks; these are his *ordinary* operations.

"In other very much rarer cases, the devils reveal their presence by troublesome vexations, which are more terrifying than painful; they cause a great noise, they move, transport, knock over and at times smash certain objects; this is what is called *infestation.*"

Infestation is the first among extraordinary diabolical operations. It is the one from which the holy Curé d'Ars suffered almost exclusively. Only on a few very rare occasions was he the victim of *external obsession,* during which the devil attacks, beats, and hurts the person obsessed. He never complained of having experienced *internal obsession,* in which the fallen spirit, by influencing the imagination in particular, seems to force upon a poor soul something of his own sentiments; nor of *possession,* properly so-called, in which Satan "seizes upon the human organism and makes use of its members, its tongue, in fact, of the whole body, which he moves according as he pleases." (*Cf.* A. Saudreau, *The Mystical State.*)

The Curé d'Ars, in the course of his ministry, encountered many such cases, and in many instances he set free the soul, and even the body, of those who were undergoing the persecution of the evil spirits.

3. Abbé Toccanier, *Procès de l'Ordinaire,* p. 181.

ted to him, he always proceeded with the utmost caution. M. Dufour, a missionary of Belley, relates how he once asked him for his opinion about a person who was seized with fury at sight of a priest or a crucifix. He replied: "It is a case of a little nerves, a little madness, and a little of the *grappin*."[4] *Grappin* was the nickname by which he generally designated the devil. As for himself, a man who in the midst of incredible labors remained ever absolutely self-possessed, could not, assuredly, be described as the victim of hallucination.[5] Opposed to every form of falsehood and far too serious to invent idle tales, he would never have spoken of those diabolical obsessions had they not been real. Such, in fact, was the conviction of all who knew him.[6]

Soon, in the silence of the night, blows were struck against doors, shouts were heard in the yard in front of the presbytery. Perhaps they were the act of thieves, who were after the rich offerings of the Vicomte d'Ars, which were kept in the large cupboard in the attic! M. Vianney boldly came downstairs, but saw nothing. Nonetheless, on

---

4. *Procès apostolique in genere,* p. 360.
5. Doctor J. B. Saunier, who for seventeen years was physician to the Curé d'Ars, has left the following statement concerning the perfect physical and moral balance of his illustrious patient: "*We have only one thing to say of the alleged physiological explanations of phenomena of this kind.*" The doctor had been questioned about the nocturnal disturbances at the presbytery, and by way of accounting for them the word hallucination had been whispered in his hearing: "*If explanations such as these be admissible when we have to account for facts accompanied by pathological circumstances that reveal their nature, and which are rarely wanting*—such as hebetude, convulsions, signs of folly—*it is quite impossible to attribute to them the same cause when they are accompanied, as in the case of M. Vianney, by perfect regularity of all the functions of the organism, by a serenity of ideas, a delicacy of perception, a sureness of view and judgement, a mastery of all his powers, and the maintenance of that miraculous health which hardly ever failed him, notwithstanding the incessant labor that absorbed his life.*" (*Procès de l'Ordinaire,* p. 1112).

   On his part, Dr. Aimé Michel of Coligny (Ain), when asked for his opinion during the same process, made the following statement, May 31, 1864: "*All that I have seen or heard of M. le Curé d'Ars strengthens my conviction that he was absolutely self-possessed and endowed with great soundness of judgement. Nothing could persuade me that he was the victim of delusions or hallucinations. As regards demoniacal attacks, I have heard of them, and if M. Vianney affirmed that he experienced them, I believe them to have taken place.*"
6. "At Ars nobody doubted the fact that those noises were caused by the devil. I never entertained a doubt myself; neither time nor reflection has altered my conviction in this respect. The idea of a fraud cannot be entertained for a moment. If these occurrences had been merely a bad joke, or the act of persons who deemed it to their interest, they would have been promptly unmasked." (Abbé Chaland, *Procès apostolique continuatif,* p. 650).

subsequent nights he was afraid to remain alone.

The following is the deposition of André Verchère, the wheelwright of the village, a hefty fellow, then twenty-eight years old:[7] "For several days M. Vianney had heard strange noises in his presbytery. One evening he came to look for me, and said: 'I wonder whether or no it is a case of thieves . . . will you come and sleep at the presbytery?' 'Most willingly, M. le Curé, and I will load my gun, too.' At nightfall I went to the presbytery. Until ten o'clock I sat by the fire warming myself and talking to M. le Curé: 'Let us go to bed,' he said at last. He gave up his room to me and went into the one adjoining it. I was unable to sleep. At about one o'clock I heard a violent shaking of the handle and lock of the front door. At the same time heavy blows were struck, as if with a club, against the same door, whilst within the presbytery there was a terrific din, like the rumbling of several carts.

"I seized my gun and rushed to the window, which I threw open. I looked out but saw nothing. For nearly a quarter of an hour the house shook—so did my legs. I felt the effects of that night for a fortnight. As soon as the noise had started, M. le Curé lit a lamp. He accompanied me.

"'Have you heard?' he asked.

"'You can see that I have heard, since I am up and have my gun.' And all the time the presbytery was shaking as in an earthquake.

"'So you are afraid?' he asked.

"'No,' I replied, 'I am not afraid, but I feel my legs giving way under me. The presbytery is going to crash to the ground.'

"'What do you think it is?'

"'I think it is the devil.'

"When the uproar ceased we returned to bed. The following evening M. le Curé came again to ask me to keep him company. I replied: 'M. le Curé, I have had quite enough.'"

---

7. He died at Ars in 1879, at the age of eighty-one.

Subsequently, at the *Providence,* M. Vianney, mimicking the perplexity of his first protector, "laughed heartily at his terror." "My poor Verchère," he told the directresses, "was shaking with fear, though he was holding his gun in his hand. He no longer knew he had a gun."[8]

The wheelwright having refused, M. Vianney appealed to the Mayor, who sent to the presbytery his son Antoine, a big lad of twenty-six, and an additional companion-in-arms in the person of Jean Cotton, gardener at the château of Ars, and two years younger than Antoine. These two defenders went to the presbytery after night prayers and remained on duty for about twelve nights. "We heard nothing whatever," was Jean Cotton's report. "Not so M. le Curé, who slept in an adjoining room. More than once his rest was disturbed, and he called out to us: 'Children, do you not hear anything?' We answered that not a sound had reached us. At one moment, however, I heard a sound resembling that which would be made if a water jug were rapidly struck with the blade of a knife . . .We had hung up our watches near the looking-glass in his room. 'I am greatly surprised,' M. le Curé told us, 'that your watches are not smashed.'"[9]

Several other young men, among whom was Edme Scipiot, steward at the château, posted themselves as sentries in the church tower. They, too, heard nothing, except that one night, according to Magdeleine Scipiot, Edme's daughter, they saw a tongue of fire, which precipitated itself upon the presbytery.

Whence exactly proceeded these noises? M. Vianney, anxious but cautious, did not as yet dare to form a definite opinion. One night, when the ground was covered with snow, shouts were heard in the yard. "It was like an army of Austrians or Cossacks who were talking all together in a language he was unable to understand."[10] He opened his door. On the white surface where objects can be distinguished even during moonless nights, he

8. Jeanne-Marie Chanay, *Procès de l'Ordinaire,* p. 685.
9. *Procès de l'Ordinaire,* p. 1382.
10. Catherine Lassagne, *Petit mémoire,* troisième rédaction, p. 93.

could detect no footprints. His mind was now made up. These were not human voices; nor could there be question of anything angelic or divine, but rather of something horrible, with the horror of Hell itself. Moreover, those shudders of terror which he experienced gave him an adequate cue as to the identity of the mysterious personage. "I came to the conclusion that it was the devil because I was afraid," he admitted later on to Mgr. Devie; "the good God does not frighten us." Knowing that neither gun nor pitchfork availed in such a contest, "he dismissed his bodyguard and remained alone on the field of battle."

It was indeed a battle, and in order to fight it the holy man had no other resource than patience and prayer. "I sometimes asked him," his confessor relates, "how he repelled those attacks. He replied: 'I turn to God; I make the Sign of the Cross; I address a few contemptuous words to the devil. I have noticed, moreover, that the tumult is greater and the assaults more numerous if, on the following day, some big sinner is due to come.'"[11]

This knowledge was his comfort during sleepless nights. "At the beginning I felt afraid," he confessed to Mgr. Mermod, one of his friends and faithful penitents; "I did not then know what it was, but now I am quite happy. It is a good sign: there is always a good haul of fish the next day." "The devil gave me a good shaking last night," he would say at times; "we shall have a great number of people tomorrow. The *grappin* is very stupid: he himself tells me of the arrival of big sinners . . . . He is angry. So much the better!"

It was now the time of superhuman toil when M. Vianney spent the greater part of his day in the confessional. Although utterly exhausted when evening came, he would not go to bed without first reading a few pages from the *Lives of the Saints*. It was likewise the hour when at close intervals he inflicted on himself bloody disciplines. When that was over he stretched himself on his thin straw mat-

11. Abbé Beau, *Procès de l'Ordinaire,* p. 1191.

tress and sought repose. Just as he was about to fall asleep he would start up, awakened by shouts, mournful cries, and formidable blows. It seemed as if the front door were being battered in with a sledgehammer. Suddenly, without a latch having been moved, the Curé d'Ars perceived with horror that the devil was close to him. "I do not ask him to enter," he used to say, half laughing, half annoyed, "but he comes in all the same."

The uproar now began. The evil spirit remained invisible, but his presence could be plainly felt. He threw over the chairs and shook the heavy furniture of the room.[12] With a fearful voice he shouted: "*Vianney, Vianney! potato eater!*[13] *Ah! thou art not yet dead! I shall get thee all right.*" Or roaring like a beast, growling like a bear or snarling like a dog, he rushed at the curtains of the bed, which he shook violently.[14]

Borrowing from the accounts of Catherine Lassagne and from his own recollections, Frère Athanase relates that the devil "reproduced the sound of a hammer driving nails into the wooden floor, or that of hooping a cask; he drummed on the table, on the chimney-piece, on the water jug; or he sang with a shrill voice, so that M. le Curé used afterwards to tell us derisively: 'The *grappin* has a very ugly voice indeed.'

"On more than one occasion M. Vianney experienced a sensation as of a hand passing over his face or of rats scampering over his body.

"One night he heard the buzz of a swarm of bees; he got up, lit his candle, and was about to open the window to let them out—but he saw no bees.

"Another time the *grappin* endeavored to throw him out of bed by pulling away his straw mattress. More fright-

12. He one day told the Abbé Tailhades, who repeated it to me: "Look at this piece of furniture; I do not know how it is that it was not smashed." (Comtesse des Garets, *Procès de l'Ordinaire,* p. 783).
13. "*Mangeur de truffes!*" In the country districts round Lyons potatoes are called *truffes.* The Curé d'Ars himself used the word.
14. These details and those that follow are taken chiefly from the depositions of Frère Athanase at the *Procès de l'Ordinaire* (pp. 807-809). These facts were for the most part recorded day by day, from 1841 to 1842, in the first rédaction of Catherine Lassagne's *Petit mémoire,* pp. 16-20.

ened than usual, M. Vianney crossed himself, and the devil left him in peace.

"One evening he had been in bed for a few moments when all of a sudden it seemed to him that his couch, which was hard enough, to be sure, was becoming exceedingly soft, and that he was sinking into it as into a feather bed. At the same time a mocking voice kept repeating: '*Ha, ha!* . . . Allons, Allons,' and other ironical exhortations, by which it sought to lead him to sensual indulgence. In his terror M. Vianney crossed himself and it ceased."[15]

The spirit of darkness displayed much resourcefulness in inventing ever new tricks; he seemed to multiply his presence and to wander over the whole presbytery. In the sleeping-room a hideous brood of bats flapped their wings under the roof beams or clustered on the curtains of the bed. In the attic, for hours on end, was heard the uninterrupted, exasperating tramp of a flock of sheep. Below the bedroom, in the so-called dining-room, a noise went on as of a prancing steed, which, leaping to the ceiling, apparently dropped to the floor on its four iron shoes.

This hellish farce wearied the poor Curé d'Ars; it never discouraged him. His dreadful sleeplessness notwithstanding, so soon as the clock in the church tower struck the midnight hour, his thoughts went to his penitents who awaited him, and of whom there were always fresh relays. So he rose promptly and went to the church. But at what a cost! "In order to encourage us he came to our singing practices," a woman of the parish related. "At times he looked ghastly pale. We asked him if he were ill. 'No,' he would say, 'but the *grappin* bothered me to such a degree that I have not slept a wink all night.'"[16]

At times the presence of this sinister visitor led to some alarming encounters. "One day," relates a missionary of Pont-d'Ain, "whilst making me go up the stairs in front of him, M. le Curé remarked: 'Oh my friend, this is not like yesterday; then the *grappin* went up before me; he

15. Abbé Beau, the saint's confessor, *Procès de l'Ordinaire,* p. 1191.
16. Marthe Miard, *Procès apostolique continuatif,* p. 843.

looked as if he had boots on.' "[17]

One morning in December, 1826, long before dawn, the Curé d'Ars set out on foot for Saint-Trivier-sur-Moignans, where he was to preach the exercises of the jubilee. He said his Rosary as he walked along. All around him the air seemed full of sinister lights. The atmosphere appeared to be on fire, and the bushes on either side of the road looked as if they were burning. This was Satan's work: he, foreseeing the success M. Vianney was about to achieve, pursued him step by step, enveloped in the element that devours him, hoping thus to terrify and discourage the servant of God. But M. Vianney quietly pursued his way.[18]

The Curé d'Ars invariably covered with a veil of silence those things that might have procured him honor, but he readily recounted, even in his catechisms in church, the pranks which the evil one played on him. Everyone knew M. Vianney to be incapable of telling a falsehood, and that, notwithstanding his unheard-of labor, he was yet perfectly sound in mind and body. Nevertheless, more than one, even among his intimates, might have wished for other proofs besides his word, and the testimony of Verchère, the wheelwright. The Abbé Raymond, who was his assistant during eight years, the Abbé Toccanier, who held the same post during six, never heard anything unusual. "Listen to the *grappin*," the Curé would sometimes say to the Abbé Raymond; but the latter strained his ears in vain. Why was the Curé d'Ars the only person at that time to hear those hellish noises? Surely because the vexations of Satan were aimed at him alone.

However, others in every way worthy of credence have, under exceptional circumstances, obtained personal proofs of these infernal *infestations*.

About the year 1820, M. Vianney removed, from the church to the presbytery, an old canvas representing the Annunciation. The picture was hung on the wall at a place

17. Abbé Dufour, *Procès apostolique in genere,* p. 359.
18. The distance between Ars and Saint-Trivier is twelve kilometers.

where there is a bend in the staircase. Upon this holy image the devil now vented his rage by covering it with filth. It became necessary to remove the picture. "Many witnessed these odious profanations," M. Monnin writes, "or at least saw the material traces of them. M. Renard testifies to having seen the picture most foully besmirched so that the figure of Our Lady was unrecognizable."[19]

Marguerite Vianney, the Gothon of his childish days, was in the habit of paying an occasional visit to her saintly brother. During one of the nights that she thus spent at the presbytery, she heard her brother leave the house to go to the church before one o'clock in the morning. "A few moments later," she relates, "a tremendous noise was produced apparently close to my bed, as if five or six men had been striking heavy blows upon the table or the cupboard. I was terrified and got up. I had strength enough to light a lamp, when I discovered that everything was in perfect order. I said to myself: 'I must have been dreaming.' So I returned to bed, but no sooner had I lain down than the noise began again. This time I was even more alarmed, so I dressed quickly and ran over to the church. When my brother returned to the presbytery I told him what had happened. 'Oh my child!' he replied, 'you should not have been frightened: it is the *grappin*. He cannot hurt you: as for me, he torments me in sundry ways. At times he seizes me by the feet and drags me about the room. It is because I convert souls to the good God.'"[20]

Mlle. Marie Ricotier of Gleizé, in the province of Lyons, who had settled at Ars in 1832, used to hear from her house certain noises that apparently originated in the presbytery. Once in particular, when the hubbub seemed to be greater than usual, she went early in the morning to speak to M. Vianney about it: "I, too, have heard it," he replied; "no doubt at this very moment there are some sinners on the road to Ars."[21]

---

19. This picture was taken away from Ars by a painter who made a copy of it, which is now in the chapel of the *Providence*. The artist, however, did not have the honesty to return the original.
20. *Procès de l'Ordinaire,* p. 1026.
21. *Ibid.,* p. 1335.

M. Amiel, a plasterer of Montmerle, one day told François Pertinand, the famous hotel-keeper: "I cannot understand how anyone can go to bed in a presbytery where such terrifying noises are heard. I stayed there for several nights, at the time when M. Vianney commissioned me to make some statues for him."

One day in 1838 Denis Chaland, of Bouligneux, then a young student of philosophy, went to Confession to the Curé d'Ars. By a special favor he was admitted to the saint's own room. He himself related what happened: "I knelt on his prie-Dieu. Suddenly, when I was about half through my Confession, a general convulsion shook the room; my prie-Dieu trembled like everything else. Full of terror I tried to stand up. M. le Curé kept me down by seizing my arm. 'It is nothing,' he said, 'it is only the devil!' At the end of this Confession M. Vianney decided my future career: 'You must become a priest.' My excitement was still very great, and I must admit that I never again went to Confession to the Curé d'Ars."[22]

This same Denis Chaland had boarded, ten years earlier, at the house of the schoolmaster of Ars. On certain evenings, curiosity proving stronger than fear, he used to go with some of his fellow-students and glue his ear to the presbytery door in order to listen to the noises which people said were caused by the devil. On more than twenty different occasions, mostly at nightfall, these children heard a guttural voice repeating: *Vianney, Vianney!*[23]

In 1842 a gendarme of Messimy, Provost-marshal Napoly, who was undergoing some severe trials, wished to consult the Curé d'Ars. He arrived in the village late at night. Now, at about midnight, as he was waiting at the door of the presbytery, he, too, heard the repeated and terrifying shout. A feeble light appeared in the saint's room! shortly afterwards he came out of the house, guiding his steps with the help of his lantern. "Monsieur le Curé, it seems that you are being attacked," exclaimed the good Napoly. . . . "But I am here to defend you!"

---

22. Abbé Denis Chaland, curé of Marlieux, *Procès apostolique continuatif,* p, 656.
23. *Ibid.* p. 655.

"Eh! my friend, it is nothing; it is the *grappin.*" So saying, M. Vianney took the hand of the gendarme—it was a trembling hand. "Come with me, my friend," he added, whilst he led the would-be defender into the sacristy, where, to quote Frère Athanase, "without doubt everything was settled satisfactorily. I have since learned that the man became an excellent Christian. M. le Curé used to tell me concerning him that, for a gendarme, he was not very bold."[24]

In March, 1852, a young nun of the congregation of the Child Jesus—Sister Clotilde—in the world Jeanne Coiffet, of Leigneux (Loire), wished to go to Confession to the saint. A day went by. When evening came she, like many other penitents, was compelled to take shelter in the vestibule of the tower. At about half-past one in the morning M. Vianney opened the door. They all rushed after him, when he, suddenly turning round, pointed his finger at the unknown religious whose shyness had kept her in the darkest corner of the room: "Let that child come," he commanded. Sister Clotilde followed him. Now the saint had no sooner entered the nave than strange noises were heard in it, as of angry men quarreling among themselves. "It is nothing," the Curé d'Ars whispered into the ear of the trembling sister; "it is the devil who is doing this."

One event which might possibly be explained through natural causes, but in which M. Vianney and the crowds saw a particularly virulent agression of the evil one, caused immense excitement among the pilgrims and strengthened them in their conviction that the devil attacked the Curé d'Ars even outwardly.[25] It was either on the Monday or Tuesday during the Forty Hours' Prayer—February 23 or 24, 1857. That morning the saint had started hearing Confessions at an unusually early hour, by rea-

24. *Procès apostolique in genere,* pp. 209-210.

25. In a book entitled *Ars et son pasteur,* published at Ars—without the sanction, it should be stated, of M. Vianney—the very year in which the event took place, Michel Givre suggests that a match struck by M. le Curé, for the purpose of lighting his lamp, may have caused the fire which we are about to describe. In that case the fire would have smouldered unnoticed for more than five hours. . . . However this may have been, the hypothesis of crime must be eliminated, since the room was locked and the key was in M. Vianney's pocket.

son of the great crowds assembled in the church, where the Blessed Sacrament was exposed. A little before seven o'clock some persons were passing by the presbytery when they noticed a fire in M. Vianney's room. He was promptly informed, just as he was about to leave his confessional to say Mass. "It would seem, Father, that your room is on fire!" He just handed the key to those who had brought the information, so that they might put out the flames, and without any excitement he simply said: "The villainous *grappin*! he could not catch the bird, so he burns the cage." He left the church, however, and passed into his courtyard, where he met with the men who, at that very moment, were carrying out of the house the smoking remains of his poor bed. He asked no questions, went back to the church, and once more entered into the sacristy. As may be imagined, some commotion had been caused among the women pentitents who crowded the nave of the church. Frère Jérôme, the watchful sacristan, thought that perhaps the saint was as yet unaware of the cause of the excitement. "M. le Curé, it is your bed that has been burnt." "Ah!" was all he said, in a tone of utter indifference, then, calm as he always was, he went to say his Mass.

M. Alfred Monnin, a young missionary of Pont d'Ain, was at that time supplying for the Abbé Toccanier, who was engaged in giving a mission at Massigneux, near Belley. This priest rushed into the room at the first signal of alarm and at once noticed the mysterious character of the fire. "The bed, the tester, the curtains of the bed, and everything near—everything had been consumed. The fire had only halted in front of the reliquary of St. Philomena, which had been placed on a chest of drawers. From that point it had drawn a line from top to bottom with geometrical accuracy, destroying everything on this side of the holy relic and sparing all on the other. As the fire had started without cause, so it died out in like manner, and it is very remarkable, and in some ways truly miraculous, that the flames had not spread from the heavy serge hangings to the floor of the upper storey, which was very low, old, and very dry, and which would have blazed like straw.

"At noon, when M. le Curé came to see me at the Providence, we spoke of the event. I told him that it was universally looked upon as a bad joke of the devil, and I asked him whether he really thought that the evil one had had something to do with it. He replied very positively and with the greatest composure: 'Oh! my friend, that is plain enough. He is angry; that is a good sign; we shall see many sinners.' As a matter of fact, there followed an extraordinary influx of people into Ars, which lasted for several days."[26]

Thirty years earlier another occurrence, the accuracy of which it seems impossible to question, had made a deep impression on the clergy of the neighborhood in particular. In 1826 it was rumored in the various presbyteries that during a mission at Montmerle the devil had dragged across the room the bed in which the Curé d'Ars slept. The priests laughed, and the story met with unbelief. But the following winter their minds underwent a great change.

A jubilee was being preached at Saint-Trivier-sur-Moignans, and M. Vianney was invited to lend a hand. This he gladly consented to do. The very first night strange noises disturbed the habitual peace of the presbytery. The priests who slept in the house accused M. Vianney of being the cause of the disturbance, for no sooner had he retired than the noise began and it proceeded from his room. "It is the *grappin*," M. Vianney said; "he is wroth because of the good that is being done here." But his colleagues refused to believe him. "You do not eat," they said, "you do not sleep; it is your head that plays you tricks! . . ." One night these reproaches were particularly sharp, and this time the servant of God remained silent.

The following night a noise was heard like the rumbling of a heavy cart, and the presbytery shook. It seemed as if the house were about to crumble. Everybody got up

---

26. *Life of the Curé of Ars,* p. 195, English translation.

terrified, M. Grangier, curé of Saint-Trivier, M. Benoît, the vicaire, M. Chevalon, an old soldier of the Republic and now a diocesan missionary, not to forget Denise Lanvis, the housekeeper. At that moment such an uproar arose in M. Vianney's room that M. Benoît exclaimed: "The Curé d'Ars is being murdered!" Everybody rushed in the direction of the Curé's room, but when the door was opened all that they saw was the holy man lying peacefully in his bed, which invisible hands had dragged into the middle of the room. "It is the *grappin* who has dragged me thus far," he said with a smile, "it is he who has caused all this tumult. It is nothing. . . . I am sorry I forgot to warn you beforehand. However, it is a good sign: there will be a big fish tomorrow."

"A big fish." By this familiar expression, which he frequently used, the Curé d'Ars meant to hint at the conversion of some big sinner. The priests still doubted, believing him to be the victim of an hallucination. The next day they caused the approach to a certain confessional to be carefully watched. Nothing out of the way happened all day. It was plain that good M. Vianney had had a nightmare. But what a joyful surprise for the parish priest and the missioners when, after the sermon, they beheld M. des Murs going across the church to ask the Curé d'Ars to hear his Confession. That nobleman had long neglected all religious practices, so that the example he thus set made a deep impression upon the people of Saint-Trivier. M. Chevalon, who had perhaps been the first among those who had laughed at M. Vianney, ever after looked on him as a great saint.[27]

It would seem that on more than one occasion the devil likewise attacked the *Providence.* On certain nights both mistresses and pupils were roused by strange noises. At other times the evil spirit endeavored to disturb their souls.

"One day," Marie Filliat relates, "after thoroughly cleansing the saucepan, I filled it with water for the soup. I

27. Catherine Lassagne, *Petit mémoire,* troisième rédaction, p. 66.

noticed little bits of meat in the water. Now the day was one of abstinence. I emptied the saucepan, rinsed it, and filled it once more with water. When the soup was ready to put on the table I saw that there were bits of meat in it. M. le Curé, on being informed, told me, 'the devil has done this thing; serve the soup just as it is.'"[28]

Thus did Satan's fury spend itself in futile efforts. Eventually M. Vianney became quite used to his visits. "You must be very much afraid?" the Abbé Toccanier asked him, alluding to those revolting interviews.

"One gets used to everything, my friend," was the gentle reply. "The *grappin* and I are almost comrades."[29]

He treated him accordingly. On December 4, 1841, he related the following incident to the mistresses of the orphanage: "Listen to this: last night the devil came into my room whilst I was reciting my breviary. He was blowing hard, and seemed to vomit on my floor, I know not what, but it looked like either corn or some other grain. I told him: 'I am going over there (to the *Providence*) to tell them of thy behavior, so that they may despise thee!' and he stopped at once."[30]

One night, as the Curé was trying to get some sleep, the hellish disturber of the peace signified his presence by shouts such as: "*Vianney, Vianney,* I shall get thee, yes, I shall get thee! . . ." But from the dark corner where his bed stood the meek saint merely answered: "I do not fear thee much."[31]

It is now easy to understand that the mastery which the servant of God had acquired over the devil should have been taken advantage of by people who asked him to deliver possessed persons. Mgr. Devie had authorized him to use his powers as exorcist whenever circumstances required. Here also we have the testimony of many witnesses.

Jean Picard, the village farrier, witnessed some extra-

28. *Procès apostolique ne pereant,* p. 1094.
29. "Le *grappin* et moi, nous sommes *quasi camarades.*" (*Procès apostalique ne pereant,* p. 202).
30. Catherine Lassagne, *Petit mémoire,* première rédaction, p. 20.
31. *Procès de l'Ordinaire,* p. 729.

ordinary scenes. A wretched woman had been brought by her husband from a considerable distance. The woman was raving, and uttered inarticulate shrieks. M. le Curé was summoned, but after examining her he declared that she must be taken back to the Bishop of the diocese. "Good, good,"exclaimed the woman, suddenly recovering her speech, though the sound of her voice froze the listeners with horror, "the *creature* shall go home! Ah, if I had the power of Jesus Christ I should plunge you all into hell."

"*Tiens,* thou knowest Jesus Christ," M. Vianney replied, "very well, let her be taken to the foot of the high altar."

Four men carried her there, notwithstanding her resistance. M. Vianney then placed his reliquary[32] on the head of the possessed woman, who became rigid like a corpse. After a while, however, she stood up of her own accord and walked rapidly towards the door of the church. She returned in an hour's time, perfectly calm now, took holy water, and fell on her knees. She was quite cured. During the three days that she spent at Ars, she was the edification of all the pilgrims.[33]

One poor old woman from the neighborhood of Clermont-Ferrand particularly excited the compassion of Pierre Oriol, one of the men who constituted "the bodyguard" of our saint. The wretched woman, he tells us, sang and danced the whole day in front of the church. They made her drink a few drops of holy water, whereupon she flew into such a rage that she began to bite into the walls of the church. Her son accompanied her, but he was helpless. A priest then led her to a spot between the presbytery and the church which M. Vianney would have to pass. The saint, indeed, soon appeared. He contented himself with giving his blessing to the poor woman, from whose mouth blood was flowing. She instantly became quite calm. Her son then related that his mother had been in her previous pitiful state for forty years, but that

32. "The Curé d'Ars always carried in his pocket a large silver reliquary containing several relics of the Passion, and, I believe, of a few saints." (Abbé Tailhades, *Procès de l'Ordinaire,* p. 1508).

33. *Procès de l'Ordinaire,* p. 1312.

she had never before shown herself either so furious or so calm. She was presumed to be possessed. Her dreadful fits never returned.[34]

On the evening of December 27, 1857, a vicaire of Saint-Pierre of Avignon and the Superior of the Franciscan nuns of Orange, brought to Ars a young school-mistress who showed every symptom of diabolical possession. The Archbishop of Avignon had personally studied the case and his advice was that she should be taken to M. Vianney. The very next morning after her arrival she was taken into the sacristy just as the saint was about to vest for Mass. The possessed woman, however, made at once for the door. "There are too many people here," she exclaimed. "Too many people?" the saint asked; "very well, they are going to leave." At a sign from him the assistants withdrew so that he found himself alone with the unfortunate victim of Satan.

From within the church only confused sounds could at first be heard. All at once the voices became louder. The vicaire of Avignon, who had remained close to the door, was now able to follow part of the dialogue:

"You absolutely insist on going out?" the Curé d'Ars asked.

"Yes!"

"And why?"

"Because I am with a man whom I do not like."

"So you do not like me?" M. Vianney said in a tone of irony. A strident *"No"* was the only reply of the spirit who abode in the unhappy girl.

Almost immediately the door was opened. The power of the saint had prevailed. Collected and modest, weeping tears of joy and boundless gratitude, the young schoolmistress appeared on the threshold. For an instant, however, fear showed itself once more in her looks. Turning towards M. Vianney, she said: "I fear lest he should come back." "No, my child, at any rate not for a long while." In fact, he did not come back, and the girl was

34. Pierre Oriol, *Procès de l'Ordinaire,* p. 751.

able to resume her teaching activities at Orange.

On July 25, 1859, the eve of the day on which the saint took to his bed never to leave it again, they brought to him, with much difficulty, towards eight o'clock at night, a woman who was thought to be possessed. Her husband accompanied her, and he alone entered with her into the courtyard of the presbytery, whither M. Vianney followed them. M. Oriol and a great number of strangers were standing at the gate. The moment the woman came out again, now free and quite happy, "a noise was heard in the yard resembling that of branches of trees being violently broken. The crash was such that the witnesses were terrified. But," adds M. Oriol, "when I went to the presbytery after night prayers, I saw that the elder-trees were unhurt."[35]

Another wretched woman could not be got into the church, so great was her resistance and the aversion she showed for M. Vianney. The saint was therefore asked to come to the house where she was lodging, but at a moment when she was not at home. He awaited her return in another room. Needless to add, the possessed woman was in complete ignorance of his presence. Suddenly, as she was approaching the house, she was seized with violent convulsions: "He is not far away, the *calotin!*" she shrieked. In her favor also the saint was able to exercise his healing power.

A truly amazing incident happened one afternoon—January 23, 1840—in the very confessional of M. Vianney. A woman from the neighborhood of Puy-en-Velay, and about whom nothing out of the ordinary could be noticed, had just knelt down at the feet of the saint. At that moment some ten persons, among whom were Marie Boyat and Geneviève Filliat, of Ars, were standing in a group near the chapel of St. John the Baptist, awaiting their turn to go to Confession: though they saw nothing, they could thus hear everything. M. Vianney repeatedly urged the woman to begin the avowal of her sins, but she per-

35. *Procès apostolique ne pereant,* p. 1108.

sisted in a sullen silence. All of a sudden a loud, strident voice was heard:

"I have committed only one sin, and I share its beautiful fruit with all those who wish for it. Raise thy hand and absolve me. Ah! it does happen at times that thou raisest it for me; for I am often close to thee in the confessional."

"Tu quis es? (Who art thou?)" the saint asked.

"*Magister caput* (The Master, the Chief)," the devil replied—then proceeding in French, he exclaimed: "Ah! black toad, how thou tormentest me! Thou art always talking about going away. Why dost thou not do so? There are black toads that torture me less than thou."

"I shall write to the bishop to make thee go out of this woman."

"Yes, but I shall cause thy hand so to tremble that thou shalt be unable to write. I shall certainly get thee, *va!* I have defeated those that were stronger than thou. And thou, thou art not yet dead. Without that . . . (here he used a word of repulsive coarseness to designate Our Lady) who is up above, we should have thee for certain; but she protects thee, together with that great dragon (St. Michael), who is at the door of thy church. . . . Say, why dost thou get up so early? Thou disobeyest *purple robe* (the bishop). Why dost thou preach so simply? That also makes thee pass for an ignorant man. Why not preach in the big style, as they do in the towns?"[36]

These diabolical invectives lasted for several minutes; they were aimed in turn against Mgr. Devie, Bishop of Belley, Mgr. de Bonald, Bishop of Le Puy, who was about to become Archbishop of Lyons; certain categories of priests and finally, once more against the Curé d'Ars himself. Now the evil spirit, who discovered matter for blame in all the above mentioned, was yet compelled to proclaim the irreproachable virtue of the servant of God, even as he had been forced to do once upon a time in the Gospel, with regard to the person of Our Lord.

---

36. This part of the dialogue is taken from the account of Catherine Lassagne (*Petit mémoire,* troisième rédaction, p. 95).

The Curé d'Ars, whose eye could penetrate into hidden things, showed himself at all times most severe towards those who dabbled in occultism or spiritualism. "What causes tables to turn and to speak?"some people one day asked a possessed woman who stood in the village square insulting the passers-by. "It is I," answered the woman, whom an evil spirit tormented . . . "all that is my work." The Curé d'Ars judged that on that day the father of lies had spoken the truth.

Comte Jules de Maubou, who owned estates in the Beaujolais, near Villefranche, but who spent part of the year in Paris, loved to visit M. Vianney, for he was the Curé's penitent and his friend.

It was about 1850. Now at that period—history ever repeats itself—spirits, mediums, and table-turning were the fashion. Parisian society, even families that had remained true to their faith and religious practices, freely indulged in what was considered to be a fashionable amusement. One day M. de Maubou was invited to an evening party at the house of a relative, where he took part in divers experiments: the usual phenomena took place under his eyes: the table lifted itself and delivered its answers by striking the floor.

Two days later the Count, having returned to the Beaujolais, set out for Ars, rejoicing at the thought of once more seeing his venerated and holy director. At the moment of the nobleman's arrival M. Vianney just happened to be standing on the threshold of his church. With a smile on his face and outstretched hand M. de Maubou ran towards his friend. But what a surprise! Without even returning his greeting, the Curé d'Ars stopped him and spoke to him in sad and severe accents.

"Jules, stop! The day before yesterday you had dealings with the devil. Come to Confession!"

The young Count readily complied, and promised never again to indulge in a pastime thus judged and condemned.

Some time after this incident the Count returned to Paris, when he found himself in another salon. He was asked this time also to assist in making a table turn. But he remembered his promise, and remained inflexible in his refusal. The guests decided to proceed with the experiment, leaving the scrupulous nobleman alone in a corner. Meanwhile M. de Maubou made internal protestations of his utter abhorrence of all such games. So great and so unforeseen was the resistance of the table that the medium could not help saying: "I cannot understand this; there must be a superior power present which paralyzes our action!"[37]

At about the same period M. Charles de Montluisant, then a young captain, who eventually attained to the rank of a general of division and died in his château of Marsanne (Drôme), was in a position to satisfy himself whether M. Vianney had any knowledge of the mysteries of the unseen world. Having heard people talking of the marvellous happenings at Ars he resolved, together with three brother officers, to make a searching inquiry into the accuracy of these reports. On the way to Ars the friends agreed that they should each of them ask M. Vianney a question. M. de Montluisant, however, bluntly declared that since "he had nothing to tell him he would tell him nothing."

At the hour of the interview he walked into the sacristy behind his friends, determined to remain dumb, when one of them introduced him at once to the Curé with the words: "M. le Curé, this is M. de Montluisant, a young officer with a future, who would like to ask you something." Thus taken by surprise, he decided to face the situation and ask something or other at random: "Come now, M. le Curé, those tales of diabolical trickeries which circulate in connection with your name, they are not true, are they? They are all imagination, are they not?" M. Vianney looked his interlocutor straight in the face, and his answer came, short and incisive: "O my friend, you know something about it right enough. . . . Had you not

37. This narrative is based in its entirety upon some notes written on May 16, 1922, at the presbytery of Ars, by M. de Fréminville, of Bourg, a grand-nephew of M. de Maubou. M. de Fréminville has authorized the present writer to make use of his own name and that of his great-uncle.

done what you did, you would not have succeeded in ridding yourself of *it*." Nonplussed by this reply, M. de Montluisant was unable to utter a word, to the astonishment of his companions.

On the return journey he must needs explain. Either the Curé d'Ars had spoken at random, or . . . What had happened? The officer had to own that whilst he was pursuing his studies in Paris, he had become affiliated to a certain group which, under the guise of philanthropy, was in reality an association of spiritualists.

"One day," he related, "as I was returning to my room, I experienced a feeling that I was not alone. Perturbed by so strange a sensation, I looked and searched everywhere. There was nothing to be seen. The next day the same thing happened. Moreover, it seemed to me as if an unseen hand were seeking to strangle me. . . . I had the faith. I went to fetch some holy water at Saint-Germain-l'Auxerrois, my parish church. I sprinkled every nook and corner of my room. From that moment every impression of a super-sensible presence vanished. After that I never again attended a séance. I doubt not that this is the incident, now long past, to which the Curé d'Ars was alluding." No comment was offered and the officers hastily changed the subject.[38]

As the Curé d'Ars advanced in years these diabolical vexations decreased both in frequency and in intensity. The evil spirit, far from succeeding in disheartening that heroic soul, was himself the first to lose heart. By degrees he gave up the contest, or more accurately, it was the Will of God that an existence so beautiful, so pure, apparently so calm and yet so much tried, should end in profound peace.

From 1845 until the day of his death, M. Vianney was hardly ever disturbed by the devil at night. Nevertheless, sleep had become well-nigh impossible, for, instead of the *grappin*, an obstinate cough now kept him awake. For all

38. The experience of the officer is recorded in the archives of the presbytery at Ars. General de Montluisant died a pious death on May 11, 1894.

that he refused to give up his interminable sittings in the confessional. He used to say: "So long as I can get an hour's, or even half an hour's, sleep during the day, I am fit to resume my work."[39] That hour, or half-hour, he spent in his room, immediately after his midday meal. He stretched himself on his straw mattress and tried to sleep. Now this was the moment which the devil occasionally chose, even now, to tease him.

Mme. Marie de Lamartine, of Grau-de-Roi, *département* of the Gard, was one day waiting, with M. Pagès, for the moment when M. Vianney would come out of the presbytery. It was about one o'clock in the afternoon. "Suddenly," she relates, "we heard the sound of shouts and groans." "That is the devil," M. Pagès informed me, "who is playing his pranks, and who is now being put in his place by the good Curé."[40]

At last the evil one kept away for good, and M. Vianney felt no regrets at parting with a comrade of that ilk. He did not torment him in his agony as he has tormented other saints. Even before the close of his earthly life the Curé d'Ars had inflicted on Satan a decisive defeat.

---

39. Abbé Toccanier, *Procès apostolique ne pereant,* p. 315.
40. *Letter* of September 18, 1907 (archives of the presbytery of Ars).

Chapter 12

THE PILGRIMAGE TO ARS
I. The Beginning—St. Philomena

THAT even during his lifetime a man should be the object of a pilgrimage, and that crowds should pay him the veneration usually bestowed on the relics of saints, is assuredly a rare occurrence, and one that reminds us of the Fathers of the Desert and their far-away Thebaid. Now, it is a fact that for a period of thirty years the humble village of Ars witnessed the marvellous spectacle of ever-fresh crowds prostrating themselves at the feet of its holy parish priest. From 1827 until 1859 the saint's church of Ars was never empty.

However, those who first spread the Curé's fame were, without exception, "simple and devout people." Those first rumors were subsequently re-echoed "by persons whose opinion was the more weighty by reason of their character, age, and condition."[1]

At Dardilly, where M. Vianney was born, and at Ecully, where, for three years, he had been vicaire, he had left behind him a fragrance of sanctity. As early as 1818 visitors came to Ars from both those villages; some even came from as far as Les Noës. A journey of a hundred kilometers could not damp their eagerness to behold, once more, "M. Jérôme, now a priest and a curé. The majority of these visitors made a retreat under his direction; three or four eventually settled in the village.

From that time onward the fame of M. Vianney spread rapidly. "In 1822," Mgr. Mermod relates, "I was a professor at the Petit Séminaire of Meximieux. One day M. Vianney came to pay a visit to M. Loras, a former fellow

1. Pierre Oriol, *Procès de l'Ordinaire,* p. 757.

student of his, and at that time superior of the establishment. He crossed our playground and went at once into the chapel to visit the Blessed Sacrament, after which he called on M. le Supérieur. The moment he appeared on the playground, Antoine Raymond, then one of the students, and destined later on to be his assistant, exclaimed: 'It is the holy Curé d'Ars!'"

Instantly play was stopped, all eyes being fixed on him. Antoine Raymond, a native of Fareins, was then sixteen years of age. At home he had heard people talk of M. Vianney, for the protestations, insidious or violent, of some of the people of Ars, and the enthusiastic admiration of others, could not fail to find an echo in the neighboring villages. Everybody wanted to know this curé of whom his flock had so much to say that was good—or bad. Well-disposed persons had no difficulty in finding out on which side lay uprightness and truth.

Trévoux, the chief town of Les Dombes, was not slow in forming a most favorable opinion of M. Vianney. We have already seen how, during the great mission of 1823, the majority of those who went to Confession crowded round his confessional. The same scenes were re-enacted in 1826, on the occasion of the universal jubilee granted by Pope Leo XII. The priests of Savigneux, Montmerle, Saint-Trivier, Chaneins, Saint-Bernard, and many others, to whom he lent his aid both in the confessional and in the pulpit, wondered at the success he obtained, and loudly proclaimed his great virtues. They did not as yet foresee that on the eve of holidays, and even oftener, many persons, and those the best of their parishes, would soon undertake the journey to Ars so as to enjoy a continuation of M. Vianney's guidance.

As early as 1827 people began to come from a distance in order to seek the advice of the enlightened priest. "In that year," Mgr. Mermod records, "I was appointed curé of Chaleins. Everyone was speaking of the sanctity of M. Vianney. Several persons of my parish were in the habit of going to Confession to him, and I must say they were a source of edification to all."[2] In 1827, according to Jean

2. *Procès de l'Ordinaire,* p. 1032.

Pertinand, the number of daily visitors to Ars amounted to twenty people.[3] During the Octave of Corpus Christi the young Comtesse Laure des Garets made a first stay in the old château, in which she definitely took up residence in 1834. Every evening she went to Benediction. "The little church of Ars," she wrote to her father, M. du Colombier, "was full of people, many strangers being among the congregation. . . . The walls draped with the canopy and with banners, the tabernacle resplendent with its gilding, the monstrance glittering with precious stones, a multitude of candles, a priest worn out by fasts and night-watches, reciting in feeble tones a prayer in which he gives utterance to his love; such is," the pious lady wrote, "the thrilling spectacle exhibited before our eyes night after night."

From the testimony of old inhabitants we know that already in 1828 the pilgrimage was large. The following year clinched matters; henceforth the saintly priest was to be the slave of souls; death alone would free him from this holy servitude. M. Mermod, the curé of Chaleins, was wont to pay him an occasional visit. "Your good angel," M. Vianney told him one day, "put a happy thought into your mind when he prompted you to come and see me." The other replied: "It seems that your angel never suggests to you to return my visit." "I cannot; all my time is taken up."[4]

All those who visited Ars did not come for the purpose of going to Confession. Curiosity was a factor in the movement. Was it not rumored that the Curé d'Ars could read people's consciences and that he wrought miracles? To think that in a corner of France there lived a *saint,* a real saint! The desire to gaze on him set the crowds in motion. "Men—unbelievers even—feel the need of holiness to such a degree that they flock to it as soon as they know where it is to be found," says René Bazin.[5] But the grace of God knows more than one approach to the heart

3. *Ibid.,* p. 368.
4. *Procès de l'Ordinaire,* p. 1035.
5. *Pélerinage à Ars,* Annales d'Ars, Avril, 1908, p. 322.

of man. At the beginning of the pilgrimage the curious were fairly numerous, but many of them came away shriven and converted. Moreover, if some sinners felt themselves drawn to Ars by an attraction for which they were unable to account, others went there in the hope of finding, at the feet of a saint, the courage to avow their sins and a remedy against a future relapse.

"Monsieur le Curé," Catherine Lassagne told him naively, "other missionaries run after sinners, even into foreign countries, but as for you, it is the sinners who are after you." And, full of a supernatural joy, for he saw the truth of the assertion, he replied in the same strain: "It certainly looks very much like it—*c'est bien quasi vrai.*"[6] He had early proofs of the accuracy of Catherine's assertion, notably on a certain evening, either in 1828 or 1829. Night prayers had been recited in church, and M. Vianney had just gone up to his room. Suddenly a powerful fist was heard thundering against the gate of the courtyard. After two or three summonses, repeated with increasing energy, the holy man, who, to be sure, had excellent reasons for caution, decided to go down and open the door. He saw, waiting there, a carman who had left his horse and cart standing in front of the church porch. "Come," said he, "the thing is quite simple: I want to go to Confession, and at once!"

At what period did people begin to attribute a miraculous efficacy to the prayers of M. Vianney? Without doubt the very first prodigies—viz., the multiplication of the corn and the flour, which had taken place about the year 1830—soon came to the knowledge of the inhabitants and of the strangers who already flocked to Ars in considerable numbers. The stir caused by those extraordinary events worried the Curé; he trembled lest men should attribute to him the glory of having been their author.

At an early date the sick and infirm were found mingling with the crowd. After they had asked the prayers

6. Catherine Lassagne, *Petit mémoire,* troisième rédaction, p. 56.

of the Curé d'Ars, some of these testified to a feeling of relief, and not a few were completely cured. These things, of course, got talked about. "However," says Pertinand, the schoolmaster, "M. le Curé recommended silence, so that people were afraid to give him pain by proclaiming the favors they had received. But a change took place when the cult of St. Philomena came to be established in the parish. From that moment the servant of God gave to her all the credit of the marvels that were being accomplished, so that he took delight in proclaiming them. To her he attributed all the prodigies that made the pilgrimage so famous. Thanks to him, devotion to the youthful saint spread rapidly, both in the surrounding district and all over France.'"[7]

It is likely enough that if the Curé d'Ars had not sounded her praises for the space of thirty years, St. Philomena would not have enjoyed the immense popularity that came to her in the nineteenth century.[8] Prior to 1830 very few people had heard her name. As recently as May 24, 1802, a workman, whilst engaged in clearing a gallery in the catacomb of St. Priscilla, in Rome, had discovered her tomb—viz., a *loculus,* or cavity, hewn out of the live rock and closed with three bricks, on which was to be read the inscription, written in minium:

PAX TECUM FILUMENA.

The bones were those of a girl between fourteen and fifteen years of age. Near the head was found, shattered into several fragments, the glass phial which, no doubt, had contained a few drops of blood, and which the Church holds to be a proof of martyrdom. The remains of *Filumena* were translated to the *Custodia* of the Sacred Relics. They were destined to remain there, in comparative oblivion, until June, 1805, when they were given to Don Francesco di Lucia, a missionary of Mugnano. At Mugnano, a small village in the kingdom of Naples,

7. *Procès de l'Ordinaire,* pp. 375, 159, 236.
8. About the extraordinary devotion of the Curé d'Ars to this saint, see our book, *Sainte Philomène,* ch. vi.

Filumena, whose arrival had been honored by the entire population, at once displayed her power by astounding prodigies.

However, the echo of these marvels only reached France about 1815. At that time the *Benfratelli,* or Brothers of St. John of God, having been expelled by the revolutionary storm, were visiting the villages and towns of the whole of France. They were on a begging tour in behalf of their work, but whilst asking for alms they likewise sang the praises of St. Philomena. Their superior, Père de Mongallon, passed through Lyons, where he enjoyed the hospitality of the wealthy Jaricot family. Yielding to the entreaties of Pauline Jaricot, then seventeen years of age, he gave her a relic which he had brought from Mugnano. Of this relic M. Vianney in turn obtained a small fragment. In this way, very humbly indeed, little *Filumena* entered Ars, where she was destined to play a twofold role—one public, the other private and intimate. In the eyes of the crowd she would be the heavenly wonderworker at whose intercession any miracle would be granted, but, in addition, a pure and mysterious affection was to link her to the saintly parish priest; she would be "his Beatrice, his ideal, his sweet star, his guide, his comforter, his pure light."[9] This mystic friendship was destined to become so strong and so deep that it could be described in the following astonishing lines: "From the start the beloved saint responded to the affection of her servant. As time went on the harmony between their hearts also grew, so that, in the best years of his life there obtained between them not merely a distant relationship, but a close and direct intercourse. Henceforth the saint on earth enjoyed with the saint in Heaven a most sweet and intimate familiarity. On the one hand we see a ceaseless invocation, on the other a sensible assistance and a kind of real presence."[10]

This "ardent and almost chivalrous love" could not remain hidden in his heart. The pilgrims were admitted

9. Chanoine Poulain, *Les Parfums d'Ars,* Annales d'Ars, August 1922, p. 78.
10. Monnin, *Life of the Curé d'Ars.*

to the secret; they reaped its benefits. Many times a day, in the pulpit, in the confessional, in the square in front of the church, M. Vianney exhorted his hearers to call upon his *dear little saint,* his *consul,* his *representative,* his *agent with God.*

Thus it came about that whilst he was still misunderstood and contradicted by men and subjected to the vexations of the devil, the Curé d'Ars, visited and comforted by his immortal friend, retained even in extreme old age that moral vigor, that freshness of the heart which in him were the presage of the unfailing youthfulness of the elect.

Chapter 13

THE PILGRIMAGE TO ARS *(continued)*

II. The Contradictions of the Clergy

THE clergy went for very little in the great movement which swept the crowds into the village of Ars. The priests, even the most zealous among them, deemed it abnormal that people should go to consult the curé of a parish of two hundred souls! "He is not like other men," was the refrain of the populace. They knew it only too well, to be sure. His outward appearance sufficiently showed what he was in reality—an eccentric who would be acting wisely were he simply to behave like everybody else!

The fact is that at first some of his brother priests judged his appearance with severity and refused to believe that certain of his actions were anything but the fruit of a deliberate and cherished eccentricity. They considered as oddities actions which, considering the purity of his intentions, were in reality proofs of his holiness and perfection.

Jeanne-Marie Chanay, the laundress of the orphanage and the presbytery, has stated that "M. le Curé had a natural love for neatness and cleanliness"; this is proved by the fact that "he very frequently changed his personal linen."[1] But the public was ignorant of this detail, and, "if M. Vianney loved cleanliness, his outward destitution seemed unfavorable to such an opinion of him."[2] Deliberately, from a motive of mortification and humility, he wore a shabby cassock, an old hat, shoes patched and

1. *Procès de l'Ordinaire,* p. 708.
2. Baronne de Belvey, *Procès de l'Ordinaire,* p. 224.

always innocent of polish. "Even at clerical conferences," the only gatherings that he attended at any time, "he always appeared poor and contemptible," says Catherine Lassagne.[3]

It is easy to understand that such meanness in his dress, the deep reason of which remained hidden, had not the good fortune to please all the members of the clergy. The priests of the province of Lyons are noted for the dignity of their external deportment. M. Vianney's contemporaries condemned as reprehensible a neglect that they called by the name of slovenliness. Some charged him with avarice. Could he not, even though his means were slender, get himself more suitable clothes? Some thought that they discovered in him symptoms of faulty judgement; others hypocrisy, a hidden ambition, a secret desire to attract attention. Hence he was the object of certain antipathies and dislikes which on occasion showed themselves by words and even by deeds. At the monthly conference a neighbor refused to remain near him unless he put on a cleaner hat.[4]

He became the butt of mild jests, which, as a matter of fact, he took with much good humor. "That is a good one for the Curé d'Ars," he would say; "when you have said 'the Curé d'Ars' you have said everything."[5] At times a note of bitterness crept into this banter, which was always so good-naturedly endured. Mgr. Devie, at least on one occasion, was able to see it for himself.

One day the Bishop of Belley presided at a dinner which marked the close of a mission at Trévoux. By his command the Abbé Vianney was placed by the side of the prelate. There can be no doubt that his intention was to give public expression to his esteem for the humble priest whose reputation calumny was even then endeavoring to tarnish. The Bishop had discovered that in that poor priest there were aspirations whose spring is not in Nature, seeing that they are such as to lead a man to the practice

3. *Petit mémoire,* troisième rédaction, p. 85.
4. Catherine Lassagne, *Petit mémoire,* première rédaction, p. 14.
5. *Ibid.*

of heroic virtue. Now, at the very beginning of the meal one of the guests so far forgot himself as to mutter, loud enough to be heard by all: "The Curé d'Ars, who is quite close to Monseigneur, does not even wear a sash." (At that time, presumably, the sash was not considered an essential item of clerical attire.) The prelate listened without saying a word, and the pastor of Ars likewise remained silent. The answer came from one of the older priests, and his retaliation was terse and to the point: "The Curé d'Ars, even without a sash, is worth as much as any other, though he may wear a sash." "Well spoken," observed the Bishop. The saint was now left in peace.[6]

M. Vianney never seemed to mind recriminations which only concerned his dress, for he had espoused the lady Poverty, and, like Francis of Assisi and Benedict Labre, he wore her livery. But from his brother priests other attacks proceeded which caused him much pain. Had he not already known hours of anguish enough when, at Ars and the surrounding villages, evil-minded persons sought to ruin his reputation as a pure and austere priest? Now efforts were being made to keep souls away from him.

His carelessness in the matter of his outward appearance would have been forgiven had he been a learned priest, banished by a love of study into this obscure corner. Alas! his colleagues had excellent memories. No doubt M. Vianney was a very good man, gentle, ready to render service, keen. . . . But what about his theological studies? Five months spent, more or less profitably, at Saint-Irénée; practically no knowledge of Latin; a dismissal in the very middle of term, then studies after a fashion at the presbytery of Ecully; and, in the end, the very last parish in the diocese! Poor M. Vianney! And it was he whom so many people naïvely went to consult! What was there so very extraordinary in his direction? The same advice—and that the result of a longer experience in the cure of souls—people had at hand in their respective parishes. "He is no more a wizard than we

6. Catherine Lassagne, *Petit mémoire,* troisième rédaction, p. 65.

are,"[7] a priest once said, speaking of M. Vianney in the presence of Mme. de Cibeins.[8] Really this persistent movement towards Ars, which was assuming the appearance of a pilgrimage, had become a scandal. The time had come to enlighten those simple-minded people, and, if need be, the higher authorities would have to be invoked. And it was done. Several priests forbade their penitents, under threat of a refusal of absolution, to go to Ars. Others even fulminated the prohibition from the pulpit. Some seized their trusty pens in order to inform the Bishop of the fresh peril that threatened so many poor souls! And the accusers as Catherine Lassagne put it, "no doubt believed that they had excellent reasons for acting as they did." However, all these "good reasons" were ultimately reducible to one—the incapacity of the Abbé Vianney. Now since we have mentioned the word, it seems to us indispensable, before we go further, to clear up once for all this question of the alleged ignorance of the Curé d'Ars, for in this matter a legend has grown up which must be refuted.

Let us admit at once and without evasion that our saint never experienced what is called a *literary curiosity.* During the whole of his priestly life he never indulged in any light reading, not even that of the newspaper. The *Annals of the Propagation of the Faith* are the only periodical that he ever perused.

His studies as a boy and a young man—hasty, mutilated, so often interrupted, and resumed so many times with heroic constancy—reacted on the whole of his subsequent career. He was the victim of circumstances; it is not possible to remain intellectually stagnant until the age of twenty and not to suffer for it. No doubt he knew at least the names of the great poets, the great dramatists, the great orators. At Ecully, in M. Balley's library, he may have read extracts of their works, but apparently such reading left no trace in his memory; in all his sermons there occurs not one quotation from a profane author.

This much being granted, we affirm that the intellec-

7. "Il n'est pas plus sorcier que nous."
8. Mme. Christine de Cibeins, *Procès apostolique continuatif,* p. 166.

tual insufficiency of the Curé d'Ars has been greatly exaggerated. On this point, moreover, has he not, by an excess of humility, furnished his enemies with arguments against himself? "He deemed himself very ignorant," Catherine Lassagne writes. "What do you expect?" he used to say. "I have made no studies; M. Balley did indeed try during five or six years to teach me something; it was all in vain; he could not get anything into my bad head."[9] In fact, he loved to "pile it on," so to speak, when mentioning his education. "When I am with other priests I am like Bordin (the village idiot). In every family there is always one child that is less intelligent than its brothers and sisters; well, in our family I was that child." In his old age he one day saw a portrait of himself, more or less accurate and drawn at haphazard. He remarked with a smile: "It is I right enough. See how stupid I look!"[10]

Such excessive distrust of his own judgement might conceivably have paralyzed and even utterly crushed him if the love of God and man had not compelled him to show himself as he really was. But even so, in the discharge of his professional duties, he sometimes endeavored to impose on people, so to speak, lest their opinion of him should be too favorable. "In the confessional," says the Baronne de Belvey, "he spoke correct French (I know it from personal observation), whereas in his catechisms he appeared deliberately to slip in a few mistakes, especially if people of mark happened to be among the audience."

If we consider his persistent toil, his power of observation, the freshness of his imagination, the smart and pointed turn of his remarks, we must conclude that, had M. Vianney been placed in normal conditions, he would have made excellent humanities. The lady whom we have just quoted, herself a very cultured person, who knew him well, has likewise stated "he did not possess what is

9. "Il y a perdu son latin et n'a rien pu loger dans ma mauvaise tête." (Abbé Raymond, *Vie MSS.,* p. 62).
10. "Voyez comme j'ai l'air bête!"*(Procès apostolique ne pereant,* p. 174, and *Procès de l'Ordinaire,* p. 245).

commonly called genius, but there was much clearness and distinction in his mind." And Catherine Lassagne records with admiration how she has heard him relate things that she had never read in books.[11]

His arduous personal preparation of his sermons had borne fruit: people admired the accuracy of his pulpit pronouncements, and he exacted a like soundness of doctrine in the priests whom he invited to preach in his church. On one occasion he did not hesitate to rebuke discreetly a certain preacher for having drawn too fanciful a picture of Purgatory.[12]

Moreover, until the very end he imposed on himself the duty of going over his textbooks. No doubt, when the crowd of pilgrims confined him to the confessional, he had perforce to forsake his books, but when the wintertime provided him with a few moments of leisure he resumed his studies every evening. "To this end," says M. Raymond, his first curate, "I myself procured for him the *Examens* of Valentin and Gousset's *Théologie Morale,* which were the books with which he began. He re-read these works every subsequent winter."

Slowly, by the sweat of his brow, he had assimilated the knowledge of theology. On the Eucharist, on the advantages and grandeur of the Catholic priesthood, on the mediation of Our Lady, he had views that were luminous, profound, and at times worthy of a Father of the Church. What more could be asked of him? He possessed a priest's professional knowledge; but souls came to him in the hope of something higher and of an order other than mere human wisdom.

Over and above the knowledge acquired by study, the mind of the saints is often enlightened by a direct intervention from above. "There is holiness in the Curé d'Ars," somebody said in the presence of a learned professor of philosophy; "there is holiness, but there is nothing else." And the other replied: "He is possessed of great lights; these lights irradiate his discourses on every kind of sub-

11. *Petit mémoire,* troisième rédaction, p. 104.
12. Frère Athanase, *Procès de l'Ordinaire,* p. 845.

ject. Oh, the clear, the beautiful vision of him who sees through the Holy Ghost! And to what heights of feeling and understanding faith raises us!"[13]

Catherine Lassagne, a simple soul without philosophical pretensions, has expressed the same thought with uncommon felicity. "M. le Curé," she wrote, "was so small, so utterly nothing in his own eyes, that the Holy Ghost loved to fill with a wonderful abundance of lights the void thus made by his selflessness."[14]

Père Cyrille Faivre, a missionary of Saint-Claude, relates the following incident: "A priest, a friend of mine, went to consult M. Vianney on a most knotty theological problem. This priest could not get over the ease with which the servant of God gave him a solution of wonderful accuracy."[15]

The Curé d'Ars himself gives a key to the enigma when he says in one of his catechisms: "Those who are led by the Holy Ghost have true ideas. That is why there are so many ignorant people who know far more than the learned."[16]

All this is true, no doubt; but the Spirit of God works in the innermost recesses of the soul, without outward show, without haste or violence; hence it came about that for a long time, and for many of his colleagues, there clung to the Abbé Vianney a reputation for incapacity, due, in the past, to notable failures. Although a few enlightened priests kept repeating what the humility of the saint strove to hide, not a few among the clergy still refused for a long time to see in him anything but a man in whom ignorance was capped by rashness. He decided certain cases of vocation against all plausibility; he solved the most thorny problems of casuistry as if they were a game to him; certain penitents were treated with extreme indulgence, others with excessive rigor. It all seemed incomprehensible! Truth to tell, all this presbytery gossip was

13. Abbé Monnin, *Procès de l'Ordinaire,* p. 1102.
14. *Petit mémoire,* troisième rédaction, p. 81.
15. *Procès de l'Ordinaire,* p. 1495.
16. Spirit of the Curé of Ars, p. 48 (English translation).

based on hearsay, for, as may be imagined, M. Vianney's critics had not had the honesty to consult him themselves or to kneel in his confessional. It happened, however, "that some persons of little education, misunderstanding his answers, made him say things that had never presented themselves to his mind."[17]

Who were those persons? "Over-enthusiastic,"[18] or simply weak-minded and scrupulous people; women for ever dissatisfied with the direction given them, on the ground that it does not tally with their dreams. Such women mingled with the crowds of pilgrims just as wasps mingle with the bees. The holy priest never harshly repelled anyone, but he did not succeed in satisfying everybody. In his dealings with certain weak heads he was always short, and he dismissed them after giving them appropriate advice. His discretion went even further: if he foresaw

---

17. Abbé Toccanier, *Procès apostolique ne pereant,* p. 333.
18. Chanoine Morel, *Procès apostolique in genere,* p. 452. It will be readily believed that there also came visionaries and adventuresses who abused the name and fame of the Curé d'Ars, and that until the end of his life. On this subject we possess several interesting documents.

"A lady of the name of Carlat," says the Abbé Faivre, missionary of Saint-Claude (*Procès de l'Ordinaire,* p. 1495), caused some stir in the neighborhood of Lons-le-Saulnier by alleged revelations and by the prestige she obtained by speaking of her relations with M. Vianney as her director. Things came to such a pass that I deemed it imperative to write to the servant of God. He answered with the following letter:

"ARS,
"September 24, (1844?).

"Most Honored Sir,

"Be sure and tell Mme. Carlat that all she says of the Curé d'Ars is utterly untrue. Never have I approved of her but always have I condemned her. This is the first news I have that she makes me the recipient of the revelations of her Guardian Angel. How is it possible that a priest can take notice of such dreams? "My most humble respects."

In addition we give the text of an anonymous note which was handed to M. Toccanier shortly after the death of the servant of God:

"PARIS,
"November 16, 1859.

"M. Toccanier is hereby informed that the woman named Marie Bogre is endeavoring even now to pass herself off as a niece of the holy and venerated Curé d'Ars, and is injuring his memory by her evil conduct and the absurdities she relates. If M. Toccanier wishes for further information, he may write to Père Richard, a Franciscan living at 150, rue de Vaugirard.

"Marie Bogre has promised to the Fathers her uncle's blessing on the Friday of each week, and she continues to get money for Masses under pretext of sending it to Ars. You surely remember her."

anything like unseemly or ridiculous importunities, he knew how to refuse to see people. "Save me from that person," he said in a calm tone of voice to one of the women attendants; "get her to leave the church; she is deserving of compassion."[19]

Great and sorrowful was the surprise of the holy director when the echo of those complaints and murmurs reached his ears. "Poor little Curé d'Ars!" he groaned. "What do they not make him say, what do they not make him do! At present it is on him they preach, and no longer on the Gospel!"[20] Letters began to reach him, anonymous for the most part, "accusing him of untimely zeal and of attracting to his church women devoid of common sense who had much better stay in their own parishes.

That was also M. Vianney's opinion. "Eh! It is not I who ask them to come!" he would say.[21]

One priest, who prudently left his letter unsigned, wrote to him in the name of several of his colleagues: "They say you are a saint, yet all those who go to see you do not come back converted. You would be well advised to moderate your ill-judged zeal, otherwise we shall feel compelled, much to our regret, to inform the bishop."

The victim of these accusations replied directly to the author of the epistle, for his handwriting had betrayed him:

"Monsieur le Curé, I thank you most sincerely for the kind advice which you have the charity to give me. I acknowledge my ignorance and my incapacity. If the people of neighboring parishes have not been converted after receiving the Sacraments at my hands, I am deeply grieved. If you think fit, you may write to the Bishop, who, I trust,

---

19. Abbé Raymond, *Vie MSS.*, p. 177.

20. Frère Athanase, *Procès atostolique in genere,* p. 208. Only an inexperienced reader could wonder at this sly guerrilla warfare waged against the Curé d'Ars by some of his brother priests. It was one way of paying toll for his sanctity. "Where is the apostle, the founder of an Order, the man who revealed or introduced a new devotion destined to become universal, the reformer, who had not to suffer, I do not say at the hands of his enemies, but at those of his friends, his brothers and sisters in the faith? The truth is that whatever is great, be it genius or holiness, alarms and shocks at first those that live in mediocrity and routine." (Henri Joly, *Le Psychologie des Saints,* p. 36 of French text).

21. Abbé Dufour, *Procès apostolique in genere,* p. 341.

will have the goodness to rebuke me. Pray to God, please, Monsieur le Curé, that I may do less harm and more good."

A reply of this kind had the result which it could not fail to achieve. "The author of the anonymous letter hastened to apologize to M. Vianney, and this time he did not forget to sign his letter."[22]

In this way all the prejudices which existed against the Curé d'Ars were dispelled little by little. To be won over, it was enough to come into contact with him, or simply to get to know him better. "A certain religious arrived in the village, treating as a *fanatic* him whom others already styled a *saint;* he left full of admiration for his supernatural illuminations and his virtues."[23]

"I used to know M. l'Abbé Tournier," the Baronne de Belvey relates, "who, at the time of his death, was curé of Ceyzeriat. He frequently indulged in jests at the expense of the servant of God, whom he had never met. At last he happened to come to Ars. He no sooner heard the saintly preacher than he burst into tears. From that moment he never suffered either himself or anyone else to utter a word against M. Vianney. . . . Another time," relates Mlle. de Belvey, "I urged one of the saint's opponents, who had strongly opposed him for the space of sixteen years, to go and judge for himself. Having occasion to pass through Ars, that priest assisted at the catechism. He was so impressed that he knew not how to express his admiration, nor did he wonder any longer at the crowds that flocked to the village."[24]

"A lodging-house keeper of Ars," Catherine Lassagne recounts, "related to me that a priest who put up at her house confessed to her that he had come for the purpose of testing M. Vianney. He had, in fact, seen him in the sacristy, when he was fully determined to embarrass him by his questions; however, when he found himself in the saint's presence he felt so upset that he did not know

22. Abbé Tailhades, *Procès de l'Ordinaire,* p. 1514.
23. Marthe Miard, *Procès apostolique continuatif,* p. 850.
24. *Procès apostolique ne pereant,* pp. 174-175.

what to say. 'I have preached before bishops,' the priest declared; 'never have I felt intimidated to such a degree.'"[25]

The truth is that the strong and direct attacks which M. Vianney had to encounter were isolated facts which took place at ever-wider intervals, approximately between 1827 and 1840.[26] The last, the echo of which has reached our times, ended also in the happiest manner possible. The story is worth telling. The culprit, who died in 1872, will surely forgive us if we mention his name, the more so as he generously repented, obtained the saint's forgiveness and friendship, and became one of his most fervent admirers.[27]

The Abbé Jean-Louis Borjon, born in 1809, and consequently M. Vianney's junior by twenty-three years, had been appointed curé of Ambérieux-en-Dombes on May 17, 1837. We are told by M. Nicolas, a neighbor of his who, at that time, was cure of Saint-Trivier, that with the inexperience of youth he combined "a brusque and haughty manner and an extreme outspokenness." At the time of his appointment to the parish, the pilgrimage to Ars was already an established fact, the distance between the two villages being less than eight kilometers. This constant exodus, the objective of which was a *saint* whom he did not know, displeased the young curé. The Abbé Borjon, in consequence, placed himself in the ranks of those who, occasionally, forgot to preach on the Gospel and spoke, instead, of the Curé d'Ars. Complications resulted which served to fan the flame.

If we may believe the Abbé Nicolas, of Saint-Trivier, "some pious women of Ambérieux took it into their heads to organize, under the auspices of M. Vianney, a religious confraternity and to collect contributions from members, without having asked leave from their parish priest. The latter was already angry with these good women because,

25. *Procès de l'Ordinaire,* p. 486.

26. There is, therefore, an obvious exaggeration in statements such as the following: "During thirty years he met, at the hands of equals and superiors, with nothing but contradiction, criticism, and contempt" *(Annales d'Ars,* Janv. 1906, p. 312). Nor does the attitude of Mgr. Devie justify such strictures, as we shall presently see.

27. Frère Athanase himself gave his name in the *Procès apostolique genere,* p. 208.

without, of course, telling him of their intention, they had got him to say a Mass in order to obtain his own removal from Ambérieux and his being replaced by M. Vianney! Hence, one fine Sunday, he thundered against them, pouring on them the vials of his wrath and not refraining from personal allusions.[28] Of course, everybody understood who was the real objective of those invectives.

It was not long before M. Vianney heard more than the echo of that philippic. Poor M. Borjon, incapable of seeing things as they were, attacked the saintly Curé, going so far as to write him a letter as cruel as it was unjust; it contained, among others, the following sentence:

"M. le Curé, when a man knows as little theology as you do, he should not go into the confessional."[29]

He who read this letter was far from being indifferent to the contents. The poor saint, with a view, perhaps, to forgetting a little, went and confided his grief to a parishioner who was particularly dear to him, old *Père* Mandy. "Without any doubt," the old Mayor declared, "this letter comes from some boorish person, so you must not attach any importance to it."

"Alas! no; it comes from an educated person." He finally admitted that it had been written by the hand of a priest. "But," he added, "I should not be pained at all could I but believe that God is not thereby offended."[30]

He returned to his room and seized his pen—he who hardly ever wrote now—and his heart dictated the following simple and sublime answer to the young priest:

"Most dear and most venerated confrère, what good reasons I have for loving you! You are the only person who really knows me. Since you are so good and kind as to take an interest in my poor soul, do help me to obtain

28. Letter of M. Nicolas to Mgr. Devie, dated December 16, 1841. In this letter the Abbé Nicolas does not make himself the mouthpiece of M. Borjon. He says, in fact, that "if hotheads have cooled down, it is in the hope that M. le Curé will himself ask for a change; for he has many adversaries. . . . But time may settle the affair." This is exactly what happened.

29. This sentence—the only one that contemporaries have preserved, the saint, no doubt, destroyed the original—is quoted from memory by the Abbé Monnin in his *Life* of the Curé, and by divers witnesses at the process of canonization.

30. J. B. Mandy, *Procès apostolique in genere,* p. 243. His father died at the age of seventy-four, January 27, 1846.

the favor for which I have been asking for so long a time, that being released from a post which I am not worthy to hold by reason of my ignorance, I may be allowed to retire into a little corner, there to weep over my poor life. What penances there are to be undertaken! how many expiations to be offered! how many tears to be shed!"

This is not the language of mock humility. False or even ordinary virtue would have found no such accents. To speak in this way a man must have kissed his crucifix long and ardently. In fact, the sorrowful mysteries of the life of Christ had become the habitual subject of M. Vianney's meditations; we can gather this from the tone of his letter. Its effect on the Abbé Borjon was such that he seized the earliest opportunity of hurrying to Ars, where he threw himself at the feet of him whom he had so grievously hurt. The Curé d'Ars, who had already forgotten everything, opened his arms and, with a heavenly smile on his face, pressed him to his heart.[31]

Subsequently the curé of Ambérieux showed himself worthy of so noble a forgiveness. He often returned to Ars, in order to be edified by M. Vianney's example and guided by his counsels. "Since that time I have seen him at work," he declared to Mgr. Mermod, "and I have very much revised my opinion." Henceforth, every year, he led his first communicants to Ars so that they might get the blessing of its holy Curé. In June, 1852, he became curé of Saint-Andre-d'Huiriat. Eventually his was the enviable privilege of testifying at the *cause* of the beatification of the servant of God when, after a solemn oath, he protested that "he entertained towards him sentiments of great friendship, great esteem, and great veneration."[32]

M. Vianney was not ignorant of the fact that he had been denounced to his Bishop. More than once clerical friends entreated him to speak in his own defense. He preferred to say nothing, accounting for his silence by a legend borrowed from his bedside book, *The Lives of the Saints.*

31. Catherine Lassagne, *Petit mémoire,* troisième rédaction, p, 84.
32. *Procès de l'Ordinaire,* p. 1269.

"A certain saint once commanded one of his religious: 'Go to the cemetery and speak as much evil of the dead as you can.' The religious obeyed. On his return the saint asked him: 'What did they answer?' 'Nothing.' 'Well, go back now and pay them a great many compliments.' The religious obeyed once more and returned to his superior. 'Surely this time they said something by way of reply?' 'Again nothing.' 'Very well,' said the saint, 'if people rebuke you, if they praise you, do as the dead.'"[33]

"Today I had two letters," he related in one of his catechisms; "In one I am told that I am a saint, in the other that I am nothing more than a quack. The first letter gave me nothing, the second took nothing from me."[34] It was after the perusal of an epistle of this kind that he said, almost joyfully: "Here is someone who knows me well! Were I tempted to pride, there would be a remedy to cure me."[35]

The Curé d'Ars did more than put up with blame with truly supernatural philosophy. The persecutions of some of his brother priests provided him with the opportunity of climbing another rung of the ladder of humility. He countersigned and himself sent to the bishop's house a letter of denunciation which chance had caused to fall into his hands. "Now they have my signature," he observed, "so there will be no lack of material to lead to a conviction."[36]

Mgr. Devie, who was indeed a great and holy bishop, was also the man least disposed to allow himself to be taken in by false reports. In his anxiety to base any decision he might have to come to upon the fullest information possible, he despatched to Ars his Vicar-General, Chanoine Ruivet. This "rigid zealot for discipline, firm to the extent of appearing hard, but whose austerity of manner and speech in reality hid a kindly and sympathetic heart, was only too glad to seize upon any pretext for leniency."[37] With the Curé d'Ars it was enough that he

33. Jeanne-Marie Chanay, *Procès de l'Ordinaire,* p. 701.
34. R. P. Monnin, *Procès apostolique ne pereant,* p. 988.
35. Abbé Rougement, *Procès apostolique continuatif,* p. 768.
36. Abbé Toccanier, *Procès apostolique in genere,* p. 157.
37. J. Cognat, *Mgr. Devie,* t. I, p. 459.

should be just. M. Vianney explained that people came of their own accord and that he went in search of no one; that once face to face with his penitents he acted for the best, according to his conscience; that, moreover, the cure of souls, considering his ignorance and wretchedness, weighed heavily on him; he had already asked Monseigneur to take the burden from his shoulders.

Only a saint could cherish hopes such as these; the Curé d'Ars sincerely believed that this fresh inquiry would induce the Bishop to allow him to resign. Great, therefore, was his disappointment when he heard M. Ruivet, unaware of his presence, addressing these words to someone: "If the denunciations were based on facts, we should not see so many pilgrims here, and among them both religious and priests."[38] After that the Vicar-General could not send in to the Bishop a report other than favorable.

Later on, for the sake of satisfying himself more fully, the prelate "desired the Curé d'Ars to submit to the Episcopal Council the difficult cases with which he met in his apostolate, together with his solution of them. The good priest willingly complied with this injunction, and in this way he sent in more than two hundred cases of conscience within the space of a few years.[39] From a searching examination of these letters Mgr. Devie came to the conclusion that M. Vianney's verdicts were invariably accurate and that no fault could be found with his line of action."[40] "One day," Mme. des Garets relates, "I took the liberty of remarking in the presence of the Bishop of Belley: 'The Curé d'Ars is not generally considered to be very learned.' 'I do not know whether he is learned or not,' his lordship replied, 'but what I do know very well is that the Holy

38. Abbé Toccanier, *Procès apostolique in genere,* p. 156.
39. Of all the letters in which the Curé d'Ars exposed his difficulties to Mgr. Devie, only one has been recovered—it deals with a question of restitution. We have yet another, addressed to Mgr. Chalandon, the coadjutor and eventually the successor of Mgr. Devie, in which M. Vianney asks if it be lawful to admit to the grace of the sacraments the doorkeepers of comedians.
40. J. Cognat, *Mgr. Devie,* t. II, p. 20. "He (Mgr. Devie) did not like rigorism, neither in practice nor in theory, and he always felt that the theological rigorism of the previous century had brought about the estrangement of many people from the practice of religion" *(ibid.,* t. I, p. 221). If, then, the Bishop of Belley approved of the decisions of the holy Curé it must have been that they inclined towards leniency.

Ghost enlightens him.'"[41] Several ecclesiastics having ridiculed the rather uncommon way of living of M. Vianney, and even uttered the word "madness" in connection with him, Mgr. Devie was much pained when he came to hear of it. When his priests were all gathered together for the annual retreat, he told them of the occurrence, adding: "Gentlemen, I could wish that all my clergy had a small grain of the same madness."[42]

Mgr. Devie had not waited ten years before giving M. Vianney proofs of his confidence. On September 15, 1832, most likely during the clergy retreat, the Curé d'Ars had asked for faculties to hear Confessions and to absolve even reserved cases in the parish of Chaneins, where a mission was to be given. Not only did the wise Bishop grant the petition, but he added in his own handwriting on the faculty paper: *Item pro tota dioecesi* ("Likewise for the whole diocese").

The attitude of the prelate towards the Curé d'Ars proved a revelation and a lesson for a number of his critics. The time came when, with the exception of an occasional complaint about small matters, the name of the saint invariably raised among his brother priests a unanimous concert of praise. Those who had been influenced by false reports saw their prejudices vanish on their first acquaintance with Ars, "The clergy of the neighborhood, who knew M. Vianney well, esteemed and loved him," says the Comte des Garets.[43] The curés of more distant parishes, "who had had some misgivings as to his competence, ended by changing their minds and feeling the greatest confidence in his knowledge."[44]

A single fact, of great significance, is sufficient proof that those who opposed the saint were soon reduced to an insignificant minority. At the very last clergy retreat that he attended—in 1834, at the Grand Sèminaire of Bourg—Mgr. Devie included the Curé's name in the official

41. *Procès de l'Ordinaire,* p. 903.
42. Frère Athanase, *Procès apostolique in genere,* p. 208.
43. *Procès de l'Ordinaire,* p. 949.
44. *Ibid.,* p. 1033.

list of confessors. Now so many priests addressed themselves to him that he had not a moment for private prayer and meditation, or even to attend the instructions of the preacher of the retreat. "This shows,"the excellent Catherine Lassagne concludes, "that he was already appreciated as a good servant of God."[45]

45. *Petit mémoire,* troisième rédaction, p. 68.

Chapter 14

THE PILGRIMAGE TO ARS
(continued)
III. The Curé d'Ars as a Confessor

DURING the space of thirty years, ever changing crowds of pilgrims invaded the old church of Ars, the flags of which became polished and worn by the feet of visitors, even as the boulders over which the waves of the sea pass and repass without ceasing.

And let no one imagine that there was an appreciable diminution in the number of visitors during the winter months when the cold makes itself so cruelly felt on the uplands of La Dombes. From November to March, M. Vianney spent not less than eleven or twelve hours each day in the confessional.[1] "Even were he never to leave the church at all," Catherine Lassagne writes, "he would not be able to satisfy all those who come. For this reason he always keeps on his rochet when going out, for, were he to enter the sacristy to take it off, he would have to remain, because of the crowds that would at once press round him." On the margin of Catherine's manuscript the Abbé Renard has jotted down this commentary: "The narrative of the directress is quite according to facts; I have often come to Ars in the summer, the spring, the autumn, and even the winter, and have myself witnessed what she describes."[2] M. Dufour, missionary of Pont-d'Ain, writes: "The first time that I entered the church of Ars—it was in 1851—there were two rows of women penitents, from the chapel of the Blessed Virgin to that of St. John the Baptist, and I never saw a gap in those two rows."

1. *Procès de l'Ordinaire,* p. 300.
2. *Petit mémoire,* première rédaction, p. 8.

M. Jean-Félix des Garets, brother of the Mayor of Ars, writes in his turn: "The concourse of pilgrims increased steadily between the years 1830 and 1845, in which year it reached its climax. At that time the number of daily arrivals amounted to some three or four hundred. At the railway station of Perrache, the most important of Lyons, a special booking-office was always open for the sole purpose of issuing tickets for Ars. These tickets were good for eight days, for it was generally known that it took all that time before a pilgrim's turn would come to see M. Vianney for the purpose of obtaining from him a word or an absolution."[3]

For the unbeliever who did not know that "the true history of the world is the history of God's grace in the world,"[4] such eagerness remained an enigma. All that multitude was made up of souls longing for pardon, for greater spiritual illumination, for more profound abnegation.

"The overwhelming majority of visitors," M. des Garets adds, "were attracted by faith, piety, or repentance, and if a few sightseers mingled with the crowd, the indifferent were often won over to God by a gesture, a look, or a tear of the venerable Curé. Persons of every age and condition formed that throng: bishops, priests, religious—many Jesuits and Marists, Capuchins, Franciscans, Dominicans—nobles and plebeians, learned and ignorant, some accustomed to discussing the weightiest of problems, others impelled solely by the simplicity of their faith. Among the last named I have seen whole families of peasants come in carts from distant provinces, even from as far as the mountains of Auvergne, in order to visit the servant of God and to perform their devotions in the church of Ars. For the surrounding district Ars was a centre to which people journeyed on foot and by carriage, by road and by river."[5]

One whose information was reliable, François Pertinand, hotel-keeper and carter at Ars, states that in 1836

3. *Procès apostolique in genere,* p. 413.
4. Louis Perroy, *L'humble Vierge Marie,* Paris, Lethielleux, p. 75.
5. *Procès apostolique in genere,* p. 414.

a service of conveyances between Ars and Trévoux was organized and ran on three days in the week. In 1840 a daily service was introduced between Ars and Lyons. Finally, according to a report of M. de Castellane, *sous-préfet* of Trévoux, dated June 28, 1855, starting that year, "two omnibuses performed the journey between Ars and Lyons each day; two others went twice a day to the station of Villefranche to meet the trains on the Paris-Lyons line; a fifth omnibus, which ran between Villars and Villefranche, called at the place of pilgrimage itself." During the last year of the saint's life (1858-1859) "the number of pilgrims," according to François Pertinand, "reached 80,000, counting those only who travelled by public conveyance. As for the total number of pilgrims, I reckon it to have been between 100,000 and 120,000."[6]

In the meantime the village of Ars had not grown in proportion to the spread of its fame, hence the crowd had to find lodgings as best it might. There were, indeed, five houses dignified by the pompous name of hotel, but they could barely accommodate a hundred and fifty persons. The others quartered themselves "on the natives"; and the quarters were not luxurious. "On our arrival at Ars, on May 8, 1845," Chanoine Camille Lenfant relates," we found all the hotels full. Everyone had to shift for himself. As for me, Providence took me to the house of Mlle. Ricotier, a woman full of faith and simplicity. In exchange for two francs and a half a day, she gave me board and lodging; I must say I had my money's worth."

In May, 1854, the Bishop of Birmingham[7] heard it rumored that "some penitents spent the whole night lying in the meadows, to the number of as many as fifty persons, either in order to get an earlier chance of going into the confessional, or because there was no room for them in the hostelries."[8]

At no time were the crowds noisy or troublesome. They had come to see a saint, to go to Confession to him, to

6. "Un pèlerinage à Ars en 1858," *Annales d'Ars,* Février, 1906, p. 342.
7. Bishop Ullathorne, O.S.B.
8. Marie des Brulais, *Suite de l'Echo de la sainte Montagne,* Nantes, p. 175.

fulfill some vow made to St. Philomena. A spirit of recollection, made up of expectation and hope, brooded over this unique village. There were those who entered it as people enter a sanctuary. So soon as they espied the brick tower of the church, many pilgrims bared their heads or made the Sign of the Cross. Even though the church was only closed between nine o'clock in the evening and midnight, it was not easy at any time to get inside. In March, 1859, Georges Seigneur, editor of the Croisé newspaper, had perforce to arm himself with patience as he very slowly mounted the flight of steps that lead to the great door. "Strangers in great numbers were standing in the old cemetery, and even in the lanes nearby, awaiting their turn. . . . They bought medals and rosaries which they intended to have blessed, or candles destined to burn before the altar of St. Philomena. In order to while away the time of waiting, several of them were contemplating the portraits of the holy priest, or they conversed together about him as children might talk of their father, though they had not as yet seen him."[9]

These portraits of the Curé d'Ars were exhibited everywhere, in shop windows, on the low wall of the cemetery, in the baskets of small tradeswomen who mingled with the pilgrims. They were of every shape, from the diminutive engraving destined to be placed in the pages of the missal to the brightly colored *"Epinal"* image, which showed divers episodes of the saint's life, reproduced with very little regard for accuracy. The likeness, it will be readily understood, could only be approximate, for M. Vianney always refused to pose for his portrait.[10] But what did that matter! Every pilgrim wished to take away with him "the portrait of the *saint*" as a precious remembrance of the pious journey.

However long they might have to wait before finding a place in the church, the visitors, with rare exceptions, never gave in to weariness. Cost what it might, they were

9. *Le Croisé,* 20 Août, 1859, première année, No. 3.
10. Comtesse des Garets, *Procès de l'Ordinaire,* p. 917.

determined to hear the saint, and for the majority, the main, if not the only motive of their pilgrimage was to have a private interview with him in the confessional.

Once in the church, a fresh period of waiting began. It should be stated that "M. Vianney devoted to each Confession only the time strictly required,"[11] that when he had a long day he heard Confessions for as many as sixteen and eighteen hours; yet for all that the majority of pilgrims were compelled, during the last ten years of his life, to wait thirty, fifty, seventy hours before reaching the blessed tribunal. "It happened many times that visitors paid some poor persons to keep their places for them."[12] All were not able to do this, so they just waited in the church, which was stiflingly hot in summer and icy cold in winter. People who wanted to go outside and yet not lose their place made suitable arrangements either with those next to them or with the guardians of the church. At night there was nothing for it but to leave, since the church would be locked. People numbered themselves in order not to miss their turn, and went to spend in the open or in the vestibule close to the tower, the few hours that intervened between the rising of the Curé d'Ars and his going to bed.[13]

Mlle. Sophie Gros, of Besançon, was able to recollect in her old age how her maid, Clémentine Viney, had been obliged, in July, 1853, to wait two days, with a basket of provisions on her arm, before her opportunity came to present herself in the confessional. During the course of the year 1855, a demoiselle Louise Dortan, of l'Hôpital (Puy-de-Dôme), who later on became a nun under the name of Sister Marie de Jésus, came to consult the Curé d'Ars on the subject of her vocation. She waited three whole days for her turn. At last, in despair of ever getting as far as the confessional, she was about to leave,

11. Abbé Toccanier, *Procès apostolique ne pereant,* p. 266.
12. Guillaume Villier, *Procès de l'Ordinaire,* p. 636.
13. Mme. Christine de Cibeins, *Procès apostolique continuatif,* p. 144. As many as eighty persons have been known to spend the night in the porch or in the neighborhood of the church, so as to retain their place for the following day." (Abbé Dufour, *Procès apostolique in genere,* p. 340).

in a flood of tears, when M. Vianney spoke to her as he came out of the chapel of St. John the Baptist, "You are not very patient, my child: you have been here only three days and you want to go home? You must remain fifteen days. Go and pray to St. Philomena to tell you what is your vocation, and after that come and see me." The girl followed the advice and was the better for it.

At about nine o'clock in the morning the saint set aside some time for interviews with religious and priests. As a rule he heard them in a confessional placed behind the high altar. "A bishop, and it was the diocesan, has been seen awaiting his turn just like the others."[14]

At times it looked as if the Curé's task were done at last; as if he might take a little rest, were it only for one day. It was a vain hope! One evening in May, 1853, three nuns and a lady, who had recently lost her husband, drove up in François Pertinand's carriage, and went rapidly up the steps that lead to the church. It so happened that M. Vianney was leaving his confessional after absolving the very last penitent. The nave was emptying. The lady in deep mourning went up to the saint, who at once consented to hear her. "Would you also like to speak to M. le Curé now that he is disengaged?" someone asked the three nuns. "No, tomorrow," they answered, "for we must look for lodgings." "Oh! tomorrow," they were told, "perhaps tomorrow will not be like today."

"It happened, in fact," one of the nuns, Sister Dosithée, of the Providence of Vitteaux, relates "that the following day there was such a concourse of pilgrims that I was carried, rather than walked, up to the confessional. At last I was able to speak to M. le Curé, for, knowing that I was ill"—she was in consumption and had attacks of hemorrhage—"he saw me before my turn."

It is true that if M. Vianney, once he had taken his seat in the tribunal of mercy, "showed no favor to anyone, he nevertheless made exceptions for his own people, for the sick and infirm and others who were unable to

14. Catherine Lassagne, *Procès apostolique in genere,* p. 111.

wait." Here the gift of intuition which God had bestowed on him in so large a measure guided his eyes. "I have heard it said of a great number of former pilgrims," relates M. Claude Rougemont, who was vicaire at Ars in 1871, "that M. le Curé had singled them out from among the crowd and summoned them either into the confessional or the sacristy because, though he had no other knowledge of them, he had seen by means of an interior light that it was necessary that these persons should speak to him without further delay." Such was the saint's prestige that only on rare occasions did this exceptional treatment give rise to murmuring. "Let it be!" he said to Frère Athanase, who, no doubt, had repeated to him the echo of some complaint, "I am accused of being somewhat easy with certain pilgrims. Surely I must take into account the trouble it costs them to come from so far and the expense to which they are put. There are some who come secretly and who do not wish to be recognized; these are in a great hurry to leave."[15]

A woman who was the mother of sixteen children had succeeded in getting a place in the middle of the nave. Suddenly the saint appeared outside his confessional, and, pointing his finger towards her, he said: "You, madame, you are in a hurry. Come at once!"[16]

In 1833, or thereabouts, Marguerite Humbert, of Ecully, now Madame Fayolle, paid a visit—the first in fifteen years—to her cousin, Jean-Marie Vianney. He had asked the daughters of the *Providence* to treat her well, because she had taken good care of him during the time of his studies. "Now, before leaving," Marguerite tells us, "I returned to the church, and I asked myself whether I should go to Confession to my cousin. At that very moment someone came to tell me that he was waiting for me. I was greatly surprised because he could not see me where I was. . . . I left Ars full of a great interior joy."[17]

"One day the servant of God was hearing Confessions

15. Frère Athanase, *Procès de l'Ordinaire,* p. 1013.
16. *Annales d'Ars,* Juillet, 1905, p. 91.
17. *Procès de l'Ordinaire,* p. 1325.

in the sacristy," M. Oriol records. "All of a sudden he appeared on the threshold, and, addressing me, he said: 'My friend, get a lady who is quite at the back of the church to come to me.' And he told me how I should know her. Now, I could not find the lady at the place to which he had directed me, so I returned and told him. 'Run quickly,' said he, 'she is in front of such a house.' I ran and overtook the lady, who was going away, grievously disappointed, for she could wait no longer."[18]

A poor woman, whose timidity had evidently caused her to miss her turn for Confession two or three times in succession, had been at Ars eight days without succeeding in seeing M. Vianney. Finally the saint himself summoned her; more than that, he went to fetch her, and led her through the crowd to the chapel of St. John the Baptist. "Quite happy now, she held on to his cassock and slipped through the passage he opened for her."

The saint knew from personal experience that grace has its moments; and that it may go by without coming back. Hence, on occasion, he literally caught souls "on the wing."

About the year 1853 a cheery band of young men set out from Lyons to go on pilgrimage to Ars. They were good Christians; all save one, an old man who had joined the group "solely to please the young people." The village was reached at about three o'clock in the afternoon. "Go to church, if you like," said the unbeliever on leaving the carriage; "as for me, I shall order dinner." He walked a few yards, then stopped. "No, on second thoughts, I will go with you," he said, "you will not be long!" So the whole band filed into the church. Now at that very moment M. Vianney came out of the sacristy and entered the chancel. He knelt down, stood up and turned round; his eyes were looking for someone in the direction of the holy water basin, and finally he signalled to someone to come up. "It is you he wants," the youths told the astonished unbeliever. So he walked up, obviously feeling very embar-

18. *Procès de l'Ordinaire,* p. 759.

rassed, we are told by the nun to whom we owe this story. "As for us, we were chuckling inwardly, for we understood that the bird had been caught. M. le Curé shook his hand, saying: 'It is a long time since you were at Confession?' 'My good Curé, it is something like thirty years, I believe.' 'Thirty years, my friend? Just think. . . . It is thirty-three years; you were then at such a place. . .'

"'You are right, M. le Curé.'

"'Ah, well, so we are going to Confession now, are we not?'

"The old man confessed afterwards that he was so taken aback by the invitation that he dared not say no; but he added: 'I at once experienced a sensation of indefinable comfort.' The Confession took twenty minutes, and made a new man of him."[19]

The way in which another sinner was won over is quite typical. About the year 1840 a certain *Père* Rochette took his son, who was sick, to the wonder-worker of Ars. His wife accompanied him; she went to Confession and received Holy Communion. As for *Père* Rochette, he had but one concern—namely, to obtain the cure of his boy. He paid, indeed, a few visits to the church, but he kept in the neighborhood of the holy water stoup. There he was when the saint, coming from behind the altar where he was hearing the Confessions of priests, began to call him. He refused to budge. At that moment his wife and his son were close to the altar rails. "Is he then such an unbeliever?" M. Vianney asked the wife. At last, at the third summons, the man decided to walk up the nave. "After all," he thought, "the Curé d'Ars will not eat me!" He went with M. Vianney behind the altar. There was no time to lose. "This is for both of us, *Père* Rochette," said the Curé, and, pointing to the confessional: "Put yourself there," he said.

"Oh!" the other replied, "I don't feel like it." "Well, begin."

Incapable of offering resistance to so sudden an attack, *Père* Rochette had fallen on his knees.

---

19. *Letters* of an Ursuline of Cracow to Mgr. Convert, June 1, 1902.

"My father," he stammered, "it is some time . . . ten years. . . ."

"Make it a little more."

"Twelve years. . . ."

"Yet a little more."

"Yes, since the great jubilee of 1826."

"Ah! there we are! One finds by dint of seeking."

Père Rochette made his Confession like a child. The following day saw him kneeling by the side of his wife at the altar rails. Their boy, the faithful chronicler adds, left in the church of Ars two crutches, for which he had no further use.[20]

Thus for countless souls the road to Ars became the road to Damascus, nor should anyone imagine that, in addition to his personal prayers and penances, the saint had recourse to any unusual means to bring about their conversion. They were moved, at first, by the fire of his preaching, so that, when he came to close quarters with them in the privacy of the confessional, a few words were enough to deal them the blow that prostrates the spirit of man in order to raise it again. Moreover, except in special cases, such as a general confession, he was expeditious, and he required a like conduct from the penitent. "Five minutes sufficed to pour out my soul into his," said *Père* Combalot on leaving the confessional of the Curé d'Ars. He did not mince matters in dealing with sinners; his sublime faith raised him far above the fear of men, and, putting all his trust in God alone, he knew, when necessary, how to say to men, irrespective of their condition: "It is not lawful!" Who can tell the number of souls whom the lancet of his word freed from the hidden virus that poisoned their life? He knew the spot which it was necessary to touch, and he rarely missed his aim.

"Ah! if God were not so good," he sighed; "but He is so good!" Or: "Save your poor soul! What a pity to lose a soul that has cost Our Lord so much! What harm then

20. *Annales d'Ars,* Janvier, 1915, pp. 254-255.

has He done to you that you treat Him thus?"[21]

"Alas!" the holy confessor said to M. Valpinson, a merchant of La Ferté-Macé, "you have a vice that will be your damnation—namely, pride." The penitent owned to it and began to reflect. That simple word changed his soul, and his life became that of a meek and humble Christian. He could never recall his memories of Ars without shedding tears.[22]

In order to move big sinners, M. Vianney, without other exhortation, contented himself with uttering one phrase, simple but terrible on the lips of one who read the future: "My friend, you are damned!" It was short, but it was eloquent. Obviously the saint intended to speak conditionally, and meant to say: "Unless you avoid such an occasion, if you persist in such a habit, if you do not follow such and such advice, you will be damned."[23] "What, I damned! I cursed by God! forever!" François Bourdin, of Villebois, kept repeating to himself on coming out of the confessional. In 1856, in consequence of bad business transactions, this man, though still young—he was thirty-five years old—had gone, full of despair, to live with his father-in-law at Ambutrix. A mission happened to be taking place at the time, but, notwithstanding the entreaties of his family, he refused to attend it. His faith, nevertheless, was far from extinct, but the despairing thoughts that haunted him turned him away from God. In the end he was touched by grace: "I want to go to Confession," he announced, "but to the great confessor, the Curé d'Ars." Yet by way of encouragement, after the avowal of his sins and miseries, all he heard was the terrifying answer: "My boy, you are damned!" But the threat became a flash of

---

21. Abbé Monnin, *Procès de l'Ordinaire,* p. 1122.
22. *Annales d'Ars,* Janvier, 1901, p. 251. From some of the facts that we relate here, certain readers might suspect that the Curé d'Ars had violated, more or less directly, the most sacred seal of Confession; this would be a monstrous error. Let them reassure themselves! It was the persons most concerned who, sooner or later, after their Confession to the Curé, made these revelations and allowed them to be divulged for the honor of the servant of God.
23. *Procès apostolique in genere,* pp. 347 and 391. "One day," the Abbé Raymond relates, "I brought to him a woman who fancied she had heard him declare that she would be damned. The good Curé had no difficulty in reassuring her." *(Procès de l'Ordinaire,* p. 306).

light. The man was converted, and to the end of his life remained a fervent Christian.[24]

As a rule the direction of pious souls did not demand many more words. But here also his utterances were fiery darts that buried themselves in the heart for all time. "Love your priests much!" was all he said to Mgr. de Langalerie, his own Bishop, when he knelt at his feet.[25]

"I have been somewhat careless when doing such-and-such a thing," Frère Athanase told him in Confession, "but in the main, my intentions are good." "O my friend, good intentions! Hell is paved with them." That was all.

Frère Amédée, the future Superior-General of the Brothers of the Holy Family, had just concluded his Confession: "Oh! love, love the good God very much!" exclaimed M. Vianney, at the same time folding his hands; and he gave him absolution without adding another word.

"He twice heard my Confession," says the Abbé Monnin. "Everyone of my accusations provoked on his part this exclamation of faith, commiseration, and horror for the smallest sin: 'What a pity!' I was particularly struck by the accent of tenderness with which he uttered the words. That simple 'what a pity!' in all its beauty showed what damage sin had done to the soul."[26]

The Abbé Denis, who lived in retirement at Neuville-sur-Saône, addressed himself fairly often to the saintly confessor: "He was short, very short," he declared; "a word of exhortation and it was over."

It was the holiness of the Curé d'Ars that imparted to his words their power and efficacy; on the lips of other men they might have seemed commonplace, but with what expression he uttered them! In addition to words, there was about M. Vianney something even more irresistible—namely, his tears. To soften a hardened heart, it was at times enough for him to point, in the midst of his tears,

24. We owe these details to M. l'Abbé Joly, curé of Benonces (Ain), who had them directly from François Bourdin himself (*Relations,* in the archives of the presbytery of Ars).

25. Mgr. de Langalerie, when Archbishop of Auch, related the incident during the clergy retreat.

26. *Procès de l'Ordinaire,* p. 1089.

to the crucifix that hung on the wall. "From his confessional proceeded groans and sighs that escaped him against his will, and which moved the penitent to repentance and love."[27] "One day," we are told by the Abbé Dubouis, curé of Fareins, "some priests of a neighboring diocese indulged in criticism of certain directions given by the servant of God. A magistrate, who had been a penitent of M. Vianney's, was present at the conversation. 'There is one thing of which I can assure you, gentlemen,' he said, 'it is that the Curé d'Ars weeps and one weeps with him; that does not happen everywhere.'"[28]

"Why do you weep so much, Father?" the saint was asked by a sinner kneeling by his side.

"Ah! my friend, I weep because you do not weep enough."[29]

The Rev. F. Cyril Faivre, himself a great confessor, relates how persons converted by the Curé d'Ars had told him that what had most deeply impressed them was to behold the man of God weeping for their sins.

Small wonder after this that both "men and women came out of his confessional with their eyes full of tears; some there were who even broke out into loud sobs and cries."[30]

In a corner of the sacristy the pilgrim venerates to this day the rude seat with its high elbow-rests on which the saint sat to hear the men's Confessions. This dark corner witnessed some very moving scenes, for it was perhaps here that the greatest number of returns to God took place, for, in the words of Mgr. Devie, "the good Curé had received from God a special gift for converting men."

In order to make sure of an audience, the men ranged themselves as close as possible to the sacristy; in fact, they penetrated even into the chancel, where benches were specially reserved for them. They never came in such numbers as the women, hence they had not so long to

27. Catherine Lassagne, *Procès apostolique in genere,* p. 123.
28. *Procès de l'Ordinaire,* p. 1238.
29. Frère Athanase, *Procès apostolique in genere,* p. 224.
30. Abbé Tailhades, *Procès de l'Ordinaire,* p. 1508.

wait for their turns; but even they were forced to spend long hours in church. Frère Athanase relates that "Frère Jérôme, the sacristan, has counted as many as seventy-two waiting together, and I myself have seen a man wait for his turn from five o'clock in the morning until the same hour in the evening."[31]

Several devoted women acted as guardians, and took up their post among the ranks of the women. In like manner for the men also, a kind of police arrangement was set up, thanks to certain men of good will who never failed. Several excellent men who were free to dispose of their time—such as MM. Thèbre, Oriol, Pagès, Viret, and others—went on duty in relays, from seven o'clock in the morning until night. One of them stationed himself between the kneeling-stools that stood on either side of the door. An iron rod barred the way. As soon as one penitent came out, the watchman on duty let in another.

On the walls of the present-day basilica, a fresco of powerful draughtsmanship evokes memories of those days, already far off, when in that darksome corner divine grace wrought such marvels. Men of every rank are there, gathered from every part of France, their cloaks still powdered with the dust of the long journey. On the faces of some we may read the effects of grace—they are prepared for every avowal, for every expiation; others, led thither by remorse, by the prayers of a beloved wife or daughter, hesitate; perhaps they even draw back and are about to take once more the shameful road of sin. . . . Perhaps it is in that very group that we may look for that libertine who hoped, on entering the church, to find indeed the Curé d'Ars, but dead![32] Suddenly, within the frame of the redoubtable door, a white figure appears. An old man, emaciated, worn out by his penances, fixes on the waiting men a look by which his whole personality seems, as it were, to express itself. He has espied the soul on which pardon is about to descend, as the eagle swoops down upon its prey. The man thus marked rises. The door is

---

31. *Procès apostolique in genere,* p. 207.
32. Comte des Clarets, *Procès de l'Ordinaire, p.* 989.

shut upon him and the Curé d'Ars. Will he be the same sinner when he reappears? No, the man we behold is a penitent whose breast is shaken by his sobs, and who, having found the way home to God, hastens to throw himself at the feet of Our Lady of Ars, who, close by, holds out her arms to him.

"The great miracle of the Curé d'Ars," someone has said, "was his confessional, besieged day and night."[33] It might be said with equal truth that his greatest miracle was the conversion of sinners: "I have seen numerous and remarkable ones," the Abbé Raymond assures us, "and they form the most beautiful chapter of the life of the Curé d'Ars. 'Oh, my friend,' he often told me, 'only at the last judgement will it become known how many souls have here found their salvation.'"[34] "In reality," Jeanne-Marie Chanay writes, "he made but small account of miraculous cures. 'The body is so very little,' he used to repeat. That which truly filled him with joy was the return of souls to God."[35] How many occasions he had for such joy! M. Prosper des Garets relates: "I asked him one day how many big sinners he had converted in the course of the year. 'Over seven hundred,' was his reply."[36] Hence it is easy to understand the wish expressed by a curé who made the pilgrimage to Ars: "Those of my parishioners who go to M. Vianney become models. I wish I could take my whole parish to him."[37]

"The Curé d'Ars felt a special attraction to the work of converting sinners,"[38] says M. Toccanier. He loved them, we might say, with all the hatred which he felt for their sins. He loathed evil, and "spoke of it with horror and indignation," but for the guilty ones he felt boundless compassion, and his lamentations over the loss of souls

33. *Sermons* of Mgr. Martin, preached on August 4, 1865, on the occasion of the blessing of the basilica of Ars.
34. *Procès de l'Ordinaire,* p. 337.
35. *Ibid.,* p. 709.
36. *Ibid.,* p. 988.
37. *Ibid.,* p. 369.
38. *Procès de l'Ordinaire,* p. 137.

were heartrending: "My God," he cried out in his room one day in Lent, 1841, "my God, is it possible that thou shouldst have endured so many torments for their salvation and that they should nevertheless be damned!"[39] And in his catechisms he said: "What bitter grief to think that there are men who will die without loving God!" Day after day his sobs were such that he was hardly able to recite the phrase which occurs in the night prayers: *"My God, who willest not the death of the sinner."*[40] *"Ah! the poor sinners!"* and one should have heard the accents in which he uttered those two words—"if only *I* could go to Confession for them!"[41] And Mme. des Garets shuddered when she one day heard him from the pulpit "conjure those of his listeners who wished to be damned to commit as few mortal sins as possible, so as not to add to their everlasting punishments! To the end of my life," the pious countess adds, "I shall remember the instruction on the last judgement in which he repeated several times: 'Cursed by God! cursed by God! What a misfortune! what a misfortune!' It was no longer words we heard, but sobs that brought tears to the eyes of all present."[42]

The *poor sinners!* It was when one of them refused to surrender that the saint redoubled his prayers and penances. "I am only content when praying for sinners," was a charming remark of his.[43] At the approach of the great feasts, and especially during paschal time, he imposed upon himself extraordinary fasts. It was assuredly his zeal for the salvation of so many sinful souls "that made him undertake, during the whole of a long life, a crushing ministry, that knew no interruption, no relaxation, no mitigation; it was his zeal that compelled him to rise at midnight or one o'clock in the morning, and only to leave the church late at night; it was his zeal that robbed him almost completely of sleep, and that enabled him to preserve an unfailing patience

39. Catherine Lassagne, Petit *mémoire,* première rédaction, p. 7.
40. Mlle. Marthe des Garets, *Procès apostolique in genere,* p. 297.
41. *Procès de l'Ordinaire,* p. 584.
42. *Ibid.,* pp. 780-781.
43. *Procès apostolique ne pereant,* p. 301.

in the midst of the most trying importunities." Thus M. le Comte des Garets, Mayor of Ars.[44]

Let it not be imagined, however, that the gentleness with which M. Vianney welcomed sinners degenerated at any time into weakness. He absolved them only after he had assured himself of the sincerity of their contrition. Until 1840 he certainly followed the *rigorism* which at that time prevailed in most of the confessionals in France. He still applied the principles that were taught in 1815 in the Grand Séminaire of Lyons. From 1840 onwards, thanks to some conversations with M. Tailhades, a pious priest, and one inclined to leniency; thanks to the counsels of M. Camelet, superior of the diocesan missionaries, who, whilst evangelizing the country, had acquired a profound experience of souls; above all, thanks to a study of the theology of St. Alphonsus, which had just been published in French by Cardinal Gousset, the Curé d'Ars showed himself sensibly less strict:[45] barring quite extraordinary cases, it never again happened, as it had in former days, that the same sinner was compelled to return to his confessional as often as five, six, or seven times. Moreover, so many Confessions had shown him "the misery of man"; it was the object of his most profound pity; he understood at last that when dealing with men kindness is required above all else. "As we advance in life," the saintly Cardinal Richard said, "we have not the conception of virtue which we had formed when we were younger."[46]

However, to the very end of his life, before he would consent to absolve an inveterate sinner, M. Vianney always insisted on adequate signs of conversion. According to the testimony of a priest, "those who obstinately refused to give up circumstances which for them constituted a state of damnation, found him inexorable. He rigorously imposed the necessary sacrifices. Thus he obliged a lady of Paris

44. *Procès de l'Ordinaire,* p. 958.
45. The interpretations of St. Alphonsus must have come to his knowledge by word of mouth or, maybe, someone lent him the works of that eminent moralist. The edition of Gousset *(Théologie morale à l'usage des curés et des confesseurs,* 2 vols. in 8, Paris, Lecoffre), which the Curé d'Ars had on his bookshelves, bears the date 1845.
46. Mgr. Odelin, *Le Cardinal Richard,* Paris, de Gigord, p. 25.

to consign to the flames all the bad books in her library before he consented to give her absolution.

Another lady, likewise of Paris, passed through Ars on her way home from the South, where she had been on a holiday. A priest who knew of her irregular life had suggested that break in the journey: "There, madame, you will see something altogether out of the common: a country priest whose name is known throughout the world. You will not regret having gone out of your way." Now this prophecy came true in a strange manner. In the course of the afternoon the lady was walking up and down in the village square with a stranger whom she had chanced to meet. M. Vianney passed them on his return from a sick-call. "You, madame," he said to the Parisian lady, "follow me"; and to the other: "You may go, you have no need of my ministrations." Having taken the sinful woman apart, he revealed to that new Samaritan all her shameful life. Thunderstruck at such penetration, she kept silence. At last she said: "M, le Curé, will you hear my Confession?"

"Your Confession would be useless," was his reply. "I can read in your soul, and there I see two devils that enslave it, the devil of pride and the devil of impurity. I can only absolve you on condition that you do not go back to Paris, and, seeing your dispositions, I know that you will return thither."

And then, in the spirit of prophecy, the man of God showed her how she would sink down to the very lowest depths of evil.

"But, Monsieur le Curé, I am incapable of committing abominations such as these! So I am damned!"

"I do not say that, but, from now onwards, how hard it will be for you to save your soul!"

"What, then, must I do?"

"Come tomorrow morning and I will tell you."

During the night that followed, that he might prevent the loss of a soul which God had created for the heights, but which was engulfed in the mire, the Curé d'Ars prayed for a long time and scourged himself to the blood.

In the morning he admitted this unusual penitent before her turn and gave her his answer:

"Well, you will leave Paris against your will, to return to the house from which you have now come. There, if you wish to save your poor soul, you must practice such-and-such mortifications."

The lady departed from Ars without absolution. For a moment Paris claimed her once more, and she saw with horror that the abyss of sin was again yawning under her feet. Seized with loathing, she cried to God and fled. Hiding herself in her villa on the Mediterranean, she resolved to pursue the straight road, notwithstanding the rebelliousness of a nature spoiled by passions that she had too long gratified. She recalled to memory the counsels of the Curé d'Ars. A strong interior grace spurred her on and helped her to carry them into practice. "On the road of abnegation," M. Vianney was wont to say, "it is only the first step that is difficult; once we have started we go on almost mechanically."[47] Our penitent had the happiness of experiencing the truth of those words. "At the end of three months," says Chanoine Ball, who collected the details of this story, "her conversion was so complete, the dispositions of her mind and heart were so profoundly altered, that she felt unable to understand how she ever could have loved that which now filled her with such loathing."[48]

When once the Curé d'Ars had obtained from his penitents the indispensable signs of amendment, he showed himself exceedingly gentle in the application of the sacramental penance. "They reproach me with it," he confided to Frère Athanase, "but can I really be hard on people who come from so far, and who, in order to do so, have made so many sacrifices?"[49] "Were I to impose severer penances, I should discourage them," he said another time. "But how can we strike a happy middle course in this matter?" a brother priest inquired. "My friend," the saint

47. *Spirit of the Curé d'Ars,* p. 209.
48. Archives of the presbytery of Ars.
49. *Procès de l'Ordinaire,* p. 832.

replied, "here is my receipt: I give them a small penance and the remainder I myself perform in their stead."[50] We can guess what that must have meant.

Nevertheless, M. Vianney by no means forgot that the sacramental penance must be *medicinal.* In this matter the saint exhibited great ability in touching the weak spot: such a sin had to be expiated, such a defect had to be corrected—very well, an appropriate expiation must be undertaken.

In the case of young people capable of attaining to great heights of virtue, vanity and unconscious pride may just prove the one obstacle on the road of perfection. In such souls M. Vianney sought to cut asunder the last remaining ties of self-love. A choice soul, but of excessive sensitiveness, Mlle. Caroline Lioger, of Lyons, who, under the name of Mère Marie-Véronique, was to become the foundress of the "Soeurs Victimes du Sacré-Coeur," came with her mother several years in succession, to stay for a time at Ars. Now M. Vianney sought to fit this young girl for a great mission, and with this end in view he took pleasure in testing her humility, and he did so unsparingly. Among other things, he commanded her to kneel on the threshold of the church, with her arms extended crosswise, at the time when people came out from Mass.[51]

Generally speaking, men sin a great deal through human respect. The Curé d'Ars, after hearing their Confession, used to tell them to go into the church to pray publicly.

"What a touching sight it was," writes the Abbé Raymond, "to see white-haired men, who had deserted the Church, neglected prayer and devotion to Mary, holding their rosary proudly and reciting it with fervor. Not one of them could remain deaf to the injunction of the holy priest, always to carry a rosary on their person, and to make use of it. It was useless for a man to object that he no longer knew how to use it; that, after all, he was able to read. . . . 'My friend,' M. Vianney would reply, 'a good Christian is always armed with his rosary: mine

50. *Procès de l'Ordinaire,* p. 1140.
51. *"Le Curé d'Ars et la Mère Véronique," Annales d'Ars,* Juillet, 1904, p. 62.

never leaves me; go and buy one. I will attach to it the indulgences of which you are in such great need in order to supplement an inadequate penance.' In fact, he generally presented the men with a rosary, which all accepted as a precious keepsake."[52]

"Do you live in your native town?" the Curé d'Ars asked after hearing the Confession of M. Georges L____, a worldly young man of twenty-six years of age.

"Yes, Father."

"What is its population?"

"Twenty-five thousand inhabitants."

"You are known there?"

"Quite well, and by nearly everybody."

"Very well, my child. For your penance you will say, before you leave this church, the acts of faith, hope, and charity. That is not all. On one of the two Sundays, when the procession of Corpus Christi takes place in your town, you will walk in the procession, taking care to secure a place immediately behind the canopy. Go, my child." The young man did not dare to protest: surprise and emotion held his lips. Now he was a victim to human respect; but he had the faith: here was his penance! When the Sunday of the first procession arrived, he put it off until the following week. When that day came round, the rain, for which he had hoped, refused to fall; so there was nothing for it but to obey. "Were I to live a hundred years," he stated later on, "I should never forget those two hours spent by me walking behind the canopy. Cold perspiration bathed my forehead; my knees shook under me. From time to time I roused my faith and endeavored to pray. My lips alone uttered the words of the liturgy." But this act of courage drew on him the attention of his Catholic fellow-citizens. Two years later, when he had become a fearless Christian, he found himself at the head of a conference of St. Vincent de Paul, which comprised thirty young men, every one of whom had been won over by his example.[53]

---

52. *Vie MSS.*, p. 168.
53. *Documents,* Ball (Archives of the presbytery of Ars).

When we remember the weakness of human nature we can understand that it would have been too much to expect that all M. Vianney's penitents would display the perseverance of this young man. Yet we may take it for granted that in nearly every instance the impression made was so deep, the blow dealt by grace so strong, that they remained faithful to duty. It is certain that the saint triumphed in cases of extreme difficulty and obtained perseverance in instances where, as a rule, one dared not so much as hope for it.

"M. Niermont, Superior of the Grand Séminaire of Brou, asked me one day," the Abbé Toccanier relates, "to question M. le Curé as to whether he had ever converted a drunkard. I carried out my commission in the sacristy, in the presence of several witnesses. This is the answer I received: 'Yes, my friend, only quite recently a woman came to thank me in the following terms: "Until lately I lived very unhappily with my husband; I received more blows than kind words. Well, since he has been to see you he has become as meek as a lamb."' A vicaire who had listened to this account related in his turn a similar case: a man of his parish, formerly addicted to drink, had recourse, since his pilgrimage to Ars, to heroic means to bring about his amendment. When he went to Mass he always went a long way round, so as to avoid passing the tavern, the sight of which was a constant temptation to him."[54]

In the *Procès,* Mgr. Mermod, who was curé of Gex at the time, relates the following incident: "An incorrigible drunkard of Chaleins, my former parish, was converted by M. Vianney. During the three years that he lived afterwards that man never drank a drop of wine, and led an exemplary life. Now a striking thing happened. One day the good man called at the presbytery; he was quite well, yet he wished to go to Confession, giving as his reason that he was going to die. As he persisted in his request, I gave him absolution and Holy Communion. An hour later he was dead."[55]

54. Abbé Toccanier, *Procès apostolique in genere,* p. 153.
55. *Procès apostolique ne pereant,* p. 951.

Thanks to the Curé d'Ars, divided households recovered their harmony, proud skeptics became humble believers, libertines died like the predestined or sought the holy solitude of the cloister.

An architect of Lyons was frequently the object of only too well-deserved reproaches on the part of his wife. One morning, after a sharp quarrel, the guilty husband exclaimed: "You shall not see me again!"On this he slammed the door and went out into the square. There he saw an omnibus that had just come to a standstill; it bore the inscription: *Correspondance d'Ars.*[56] "What place is that?" he asked a passer-by. Ars, he was told, was a village in the Ain to which people went in order to see an extraordinary curé. Feeling that he needed a change to calm his nerves, even more than to satisfy his curiosity, the man took his place in the coach, which started almost immediately. The moment of departure was arranged so as to enable travellers to reach Ars a short time before the eleven o'clock catechism.

Our architect entered the church, saw the saint, and listened to his words. When he came out he was profoundly moved by what he had seen and heard. "Monsieur," he said to the Abbé Toccanier with whom he presently fell in, "that priest is so plunged in the love of God, his words are so burning, that, if I hear him another time, *I, too, shall take the plunge* just like the others!" The good missionary assured him that he saw no objection to such a course, far from it. In the afternoon the man took up his post in the queue of penitents. When he issued from the sacristy he felt transformed and the happiest of mortals; he hastened back to Lyons, where, like the prodigal, he threw himself into the arms of the woman who was *not to have seen him again.* He was, in fact, no longer the same man.[57]

Some twelve or fifteen years earlier—it was certainly before M. Toccanier's appointment to Ars—another conversion had caused a great stir in the city of Lyons. M. Mais-

56. Coach connecting with Ars.
57. Abbé Toccanier, *Procès apostolique in genere,* p. 152.

siat, a drawing-master in the school of Arts and Crafts, was likewise a geologist of note; he loved to describe himself as a *philosopher,* by which he meant to let people know that he was guided by reason alone. His first Communion was made devoutly, at the very height of the Terror, but he subsequently abandoned the Catholic Faith to embrace in turn the tenets of Mohammedanism, Judaism, Protestantism, spiritualism, Saint-Simonianism, and finally communism. His life was truly a romance.

One day in June, 1841, our *philosopher* set out from Lyons for a month's tour among the hills of the Beaujolais. In the coach for Villefranche-sur-Saône he met an old friend who was going from that town to Ars. "Come with me," the friend said; "you shall see a priest who works miracles."

"Miracles!" the geologist exclaimed with a sneer, "I do not believe in them."

"Come, I say, you shall both see and believe."

"Very well! I do not mind making a trip to Ars!"And, playing on the words, he added: "*Ars* is a name that pleases me, for I am an *artist.*"

The following morning M. Maissiat, out of curiosity, assisted at M. Vianney's Mass. On his way from the sacristy to the altar the saint fixed his glance on the skeptic. Mass was no sooner over than he made straight for him, and, placing his bony hand on his shoulder, signed to the man to follow him. On entering the sacristy our philosopher beheld the confessional, but when a gesture of the Curé invited him to kneel down in it: "Oh! as for that," he exclaimed, "no!" All this time the man of God never took his eyes off him. M. Maissiat finally went on his knees. After all, what did it matter? He was alone with that priest; so he might as well tell him coldly, like a man who relates a tale, the miserable story of his soul. The holy confessor listened, but without any illusion as to the real feelings of this strange penitent. "My friend, come back and talk to me tomorrow. In the meantime go before the altar of St. Philomena and tell her to ask Our Lord for your conversion."

M. Maissiat uttered no protest, but went and stood erect on the appointed spot. But, oh mystery! Suddenly he was overcome with tears. Why? He could not explain. Rushing through the crowd, he left the church bathed in tears. "Oh! what sweetness there was in those tears!" he subsequently confessed.

There was no longer question of the projected trip to the hills of the Beaujolais. On the following morning the geologist found himself once more at the feet of the Curé d'Ars. "Father," he said, already overcome by grace, "I do not believe in anything. . . . Help me!" And the saint helped him so effectively that after nine days spent with him, M. Maissiat returned to Lyons full of faith. The Abbé Raymond, who knew him well, assures us that when he rejoined his colleagues, who did not share his beliefs, he set human respect at defiance and proved himself one of the most fervent and zealous Catholics of Lyons. Another of his friends, M. Gaillard, curé of Montagnat, tells us that he died in the beautiful dispositions which can only spring from Christian piety.[58]

About the middle of November, 1855, a young man of Clermont-l'Hérault, Sylvain Dutheil by name, and his mother, took rooms at the hotel Pertinand. At the age of only sixteen Sylvain had enlisted in the army, but in consequence of his excesses, he contracted a pulmonary disease that compelled him to return home. Some strange occurrences had impelled him to undertake the long and painful journey to Ars.

"One day, as he passed through a street of Montpellier," Frère Athanase relates, "the young man noticed a portrait of the Curé d'Ars and made fun of it. His sister, who was with him, rebuked him, and when she added: 'You might obtain your cure were you to put your trust in that holy man!' the young man scoffed only the more. That night the holy Curé appeared to him, holding in his hand an apple more than half rotten. The dream made an impression on the youth, and he asked to be taken to Ars.

58. *Procès de l'Ordinaire,* pp. 1427-1429, and Abbé Raymond, *Vie MSS.,* p. 158.

"His mother took him thither. Every day M. Vianney visited him at the hotel. On the morning of December 8, the feast of the Immaculate Conception, Sylvain, at last converted and absolved from his sins, was carried to the foot of the altar. The temperature was icy cold. After his Communion the sick man, now quite exhausted, was carried into the sacristy and placed near the stove. 'Oh! how happy I am,' he exclaimed; 'never in all my life have I felt such happiness.'

"When he had been taken back to the hotel, he threw himself into the arms of his mother and told her amid his tears: 'The joy of this Communion makes me forget all my sufferings. I do not wish to leave this holy man; I want to die here!' He did, in fact, die that same night."[59]

In 1859 an old boatman on the river Saône, who was a hardened sinner, was inveigled into the village. When he beheld the church full of pilgrims and the confessional beleaguered by penitents, he understood that he had been tricked, so he started cursing, and was for leaving on the spot. The objection was raised that the hour was late, that, willy nilly, he would be forced to spend the night in the hateful village. In the meantime someone had succeeded in letting M. Vianney know of the arrival of this "big fish."

At nightfall the Curé d'Ars called at the room occupied by the boatman. "I have not come here to play the devotee," shouted the infuriated man. "Leave me in peace! I am anxious to be off."

"So you do not want to have pity on your soul, my friend," was M. Vianney's gentle reply, whilst at the same time he grasped his hand.

Having uttered these simple words, he left him. What happened during the night? No one knows; but in the morning the saint found *his* sinner, weeping and grasping a crucifix. "His conversion was a complete and signal one." M. Vianney told him—at least so rumor had it—that confessor and penitent would follow each other to

59. *Procès de l'Ordinaire,* p. 871.

the grave. Be this as it may, "shortly after the death of the servant of God the old boatman was found kneeling on his bed, dead."[60]

One day during the autumn of 1852 François Dorel, a plasterer, of Villefranche-sur-Saône, was walking with a friend on the road to Ars. Dorel was a jovial young man of thirty-two years. No one seeing him, accoutred as he was, would have taken him for a pilgrim. Gaitered, with a gun slung over his shoulder, he whistled every now and again to a magnificent hound. The fact was that our man had no desire at all to be taken for a devotee in quest of a confessor. His friend had casually asked him the day before: "Will you come to Ars tomorrow? There is a curé there who works miracles, and who hears Confessions night and day. It is worth seeing."

"So you, too, have a mind to? . . ."

"Eh? why not?"

"As you like. Listen: I am willing enough to go with you, but I shall take my gun and my dog. And after seeing that wonderful curé, I shall shoot a few ducks on the ponds of La Dombes. As for you, well, if it gives you pleasure, you may go to Confession!"

The two travellers entered the village just in time to see the Curé cross the square between two rows of pilgrims. He advanced slowly, as usual, blessing the people. François Dorel, full of curiosity, had mingled with the crowd. What a surprise awaited him! When he came to him, the holy old man stood still, and, looking in turn at the dog and the sportsman, he gravely said to the stranger: "Monsieur, it is greatly to be wished that your soul were as beautiful as your dog!"

The man blushed and hung his head. His dog had remained what God had made him, faithful; but he, a Christian, had spoiled the work of God in his soul! Terrified by this unexpected revelation, he reflected for a long time. At last, entrusting to some villagers both gun and dog, he entered the church and went to Confession

60. *Procès apostolique in genere,* p. 153.

to M. Vianney. "Such was his repentance that he burst into tears. Realizing at last the value of his soul, the vanity of the world, and the seriousness of life, he decided to enter religion. "Go to La Trappe!" the Curé d'Ars told him authoritatively. Thus it came about that on December 18, 1852, François Dorel presented himself at Notre Dame d'Aiguebelle, where he took the habit a year later; after a delay of sixteen years he made his solemn profession under the name of Frère Arsène. He died a holy death on December 18, 1888.[61]

61. From an *Account* of eight Trappist vocations inspired by the Curé d'Ars, addressed to Mgr. Convert on May 21, 1901, by the Abbot of Aiguebelle.

Chapter 15

THE PILGRIMAGE TO ARS *(continued)* IV. The Curé d'Ars as a Spiritual Director

VERY fascinating pages might be written on the way in which M. Vianney treated souls according as they were only just given to piety or already advanced in perfection.

A few instances are quoted, it is true, when he refused to hear the Confessions of persons whom he knew to be in a state of grace.

"One of my aunts, a Marist Sister," the Abbé Rougemont relates, "came with her superior to ask his advice on a matter that concerned their community. Even before they opened their mouths he told them what line of action they were to take, but when they expressed a wish to go to Confession, the holy Curé said: "You do not need it; leave the time free for those who do."

In January, 1853, Mlle. Claire Dechamps came with her uncle, the Cardinal Archbishop of Mechlin, to consult him. He allowed her to make the Sign of the Cross, when he suddenly said: "Yes, my child, you are destined for the community of the Sacré-Coeur; go to Holy Communion without absolution." And she went full of joy.[1]

Cases of this kind were exceptional, and the Curé d'Ars had his reasons for acting thus. To all his penitents he gave the necessary minutes, even to children towards whom he showed himself genial and fatherly. The two Abbés Lémann, converts from Judaism, confessed them-

1. *Memoire* of M. l'Abbé François, chaplain to the Redemptoristines of Grenoble (Archives of the presbytery of Ars).

selves to him in their youth. "During those moments," they relate, "he allowed us to hide our faces against his long white hair; we wished to have the happiness of being, as it were, impregnated with his sanctity."[2]

However harassed he may have been, "he never encountered an ignorant person whom he did not enlighten, nor a just soul that he did not encourage and urge on towards perfection."

The holiness of his life and the superhuman wisdom of his decisions inspired the souls of the devout with unbounded trustfulness. "In the course of my work as vicaire at Ars," the Abbé Claude Rougemont declares, "I have met with a number of persons who looked upon M. Vianney as an unequalled and divinely inspired director," and Mme. Christine de Cibeins declared that, "in the confessional as in the pulpit he was to me both the law and the prophets."[3]

His directions, as a rule, were clear and prompt: "He would lift his eyes to heaven, and then give his decision not only without hesitation but with much assurance."[4] People, however, consulted him on such a variety of topics that he occasionally appealed for time either for personal reflection or to take counsel with a brother priest. "Although I was quite a young priest at the time," the Abbé Dufour relates, "he was humble enough one day to ask for my advice on a question of restitution that he had to solve."

More than one penitent of the Cure d'Ars felt disappointed because they had hoped to hear extraordinary things from him. His decisions were free from all excitement or exaggeration; they were characterized by wisdom and circumspection. He was able to disentangle the secret motives, conscious or unconscious, of certain aspirations, certain dreams, and he helped souls to find their level. A certain girl longed for the cloister: he asked her to settle down in the world; before the eyes of another

2. *Letter* to Mgr. Convert, August 11, 1908.
3. *Procès apostolique continuatif,* p. 155.
4. *Ibid.,* p. 137.

who deemed herself called to the married state, he opened wider, more serene horizons. He urged souls forward or kept them back, according to the exigencies of each particular case.

Moreover, he refrained from offering advice when he was aware that others might have more authority to give it. Thus, when a lady of Grenoble asked him whether or no, in order to pay for the education of her children, she might open a café, he sent her to her own parish priest.[5]

Mlle. Louise Martin, of Saint-Rambert, Ain, a lively and even frolicsome but noble-hearted girl, had at the age of eighteen, felt an attraction towards the religious life. Her parents called her foolish. One day she went to pay a visit to some cousins, who were boarders at the convent of the Visitandines of Montluel. On entering the parlor she caught a glimpse of the grille of the cloister. "Oh!" she exclaimed, "it is not I who would care to live in there!" Shortly after this visit she felt troubled, and anxiously asked herself: "What if, after all, God is calling me to a convent of contemplative nuns?" Her grandmother had been made the confidant of these interior struggles. With her, unknown to her parents, she set out for Ars. After a long period of waiting in the church, her turn came at last to enter the confessional. Alas! at that very instant M. Vianney came out of it, to go into the sacristy, for it was St. Mark's day, April 25, 1843, and he was to take part in the procession. Louise Martin rushed after him: "M. le Curé, I want to receive Holy Communion at your Mass, and I have not been to Confession." At that moment the crowd that filled the church overflowed even into the sacristy, so that its door could only be shut with difficulty.

"Are you self-conscious?" the holy Curé smilingly asked the girl.

"Oh! no, Father."

"Very well, kneel down and make your Confession."

She made her Confession, told him of her anxieties. . . .

5. *Ibid,,* p. 854.

"Your vocation comes from Heaven, my child. Enter at once at the Visitation."

Louise's parents resisted no longer, and Sister Marie Anastasie gave herself to God with all her ardent nature.[6]

About the year 1836 M. and Mme. Millet, of Mâcon, decided to spend a few days at Ars in order to confer at leisure, as they imagined, with the holy Curé. In fact they did succeed in obtaining an interview; but their daughter, Louise-Colombe, whom they had taken with them, would not on any account approach the servant of God. Yet she was a good and pious girl. When the pilgrims were about to leave Ars after a week's stay, they went to pay a last visit to the church. M. Vianney was just then entering the sacristy. Prompted by a supernatural intuition, he cast a searching glance upon the crowd, and finally pointed his breviary in the direction of Louise Millet. She understood; there was nothing for it but to surrender. The crowd made way for her to pass. The saint pointed to the confessional. The girl fell on her knees, and, after a brief conversation, she heard the words that gave to her life its true direction: "My child, you will be a religious of the Visitation, at home, in your own town. The good God wills it . . . the good God wills it!" The penitent protested in vain, for the third time the Curé repeated: "My child, the good God wills it!" The difficulties that had to be overcome seemed wellnigh insurmountable, yet they vanished of their own accord, and, freed from every earthly tie, Louise-Colombe took wings like a dove and flew into the ark.[7]

A young girl, destined to become Sister Marie-Mechtilde, at the Ursuline Convent of Avignon, was at school at Troyes when, in July, 1856, a relative came to fetch her to make a visit to Ars. "At the moment of departure," so she herself related in 1916, "I met a friend who told me in confidence: 'I am glad you are going there; the holy

6. Extract from the *Circular Letters of the Visitation of Montluel (Annales d'Ars,* August, 1909, p. 94).

7. *Circular Letter of the Visitation of Mâcon,* November 21, 1910. Sister Louise-Colombe Millet died in the monastery on August 20, 1908, full of merits and years, for she was eighty-nine years of age and had been sixty-four years professed.

Curé will tell you what is your vocation. He told me mine.' 'Father, I have brought you a little blue-stocking.' That was how I was introduced to M. Vianney. He replied: 'So much the worse! One act of the love of God is worth more than all that.' 'But, Father, what will become of the child?' queried my relative. At these words the saint looked at me for a while; he seemed to read the secrets of my soul in my eyes. 'A religious,' he said at last.

"I exclaimed quickly and with vivacity, knowing that it would mean leaving my mother, my brother, and my beloved studies: 'No, never! no, no, no!' But he, smiling indulgently at my repeated *'noes,'* exclaimed in his turn: 'Yes, yes, yes!' I then followed him into the confessional. My only thought had been to win diplomas; he gave another turn to my mind and to my heart.

"Three years later, in 1859, the very year of his holy death, I made my profession, and now I have been a religious for the space of fifty-eight years."[8]

In this way did the Curé d'Ars direct towards the summits good, but weak or troubled souls, who, but for him, would have failed to give themselves wholly to God. But, skillful in discerning the plans of Providence, he dispelled the dreams of an illusory perfection entertained by certain generous souls.

"I saw," writes the Abbé Dufour, "a colonel in uniform serve his Mass and accompany him, candle in hand, whilst he distributed Holy Communion. Afterwards the officer asked him whether he should not enter religion, seeing that he was not engaged in the bonds of matrimony. "Be sure you do no such thing," replied the servant of God, "the army has too great a need of an example such as you give."[9]

"Father," a priest besought him as he knelt at his feet, "shall I foster in my soul the desire for the religious life which I have felt so keenly ever since my second year at the Grand Séminaire—that is, for close on twenty years?"

---

8. *Letter* written to Mgr. Convert, in 1916, by Sister Marie-Mechtilde, at the Ursuline Convent, via Nomentana, Rome.
9. *Procès apostolique in genere,* p. 341.

He answered unhesitatingly: "Yes, my friend, that thought is of God, and you should cherish it."

"In that case, Father, you give me leave to resign the post I hold" (the priest was a professor at a Petit Séminaire) "and to enter a religious Order? And which one, if you please?"

"Not so quickly, my friend! Stay where you are. You see, the good God at times inspires us with desires of which he will never ask the fulfillment in this world."

And he made the priest, who was engaged in the work of education, realize that his aspirations towards the monastic life were of this kind; and that, if they were carefully cherished in his heart, they would prove both a preservative against worldliness and a stimulus to the practice of every priestly virtue. Three years later, still tormented by the attraction of the cloister, the same priest returned to the charge. From the Petit Séminaire he had been transferred to a Catholic college. "Now that I am there, what do you advise, Father?" The Saint smilingly replied: "Exactly the same thing!" And, in a graver tone, he added: "Be sure you never become a curé. The most beautiful task anyone can perform in the century in which we live is the Christian education of youth."[10]

Many persons asked the Cure d'Ars to guide them in their choice of devotions. He was an enemy to the little devotions which encumber certain lives and render them fruitless, for he discovered in them a measure of egotism in disguise. The recitation of the Rosary, the *Angelus,* ejaculatory prayers, above all, assistance at Mass and other services—these practices, which the Church has approved and recommended, were also those he extolled. He preferred public to private prayers. "Private prayer," he used to say, "resembles straw scattered here and there over a field; if it is set on fire, the flame is not a powerful one; but if you gather those scattered straws into a bundle, the flame is bright, and rises in

10. From a *Letter* addressed on September 1, 1864, to R. P. Faivre, missionary of Saint-Claude, by M. l'Abbé Cornu, Superior, at the time, of the Petit Séminaire of Nozeroy (Jura).

a lofty column towards the sky: such is public prayer."[11]

M. Vianney likewise endeavored to inculcate upon souls eager to go forward on the road of perfection the habit of daily mental prayer, and he taught them how to go about it. To those who felt unable to apply themselves to methodical meditations he simply recommended to think frequently of God. "He drew my attention," says Marthe Miard, the little shopkeeper, "to the fact that I had in my house so many statues of Our Lady, so many pious objects, that I had only to look at them to find inspiration for my prayers."[12] If he were asked what reading would help the soul's advancement, he recommended the *Gospel,* the *Imitation of Christ,* and the *Lives of the Saints.*[13]

It is likewise noteworthy that the prudent director invariably commanded all persons, without distinction, to begin by doing that which is of obligation. "It would be impossible to say," writes Mlle. de Belvey, "with what admirable judgement he discerned the need in each individual case, whether of precept, obligation, or simply of counsel: he rejected what was prompted by self-love or was but the inspiration of ill-regulated zeal."[14] What he taught in his catechisms he repeated in the confessional:

"Religion is sometimes misunderstood. For instance, my children, here is a person who has to do a day's work. She has an idea of performing great penances, to spend

---

11. Baronne de Belvey, *Procès de l'Ordinaire,* p. 206. In order to make sure of a good sale several devotional books were published under the name of M. Vianney, notably one entitled *Considérations sur la nécessité de connaître Jésus Christ et d'imiter ses vertus* (Lyon, Guyot, 1851). The publisher, perhaps himself deceived about the identity of the author, was bold enough to say in his short preface: "The favorable reception recently given to the *Guide des âmes pieuses* of M. le Curé d'Ars, and the considerable sale it obtained, are sufficient guarantee of the success which is sure to be achieved by this new work which he kindly permits us to bring out."

The *Guide des âmes pieuses* had for its author M. Peyronnet, Chanoine of Fourvière.

The truth is that "M. Vianney allowed the inclusion in the *Guide des âmes pieuses* of three or four prayers written at his dictation by Catherine Lassagne. He had likewise composed a prayer to be said by priests on taking possession of their parishes." (Baronne de Belvey, *Procès de l'Ordinaire,* pp. 258 and 202).

12. *Procès apostolique continuatif,* p. 845.
13. *Procès de l'Ordinaire,* p. 738.
14. *Ibid.,* p. 228.

half the night in prayer; if she is well instructed she will say to herself: 'No, I must not do these things or I shall not be fit to do my duty tomorrow: I shall be sleepy, and the least thing will make me irritable; I shall be cross all day; I shall not do half the work I should have done had I had a night's rest.' A well instructed person always has two guides: counsel and obedience."

"M. le Curé," says Catherine Lassagne, "would not have a mother neglect the management of her house on the plea of going to church when there was no obligation to do so. On one occasion, at the beginning of Lent, he forbade me to fast." "But you, M. le Curé," I replied, "you fast." "That is true," he replied, "but though I fast I can do my work, but you would not be able to do yours."[15]

Married people were shown the nobility of their calling, and he exhorted them to fulfill holily its duties. A lady of the name of Ruet, of Ouroux, in the *département* of the Rhône, had already a large family, and was about to become a mother once more. She came to Ars in order to seek courage at the feet of its holy Curé. She had not long to wait, for M. Vianney summoned her from amid the crowd. "You look very sad, my child," he said, when she was on her knees in his confessional. "Oh! I am so advanced in years, Father!" "Be comforted, my child. . . . If you only knew the women who will go to Hell because they did not bring into the world the children they should have given to it!"

"Come now, my little one," he said with fatherly kindliness to a woman who confided to him her anxiety because of her large family, "do not be alarmed at your burden; Our Lord carries it with you. The good God does well all that He does: when He gives many children to a young mother it is that He deems her worthy to rear them. It is a mark of confidence on His part."

As for his brother priests, M. Vianney besought them to strive unhesitatingly after the perfection of the evangelical counsels. From some whom he deemed capable of

15. *Ibid.*, p. 498.

making them, he at times exacted sacrifices, small enough apparently, yet important, doubtless, in the eyes of God and His servant. A priest, who has since become a religious of the Sacré-Coeur d'Issoudun, made a retreat under the guidance of the Curé. As he came to the end of his Confession he asked himself: "Shall I accuse myself of that?" as he thought of the hours of leisure he spent in playing cards with other priests. To satisfy his conscience he mentioned the matter just as it was.

"You must not do that," said the holy confessor. "But, Father, a game may be a lesser evil. When we meet. . . ."

"Oh! in that case, there is no need to meet." "But, Father, at times one is called upon to render service to a brother priest—and afterwards. . . ."

"When the service has been rendered one comes away."

The saint's decisions were short, clear, and uncompromising. The penitent on the other side of the grille could not make up his mind, for such strictness appeared to him untraditional and beyond his strength when, raising his head,

"Very well, Father, I promise you never again to play, but you will help me by your prayers."

"That will do!" replied M. Vianney, and he gave him absolution. On leaving the confessional the penitent entered the chapel of St. Philomena, and there wrote down his resolution, resting his notebook on the altar. A short time afterwards, when his accustomed partners invited him to take a hand at cards, he said: "I will look on for a while, but I shall not play; I have just come from Ars, and I promised M. le Curé to give up playing." Not another word was uttered.[16]

Obviously, under different circumstances, the saint recommended to priests sacrifices of a more heroic kind. One day a parish priest came to him lamenting the indifference of his people and the fruitlessness of his labors. M. Vianney replied in words that may sound harsh, but he to whom they were addressed was, no doubt, strong

16. *Annales d'Ars,* February, 1901, p. 269.

enough to bear them: "You have preached, you have prayed; but have you fasted? Have you taken the discipline? Have you slept on the bare floor? So long as you have done none of these things you have no right to complain."

With the scrupulous the saint insisted on trust in God and obedience to the confessor. "As a matter of fact, one word from him was enough to restore calm to anxious and troubled souls. The fearful and timorous were roused to action and self-sacrifice. Adèle Conil, a young woman of Mormoiron (Vaucluse) had been offered the honor of acting as godmother. The exiguous responsibilities of the office alarmed her—though it must be said that in those days these duties were taken more seriously than they are today, as was only right. The girl refused. Not long afterwards she made a pilgrimage to Ars, and went to Confession to the holy curé. 'You have not done well in refusing to be sponsor,' M. Vianney told her, although there had been no allusion at all to a baptism; 'my child, we must not be afraid of doing good, even if it costs us something. Come now! another time you will do better.'"[17]

Before all else M. Vianney urged pious souls to a frequent reception of the Sacraments. He used to say that "all those who receive them are not saints, but the saints are always taken from the ranks of those who receive them frequently."[18] Thus at a time when frequent Communion was almost unknown in France, he became one of the first promoters of that holy practice.[19] But here also he ever acted wisely; he wished people to make an earnest preparation for, and endeavor to draw as much fruit as possible from, the Sacraments. And, since neither absolution nor Communion can make up for a lack of personal effort in fighting against our nature, he always showed himself rather severe with recidivists. Nor could he put up with lukewarmness in the soul of a Christian. "Thus, then, my poor child," he said to a lady of Lyons,

17. *Annales d'Ars,* September, 1919, p. 111.
18. Jeanne-Marie Chanay, *Procès de l'Ordinaire,* p. 686.
19. *Procès apostolique ne pereant,* p. 282.

"you do not want to be converted? You go to Holy Communion, but there is no amendment in your life! You remain always the same, hot-headed, passionate!" The lady's daughter related the incident, and she added: "My poor mother shook in all her limbs as she perceived that the Curé d'Ars had read her soul clearly. When she at last dared to raise her eyes, which were full of tears, she thought M. Vianney's face was all on fire."[20]

One morning in 1845 Mlle. Etiennette Poignard, of Marcy, near Villefranche-sur-Saône, took her place, with a few cheery girl friends of hers, in a conveyance bound for Ars. They chatted during the whole of the journey. Etiennette, who was a pious girl, went straight to the church, where M. Vianney was just beginning his Mass. At the moment of the Communion she went and knelt at the altar rail. The Curé gave Holy Communion to those who knelt there, but when he came to the young girl he took a Host, raised it above the ciborium, and began the formula: *Corpus Domini nostri . . .* when, without finishing the sentence, he stood quite still.

The girl suffered indescribable anguish. The man of God wished to give her a lesson for the whole of her life. Not knowing what to do, she mentally made the acts of faith, hope, and charity. When she had ended, the Curé d'Ars placed the Host on her tongue and passed on. "My child," he said, when he met her again, "a person who has not said her morning prayers and who has been frivolous the whole time of the journey, is not very well prepared for Holy Communion!"[21]

Before admitting people to frequent Communion, over and above a certain degree of piety, M. Vianney likewise required sufficient knowledge. Mme. Maduel, of Lurcy, a pious but rather ignorant person, once asked him, before receiving absolution, for permission to receive Holy Communion several times a week. "Yes, my good woman," the saint replied, "but for your penance you will go to *your*

---

20. *Documents,* Ball (Archives of the presbytery).
21. This fact is taken from an oral account of Mlle. Marie Brizard, of Ars, an intimate friend of Mlle. Etiennette Poignard.

curé"—and he emphasized those words. "You will ask him to explain to you the teaching of the catechism on Holy Communion and on the dispositions you should bring to it."

Rather than be catechized by her parish priest, the poor woman would have wished to forego frequent Communion. But it was *her penance!* Willy nilly, she must address herself to M. Bernard, curé of Lurcy. With a view to sparing the susceptibilities of his parishioner, M. Bernard contented himself with lending her two books on spirituality and pointing out the chapters she was to read. She read and pondered them. "Ah!" she said to M. Bernard when returning the books, "how glad I am that I was given such a penance! In this way I have learned things of which I had no notion and which will be of the greatest help to me."

M. Bernard subsequently related this incident to some brother priests who reproached the Curé d'Ars with being ignorant of the science of direction and with pandering to the whims and fancies of false devotees.

On the other hand, when he met with true piety, M. Vianney was lavish in encouragements. He loved to whet the spiritual appetite of well-disposed souls. His catechisms on frequent Communion are punctuated with fervid appeals, and cries from a heart all on fire: "My children, every creature in the universe requires food that it may live; for this purpose God has caused the trees and plants to grow. It is a well-appointed table to which all the animals come for the food that suits them. But the soul must also be fed. Where, then, is its food? . . . My children, when God resolved to provide food for our soul so as to sustain her on the pilgrimage of life, He examined the whole of creation, but found nothing that was worthy of her. So He looked at Himself and resolved to give Himself. . . .

"O my soul, how great thou art! God alone can satisfy thee! The food of the soul! what is it but the Body and Blood of God! O beautiful food! God alone can be the food of the soul! God alone can suffice her! God alone is able to fill her! God alone can allay her hunger! She feels an imperative need of her God! How happy are pure souls that unite themselves to Our Lord in Holy Communion! In Heaven they will sparkle like beautiful diamonds because God will shine through them, O blessed life! to feed on God! O man, how great thou art! nourished and refreshed as thou art with the Flesh and Blood of God! Go then to Holy Communion, my children! . . ."[22]

In the confessional and as a director, the Curé d'Ars spoke in a like strain. One morning in 1846 he had summoned from among the crowd of women penitents the Reverend Mother Elisabeth Giraud, foundress of the Sisters of the Holy Rosary, at Pont-de-Beauvoisin of Isère. After a word or two about the heavy burden she had assumed, he added: "You do not receive Holy Communion often enough; do go to the holy table more frequently! It is now the hour of my Mass: I want you to have the joy of receiving Our Lord today." "I have always been a great coward," humble Mother Elizabeth confided to some friends. "At that time I used to communicate once a week, and I imagined it was too often."[23]

In one of the villages of the Beaujolais there lived a devout person who communicated but rarely. After much persuasion M. Vianney prevailed upon her to receive the Holy Eucharist once a fortnight. This woman made several pilgrimages to Ars, and each time she was told to communicate more often. Although she obeyed, the woman objected that practices of devotion were not in honor in her parish, and she did not like to be singular.

"You have a good many friends," the holy Curé said at last; "choose the more virtuous from among them and bring them to me; then you will no longer be alone."

She returned with two companions. "You will come back in six months," the man of God said to each of them, "but not alone; you must win over two or three others."

At the end of six months twelve women of the Beaujolais set out for Ars. All were taught by the saint to

22. *Instructions de onze heures, MSS.*, de la Bastie, pp. 52-55, *passim.*
23. Archives of the presbytery of Ars: *Documents,* Ball.

receive Holy Communion frequently. Their own parish priest soon began to wonder at the happy transformation of his parish, and wished to know the cause. When he was told the story, he, too, journeyed in all haste to Ars, to thank his zealous and far-seeing confrère.[24]

How many souls, how many parishes besides these owe to the holy Curé whatever progress they may have made? What we know of his influence as a confessor and director of souls is very little in reality; for the most part it remains the secret of God and will be revealed in due time. "M. Vianney," says the Comtesse des Garets, "has felt obliged to confess that only the day of judgement will reveal all the good that has been wrought by his ministry."[25] So we can well understand that the devil, the implacable enemy of souls, should have exclaimed by the mouth of a possessed woman: "How thou makest me suffer! If there were three men on earth like thyself, my kingdom would be destroyed."

---

24. *Documents,* Ball, and *Notes MSS.,* of Mgr. Convert, Cahier I, n. 5.
25. *Procès de l'Ordinaire,* p. 791.

Chapter 16

THE PILGRIMAGE TO ARS
(continued)
V. A Typical Day of the Curé d'Ars—His Interior Life

EXCEPT for the five days of the annual retreat, which, until 1835, he spent at Meximieux or at Bourg-en-Bresse, and for one week of so-called repose which he took with his family in 1843, from the year 1830 the Curé d'Ars never left the village of his adoption. But for a few of the more striking incidents, which some faithful memories have preserved for us, from that year onwards his existence became one of sublime monotony. At all seasons he was on his feet twenty hours out of the twenty-four, if not more, and to the confessional he devoted from fifteen to sixteen hours in summer, and from eleven to thirteen even in the heart of winter.[1]

From the time of his appointment as vicaire of Ecully, M. Vianney had got into the habit of going into the church as early as four o'clock in the morning. Once Curé d'Ars, he went there at an even earlier hour, solely from devotion, because the tabernacle attracted him irresistibly. Then, as the parish improved, people were not afraid to ask him, long before dawn, to hear their Confessions. The habit of attending *veillées* had not as yet wholly disap-

1. Jean Pertinand, *Procès apostolique ne pereant,* p. 866. The horarium of the Curé d'Ars was not absolutely uniform; this chapter only describes the manner in which he most commonly spent his day, especially from the time when M. Raymond became his assistant. Our description of a typical day of the holy Cure is based on a harmony of the descriptions of several witnesses: the Abbé Beau, his confessor, *Procès de l'Ordinaire,* p. 1198; Catherine Lassagne, *Petit mémoire,* première edition, p. 7, and troisième, p, 22; Pierre Oriol, *Procès de l'Ordinaire,* p. 734; Abbé Toccanier, *ibid.,* pp. 139-140; Abbé Tailhades, *ibid.,* pp. 1505-1506; Frère Athanase, *ibid.* p. 824.

peared, but now they were conducted with perfect propriety. They began and ended with prayer. Now, "on their way home, at midnight or one o'clock in the morning, the women went to see M. Vianney in his confessional; they loved those Confessions at night-time; at that hour M. le Curé was not yet wearied and harassed by the crowd. He received them with most touching kindness, gave them as much time as they desired, and finally dismissed them with a few words marked by the most fatherly affection. 'Come now, my little one, go and take your rest; you are very sleepy.' The good women kept grateful and tender memories of those Confessions, so that twenty years after the saint's death they still exclaimed: 'Oh, how lovely it was to go to Confession at that moment!'"[2]

Later on the pilgrims began to arrive. From that time onwards M. Vianney himself rang the Angelus at about an hour after midnight, thus letting people know that the church was open and the priest at the disposal of those who might wish to go to Confession. Whilst waiting for his penitents he remained in prayer, kneeling before the altar, or he recited his Office. "What a beautiful and edifying spectacle it was," Catherine Lassagne writes, "to see, by the light of his candle, that figure emaciated by penance! He prayed with so much recollection! From time to time he raised his eyes to the tabernacle, smiling so sweetly that one might have thought he beheld Our Lord."

When the crowds became so vast that M. Vianney could not have coped with them even by hearing Confessions day and night, he sometimes arose even before midnight, and this during the hottest weeks of the summer. One of the directresses of the *Providence,* Jeanne-Marie Chanay, laughingly told him one day: "M. le Cure, you did not say your morning prayers today!" The same witness tells us that on such occasions "he coaxed his body by promising it a few moments' rest during the day," but those moments never came. The poor "corpse"—it was his word—had perforce to wait until the following night before it could rest

2. Mgr. Convert, *A l'école du Bienheureux Curé d'Ars,* p. 256.

itself for a while. "I catch it!" ("Je l'attrape!") the incorrigible ascetic used to say, treating the thin outward shell of his soul as if it were not merely a stranger, but an enemy.

However early M. Vianney might be, some women penitents were even earlier. For a long time there was no shelter of any kind for the pilgrims. They were compelled to wait in the little cemetery, or in the open space before the church. That in itself was already no slight penance. Eventually, in about 1845, a kind of lobby was built on the left-hand side, close to the tower. It sheltered the women, for, at an early period, women alone were allowed to come to Confession during the hours of the night.

Presently M. Vianney would come along, guiding himself by means of his lantern with its cracked glass. Wearing his surplice and purple stole, he passed through the lobby and opened the door of the church. This was the signal for the penitents to make a rush for his confessional. It must be owned that for a few minutes there was a certain amount of noise in the holy place, but some ladies of good will—about ten of them, who took it in turns night after night—volunteered to keep order. They lighted the lamps, rang the Angelus, for M. Vianney had given it up by now, and found a place for everyone as they arrived.

In the meantime the Curé d'Ars had gone to kneel on the altar step. In a rapid flight his soul winged itself up to God; to Him he offered all the labors of the day, the dawn of which was not due for a long time, and he besought Him to have pity on poor sinners. Then he entered his confessional.[3]

Towards six o'clock in summer, seven in winter, M. Vianney came out of the confessional to say Mass.[4] He

3. The two foregoing chapters have described the Curé d'Ars in the confessional; hence in this chapter no details are given about his work as a spiritual director.
4. If we may believe a letter of M. Sionnet, of Nantes, written to M. Toccanier, May 4, 1861, an association had been formed, with the approval of the Cure d'Ars, of pious persons who, at seven o'clock each morning, united themselves to his Mass, wherever they happened to be at the time.

who was so unpunctual when it was question of food or sleep, was intolerant of delay at that moment, the most sacred of his day. "One evening one of the most prominent persons of his parish sent word to ask him to wait a little, on the following day, for her. 'Tell her that it is impossible,' replied the saint. 'Let her get up! I cannot, for her sake, be the cause of any one of my parishioners missing Mass.'"[5]

At the time of his Mass he appeared as if lost to the world; his face no longer showed even a shadow of sadness. He once said: "I should not care to be curé in a parish, but I am very happy to be a priest because I can say Mass."[6] According to a remark of his confessor, "all that he had done from the moment of his rising until then could be considered as an excellent preparation;" nonetheless, he was anxious to collect himself for a few minutes before approaching the altar. Hence "kneeling on the flags of the chancel, he remained immovable, with his hands folded and his eyes fixed on the tabernacle. Nothing could now distract his attention."[7] However, on his return to the sacristy he permitted a few words to be addressed to him if absolutely necessary. The pilgrims who wished to recommend themselves to his prayers endeavored to speak to him as he put on his vestments, but his only answer was a nod, and he was able, by a simple gesture, to dismiss the inconsiderate. Besides, Frère Athanase stood near him to prevent his being mobbed. But even so, at his very elbow, discussions would arise. The question was: who from among the devout laity, or even from among the priests, would serve his Mass?

He never deemed the vestments too magnificent. He would have wished the chalice to be of solid gold, because "even the best that he had did not seem worthy to contain the Blood of Jesus Christ."[8] He loved the high altar with its marble base, ornamented with sculptures of the

5. *Procès apostolique in genere,* p. 266.
6. *Procès de l'Ordinaire,* p. 474.
7. *Procès de l'Ordinaire,* p. 814.
8. Frère Athanase, *Procès apostolique in genere,* p. 317.

Lamb, St. John the Baptist (his patron saint), St. Sixtus (patron of Ars); with its tabernacle of gilded and embossed brass, and its lofty *baldacchino* adorned with white plumes. But for him the chief glory of the church was the irreproachable behavior of the people.

As a rule the Curé d'Ars was not longer than any other priest in saying his Mass; it took him half an hour. All his life he followed the peculiar rite of the Church of Lyons.[9] According to that rite, after the elevation the celebrant stands still for a while with outstretched arms. M. Vianney prolonged this ceremony; the beholders were impressed by it. In 1827 a little schoolboy, himself destined to become a priest, used to assist him in the capacity of altar boy. "I was impressed," he relates, "when I saw how, after the Consecration, he lifted both his eyes and hands and remained for nearly five minutes in a kind of ecstasy. We used to say, my comrades and I, that he saw the good God."[10] "Before the Communion he again paused for a moment, seemingly to converse with Our Lord, and then consumed the sacred species."[11]

"How beautiful he was whilst saying Mass!" exclaimed Frère Athanase. "I thought I was beholding another St. Francis de Sales."[12] And his confessor, the Abbé Louis Beau: "I have seen the servant of God say Mass: each time it seemed to me as if an angel stood at the altar."[13]

People came to church on purpose to see him and to be edified. Guests staying at the château, who otherwise would not have troubled to assist at the sung Mass, went to it in order to get an opportunity of studying him. "Someone in the village," says Baronne de Belvey, "once told me: 'If you want to learn how to assist at Mass with profit, place yourself so as to be able to see our holy Curé at the altar.' So I went into a corner whence I could watch

9. The Diocese of Belley adopted the Roman rite in 1867.
10. Denis Chaland, born at Villeneuve in 1817, curé of Marlieux, *Procès apostolique continuatif,* p. 654. "At the more sacred moments he remained still, as if lost in a loving contemplation." (Mme. Christine de Cibeins, *ibid.,* p, 115).
11. *Procès de l'Ordinaire,* p. 587.
12. *Ibid.,* p. 814.
13. *Ibid.,* p. 1186.

him. I noticed something heavenly on his countenance; he shed tears during nearly the whole time of the Holy Sacrifice. The same thing happened every time I went to Ars."[14] An artist declared the expression of his face to be simply indescribable.

He showed no sign of distraction. His outward appearance revealed that which took place within the recesses of his soul. An enemy to every form of affectation, he indulged in no exaggerated or useless gestures, but his eyes, now raised, now lowered, pleaded and contemplated, and his hands, whether extended or folded, were themselves a supplication. The whole scene was an exhortation, silent, but supremely persuasive. "The spectacle of the Curé d'Ars saying Mass has converted more than one sinner." A Freemason, having consented to enter the church, "had no sooner seen him at the altar than his heart was changed."[15] Everything about him breathed the spirit of adoration. The onlookers had a sensible impression that he was not alone at the altar—that Jesus Christ was there with his priest. His movements, his looks, his whole attitude expressed in turn the emotions of self-effacement, yearning, hope, and love.

As he stood at the altar all those feelings came crowding in upon him, and, strangely enough, they were not unmixed with fear and even temptations to despair. One morning the thought of Hell so harassed him with a fear of losing God forever that he groaned within himself: "At least leave me the Blessed Virgin!"[16] One Christmas, during the midnight Mass, a fairly long hymn was sung after the consecration. According to the rubrics of the rite of Lyons, M. le Curé, who was the celebrant, had, at a certain moment after the consecration, to hold the sacred Host over the chalice until the *Pater Noster*. "I saw him look at the Host now with tears, now all smiles," says Frère Athanase. "He seemed to speak to it; then the tears began again, to be followed by yet more smiles. On our return to

14. *Ibid.*, p, 203.
15. *Ibid.*, p. 870.
16. Catherine Lassagne, *Petit mémoire*, première rédaction, p, 31.

the sacristy after Mass we apologized for having kept him waiting. 'Oh, I did not find the time long,' was his reply.

"'But, Monsieur le Curé, what were you doing whilst you held the sacred Host? You seemed to be greatly moved.'

"'So I was. A curious idea came into my head. I said to Our Lord: "If I knew that I should have the misfortune to be deprived of seeing You throughout all eternity, now that I hold You in my hand I should never let You go."'"[17]

After his Mass, M. Vianney resumed his rochet and stole and went once more to kneel before the altar to make his thanksgiving. It frequently happened that some pilgrims did not shrink from approaching quite close to him, to stare at him with curiosity; nay, even to pass remarks about him; but he appeared to be insensible to things earthly; he had neither eyes nor ears for them, but was wholly lost in God. "When we have been to Holy Communion," he exclaimed in one of his catechisms, "the balm of love envelops the soul as the flower envelops the bee."

His thanksgiving ended—if that burning heart ever ceased giving thanks—M. Vianney returned to the sacristy. The brother sacristan had already placed on the vestment press the objects he was asked to bless, the pictures he was requested to sign. The initials J.-M. B. V. were soon scrawled, and the blessings took but little time. However, there were always some persons waiting, those in affliction who looked for a word of comfort. The saint did not turn them away, but very few words indeed must suffice to lull or heal their afflictions, because the men, whose turn it now was, were already taking their places, in ever-increasing numbers, in the nave and all round the chancel.

From 1827, out of obedience to his physician and his Bishop, M. Vianney took a little milk towards eight o'clock; but on fast-days he deprived himself even of that much. He could thus snatch a few minutes to go to the *Providence;* it was not long, however, before he was once more in the confessional, but this time in the sacristy.

At about ten o'clock he would look for a favorable

17. *Procès apostolique in genere,* p. 213.

moment in which to say the morning Hours—that is, from Prime to None. If a new penitent happened to come in, he pointed to the *prie-Dieu* and told him to go on with his preparation. He then knelt down on the flags of the sacristy and recited his Office.

"What happiness," he exclaimed, "to be able to relax a little in this way!"[18] He relished the beauty of the psalms, and, though he understood Latin but imperfectly, a special grace enabled him to penetrate their deep meaning. "When I think of those beautiful prayers," he declared, "I am tempted to cry out, 'Happy fault!' for if David had had no sins to lament we should be without them." From the psalms his love passed on to the very book that contains them. "He so loved the volume of his Breviary," says the Abbé Tailhades, "that as he went to and fro he nearly always carried it under his arm. On my asking him the reason why, he replied: 'The Breviary is my constant companion; I could not go anywhere without it.'"

One day a lawyer of Lyons watched him for a long time whilst he was saying his Office. "His countenance," he writes, "reflected the lofty sentiments of his heart; his mouth appeared to relish what his mind perceived; his eyes were bright and radiant. He seemingly breathed a purer atmosphere than that of earth, and, deaf to the din of this world, he heard no accents other than the voice of the Holy Ghost."[19]

There he knelt, rigid as a statue, without any outward distraction, and we may be very sure that there were none in the sanctuary of his soul. Speaking of people who are distracted whilst at prayer, he said in one of his catechisms: "Flies do not settle on boiling water; they only fall into cold or tepid water."[20]

His Breviary ended, M. Vianney resumed the Confessions until eleven o'clock, when he came out of the sacristy

18. Most of the details concerning the Breviary of the Curé d'Ars are from the Abbé Alexis Tailhades, *Procès de l'Ordinaire,* pp. 1507-1508.
19. Brac de la Perrière, *Souvenirs de deux pèlerinages à Ars,* p 6.
20. *Procès apostolique in genere,* p. 170.

and went to the *catechism stall.* This name designated a kind of small pulpit, consisting of a wooden seat, a rest for the elbows, and another for the feet, the whole surrounded by an open-work barrier. Here, for a period of fifteen years—from 1845 to 1859—every weekday at eleven o'clock M. Vianney came and took his seat to give the pilgrims nothing more nor less than a simple catechism lesson.

It will readily be understood that his overwhelming occupations did not permit of his preparing either his *eleven o'clock instructions* or the Sunday homilies. "From the day," says Pertinand, the schoolmaster, "when the influx of pilgrims no longer left him the requisite time, he made a novena to the Holy Ghost to obtain the grace to be able to speak without study. At the close of the novena he went up into the pulpit, trusted to inspiration, and ever afterwards acted in this way.[21]

His church was thronged by all kinds of people, by good and fervent Christians, but likewise by the intellectuals who knew everything, so they thought, yet were ignorant of their religion. Priests and even bishops were to be seen mingling with the faithful. M. Vianney's only preoccupation was souls, and he went about it with charming simplicity. Had he seen the Holy Father and the College of Cardinals seated before him, he would not have altered his manner. As a matter of fact, people listened to him not as one listens to an ordinary preacher; they hearkened to him as to a messenger from God, a new John the Baptist who knew the secrets of the world to come. He began by reading out of the book one or two questions with the answers, after which he laid the catechism on the board beside him. How often did that little volume disappear, snatched by an indiscreet but pious hand and treasured as a relic! He then outlined his explanation of the text. However, he soon lost sight of the subject-matter of the lesson, and, with one bound, his mind passed on to those "mother thoughts" *(pensées mères)*—as a priest once put it[22]—which were the life

21. *Procès de l'Ordinaire,* p. 367.
22. "The curé of one of the large parishes of Lyons." (Abbé Dubouis, *Procès de l'Ordinaire,* p. 1234).

of his soul and the habitual subject of his contemplation. His words had in them a ring that seemed to belong to another world. His fiery gaze was fixed now on this one among the listeners, now on that, as if he wished to drive home into their hearts the sword of his words. Vice was castigated, sin cursed, but most often he sang the beauty and happiness of divine love.

His low, harsh voice was not heard by all, but his groans and sighs were enough to stir souls to their depths. In September, 1845, Soeur Marie-Gonzague, a sister of the Congregation of St. Joseph, came to Ars against her will, for, far from believing all the marvellous things that were being reported about him, she felt a certain aversion for M. Vianney.

"At the very moment when we left the carriage," she herself has related, "the catechism bell was ringing. My superior wished to attend it, so I followed her. As I entered the church I saw M. le Curé go up into his little pulpit. My eyes met his. Seized with a kind of vertigo and greatly moved, I fell on my knees. An instant later I felt myself being pulled up by a woman, whom I believe to have been Mlle. Catherine Lassagne. She took me by the hand and told me to go nearer, because I should be unable to hear from the place where I was. So she made me go up right in front of the little pulpit. I was able to grasp a few words about the will of God and the value of suffering. I wept the whole time: my feelings towards the saint were completely changed."[23]

At about the same time a doctor of Lyons came to Ars with a party of relatives and friends. He was not an unbeliever, and had been carefully brought up, but he had not the faintest notion of what a saint was like or of the spectacle that awaited him. Presently the catechism began, and at the very first words this particular listener was seized with fits of laughter. What was he to do? He was being watched; he was creating a scandal. So he cov-

23. From a *Letter* of October 2, 1874, written to M. Toccanier by Soeur Marie-Gonzague (in the world Mlle. Richard-Heydt).

ered his face with his hands the while M. le Curé went on with his lesson. Soon the laughter ceased; at the end of five minutes a flood of tears, which he did not seek to hide as he had tried to hide his laughter, began to stream down the physician's cheeks.

M. Pierre Oriol, a prosperous landowner of Pélussin, in the *département* of the Loire, who was one day to settle in the village of Ars, in order to become one of M. Vianney's "guards," also saw him for the first time during a catechism lesson. "The first word that I heard," that good man confessed afterwards, "went straight to my heart and rebuked me because of my previous life."[24]

The audience was moved and wept, though less than the speaker himself. One day, as he lamented the wretchedness of sinners, he began to weep as usual, whereupon a lady in the congregation involuntarily exclaimed: "O my God, give me such tears!"

Truth to tell, not everyone was gripped after this fashion, for impressions always vary according to the dispositions of each one. "Ah! that catechism to which I had been looking forward with so much keenness, I confess that I did not understand much of it. At every moment I caught myself saying: 'But what is he going to tell me?'" So spoke the Abbé Théodore Wibaux, of Roubaix, afterwards Superior of the Grand Séminaire of Saigon and Protonotary Apostolic. Such a state of mind, however, will be readily accounted for if we bear in mind that when M. Wibaux visited Ars in 1857 he was very troubled about his future, and, whilst the saint spoke, he was wondering what he would tell him in the interview which was to take place at the close of the catechism.

On the other hand, there were pilgrims, and those not among the least distinguished, who never wearied of listening to those familiar instructions of the saint. Mgr. Allou, Bishop of Meaux, who spent eight days at the Château d'Ars, did not once miss the catechism, and "he marvelled on leaving."[25] The missionaries who came to help the Curé

24. *Procès de l'Ordinaire,* p. 727.

when the pilgrimage was at its height, unless they were unavoidably prevented, never failed to sit among the audience which was being catechized by the holy Curé, and though he always repeated himself they always found him fresh and original.[26]

The most amazing and stirring moment of M. Vianney's day was, perhaps, that when he left the church in order to take his meal. Kneeling before the altar, he had just recited the midday *Angelus*. He had now to go to the presbytery—that is, to cross a space of barely ten meters. Now, this journey took him at least a quarter of an hour daily. Pilgrims were lined up on either side of the way, from the lobby of the belfry down the narrow passage to the door of his house. Those who had not come for the purpose of Confession and who only wished to exchange a word with him, or to make a request, grouped themselves there in order to be among the first to get near him. Carried by their relations or friends, the sick or infirm who were unable to penetrate into the narrow nave of the church waited here, leaning on crutches or resting on stretchers. Here also were placed the children who were not able to remain long in church.

The saint appeared, taking in at a glance all those strangers who, for the most part, had not seen him as yet, and who now, of their own accord, fell on their knees. After a few moments' silence, due to their emotion, they burst into uncontrollable exclamations: "Good Father! Holy Father! Bless me! Pray for our sick! Cure this poor little one! Convert my father . . . my husband!" To many of these supplications he could only reply with a look, a smile, or tears. He uttered a word, perhaps, or pointed to heaven. He fondled the children and placed his venerable hands on their heads. At the age of seventy-five, M. Monnet, a priest living in retirement at Ars, still remembered with a thrill how the holy old man placed his trembling hands on his boyish head, bestowing on him the blessing to which he attributed his vocation to

25. Frère Athanase, *Procès apostolique in genere*, p. 205.
26. Abbé Dufour, *Procès apostolique in genere*, p. 339.

the priesthood.

More than once, in order to clear the presbytery door, so as to enable him to go in alone—for at that moment he suffered no one to enter with him—he had recourse to an innocent ruse, one, moreover, that greatly delighted the pilgrims: taking a handful of medals from his pocket, he threw them among the crowd, and whilst they were being gathered up he entered his courtyard and closed and locked the gate.

In his room he found awaiting him the portion of food that had been brought over from the *Providence.* We have already described his régime, so we need not return to it here. He partook of his food standing, whilst he examined his correspondence, which had previously been laid near the china porringer in which his broth and vegetables were served. "The meal was so rapid," says Frère Athanase, "that the Curé once told me: 'It has happened that between noon and one o'clock I have been able to dine, sweep my room, shave, take a siesta, and visit my sick people.'"[27]

M. Vianney had always loved to visit the sick. From 1845 he had handed over to his assistant all external parochial activities, with the exception of this one. By the *sick* we must understand not only those of Ars, but likewise the strangers who, though obliged to keep to their beds in the hotels or in private houses, were yet anxious to hear and see the saint. Among them there frequently happened to be persons already grievously stricken, who had had themselves carried to Ars, where they hoped to die, assisted and comforted by his presence.

When, at about half-past twelve, M. Vianney issued from the presbytery to visit some sick person, he was promptly surrounded by the crowd that had been waiting for him. He could not walk down the steps of the church, cross the village square or advance along the street, except slowly and protected by two or three men

---

27. *Procès atostolique in genere,* p, 222.

of good will—"his bodyguard." These men walked in front of him with outstretched arms, so as to protect the saint from being subjected to the indiscreet veneration of the crowd. Notwithstanding these precautions, people slashed his cassock and surplice whilst kissing them; they cut locks of his hair; sometimes boldness went the length of hastily snatching away his Breviary, only to return it at once, after the subtraction of a few pictures, and sometimes it was not restored at all. M. Vianney suffered these thefts without complaint; he had become inured to the indiscretions of the crowd. Amusing mistakes occasionally occurred.

The Abbé Dufour, who was frequently told off to keep order, relates the following incident: "The eagerness of the faithful to seize upon objects belonging to the servant of God led, at least on two occasions, to my being robbed because they mistook me for M. le Curé. One fine day I had my Breviary snatched from me. However, it was promptly returned by post from Saint-Etienne. I complained to M. Vianney, who laughingly replied: 'That has already happened to me several times.' Another day a piece was cut out of my cassock. It was evening, and darkness had favored this glorious mistake."[28]

Thus it was impossible for the Cure d'Ars to show himself without at once being surrounded and mobbed. "People only left the church or its vicinity in order to cling to his footsteps," Frère Athanase relates; "they even accompanied him on his sick calls."[29] Priests besought him as a favor to allow them to go with him to the bedside of the sick, for the sake of edification and instruction. "Twice," says the Abbé Tailhades, "I have had the happiness of seeing him administer the last Sacraments. Never have I heard anyone speak of the next world with such faith, such conviction. One might have thought that he beheld with his eyes the things he described. He comforted the poor invalids and quickened their confidence. They would have wished to die in his arms."[30]

28. *Procès apostolique in genere,* p, 362.
29. *Procès de l'Ordinaire,* p. 823.

On leaving the house of the sick he found the crowd waiting outside. Did not everybody know that his pockets were full of rosaries, crucifixes, and medals? What happiness to receive one of these from his own hand! Hence the more knowing ones were seen to kneel down in several places in succession along the road he must needs take. They did so, no doubt, for the purpose of receiving a repeated blessing, but also in order to have a share in fresh distributions. It was thanks to a maneuver of this kind, of which the saint, as a matter of fact, was well aware, that a little girl of Lyons succeeded in collecting quite a rich treasure. She had come to spend three days at Ars, and whenever chance favored her she held out her hand to the good Curé as he went by. Later on, when she had become a nun, she related that on the third day he gave her a crucifix and a medal, telling her at the same time: "'Little one, that makes seventeen.' I counted my store and found that during those three days I had indeed received seventeen medals."[31] It will be readily understood that the saint quickly ran out of stock. But that did not worry him, for generous persons among the pilgrims saw to its being promptly replenished.

The two brothers Lémann, the young convert Jews whom, as we have seen, M. Vianney received with so much tenderness, were on the point of leaving Ars.

"On our way out of the village," they relate, "we saw a crowd coming from the opposite direction: it was M. le Curé returning from a sick call, and, as in the days of Our Lord, groups of people pressed round him. As we went by he recognized us. Youth knows no hesitation. 'Good Monsieur le Curé,' we told him, 'you have already given us medals, but we want more.' He smiled, and seeing the owner of a little shop at her door, he said: 'Please bring me a gross of medals.' She handed them to him, he blessed them, and gave us a handful; then turning to the woman he said: 'You will get yourself paid by whom-

30. *Procès de l'Ordinaire,* p. 1507.
31. *Letter* of an Ursuline nun of Cracow to Mgr. Convert, June 1, 1902.

soever you like.' Happy to have had the 'custom' of her pastor, the woman bowed. It was evident that she felt quite sure she would suffer no loss and that she had often done business along these lines."[32]

Very often, unless the case was urgent, these visits to the sick had been preceded by another visit which M. Vianney had at heart to make every day, for his children of the *Providence* were eager to see him in their midst. We have already described the mutual happiness of father and children during those visits. When, after September, 1853, that part of the house which was contiguous to the chapel came to be occupied by M. Toccanier and other temporary colleagues, the Curé d'Ars took particular care not to forget his "dear missionaries," his "comrades," as he familiarly called them. He would look in towards the end of their luncheon, and, whilst watching them enjoy those delicious fruits which he himself liked so much, but from which a love of penance always caused him to abstain, he remained standing, leaning against the door, and practically monopolizing the conversation so as to cut short all possible remarks of a flattering nature. His manner was most genial and kindly, and at times he would even mildly tease his dear confrères. The only thing he ever consented to accept was an occasional cup of coffee; he took it without sugar, and found it particularly bitter.[33]

In the afternoon, at the earliest moment possible, M. Vianney returned to the church. Kneeling on the pavement, before the high altar, he recited Vespers and Compline with angelic fervor. Immediately afterwards he went to the *poor sinners.* "He heard the Confessions of the women until about five o'clock, went to his house for five minutes," says M. Oriol, "and then shut himself in the sacristy, where he heard the men's Confessions until half-past seven or eight o'clock. At that hour he went into the pulpit to recite the chaplet of the Immaculate Concep-

32. *Letter* to Mgr. Convert, August 11, 1908.
33. Abbé Toccanier, *Procès de l'Ordinaire,* p. 163.

tion and night prayers. This over, he returned to the presbytery, where he gave interviews to a few more people—for instance, to the missionaries, the brothers, to priests and laymen who came from a distance. With all these he conversed in a very cordial manner, but when they also were gone he locked himself in his room. What did he do during the hours of the night? I cannot tell, but I believe that he spent most of the time in prayer."[34]

Such is the description of the second half of our saint's day as set down by one of his intimates who was often present at those evening conversations. He did not tell us how M. Vianney recited night prayers, so we must listen to yet another witness.

"I did not see him, and it was with difficulty that I heard him," writes M. Brac de la Perrière. "The nave was but dimly lighted. The feeble voice of the saintly priest could be heard only with difficulty by those of the faithful who were placed at some distance. However, after a little while the silence that prevailed enabled the ear to accustom itself to the low sound of the prayer, even as the eye became used to the mystic dimness of the sanctuary. We heard a gentle murmur, now interrupted, now lasting for periods of equal duration. Before long we were overwhelmed by this ineffable colloquy, and, without being aware of it, we entered into a profound recollection which expanded the soul and disposed it to pray in unison with those present."[35]

M. Oriol likewise failed to tell us how the holy Curé d'Ars spent his time when he at last found himself alone in his poor room. Though worn out by now, he yet recited Matins and Lauds for the following day, and concluded by reading a few pages from his bedside book—*The Lives of the Saints.* What heroism it required, night after night, to make him go through with his reading! Frère Athanase declares that "he was often so exhausted that, on returning to his house, he was hardly able to walk upstairs,

34. *Procès de l'Ordinaire,* p. 734.
35. *Souvenirs de deux pèlerinages à Ars,* op. cit., p. 4.

and I have seen him fall against the wall. But such was his spirit that his weakness provided him with matter for good-humored remarks. Occasionally, when alluding to some ill-natured observation made about him, he would say: 'Well, well! The old wizard has done good business today!' "[36]

Apparently he did not spend more than three hours in bed. "When did he sleep?" a good man of Ars asked himself, for he was always seen up and about. "There was nearly always a light in his window," said another. The fact was that during his dreadful disciplines, and, later, when sleep refused to visit him and the devil did not torment him too much, he let his candle burn so that he might contemplate the images of the saints which covered one of the walls. "When I cannot sleep," he said, "I take pleasure in looking at my pictures." And if he happened to fall asleep he no sooner opened his eyes again than he turned them in that direction. "I am in the company of the saints," he once told Mme. des Garets. "At night, when I wake up, it seems to me that they, too, look at me as if to say: 'What, lazy man, you sleep, whereas we used to spend the time watching and praying to God!' "

What he forgot to mention were his nightly sufferings caused by the excessive strain on his nervous system, which arose from the oppressive labors of the day, the fever that shook him as he lay on his pallet, the cough that forced him to get up several times within a single hour. Nevertheless, when the appointed moment came for going to the church, he forsook his hard mattress in order to take up where he had left off the interminable and holy task of his life.

One of the marvels of a life so completely dedicated to the service of the neighbor was the fact that it was spent at one and the same time amid the ceaseless coming and going of multitudes and in the most profound recollection. "The holy Curé was disturbed in every conceivable

---

36. "Allons! le vieux sorcier a bien fait marcher son commerce aujourd' hui!" *(Procès de l'Ordinaire,* p. 824).

manner, yet nothing seemed to upset his interior life."[37] Whence did he derive such marvellous calm and self-control? A reliable witness shall give us the secret. The devout Chanoine Gardette, chaplain to the Carmel of Chalon-sur-Saône, testified as follows: "M. Vianney once expressed himself thus in my presence: 'Oh, how I wish I could lose myself, never again to find myself except in God!' Well, watching him at work, one could see that his wish had been fulfilled. Indeed, he knew so well how to abandon himself to God's good pleasure that amid the manifold and laborious activities of his ministry he appeared as recollected as when engaged in his religious exercises. He always seemed to have but one thing to do—viz., the duty of the present moment. The keenness he displayed was that of apostolic zeal, never that of merely natural love of activity. Thus, whether one watched him in the morning, at noon, or at night, he invariably exhibited true liberty of spirit, meekness of disposition, and interior peace. It seems to me that here we have the realization of the ideal of union with God—that is, the fullest possible development of perfect love."[38]

A soul not united to God as to its center may indeed perform a series of holy actions and yet not itself be holy. To avoid such a danger the Curé d'Ars constantly lifted up his heart to God—in the pulpit, in the confessional, in the midst of conversations and the most varied occupations. "He had acquired the habit of the saints, which consists in leaving God for active work, when this was required of him, and returning to God by prayer at the earliest possible moment."[39] Prayer was the greatest joy of his soul and his habitual refuge. "Prayer is a fragrant dew," he used to say; "the more we pray, the more we love to pray." In fact, if all his life he longed so earnestly for solitude, it was that he might give himself up wholly to prayer and the contemplation of the things of God. Alas! the time had come when he could no longer give himself,

---

37. Frère Athanase, *Procès de l'Ordinaire* p. 820.
38. *Procès apostolique ne pereant,* p. 923.
39. *Procès de l'Ordinaire,* p. 407.

as did his brother priests, even to the refreshing exercises of the annual retreat. On the very last occasion when he thus hoped to quicken his spirit—it was in 1835, at the Seminary of Brou—Mgr. Devie sent him back to his parish even before the opening exercise. "You have no need of a retreat," the prelate declared, "whereas over there sinners want you." And he went home without a word.[40]

There were times, however, when he was heard to groan as he remembered the far-off days when he lived in the solitude of the fields. "Oh, how happy I was then! Then my head was not racked as it is today; it was so easy to pray!" And he would add with a smile: "I believe my vocation was to remain a shepherd all my life."[41] Yet when he became a priest—a shepherd of souls—he was able, at least during the first years, to indulge his holy passion for prayer. At that time he had assuredly attained to that exalted degree of prayer which is called "the prayer of simplicity," "where intuition replaces, for the most part, discourse or reasoning, where affections and resolutions vary but little and are expressed in but few words."[42] "Before the great work of the pilgrimage began," says the Abbé Claude Rougement, vicaire of Ars, "according to the testimony of the old inhabitants, M. Vianney was forever to be seen in church, on his knees, and praying without using a book." "His prayer was *affective,*" says the Baronne de Belvey, "rather than made up of reflections and reasonings."[43] He gazed at the tabernacle and never ceased from assuring Our Lord that he loved Him. In this he followed no other method than that of *Père* Chaffangeon: "I look at the good God, and the good God looks at me."

Frère Jérôme declares in his turn that "when the influx of pilgrims put an end to his long hours of prayer, M. le Curé accustomed himself to choosing, in the morning, a subject of meditation to which he referred all the actions

40. Abbè Cognat, *Monseigneur Devie,* t. II, p. 281.
41. *Procès de l'Ordinaire,* p. 666.
42. Paulain, *The Graces of Interior Prayer,* ch. ii.
43. *Procès de l'Ordinaire,* p. 237.

of the day."[44] "I once asked him for advice on mental prayer," says the Abbé Dufour. "'I no longer have time for regular prayer,' was his answer, 'but at the very first moment of the day I endeavor to unite myself closely to Jesus Christ, and I then perform my task with the thought of this union in mind.'" "From which I infer," adds M. Dufour, "that his life was one long prayer."[45]

In this way he concentrated the attention of his heart upon some scene of the life of Our Lord, our Blessed Lady, or upon one of his favorite saints. His preferences were, however, for the sorrowful mysteries, and he usually accompanied Our Lord throughout the divers phases of His Passion. That he might the more readily recall them to mind, he asked Catherine Lassagne to write them down in the margin of his Breviary;[46] in this way, whilst reciting his Office, he lived over again, with tearful emotion, every one of the stages of the work of our redemption.

As he walked among the crowds he frequently bore the appearance of one who feels quite alone, so deeply was he absorbed in holy considerations. Hence, whilst living a most active life, he ever remained the contemplative that he had wished to be. "That is real faith," he used to say, "when we speak to God as we would converse with a man." This ideal was fully realized in his own life.

Gradually the years, and even more so the fatigues so heroically endured, bent his shoulders and wrinkled his brow, but his heart retained its youthfulness; that heart, in fact, never knew but one season—that of an endless spring-tide. He himself says, in a phrase that has all the beauty and melody of poetry: "In a soul united to God it is always springtime."

---

44. *Ibid.*, p. 547.
45. *Procès apostolique in genere,* p. 547.
46. These devout mementoes, as we have transcribed them from the saint's Breviary, are as follows: *At Matins:* Jesus Christ in prayer in the Garden of Olives. *At Lauds:* Jesus Christ in agony—the sweat of blood. *At Prime:* Jesus Christ crowned with thorns, scourged, crushed under foot. *At Terce:* Jesus Christ condemned to death and carrying His Cross to Calvary. *At Sext:* Jesus Christ crucified. *At None:* Jesus Christ dies—His Heart is pierced. *At Vespers:* Jesus Christ is taken down from the cross and placed in the arms of His holy Mother. *At Compline:* Jesus Christ is laid in the sepulchre. The sorrow of Mary as she leaves the tomb.

SHRINE OF ST. PHILOMENA AT ARS

THE CURÉ D'ARS AMONG THE SICK

THE CURÉ D'ARS
calling penitents to the confessional

These illustrations reproduced from the frescoes of M. Borel in the Chapel of the Shrine at Ars.

The realization by him of the presence of God gave rise, at times, to real transports of joy. "When I saw him with that air of extraordinary happiness," Catherine Lassagne naïvely relates, "I used to say to Frère Jérôme: 'M. le Curé has a great deal of love for God today.' Assuredly he did not desire those sweet delights for their own sake. 'When we experience no consolations,' he was wont to say, 'we serve God for His own sake; when we have them, we run the risk of serving Him for our own sake.' Nonetheless, those intimate joys made his life bearable. They were to him a token of God's friendship and of His adorable condescension, and he realized that, being thus admitted, whilst yet a servant, into familiar intercourse with God his Master, his influence with Him would be all the more powerful. He himself said that 'God was so united to His saints that it looked as if, instead of His own, He was doing their will.' When someone drew his attention to the fact that St. Philomena refused him nothing, but seemed to obey him, 'What is there to marvel at in that,' he replied, 'since God himself obeys me at Mass?'"

But let not the reader imagine that in those hours of holy joy M. Vianney suffered any loss of his charming simplicity. In those moments "there were no affected attitudes, no 'Ohs!' and 'Ahs!' no sighs and transports,"[47] in fact, nothing beyond an indescribable and truly heavenly smile which those who beheld it could never forget.

---

47. *Procès de l'Ordinaire,* p, 237.

Chapter 17

THE CURÉ D'ARS' YEARNING FOR SOLITUDE—GRAVE ILLNESS AND FLIGHT OF 1843

WITH the exception of his most intimate friends, none of those who saw the Curé d'Ars amongst the pilgrims, all smiles and full of graciousness, would have imagined that he was forever pursued by a desire for solitude. Catherine Lassagne's remark must, at first sight, appear exaggerated when she affirms that: "He remained in the parish of Ars for a period of forty-one years, but *always against his will.*"[1] One day in 1843 he made this confession to the Comte des Garets, Mayor of Ars: "Since the age of eleven I have been asking God to let me live in solitude: my prayers have never been answered!"

He conceived this desire in his early childhood through his love of prayer. Even at that tender age he understood that silence and recollection help the soul in its flight to God. When he became a parish priest, a new incentive was added to the old one. Ignorant and incapable as he believed himself to be, had he not committed the sin of presumption, when he undertook the cure of souls? "Ah!" he said, with a sigh, "it is not the labor that costs; that which terrifies me is the account to be given of my life as curé!"[2] This perspective alarmed his soul until the very end. In 1858—he was then seventy-two years of age—during a mission given in his parish by the Abbé Descotes, he approached the preacher with an air of joy, just as the latter was preparing to leave the sacristy to go up into the pulpit. "Oh!" said he, "this time you are going to

1. *Petit mémoire,* troisième rédaction, p. 80.
2. Marthe Miard, *Procès apostolique continuatif,* p. 753.

convert us." "Oh! as for you, M. le Curé," replied the missionary in a like strain, "you have nothing to fear—I will answer for you." "Ah! my friend," sighed the Curé, becoming suddenly grave, and with an expression almost of anguish: "You do not know what it is to pass from the cure of souls to the tribunal of God."[3]

This yearning for solitude, for "a little corner where he might weep over his poor life," haunted him from the very first years of his life as a priest. Catherine Lassagne remembered having heard him speak of it "when he had been barely two years in the parish." We have seen how, in 1827, M. Vianney made a personal appeal to the Bishop for permission to leave Ars. Doubtless he was worried and upset over the calumnies that had been spread about him. But he was really far more harassed by another thought: the Bishop would perhaps allow him to explain, and if so he would confide to him the secret that weighed so heavily upon him. The Bishop offered him Fareins; he hesitated: his secret prayer had not been granted, so in the end he decided to remain at Ars; by staying on he might perhaps obtain a more willing consent to his departure for La Trappe or La Chartreuse?

In 1830, when he was already besieged by the crowds, his feelings in the matter were the same, except that his aspirations were even keener. His neighbor of Chaleins, the Abbé Mermod, came to him for guidance on the road to perfection. "A man should not remain a curé until the end of his life," M. Vianney told him, "he should reserve some time for himself, so as to prepare for death." Twenty-five years later Chanoine Camelet, superior of the missionaries of Pont-d'Ain, was the recipient of a like confidence: "I should not like to die a curé, because I know of no saint who died in a like position. I should like to have two years in which to weep for my poor life. Oh! it seems to me, I should then indeed love the good God!"[4]

The Bishop of Belley often heard an echo of those wishes

3. Abbé Descotes, *Procès de l'Ordinaire,* p. 1344.
4. Chanoine Camelet, *Procès de l'Ordinaire,* p. 1375.

and those sighs; but he invariably turned a deaf ear to them. The persistence, however, with which M. Vianney pleaded for his *exeat* shows that he never quite gave up hope of being heard one day. "With him that hope was a need," Mme. des Garets affirmed. When he had to write to his Bishop to consult him about the solution of a case of conscience, he rarely did so without alluding to the all-important subject. The following characteristic passage is from a letter written in 1851 to Mgr. Devie, who was about to retire, Rome having appointed Mgr. Chalandon coadjutor:

"Monseigneur, knowing that you are fortunate enough to be preparing to retire so that you may think only of Heaven, I beseech you to procure the same happiness for me. Were you to leave without consenting to do so, I should die of grief.

"May your kind heart forgive me, Monseigneur, for all the trouble I have caused you. I entertain great hopes that your lordship will grant the favor I ask. You know that I am only a poor, ignorant man. Such, indeed, is everybody's conviction. . . ."

And he signed in all humility: "Jean-Marie VIANNEY, the poor parish priest of Ars."[5] The letter was unsuccessful. A few years later Mgr. Chalandon, now Bishop of Belley, received the following urgent request:

"Monseigneur, I am becoming more and more infirm. Unable to rest for long in bed, I am compelled to spend parts of the night in a chair. I have attacks of dizziness in the confessional, when I lose myself for two or three minutes at a time.

"Considering my infirmities and age, I should like to bid farewell to Ars for ever, Monseigneur. . . ."

---

5. This letter, like the one we are about to quote, and most of the letters written by M. Vianney, bears no date on the original. The context, however, indicates with tolerable clearness at what time the letters were written.

This time he signs: "VIANNEY, *a poor unfortunate priest.*"

At every episcopal visitation these requests were repeated by word of mouth. The days immediately preceding the visitation saw an increase of penances; he prayed, wept, sighed, and fasted before presenting his request. As soon as the Bishop came in sight, he felt a new quickening of the hopes that had so often been shattered. One fine day M. Oriol saw him enter the sacristy, radiantly happy: "Monseigneur is coming," he whispered into his ear. "Monseigneur is coming, and I am going to ask him, you know what."[6]

Monseigneur did come; in fact, he paid fairly frequent visits to his holy friend; but M. Vianney always remained parish priest of Ars. Mgr. Devie, as well as Mgr. Chalandon who succeeded him, opposed with energy the Curé's request for permission to retire. Mgr. de Langalerie, who was raised to the See of Belley in 1857, must also have received more than one request of a like nature, for, strange as it may seem, the holy Curé never appears to have been willing to die in harness. Even in the last month of his life he still spoke of retiring. On this subject we have the authority of Mgr. de Langalerie, who spoke as follows in his discourse pronounced at the funeral of M. Vianney:

"'Ah! Monseigneur,' he told us hardly a fortnight ago, 'in a little while I shall ask you to let me take my leave so that I may weep for the sins of my life.' 'But, my good Curé,' we answered, 'the tears of the sinners whom God sends to you are surely worth as much as yours. Do not speak to me in that strain, otherwise I shall no longer come to see you.' But our words of affection and encouragement seemingly failed to convince him."

So persistent a desire for solitude is not to be wondered at in a man like M. Vianney, who would gladly have spent his whole life kneeling before the tabernacle. When we look into it closely, however, a subtle tempta-

6. *Procès de l'Ordinaire,* p. 723.

tion, which the saint himself ended by divining, disguised itself under the form of an attraction than which none appeared more legitimate. The testimony of several persons who were most intimate with him—and they were persons of weight—is to the same effect. "The Curé d'Ars," M. Monnin declared, "owned himself that there was something intemperate in this desire, and that the devil made use of it to tempt him. He subdued and resisted it, but all his life he had to fight against the attraction."[7]

The testimony of M. des Garets, the Mayor of Ars, is even more precise and explicit: "I have always known of M. Vianney's desire for solitude. I now discern three motives for his inclination: he wanted, in the first place, to decline the responsibility of a parish; secondly, he sought an opportunity to weep over what he called his *poor life;* thirdly, he wished to escape from occupations that were too prolonged, and to have leisure and freedom in order that he might yield to the attraction which prayer and meditation had for his soul. These were the motives of which the good Curé himself was conscious. My conviction is, however, that behind them there was a real temptation on the part of the devil of which he remained unaware, notwithstanding his experience in the ways of God. The devil was perfectly cognizant of all the good M. Vianney was doing through the pilgrimage to Ars, and the greater good that might yet result from it in the future; so he had every interest in turning aside, under specious pretexts, the heart of the servant of God."[8]

On his part Frère Athanase, one of the saint's great confidants, declares that M. Vianney suffered much in his soul. He was particularly tormented by a craving for solitude, of which he often spoke. It was like a temptation that beset him by day and even more so by night. "When I cannot sleep," he told me, "my mind travels: I am with the Trappists, or the Carthusians; I look for a corner where I may weep for my poor life and do penance for my sins."

---

7. *Ibid.,* p. 1115.
8. *Procès de l'Ordinaire,* pp. 947-948.

Such had been, once upon a time, the sighs of St. Catherine of Siena, the wonder worker, as the crowds hailed her. "Why, O Lord, do you allow me to be made everybody's plaything?" she groaned. "All thy servants are permitted to live in peace in the midst of men, all except me!" In this respect the poor Curé met with a like treatment; God would not listen to his prayer, and he knew it.

"I have heard him say in private," Catherine Lassagne relates: 'The good God grants me nearly all that I ask, except when I pray for myself.' 'The reason is,' I replied, 'that you ask the good God to take you away from Ars, and that is not His Will.' He did not answer a word."

As a matter of fact, this hunger after recollection and solitude, which was never assuaged, was not merely a temptation of the evil one, it was likewise a trial sent by God Himself. The Abbé Monnin knew this well. "I also think," he said, "that in all this there was a secret disposition of divine Providence: by sacrificing his tastes to obedience, his pleasure to duty, M. Vianney found hourly occasions to crush underfoot his own will."[9]

M. Vianney's attraction for solitude, however, was balanced by that for the apostolic life, and, by a divine permission, his heart fluctuated forever between these opposites. He was certainly terrified at the responsibility attaching to the cure of souls. One day a young seminarist of Lyons was making his Confession to him when he asked him whether he was in Holy Orders. "Yes," was the reply, "I am a deacon, and I have only three months to wait before I become a priest." "Oh! my child," exclaimed the saint, "do not speak thus: one always becomes a priest too soon!" On the other hand, he understood that souls have need of the priesthood, and that "to feed the flock of Christ is a work of love,"[10] excelling all others. He sighed for peaceful solitude, yet he was never happier than on the days when the crowds surged all round him! According to Mme. des Garets, he should have convinced himself once for all that he was made for that kind of

9. *Procès de l'Ordinaire,* p. 1115.
10. *Sit amoris officium pascere Domini gregem* (St August., *Tract. in Joan., CXVIII*).

work: as soon as the multitude subsided, he looked sad and made novenas for them to come back. Once they had returned, were he asked to take a little rest, he would reply that "it would not be right to detain those poor people who had come from so far and who spent whole nights waiting for their turn to go to Confession. "The good God should give me the faculty He bestowed on several of the saints, that of being in more than one place at a time. If I already had my foot in Heaven and were told to return to earth to work for the conversion of one sinner, I would gladly return; and if, to obtain that end, it were necessary for me to remain here till the world's last day, to get up at midnight and to suffer all that I now suffer, I would agree to it with all my heart."[11]

One day, whilst catechizing in the church, he exclaimed: "Oh! had I known what it means to be a priest, I would promptly have taken refuge at La Trappe." To which a voice from the crowd replied: "My God! what a loss that would have been!"[12] This cry of the heart was both an encouragement and a lesson to the saint.

On three separate occasions the Curé d'Ars tried to leave his parish. This shows the powerful hold the hunger for solitude had over him. He thought he saw in it, even if not very clearly, an expression of the will of God as opposed to that of his Bishop, whose consent he always hoped, some day, to win.

To the year 1840 or thereabouts, we must assign a first departure which passed unnoticed and which M. Vianney only betrayed at a much later date. He left his presbytery on a very dark night—it may have been at two o'clock in the morning—and alone he took the road to Villefranche. Whither was he going and what were his intentions? This he never revealed. He walked for a while, but when he came to the cross of Les Combes, not far from Ars, he stopped and began to think: "Is it really the will of God that I am doing now? Is not the conversion of even one

11. *Procès de l'Ordinaire,* p. 883.
12. *Procès de l'Ordinaire,* p. 1115.

soul of greater value than all the prayers that I might say in solitude?" He thereupon retraced his steps. The souls that were waiting for him quickly closed round him. "He had suddenly been seized by a temptation to flee," says the Abbé Toccanier, to whom we owe the story.

The tempter—for he was surely at the root of the matter—would not admit defeat, but deemed the indispositions and maladies of the holy man a priceless occasion for revenge.

In 1835, the Abbé Vianney still suffered from the effects of his "youthful follies"; facial neuralgia, excruciating toothaches, and violent abdominal pains reminded him fairly frequently that a man may not, with impunity, spend the nights on the damp flags in one of the lower rooms. The Curé's letters to his doctor supply us with ample proofs of his ailments. There was no doubt that he needed help; it would enable him to take a little rest from time to time. But apart from M. Alexis Tailhades, of Montpellier, who stayed with him as his guest and disciple during the winter of 1839, no priest was appointed as his coadjutor before the year 1843. Mgr. Devie, having no priest to give him, could do no more than exhort the priests in the vicinity of Ars to help as best they could an overworked colleague. Thus it came about that, out of sheer good will, M. Dérognat, curé of Rancé, and M. Raymond, curé of Savigneux, occasionally lent him assistance in the discharge of the different functions of his ministry.

In 1843, M. Vianney believed his end to be near at hand. Two years previously, when he was almost worn out with fatigue, he made a will, in which he bequeathed "his sinful body to the earth and his poor soul to the three Persons of the adorable Trinity."[13] *The month of Mary* had only just begun. For sixteen years, unaided, he had led the May devotions. He generally began by reading a passage out of a book, upon which he afterwards commented, "and once started he spoke for a long time,"

13. *Testament,* dated December 2, 1841.

says Catherine Lassagne. On the evening of May 3 he began to read when he was stopped by a fit of choking. He knelt down to recite the usual prayer, but was hardly able to utter the opening words. A violent fever shook him. The people thronged round him; eventually he was carried into a room near the one he usually occupied, where it would be easier to attend to him. The wooden bed on which M. Balley died was kept here and venerated as a relic. It was hurriedly made ready, M. Vianney's *paillasse* was fetched, and the sick man, who had swooned away, was laid upon it.

Dr. Saunier, who had been summoned with all haste, diagnosed the case as one of pleuro-pneumonia. The Comte des Garets likewise hastened to the presbytery. When he beheld his poor parish priest stretched on that bed of straw which rested on hard planks and was no thicker than a man's fist, he offered him a good mattress. After much insistence the saint consented to accept it. It was high time he received proper treatment. Already on May 6—the day on which M. Vianney entered upon his fifty-eighth year—the doctor judged his condition to be hopeless. Such was the popularity of the Curé d'Ars that three other doctors answered a summons of Dr. Saunier. A consultation took place, in which it was decided that the patient should refrain from speaking. Above all, he was to be spared every kind of emotion, for the heart only did its work with the utmost difficulty.

M. Vianney, nevertheless, still retained his sense of humor, of which he gave proof then and there. "When he saw the representatives of the medical faculty standing round his bed, he said laughingly:

"'I am keeping up a great fight at the present moment.'

"'Eh! and against whom, M. le Curé?'

"'Against four doctors. Should a fifth join them, I am lost!'"[14]

This pleasantry should not make us overlook the fact that during this grave illness, the Curé d'Ars trembled

14. *Letter* of Mme. des Garets, May 14, 1843.

at the thought of the judgements of God. To M. des Garets, who lived and even slept at the presbytery whilst the life of his pastor hung in the balance, he confessed: "I should like to live longer in order to weep for my sins and to do a little good." At night he was at times greatly agitated and troubled by fearful nightmares. One morning he said: "Last night I thought I heard the devils shouting triumphantly: 'We have him! We have him! He is ours!'"

These temptations, however, did not cause him to lose either his patience or his trust in God. "He never complained," says Jean Pertinand, the schoolmaster, who had taken on the duties of a nurse; "he accepted, from a motive of obedience, every remedy[15] and bore his sufferings with perfect submission to the divine will, which he saw in everything that befell him."

In the meantime it seemed as if death had visited every house in Ars. The pilgrims wandered round the church like sheep without a shepherd; there were two or three hundred there who had not yet finished their Confessions and who refused to go to the good Abbé Lacôte, curé of Saint-Jean-le-Vieux, and M. Vianney's "supply." They were told to go to Confession to the priest whom the Curé had asked to replace him. "I have not the courage to begin all over again," said a lady to whom the Abbé Renard gave that advice; "let me at least kneel on the threshold of his room, that he may see me and give me his blessing; that will somewhat calm my soul!" The people had brought baskets filled with medals, rosaries, crosses, and pictures, which were taken to the bedside of the dying priest—for everybody believed the end to be near. M. Vianney raised his hand and blessed these objects that would be so jealously cherished. "I do not know," the Comtesse des Garets wrote, "whether as many objects are blessed by all the bishops of France taken together."

15. On May 13, the physician had prescribed chicken broth. It required the authority of M. Dubouis to make him take it. M. Dubouis "scolded him, whereupon he took the broth without another word." (Comtesse des Garets, *Letter* of May 14, 1843).

Hope was no longer possible unless Heaven intervened; hence the crowds, unable now to approach the saint's confessional, surged round the altar of St. Philomena, where many candles were kept burning, and at which some priests had begun a novena of Masses. Nonetheless, the church seemed empty without *him!*[16]

In the evening of May 11 his agony appeared imminent. Seven priests were in the room. There was no time for further delay, and it was resolved to give the sick man the last Sacraments. His confessor, M. Valentin, curé of Jassans, who undertook this office, thought it more prudent to keep both parishioners and pilgrims in ignorance of the ceremony that was about to take place. "No, no! Ring the bell," said the dying man, "a parish priest. needs all the prayers he can get!" So the bell began to toll, and all at once the steps and the courtyard of the presbytery were invaded.

"Do you believe all the truths that the Church teaches us?" the curé of Jassans asked him in an unsteady voice. "I have never doubted them," replied the saint. So he received the last Sacraments with a faith that deeply impressed those who were present. After their departure, when M. Dubouis, curé of Fareins, alone remained by his bedside, the dying saint "consecrated himself to St. Philomena, promised to have a hundred Masses said in her honor, and asked that a big candle might be lighted before her image."[17]

He then almost immediately fell into a state of coma. Those who watched were on their knees. Dr. Saunier stood by his bed, convinced that the end had come. But the holy Curé, whose eyes were closed, heard the doctor pronounce his sentence. "My poor cousin," he said, addressing himself to Marguerite Humbert, of Dardilly, a few months later, "when I was at my last gasp and Extreme Unction had been given me, the physician said, as he felt my pulse: 'He has only thirty or forty minutes to live.' And I thought within myself: 'My God, I shall then have to appear before

16. *Letter* of Mme. des Garets, May 10, 1843.
17. *Procès de l'Ordinaire,* p. 290.

Thee empty-handed!' And I turned to the Blessed Virgin and St. Philomena, saying: 'Ah! if I can still be of use in the saving of a few souls!' And he added: 'My good cousin, when you assist the dying, read loudly, because the sick can hear even when they appear to be unconscious.'"[18]

Now, no sooner had M. Vianney interiorly invoked Mary and his "dear little saint, than the sickness abated. He opened his eyes and recovered his speech." He then had three hours of calm, during which he remained immovable, with hands folded, praying with angelic fervor. Unfortunately, a violent fever seized him once more.[19] The doctor would not commit himself, it being his opinion that death was only staved off for a few hours. It was decided, however, that if he lived through the night, M. Dubouis should celebrate, at St. Philomena's altar, the first of the hundred Masses promised by the Curé d'Ars.

At dawn, on May 12, the sick man was still breathing. When the news spread, the church filled and the promised Mass began. Never were more fervent prayers sent up from Ars to Heaven. In the meantime the schoolmaster kept watch by the bedside of his pastor. In addition to a dreadful fever, M. Vianney seemed to be a prey to some great anxiety. Pertinand expected every moment to receive his last breath, when all of a sudden he became calm, as if he had been reassured by a vision which he contemplated attentively, and which filled him with rapture. The Mass was hardly ended when he exclaimed: "My friend, a great change has taken place in me: I am cured!" A few moments before, whilst he appeared to be in an ecstasy, he had repeatedly pronounced the name of Philomena. Everybody felt convinced that his "dear little saint" had appeared to him. He himself attributed to her his unexpected recovery. His strength, in fact, returned "with a rapidity that his doctors described as *marvellous.*" "Say *miraculous,*" was his rejoinder.[20]

---

18. Marguerite Humbert, *Procès de l'Ordinaire,* p. 1325.
19. *Letter* of the Comte des Garets to M. Guillemin, Vicar-General of Belley. The latter had written to the Mayor in the name of Mgr. Devie to ask for relics, "if the Curé should die."
20. Comtesse des Garets, *Letter* of May 17, 1843; *Procès l'Ordinaire,* p. 900.

Finally, after sixteen days, which, to his heart, seemed interminable, he at length beheld the church and the tabernacle. As early as Saturday, May 20, leaning on the arm of his faithful Pertinand, he began once more to say Mass. Too weak to fast long, he had to say it towards two o'clock in the morning. "Notwithstanding the early hour," Mme. des Garets relates, "the whole parish was gathered in the church. He chose the altar of Our Lady, as was his habit on all Saturdays. I should have loved to see all those dear to me in that chapel, so remarkable was the expression of the holy Curé's countenance. What unforgettable memories! It felt like assisting at a Mass in the catacombs."[21]

M. Vianney deemed his convalescence already well advanced; the doctor, however, forbade him to resume his task until his recovery was complete. He obeyed, but at what a cost! Every time he entered the church he cast longing eyes in the direction of his confessional, and for the moment his keenest wish, apparently, was speedily to recover his wonted strength.

Meanwhile a fresh anxiety began to vex the minds of the people of Ars. On May 17 the Comtesse des Garets wrote to her mother: "What is he going to do with his life, for the prolongation of which he prayed so earnestly? How does he intend to expend the strength, the return of which he desired so eagerly? These questions are on everybody's lips. We now fear that our holy Curé meditates leaving Ars, so that our joy at the recovery of one whom Heaven has allowed to remain on earth is greatly troubled by apprehensions of so painful a nature."

Ten days later there was no room left for uncertainty. M. des Garets went to see the convalescent saint. He found him in his room, sitting on the bed and weeping copiously. "What is the matter?" exclaimed M. des Garets. "Oh!" M. Vianney replied, "no one knows how many tears I have shed on this pallet, I who, since the age of eleven,

21. *Ibid.*

have only asked for solitude. And it has always been refused me," he sobbed.[22]

After describing that sick call, the châtelaine writes: "We fear, we greatly fear, lest our saintly Curé should escape us and we should have to mourn him alive, after the great joy of his resurrection. We cannot disguise from ourselves the fact that the holy man imagines his day's work is done. 'I shall go on until I collapse,' he had said. And collapsed he has. If he has prayed for a prolongation of life, he has done so for his own good, that he may prepare for death in silence and solitude. Life has been restored to him. Together with his cure, he thinks Heaven has also granted him his freedom. That is what he thinks; that is what he yearns for. People told us that we were too proud of our Curé, and that God would punish our arrogance: they were right."[23]

Weeks went by; the suspense remained, but M. Vianney made no preparations for departure. He was fully resolved to go some day, but was at present content to wait until he had regained his strength. It goes without saying that from his bed he had removed the mattress henceforth judged useless. No sooner had the doctor given his consent than he returned to his confessional, and that at one o'clock in the morning. It was in vain that the good Pertinand endeavored to stop him. "*Mon Jean,*" the Curé said, "whilst I was ill, I did God's will and obeyed; at present it is for you to obey; go to bed like a good man." The doctor thought it wiser to shut his eyes to such imprudence: the saint's penitents were infinitely grateful to him. On one point, however, Dr. Saunier remained unflinching—namely, the Curé's diet. Until his recovery was complete, M. Vianney was to make two meals daily; at the midday meal he was to eat a little meat and—Oh, scandal!—to drink a quarter of a glass of old claret. The good saint felt very guilty; however, Mgr. Devie had added his authority to that of the doctor, so, whether he liked it or not, there was nothing for it but to obey.

---

22. *Procès de l'Ordinaire,* p. 894.
23. Comtesse des Garets, *Letter* of May 27, 1843.

And whilst his friends could not help smiling, he groaned: "I have become a glutton![24] We obtain fewer graces.[25] I do not feel quite at ease when I go to Confession!"[26]

Unhappily, the poor saint was neither less wan nor less emaciated than in the past. He was only fifty-seven, and he had the appearance of an old man. On August 17 of that same year the Abbé Faivre, of the Diocese of Saint-Claude, had occasion to visit the Curé. "His mortified and penitential life," he relates, "was such that it seemed to me, as a missionary who knows what it means to spend whole days hearing Confessions, preaching, catechizing, that, humanly speaking, he could not live three months."[27]

Nor were the physicians less pessimistic. They considered it imperative that M. Vianney should have a change of air and—this they probably did not dare to tell him—that he should give up the confessional for good. On his part Mgr. Devie had written, authorizing him to take a rest. As a matter of fact, he was free to absent himself for a fortnight, without special leave of his Bishop, so long as he provided a substitute. Now M. Raymond, of Savigneux, was more often at Ars than in his own parish—so the "supply" was found. Always hesitating and wavering on this point, when he was so firm and decided on all others, M. Vianney longed to escape for a few weeks from the throngs of pilgrims—and there was surely nothing blameworthy in the desire—but with the longing was linked a subtle temptation. Once away from Ars he would bury himself in some secluded spot never again to forsake it. At all events, he wrote to his brother François asking him to prepare a room for him in the dear home at Dardilly.

On Monday, September 11, he confided his project to the Abbé Raymond. The curé of Savigneux did not raise many objections, for he secretly aspired to become parish priest of Ars. He promised to take the letter with which M. Vianney entrusted him as soon as possible to the Bishop. In it his lordship was besought to assign to the

24. *Procès de l'Ordinaire,* p. 162.
25. *Ibid.,* p. 438.
26. *Ibid.,* p. 1254.
27. *Ibid.,* p. 1495.

"poor Curé d'Ars" the chapel of the Minims of Montmerle, where his only duty would be to say Mass—a post that would just suit him.[28]

During the night of September 11 to 12 the Curé d'Ars fled. However, he had not been able to resist the desire to bid farewell to his beloved and regretted *Providence.* This threatened to spoil all his plans. Before ten o'clock that night—of course, Catherine and the others had promised secrecy—the whole parish was on the alert, for they had found out the secret, and a few persons were posted round about the presbytery. A little before one o'clock someone was heard making his way cautiously through the quickset hedge of the garden. It was M. le Curé. He had his Breviary under his arm and a small parcel in his hand. Several people endeavored to detain him, they even offered him pious objects which they asked him to bless. He would not stop, but, hastening his steps, he went down towards the footbridge of the Fontblin. He crossed it and disappeared in the darkness. Jean Pertinand, the schoolmaster, was summoned. "He must run after M. le Curé." The young man eventually succeeded in overtaking him at some distance from the village, for he had lost his way in the fields.

"Monsieur le Curé," Pertinand exclaimed, "why are you leaving us like this?"

"Come," the fugitive replied, "do not let us lose time. I have written to Monseigneur asking for permission to retire, and I shall await his answer at Dardilly. I shall say Mass at Fourvière, to the end that I may see God's Will more clearly. If Monseigneur consents, my wish will be accomplished; if he wants me to go back, I shall go back. As for

28. Montmerle is a market town of 1,500 inhabitants, situate on the left bank of the Saône, twelve kilometers northwest of Ars. It was famous for its fair of the *Nativity,* as it was called, which lasted from August 15 to September 30. Every imaginable thing was sold, and the whole countryside flocked to it. Since 1870 it has lost much of its importance, and is like any other fair; but whilst it was at the height of its fame a Mass was said daily in the chapel of Notre-Dame des Minimes, and there was a great concourse of people each day. At the period to which we refer there were but few traces left of the pilgrimages to Our Lady's sanctuary which, at one time, had been much frequented. Did the Curé d'Ars dream of reviving the pilgrimages? It is not unlikely. His great desire, nevertheless, was to find at Montmerle more solitude and more time for recollection than he enjoyed at Ars.

the parish, it will not suffer; I have seen to everything."

So M. Vianney and Jean Pertinand started off in the direction of Dardilly. Suddenly the fugitive halted. During his long imprisonment in the confessional the roads had been improved, with the result that he was unable to recognize them. "*Mon Jean,*" he said with some sharpness, "you are deceiving me!" The young man had no difficulty in showing that it was not so. The two travellers pursued their way, praying and conversing. "We certainly said ten Rosaries during the seven hours that the journey took us," Pertinand related.

They reached Trévoux at such an early hour that, out of kindness, M. Vianney would not rouse the sleeping guardian of the bridge.[29] At Neuville, where our weary travellers crossed the Saône, the saint, who had set out without any money, offered to pay for a breakfast for his companion, who was likewise penniless. He spoke of pawning his watch: the schoolmaster refused point-blank. A like transaction was suggested to the toll-gatherer at Neuville, who said: "You can pay me another time."

At last the Curé d'Ars crossed the threshold of his old home. He was so worn out, however, that he was compelled to go to bed almost immediately. When Jean Pertinand had also taken a very much-needed rest, the Curé bade him "return to Ars; but come back on the Friday of next week, for on Saturday we will go together to Fourvière. After that we shall see."

The previsions of the holy man were not to be realized, On the morning of September 12 consternation was written on the countenances of the inhabitants of Ars. It was only too true; M. le Curé had entered at the Chartreuse, and that for ever! With him all life, all joy, and all courage seemed to have vanished from the village. Two days after his departure Mme. des Garets wrote as follows:

"*La Providence,* the school for little girls, resounds with

---

29. This delicate attention, which reveals the saint's goodness of heart, obliged him to follow the course of the Saône, on its left bank, as far as the next bridge. There being a bend in the river between the two bridges, the Curé's journey was lengthened by several kilometers.

groans and sobs; half of their number, at least, have already been driven away by their grief. The flood of pilgrims has ebbed away. The church is almost empty. At long intervals some poor girls may be seen praying before an altar at which a taper is burning. I cannot describe the sadness that oppresses the heart at sight of such a transformation. It is a real passage from life to death.

"We were wont to have a chapter of the *Lives of the Saints* enacted before our eyes, day by day. Now the book is closed."

In the meantime the Abbé Raymond, whilst retaining the title of curé of Savigneux, had installed himself permanently at Ars! But this priest, who had dreamed of directing the pilgrimages to Ars, must have understood the lesson he got. The presence of M. Vianney was the sole reason for the great movement. As a matter of fact, as soon as his hiding-place became known, "Ars was no longer Ars," as someone expressed it.

Already on Thursday, September 14, on being informed by Jean Pertinand of the Curé's whereabouts, the Comte des Garets had hastened to Dardilly. François Vianney had recourse to a subterfuge and declared that his brother had left for an unknown destination, so M. des Garets had to content himself with leaving a note for his holy parish priest.

"Do not decide anything yet," he told him. "You are in need of rest; I know it better than anyone. Stay with your brother for as long a time as you think necessary, but do not forget your poor parish of Ars. Think of all those holy souls to whom you were showing the way to Heaven, and of all those who have forsaken that heavenly road and whom you will bring back to it. Think of your *Providence,* of which you are the soul and stay, and which can only exist through you. Lastly, think of the good of religion itself, which God has called upon you to sustain and to glorify."

Whilst M. des Garets wrote these appealing lines, M. Vianney, wholly ignorant of his presence, was praying in the room above the living-room, in which the Mayor was writing. He was only informed after the latter's departure, and he was greatly moved as he read and re-read the letter. Other communications likewise reached him: one from Catherine Lassagne contained bad news—only fifteen children remained at the *Providence;* M. Raymond had seen Monseigneur, and Monseigneur had affirmed that he would never allow the Curé d'Ars to leave the Diocese of Belley. Another missive was from an innkeeper who had opened business at Ars against the will of M. Vianney. The man was hit in a vital spot, for business was at a standstill. The following is the burden of his message:

"Monsieur, I hasten to beseech you not to forsake us. You know what I have always told you, and I now repeat it with all my heart: if there is anything in my house that does not please you, I submit wholly to your will."

But what was the amazement, nay, the embarrassment of M. Vianney when, in the course of Friday, he saw arriving at Dardilly . . . the pilgrims of Ars! The swarm of ants had found its old path. What was he to do? Send them away? He did not so much as think of it, but as soon as he had obtained faculties from the Archbishop of Lyons, he installed himself in one of the confessionals of the church of his native village. He could no longer be expected for meals. Strangers knocked at the door of his brother's house at every moment. "If he remains here," François declared, "I shall be obliged to summon assistance: I am no longer master in my own house!"

On the evening of Saturday, September 16, François Pertinand, the hotel-keeper and brother of the schoolmaster, took along with him to Dardilly twenty-three young men of Ars. They presented themselves at the Vianneys' farm at dawn, but the saint's relatives refused to open the door. All at once a gentle, familiar voice was heard. Their beloved pastor stood at the window, calling to them. He had been up for hours, and he now made them come into his room, recited the Rosary with them, and finally led them to the church, where they assisted at his Mass. M. Vianney pressed them warmly to stay to breakfast. Discretion caused them to refuse. During the night of Sunday to Monday they started on their return journey. M. Vianney recommended them all to assist at Mass on Tuesday on their return home: "I shall say my Mass at Fourvière that same morning in order that I may at last know God's Will—and you, too, will pray for me."

The Will of God manifested itself by other means. On Saturday evening, September 16, a traveller charged with a special mission from the Bishop of Belley arrived at Dardilly. Lest he should rouse suspicion, the Abbé Raymond—for he it was—presented himself at the village presbytery at about eight o'clock. His reception was frigid: no doubt this priest, who declared he had a mission from his Bishop, had come to take M. Vianney away. M. Raymond was taken aback, but, in the hope of appeasing the parish priest, he offered to sing the public Mass on the following day. To this the curé of Dardilly offered no objection, and it was agreed that after the sung Mass Monseigneur's messenger should have an interview with M. Vianney.

And so it all happened. The saint assisted at the parochial Mass, after which he insisted on taking the curé of Savigneux to his brother's house, which, as a matter of fact, was close to the church. Mgr. Devie's reply! . . . How eager he was to know its nature! He read the letter of which M. Raymond was the bearer, and for a moment disappointment could be seen depicted on his countenance, but he made no comment of any kind.[30] After

30. We have not been able to recover the Bishop's letter to the saint, but the following is the text of the one he wrote to the Mayor of Ars, Comte des Garets:

"BOURG,
"*September* 13, 1843.

"MONSIEUR,

"At the moment of receiving your holy Cure's letter, I likewise received the one which you have done me the honour of addressing to me. I entrust my reply to each of these letters to M. le Curé of Savigneux.

"I have told the good Curé that I wish him to remain at Ars, notwithstanding the motives he sees for going elsewhere; I hope that he will yield to my reasoning.

"However, in order not to hurt him too much, I have mentioned two other posts to which I might appoint him. It is precisely by acting in such a manner that I persuaded him, a few years ago, to give up the project he had formed of leaving Ars. I now cherish a hope of achieving a like success. Your insistence, that of your parishioners *(sic),* and of the neighboring curés will help, I trust, in determining him to remain at Ars. In any case, he knows by now that I shall never allow him to leave the Diocese of Belley; I should feel that I was losing a treasure.

"Your most humble and wholly devoted servant, ALEXANDRE-RAYMOND,
Bishop of Belley."

M. Raymond's departure, he came downstairs in order to soothe François, for his brother, finding himself surrounded by a constant influx of people from Ars, complained bitterly of their importunity towards their curé.

M. Raymond lunched at the presbytery. "I beg of you," the curé of Dardilly said to him, "to go away as quickly as possible; people know what you have come for; you had better leave M. Vianney alone, else they will do you an ill-turn." However, the episcopal delegate stuck to his guns: he was now determined to restore the Curé d'Ars to his flock, for in an interview he had had with M. des Garets, before he undertook this journey, the latter had made it quite clear that it was useless for him to cherish the ambition of becoming M. Vianney's successor. So the Abbé Raymond assisted at Vespers, at which the saint was the celebrant. After Benediction of the Blessed Sacrament the curé of Dardilly began once more to blame his unhappy colleague of Savigneux. "Many people here," he said to M. Vianney, "look askance at him." To which the saint replied: "Do not worry about M. Raymond; he is a horse that is used to the sound of the trumpet; he is not afraid of noise!"

The Curé d'Ars, in the meantime, had come to a decision: the Bishop offered him the chaplaincy of Notre-Dame de Beaumont, but asked him to weigh the proposal before deciding. Very well, he would go to Beaumont, and Our Lady, who was honored there, would surely help him to come to a right decision. But how was he to elude the watchfulness of the people of Dardilly, who were already mounting guard over the Vianneys' house?

It so happened that on the evening of that very Sunday, just as M. Vianney was about to take his rest, for the last time, under the roof of the old home, a delegation of the leading inhabitants appeared in the courtyard. The saint had perforce to go downstairs and to listen to their request. "Make up your mind to live here in retirement," the good people urged; "we will obtain the necessary authorization." To this proposal M. Vianney meekly replied: "O my friends, if you succeed I shall be only too glad!" This answer calmed their fears, and the deputation withdrew.

The good people! had they but known what was in the air, they would have remained until dawn. A plan for his escape had been concerted between M. Vianney and M. Raymond. Before nightfall, M. Raymond set out from the presbytery of Dardilly. He pretended that he was going to take M. Vianney's reply to the Bishop; in reality, he did not intend to go farther than the village of Albigny, whose curé, M. Martin, was an intimate friend of his. It was there that the Curé d'Ars was to join him. François had been admitted into the secret. That good man's patience had been so sorely tried by the many visitors of the preceding days that he gladly consented to further this "evasion."

On the morning of Monday, September 18, the two brothers rose early and started off in the darkness for the village of Albigny. The saint rode, for the first part of the way, on the farm horse, which François led by the bridle; but as they neared Albigny he expressed a wish to proceed on foot. He alighted, bade adieu to his brother, and entered the village alone. His first impression could not have been more unfortunate. The day before had been the *vogue* of the district, and dancing was still going on in the early hours of Monday. M. Vianney found M. Raymond, said his Mass, and was for pursuing their journey at once.

Beaumont, a village lost amid the ponds of La Dombes, and some fifty kilometers distant from Dardilly, was not easily reached. M. Raymond hoped that after crossing the Saône at Neuville they would find a conveyance. He was doomed to disappointment. After traveling five leagues on foot they arrived at Saint-Marcel, where the Mayor happened to meet them and to recognize M. Vianney. There was nothing for it but to halt and rest for a while, However, no sooner was the news of the saint's arrival noised abroad, than the little church of Saint-Marcel filled with people. M. Vianney was compelled to go into the pulpit. He preached on detachment from the things of this world, on the shortness of life, and the happiness of Heaven. A carriage was at length procured, and at nightfall the travellers reached Marlieux, the parish of which Beaumont was a dependency.

During the summer months Notre-Dame de Beaumont, a rustic sanctuary looking out upon immense swamps, attracted a goodly number of pilgrims. Local tradition had it that more than once Our Lady listened to the prayers of sorrowing parents and brought back to life little children who had died without Baptism, prolonging the life thus restored until the little ones had received the Sacrament which opens the gate of Heaven. On the morning of Tuesday the curé of Marlieux conducted his guests of the previous night to the old chapel. "M. Vianney," says the Abbé Raymond, "said Mass, his intention being that of obtaining the light of the Holy Ghost. At the end of Mass I asked him: 'Well, what is your decision?' 'I have come to no decision as yet,' he replied, 'I shall go on praying whilst serving your Mass.' As soon as I returned to the sacristy, even before I took off the sacred vestments, he told me: 'The good God does not want me here.' 'Well, where do you wish to go?' 'Let us return to Ars!'"

His mind was made up at last.

Without further delay the Abbé Raymond made arrangements for the return journey. A conveyance took the travellers through the melancholy stretch of swamps and ponds as far as Ambérieux-en-Dombes. At times M. Vianney wept, and he prayed without ceasing. At Ambérieux he said: "The carriage tires me too much; I shall make the remaining part of the journey on foot." Only seven kilometers now separated him from the tiny village, always so dear to his heart, from which he fled that he might the better find God, and to which the will of God now restored him. At Savigneux, by the advice of his fellow-traveller, he entered the church for a visit to the Blessed Sacrament and a few moments' rest. A courier was then despatched to Ars, which was quite near, with the tidings: "M. le Curé is coming back; he will be with you within an hour."

The joyful news was no sooner broadcast than the bells rang out a festive peal. "Joy was universal," Catherine Lassagne writes. "The people quickly assembled in order that they might behold him whom they had lost for eight days; even those who were threshing the corn came in their working clothes."

Towards five o'clock, amid the pealing of the bells, the Curé d'Ars appeared. Leaning on a stick, he walked to the square where his flock awaited him. "And so all was lost?" he exclaimed; "well, and now all is found! I shall never leave you again, my children. . . . I shall never leave you again!" He could not utter another word, for he was overcome by emotion; but his eyes raised to heaven, and the gestures of his trembling arms sufficiently testified to his happiness. "Supported by M. Raymond, he walked several times through the square, blessing his people, who could do nothing but weep, stammer a few words, or throw themselves at his knees."

The saint paid a brief visit to the *Providence,* where there was an outburst of joy; they had at last recovered their father! But he was faint from fatigue, so the hour of night prayers was advanced. He insisted on reciting them himself in presence of the whole parish.

Catherine Lassagne writes in her *Petit mémoire:* "So our holy Curé was restored to our affection, Whilst he had been away the crowds had dispersed. Their absence enabled him to take a few days' rest. But very soon he went back to his ordinary duties amongst us. When the news of his return spread, penitents came from all parts, so that he resumed his former mode of life."

"What would have become of so many sinners?" he himself said in all simplicity. And the Comte des Garets adds: "Thenceforth he understood better that God wanted him to remain with us."

Chapter 18

INCIDENTS OF THE LAST YEARS

I. Suppression of the Orphanage—Foundation of the Day School and of the Boarding-School of the Brothers—Decennial Missions

THE hopes which the Curé d'Ars had founded on his house of *Providence* were doomed to partial disappointment. From 1827 he took his meals there; and there also he hoped to end his days when he should have resigned the parish into other hands. Man proposes, but God disposes, often against man's wishes, even if he happens to be a saint. Unexpected events thwarted the realization of M. Vianney's pleasant dream. He was even refused the consolation of seeing his work of preservation and charity continued on the lines on which he had planned it. As we have seen, the *Providence* was both a school and an orphanage; as an orphanage it was doomed to extinction.

This suppression has been represented as the result of a dark plot between the Bishop of Belley and a congregation of nuns. The chapter in which M. Monnin fancies he is giving a true description of the affair, is entitled: "*Conspiracy against the Institution of the 'Providence' and the circumstances that brought about its fall.*"[1] If there

1. As soon as M. Monnin published his book (1861) his attention was drawn to the rather shocking nature of this title. He modified it in subsequent editions, but only in the Index! *"Of the Circumstances that Led to the Downfall of the Providence."* He also altered the text of the chapter by making many excisions.

In that chapter (the seventh of the third book in the edition of 1861) Mgr. Devie is hardly mentioned at all, nevertheless the reader gets the impression that he was the instigator of a *conspiracy* of which M. Guillemin, the Vicar-General, and Mère Saint-Claude were the moving spirits. In ch. iv, p. 462—and the sentence was not suppressed in any edition—M. Monnin says: *"Mgr. Devie,* by a special dis-

was a fall of some sort, there certainly never was a conspiracy. The true story of the event is not so black.

The *Providence,* as it had been conceived and set on foot by the Abbé Vianney, was an undertaking of so peculiar a nature, that it seemed impossible for it to survive him. Now, after the twofold alarm of 1843—viz., the grave illness and the "flight" of M. le Curé—some of his entourage began to ask themselves whether Ars would possess him much longer. Should an undertaking be suffered to collapse which had been up till then an immense boon to the whole countryside? M. Vianney, indeed, realized that Catherine Lassagne, Marie Filliat, and Jeanne-Marie Chanay were not immortal, and he had added to their number three young women of Ars who were at first to assist and eventually to replace them. However, in his humility the Saint failed to see that it would be a waste of energy to train new mistresses if at the same time the *Providence* were not to have the support of a man like himself. Apparently the wisest and simplest thing would be to entrust the work to a religious congregation which would assure its continuity; such, at least, was the opinion of several persons who were intimate with M. Vianney. "I was one of those who urged him to send for some Sisters," says the Abbé Raymond, his first assistant. And again, without undervaluing the merits of Catherine Lassagne and her companions, certain mothers who sent their daughters to the school made no secret of their opinion that if nuns were in charge the house would be cleaner and the children would be better taught. A few went even further, objecting to their children mixing with those poor creatures who had been picked up in all sorts of places.

These mutterings ended by reaching the ears of M. Vianney, and they did not find him insensible; in fact, he

---

position of Providence, *never did anything to encourage the works inspired by his zeal* (M. Vianney's); on the contrary, he did, unintentionally, several things to hinder them." *Several things?* What were they? And at what period of the saint's life? M. Monnin makes accusations which he does not substantiate. M. Cognat is nearer the truth when he writes: "Mgr. Devie did not content himself merely with defending the Curé d'Ars against the prejudices of which he was the object; *he seconded, as much as he could, his works of zeal. . . . He helped him with his counsel and his moral support in his various institutions"* (*Mgr. Devie,* t. II, pp. 280-281).

was pained. Since the work achieved the end which he had in view when he founded it, he could not understand why people should wish for something else. If the Académie wanted qualified teachers for its schools, that was its own lookout; but was it necessary that the daughters of the good people of Ars should be so very learned, since when they reached the age of twelve, they would have to work in the house and in the fields? Moreover, if people preferred nuns, Catherine, Marie, and Jeanne-Marie were there: "they only needed to be dyed," as he expressed it.[2]

The diocesan authorities who professed a profound veneration for M. Vianney were not ignorant of anything that happened at Ars. Mgr. Devie himself was anxious about the future of the *Providence.* He commissioned M. le Chanoine Perrodin, the Superior of his Grand Séminaire, to sound the saintly Curé as to his intentions. With the help of the Sisters of St. Joseph, M. Perrodin had founded a Providence at Bourg, which had proved a great success. During repeated visits, he explained to the servant of God that it would be of great advantage to entrust his institution to those Sisters. M. Vianney yielded, but only after many entreaties.[3]

In May, 1847, the Reverend Mother Saint-Claude, Superior-General of the Sisters of St. Joseph, visited the schools of her congregation at Villeneuve, which is close to Ars. She informed the saint that she would be passing through the village, and asked for an interview. This interview seemed to be the result of pure chance; in reality it had been previously concerted between the Bishop and the mother-house of the Sisters. Whilst the venerable Superior was staying at Villeneuve, M. Guillemin, the Vicar-General of Mgr. Devie and an old friend of M. Vianney, likewise set out for Ars in order to be there at the same time as Mère Saint-Claude.

M. Vianney, who had not been notified of the arrival of the Vicar-General, showed much emotion: he understood that the authorities wished to precipitate matters.

---

2. Marthe Miard, *Procès apostolique continuatif,* p. 843.
3. Baronne de Belvey, *Procès de l'Ordinaire,* p. 242.

After a preliminary exchange of ideas with M. Guillemin and the Reverend Mother, an eventual transformation of his orphanage was accepted by him in principle.

Great was the grief of Catherine Lassagne and her fellow-workers when they heard of the project. So they were not to end their days among their adopted children in a house that was so dear to them! They were still comparatively young—Catherine was only forty-one, Jeanne-Marie Chanay forty-eight, and Marie Filliat thirty-nine—what was to become of them, deprived, as they would be, of an interest which was their very life, to which they had sacrificed everything, their time, their labor, their health, their future? The poor founder saw their tears and heard their lamentations. Touched by a grief which he had not expected to be so deep and demonstrative, he endeavored to comfort these excellent women by those supernatural considerations which were the stay of his own life.

Negotiations between the saint and the mother-house of Bourg were protracted over the following six months. At length, on November 5, 1847, a deed was drawn, signed, and sealed as "between M. Vianney, parish priest of Ars, on the one part, and Mme. Louise Monnet, in religion Soeur Saint-Claude, Superior-General of the Congregation of St. Joseph, of which the novitiate is at Bourg, on the other." By this deed M. Vianney conveyed the round sum of 53,000 francs to the Congregation of St. Joseph, which, in return, undertook to continue, just as it was, the entire work of the *Providence*—that is, the parochial school and the orphanage, both of which were to remain gratuitous.

On December 13, 1847, the administrative council of St. Joseph confirmed the transaction in the name and by the authority of the Bishop of Belley. On November 5, 1848, exactly one year after the signing of the contract, the sisters took possession of the house.

At the time of the arrival of the Sisters, the orphanage was but a shadow of its former self: only two children were left, and even these did not stay long. What had happened? Here we come to an obscure part in this history, and no documents throw light upon it.

In the course of the unheard-of panic which seized both pilgrims and parishioners at the time of the saint's "flight" to Dardilly in September 1843, the orphanage gradually emptied. This proves that no one thought the institution could survive M. Vianney. We have seen how Catherine wrote to tell him that only *fifteen little ones* were left in the house. On the other hand none of the *big girls* seem to have been upset. It goes without saying that as soon as the alarm was over the children who had been withdrawn by either parents or teachers promptly returned. What was the number when, four years later, a radical change was brought about in the management? Catherine's notes give us no definite information. She speaks vaguely of some sixty children, and we have seen that she did not trouble to count heads; but she never mentions that there was a gradual falling off in numbers, until she suddenly writes that in this year 1848 "the *big girls* were put into situations and the few little ones that remained were sent away, except for one or two." Hence we conclude that the majority of the poor mites had already been returned to their parents or placed with charitable persons.

Towards the end of 1847, the personnel of the *Providence* was likewise reduced. At the request of M. Vianney, the three young women on whom he had relied for the continuation of the work, entered the novitiate of St. Joseph of Bourg. Two of them returned to their families a few weeks later; the *"Journées de février,"* 1848, had their repercussion even as far as Bourg, for, when some disorders broke out, most of the novices left the motherhouse; when order was re-established the two postulants of Ars did not return to the novitiate. The departure of the orphans and the reduction in the personnel chosen by M. Vianney obviously meant a winding up of affairs.

But how reconcile this "liquidation" with the undertaking entered upon by the Sisters of St. Joseph to continue purely and simply the work of the *Providence?* The heavy task that they were assuming must have frightened them from the very start. Assuredly they had no wish to see the extinction of the *Providence,* but they were chiefly interested in the school for little girls to which they intended some day to add a small boarding-school. It is likely enough that they explained to M. Vianney by word of mouth—no written document has been preserved—that it would be a good thing to leave the work of the *Providence,* properly so-called, in abeyance, at least for a time, subject to its being resumed on a new basis and under better conditions. He may even have been given a hint that such was the mind of the Bishop of Belley.

The Curé d'Ars, who only sought the good of souls, could not come to a decision. He had recourse to prayer, and an interior voice seemed to urge him not to yield on this point: the orphanage suppressed, his work, it appeared to him, was destroyed.[4] "The Bishop," he groaned, "sees the will of God in all this, but I fail to see it." At length he agreed to all that was asked of him, and he did so gladly and wholeheartedly. On October 24, twelve days before the arrival of the Sisters, he wrote to Mgr. Devie: "I always cherish the blissful hope that you will have the great charity to bless our chapel and to install our good Sisters, to whose arrival the whole parish, as well as myself, looks forward with impatience." Better still, he instilled a like resignation into the hearts of his devoted helpers. On that same October 24 Catherine Lassagne expressed herself, with regard to the new teachers, in the following terms: "We trust that they feel as eager to come as we are to receive them."[5]

In the meantime M. Vianney had hastened the completion of the chapel. The morning of November 5, which was a Sunday, saw it adorned with statues, pictures, and reliquaries. Mgr. Devie, still very active notwithstanding his eighty years, insisted on personally installing the new

4. "He was most anxious for his *Providence* to be preserved in its original character." (B. de Belley, *Procès apostolique ne pereant,* p. 208).
5. *Letter* to Rev. Mother Saint-Claude.

Superior, Soeur Marie Séraphie, and her companions. On that day the Bishop blessed the new chapel, which was dedicated to the Holy Family, and he also erected the Stations of the Cross. It was a holiday for the whole village. The Mayor, M. Prosper des Garets, had his place in the humble sanctuary, beside M. Vianney, and the people of Ars filled the small nave. All conspired to give the Sisters a most hearty welcome.

With their advent a new era began for the *Providence* of Ars. Deprived of its orphans, it was difficult for the house to recover the exuberant vitality of former days. In the deed of transfer of November 5, 1847, it had been stipulated that Catherine Lassagne and her companions should live for the rest of their days with the Sisters and co-operate with them. But it was easy to foresee that such a scheme would not work.

Catherine Lassagne, a devout woman but highly strung, certainly did display some resentment when she had to resign her authority. On the arrival of the nuns in the afternoon of Saturday, November 4, she stood on the threshold of the house. Handing over the keys, she said coldly: "This is your home!"[6] For all that, she remained where she was, and both she and her companions stayed on for several months. On the December 25, Soeur Marie-Séraphie wrote to her Superior-General: "Those ladies are making friends with us. Jeanne-Marie, it is true, treats us from time to time to some sharp words, but this is, I believe, the result rather of her temperament than of her will. Everything is sure to go well." Nevertheless, the end of 1848 and the opening months of 1849, which were a period of transition and trial, proved really difficult for everybody. The premises of the *Providence* had been neglected; they clamored for brush and broom; the walls, which were very damp, had become dilapidated, so that the masons had to be called in.

It was to be expected that the old mistresses would part company with the new ones, but they did so ami-

6. "Vous êtes chez vous!"

cably.[7] Jeanne-Marie Chanay went to live in the village with one of her sisters, whilst Catherine Lassagne and Marie Filliat settled down in two small rooms contiguous to the presbytery. Their occupations, henceforth, were to look after the vestments and the church linen, the decoration of the altars and the preparation of the Curé's meals; between-whiles they did some spinning or they visited the sick. Catherine, far from sulking, often visited the sisters. After that first moment of ill humor, which she promptly repressed, she initiated the newcomers into their task and was always disposed to help them. Each month she presided over the meeting of the Associates of the Living Rosary, which was held in their chapel.

During the first fortnight following upon the installation of the Sisters, M. Vianney maintained a reserved and, as it were, expectant attitude. He had ceased taking his meals at the *Providence;* henceforth, until his death, he would be served in his own room. He was now sixty-two years of age. It is a trying thing for all men, even for a man of consummate holiness, to change old habits. He uttered no complaint, but it was obvious that he suffered. The only regret that he expressed was that of no longer seeing his beloved orphans around him. By their prayers they had had a share in all his undertakings; how many graces he attributed to their intercession! "The *Providence* has been reproached with many things," he one day confided to M. des Garets; "it was said that the children were not well looked after, and yet God wrought miracles in its behalf."[8]

At the end of a fortnight, at the one o'clock recreation, the saint appeared once more among his children. He spoke to them with his accustomed playfulness, and both the children and their new mistresses rejoiced at the sight of him. Henceforth he visited the school occasionally, but he was no longer responsible for its existence,

7. Catherine writes as follows at the conclusion of some notes she has compiled on the *Providence:* "Then the former directresses made way for the nuns, and withdrew in order to prepare for death. May God be praised for everything! Amen."
8. *Procès de l'Ordinaire,* p. 908.

since the Sisters were now in sole charge. Other works of great importance also attracted his attention and benefited by his generosity.

M. Vianney, therefore, left the Sisters full liberty of action. They had their superiors, their rules, their peculiar customs—that must suffice them. To himself he only reserved the spiritual direction of the pupils.[9] However, from the day when the missionaries took up their residence in the rooms adjoining the school, he resumed his custom of a daily visit to the pupils of the Sisters. As they returned to their classrooms, towards half-past one, he loved to bless now one, now another, by tracing a cross on their foreheads.

In order to give a practical demonstration of his sympathetic attitude towards the new teachers, who, almost from the first day, took in boarders, he had one of his grandnieces entrusted to them. There was a vein of roguishness in the child. One day complaints were made to the great-uncle that the child was continually in mischief. "What do you expect?" he said with a smile; "we are none of us any good in our family." Nevertheless, as Soeur Saint-Lazare tells us, it was this naughty pupil who once had the honor of presenting the Curé with the bouquet that was always offered to him on the Feast of St. John the Baptist. "Ah! my child," he said as he accepted the flowers, "an *Ave* is worth more than all this."

"When I opened a shop in the village," Marthe Miard relates—it was about 1850—"the zeal of the Sisters for cleanliness and beauty caused the *Providence* gradually to lose its former bareness. I have an idea that M. le Curé was pained; but he never showed any resentment." He had organized that institution after the model of his own life, and miracles had demonstrated that God accepted the prayers that rose up from amid such poverty and dilapidation. But the saints, who are all more or less sublimely eccentric, have their own conception of things. As for the nuns, they only did their duty in keeping the

9. On May 7, 1849, Soeur Marie-Séraphie wrote to her Superior-General: "We hope that M. le Curé will not always remain inactive as regards his beloved *Providence.*"

school clean and neat.

One fact plainly shows the curé's esteem for the Congregation of St. Joseph. In 1857, owing to his personal intervention, one of his nieces entered it as a postulant.

Every year, on July 2, the Feast of the Visitation of Our Lady, it was his happiness to officiate at the ceremony of the renewal of vows in the chapel of the *Providence.* "The feast of today deserves special mention," the Abbé Toccanier jotted down in his diary on the evening of July 2, 1855. "The Mass was said by M. le Curé, when he wore the splendid chasuble of the Immaculate Conception. Twenty-two Sisters of St. Joseph renewed their vows in the presence of the servant of God. The number of parishioners and pilgrims who communicated at his Mass was so great that he emptied a whole ciborium." As he left the chapel that morning the saint could not restrain his gladness. "Oh! how beautiful is religion!" he exclaimed. "I was thinking a little while ago that between Our Lord and these good religious, His mystic brides, there took place a contest in generosity. But, do what they may, Our Lord invariably proves the winner. The Sisters said: 'I renew my vows of poverty, chastity, and obedience.' Yet it was they who received most, for I, in my turn, said: 'May the Body of our Lord Jesus Christ keep thy soul unto life everlasting.'"[10]

All through his long ministry, the Curé d'Ars took as much interest in the education of boys as in that of girls. About 1835 he had once, when in conversation with the Mayor, Michel Sève, insisted on the post of schoolmaster being filled by a man of Ars, one Jean Pertinand, a nephew of the Abbé Renard. Thus in 1838, this young man of twenty, who was provided with all the necessary qualifications, became the schoolmaster of his native village. He acted as such for the space of eleven years. "M. le Curé,"

10. *Procès de l'Ordinaire,* p. 1904. The Curé d'Ars did not live to see the resurrection of his orphanage, for it was only reopened in 1863. "May God bless this resumption of the work of the holy Curé; he was so devoted to his beloved *Providence!*" Mgr. de Langalerie, Bishop of Belley, wrote to the Abbé Toccanier on April 13, 1864.

he relates, "often visited my class, and every one of his visits produced an excellent effect on the children; a word from his lips was sufficient to make them good and docile for several days. He himself paid for the small boys whose parents were said to be poor."

But his dream was to see the school kept by religious and wholly gratuitous. On March 10, 1849, the dream became a reality. M. Vianney having made himself personally responsible for the board and lodging of the teachers, Jean Pertinand saw himself replaced by three Brothers of the Holy Family of Belley.[11] Their superior was a religious aged twenty-four, named Frère Athanase,[12] who was destined to play an important role in the life of our saint. To the small school, to which only the children of the village were admitted, the zealous headmaster soon resolved to join a boarding-school for the benefit of the well-to-do families of the district. With some trepidation he confided the project to his saintly Curé. "Yes, my friend," was M. Vianney's unhesitating reply, "do open a boarding-school; you will succeed; you will see that you will snatch many youthful souls from the *grappin.*" Many boarders did, in fact, apply for admission, so that it became necessary to think of the erection of new buildings. On May 28, 1856, the Curé d'Ars, radiantly happy, blessed

11. At first there was only a verbal agreement. Six years later, on February 13, 1855, by a deed drawn up and signed in due form, M. Vianney endowed the boys' school. He at once handed to Frère Gabriel, Superior-General of the Holy Family of Belley, the sum of 10,000 francs. Soon afterwards he added to this sum another 10,000 francs. The school was to be entrusted for all time to the Brothers of the said congregation. The Commune of Ars undertook to provide lodgings, carry out the more important repairs, and pay annually the sum of one hundred francs to each of the teachers.

12. Jacob Planche, in religion Frère Athanase, was born at Chalon-sur-Saône on January 2, 1825. He conducted the school of Ars for forty-one years. By his knowledge, his authority, and his virtue he proved himself wholly equal to his task. During a period of ten years he was the "comrade" and one of the secretaries of M. Vianney, hence one of the witnesses of the ten most important years of his wonderful life. He played the organ, sang at the lectern, taught plain-chant, trained the altar boys, and, if need be, took their place. He was secretary to the Mayor of Ars from 1849 until 1910, when his great age compelled him to resign that office. He was very popular in the village, and the pilgrims loved to call on him. After M. Vianney's death, Frère Athanase remained the living chronicle of the holy Cure's days. He spoke of him with enthusiasm and admiration. He died on June 17, 1912, at the age of eighty-eight. Whilst the last Sacraments were being administered to him he still managed to relate to those who were present three or four incidents of the life of the Curé d'Ars.

the foundation-stone of the new edifice.[13]

Himself a schoolmaster during the time he lay hid in the far-off village of Les Robins, M. Vianney would have liked to spread far and wide the benefits of education. No one, assuredly, could tax the holy priest with *obscurantism,* though he was unversed in human science. Thanks to the daily alms that were given him for his various undertakings, he was able to co-operate in the foundation of schools in other villages, such as Jassans, Beauregard (the home of the Abbé Raymond), and Saint-Euphémie, in the Diocese of Valence. He encouraged and assisted the foundation of Saint-Sorlin (Rhône) for foundlings. To the schools of Dardilly, his native place, he gave 2,000 francs. "They will prosper and do much good," he declared to the curé of Dardilly who was anxious about the future. "This prediction," the latter admitted, "was fulfilled in a truly providential manner when, in 1880, everything seemed ready for the conversion into a penitentiary of both day-school and boarding-school."

The Curé d'Ars was of opinion that no sacrifice was too great for the sake of a good education. The mother of a family told him one day: "I have now spent all I possessed in procuring a good education for my children; nothing is left to me except my house." "Sell it," the saint replied, "and complete your work." In point of fact the house was sold, but, by an unexpected turn of fortune, the purchaser made his will in favor of the mother of the children. He died shortly afterwards, and thus she inherited the home of which she had so generously made the sacrifice.[14]

That same year, 1849, in addition to the school for boys, M. Vianney interested himself in an undertaking of more universal interest and one destined to yield even

---

13. In 1872, during the pastorate of M. Toccanier, the number of boarders continuing to increase, Frère Athanase proceeded with the enlargement of the premises, and gave them their present appearance. In the days of its prosperity the school accommodated as many as eighty children. Such was the institution, the work of a saint, which, in 1903, fell under the blows of the Waldeck-Rousseau law.
14. Catherine Lassagne, *Procès apostolique in genere,* p. 114.

more far-reaching results. Experience had taught him the great utility of missions, even in the most forsaken parishes. Had he not decided, as early as 1819—that is, the year after his arrival at Ars—to have a mission given to his flock by two priests of the Chartreux of Lyons?

The Diocese of Belley had, by now, its own diocesan missionaries. In 1833, at the instigation of Mgr. Devie, MM. Mury and Convert had founded a small society of preachers at Bourg. The two founders quickly wore themselves out, and died in harness, within six months of each other, seven years after the foundation. At their death the work was entrusted to Chanoine Camelet who transferred the headquarters to Pont-d'Ain. When M. Vianney, having given up the *Providence* to the Sisters of St. Joseph, had no longer to provide for the upkeep of that establishment, Mgr. Devie asked him to think of his missionaries. "I will consult the good God," the saint replied. A few days later he handed to the Abbé Raymond 6,000 francs, the income of which was to defray the expenses of a mission to be held every ten years in two different parishes. This foundation gave him a taste for more: was it not for the conversion of sinners? At the time of his death he had founded close to one hundred decennial missions. Thus, even after his death, he still went on with the work of bringing souls back to God.[15]

"Oh! how I regret having thought so late of so beautiful a work!" he would say from time to time. He conceived a real passion for it; he spoke of it unceasingly, saving up sou after sou so as to be in a position to found yet another mission. "I am becoming a miser for the sake of the good God," he often smilingly observed, and when he had scraped together sufficient money to found yet another, he experienced something like the joy of a landowner who has just increased his estate. "I love the missions to such an extent," he exclaimed in the pulpit, "that if, by selling my body, I could establish another, I should sell it."

15. Of course Ars was not forgotten; the decennial mission, which M. Vianney founded for his village, was given for the first time in 1851.

One fine day in July, 1855, he, in great glee, entered the room in which several missionaries of Pont-d'Ain were taking their midday meal. "How radiant you look, Monsieur le Curé!" said M. Alfred Monnin.

"I should think so! This morning, I discovered that I am the possessor of as much as 200,000 francs. . . . And this capital is placed with the safest bank in the world; I have lent it to the three wealthiest persons it is possible to find."

"And who are those three persons?"

"The Persons of the most Holy Trinity."[16]

How did the Curé d'Ars come to command resources so considerable for the work of the missions? In the first place, by the charity of others.

"One morning," Frère Athanase relates, "he said to me in the sacristy: 'Comrade, did you get up early this morning?'

"'At the usual hour,' I replied.

"'So much the worse!' he said with some vivacity; 'had you imitated me you would have had an excellent day: I have been given money for the foundation of a mission, and even more than is required. As I came out of the presbytery last night, I met a young man who was waiting for me, and he gave me 1,000 francs for this work; then in the chapel of St. John the Baptist another person gave me a like amount; finally, a third donor arrived who more than completed the sum.'

"It was only seven o'clock in the morning when M. le Curé told me this story!"[17]

"One day," the Abbé Raymond relates, "a pious lady came to see him in the sacristy. 'Father,' she said, 'have you received a letter in which I inform you of the despatch of fifty francs as a contribution towards your charities?'

"'Yes, my dear Madam, I have received it, but shortly after I fell in with a charitable man who gave me 5,000 francs for a work I have very much at heart because it is calculated to contribute greatly to the salvation of souls.

16. Abbé Monnin, *Procès de l'Ordinaire,* p. 1130.
17. *Procès de l'Ordinaire,* p. 828.

That big sum has somehow caused me to forget yours; that is the reason I have not acknowledged it.'

"'But, Father, what is the work to which you seemingly attach such value?'

"'Ah! Madam, it is the work of the missions.'

"'Might I not have some share in it, my good Father? How much do you want for a mission?'

"'Three thousand francs, my dear Madam.'"

So the Curé d'Ars got this lady, a widow of Lyons who had an income of 10,000 francs, to found not one, but two missions.

Truly this, his favorite undertaking, rendered M. Vianney "miserly" for the time being. Previously to this time he had taken delight in enriching several parishes, less favored than his own, with sacred vestments and vessels, statues and banners. Among the beneficiaries of his bounty were the villages of Beauregard, Saint-Euphémie de l'Ain, Saint-Jean-de-Thurigneux, Toussieux, Frans, Ambérieux-en-Dombes, Saint-Didier-de-Formans, Sainte-Euphémie in la Drôme, and others also. To the curé of Dardilly, his native village, he gave a ciborium and a chalice of great value. But from 1849 onwards the saint began to study economy.

"The curé of a poor parish," the Abbé Etienne Dubouis relates, "had requested him to ask Vianney for the sum of about eighty francs to enable him to acquire a statue or a banner. 'Oh! no,' he replied, 'it is impossible. All my resources are ear-marked for the work of the missions.'"[18]

On June 14, 1855, he sent M. Toccanier to Bourg with the money for three of these pious foundations; but he had been obliged to borrow in order to complete the sum required for the third of these missions. That same evening he said to Frère Athanase and Frère Jérôme "I have borrowed money because I did not wish to leave this foundation unfinished. If no one helps me to refund the sum, well, I shall sell my *rags,* and if that is not enough, they can send me to the prison of Toulon!" He was joking, of course.

---

18. *Ibid.,* p. 1243.

"One fine day," says Marie Ricotier, "M. le Curé came to me with a parcel in his hand, saying: 'I have to send away the money for a foundation (of a mission) but I am 200 francs short. Would you give me that sum for this alb which belongs to me?' The bargain was clinched. In this way I came into possession of a multitude of objects which I bought by way of concurring in his charities."[19]

In addition to the missions M. Vianney likewise founded a great number of Masses in perpetuity, the fees for which were assured by investments in the State bank. In 1855, he had already invested nearly 40,000 francs for this object, and the church of Ars alone was by then provided with two hundred and eighty annual Masses. And because he had very much at heart the work of the *propagation of the faith*—his little parish mustered ten circles of ten members each—he had founded seventy of those Masses with a view to securing for the missionaries the protection of the Blessed Virgin Mary. Most of the others were to be offered up for the conversion of sinners.[20]

19. *Procès de l'Ordinaire,* p. 1338.
20. The money thus invested by the Curé d'Ars has been confiscated by the State, in virtue of the law of separation of Church and State, and the law of April 13, 1908, so that the Masses are no longer said.

Chapter 19

INCIDENTS OF THE LAST YEARS
(continued)
II. La Salette

IN the course of the evening of Tuesday, September 24, 1850, François Pertinand, the carrier of Ars, brought, as far as the steps of the church, a party of five travellers, three men—viz., MM. de Brayer, Verrier, and Thibaut—a girl of the name of Angélique Giraud, and a boy of fifteen, Maximin, Angélique's brother. With the exception of M. Thibaut, who was ailing, and for that reason followed Pertinand to the hostelry, the strangers went at once into the church to look for M. Vianney.

With his slender and delicate body, round face, and a complexion bespeaking perfect health, and large, beautiful eyes full of expression, Maximin Giraud looked younger than his years. He was one of the *voyants* of La Salette. Four years earlier, on September 19, 1846, on the alpine mountains of that name, he and Mèlanie Mathieu, a shepherdess of fourteen, tended the cows of a farmer with whom he had taken service only the day before. At about three o'clock in the afternoon, a beautiful Lady, so the shepherds related, appeared to them in the midst of a wonderful brightness. Seated on a rock, close to the banks of a streamlet, called the Sézia, the Lady wept whilst she covered her face with her hands. Presently a gentle voice bade the children approach without fear. The Apparition stood up and spoke to them, the burden of its message being the anger of God against blasphemers and desecrators of the Sunday, calamities that were impending, and the need of penance and prayer. At the end of about half an hour the beautiful Lady rose upwards and gradually vanished in the sky.

During four years, though harassed by a thousand queries from both wise and foolish people, neither Mèlanie Mathieu nor Maximin Giraud wavered at any time; nor did they contradict each other in their respective statements. Both were endowed with the honesty of simple people, hence their story of the apparition met with very little incredulity in their immediate neighborhood. The Bishop of Grenoble prescribed a rigorous control of their asseverations. However, at the time of Maximin's journey to Ars in September, 1850, Mgr. de Bruillard's pastoral letter on the facts of La Salette was only in course of preparation—it was published a year later, on September 19, 1851. This detail is important. Hence in 1850 there was as yet no official pronouncement concerning the truth or falsehood of the apparition.

As soon as the snow began to melt, in the spring of 1847, pilgrims went up to La Salette. On their return many of their number passed through Ars, and from them M. Vianney received early information of the wonderful occurrence. "From the very first he believed in the apparition of our Blessed Lady," says M. le Comte des Garets, with some reserve, however, for in matters of this kind he always went by the authority of the bishops."[1] Now his Bishop, Mgr. Devie, whom, assuredly, he consulted in a matter of such importance, maintained, until 1851, an attitude of expectancy. So the Curé based his conduct on that of the prelate, but in practice he recommended the pilgrimage to those who showed a wish to make it. He spoke of the apparition in his catechisms, signed pictures and blessed medals that represented it; an engraving of it was hung on one of the walls of the presbytery; he had some water from the miraculous source and distributed it among his friends. All this he did notwithstanding the

1. *Procès de l'Ordinaire,* p. 964. Absorbed as he was by his work in the confessional, the Curé d'Ars had obviously not been able to look into the subject for himself. "Judging by what the servant of God told me," says the Abbé Toccanier, "I understood that he believed in the Apparition by reason of his great devotion to the Blessed Virgin. He took the occurrence to be true because he saw serious persons believing in it. "*(Procès apostolique ne pereant,* p. 309).

objections of his assistant, the Abbé Raymond. The latter, indeed, did not believe in La Salette. He had climbed the mountain on a certain day when Maximin himself had gone up. Now the boy had refused to answer the questions put to him by the vicaire of Ars, and this conduct seems to have excited the spleen of M. Raymond, who was choleric by nature. Thus an incident, trivial enough in itself, had sufficed to prejudice M. Vianney's vicaire against the whole affair.

By what right and for what purpose had MM. de Brayer and Verrier taken young Maximin Giraud to the Curé d'Ars on that evening of September 24, 1850? Mgr. de Bruillard, the prudent Bishop of Grenoble, had urged upon M. Mélin, the curé of Corps, Maximin's birthplace, to keep the child at all costs within the boundaries of the diocese. The inquiry into the facts of La Salette not being as yet concluded, the witnesses of the apparition must needs be within reach. Moreover, it was not seemly that either Maximin or Mélanie should be exhibited as objects of curiosity; whatever the notoriety they had gained, it was necessary that they should both of them remain in the background. This was not understood by MM. de Brayer, Verrier, and Thibaut. These gentlemen, whose intentions were perfectly honorable, though their conduct was imprudent, had taken Maximin away from his mountain village, despite the opposition of M. Mélin and the prohibition of Mgr. de Bruillard. Ostensibly the boy came to consult, on the subject of his vocation, a priest who was a saint and who could read the hearts of men; but the real purpose of the journey was quite other: M. de Brayer and his friends had come to Ars with aims and intentions that were political rather than religious.[2]

---

2. Mgr. Giray, *Les Miracles de la Salette,* t. II, p. 273. Mgr. Giray gives no explanation of those political aims. Mgr. Ginoulhiac, who succeeded Mgr. de Bruillard in the See of Grenoble, and eventually became Archbishop of Lyons, has not been afraid to state them publicly in a document that was to be read throughout the diocese *(Pastoral* of November 4, 1854, p. 18).

"The more zealous partisans of the Baron de Richemont, hoping that the facts of La Salette and the testimony of the two children might strengthen their cause, had gone to Corps as early as 1847, in order to win them over and to find out their secret, which, so they fancied, concerned the pretended Louis XVII.

The visitors asked to see M. Vianney; but he being in the confessional, they were received by his vicaire, who was less busy. "Having asked them to come to the *Providence* for a talk with me," says the Abbé Raymond, "I questioned them about the object of their journey. They replied that Maximin wished to consult M. Vianney on the subject of his vocation.

"'But,' said I, 'M. le Curé of Corps, who knows him and who taught him, would be in a much better position to enlighten the boy in such a matter.'

"The gentlemen persisted, however, adding, in the hearing of Maximin, that he was a rather thoughtless boy, that M. le Curé of Corps was growing weary, and that was why M. Vianney's advice was desired. 'Very well,' I replied, 'you will have that privilege tomorrow morning.'

"Presently one of the travellers asked me: 'As for you, Monsieur l'Abbé, what do you think of La Salette?' I answered that I had not as yet formed a definite opinion on the subject, and I pointed out that in some respects those concerned were not as discreet and as prudent as the Church requires. They said: 'How can anyone refuse to give credence to children who are incapable of inventing the things they relate?'"[3]

On this the conversation took a somewhat acrid tone. M. Raymond related an incident which had come to his knowledge only a few days earlier, though it had happened forty years before. Three small girls conspired to foist upon their families and the general public a belief in an alleged apparition of the Blessed Virgin Mary, and it was only in her fiftieth year that one of the pretended seers avowed the imposture. "You see," said M. Vianney's vicaire, facing little Maximin, "I receive you, though over

---

"Great was their disappointment when, after questioning Maximin, with whom they had more opportunities for conversing, they felt compelled to admit that the child did not even know whether or no Louis XVI, Louis XVII, or Louis XVIII had ever existed. After this, it seemed hardly reasonable on the part of the friends of the Baron de Richemont to persist in believing that that nobleman was the object of the secret mission of the shepherds. They were shaken by the ignorance and the obstinacy of Maximin; but soon even this seemed a mystery demanding another effort: hence the decision to drag the child to Ars."

3. *Procès de l'Ordinaire,* p. 1439.

there you refused to speak to me. However, here you will have to do with a saint, and the saints are not taken in!"[4]

Maximin, tired from the journey and irritated by the hints of these strangers, returned M. Raymond the answer which he invariably gave when people appeared to question his veracity. A year later he gave an account of this interview to Mlle. des Brulais, of Nantes. This is what he told her: "Ah! M. le Vicaire of Ars said that I had invented a tale and that I had not seen our Blessed Lady. I was not then in a good mood, so I replied: 'Well, if you like, put it that I have told a lie and that I have seen nothing!' After that I walked away."[5]

"As for me," said the Abbé Raymond, "I went to inform M. Vianney of what had taken place, and he thanked me very kindly.

"The following morning he had a private interview with Maximin, in the sacristy. What took place then? M. le Curé never breathed a word about it, but Frère Jérôme and myself noticed the next day that he no longer consented to autograph pictures or to bless medals of La Salette."

Whence came this surprising change of attitude? The simplest thing will be to hear Maximin himself, the more so as his narrative does not contradict what less authorized witnesses have affirmed, and his story has about it the ring of sincerity. On September 27, 1851, the lady of Nantes mentioned above met Maximin on the mountain of La Salette. She found him just as he had always been, bright and affectionate, and ready to relate with the utmost simplicity what he called his *little frolics,*[6] without disguise or excuse. In this way he confessed that last year *his head* led him to accompany three gentlemen who, since then, had fallen under suspicion of harbouring a desire to exploit his secret for the benefit of a political opinion. This is the conversation they had:

---

4. Abbé Toccanier, *Procès apostolique ne pereant,* p. 980.
5. M. des Brulais, *L'Echo de la sainte montagne,* p. 269.
6. "Ses petites équipées."

Query: "Why, child, did you surrender yourself into their hands?"

Answer: "Why? In order to see the world, of course."

Q.: "What a road you were entering upon, you poor, imprudent child! What were you thinking of?"

A.: "Ah! I have been very foolish, it is true."

Q.: "What took place during your interview with M. le Curé d'Ars? Will you tell me something about it?"

A.: "The three gentlemen took me to the Curé d'Ars, in order, as they said, that I might consult him on the subject of my vocation. M. le Curé advised me to return again to my own diocese. Those gentlemen were very angry because of this advice. They said I had misunderstood M. Vianney, and they sent me back to him."

At his first interview, which was exceedingly short, Maximin had seen the holy Curé behind the altar, near the confessional reserved for the clergy.

"On that occasion," Maximin pursued, "I went into his confessional in the sacristy. The Curé d'Ars is not easy to understand because he has not many teeth left. He asked me whether I had seen *the Blessed Virgin.* I answered him: 'I cannot say whether it is the Blessed Virgin or not; I have seen something . . . *a Lady.* But, M. le Curé, if you know that it is the Blessed Virgin, you should tell it to all those pilgrims, so that they may believe in La Salette.'"

Q.: "They say, my dear child, that you confessed to M. le Curé d'Ars that you had told lies. Is that true?"

A.: "Ah! I said that I had occasionally lied to M. le Curé of Corps. 'You must retract,' M. Vianney told me. 'No, I cannot retract with regard to those lies; it is not worth while.' He told me once more that I must. And I: 'As it happened a long time ago, I can no longer do so, it is too old a story.'"

Q.: "But what did you mean?"

A.: "I meant my little lies to M. le Curé of Corps when

I did not wish to tell him where I was going, or when I did not want to learn my lessons."

Q.: "Well, now I can see that M. le Curé d'Ars understood that the lies you mentioned to him were in reference to the apparition."

A.: "Oh! yes, he understood me in that way; at least, that is what has been written in the papers."

Q.: "So you were not making your Confession?"

A.: "No. I was in the confessional, it is true, but I had not said my *Confiteor,* and I had not come to Ars for the purpose of going to Confession."[7]

The interview between Maximin and the Curé d'Ars lasted about twenty minutes. The five travellers left Ars that same day, very quietly, and it would seem that their hurried passage through the village was not even noticed by the pilgrims. If, in the sequel, the Abbé Raymond had imitated the discretion of his holy parish priest, what has been called the *incident of La Salette* would, in all probability, never have arisen at all.

On the morning of September 25, M. Raymond noticed that not only did M. Vianney refuse to bless medals of Our Lady of La Salette; he also found on the sacristy table an envelope on which the Curé d'Ars had written the address of Mgr. de Bruillard. "What is this?" the vicaire asked with his wonted precision.

"I wanted to write a letter to the Bishop of Grenoble," replied the saint, "which Maximin was to have handed to him; but the youth refused." And he added with some annoyance: "I was dissatisfied with him and he was dissatisfied with me."

From that moment, M. Raymond relates, every effort to obtain further details about the interview between M. Vianney and Maximin proved futile. First M. le Curé of Voiron, then M. Gerin, parish priest at the cathedral of Grenoble, a most highly respected priest and an intimate friend of the servant of God, came to Ars for the purpose

---

7. M. des Brulais, *L'Echo de la sainte montagne,* pp. 267-269.

of getting some information: it was all in vain. Only when M. Rousselot, Vicar-General, and M. le Curé of Corps were sent by the Bishop of Grenoble and presented a note from Maximin authorizing M. Vianney to speak openly of all that he had confided to him, did the Curé d'Ars consent to give a personal explanation of the *incident of La Salette.*

What he said was inspired by the ambiguous attitude assumed by Maximin, and is brevity itself: "If what the child told me be true, he has not seen the Blessed Virgin." The reader must recollect Maximin's reply to M. Raymond: "Put it that I am telling lies and have seen nothing." Is it rash to think that these words were repeated to the Curé d'Ars and the most unfavorable construction put upon them? On the other hand, M. Vianney recalled to memory that the lad, at the end of his tale in which he spoke of a *beautiful Lady,* without mentioning the Blessed Virgin Mary,[8] had uttered the word *lies.* The Curé d'Ars, who was not assisted by the gift of intuition in every possible circumstance, thought that the boy wished to retract his previous affirmations concerning the apparition itself.[9] With that thought a distressing doubt entered his soul.

His anguish lasted eight years, and the trial was a twofold one; he doubted, and the throngs of pilgrims, who should have been in complete ignorance, knew that he doubted. "There was much excitement round his person; facts were exaggerated and distorted, as is invariably the case under such circumstances. The enemies of La Salette misused the name and authority of the Curé d'Ars. Devout souls were profoundly perturbed on learning that the

---

8. "I know," says Mme. Christine de Cibeins, "that after Maximin's visit to M. le Curé, the latter declared that the youth had told him that he had not seen the Blessed Virgin, but a *beautiful lady." (Procès apostolique continuatif,* p. 155).

9. "M le Cure d'Ars has told me himself that Maximin admitted, outside Confession, that he was a liar. Efforts have been made to explain the admission as meaning that Maximin wished to say that he had occasionally told lies, though not in this circumstance. M. le Curé d'Ars, who at one moment believed in the miracle of La Salette, does so no longer since his interview with Maximin. There is no doubt about that fact." *(Letter* of Mgr. Chalandon, Bishop of Belley, to Cardinal Billiet, Archbishop of Chambéry, August 26, 1854.

apparition could not have taken place since a saint like M. Vianney no longer believed in it. The Abbé Raymond, eager to make a display of zeal, took it on himself to order the Sisters of Pont-d'Ain, with whom he had stayed, to remove from their house a picture of La Salette; and when the nuns expressed their astonishment, M. Vianney's assistant declared that "M. le Curé has seen Maximin; since then he no longer believes in La Salette."

M. Vianney was much grieved by the publicity that was given to the incident, in consequence of the indiscretions of M. Raymond.[10] No doubt, like everybody else, he had a right to form his own opinion on an event of recent occurrence, and round which noisy controversies were raging. The Church was far from raising to the dignity of a dogma of the faith the vision with which those two children claimed to have been favored. But the Curé d'Ars, whom even bishops came to consult, could not be wholly ignorant of the moral authority and the prestige that he wielded in the world of souls. What if there was a misunderstanding, as some affirmed there was? What a pity it would be to spread an unjustifiable mistrust concerning a fact that was true and in which God's glory was in question! "I feel remorse," M. Vianney confided to the former directress of the *Providence;* "I am afraid of having done something against the Blessed Virgin. I wish the good God would enlighten me in this matter. I am going to pray much. If the thing is true, oh! I shall speak of it; if it is not true, that will be the end."[11]

So long as the Bishop of Grenoble did not pronounce sentence in favor of La Salette, M. Vianney readily eluded all questions. He simply requested all indiscreet inquirers to wait for the judgement of ecclesiastical authority. When in September, 1851, Mgr. de Bruillard issued his pastoral letter, the Curé d'Ars felt increasing anxiety. The Bishop on whom La Salette depended and whose duty it

10. "I know," M. Toccanier has stated, "that many people imagined that M. Vianney had been led into error by Maximin, but I also know that many others, on hearing that the servant of God had ceased to believe in La Salette, gave up their own belief in it." (*Procès apostolique ne pereant,* p. 310).

11. Catherine Lassagne, *Procès apostolique in genere,* p. 123.

was to decide, had given a verdict in the affirmative: the two shepherds had not been deluded themselves, and had not led others into error. M. Vianney would have wished to bow without reservation to this sentence. Alas! certain words of Maximin's obstinately haunted his memory! He denied nothing, but he was unable to recover his former conviction.

Yet, now that the Bishop had spoken, it happened even more frequently that, as the saint passed through the throng of pilgrims, men and women of the world, and even priests, asked him outright: "Father, must we believe in La Salette?" The thing became an obsession; hence he made up his mind to reply evasively, unless the position of the questioner compelled him to declare his mind. Otherwise, leaving inquirers to their own opinions, he kept his personal impressions to himself. "One day," says M. Dubouis, curé of Fareins, "the first vicaire of Saint-Sulpice asked him in my presence what he thought of La Salette. M. Vianney simply told him that we should love the Blessed Virgin very much. Three times the vicaire repeated his question, and three times the Curé d'Ars made the same answer.

At last the trial came to an end. In October, 1858—that is, some ten months before his death—M. Vianney went back to his first opinion concerning La Salette. This is how he related the story of his restored belief:

"For about a fortnight I had been experiencing a great interior trouble, and my soul felt as if it were being dragged over a rough road. Then I made an act of faith in respect to the apparition, and at once my soul recovered its tranquillity. I also desired to see a priest of Grenoble in order to confide to him what had taken place within me. The following day a distinguished ecclesiastic of that town arrived here.[12] He came into the sacristy and asked me what one should think of La Salette. I replied: 'One may believe in it.'"

"I was in need of money to complete the requisite sum

12. This *distinguished ecclesiastic* was Chanoine Gerin, parish priest of the cathedral of Grenoble. His interview with M. Vianney took place on October 11.

for the foundation of a mission. I prayed to *Our Lady of La Salette* to procure that sum for me, and I found just what was needed. I looked upon the incident as miraculous."[13]

Henceforth, whilst maintaining great reserve amid the discussions which kept arising on occasion, he encouraged the pilgrimage to La Salette, and those of his penitents who expressed a desire to do so were urged to make the ascent of the *holy mountain.* He began once more to bless and distribute medals or pictures showing *Our Lady in tears.* It is not known whether he ever alluded to the subject in his catechisms: during this supreme period of his life the Curé d'Ars was not easily heard, moreover, his preaching was now nothing but a song of love for God and for Jesus Christ in the Eucharist. However that may have been, he did not fail, as opportunities occurred, to testify in favor of the apparition.

In 1876, Chanoine Oronte Seignemartin, curé of the cathedral parish at Belley, and former curé of Saint-Trivier sur-Moignans, related how he once assisted at a gathering which was likewise attended by M. Vianney. "The conversation turned on La Salette, and I asked M. Vianney what he thought of the apparition. He replied in a grave tone of voice: 'I firmly believe in it.'"

"At the close of 1858 my mother was ill," says Magdeleine Mandy-Scipiot, "so I asked leave from M. le Curé to make a vow to Our Lady of La Salette in her behalf. He replied that that was not necessary, that I should make a vow to Our Lady of Fourvière. 'However, as regards La Salette,' he added, 'you may believe in it; I myself believe in it with all my heart.'"[14]

13. *Procès apostolique ne pereant,* p. 897.
14. *Procès apostolique in genere,* p. 271.

Chapter 20

INCIDENTS OF THE LAST YEARS *(continued)*

III. The Curé d'Ars a Canon of Belley and Chevalier of the Légion d'Honneur —The Feast of December 8, 1854.

IT may be confidently asserted that towards the year 1850 the Abbé Jean-Marie Vianney, parish priest of Ars, was the best-known and most popular priest throughout the whole of France. Some ten years earlier, at Paris, the elite of society had surged round the pulpit of Notre-Dame; at present the lowly Curé, whose church was never empty, was far better known than the eloquent Lacordaire. Yet a man so deservedly popular had had no honor or distinction of any kind bestowed upon him. "Here comes the *saint!*" people exclaimed as he went by, and it is true enough that any other distinction would have been eclipsed by that one. Accordingly, Mgr. Devie, who showed such profound regard for the Curé d'Ars, deemed it superfluous to make him a canon of his cathedral. As a matter of fact, it was not customary for a simple *desservant* to receive such an honor.

Mgr. Chalandon, who succeeded Mgr. Devie (July 25, 1852), did not share his predecessor's opinion in this respect. During the two years of his coadjutorship he, too, had learned to esteem M. Vianney; hence one of his first decisions was to give the mozetta to the most deserving priest of the diocese, even if for once tradition had to be flouted.

Three months after his enthronement in the See of Belley—Monday, October 25—the prelate, accompanied by M. Poncet, his Vicar-General, and by Comte Prosper des Garets, appeared on the threshold of the church of Ars. The Abbé Raymond, who had had warning of the visit, was there to receive him. As for M. Vianney, he was hearing Confessions in the sacristy.

Someone went to tell him of the Bishop's presence. Clad in his surplice with narrow sleeves, he hurried through the ranks of the pilgrims in order to offer holy water to the prelate, according to the rubrics of the ritual; in fact, since this was the first time he saw him as Bishop of Belley, he deemed it his duty to make a little speech. It was evident, however, that the Bishop held something hidden under his mozetta. A quick movement brought to light the mysterious object; its silken folds were shot with black and red, and the whole was bordered with white ermine. M. Vianney understood. "No, Monseigneur," he protested; "give it to my vicaire: it will look better on him than on me." His protests were useless. Helped by M. Poncet and M. Raymond, the Bishop invested M. Vianney with the insignia of an honorary canon; the mozetta, however, had slipped the wrong way over the Curé's shoulders; owing to the efforts of the holy man to get rid of it, the Bishop only just succeeded in buttoning it as high as his shoulders. In the meantime the prelate had intoned the *Veni Creator.* A last protest on the part of Canon Vianney was drowned by the words of the hymn, and the prelate entered the church.

"Our poor parish priest," writes the châtelaine, "looked like a condemned man who is being dragged to the scaffold with a rope round his neck. He took refuge in the sacristy. But M. des Garets followed him thither and found him pulling the unfortunate mozetta from his shoulders. The Mayor only succeeded in persuading him to keep it on by pointing out that to strip himself of it would be tantamount to an affront to the Bishop."[1]

"Then," says Frère Athanase, "instead of occupying his wonted place, he withdrew into the recess of the sacristy

1. Comtesse des Garets, *Procès de l'Ordinaire.* p. 918.

door, as if he felt ashamed and wished to hide himself. Thereupon I whispered into his ear: 'Do not stay here, I beg of you, Monsieur le Curé; you are in a draught.' 'I am all right; leave me alone,' was his reply."

A short ceremony took place in the church, in the course of which the Bishop addressed the congregation. He, of course, proclaimed the elevation of the holy Curé to the dignity of an honorary canon. The new dignitary, however, felt so abashed that he quite forgot to straighten his mozetta, which was becoming more and more disarranged. "One might have thought that M. le Curé had thorns on his back," says Jean-Baptiste Mandy, the son of the former Mayor. At last he must needs return to the presbytery, in this array, by the side of the Bishop. Magdeleine Mandy-Scipiot, one of his penitents who probably had not been previously informed, "failed to recognize him." If we may believe her, "he had the look of a condemned man." According to Mme. des Garets, it was the most amusing scene that could well be imagined.[2]

After the Bishop's departure, when the excitement had abated, it occurred to Canon Vianney that the prelate had bestowed a fine present upon him. Thereupon he at once resolved to take advantage of it for the benefit of his charities; he began to look for a purchaser.

"I had just returned from Villefranche," says Mlle. Marie Ricotier, "and was giving M. le Curé an account of a commission with which he had entrusted me. 'You come at the right moment,' he said. 'I want to sell you my mozetta. I have already offered it to M. Borjon, the curé of Ambérieux, who would not give me twelve francs for it; but you, surely you will give me fifteen?'

"'It is worth more than that.'

"'Twenty, then?'

"I put twenty-five francs into his hand, adding: 'That is not yet its real price; but I will make inquiries.' Eventually I learned that it had been made at the novitiate house of the Sisters of St. Joseph, at Bourg, and had cost

2. *Procès de l'Ordinaire,* p. 918.

fifty francs. So I paid another twenty-five francs, telling him at the same time: 'Your canon's mozetta is now my property, but you may have the use of it.' On hearing this, M. le Curé was so pleased that he exclaimed: 'Oh, let Monseigneur give me another one! I shall make money by it!'

"He wished me, however, to carry away my purchase. 'If the Bishop compels me to put it on, I can always find it at your house.'"[3]

Having thus eased his conscience, he wrote to his Bishop ten days later, to inform him of his good fortune:

"Monseigneur, the mozetta which you have had the great charity to bestow on me has given me much pleasure, because, being in want of money to complete a foundation, I have sold it for fifty francs. That price completely satisfied me."[4]

Notwithstanding the most pressing solicitations, M. Vianney would at no time consent to appear in the dress of a canon, not even in the presence of his Bishop. The Abbé Toccanier having asked him one day why he did not wear his mozetta, he replied with a smile: "O my friend, you see, I am cleverer than people imagine; they were preparing to laugh at me when they saw it on my shoulders. They have been well caught!"

"But you should wear it for the sake of Monseigneur. You are the only one whom our new Bishop has thought of honoring; since then he has appointed no other canon."

"Ah!" replied the humble priest, "that is because Monseigneur was unlucky the first time; he did not care to try again."[5]

The public authorities were by no means uninterested in the ceaseless flow of pilgrims to Ars. The civil

3. *Ibid.*, p. 1337.
4. *Letter* of November 4, 1852.
5. Abbé Toccanier, *Notes MSS.*, p. 27. The above dialogue took place before May 19, 1856, because on that day Mgr. Chalandon bestowed the dignity of canon upon the famous Abbé Gorini, *desservant* of Saint-Denis and author of a work entitled *Défense de l'Eglise.* On May 19 the Bishop wrote to the Abbé Gorini as follows: "In order to honour piety I have appointed M. le Curé d'Ars an honorary canon; to honour clerical science, I grant you a like distinction." (Abbé Martin, *Vie de M. Gorini, curé de la Tranclière et de Saint-Denis,* Tolra, Paris, 1863, p. 238).

administration of the *département* of the Ain looked upon M. Vianney as one whose popularity made him a public benefactor. On June 30, 1855, the Sous-Préfet of Trévoux, the Marquis de Castellane, wrote the following letter to the Bishop of Belley:

"MONSEIGNEUR,

"I have the honor to send you herewith a copy of the report which I have just submitted to M. le Préfet, with the view of obtaining for the deserving Curé d'Ars some mark of recognition.

"I have no doubt that the Government of the Emperor, in its eagerness to reward true merit, will consider the eminent services rendered daily by M. l'Abbé Vianney."

The report of the Marquis de Castellane opened thus:

"MONSIEUR LE PRÉFET,

"In a small commune of my arrondissement, the population of which numbers 510 souls, there is a *desservant* whose evangelical holiness and lofty piety have gained for him a European reputation.

"This description, however vague it may be, can only apply to M. Vianney, Curé d'Ars.

"The commune of Ars, formerly the most obscure in my arrondissement, witnesses a daily influx of a prodigious number of pilgrims.

"Transport facilities have had to be organized; these have been functioning regularly for a considerable time.

"This concourse, now of long standing and wholly due to the reputation for sanctity of a humble priest, constitutes a truly marvellous event in a century which has inherited so many doctrines that are anti-religious and hostile to the Christian faith.

"The confidence of the people in M. le Desservant of Ars is unlimited; it is the faith that transports mountains, spoken of in the Gospel.

"Hence more than one occurrence is mentioned which it would be difficult to explain by purely natural causes.

"The limited space at my disposal does not permit of an enumeration of them: but it is enough to state that in the procedure of the venerable Curé d'Ars there is nothing that savors of charlatanism.

"M. Vianney is another St. Vincent de Paul, whose charity works wonders."

After enumerating the various undertakings due to the initiative of the holy Curé, the Sous-Préfet of Trévoux concludes:

"Wherefore, even from a purely material point of view, he is a most valuable man.

"For all these reasons, M. le Préfet, I have the honor to request that you will have the kindness, on the occasion of the forthcoming feast day of His Majesty, to propose M. Vianney, Curé d'Ars, for the rank of a knight of the Imperial Order of the Légion d'Honneur."

On receipt of this memorandum, the Préfet of the Ain, the Comte de Coëtlogon, took the necessary steps with M. Fortoul, the Minister of Public Instruction and Worship. On August 11 the latter had the satisfaction of being able to inform Mgr. Chalandon that, by a decree of the same day, a knight's cross was being awarded to the Curé d'Ars.

When the August 15 list of honors appeared in the newspapers, the nomination of M. Vianney was hailed with delight and satisfaction.[6] The Mayor, M. des Garets, broke the news to the Curé. "Is there a pension attached to that cross? Does it mean money for my poor?" asked the saint, betraying neither satisfaction nor surprise.

"No; it is just a distinction." "Very well, since the poor have nothing to gain by it, tell the Emperor, please, that I do not want it."[7]

It goes without saying that M. des Garets refused to comply with so singular a request. Presently a painter,

6. August 15, Feast of the Assumption, was also the Feast of St. Napoleon.
7. Frère Athanase, *Procès de l'Ordinaire,* p. 830.

feeling sure of an eager welcome, came and offered his services to *M. le Chanoine Vianney, chevalier de la Légion d'honneur.* The poor artist departed a disappointed man. On August 28 Mme. la Comtesse des Garets wrote: "Everybody wants M. le Curé's portrait to be painted, but he refuses his consent. He said laughingly: 'I advise you to paint me with my mozetta and my cross of honor, and to write underneath: *"Nothingness, pride!"*'"

A little later, alluding to that mozetta and that cross, a priest chaffed him mildly: "Monsieur le Curé, all the authorities on earth honor you: God will surely not fail to honor you in Heaven."

"That is what fills me with fear," replied the saint in a grave tone of voice: "what if, when death comes and I present myself with these baubles, God were to say to me: 'Begone: you have had your reward'?"[8]

In his capacity as an officer of the Légion d'honneur, Mgr. Chalandon was requested to pin the cross on the breast of the Curé d'Ars. For reasons of which we are ignorant, the ceremony was put off until November. In the meantime, however, M. Vianney received a communication from the *Grande Chancellerie* requesting him to forward twelve francs to pay for the postage of the cross and the certificate! He was startled: "No, never!" he exclaimed; "have I not refused it? I prefer to spend that money today in feeding twelve poor persons!"[9] The small bill was taken to M. Toccanier, who paid it without letting the holy man know. "I did not send the money," he said later on, "and yet *they* have sent me the cross all the same."

In October the Préfet, a practicing Catholic, came to Ars to offer his personal congratulations to the new chevalier. They met in the village square. After the preliminary compliments, the saint said: "Oh! Monsieur le Préfet, I beseech you, take your cross to someone more deserving. I would rather have something for my poor."

"But," replied M. de Coëtlogon, "if the Emperor has

8. *Procès de l'Ordinaire,* p. 176.
9. *Procès de l'Ordinaire,* p. 830.

given you the cross, it is not so much to honor you as it is to add lustre to the Légion d'honneur. . . ."

M. Vianney cut short the compliment by remarking with a smile: "Monsieur le Préfet, I shall pray God to keep you for a long time in the *département* of the Ain, so that you may do good there by your wise counsel and, above all, by your good example." With these words he gave the Comte de Coëtlogon a medal of the Blessed Virgin, saluted him, and went into his confessional.

November came. In the interval, Mgr. Chalandon, who had been officially delegated to perform the investiture, bethought himself of the beautiful new mozetta with which he had invested Canon Vianney three years earlier. He deemed it no rash judgement to suspect that the cross of honor would likewise pass into the hands of the poor. Was it worthwhile for the head of the diocese to displace himself in order to present that incorrigible Curé d'Ars with a trinket which would be turned into money, probably the same evening? So the prelate judged it wiser to subdelegate his duties to the excellent Abbé Toccanier, M. Raymond's successor.

In this way the small box, bearing a large red seal and containing the vermeil star, was duly despatched to M. Toccanier, who, one fine afternoon, presented the casket sealed with the imperial seal to M. Vianney at a moment when the latter happened to be alone in his room. Frère Athanase, the teachers Catherine Lassagne and Jeanne-Marie Chanay, to whom word had been sent, were waiting outside on the landing. As soon as M. Toccanier began to speak, they appeared on the scene. "Monsieur le Curé, perhaps someone has sent you some relics," the vicaire began.

The servant of God did not see the trick, but, eager to venerate the sacred remains, he broke the wax seal.

"Oh, it is only that!" he exclaimed, as he uncovered the beautiful trinket. "M. le Curé, please note that the decoration is surmounted by a real cross; will you bless it?" When he had made over it a big Sign of the Cross, the Abbé Toccanier proceeded: "Let me now place it for a moment on your breast."

"O my friend, I shall take care not to let you do so. I should have the same words addressed to me which St. Benedict spoke to the equerry of King Totila who approached him wearing the purple of his master: 'Take off those trappings of a dignity which is not yours.'" And placing the decoration in the hand of the episcopal subdelegate, he said: "Take it, my friend, and may you have as much pleasure in receiving it as I have in giving it to you."[10]

That is how "the poor Curé d'Ars" was decorated. He refused to have the cross pinned to his cassock, so that the only time he ever wore it was when it was placed on his coffin.[11]

What is the explanation of so profound a contempt for the honors and interests of this world? It has been said that "all that concerned the supernatural order, all that could spread the kingdom of God, passionately stirred his heart."[12] Hence his joy and repose consisted in things appertaining to religion. The only festivities that appealed to his soul were those of the Church.

Even in their extreme old age, some men of Ars still cherished the remembrance of a unique festival, when M. Vianney displayed an extraordinary, enthusiastic, and overflowing joy. In November, 1854, whilst Rome was about to celebrate, with the utmost magnificence, the definition of the dogma of the Immaculate Conception, the Curé d'Ars equally prepared himself to honor this great event with due solemnity. "A few days before the definition of the dogma," writes Baronne de Belvey, "I heard the servant of God deliver a special sermon in which he recalled with transports of joy all that he himself had done for Mary Immaculate. The whole congregation was thrilled when he exclaimed: 'If, by selling myself, I could give

10. These details are derived from two depositions of the Abbé Toccanier: *Procès de l'Ordinaire,* p. 175, and *Procès apostolique in genere,* p. 168. In order to cut short any litigation after his death, on the subject of this cross of honor, the Curé d'Ars gave it to M. Toccanier by a will written in his own hand.

11. *Procès apostolique ne pereant,* p. 901.

12. Abbé Monnin, *Procès de l'Ordinaire,* p. 1123.

something to the Blessed Virgin, I should sell myself!' "[13]

The impending solemnity provided the saint with an exceptional opportunity of proving to Our Lady his love, now more than sixty years old. He had loved Mary from the cradle. As a priest he had exerted all his energy in spreading her glory. To convince themselves of it, the pilgrims had but to look at the small statues of her that adorned the front of every house in the village. In each home there was also a colored picture of the Mother of God, presented and signed by M. le Curé.[14] In 1844 he had erected a large statue of Mary Immaculate on the pediment of his church. Eight years earlier, on May 1, 1836, he had dedicated his parish to Mary conceived without sin. The picture which perpetuates this consecration, says Catherine Lassagne, is placed at the entrance to the Lady Chapel.[15] Shortly afterwards he ordered a heart to be made, in vermeil, which is, even to this day, suspended from the neck of the *miraculous Virgin.*[16] This heart contains the names of all the parishioners of Ars, written on a white silk ribbon. On the feasts of Our Lady, Communions were numerous, and the church was never empty. On the evenings of those festivals the nave and the side chapels could barely contain the congregation, for no one wished to miss M. Vianney's homily in honor of Our Blessed Lady. The hearers were enthralled by the enthusiasm with which he spoke of the holiness, the power, and the love of the Mother of God.

---

13. *Procès de l'Ordinaire,* p. 235.
14. These rather crude lithographs, published at Lyons, are still preserved in many of the houses of Ars.
15. This large picture, with a blue background, bears the following inscription in letters of gold: *Consecration of the parish of Ars to Mary conceived without sin, made on May* 1, 1836, *by M. Jean-Marie Vianney, Curé d'Ars.* A smaller reproduction of this picture may be seen at Lyons, in the choir of the old chapel of Fourvière. As a matter of fact, it would seem that, when M. Vianney consecrated his parish to the Blessed Virgin, he was thinking of Fourvière. (At one time he had conceived the plan of leading his parishioners to that shrine, on an annual pilgrimage; once only, on August 6, 1823, did he carry out this dream so dear to his heart.) Hence his idea of presenting the famous chapel with a commemorative picture.
16. Catherine Lassagne calls the statue of Our Lady of Ars *miraculous,* either by reason of the marvellous conversions that took place before its altar, or because it is a copy of the Madonna of the *Miraculous Medal.* The former explanation appears to be the more plausible of the two.

But M. Vianney surpassed himself on the unforgettable date of December 8, 1854, when Pius IX, in virtue of the authority of the holy Apostles Peter and Paul, and of his own, defined that "the Blessed Virgin Mary was preserved from all stain of original sin, from the first instant of her conception." Notwithstanding his exhaustion, he insisted on singing the parish Mass that day, and with much joy he wore for the first time a splendid vestment of blue velvet figured with gold, which the architect Bossan had designed.[17] The nave and sanctuary were adorned with their brightest ornaments.

In the afternoon, at the conclusion of Vespers, the whole parish walked in procession to the school of the brothers, where M. le Curé blessed a statue of the Immaculate, erected in the garden and given by himself. In the evening the tower, the church, and the front of the houses were illuminated. There was, of course, a final service in the church, during which M. Vianney delivered an address. "What happiness! what happiness!" he exclaimed at the beginning of his homily. "I have always thought that one ray was wanting to the splendor of Catholic dogma; it was a void in religion that had to be filled."

Illuminations! These were a novelty for both people and priest. Before going out to contemplate the marvellous spectacle, the saint himself started the ringing of the bells. They were rung for a long time; so long, indeed, says Catherine Lassagne, "that people came in haste from the neighboring villages, in the belief that there was a fire." In the meantime "M. le Curé was joyfully walking about, by the light of the torches, with the priests who had come for the feast and the Brothers."[18] This day was, assuredly, one of the happiest of his life; though nearly seventy years of age, he looked like a youth of twenty.

17. The vestment, which cost 1,400 francs, was a gift from the parishioners to their pastor. All wished to contribute towards the cost. "Its acquisition was indeed an offering of the poor," says Catherine Lassagne. "Some people may wonder that M. Vianney should have allowed the making of a vestment with a blue foundation for the Feast of Our Lady. However, the Bishop of Belley, having examined it, found it so heavily gilt that he authorized its use as though its foundation had been of cloth of gold" (*Procès apostolique in genere,* p. 354).

18. *Petit mémoire,* troisième rédaction, p. 49.

Never did a child enjoy its mother's triumph as he enjoyed the triumph of his heavenly Mother; and he it was who had prompted and organized "this immense manifestation of joy."[19]

19. Comtesse des Garets, *Procès de l'Ordinaire,* p. 900.

Chapter 21

INCIDENTS OF THE LAST YEARS *(continued)* IV. Towards "La Trappe" of La Neylière

NOTWITHSTANDING their Cure's promise never again to leave them, the inhabitants of Ars could not forget their alarm of September, 1843. Five years after that date Père Léonard, a venerable Capuchin of the convent of Les Broteaux, of Lyons, enrolled M. Vianney in the third Order of St. Francis. The incident was enough to give rise to lively anxiety in the village: "they thought he was going to become a Capuchin," says Mme. des Garets. The rumor was not altogether groundless. The fact is, M. Vianney had expressed to Père Léonard, who heard his Confession on several occasions, a desire to be admitted to his Order. But that good religious, far from allowing himself to be dazzled by the prospect of so splendid an acquisition, represented to him that he would do far more good by remaining in his parish than by entering a monastery. As the Curé persisted, Père Léonard spoke to him of the third Order and gave him the rules: shortly afterwards M. Vianney asked for the habit of a tertiary. . . . In this he was followed by the more fervent among his parishioners.

Two years earlier, on December 8, 1846, Père Eymard, a Marist who was destined to become the founder of the Congregation of the Blessed Sacrament, had affiliated M. Vianney to the Third Order of Mary.[1] This Third Order was a recent institution of Père Jean-Claude Colin, a fel-

1. At that time it was still lawful to be affiliated to several third Orders.

low-student of M. Vianney's at Verrières and at Saint-Irénée of Lyons. Those who trembled lest the saint should again forsake them, little suspected that the real danger came from that quarter.

Jean-Claude Colin, raised by God for the purpose of establishing in France and throughout the world the Society of Mary, had remained profoundly attached to Jean-Marie Vianney. Both had an innate taste for self-effacement and simplicity, and a tender devotion to Mary; time had not interrupted their friendly relations. Père Colin frequently sent his religious to see his friend at Ars, whilst the holy Curé heartily applauded the various undertakings of the founder of the Marists. When the first missionaries set out for Oceania, as it was then called, M. Vianney helped them by his prayers and sought to procure for them pecuniary aid.

Nevertheless, in the midst of his apostolic labors, he was still harassed and tormented by a vision of life in the wilderness where he might pray to his heart's content. But where was such a desert to be found? Had not Mgr. Devie stated that, during his lifetime, M. Vianney should never leave the diocese? But a new ray of hope had just appeared on the horizon. As early as 1842, the venerable Père Colin had dreamed of a new foundation—a house of Perpetual Adoration, in which recluses would give themselves up to prayer and penance. A start was made at Marcellange, in the *département* of the Allier, but it came to nothing. In 1850, however, the Society of Mary acquired a property called La Neylière, situated at Saint-Symphorien-sur-Coise, forty-five kilometers from Lyons. Far from the noise of the world and nestling among beautiful hills, La Neylière was an ideal retreat for contemplatives. Encouraged by several bishops, notably by Mgr. Devie, Bishop of Belley, Père Colin made all preliminary preparations for installing on this *Thabor* a dozen of his religious. They were to be joined by several priests from various dioceses of France and even from England, who had begged for the privilege of taking part in the new

2. *Le Très Révérend Père Colin,* Lyon, Vitte, 1900, p. 395.

venture.[2] On Sunday, May 16, 1852, seven fathers and five coadjutor brothers shut themselves up at Notre-Dame de la Neylière and began to keep that perpetual silence which was to be one of the cardinal points of their observance.

When M. Vianney heard of these things he became pensive. An event which was not altogether unexpected came to quicken his hopes. In 1850, Mgr. Devie, weighed down with years—he was eighty-four—and worn out by thirty years of a laborious episcopate, had asked the Holy See to give him a coadjutor. His request was granted, and Mgr. Georges Chalandon, Vicar-General of Metz and a native of Lyons, was consecrated at Belley on January 12, 1851. "On learning this news," says the Baronne de Belvey, "M. Vianney evinced much joy: 'I hope that the new Bishop will allow me to retire,' he said." On July 25, 1852, two months after the inauguration of the *mitigated Trappe* of La Neylière, Mgr. Devie passed away, and Mgr. Chalandon, until now Bishop of Thaumacum *in partibus,* became Bishop of Belley. Believing that there were now no further obstacles in the way, the Curé d'Ars at once bethought himself of a new "flight." He would seek the shelter of La Neylière in order to weep over his "poor life," and end his days in prayer and penance. Père Colin, who was informed of the project, advised him not to act too hastily; both, therefore, awaited a favorable opportunity to carry out their concerted plan.

Such an occasion seemed to present itself in September, 1853. For several months M. Vianney had felt that before long his assistant would be taken from him. The people of Ars desired the removal of a priest whose character was so unaccommodating, and M. Raymond himself, understanding at last that the parish of Ars would never be given to him, had petitioned for a change. To replace him Mgr. Chalandon looked to the youthful society of missionaries established at Pont-d'Ain, whose superior was M. le Chanoine Camelet. M. Camelet was in great favor with M. Vianney, who, during the jubilee of

1847, had much appreciated his talents and his zeal. The Bishop of Belley rightly judged that the Curé d'Ars, round whom surged ever increasing crowds, needed an assistant who would be suited to this kind of work and who, when the pilgrimages were at their height, could appeal to colleagues who would be ever ready to help. Mgr. Chalandon chose the Abbé Toccanier, whom M. Camelet had singled out as being the best fitted for so delicate a post. In 1853 M. Toccanier was thirty-one years old. He was robust in appearance and his healthy complexion provided a vivid contrast to the emaciation of his holy Curé; but the style of his preaching, which was quick, direct, personal, and very much to the point in its simplicity, recalled the manner of M. Vianney. Moreover, he was most devout, kind, and affable. He was certainly the right man to take his place beside our genial saint.

The clergy retreat of that year opened on Monday, August 29, at the Grand Séminaire of Brou. There the Abbés Toccanier and Raymond met. M. Poncet, the Vicar-General, informed the Abbé Raymond that he was appointed to the parish of Polliat, whilst M. Camelet, on his side, told M. Toccanier that he was to be the resident auxiliary of the Curé d'Ars.

If we are to believe Catherine Lassagne, M. Vianney was still in ignorance of "these expedients" when, on Thursday, September 1, he told her, when she brought his small midday meal to his room: "I have been thinking that this time I must go. Melin, my brother-in-law who lives in the parish of Saint-Irénée (of Lyons), expects me. I shall leave on Monday, during the night: keep this to yourself."

"Oh! Monsieur le Curé, you must not go away," poor Catherine replied. And she reminded him of the story of ten years before: his stay at Dardilly, the crowds in pursuit, the moving circumstances of his return to Ars. He was not impressed. What was decided was decided. "Monseigneur will not be inconvenienced because of me, he

3. The details of this third attempt at flight are drawn from the various *processes*, to which it would be tedious continually to refer.

has plenty of priests!"[3]

In the course of Saturday afternoon, M. Poncet, the Vicar-General, arrived with MM. Raymond and Toccanier. "The good Curé," the last named relates, "gave us a kindly reception, but he looked worried." In the evening M. Poncet explained to him the wishes of the Bishop regarding the future: henceforth the Curé d'Ars would have at his disposal as many assistants as possible. To this the saint offered no objection. Then M. Raymond saw him in order to explain on what terms he would introduce his successor, during the parish Mass on the following day.

On Sunday morning M. Toccanier officiated and M. Raymond delivered the address that he had prepared. In the afternoon, the Vicar-General left for Trévoux where he was to preside at the conclusion of a nuns' retreat, and the saint's former auxiliary set out for Beauregard, his native village, which was not far from Ars. "That day," Catherine writes, "everybody in the parish was happy in the knowledge that a missionary was coming to help our holy Curé; but how sad I was!"

The secret weighed heavily upon the good woman, just as it had done ten years earlier. Hence, towards eight o'clock that night, she asked M. Vianney's permission to take the discreet Marie Filliat into her confidence. "As you wish," he replied. The two women soon came to him bathed in tears. "Do not go away," they pleaded, "do not go away!" He replied that his determination was final and he entrusted Catherine with a letter for Mgr. Chalandon. Even with his new Bishop the Curé d'Ars deemed it necessary to precipitate matters. His first illusions had already vanished; Mgr. Chalandon would be as unyielding as Mgr. Devie, for had he not just lately replied to a request of the saint whom he had come to see: "I let you go, Monsieur le Curé! But that would be so big a sin that no one would give me absolution!"

After their futile efforts, Marie and Catherine had remained in conversation near the gate of the presbytery garden. "What is to be done?" one of them said; "feeble as he is at his age—he was over sixty-seven—he cannot go on foot to Lyons. You, Marie, you can carry the basket of provisions. But what if he should be taken ill on the way? We should have to take him in a carriage."

"But there is not one man here at this moment to help us." Just then Frère Jérôme, the sacristan, happened to go by. He seemed surprised at finding Catherine and Marie out of doors at that hour. A minute later he knew everything! He ran to inform Frère Athanase and together they went to M. Toccanier who lodged in an annex belonging to the *Providence.* The vicaire thought that it was a sick call. "Imagine my surprise," he writes, "when I heard the tale the good Brothers had to tell; I could hardly bring myself to believe them. 'Stand on guard in front of the presbytery,' I told them, 'and if M. le Curé really means to escape call me.' At midnight there were three hasty knocks on my door. I was reclining on my bed fully dressed. I soon found myself in the little square with the two Brothers spying on the movements of our holy Curé who, thanks to the light of his lamp, could be seen in his room seizing his hat, his Breviary, and his umbrella. 'We must let him come downstairs,' I said to the Brothers. He did come down and walk towards Marie Filliat and Catherine Lassagne, who were to accompany him. We listened attentively. 'Are you ready?' he asked. 'Very well, let us go!'

"He came out, followed by Marie, who carried the provisions, and by Catherine, who held a lantern in her hand. Suddenly he found himself confronted by us. He looked sternly at Catherine, who burst into tears. 'You have sold me,' he told her. But Frère Athanase broke in at once: 'Where are you going, Monsieur le Curé? You wish to forsake us! Very well, we shall ring the tocsin.'

"'And we shall follow you in procession!' M. Jérôme added.

"'Do so by all means, only let me go!' was M. Vianney's brief and firm reply.

"'Let us fall back and then follow him,' M. Toccanier whispered to his two acolytes. Meanwhile Frère Jérôme had relieved Catherine of her lantern and, whilst pretending to guide M. Vianney in the darkness, he led him, not in the direction of the footbridge which spans the Fontblin, but towards the road to Villeneuve. The vicaire had calculated that by making a tour of the village the saint would find himself at the spot from which he had started. Notwithstanding the darkness of the night the Curé d'Ars soon noticed that he was being deceived. By now quite a crowd had collected round him; it was made up of the pilgrims who, as usual, were spending the night in the lobby of the bell-tower, and of the villagers who, having been roused by the cries of the strangers, hurried to the scene, appealing loudly to him as to their confessor or their director. In the midst of a veritable tumult, M. Toccanier endeavored to argue with the fugitive. In this way they came to the frail bridge of planks which had been thrown across the brook.

"M. Toccanier thought that, once the Fontblin crossed and M. Vianney started on the Lyons road, it would be more difficult to bring him back. The missionary resolutely placed himself in front of him just as he was about to set foot on the bridge. 'Let me pass, let me pass!' the saint pleaded in a voice of anguish. He had his Breviary under his arm. M. Toccanier snatched it from him unexpectedly and handed it to the nearest among the bystanders, who was none other than Catherine Lassagne. 'Go away and do not come back,' the missionary whispered in her ear. 'Give me back my Breviary!' the Curé exclaimed. However, on second thoughts, he signed to Marie Filliat to proceed: 'Go on! I shall say it when we get to Lyons.'

"'Eh! what, Monsieur le Curé, you intend to let the hours of the day go by without saying your Office! What an example!'

"A scruple was thus started in the mind of the saint. There was a moment of silence. 'I have another Breviary in my room, that of Mgr. Devie,' he said at length. 'Let us go and fetch it,' suggested the Abbé Toccanier, who, though he did not as yet realize it, had won the day. M. Vianney turned and, followed by an ever-increasing throng, retraced his steps to the presbytery.

"He had not yet covered thirty meters of the road when the church bell sounded. It was the tocsin! How lugubrious it sounded in the gloom! 'Monsieur le Curé, the Angelus already!' And the poor saint, always guileless and trusting, fell on his knees and recited the "Hail Marys" with angelic fervor. 'Monsieur le Curé,' added the wily vicaire, 'what if we were to recite a decade of the Rosary that you may have a safe journey?' He was anxious to gain time. But this once M. Vianney suspected the trap. 'No,' he replied, 'I can say my Rosary on the way.'

"The Curé d'Ars having risen from his knees," M. Toccanier relates, "advanced with rapid strides, rushed into the courtyard and went up to his room, whither I followed him alone. On the way Frère Athanase informed me that the Mayor had been warned and would be on the spot in a few moments. In order to give the Comte des Garets more time, I changed the order of the eight volumes of the big *in octavo* Breviary on the shelf where they stood. These volumes were a treasured souvenir of the aged Bishop who had died but a short time before. At the moment when M. Vianney finally put his hand on the right volume, my eye caught sight of a portrait of Mgr. Devie which was hanging on the wall. I called to mind that the prelate had prevented previous flights. An inspiration came to me. 'Monsieur le Curé,' I cried in a firm tone of voice, 'see how Mgr. Devie frowns at you from heaven above. The will of a bishop must be respected during his lifetime, and even more so when he is dead. Remember what he told you ten years ago.'

"This apostrophe upset M. Vianney, and he answered me with the naiveté of a child afraid of a scolding from its father: 'Monseigneur will not reproach me; he knows very well that I have need to go and weep for my "poor life!"' And, impatient of further delay, he seized the big Breviary bound in dark green morocco and started to go downstairs. At the bend in the staircase he nearly collided with M. des Garets. 'At that moment,' the Mayor related, 'I found him looking agitated, sad, almost sombre.' In fact, our good Curé, who used to be so affable towards that old and loyal friend, now hardly listened to him, so that M. le Comte said to me: 'He must surely have a presentiment that his end is near.'"

Now, whilst the women were praying in church "that God would change the mind of his servant," as Catherine Lassagne puts it, the men had invaded the narrow courtyard of the presbytery. Roused by the tocsin, many imagined that the alarm was sounded because of a fire or an attack by robbers, so they came armed with buckets, forks, and sticks. All these people were talking and gesticulating in the dim light of the lanterns. When M. Vianney appeared they barred his way, beseeching him not to go away. But he, with his mind fixed on finding an exit, went from one door to the other, repeating: "Let me pass! let me pass!" "What a touching scene it was!" the devout Catherine remarks: "it was so vivid a picture of Our Lord's capture in the Garden of Olives!" "I was posted at one of the exits," says Michel Tournassoud, the village cobbler. "M. le Curé seized me by the arm, half smiling, half crying, and pushed me on one side. But he did not succeed in opening the door."

By dint of supplications he ended by being allowed to cross the threshold. Having reached a spot between the presbytery and the church, his eyes seemed to calculate the distance. "He was certainly still in a mood to escape for good," says M. Toccanier, when a fresh incident came to alter the face of events.

The women came out of the church and, joining the men, they fell on their knees before the saint. They were for the most part strangers who had come from a distance to make their Confession to him. They exclaimed with tears: "Father, before you go, hear me! Let me finish my Confession! Oh! no, kind Father, do not forsake us!"

"It was then," says M. Toccanier, "that I made a supreme effort and addressed him in words which I could not have uttered in cold blood: 'What! you, Monsieur le Curé, who know by heart the *Lives of the Saints*—you forget the zeal of St. Martin, who, having his crown already within his grasp, exclaimed: "*I do not refuse to work.*" You would leave the field of battle! And what about the example of St. Philip Neri, who said that were he to stand on the threshold of Paradise and a sinner claimed his ministrations, he would gladly leave the court of Heaven in order to hear that Confession. And you, Monsieur le Curé, you would dare to leave unfinished the Confessions of these men, of these women who have come from so far?' When I ceased the pilgrims redoubled their supplications."

M. Vianney understood that these eager entreaties were a manifestation of God's Will. "Come to the sacristy," the Comte des Garets whispered into his ear; "I have something to say to you." "Very well," he replied, and addressing the crowd, he said: "Let us go to the church!"

He was the first to enter; he prayed for a long while, and finally went into the sacristy. There M. des Garets was about to recapitulate M. Toccanier's arguments, but he was not given time. "M. Vianney abruptly turned his back on me without answering," the Comte related afterwards, "put on his surplice and made for the confessional." "He did not walk so much as the people carried him to it," says M. Toccanier. As was his practice every morning on first entering the church, he knelt on the altar step, recited five *Paters* and *Aves* with the people, and began to hear Confessions.

On the Monday morning, at about seven o'clock, he said the first Mass. "M. Poncet is there, is he not?" he asked M. Toccanier on his return to the sacristy. "Yes, he wished to see you again." "Ah! very well." When he had made his thanksgiving he went to present his respects to the Vicar-General as tranquilly as if nothing out of the ordinary had happened but a few hours before. M. Poncet had been fetched from Trévoux during the night by one of the carriers. He now assured M. Vianney once more that the will of the Bishop was that he should stay in the diocese. The Abbé Beau, curé of Jassans and the saint's confessor, and the Abbé Raymond, who had also been summoned, arrived a little later, and together they saw the servant of God.

"We had already been informed of the events of the

night," M. Raymond writes. "When he found himself, as it were, trapped in his courtyard, he had shown some impatience, but his excitement was so great that he may well be excused from all blame, for, without a doubt, he was no longer master of himself. This had been one of the sharpest trials of his life: by permitting it Providence added to the perfection of his virtues. When we saw him on the morning of that fifth of September, he had recovered his wonted serenity and his absolute submission to God's Will as manifested by that of his Bishop. We alluded to the incidents of the night, to which his only answer was: 'I behaved like a child; *l'ai fait l'enfant!*'"

The most amazing feature of the whole affair was assuredly the indecision and want of foresight of the Curé d'Ars. During that tragic night, he hesitated like one feeling his way, he confided his secret to two persons who had already *sold him* ten years earlier and who could do no other than betray him again. He might so easily have asked François Pertinand to drive him to Lyons; but the thought does not seem to have occurred to him.

Had he succeeded in making good his escape, what would have become of him on that September day? After examining existing documents we are driven to the following conclusions: Relying rather on his energy of will than on his actual strength, M. Vianney hoped to reach Lyons at about nine or ten o'clock in the morning. A little later, a carriage was to meet him at the house of Melin, his brother-in-law, and to take him to Notre-Dame de la Neylière.

One thing which seems quite certain is that at La Neylière, Père Colin had a room ready for the Curé d'Ars, and that he personally awaited his arrival.[4] At the hour when he might be expected, the venerable founder remained for a considerable time on the threshold of the

4. Père Colin definitely took up residence at La Neylière only in the following year—viz., 1854. Two years later, for reasons which the saintly founder deemed *very weighty,* the contemplative branch of the Society of Mary ceased to exist *(P. Colin,* p. 395).

house, and he even expressed his astonishment to Père Jobert, one of his religious, when he saw no sign of an approaching carriage. We know why M. Vianney never reached La Neylière.

According to the evidence of reliable witnesses, "the wise and prudent Père Colin had at first advised M. Vianney to stay where he was because there he could do more good." From a like motive Père Léonard had dissuaded him from entering at the Capuchins of Lyons. For these reasons this third "escape" of the Curé d'Ars is a painful, mysterious, and perturbing incident in his life. "He imagined he was doing the will of God by going away," says Catherine Lassagne. Not long after he received a letter from a priest in which it was pointed out to him that his longing for solitude was a temptation of the devil. The letter made a deep impression on his mind.

"One result of his latest attempt at flight," says Comte Prosper des Garets, "was to enlighten him as to the future. Henceforth he never entertained the idea; at any rate, he never mentioned the subject. He threw himself wholly and without reserve into his ministry; in fact, he went to the church at an even earlier hour and remained a longer time in the confessional."[5]

If he himself made no further effort to leave his parish of Ars, there were those who endeavored to snatch him from it. One night in 1854, about half an hour before midnight, a carriage and pair stopped in the open space behind the apse of the church. Some men alighted and posted themselves at the presbytery door. When, towards midnight, M. Vianney appeared on the threshold, one of the men seized him by the arm. "If you wish to leave," he said, "here is a carriage ready for you."

"I have not the permission of my Bishop," said the saint, shaking off the stranger. And he hurried into the church porch.

At Christmas of that same year, alarming news reached

5. *Procès de l'Ordinaire,* p. 793.

him from Dardilly: François *l'ainé* was seriously ill. The saint had ever cherished a tender affection towards his former fellow-laborer, this big brother who, since the death of their father in 1819, was the master of the old home. He was an excellent Christian, moreover: never, even at harvest-time, had he been seen working on Sunday. "He who has permitted the rain to moisten the earth, will know how to dry it," he used to say. Perhaps he had gathered the phrase from Jean-Marie's lips. The holy Curé, on hearing of his brother's illness, was very grieved and wrote to him as follows:

"I have had news of you. It had been kept from me and I am much pained. I earnestly entreat you to let me know how you are. I should have set out (to see you) were it not that it is the Octave (of Christmas).

"Send me word at once, I beg of you, to relieve my anxiety. Farewell, my dear brother, I hope to see you soon. My compliments to my sister, who, I imagine, is in great distress."

However, the days went by and François waited in vain for Jean-Marie to come. On January 25, he asked his son Antoine to go to Ars and to bring back the much-longed-for brother. In this way it became known at Dardilly that the Curé d'Ars was coming. "What if we kept him for good this time!" they said among themselves. But let us listen to the best informed of all the witnesses. Three days after the adventure M. Toccanier wrote from Ars to the Bishop of Belley:

"MONSEIGNEUR,

"I have the honour to inform your Lordship that the care of my holy Curé will not, in future, give me any anxiety: divine Providence visibly watches over him so that we may keep him.

"These are the facts. On the twenty-sixth of this month, M. Vianney, yielding to the insistence of his nephew, who implored him to go to Dardilly to visit his sick brother, came himself to inform me of the project, adding: 'It is a pity that I have made no arrangements; I should not then come back.'

"Since I could not oppose this act of brotherly affection, I volunteered to accompany him. We got into the carriage—that is, his nephew, the driver, and Frère Jérôme, the sacristan, whom M. Vianney at first wished to leave behind. Some of the inhabitants of Ars and the pilgrims knelt down, eager to receive our holy Curé's blessing; they afterwards went into the church to pray for his safe journey and a speedy return. As regards the latter intention, their prayers were destined to be answered, but in a manner exceeding all their expectations!

"Little used to travelling by coach, and weakened, as he was, by the ailment you know of and which the newspapers have *so much exaggerated,* he was unable to endure for long the jolting of the carriage.[6] When we reached Parcieux, where we were still a long way from the bridge of the Saône, he said: 'I can go no further; I feel faint.' The roads were covered with snow and ice. He was already feeling sick when we climbed the Grandes Balmes. Having alighted, he proceeded to walk up the hill. He was shaking, so we tried to cut a stick from the hedge; to this he objected because it would have been 'stealing.' Presently a man passed us carrying vine-props: he gave him forty sous for one of them. In this way he travelled another three or four kilometers, very slowly, driving and walking by turns.

"At last, he decided to return to Ars with the driver and the good sacristan. As for me, knowing that I should be carrying out the dearest wish of his heart, I continued the journey with his nephew as far as Neuville, where we found another carriage. The roads were so slippery that we only reached Dardilly at nightfall. But what a disappointment for the poor brother not to see the one whom alone he desired to behold! However, my visit gave him pleasure. Towards ten o'clock that night, the curé of

6. This is the only allusion, in the existing documents, to a fresh indisposition of the Curé d'Ars. We have not been able to discover any one of the newspapers here mentioned.

Dardilly, who had already given him holy Viaticum, deemed it expedient to administer Extreme Unction.

"I longed to see my holy Curé again, so I left for Ars on the very next morning. I asked Frère Jérôme whether they had met with any untoward occurrences on the return journey. A wonderful thing had indeed happened. You know, Monseigneur, how weak M. Vianney is. Well, on that return journey he was a changed man: he had recovered all his energy and he never alighted from the carriage until it stopped at the door of his presbytery. He straightway went into his confessional, and in the evening he recited the prayers as usual,

"The following is an interesting episode of this journey: Driving up towards Trévoux, M. Vianney's carriage crossed the omnibus which plies between Ars and Lyons. It was full of pilgrims who, having failed to find him whom they sought, were now sadly returning home. Fortunately they recognized the saint. At once they all alighted, sent off the empty conveyance, escorted M. Vianney as far as Ars, and followed him into the church. We asked him whether among their number there were any old sinners. 'Oh yes, my friend, there were some who had not been to Confession for forty years.' 'You see, Monsieur le Curé, that the good God Himself stopped you, so as to bring you back at once to do the work which He loves beyond all others, the salvation of souls.' He made no reply.

"For my part, Monseigneur, foreseeing that the inhabitants of Dardilly would take advantage of his brother's illness in order to bring fresh pressure to bear upon M. Vianney, I took the precaution of asking the invalid whether he had anything special to tell his brother. 'No,' he replied, 'I only wished to see him.' On my return I related these words to my holy Curé. It was very fortunate, for two hours later the vicaire of Dardilly appeared on the scene. 'Your brother insists on seeing you,' the priest said. 'If you cannot travel by coach, you can go by train.' 'I am unable to go to Dardilly; I nearly died in the attempt.' 'But, Monsieur le Curé, your brother must have something of importance to tell you, otherwise I should not be here.' 'No, my friend, I know all about it; the missionary has given me my brother's message.'"

François' illness proved fatal. Though he lingered for many days, he was denied the consolation, to which he had every claim, of being assisted at the last by his beloved Jean-Marie. Eight days before the end he said to his daughter, who was weeping by his bedside: "Be comforted; I shall last until Good Friday." As a matter of fact, he passed away on Good Friday, April 6, 1855. On Holy Saturday his brother did not even think of attending the funeral; he wept silently in the shadow of his confessional in which, because of Easter Day, he was kept imprisoned for the space of eighteen hours.

"He made even that sacrifice," Catherine Lassagne notes in her precious *Mémoire*. "He realized that the people of Dardilly would make a further effort to detain him. . . . We must believe that in January God permitted his excessive fatigue to prevent his falling into the snare. . . . In this way does God act as He pleases, notwithstanding the machinations of men."[7]

7. *Petit mémoire,* troisième rédaction, p. 31-32

Chapter 22

PHYSICAL AND MORAL PORTRAIT

"OUTWARDLY, there was nothing remarkable about the Curé d'Ars," says an eyewitness, "apart from the functions of his ministry."[1] He was always so eager to efface himself, to pass unnoticed! Some who chanced to meet him in the village street, on his way back from the orphanage, his small can of buttermilk in his hand—for all the world like a beggar who has just received his dole—were at times not a little disillusioned. "So that is the Curé d'Ars!" a Parisian lady, exclaimed when she beheld him looking so different from the picture she had formed in her imagination. "Indeed it is," the humble priest replied with the most gracious of smiles; "your experience is not that of the Queen of Sheba when she visited Solomon: she was surprised to find so much; you are surprised to find so little."

However, those who were drawn to Ars by faith and a desire to behold a saint—that is, the genuine pilgrims, were not deceived by externals. The first glimpse of the holy man was sufficient to fill them with awe and admiration, for they saw how the beauty of his soul transfigured his outward appearance, which otherwise would have been ordinary enough.

M. Vianney was a little below medium height. Towards the end of his life, when his head had become somewhat bowed, his rounded shoulders caused him to look even shorter than he was.

A writer of the period describes him thus: "His face was emaciated almost to the extent of disfigurement, and, owing to the attenuation of his cheeks, which tapered

1. *Procès de l'Ordinaire,* p. 791.

towards the chin, it had the shape of a heart." His complexion, slightly tanned in his childhood, and, later on, much browned through exposure to the sun and air, had become pallid through the interminable hours spent in the confessional. Very early in life deep wrinkles lined his countenance; they were the outward signs of his holy vigils and heroic fatigues. His thick, straight hair, which was cut short on the crown of his head, but left rather long at the back, never became completely white.

His forehead was high, wide, and unruffled; he had prominent brows and deep-set blue eyes glowing with a strange supernatural vivacity, and a look that was frank and at the same time deep, intense, and searching. "He seemed to read me through and through," said the Abbé Denis Chaland; "his eyes, when they met mine, penetrated to the very depths of my soul. I once knew someone who confessed to being terrified by his glance." In conversation with him, the visitor was struck by the expression of his eyes, which seemed to be gazing upon another world; but, in repose, they generally had a look of gentle and resigned melancholy. The reason was, no doubt, that in those moments his thoughts went from God, who was offended, to men who outraged Him.

Hence, perhaps, the extreme mobility of his features. Not that he was addicted to peculiar tricks, or extravagant and ridiculous mannerisms; but his physiognomy rapidly passed from an expression of joy to one of sorrow, according as he thought of the lovingkindness of God or the miseries of "poor sinners." Many attempts were made to take his likeness, but the Curé would never give his consent. "I know that someone was trying to make a fool of me today," he smilingly said, "but I frustrated all his endeavors, for I kept moving all the time." In order to secure a portrait of him which was at all like, it required the quick eye, the talent, and also the obstinacy of Émilien Cabuchet.

In his youth M. Vianney gave an impression of vigor, but through his fasts, his limbs became so weakened that willpower alone enabled him to stand at all. His fleshless hands, the veins of which stood out like cords, conveyed an idea of the emaciation of his body, worn out by privations and labor.

However, his being a wiry constitution, neither age nor toil deprived his limbs of their suppleness. By a rare privilege, he preserved until the end the full use of those faculties and organs which he needed in the accomplishment of his mission. His hearing remained acute, his eyes retained their undimmed brightness, his memory lost nothing of its freshness. His step, though heavy, continued to be rapid, like that of a man who knows the value of time, and who, even when exhausted, hurries along in the service of God.

It seemed as if he were endued with extraordinary strength from Heaven. "Unaided, he was able to carry out of the church a huge, heavy banner, which any other would have had great difficulty in lifting."[2]

Beneath the covering of an attenuated, almost transparent body, the soul of the Curé d'Ars shone forth. It was reflected on his countenance, in his gaze. Now, the root qualities of this soul were simplicity, refinement, and goodness.

There was nothing in his manner that was either affected or just conventional; nothing of that purely artificial amiability of which so many people make a showy parade. He conversed with perfect ease with persons of the highest rank. When Cardinal de Bonald, Archbishop of Lyons, came to visit him, M. Vianney hastened to meet him with outstretched hands. "I was no more embarrassed with him than with a simple curé," the poor old priest declared, when he subsequently spoke of that memorable interview.[3]

After a meeting with M. Vianney on May 14, 1854, Dr. Ullathorne, Bishop of Birmingham, wrote as follows: "He gave us a charming reception, full of simplicity, humility, and charity, without a trace of obsequiousness, which

2. *Procès apostolique continuatif,* p. 157.
3. *Procès de l'Ordinaire,* p. 892.

is but a pretense of humility. His was true humility and perfect naturalness blending with the hearty courtesy of a saint."

A young man of noble birth came to make his Confession to the Curé. Afterwards, chancing to meet Frère Athanase, the schoolmaster, he asked him various questions: "Tell me, brother, what is M. Vianney's parentage . . . where did he study . . . in what society has he moved . . . what position did he occupy before he came to Ars?" The brother explained that the Curé was a peasant by birth, that he had made practically no studies, etc. The young man's astonishment seemed to increase with each answer. "Why have you asked me so many questions?" Frère Athanase said at length.

"Because I was struck by the exquisite courtesy with which M. Vianney received me. When I entered the sacristy he greeted me most graciously; he did not sit down until I was on my knees on the prie-Dieu. When my Confession was over he was the first to rise; he opened the door for me, and, after bidding me good-bye, ushered in the next penitent with equal courtesy."

Frère Athanase assured him that the Curé acted in the same manner towards everyone. "I understand," the other said, "he is a saint; he possesses charity, which is the source of true refinement."[4]

Whether he received visitors in his room or at the *Providence,* M. Vianney always insisted on their being seated, though he himself refused to sit down. His words of welcome were ever the same: "I pay my respects to you," but the tone of his voice varied according to the social position of the visitor or the degree of friendship between him and the saint.

If his threadbare cassock would have rendered a comparison with St. Francis de Sales difficult as regards externals, eyewitnesses have related charming anecdotes about him, such as would be worthy of the life of the gentle Bishop of Geneva.

4. *Procès de l'Ordinaire,* p. 836.

On his feast day, June 23, 1855, a certain person of Ars offered him a cake on which were figures representing an ox, a lion, a giraffe, and some turtle-doves. On receiving the cake, which would enable him to give pleasure to others, he made quite a little speech. "The ox," he said, "represents strength, the lion courage, the giraffe a soul that hastens with great strides towards heaven, and the turtledove a soul that rises above earthly things."

Mlle. Marthe des Garets tells us that people used to press round him so as to get a better view of him and to be able to speak to him. There were delightful moments when, having been unexpectedly caught in the sacristy, he would stop to say a few pious words in his own genial way. Mlle. des Garets, together with her brothers and sisters, loved to waylay him in the corridor. He would give the boys a fatherly pat, and smile on the little girls, repeating: "My children, O my children, love the good God very much!"[5]

André-Benoît Trève, a wealthy agriculturalist and a native of Ars, after closely observing the Curé, thus voiced his appreciation: "Despite his natural animation, which was betrayed by the keen look in his eyes, he had a most attractive manner. Had he not been venerated as a saint, he would have been loved as the meekest of men."

However, there was no trace of weakness in his gentleness. If he showed special consideration to those who needed it, he never allowed them to detain him unreasonably. Time, to him, was very precious, and when he thought he had said all that was necessary, he disliked being further pressed. "I am very busy, I am in a hurry,"[6] he would declare firmly to the importunate. To a poor or sorrowful person who needed it, he willingly granted an extra quarter of an hour, but to those of exalted rank, who merely wished to make his acquaintance, he only accorded the necessary minutes. Mme. Mandy-Scipiot

---

5. *Procès apostolique in genere,* pp. 297 and 327.
6. *Letter* of R. P. Marie-Joseph, a Capuchin, June 19, 1914 (Archives of the presbytery of Ars). This religious received just such an answer in September, 1857, because he persisted in arguing about a decision of M. Vianney's.

relates how she one day witnessed the arrival, in a carriage and four, of a very noble family, who had the privilege of being received in a tiny parlor near the entrance to the courtyard, which the saint had had furnished. The visit lasted five minutes, at the end of which the family, who had been delighted at the honor paid them by the servant of God, appeared dismayed when they saw him depart so soon.

When necessary, the Curé knew how to call people to order. One day, a man in the crowd presumed to interrupt him in a very rude fashion. "Who are you, my friend?" asked the saint. The man answered that he was a Protestant. "O my *poor* friend," replied the Curé, emphasizing his words, "you are indeed poor, very poor: you Protestants have not one saint of your own whose name you could bestow upon your children. You are obliged to borrow your Christian names from the Catholic Church." Having said it he went on his way.[7]

"I never wait anywhere, not even at the Vatican," said a great lady, who thought she could dazzle the Curé with her titles and so get to his confessional before her turn.

"Oh!" replied the servant of God, with a certain archness, "you will, nevertheless, have to wait at the confessional of the poor Curé d'Ars."

In August, 1854, a young fop came to Ars to visit the Curé. He walked up to him just as he was making his way to the presbytery, through a large crowd of pilgrims.

"Monsieur le Curé, I should like to discuss religion with you."

"You, my friend," returned M. Vianney, "you wish to discuss religion! Why, you know less of your catechism than a little child! You are an ignoramus, my friend, an ignoramus!"

"My daughter, in which month of the year do you talk least?" he inquired of someone who was wasting his time in useless chatter. "I think it would be during the month of February," he continued, "because it is three days shorter

---

7. *Procès apostolique ne pereant,* p. 1135.

than the other months." A charming smile softened the otherwise cutting remark.

According to the Abbé Toccanier, himself a most kind-hearted man, M. Vianney had been endowed by nature with a peculiarly tender heart. When he met with anyone in pain, with little orphans, a mother or a widow in deep mourning, tears would roll down his cheeks, which he made no attempt to hide. "He was highly sensitive," wrote Mlle. des Garets; "one might almost say that his was an overflowing sensitiveness. There was nothing morbid about it, however. Any other person as overworked, harassed, and jostled as he was, might have given way to nerves. His wonderful evenness of temper, still more his admirable self-control, preserved his placidity. Hence, he was always the same, always ready to oblige, however people might have behaved towards him."[8] "Never did a revengeful thought enter his mind; he only knew how to pardon, to love, and to thank," writes the Abbé Raymond, his first vicaire, who, assuredly, knew something about him.

He felt an instinctive attraction towards pure souls. Hence, his tenderness towards children, which was elicited from him by their innocence. He would stop in the street to speak to them, when he would fix on them a glance of extraordinary gentleness. He loved to be in their midst. One of his keenest joys was to watch the orphans of the *Providence* at play. Towards children his graciousness was amazing, and the little ones dared to do what they liked with him.

One day, in 1852, just as the eleven o'clock catechism was ending, a little girl, raising herself on tiptoe, took the liberty of pulling from his head a hair that was longer than the rest. "Little one, love the good God very much," was all he said with a smile.

In 1858 a lady of Lyons brought her two children to Ars. The elder of them, a boy of eleven, wanted to know

8. *Procès de l'Ordinaire,* p. 975.

his vocation. He was present at the saint's Mass. On returning to the sacristy M. Vianney, still plunged in deep recollection, was slowly taking off the sacred vestments. Priests and laymen were there, waiting for their turn to speak to him. The boy had slipped in among these grown-ups and it was he who was the object of the Curé's first look and first smile of welcome.

"What do you want, my child?" he asked in that somewhat cracked yet most gentle voice which they who had once heard it never forgot.

"Monsieur le Curé, I should like to know . . ."

"You will be a good priest," put in M. Vianney, without a shadow of hesitation.

The younger of the two children, scarcely six years old, heard of this incident. A few weeks earlier he had been given a primer, and he felt a growing disgust for a book, to him so full of mysteries. "I shall ask M. le Curé whether I need learn to read," he told his mother.

The following day, at noon, as M. Vianney was leaving the church for the presbytery, he noticed the little fellow, who evidently wanted to speak to him.

"Monsieur le Curé," the budding scholar inquired, "must I learn or shall I play?"

"Play, my child, it is the privilege of your age." No decision of the saint was ever hailed with keener delight.

"Maman," the child triumphantly exclaimed, "M. le Curé has told me to play!"[9]

M. Vianney readily responded to the sentiment of friendship, and he often acknowledged its manifestation with real effusion. The reason was that, so far from shrivelling up or narrowing the heart, holiness causes it to expand and to overflow. "The saints had a *liquid* heart," said the Curé d'Ars. "When the heart is pure," he

---

9. It is impossible to translate the child's ungrammatical phrase without spoiling its charm, "Monsieur le Curé, faut-il que j'*apprende* ou que je *jouille?"* "Joue, mon enfant, c'est de ton age!" "Maman, M. le Curé m'a dit qu'il fallait que je *jouille!"*

M. l'Abbé A. Salomon, successively curé of Meximieux and Trévoux, and who was in all probability the boy mentioned in the first part of this episode, relates it in a letter of April 28, 1905. He declares that the story is "true, down to the smallest detail."

exclaimed, "it cannot help loving, because it has rediscovered the source of love, which is God."

At the time of the cholera in 1854, his beloved Abbé Toccanier went to stay at Seyssel, his native place, for the space of three weeks. The missionary was no sooner back at Ars than, eager to behold once more his holy Curé, he went and stood in front of the confessional, in which the saint had been imprisoned since midnight. M. Vianney rose at once and embraced him tenderly. "Here you are, my good friend," he said in a low voice. "Oh! so much the better! Time has hung heavily upon me. I have been thinking that the reprobate must be very unhappy in Hell, separated as they are eternally from God; already on earth we suffer greatly when parted from those we love!"[10]

Nothing could be more delicate than his gratitude. With what touching accents did he not speak at all times of his benefactors: his mother, M. Balley of Ecully—neither of whom he could mention without shedding tears—Mlle. d'Ars and the family of the des Garets. . . . Almost all his letters to Comte Prosper des Garets contain the words: "My most venerated benefactor."[11]

To *Mère* Fayot of Les Robins he wrote on November 7, 1823: "Will you please tell all those whom I have had the happiness of knowing at Les Noës, that I express to them my sentiments of respect and gratitude; their many kindnesses to me will never be effaced from my memory."

He did not know, indeed, how sufficiently to show his gratitude towards his "dear benefactress" of Les Robins. Later on, when one of her daughters visited him at Ars, he bought her a silk umbrella, in memory of all the good care that had been bestowed upon him by her mother.

A young preacher, still at the beginning of his career, having been sent by M. Camelet, superior of the missionaries of Pont-d'Ain, to assist the Abbé Toccanier, "Where is he," inquired M. Vianney, "where is the little missionary, that I may give him a rosary?"

10. *Procès apostolique in genere,* p. 163.
11. Mlle. Marthe des Garets, *Procès apostolique in genere,* p. 299.

In 1849 the Brothers of the Holy Family of Belley took over the free school for boys, over which Jean Pertinand had presided for the space of eleven years. However, the Curé d'Ars only consented to the change after he had assured himself that it would not be "a cause of pain or loss" for that worthy man, and he sought to procure suitable employment for him.[12]

On all occasions M. Vianney showed himself grateful: a picture, a simple medal given to him appeared precious in his estimation.

The Abbé Alfred Monnin has spoken of "the power of consolation" which issued from the Curé d'Ars. The expression is one of wonderful accuracy. The victims of every form of human misery had recourse to him: fathers and mothers, brides in mourning; anguished Monicas seeking their Augustines; those tried in body or soul; the failures; broken, discouraged, despairing hearts. . . . It seemed as if he thought only of their sufferings, his own were of no consequence! He listened to their confidences and to their lamentations with sighs of compassion, whilst he raised his old and trembling hands towards heaven. It is said that "he consoled them with truly priestly tenderness; it was a joy to him to wipe away their tears." After they had poured their troubles into his great heart, the pilgrims went away more resigned, calmer and more determined to do their duty and to face whatever trials the future might have in store for them. "I have never come away from him without having been comforted," says the Abbé Borjon, who, the reader remembers, had been so nobly forgiven by our saint.

"I can say," affirms the Abbé Étienne Dubouis, whose heart was breaking because of the divisions caused in his parish of Fareins by a remnant of Jansenism, "I can say that all came away from him with a mind more serene and a spirit strengthened to fight the battle of life."

12. Jean Pertinand, one of a family of fifteen children, was only thirty-two when he left Ars. In 1863 we find him in possession of a small property at Amblagnieux (Isère); and manager of the iron-ore mines of Serrières.

When writing to M. Vianney, a certain gendarme, who was greatly tried by ill-health, gave him the apt title of *"Generous consoler of the afflicted!"* heavily underlining the words.[13]

Verily, as René Bazin says, "what a prodigious creator of natural and supernatural happiness, what a force of consolation and resurrection passed through that village!"[14] "For every sorrow the Curé d'Ars had the right word, and what others could not accomplish by long discourses, he achieved with one word." Putting aside all purely human consolations, which he nearly always deemed useless, he was solely guided by the thoughts of faith. He was not afraid to raise poor, afflicted souls above themselves. "May God's will be done!" he would exclaim. "We must will what God wills; we must be content with whatever God sends us."[15]

Marthe Miard, a humble shopkeeper of Ars, had sustained losses in her business: "Oh!" said the Curé, "far better that than sin."[16]

Marthe Miard also relates the following: "The curé of my native place—Saint-Jean-de-Bourgneuf, in Isère—refused at first to believe the marvels that I related. However, as he was suffering greatly, he, too, journeyed to Ars. After seeing M. Vianney, he seemed quite changed: he accepted his cross with complete resignation. M. le Curé had simply said to him: 'My friend, ponder the patience of Our Lord!'"[17]

In May, 1855, a lady came from a great distance to Ars, in the hope of obtaining relief from a very painful infirmity. "Finding that no cure was effected after a very fervent novena, she begged the Curé's assistant to ask him whether she would be healed. The reply of the man of God was as follows: 'This person is pious; the cross is well placed. It will be the ladder by which the poor lady will go to Heaven.'"

13. *Letter* of Gendarme Saget, at Fours (Nièvre), July 21, 1859.
14. Cf. *Annales d'Ars,* April, 1908, p. 327.
15. Marthe Miard, *Procès apostolique continuatif,* p. 845.
16. *Ibid.,* p. 844.
17. Marthe Miard, *Procès apostolique continuatif,* p. 851.

His cousin, Marguerite Humbert, came one day from Ecully to beg his prayers for one of her little daughters who was dangerously ill. "She is ripe for Heaven," he said without hesitation. "As for you, my cousin, you need crosses to make you think of God."[18]

Claudine Fayot, whom Jean-Marie Vianney had known as a tiny child when he lived hidden away in the hamlet of Les Robins, was slowly wasting away. Her mother made known her grief and alarm to the priest, whom she had loved as her own son. M. Vianney's message was brevity itself: "Earth is nothing!" was all he said. Shortly after, Claudine died a holy death.[19]

Mme. Chamonard, of Saint-Romain-les-Iles in the *département* of the Saône-et-Loire, herself an excellent Christian, was married to the most unbelieving of men. In the summer of 1851 she suggested to her husband, who was ill and in great pain, that he should consult M. Vianney. The sick man laughed at so strange a proposal. What! he, a freethinker, to pay such honor to a priest! But then, he was so anxious to get well! So he made up his mind to do so. It took all his wife's persuasiveness, however, to induce him to cross the threshold of the church of Ars. M. Vianney, who was giving his catechism lesson at the time, fixed his searching gaze upon the unbeliever. M. Chamonard hastily left the church, swearing that he would never again set foot in it, and resolved to depart at once. When the distressed wife at last succeeded in approaching the saint, she contented herself with merely asking for her husband's cure. "It is not so much his physical suffering that matters," said M. Vianney; "it is his soul that is in need of a cure. You have undertaken a mission which is only just beginning." Mme. Chamonard left Ars "filled with admiration and singularly comforted." She carried away with her "an unshakable hope." Four years later her husband died the death of the predestined.

Françoise Lebeau, a poor girl of Saint-Martin-de-Com-

18. *Procès de l'Ordinaire,* p. 1325.
19. We owe this detail to Mme. Sophie Côte Forge, of Lyons, a great-grand-daughter of Mme. Fayot, of Les Robins.

mune in the Saône-et-Loire, had become quite blind. She went with her mother on a pilgrimage to Ars. They begged their bread the whole way and slept in stables or sheds. To this poor girl M. Vianney did not fear to disclose something of the divine mystery of suffering, for his inspired gaze had fathomed her valiant spirit. "My child," he said, "you can be cured, but if the good God restores your sight, your salvation will be less assured; if, on the contrary, you consent to keep your infirmity, you will go to Heaven, and I even guarantee that you will have a high place there." The blind girl understood; she no longer asked for a cure, and left Ars in a state of perfect resignation to God's Will.[20]

Nor had M. Vianney the courage to pity the mothers whose children died in infancy. "I had the misfortune to lose one of my children aged five years," relates Mme. des Garets. "This is what M. Vianney replied to my brother-in-law who brought the news to him: 'Happy mother, happy child! What a grace for both of them! How is it that this innocent little one has merited that its time of probation should have been shortened, to enable it to enter so soon into eternal bliss?'"

On other occasions, however, he did not blush to weep with this noble Christian lady. By infinite tactfulness he had prevailed over M. Eugène, the eldest of the sons of the des Garets, to resign himself to die at the early age of twenty-five years. His edifying end, on February 1, 1855, greatly comforted his mother, and there was no need for M. Vianney to raise her spirit. But when, five months later, she lost her second and favorite son, Joanny, who fell mortally wounded at the first assault on Sebastopol, despair seized the stricken mother. Hasten-

20. From a *Letter* of the Abbé Chopin, curé of Saint-Clément-les-Mâcon and great-nephew of François Lebeau, addressed to Mgr. Convert, February 6, 1911, we learn that the blind girl had asked M. Vianney: "Shall I not one day prove a burden to my brothers and sisters?" (there were eight of them). "Do not worry, little one, your brothers and sisters will live to an extreme old age, will take care of you, and when the first of the sisters shall come to die the others will follow her one after the other at an interval of about two years." The first to die was Françoise herself (January, 1895). The others followed at the intervals foretold by the Curé d'Ars, all between the ages of eighty and ninety years.

ing to the château, and mingling his tears with those of the sorrowing mother, the saint exhorted her: "Be great! be strong! do not let yourself be crushed, but know how to accept the blow!" And in a tone of infinite compassion he called her "the mother of sorrows." In recalling this terrible hour when he had stood by her on her own calvary, Mme. des Garets said: "On leaving his presence one felt oneself reborn and capable of accepting and bearing one's cross."[21]

The afflicted who were unable to visit the Curé d'Ars wrote to him or got their friends to write on their behalf. That is why there was always a heavy post awaiting M. Vianney on the small oak table in his room, when he entered it at noon. He hurriedly looked through the letters, but even so he could not read them all. Most of them were requests for counsel and prayer, sorrowful confidences, and cries of distress. Overwhelmed as he was by his work in the confessional, he could but seldom reply to a letter personally, hence the duty of acknowledging letters devolved on those who were his familiars: at first Catherine Lassagne, and then successively Abbé Raymond, Abbé Toccanier, and Frère Athanase. To these casual secretaries he would indicate the nature of the reply, and sometimes he would affix his signature. Of various letters of consolation which the saint himself wrote, two remain, written to one of his cousins, Frère Chalovet, whom obedience had sent to the Hôtel-Dieu of Lyons, and who was greatly tempted.

"My good friend, I write these lines in haste to tell you not to leave, in spite of all the trials that the good God wishes you to endure. Take courage! Heaven is rich enough to reward you.

"Remember that the evils of this world are the lot of good Christians. You are going through a kind of martyrdom. But what a happiness for you to be a martyr of charity! Do not lose so beautiful a crown.

21. Comtesse des Garets, *Procès de l'Ordinaire,* pp. 780-781, 892-893.

"'Blessed are they that suffer persecution for my sake,' says Jesus Christ, our model. Farewell, my most dear friend. Persevere along the way on which you have so happily entered, and we shall see each other again in heaven . . . ." (Letter of July 25.)

"Courage, my good cousin! Soon we shall see it, our beautiful Heaven. Soon there will be no more cross for us! What divine bliss! to see that good Jesus who has loved us so much and who will make us so happy!" (May 17.)

Many of the letters received by M. Vianney are most moving. With a saint who had the reputation of reading the secrets of the heart, correspondents felt at their ease and laid bare their miseries, both great and small, without false shame or human respect.

The following are extracts from this spiritual correspondence, of which only a few fragments have been preserved.[22]

The pastor of a most irreligious parish wrote these sorrowful lines to his saintly colleague, who had experienced similar trials:

"MELLEREY, NEAR GIVRY (DIOCESE OF AUTUN),
"*December* 3, 1858.

"MY MOST DEAR FATHER,

"I am your penitent, your child, I come to implore the help of your prayers, in a special manner, to the end that I may be guarded against a calamity that threatens me.

"A great scandal is imminent in my parish, and I have recourse to you to prevent it. The feast of St. Nicholas,

22. The Abbé Monnin says that the Curé d'Ars "refused to read through letters that began with some laudatory phrase," that he "crumpled them up with a kind of indignation and threw them into the fire "*(Life,* ch. xxix). In like manner, M. Joseph Vianney *(Le Bienheureux Curé d'Ars,* p. 163): "He burnt, without perusing them, letters that began with complimentary phrases." The fact is probably not to be denied. It is nonetheless true that a few letters, even of this kind, have escaped destruction, indeed there are very few among those that have been preserved which do not begin with some laudatory formula. It is safer to say that M. Vianney kept no letters unless they contained requests for Masses or novenas, in which case he passed them on to one of his assistants. It is thanks to this circumstance that fragments—far too few, alas!—of the saint's correspondence have come down to us.

which is next Monday, will be the occasion for a party of vine-dressers and others to give themselves up for two or three days to the most profane diversions (dances and revelry of every kind) and they will entice many people to evil, even the children for whom I have labored so much. And all this during Advent, just before the feast of the Immaculate Conception of Mary, our good and sweet Mother! I am having a novena made to the Blessed Virgin to avert the scandal. I implore you to unite your prayers to ours . . .

"ABBÉ FERRET."

Letters concerning religious vocations, very often full of anguish and tear-stained, were certainly the most numerous of those that the Curé received. A young girl from Bourgoin wrote to him on February 2, 1859:

"When will the good God break the chains that keep me bound to this corrupt world? Oh! what sins, what bad example one beholds!

"I want to belong to God, but this is what hinders the execution of my heart's desire: the Superior-General of the Sisters of the Blessed Sacrament will not receive me. At my mother's death my poor father deserted us: he left us in order to look elsewhere for a home and work. The Superior tells me that this is a stain on our family and that their Congregation could not receive one belonging to a family on which there was such a stain.

"O my Father, if I must remain in the world, what graces I shall require to sanctify myself! Alas! I am very frivolous: you yourself have told me in the confessional that I am *too exterior.* That is quite true: I always imagine that others are looking at me. I am full of good will, however.

"Oh! pray for me, Father, for if you do I feel sure that I shall be converted."

Another young woman wrote to him from Paris:

"Good Father, I have heard people talk of you and of your miracles. . . . So I said to myself, if God would let me know His Will by the voice of the Curé d'Ars, it would be a much quicker way of obtaining this grace than by long prayers.

"In spite of my age, I am very much of a child; but Our Lord did not reject children; only I am far from having the simplicity which made them so lovable in the eyes of the good Jesus. I am sixteen years old, and I have not yet thought seriously of my vocation; but I wish to save my soul.

"As God has given you the grace of discernment of spirits, you can see what is going on in my soul. . . ."

"I am undecided, I need enlightenment," writes a child of the same age as the preceding one. "Many obstacles stand in the way of my vocation. My mother is very pious, but my father is a soldier, and I am sure it will be very difficult to obtain his consent. . . ."

Here is a letter from the father of a family, who grieves and secretly rebels at the thought of his daughter entering a very strict Order. He implores the curé to combat this wish. We do not know how the saint met this cry wrung from a father's heart.

"NIMES,
"*June* 25, 1855.

"MONSIEUR LE CURÉ,

"The fame of your virtues and of the marvellous gifts which it has pleased God to bestow upon you, has reached us; hence, one of my daughters, a young girl of twenty years, hopes, in a few days' time, to ask your advice on a matter of the greatest importance: it is a question of a decision on which the whole of her future depends.

"Although my daughter is endowed with all those qualities which would open the world to her, she has felt, already for several years, a very pronounced attraction towards the religious life. At first we looked upon this disposition as a passing phase of fervent piety and the consequence of the natural inexperience of her age. However, these thoughts persist.

"Our love for this dear child is not selfish; above all things we desire her happiness; and if it is clearly shown to us that in this world she can find it only by embracing religion, we shall know how to make the sacrifice, however painful it may prove. But it would cost us too much to see her choose so severe an Order as Carmel, which she has in view; an Order where nothing tempers the rigor of seclusion, austerity, and isolation. This is an extremity to which we shall never give our consent, and we come to beg of you to turn our daughter from it. Our beloved child, although she has not as yet the happiness of knowing you, feels the most absolute confidence in your lights and holy inspirations. She believes that God Himself is about to speak to her by your mouth, to point out to her the road she must take. It is for this purpose that she and her mother are coming to see you.

"Monsieur le Curé, in so solemn a matter, when it is a question of taking a step so decisive and in a manner irrevocable, it is well to warn her against undue precipitancy. If she is really determined to enter religion, if God calls her, as she assures us He does, why, for instance, should she not enter at the Sacré-Coeur, which she knows and where she is known, for she was a boarder at the convent of Montpellier, and they would be so happy to receive her there? Why should she bury herself alive in Carmel?

"My daughter, then, will visit you in two or three days' time. It is without her knowledge that I take the liberty of writing to you, to explain beforehand her dispositions and to beg of you to do what you can to prevent an extreme step, which would plunge us all into consternation and misery. I feel convinced that if you advise her to choose the Sacré-Coeur, where, after all, she can realize the designs of God upon her just as well as at Carmel, and make sure of her salvation, she will not hesitate to do your bidding. She is determined to listen to no one but you and to abide by your decision alone. You are at present the sole arbiter of her destiny."

We may feel quite certain that if the Curé d'Ars discerned the call of God in Mlle. Bossy's wish to enter

Carmel, he will have urged her to do so.

It will be readily understood that those in affliction, those whose hearts were rent by bereavement, found the "good Father" easy of approach.

The Baronne de Bréda wrote to him from Paris on December 3, 1858: "Monsieur le Curé, your heart has so often been touched by the lamentations of disconsolate mothers seeking the aid of your holy prayers, I come to add to their number. . . ."

Her request was that he would save her daughter, whom a mysterious illness had made "a real martyr."

On January 12, 1853, someone writes from Grenoble: "An afflicted soul comes to implore your help. A husband, a father suddenly snatched from the tender love of his family; young children left in the inexperienced hands of a brokenhearted mother. . . ." What an object of immense pity! The poor mother wished to go to Ars to seek, not, indeed, consolation (there is none for such sorrows), but at least some mitigation of her profound grief, resignation to bear her terrible misfortune, and submission to the will of God. . . .

"Amidst the sufferings of a long illness," a woman of Lyons wrote from her sickbed, "I should like to receive the consolations which those enjoy who have the happiness of approaching you. It seems to me I should suffer more patiently were I helped at least by your prayers. It is to ask this favor, to which I attach the greatest value, that I take the liberty of writing to you, my good and venerated Curé."

M. Vianney never scorned any of these requests. However, since it was not possible to present them to God, one by one, he gathered them in one great petition which he offered daily to Our Lord at the *Memento* of his Mass. Moreover, the tears of compassion which frequently escaped from his eyes as he listened to so many affecting stories were in themselves a prayer and a supplication.

We have described the heart of the Curé d'Ars—it now remains to speak of his spirit, his tact, and his exquisite judgement.

" A gentle and frank gaiety and a delightful ease characterized his relations with his friends."[23] He nevertheless showed extreme reserve towards the persons who served him. He was aware of their devotedness and of their tried virtue, but a supernatural prudence dictated this attitude. Catherine Lassagne, who was both shrewd and discreet, was quite conscious of it:

"Those (she puts the masculine *ceux* instead of *celles)* who were oftenest near his person, to render him the needful services, were seized with a holy reverence when in his presence, so that at times they were afraid to speak to him even on most pressing matters. The good God permitted this, in order that those who strove to serve His good and faithful servant should do so purely for His glory."[24]

But with his colleagues, assistants or other friends, he was glad to relax—this was, in fact, a need of his responsive and sensitive nature—especially in the evening, after the heavy strain of the confessional. He was escorted to his room by one of the Brothers, who was often accompanied by some of the missionaries, the devoted Mayor, M. des Garets, and others besides; indeed, many of the pilgrims, both priests and laymen, craved the favor of spending the last moments of the day in his company, and M. Vianney willingly received them.

He would listen to the news of the day, the events which concerned France and the Church.[25] Politics interested him only in so far as they bore on religion. "When people spoke to him of worldly affairs, he seemed to be no longer in his element." He was anxious to return to

23. *Procès de l'Ordinaire,* p. 150.

24. *Petit mémoire,* troisième rédaction, p. 91.

25. It may be that he read, at long intervals, a few numbers of the *Ami de la Religion et du Roi* (founded in 1814), and the *Mémorial catholique* (founded in 1823), which the châtelains of the district, or his brother priests passed on to him. But he never subscribed to a newspaper. No contemporary has informed us as to his opinion concerning the *Avenir,* of Lamennais, and the events which led to the apostasy of that unfortunate priest. However, certain *intuitions* show that the Curé d'Ars was not wholly ignorant of the events of his time, and that he held *views* on many subjects.

his favorite subjects.

"His only pleasure was to converse on spiritual matters," relates his confessor, the Abbé Louis Beau. When courtesy obliged him to listen to conversations on temporal matters, one felt that he took only that measure of interest which kindness demanded.

"I have witnessed the joy which he felt when some good news about the Church or the salvation of souls was brought to him, when, for example, he heard that a mission had been a great success; on the other hand, how keenly he suffered when he heard of a scandal!"[26]

"His heart was so full of the love of God," says the Comte des Garets, "that he introduced it into all his conversations, and he would often break off to join his hands and with eyes lifted up to heaven, exclaim: 'My God, how good Thou art!'"[27]

It was his habitual thought. "One day," relates the Abbé Toccanier, "I casually remarked: 'The weather is bad today, Monsieur le Curé.' 'It is always fine weather for the just,' he replied; 'it is bad weather only for poor sinners.'"[28]

M. Vianney was a stranger to all the subtleties of self-love. As a rule, "he did not speak of himself, either favorably or unfavorably. When his most intimate friends wished to ascertain certain details which concerned him and were to his credit, they had recourse to subterfuges by which they led him imperceptibly to take them into his confidence. But he no sooner noticed the trap than he became silent, and if they persisted, 'it is enough,' he would protest, 'I have already said too much!'" Nevertheless, he was very willing to be reminiscent. "But," says Frère Athanase, "whenever he related incidents, even such as reflected favorably on himself, he invariably spoke of them as if they concerned a stranger." "A favorite ruse of the missionaries when they wished to prolong the pleasure of hearing him speak," says M. Dufour, who was one of them, "was casually to mention the name of M. Balley,

26. *Procès de l'Ordinaire,* p. 1193.
27. *Procès apostolique ne pereant,* p, 375.
28. *Ibid.,* p. 295.

concerning whom he was inexhaustible. . . ."[29] However, the conversation could not go on indefinitely. "When M. Vianney," says the Comte des Garets, "had conversed for some time with unconstrained familiarity, standing the while and leaning against his humble table, he would suddenly salute us, saying: 'I have the honor to wish you good-night!' And we went away charmed with our interview."[30]

If the Curé d'Ars was simple he was also shrewd. "What wit that man had, and what a great mind!" says René Bazin.[31] He was very observant: many a shaft of mordant wit might he have dashed off, but he always refrained from doing so. However, "in the freedom of familiar conversation he occasionally dropped remarks of delightful gaiety and even piquancy; observations that were not devoid of a certain delicate irony."[32] These sallies never wounded because their sting was softened by the merry tone of his voice and the kindly expression of his face.[33]

"One of my sisters begged for some relics," Mlle. Marthe des Garets relates. "'Make them yourself,' replied the Curé, thereby wishing to insinuate that she had but to become a saint."

A nun said to him with artless simplicity: "People in general believe that you are ignorant, Father."

"They are not mistaken, my daughter; but it is of no consequence; I shall always be able to teach you more than you will ever be able to learn."[34]

M. Blanchon, curé of Bublanne, one of his friends in the diocese, who was rather stout, was one day conversing familiarly with him. "Monsieur le Curé," this worthy colleague said jestingly, "I rely upon you to get me safely up aloft. . . . When you go to Heaven, I shall try to hold on to your cassock." The answer came promptly, accompanied by a pleasant and mischievous smile: "Oh, my

---

29. *Procès apostolique in genere,* p. 329.
30. *Procès de l'Ordinaire,* p. 957.
31. *Annales d'Ars,* April, 1908, p. 324.
32. Mme. Christine de Cibeins, *Procès apostolique continuatif,* p. 155.
33. Comte des Garets, *Procès de l'Ordinaire,* p. 957.
34. "Je vous en dirai encore plus que vous n'en ferez."

friend, you had better not do any such thing: the entrance into Heaven is narrow; we should get stuck in the gate."

"What must I do to get to Heaven?" asked a good lady who was likewise of no ordinary proportions. "Three Lents, my daughter!"

"The Emperor has achieved several fine things," M. Vianney remarked one day at the eleven o'clock catechism, as some ladies, dressed in the hideous fashion of the time, were struggling to get into the church; "he has forgotten, however, to have the church doors enlarged so as to make room for the crinolines!"

Once, during a heavy shower, the holy Cure was hastening alone, without hat or umbrella, past the house of the Brothers, to visit a sick person. Frère Athanase ran after him, but overtook him only with difficulty. "Where are you going, comrade?" inquired M. Vianney. "Oh! I have brought you an umbrella." "Bah, bah, I am not made of sugar." And laughing heartily he took the umbrella and hurried on.[35]

He shrewdly appraised various preachers. M. Collet, who eventually became curé of Trévoux, loved to preach stern truths. He had preceded in the pulpit of Ars the Abbé Alfred Monnin, who preferred to speak about the more comforting dogmas of the faith, treating them in the manner suggested by his vivid and exuberant imagination. "These good men," M. Vianney afterwards observed, "lead us to Heaven, the one over a bridge of stone, the other over one of flowers."[36]

On no occasion was the Curé d'Ars ever known to offend against charity by his words. Once only did Frère Jérôme fancy he had found him at fault. However, the Brother, who acknowledged that "he was inclined to scrupulosity on his own account quite as much as on that of others," had failed to see that M. Vianney was only protesting against the practices of a ne'er-do-well, who was known throughout the district. "M. le Curé," the Brother adds, "was forever beseeching God to prevent that person from

35. Mgr. Convert, *Notes MSS.*, n. 45.
36. Mgr. Convert, *Le Curé d'Ars et les dons du Saint-Esprit*, p. 423.

being raised to the priesthood, to which he aspired."[37]

As regards speech, the saint was always most reserved; in fact, almost excessively so. Of this we have proof in one of his letters, written in 1828, and addressed to the Comte de Cibeins. Its only purpose appears to be a desire to make amends for the semblance of a peccadillo. After a somewhat vague preamble, M. Vianney, obviously embarrassed, comes at last to the point:

"There is something which troubles me sorely: when I called on you I inadvertently uttered a slander, for which I am deeply sorry, even though I did not realize I was doing wrong when I told you that I was being deceived. Had I thought at the moment that I was doing wrong, I should have preferred to lose all that I have. I beg of you, Monsieur, never to mention the matter, which has pained me very much. For the sake of the good things of the earth, we should not forfeit those of Heaven."

Such perfect contrition, for the veriest shadow of a fault, shows to what heights the Curé d'Ars had carried the refinement of his charity.

37. Frère Jérôme, *Procès de l'Ordinaire,* p. 540.

Chapter 23

AT THE HEIGHT OF SANCTITY
I. Testimonies

SANCTITY—that is, the utter renouncement of self and all that is transitory, a sustained yearning for God and heavenly realities; sanctity, as we admire it in a Curé d'Ars, the sanctity that obtains the honors of canonization, is not a universal vocation common to all Christians. Such holiness presupposes, on the part of God, gratuitous gifts of an eminent order, but by a reciprocal claim, it requires on the part of the creature, a persevering, arduous, and even heroic endeavor, so that, in one sense at least, holiness, like genius, might be described as a capacity for taking pains. Sanctity is both given and acquired: it springs from God's preventing grace, and yet it is the resultant of a human life, the happy conclusion of long sustained labor.[1]

Even though the Curé d'Ars felt, from his infancy, an irresistible attraction towards God, he was not, on that account, exempt from the law of effort, stubborn effort at that. His sails were not always filled by a favorable wind—he, too, was at times compelled to bend to his oars. Like every man coming into this world, he had to reform an impatient character, restrain tendencies that were human and overcome bitter repugnances. He knew what it was to suffer from irritation of the nerves, dryness and weariness of the soul, and even at times a prostration that bordered on despair. "Ah! it is a fine thing to be a

1. "The Church has hit on the right word when, over and above the virtues practiced by pious souls, she attributes to her saints a special degree of *heroicity.* A saint is a hero. All can be and should be holy (in the sense that all can and should possess sanctifying grace), but everybody cannot be a *saint. Sanctity* is like genius: "the one like the other pre-supposes a certain predestination for which there is no substitute" (Dom Paul Chauvin, *Qu'est-ce qu'un saint?* Bloud, Paris, p. 14).

saint, but how much it has cost the Curé d'Ars!" exclaimed one of his penitents.[2]

Assuredly all this required much labor and time, for "it is no child's play to renounce oneself perfectly."[3] He reached the goal because, even though his senses and feelings may have rebelled at times, his will never said: "I cannot"; on the contrary, its motto ever was: "I can do all things in him who strengtheneth me." (*Phil.* 4:13). Here we have the secret of his exalted holiness: an heroic will, an unflinching courage.

Jean-Marie Vianney proved himself pious as a child and exemplary as a youth, a seminarist, a priest. And then a day came, known to God alone, when he became "a saint and a great saint."[4] If it be permissible reverently to sound this mystery, we may have to look for that date at the period of his life when he had acquired that "ineffable gentleness" which charmed the pilgrims; the period when he renounced every desire that savored in the least degree of self-love; when he put away that most legitimate of dreams, the thought of a few days' repose among his own and in the home where he was born; the period when, guided by more continuous and brighter lights from above, he opened his arms wide to sinners, with a compassion and a meekness that knew no bounds. We are of opinion that it was the year 1844 or 1845 that saw the Curé d'Ars established on the heights of sanctity.

By that time he seemed to have become a wholly supernatural being, "and suffering was the only thing human about him."[5] "He attained that heroic degree of virtue which is the supreme effort of nature strengthened by grace."[6] Virtue had become in him as a second nature. His will, ever active, persevering, enamored only of that

2. Baronne Alix de Belvey, *Procès de l'Ordinaire,* p. 237. The Curé d'Ars himself says: "The saints become saints only after many sacrifices and much violent effort." *(Sermons,* t. IV, p. 145).
3. *Imitation of Christ,* III, ch. 32.
4. Abbé Dufour, *Procès apostolique in genere,* p. 422.
5. *Letter* of the Comtesse des Garets to her daughter, Marthe, *Procès apostolique in genere,* p. 306.
6. *Procès apostolique continuatif,* pp. 820-821.

which is good, tending continuously towards that which is better, passed from the perfection acquired yesterday to the higher degree held out to him by the new-born day. He knew no slackness, no routine; a constant alertness of mind and heart upheld him in the discharge of his duty.

Numerous witnesses of his life have borne testimony to this state of acquired holiness, and many of their statements bespeak profound understanding, and have about them the ring of genuine conviction.

"M. Vianney's reputation for sanctity was established first by simple and devout people," says Pierre Oriol, the Curé's loyal henchman; "but subsequently these first rumors, which originated at Ars and in the surrounding districts, were re-echoed by those whose opinion was of the greatest weight, by reason of their character, their age, and their position. I have often witnessed the admiration aroused by the spectacle of the virtues of the Curé d'Ars. . . . And that reputation grew steadily."[7] No man is a hero to his valet. M. Vianney lived in a glass house, as it were, and he suffered himself to be watched, spied upon, and discussed at leisure. Now, those who were in the closest contact with him, those who were most intimate with him, were likewise the first to proclaim his sanctity.[8] "They never discovered in his conduct a deliberate venial sin," says a priest of Ars.

Contemporary evidence is very plentiful. Rarely has there been so beautiful and so unanimous a concert of praise. The eloquent panegyrics which are annually heard

7. *Procès de l'Ordinaire,* p. 757.

8. "A great man, so great in the eyes of the crowd and of those who only see the external result of his labours, appears frequently very small indeed to those who behold him at close quarters and are acquainted with his foibles. Now a saint is especially holy in the estimation of those who watch him the closest. It is they who, having witnessed his hidden virtues, his secret gentleness, his influence with God, and his unseen action upon souls, are oftenest called upon to enlighten ignorance, and to remove the prejudices that would obscure the saint's merit." (H. Joly, *Psychologie des Saints,* p. 28). But according to the remark of Dom Chauvin (*Qu'est-ce qu'un Saint?* p. 19): "If sanctity forced itself upon men, no one would be able to resist it." Now we know that the reality is far otherwise; thus, for instance, the Abbé Raymond who, during eight years, was the "much-loved" auxiliary of the Curé d'Ars, did not treat him, as we shall see hereafter, with the respect due to his sanctity.

in the basilica or in the village square of Ars will never have a ring of more convincing or more penetrating sincerity.

To begin with, we have the testimony of the Abbé Louis Beau, curé of Jassans, who knew the saint more intimately than anyone else—he was his confessor during the last thirteen years of his life:

"I do not think that he slackened his effort for as much as a day. He discharged his duties as a priest and pastor with admirable delicacy of conscience, and he persevered until death in a strict fulfilment of all his duties. I particularly noticed the manner in which he made the Sign of the Cross, recited grace before meals, and the *Ave Maria* when the hour struck. I am still deeply moved by the remembrance of what I witnessed on those occasions. With what angelic piety he recited his Breviary! I cannot find words to express myself. I do not think it is possible to go any further in the practice of heroic virtues. When I read the *Lives of the Saints* I fail to discover in them anything exceeding that which I have witnessed in M. le Curé d'Ars. He was surrounded by a halo of sanctity. I cannot express with how much veneration and respect for his person he inspired me. It is my opinion that he had preserved the grace of his Baptism, and to that grace he was constantly adding by the eminent sanctity of his life."[9]

After his confessor, let us quote one who was his right hand in all his undertakings and the best-informed witness of his life, one whom Mgr. de Langalerie called "a living relic of the Curé d'Ars." In the chapter of her *Petit mémoire sur M. Vianney,* in which she enumerates "the benefits he bestowed on the parish," Catherine Lassagne suddenly drops her usual restraint, and exclaims:

"How good the good God is to have given us this saint whom we have had the happiness of possessing in our midst for more than forty years! It may be said that he went on his way doing good. Only on the day of judge-

9. *Procès de l'Ordinaire,* pp. 1189-1190, 1221, 1240.

ment shall we see the merits with which he must be enriched!"[10]

Let us now hear the prelate who was his Bishop for twenty-nine years. In 1839, the Abbé Tailhades, of Montpellier, went to see Mgr. Devie at the conclusion of a two-months' stay with M. Vianney. The Abbé had collected some notes about the Curé, and at one moment he even thought of publishing them. To do so he needed the consent of the Bishop of Belley. "The Bishop," says the Abbé Tailhades, "seizing this opportunity to sound me concerning M. Vianney, asked: 'What do you think of the Curé d'Ars?' 'I believe he is a saint,' I replied, whereupon the Bishop said: 'I am of the same opinion.'"[11]

"Now," as the Abbé Raymond remarks, "who is better qualified to pass judgement than the clergy, who know the obligations of the priesthood, the holiness that should adorn those who are invested with so sublime a dignity; the priests who know the labors, the fatigues, the anxieties that are inseparable from the parochial ministry, and the work of the confessional and who are able to gauge, from personal experience, the heights of virtue, self-denial and self-sacrifice to which the good Curé had attained?"

The Abbé Toccanier, his assistant for six years, has said of him: "One approached him as one approaches a relic. Never have I seen so much energy and strength of will. Nothing daunted him: neither opposition, nor infirmities, nor temptations. He always displayed equal courage in the practice of virtue and in devotion to his neighbor. So striking was this virtue that it roused to admiration those who beheld him. His was a calm strength, like the strength that comes from God, and is therefore unconquerable. The pilgrims, among them even religious belonging to the strictest Orders, used to say that they needed no other miracle than this strength to convince themselves of his holiness."

The following is the testimony of the Abbé Alfred

10. *Petit mémoire,* troisième rédaction, p. 81.
11. *Procès de l'Ordinaire,* p. 1525.

Monnin, his first biographer who, in his capacity as a missionary, stayed with him at Ars on four or five occasions, each time for several months:

"I cannot think of even one instant when his conduct did not bear the stamp of perfection. I feel that never has sanctity appeared to me under forms more manifest, more amiable, more resplendent. He said nothing, did nothing that could have been said better or done better!"

Mgr. Louis Mermod, chaplain to the Visitation Convent at Gex, a priest of great virtue, who, as a young cleric, had been a faithful penitent of M. Vianney's, writes as follows:

"After my departure from Chaleins, twenty-five years went by before I again saw the servant of God. When I had that happiness, I saw such obvious proofs of his holiness in his very countenance that I felt ashamed to appear before him."[12]

M. Jean-Louis Borjon, former curé of Ambérieux-en-Dombes, who had made him suffer and who had been wholeheartedly forgiven, bore the following testimony to the sanctity of the holy Curé:

"I found in him the virtues which make the great saints."

Other priests, who also knew him well, speak in a like strain:

"M. Vianney was the embodiment of the supernatural life."[13] "The perfection which he preached to others formed the austere rule of his own conduct. Faith was the motive power of all his actions, of his whole life."[14] "I noticed in him the perfection of every virtue."[15] "I never saw a truer picture of the divine Master."[16] "The privilege of having known him seems to me to have been a special grace from God."[17]

The celebrated Abbé Combalot, who, in his youth, had

---

12. *Procès de l'Ordinaire,* pp. 1036 and 1269. The *Life* of Mgr. Mermod has been written by the Abbé Chatelard, chaplain at the Visitation of Bourg.
13. Chanoine Jean Gardette, *Procès apostolique ne pereant,* p. 921.
14. Abbé Raymond, *Procès de l'Ordinaire,* pp. 290 and 306.
15. Abbé J. B. Descotes, *Procès de l'Ordinaire,* p. 1343.
16. Abbé Dubouis, *Procès de l'Ordinaire,* p. 1246.
17. R. P. Faivre, *Procès de l'Ordinaire,* p. 1493.

been a disciple of Lamennais and had remained one of his greatest admirers, came one day, at a very early hour, to confess himself to the Curé d'Ars. On issuing from the confessional he threw himself, bathed in tears, into the arms of the Abbé Toccanier: "My God! what a man you have here," he exclaimed; "is it possible that I should have allowed my head to turn white before coming to see him!"

"Two priests, one of whom was the postulator of the cause of Venerable de la Salle—Mgr. Estrade—and the other a religious, but both of the clergy of Rome, came to Ars whilst I was there," says the Abbé Raymond. "Having heard that there were two priests in Rome who enjoyed a reputation for great sanctity, I asked the visitors whether they knew them.

"'Yes,' they said.

"'What difference do you find between these two living saints and my good Curé?'

"'M. Vianney,' they said, 'makes a deeper impression upon us: his person seems to breathe forth even greater holiness.'"[18]

Nor have laymen been less emphatic or less enthusiastic in their tribute of admiration and praise. Let us hear some of these witnesses chosen at random from all classes of society.

Dr. Jean-Baptiste Saunier, who attended the Curé d'Ars during the last years of his life, makes the following attestation: "My dealings with the servant of God were most intimate; I always found him a perfect pattern of every virtue."[19]

The appreciations that follow come, for the most part, from inhabitants of Ars, peasants, workmen, or châtelains:

"He was, always and everywhere, in the fullest meaning of the word, a perfect priest, a model parish priest, and a true man of God."[20] "Distinguished ecclesiastics,

18. *Procès de l'Ordinaire,* p. 339; *Procès apostolique ne pereant,* p. 559.
19. *Procès de l'Ordinaire,* p. 1398.
20. Vicomte Jean-Félix des Garets, *Procès apostolique in genere,* p, 422.

men of the world, artists, have assured us that they had never witnessed anything like that burning, adoring, and pleading heart."[21] "He was a hero, not in the practice of one virtue only, but in that of all, and this not for a given time only, but all through his life."[22] "The perusal of the *Lives of the Saints* had not inspired me with so lofty a conception of holiness as did his whole conduct."[23] "I look upon him as one of the greatest saints that God has given to His Church."[24] "If he is not a saint there never will be one!"[25]

Even the great public, whose voice, it has been said, is the voice of God, made no mistake in its judgement of the Curé d'Ars. "Where is the saint?" the newcomers asked. "The saint! See, the saint is coming!" were cries that rose from among the serried ranks of the crowd so soon as the lowly priest appeared. And more than one visitor, after he had thus acclaimed him, would say to the Curé's own people: "We need see no other marvel in order to believe that your pastor is a saint."[26] And indeed, as has been stated by Cardinal Luçon, a former Bishop of Belley and subsequently Archbishop of Rheims, "if ever a man was canonized by the voice of the people, that man was, assuredly, our Curé: the sentence of the Church can only confirm the judgement of the people."[27]

A vine-dresser of the district of Mâcon was asked what he had seen in the village of Ars: "I have seen God in a man," was his reply. A young pilgrim said: "When one has had the happiness of seeing that priest, I cannot conceive how it is possible to offend the good God." A gentleman of Marseilles had so high an idea of his sanctity that he feared to appear before the Curé d'Ars without having first cleared his conscience and received Holy Communion in the chapel of Fourvière.[28]

21. *Procès apostolique in genere,* p. 319.
22. Mme. Christine de Cibeins, *Procès apostolique continuatif,* p. 158.
23. Baronne Alix de Belvey, *Procès de l'Ordinaire,* p. 250.
24. Hippolyte Pagès, *Procès de l'Ordinaire,* p. 406.
25. André Verchère, the wheelwright of Ars, *Procès de l'Ordinaire,* p. 1327.
26. Abbé Toccanier, *Procès apostolique ne pereant,* p. 325.
27. *Pastoral Letter* of October 23, 1904.
28. *Procès apostolique ne pereant,* p. 270.

In 1851, a rumor having been circulated at Lyons to the effect that M. Vianney had foretold the assassination of the Prince-President in the course of a review which he was to hold, a stranger, whose mien was not reassuring, came to see M. des Garets, the Mayor of Ars. The man was a commissary of police, and was charged with the duty of inquiring into the alleged prediction of M. Vianney. M. des Garets, somewhat perturbed, went to inform M. Vianney, and found him in the confessional: "Set your mind at ease," he said, "there is nothing to fear." He bade the commissary come into the sacristy and closed the door. The interview lasted ten minutes. "When the door opened once more," relates the Mayor, "I beheld M. le Curé coming out accompanied by the man, who was weeping copiously. I rejoined him, and, as we came out of the church, he told me, with deep feeling: 'Your Curé is wonderful: he is a saint!'"[29]

The commissary of police had been ordered to execute a disagreeable task in respect to a man whom he was only too willing to rank as a fanatic and a disturber of the peace; when he left him "he was full of admiration for his virtues." Many persons set out for Ars in a like spirit of incredulity. A saint! what an antiquated, prehistoric notion!

"In the summer of 1841," says M. Brac de la Perrière, "a friend of mine, who was seriously ill, heard some people speak of a village Curé of eminent sanctity. The pious souls who had given him this information doubted neither the miracles already wrought by the priest, nor those that he might yet perform. My friend conceived a desire to see him and asked me to accompany him to Ars.

"At first, I must own, I was but little disposed to comply. My faith in Christian holiness was absolute. I had great respect for those admirable figures of saints who rise at long intervals, and who seem to be like apparitions granted to the world for its consolation and instruction. However, whilst living in a materialistic age and

---

29. Comte Prosper des Garets, *Procès apostolique ne pereant,* p. 371.

pursuing my classical studies, I had not escaped the infection of intellectual pride. I asked myself how it would be possible for me to acknowledge as a saint one who was separated from me neither by time nor by a succession of generations; one whose merit would meet with no better judge than the poor intellect of a youth of twenty-five. I refused to undertake the journey. It was in vain that my friend insisted. Towards the end of August he declared that he would set out alone. Then the fear of seeing him leave his family at a moment when his health was precarious caused me to make up my mind to accompany him."

Now, as is proved by his long account, the young traveller who set out a skeptic, returned to Lyons full of enthusiasm about the things that he had seen and heard: "Henceforth we shall ever feel compelled to flee to our memories of Ars as unto a sanctuary, and to conjure up before the eyes of our soul the saintly figure of M. Vianney—only thus shall we find anew both encouragement and comfort."[30]

In a word, during twenty years, this concert of praise was unanimous: there was never a jarring note. "I do not know that one word was ever said to contradict this reputation for sanctity," says Mlle. Marthe des Garets. "In fact, I was astonished at the silence of irreligious newspapers in this respect, though their correspondents did not fail to visit the village in order to spy upon what was taking place there."[31]

If, however, a few scoffers were found here and there, even they paid unconscious homage to the saint: they were the personification of vice and irreligion attacking virtue. One day a man of Villefranche, one of those free-thinkers whose kind never quite dies out, made this remark, worthy of M. Homais: "It is a pity that the Curé d'Ars should have come to disturb the nineteenth century!"[32] Would there were no other disturbances in the world!

30. Brac de la Perrière, *Souvenirs de deux pèlerinages à Ars,* pp. 1 and 8.
31. *Procès apostolique in genere,* p. 327.
32. *Procès de l'Ordinaire,* p. 758.

The reader will have observed that none of these witnesses, so diverse by reason of their birth, education and station in life, but all endowed alike with a happy clearsightedness, ever associate the idea of holiness with what is merely an accessory to sanctity. Instinctively they grasp essentials. To their mind the Curé d'Ars is a saint because he had edified them by his heroic virtues, not because he had wrought miracles, was rapt in ecstasy, read the hearts of men or foretold the future—they knew that such things are not a necessary ingredient of holiness.[33]

These gratuitous gifts of God were neither desired nor asked for by the holy Curé; all he sought was God, God worshipped and loved for His own sake; that which he succeeded in acquiring, in no stinted measure, was love, the most perfect of all supernatural gifts. Now, as it has been said, "holiness is love."[34]

---

33. "In reality, it is impossible to set up a hierarchy of superiority between the twofold way, ordinary and extraordinary. It may be affirmed, however, that the common way demands more renouncement, labor, and toil. But the serious practice of virtue remains ultimately the only criterion of any value. A saint is one who has practiced virtue in an heroic degree, not one who has had ecstasies and revelations." (Dom Chauvin, *Qu'est-ce qu'un saint?* p. 42).
34. *Qu'est-ce qu'un saint?* p. 36.

Chapter 24

AT THE HEIGHT OF SANCTITY
(continued)
II. Heroic Virtues: Humility, Love of Poverty and of the Poor

WHEN the Catholic Church weighs the possibility of the beatification of one who died in the odor of sanctity, she makes a prolonged and searching examination of his life and conduct, so as to ascertain whether or not they are characterized by the perfect practice of every Christian virtue. It was such an investigation that raised the Curé d'Ars to our altars. The historian of his life is not bound to start his *process* afresh. It is enough that he should state the virtues in which his hero *specialized.*

Now among the many heroic personages whom the Church honors, what is it that constitutes the *singular* and personal merit of Saint Jean-Marie-Baptiste Vianney?

It seems to us that he has been especially heroic in the practice of four virtues: humility, love of poverty and of the poor, patience, and mortification—four exquisite flowers, the perfume of which we have inhaled at almost every page of this book. We must now relish their fragrance in a more leisurely manner.

We speak here of *heroic virtues*—that is, *habits* almost superhuman, when heroism has become the *habitual disposition* of the soul, not *heroic acts,* fitful, spasmodic, and the result of fortuitous circumstances,

Of those virtues we can admire only the outward appearance, for the unceasing action of divine grace that raised the Curé d'Ars to so lofty a degree of holiness, must remain almost entirely hidden.

Humility, chiefest of moral virtues, without which a man has but the appearance of virtue, was truly the guiding principle of M. Vianney's life and conduct. It radiated from his whole person. Mgr. de Ségur, who visited him in 1858, was of opinion that this virtue was enough by itself to obtain for him the honors of canonization. When the blind prelate returned to the château, whose hospitality he was enjoying, he could speak of nothing but the humility of the Curé d'Ars. "It seemed to him a veritable marvel," says the Comtesse des Garets, "considering the crowds that thronged around him, which might have been for the good Curé a constant temptation to self-esteem."[1]

The Abbé Raymond, who was an eyewitness of his life, and an exacting one at that, also felt compelled to do homage to this wonder: "One of the things which struck me most in the Curé d'Ars," he confessed, "is that he should have so admirably resisted the intoxication that might have resulted from the unending homage of which he was the object. He quite saw and understood that it was for his sake people came to Ars. Yet I never surprised a feeling of pride in his heart, nor a word of self-complacency on his lips."[2] A foolish and conceited man, even though he were clever, would have lost his head; no ordinary virtue could have withstood the dazzling glare of so much glory; only a saint could remain humble amid such ovations.

A penitent of M. Vianney, a lady endowed with much sound judgement and discrimination, was of opinion that her holy confessor had reached a stage when he no longer even felt the assaults of pride. "He seemed indifferent to all homage," said the Baronne de Belvey, "his only thought was the fulfillment of the various functions of his office."[3] Amid the ovations of the people he behaved like a child whose admirable candor renders it unconscious of what is taking place. The Curé d'Ars literally pursued that

1. *Procès de l'Ordinaire,* p. 916.
2. *Ibid.,* p. 320.
3. *Ibid.,* p. 246.

delightful "way of childhood" which youthful St. Therese de l'Enfant Jésus was to teach and to practice so perfectly.[4]

"One day," says the Abbé Dufour, missionary of Pont-d'Ain, "a priest addressed him, in my presence, in words of an exceedingly flattering nature. He looked at him in astonishment, and asked: 'Oh! mon Dieu! what *are* you saying?'"[5]

Ordinary humility, which is binding on all men, consists in that no one esteems himself to be worth more than he is. Such humility springs from ordinary common sense. The Curé d'Ars had gone far beyond this elementary degree: to that end, however, he, too, had needed special help from above. "M. Vianney's humility had reached an heroic degree, which, in the saints, is the fruit of peculiar graces,"[6] a free gift of God—that is, rather than the result of human endeavor.

As a matter of fact, such is the explanation he himself gave in certain moments of communicativeness. "My daughter," he said to one of his penitents, "do not ask God to give you a perfect knowledge of your misery. I prayed for it once, and I obtained it. If God had not sustained me, I should have fallen into despair that very moment."[7] He made a like confidence to Frère Athanase. "I was so terrified at sight of my wretchedness," he added, "that I immediately asked for the grace to forget it. God has heard me, but He has left me enough light on my nothingness to make me realize that I am incapable of accomplishing any good!"[8]

Though M. Vianney was not ignorant of all the good that was brought about by his ministry, he looked upon himself as no more than an instrument, and gave the glory to Him to whom it is due. "I am like a plane in the hands of the good God," he one day said to Frère Athanase. . . . "Oh, my friend, had He discovered a priest more ignorant and more unworthy than myself, He would have put

4. *The Story of* a *Soul,* ch. xi.
5. *Procès apostolique in genere,* p. 349.
6. J. de Guibert, "Humilité et vérité," *Revue d'ascétique et de mystique,* Juillet, 1924.
7. Baronne de Belvey, *Procès de l'Ordinaire,* p. 246.
8. *Procès de l'Ordinaire,* p. 804.

him in my place that so He might show the greatness of His mercy towards poor sinners."[9]

Enlightened as he was with regard to himself, the Curé d'Ars readily perceived that whatever qualities he might have possessed, whatever good he might have achieved, had its source not in himself, but in God. He likewise knew the depths into which he might have sunk had God not kept him from danger. "I am the least of men," he sighed; "what would have become of me had God not spared me?"[10]

There are those who seek the praise of men by feigning humility. "No one could be further than M. Vianney from that which he used to call 'crooked humility'—*l'humilité à crochet.* If he spoke of his own ignorance, his wretchedness, his worthlessness, he did so quite naturally, without a trace of affectation."

He was, as it were, humility personified. M. Seignemartin, former curé of Saint-Trivier-sur-Moignans, who had known him well, thus recalls his memories: "The sight, the conversation, the example of the venerable Curé d'Ars have taught me humility far more effectively than any books. If he spoke of himself as a poor sinner who needed to weep for his poor life, he did so with a simplicity, an accent of sincerity which left the hearers in no doubt as to his real feelings."[11]

He never succeeded in suppressing the unanimous concert of praise which continually gathered strength: his reputation for sanctity sprang up spontaneously and grew, notwithstanding the persevering efforts of his profound humility. However, he did not look for humiliations for their own sake. There was tact and discretion in his very humility. "When compliments were paid him in the course of conversation, he did not rebut them directly, but passed them off by some apt rejoinder."[12] The Gascon poet Jasmin, the author of *Papillotos,* wished to make the acquain-

---

9. *Procès apostolique in genere,* p. 223.
10. *Ibid.,* p. 270.
11. *Procès ne pereant,* p. 643.
12. Comtesse des Garets, *Procès de l'Ordinaire,* p. 917.

tance of the Curé d'Ars. "Monsieur le Curé," he said on leaving, "I have never seen God so near." "That is true," the saint replied, "God is not far away." And he pointed to the tabernacle.[13]

Nor should it be imagined that for humility's sake M. Vianney sought ridicule. According to Mme. des Garets, "his humility had a certain character of unction and dignity." Only with his intimate friends did he jest at his own expense, and if, at times, it happened that his appearance in public looked somewhat ludicrous, it was quite unintentional. Some pilgrims who chanced to see him crossing the square carrying his little can of milk, may have smiled; but how edified they were when they learned that this hero of charity acted thus in order to gain time so as to resume all the sooner his sublime task!

There were occasions when the Curé d'Ars suffered visibly from the praise bestowed upon him by men. It happened fairly often that strange preachers, speaking in his presence, deemed it necessary to compliment the pastor of the place. At such times his eyes would flash with momentary annoyance, "and," says the Comtesse des Garets, "he would hide himself in his stall with so pained an expression that even we felt sorry for him. . . . At the conclusion of a Lenten course of sermons a certain preacher devoted his whole peroration to a eulogy of M. Vianney. 'O my friend,' he said when he met the preacher in the sacristy, 'you have preached very well during the whole of Lent; unfortunately, the end has well-nigh spoilt everything!' "[14]

One day Mgr. Devie inadvertently thought aloud in his presence: "My *holy* Curé!" M. Vianney was disconsolate: "Even Monseigneur is mistaken in me!" he exclaimed. "What a hypocrite I must be!"[15]

Brother Gabriel, the Superior of the Brothers of the Holy Family, wrote a small book entitled: *L'Ange conducteur des pèlerins d'Ars.* He presented half a dozen

13. *Ibid.*
14. *Procès de l'Ordinaire,* pp. 896, 981.
15. *Ibid.,* p. 1156.

copies to the holy Curé, who received them with pleasure, adding that the books would do a great deal of good.

"But," the author relates, "in the preface I made the mistake of giving a brief sketch of his life, representing him as a pattern of virtue and holiness. The very next morning, as soon as he saw me in the church, he signed to me to go to him. His countenance expressed unusual sadness and sternness. I followed him into the sacristy. When he had closed the door he told me, with animation and in a flood of tears: 'My friend, I did not think you were capable of writing a bad book.'

"'Oh! Monsieur le Curé!'

"'It is a bad book! a bad book! How much has it cost you? I want to compensate you at once, and then we will burn it.'

"In my stupefaction, I asked what it was that made it a bad book.

"'Yes, yes! it is a bad book! a bad book!'

"'But, once more, Father, in what way, if you please?'

"'Well, then, since I must tell you: in that book you speak of me as a virtuous man, as a saint, when I am the least of priests.'

"'And yet, Father, I have shown the book to several learned men; the Bishop has looked through the proofs and has given his approval; it cannot be a bad book.'

"M. Vianney's tears only redoubled. 'Cut out all that concerns me, and it will be a good book,' he said.

"As soon as I was back at Belley I related the incident to Mgr. Devie. 'What a lesson in humility that holy priest gives us!' the prelate observed. 'No, no, do not cut out anything from your booklet; I forbid it.' I followed that advice. But at no time would the Curé d'Ars write his name in any copy of my book, whereas he readily autographed the various books or objects of devotion that were held out for his signature."[16]

In 1845, a new parish priest, M. l'Abbé Louis Beau, was appointed to Jassans. M. Beau wished to get in touch

16. *Procès de l'Ordinaire,* p. 1491.

as soon as possible with his colleague of Ars. On his first visit he was received and entertained at lunch by M. Raymond. M. Vianney came in towards the end of the meal and showed himself much gratified at seeing M. Beau. He embraced him and held his hands in his own for a considerable time. Finally, having led him into his own room at the presbytery, he said to him, with gentle familiarity: "Comrade, your predecessor was kind enough to hear my Confession; you will do me the same service, will you not?" M. Vianney was fifty-nine years old, M. Beau thirty-seven, and he saw himself unexpectedly in the role of a director of a saint! He was about to say "No," but the Curé d'Ars swept aside, his objections; in a manner that admitted of no reply, he pointed to the seat prepared for the confessor, and, kneeling on the boards, he began his Confession.

On June 14, 1848, Père Nègre, the director of a *patronage* of Lyons, led a number of his young people on a pilgrimage to Ars. They knew that it was M. Vianney's *feast,* and the little band had learned by heart a few couplets appropriate to the occasion. The chapel of the *Providence* was in building at the time, hence it was decided to take advantage of the moment when the saint came to look at the work to pay him the poetical compliment. M. Vianney at first showed himself most gracious, but alas! the end was to be very different from the beginning. No sooner had Père Nègre presented his youthful band than the song began. That was enough: without waiting for the second verse, M. Vianney "ran from the yard and disappeared."

The assiduities of the crowd surging round his person was at all times a cause of suffering for him. "He was truly distressed," says Mme. des Garets, "to see people endeavoring to get possession of things used by him for the purpose of treating them as relics." One day, perceiving that his cassock had been slashed, he said, with a groan: "What misguided devotion!" Whenever he had his hair cut he took care to gather and burn it himself in the fireplace in his room. True, his hairdressers were none too scrupulous, and were only too ready to yield to bribes. Jean Pertinand, the schoolmaster, made many friends, thanks to the pious thefts that he permitted himself on those occasions.[17]

The Curé d'Ars, the least suspicious of men, could not always guess the cause of the thefts of which he was repeatedly the victim. "After a mission he noticed that his candlestick had disappeared. 'What a strange thing,' he remarked, 'I thought everybody had been converted . . . and now I have been robbed!'"

When, in the course of his last years, Dr. Saunier deemed it necessary to bleed him to prevent congestion in the head, M. Vianney had the blood taken to the cemetery, "because it was Christian blood," but he insisted on its being buried in his presence. This, however, did not prevent the good Brothers of Ars from stealing some of it and distributing it as a precious relic.[18]

One of the great trials of the humble priest must have been to see his portrait put up everywhere in the village. Towards 1845 the "Épinal pictures," depicting divers incidents in his life, began to be circulated. He was much grieved thereat, and, for a time, he endeavored to suppress the pictures. But the shopkeepers implored him to permit their sale. "It was a means of earning their poor livelihood," they said. The kindly Curé allowed himself to be softened. "How much do you make on that engraving?" he asked. "Two sous, Monsieur le Curé." "Two sous! Ah! to be sure, that is dear enough for that wretched *carnaval!*"

One day, as he was passing a shop window in which his portrait was exhibited, he inquired about its price. "Five francs" was the answer.

"Five francs! Oh! you will never sell it: the Curé d'Ars is not worth so much."

"Well," he said at times, "if that poor *carnaval* recalls

---

17. Jean Pertinand, *Procès de l'Ordinaire,* p. 917.
18. There still exist a few phials containing some of that blood, which has remained liquid. One is in the treasury of Ars and another at Nantes, in the chapel of the Capuchin Fathers. The latter came probably from M. Sionnet, a great friend of the holy Curé.

to mind the counsels that I have given, it will not prove altogether useless." Nevertheless, in order to show his contempt for them, he always refused either to sign or to bless his portraits. If one were found among the pictures that he was asked to bless he brushed it roughly aside, and he would indulge in some such remark: "That only comes handy on three days in the year:" an allusion to the three days of the carnival and its masquerades. For, in sheer despair, he had decided to treat the thing as a joke. "Whilst he was one day conversing with my husband near the church," says Mme. Prosper des Garets, "he led him to the shop windows and showed him what he called his *carnaval.* In this connection he made the most comical remarks it is possible to imagine."[19] "Eh, what! you hang me up and you sell me!" he laughingly said to a young woman of the village, who carried on her business by the cemetery wall. "They have made a new portrait of me," he informed Catherine Lassagne, "this time it really is myself: I look stupid, as stupid as a goose!"[20] Seeing one of these caricatures, even more grotesque and more crudely colored than the rest, he said gaily: "Look for a moment! Would you not think that I had just come out of a pot-house?"

There was one point, however, on which he would not compromise: he never consented to pose for his picture. He was photographed only on his deathbed. In 1858, the Abbé Toccanier and the sculptor Émilien Cabuchet made up their minds to secure, at all costs, a likeness as faithful as possible of the holy Curé. The existing portraits bore no resemblance to the original, for they had been made furtively or even from memory. The aim of the sculptor was to copy the model and to make a wax bust. The difficulty was how to go about it?

Mgr. de Langalerie, who, on May 1, 1857, had succeeded Mgr. Chalandon, on the latter's translation to the archiepiscopal See of Aix, entrusted to Cabuchet a letter

19. *Procès de l'Ordinaire,* p. 917.
20. *Ibid.,* p. 520.

of recommendation, and it was in the confessional that the artist thought of presenting himself. He knelt down, and whilst M. Vianney was in the act of raising his hand to bless him, he produced the episcopal letter that was to override all obstacles. The saint, scanned it, rose up, opened the door, and dismissed the false penitent with the peremptory remark: "No, no! neither for you nor for your Bishop!"

So there was nothing for it but to resort to cunning. The Abbé Toccanier reserved for the artist a corner of the church which allowed him to study his model. Cabuchet attended the saint's catechism. Having hidden his provision of wax in his large hat, he imagined that he might now work without being noticed. Everything went smoothly until the eighth day of this maneuver, when M. Vianney suddenly addressed the artist in a voice to which he could not succeed in giving a sharp tone: "You, over there, when will you have done being a cause of distraction to me and to the others?" However, Cabuchet had had time to model his lump of wax sufficiently to catch that physiognomy so mobile, so alive, so expressive, which reflected almost simultaneously all the emotions of a most sensitive soul. When the bust was finished the sculptor brought it into the dining-room of the missionaries. The Curé d'Ars was then confronted with his own likeness. He examined it. "Ah! as for that, that is not a *carnaval,*" he said laughingly, approving yet confused. Then: "Who has done this?" Émilien Cabuchet stepped forward. "You have disobeyed me, monsieur," the saint said severely. "Must I forgive you?" The Abbé Toccanier and the brothers who assisted at the scene pleaded for mercy for the artist and for the masterpiece. M. Vianney consented not to destroy a bust that represented him so faithfully, but he exacted a promise from Cabuchet not to give it to the public during his lifetime.

Thus the Curé d'Ars retained his lowliness until the end. He would not even plead his superhuman exertions in order to claim any privilege. If, during the last years of his life, he was dispensed from his Breviary, it was as a result of steps taken by his assistant. It might have seemed, for instance, that his renown for sanctity and his experience of souls would have exempted him from the obligation of a yearly renewal of his faculties for hearing Confessions, as prescribed by the old *Rituel de Belley.* But until 1858 he had his faculty paper renewed every year, either by the Bishop or by one of the Vicars-General. We have already seen with what wonderful meekness he allowed himself to be rebuked by colleagues very much his juniors and having none of his reputation. At a time when he had won the veneration of all the clergy, he never ceased to consider himself the least of them: "He always received them with the utmost respect, showed them every mark of reverence, and recommended himself to their prayers."[21]

He beheld, seated under his pulpit, kneeling in his confessional, bishops, famous preachers, laymen of high position. However, he declared that "to these visits of famous personages he preferred that of some poor woman who came to beg for an alms." In 1850, Bérenger de la Drôme came to consult him about, apparently, inextricable difficulties. The saint solved them at once. The magistrate went away full of admiration. M. Vianney had not even asked his name. After the interview which he had in October, 1855, with the Préfet of the Ain and the officer commanding the troops of the *département,* who had come to congratulate him on his promotion to the Légion d'honneur "Oh! Monsieur le Curé," said Comte Prosper des Garets, "see how Ars is being visited by the great ones of the world." "They are bodies and souls," was the casual reply of the humble priest.

Père Pététot, the superior of the oratory, and Père Combalot, the apostolic missionary of fiery eloquence, came to him for lessons in zeal and eloquence. They went away enchanted. Mgr. Allou, Bishop of Meaux, assisted at his catechisms for eight consecutive days, lost amidst the throng of the faithful. Mgr. Dupanloup and Cardinal de

21. *Procès apostolique ne pereant,* p. 643.

Bonald journeyed to Ars for the purpose of consulting him. "He appeared not even to perceive that he was the object of their pious veneration: he accepted it as if it had been meant for another."[22]

On the evening of Saturday, May 3, 1845, Père Lacordaire, who, for some years, had wished to know the Curé d'Ars, came to the village, incognito, from Lyons. He stayed at the château. The following day he went to the church as early as five o'clock. M. Vianney manifested much joy at seeing him, embraced him with effusion, pressed his hands repeatedly, and thanked him with an ineffable smile of happiness. After that he looked for the most precious chalice and the richest vestment for his Mass. At ten o'clock the famous Dominican was present at the parish Mass, in the tribune reserved for the des Garets. M. le Curé was the celebrant, and preached on the *Gift of the Holy Ghost.* Lacordaire came back for the catechism, which was given at about one o'clock every Sunday. He sang Vespers and preached afterwards. Several newly arrived pilgrims felt disappointed, for they would have preferred to hear the saint. As a matter of fact, "Lacordaire's humility certainly caused him to tone down his style somewhat." "Whilst the great orator spoke," says an eyewitness, "M. Vianney listened with an attention which I am not afraid to call greedy and moving."[23]

On the following Monday the priests of the district met for a clerical conference and lunched at the château, Père Lacordaire being the principal guest. "You will not have thought the Curé d'Ars very eloquent," one of the company took the liberty of remarking. "He preached as a good curé should preach," was the Dominican's frigid reply. On the previous day the famous preacher had remarked, in presence of Jean Pertinand the schoolmaster: "That holy priest has uttered, in a striking manner, a thought in connection with the Holy Ghost which I myself have

---

22. *Procès de l'Ordinaire,* p. 651.
23. All these details are taken from the pamphlet, *Souvenirs de deux pèlerinages à Ars,* by M. Brac de la Perrière, who was one of Père Lacordaire's companions on his pilgrimage to Ars.

been pondering for a long time."

As for M. Vianney, he seemingly took advantage of the honor of such a visit to humble himself still more. "The day after," says the Abbé Raymond, "he said to me: 'You know the saying: "extremes meet;" well, it was realized yesterday in the pulpit of Ars, where extreme knowledge and extreme ignorance were seen.'"[24]

Truly, humility was ever the favorite virtue of our saint. "He prized it so highly," Frère Athanase records, "that he constantly spoke of it, especially in his instructions, 'Remain humble, remain simple,' he repeated unceasingly to the Brothers of the Holy Family; 'the more you are so, the more good you will do.'"[25]

He loved to relate the following anecdote:

The devil one day appeared to St. Macarius. "All that you do, I do likewise," Satan said to the solitary of the Thebaïd. "You fast; I never eat at all. You watch; I never sleep. There is only one thing you do that I am unable to perform."

"Oh! What is it?"

"To humble myself."[26]

According to the Abbé Toccanier, he frequently repeated: "Humility is to the various virtues what the chain is in a rosary: take away the chain and the beads are scattered; remove humility, and all virtues vanish."

A humble soul loves poverty and the poor.

"Of the Curé d'Ars one could truly affirm what St. Francis of Assisi was wont to say of himself—viz., that he had espoused the Lady Poverty. M. Vianney's room was poor, his furniture was poor, his dress was poor, his food was poor."[27] If an artist had wished to paint poverty itself, no more suitable model could have been found.[28]

We have already heard the rebukes administered to him by some brother priests on account of his outward

24. *Procès de l'Ordinaire,* p. 328.
25. *Ibid.,* p. 858.
26. *Ibid.,* pp. 173-174.
27. *Procès apostolique ne pereant,* p. 901.
28. Cardinal Luçon, "Panégyrique du Curé d'Ars," *Annales d'Ars,* August, 1908, p. 74.

appearance. That was in the opening years of his ministry. Whilst he could afford the time—that is, until 1827 or 1828, he mended his own clothes, and as he was no great adept in the use of the needle, we may imagine the nature of the performance. "He had darned his stockings," says Jeanne-Marie Chanay, "so often and in such a way that they must have cut his feet." One day Catherine Lassagne, who had to see him about something, surprised him in the act of patching a hole in the knee of his breeches. The good girl stood aghast on the threshold of the room. "Ah! Catherine," he said pleasantly, "you thought to find your Curé and you hit on a tailor!"

Until the time when the pilgrimage became an institution, he owned only one cassock, the many and varied patches of which ended by becoming almost innumerable. Such deliberate penury put him to great straits one winter's day, on his return from a neighboring village situate amid the ponds. He was wet to the skin, and he had repeatedly slipped and fallen into the mud. Realizing that it would be a fatal imprudence to go in such a state to his presbytery, where he would find no clothes into which to change, he sought shelter in the house of one of his good parishioners, to whom he was compelled to avow his embarrassment. The man was moved to tears, helped his Curé to divest himself, and lent him some of his own clothes whilst the dripping cassock was drying in front of a big fire of faggots.

When the number of pilgrims grew, it was represented to him that this wretched garment was no longer seemly. So he accepted the gift of two cassocks, setting the better one aside for great days, but the poorer one was the one he preferred. He wore it for a long time, and it ended by becoming very shabby. He apologized for wearing it at functions: "A bad cassock goes well with a beautiful chasuble," he observed. On the occasion of a visit from the Bishop he forgot to put on his gala dress. "I only remembered it afterwards," he told Frère Athanase: "I was sorry." He never consented to have more than two cassocks at a time. People who offered him a new cassock in exchange for his old one—it was a way of acquiring a precious relic—invariably saw their gift rejected. At times new cassocks were placed in his room without his having been told. He gave them to the Brothers. In this way Frère Athanase became possessed of as many as three cassocks.

"During the last ten years of his life," says M. Beau, his confessor, "he was always seen dressed simply but neatly in full clerical garb; but he never wore a cloak. At Trévoux, during the jubilee of 1826, somebody bought him one: he passed it on to a poor man. The same cassock did duty in December as well as in July: in winter it required no little ingenuity to line it without his noticing it.

The presbytery of Ars was in keeping with its occupant. The small yard in front of the house was overgrown with grass, like a meadow. Three elder-trees had fortuitously sprung up in it. M. Vianney laughingly styled them his *Bois de Boulogne.* It is doubtful whether he ever enjoyed their shade or breathed the fragrance of their blossoms. By degrees the walls of the presbytery lost their coating, and eventually cracks began to show themselves. By dint of pleading, M. des Garets obtained leave to have them repaired and whitewashed. But the saint would not suffer the interior to be touched. "I am quite well lodged as it is," he declared; "when a new curé comes he will do as he likes with my room and everything else, too."

The flooring of his room had partially given way. The Mayor was compelled to take advantage of his absence to see to the most urgent repairs. There was no longer any furniture in the remaining rooms, so that they were wholly neglected. The window-frames were disjointed and the panes of glass had fallen from the casements; brambles invaded the kitchen on the ground-floor; one shoot having taken root, grew up the chimney. Outside the saint's room all was in a state of utter dilapidation.

The utensils required for his personal use were reduced to a strict minimum. For his meals a bowl and a spoon sufficed. Catherine Lassagne relates that "he had been presented with three rather pretty cups. One day I looked for them in his room, but could not find them. In my own mind I blamed thieves or pious people eager for relics, when I espied fragments of china lying in a corner. Jeanne-Marie Chanay, who was with me, said to the servant of God: 'So, Monsieur le Curé, that is the way you treat your crockery!' He smiled at first, and then said somewhat severely: 'Am I never to have poverty in my own home?'"

He never paid a sou for his keep to the mistresses of the *Providence;* a few kindly persons supplied what was required for his maintenance. Not once was he known to be in any anxiety about tomorrow. And yet, how much money passed through his hands! "He received considerable sums; they were expended in good works." "Such money seemed to burn his fingers." Much of it was spent in relieving the poor. He pitied and at the same time joked about those who amassed for the sake of amassing: "They are like people filling a sack with mist, or, again, like one who lays in a store of pumpkins, and who, when winter comes, discovers that they are rotten." "Monsieur le Curé," Catherine Lassagne one day counselled, "you have some bank-notes on your table; take care you do not throw them into the fire." "*Tiens,* I have already done so!" he replied, without emotion. The evening before, to light his candle, he had used an envelope containing five hundred francs in banknotes. On meeting his friend, the Abbé Dubouis of Fareins, he told him: "Yesterday, my friend, I made ashes that are worth a great deal!" and having related the incident, he added: "Oh! there is less harm in that than if I had committed a venial sin."[29]

"His heart pitied all miseries," says M. des Garets. "He had a tender love for the victims of misfortune. For them he stripped himself of all things; he was for ever giving, giving. To enable him to bestow alms, he sold all his personal property: his furniture, his linen, any trifle

29. Abbé Dubouis, *Procès de l'Ordinaire,* p. 1235.

that belonged to him."[30]

His charity was inexhaustible. "He confided to me," says Frère Athanase, "that often, before daybreak, he had already given away in charity over a hundred francs. He laughingly called the pocket of his cassock, in which he carried the money destined for the poor, *la poche à la navette*—the shuttle pocket—because money was continually going in and coming out of it. At night he reckoned up what he called his *profits*—that is, the few coins that he might still possess. When he found himself penniless he borrowed, for he would not send the destitute away without an alms." Nevertheless, he did not squander money. If he allowed himself to be exploited—and that is the lot of all who practice charity—he placed his alms with discrimination. In this respect also he was well served by his gift of discernment, for, as a rule, he displayed a larger liberality towards those whose need was the more urgent.

Towards the end of his life he was paying the rent of at least thirty families, either at Ars or in the surrounding district. He became "miserly;" every year, a little before Martinmas, he began to save: "I must pay for *my farms,*" he used to say. More than one indigent household received from him fuel and flour. Every week, for a long period, the mother of a family came to him from Villefranche-sur-Saône to beg her children's bread.

He used infinite tact so as not to wound the susceptibilities of the poor. To some persons who came to open a small business in the village he advanced the funds they needed. When they spoke of reimbursing him: "I do not lend," he said softly, "I give. Has not the good God been the first to give to me?" Only a few shirts at a time were placed in his wardrobe; otherwise he would have given away all his linen at once. "Put in more," he firmly demanded of Catherine. The reason for this was that the ragged poor who were ashamed of their destitution were taken up to his room, and there they put on new underwear. In winter he even made a good fire for them; "and

30. *Procès de l'Ordinaire,* p. 959.

whilst warming their bodies, he endeavored to warm up their souls with the fire of divine love," says Catherine Lassagne. At times the persons of his entourage sought to relieve the poor in his place; but they wanted him. He addressed them as "my friends," in accents so sweet that they went away comforted. "How happy we are," he said, "that the poor should thus come to us; if they did not come we should have to look for them; and for that there is not always time."[31]

Every opportunity was good when it was a question of relieving the poor. One day, on his way to the orphanage for the catechism lesson, he fell in with a poor fellow who was almost barefooted. He gave him his shoes and went on to the *Providence,* endeavoring to hide his stockinged feet under his cassock. "I had given him, one morning, a new pair of fur-lined shoes," says Jeanne-Marie Chanay. "What was my surprise to see him in the evening wearing his old shoes, which were completely worn out, and which I had forgotten to remove from his room. 'You have given away the others,' I said, with some heat. 'It is quite possible!' he calmly replied."

In January, 1823, during the great mission at Trévoux, when M. Vianney practically spent the whole night and day in the confessional, his colleagues in the neighborhood bought him a pair of trousers. The material chosen was velvet, for it was meant to last a long time. One Saturday night, as the saint was returning to his parish on foot as usual, he came across a poor man who was inadequately clad and shaking with cold. "Wait a moment, my friend," said the Abbé Vianney as he went behind a hedge, reappearing almost at once, his fine trousers in his hand. The poor man made haste to put them on. A few days later mention was made of the garment at the presbytery of Trévoux, and M. Vianney was asked whether he was satisfied with the gift. "Oh yes," he replied joyfully, "I have put them to fairly good use; a poor man has borrowed them from me for an unlimited period."

31. Catherine Lassagne, *Procès de l'Ordinaire,* p. 495.

He had a tender spot in his heart for *Mère* Bichet, a blind woman of Ars who lived near the church. He felt a particular happiness in giving to her, because he could bestow an alms on her without her recognizing the benefactor. He would approach very quietly, lay his gift—either in kind or money—in her apron, and withdraw without a word. The good woman, imagining that she had to do with some neighbor, said each time: "Thank you, *ma mie,* thank you very much." And M. le Curé went away chuckling heartily.[32]

His benefactions were widespread, so that he needed the help of various agents. "I have been as far as Lyons," says Marie Filliat, "to give in his name a hundred francs to a family in need. . . . One day, regretting that he had not bestowed a larger alms upon a poor beggar woman of Saint-Didier, he commissioned me to take fifteen francs to her. I have carried out more than one such errand in the neighboring villages."[33]

The casual poor, who were often exacting and difficult to please, were well received by him. "There are impostors," M. Toccanier told him; "it must happen that you are frequently taken in if you give to all comers." "We are never taken in if we give to God," the saint replied.[34] A former boarder of the *Providence* had stolen some linen from the orphanage and money from the sacristy. She was arrested and condemned to imprisonment. M. Vianney's efforts to save her from this degradation proved ineffectual. When she came out of prison she appealed to the kindness of the Curé d'Ars. He interested himself in her, and supplied her with clothes and money.

In the light of what we have related it is obvious that the fame of the Curé d'Ars was widespread among the disinherited of this world. Ars had become a center, towards which the indigent converged. Some of the villagers, weary of entertaining those poor people, who were not all equally desirable, complained to the Mayor:

---

32. *Procès de l'Ordinaire,* p. 596.
33. *Procès de l'Ordinaire,* p. 1304.
34. *Ibid.,* p. 141.

New Church at Ars—Interior

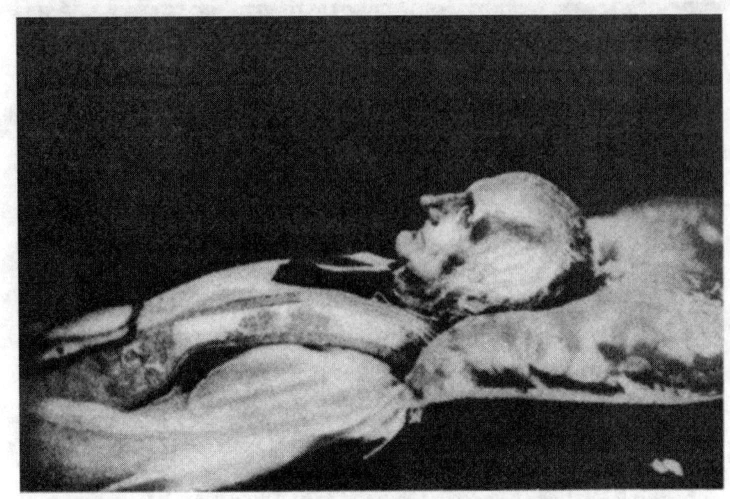

The Curé d'Ars on his deathbed

"M. le Curé is to blame," they said. Comte des Garets transmitted their grievance to the one most concerned in the matter. "Did Our Lord not say: 'The poor you shall always have with you?' was the saint's reply. And he insisted that none should be driven away."

His conduct was inspired by a love for the poor that was wholly supernatural and inspired by the Gospel. In the poor he saw Our Lord, the divine Pauper who has blessed poverty. Hence he loved to relate in his catechisms divers anecdotes telling of Jesus appearing in the guise of a beggar. He burst into tears every time he told the story of St. John of God, who, perceiving all of a sudden the stigmata in the feet of a destitute man whom he was succoring, exclaimed: "So it is you, Lord!" A final example will show with what veneration the Curé d'Ars surrounded poverty:

One summer's day, shortly before noon, M. Vianney was seated in his little pulpit catechizing the throng of pilgrims. There was a dense crowd even as far down as the threshold of the church. Presently a poor man came on the scene, laden with his wallet and leaning on two crutches. He, too, would have loved to come in; but it was not possible. M. le Curé saw his futile attempts, he suddenly rose, went through the throng, and led the mendicant through the serried ranks of the pilgrims. However, there remained not one vacant chair in the nave. Where was this pauper of Jesus Christ to rest his weary limbs? A saint is not embarrassed by so small a matter: the Curé d'Ars took the man into his pulpit and made him sit down on the seat, whence he commanded a view of all the people; then, in a joyful tone of voice, he uttered the one syllable: "*Na!*" And he proceeded with his discourse, standing the while.

A scene like this might well seem to have been borrowed from the life of the *Poverello* of Assisi.

Chapter 25

AT THE HEIGHT OF SANCTITY
(continued)
III. Heroic Virtues: Patience and Mortification

LOVE of poverty and of the poor was rooted in the very temperament of M. Vianney, for he was by nature kind. But there is another virtue—patience—with which he was apparently not endowed at birth. Had he not acquired this virtue by prolonged and heroic efforts, he would have remained brusque and violent. In the end he reached such heights of patience that the meekness of his character led people to believe that he was passionless and incapable of getting angry. However, those who saw him often, and at close quarters, noticed quickly enough that he had "a vivid imagination and a quick temper."[1]

He used to say in the pulpit: "O my children, you complain that you are unable to practice patience. But goodness me! surely everybody has a dose of vivacity."[2]

"Monsieur le Curé," the Abbé Raymond asked him, "how do you manage to remain calm with so vivacious a temperament?" "Ah! my friend, virtue demands courage, constant effort and, above all, help from on high."

"It cost him long hours of toil and much suffering before he acquired that patience which all admired," says Comte des Garets; "hence, of all his virtues, his patience amazed and impressed me most. I do not think it is possible to carry it further. I always found him the same, ready to

1. Frère Athanase, *Procès de l'Ordinaire,* p. 219.
2. *Procès de l'Ordinaire,* p. 604.

oblige, however people may have behaved towards him."[3]

"I believe," says Frere Athanase, "that if he had not been wholly dominated by virtue, he would easily have yielded to anger. It required extraordinary exertion on his part to enable him to overcome this tendency. I know it from my own personal observation, for I have watched him and have seen symptoms, slight enough in themselves, it is true. Thus, when some very tiresome people set him on edge, he used to twist the handkerchief which he was in the habit of carrying in his hand, and it was easy to see what self-restraint he imposed upon himself so as not to yield to impatience. But one had to be very intimate with him to notice such things."[4]

"He felt keenly;"[5] he occasionally experienced involuntary antipathies, but they were veiled by his charity. "We have often thought that he had to do violence to himself when in the presence of certain persons, though he never showed anything," says Marthe Miard. All that could be observed when such storms swooped down upon his soul was a fleeting alteration of his countenance and the flashing of his eyes. Such, for a moment, was his appearance on the day of his nomination as a canon, when Frère Jérôme came to ask him to go to his stall wearing his mozetta.

The holy Curé has furnished us with truly amazing proofs of his patience.

"One day," says Pertinand, the schoolmaster, "we surprised one of the village children in the act of stealing money that had been given for Masses. The Mayor and I went to inform the child's parents. The mother of the little thief, imagining that M. le Curé had denounced the culprit, came to the sacristy on the following day and heaped bitter reproaches upon him. I was standing near the door, in the church, and heard that torrent of abuse. 'You are quite right; pray for my conversion,' was all that our good pastor said by way of reply."[6]

---

3. *Ibid.*, pp. 969, 975.
4. *Procès de l'Ordinaire,* p. 848.
5. *Ibid.*, p. 957.
6. *Ibid.*, p. 383.

"I have heard it stated," Catherine relates in her *Petit mémoire,* "that at the beginning (of M. Vianney's ministry) a man of the village went to his house and overwhelmed him with insults. He listened without a word; when the man had finished he courteously accompanied him to the door and embraced him before parting. But the strain had been so intense that, returning to his room with great difficulty, he was forced to lie down on the bed. In a few moments his whole body was covered with pimples."

More than once, when someone spoke to him harshly, he remained quite calm, but shortly after his whole being was seen to tremble. "When the passions have been mastered one's limbs must be allowed to shake,"[7] he would say.

One day something very provoking happened at the *Providence,* says Jeanne-Marie Chanay: "If I were not keen about my conversion," he said, "I should be angry." Whilst uttering these words he retained all his usual calm.

"It has come back to my mind," says André Trève, "though I can fix neither the place nor the time, that he was once struck in the face, when he said: 'My friend, my other cheek is jealous!'"[8]

His admirable patience shone forth especially when the crowds surged round him. Here he found constant opportunities for self-repression. Those who wished to gain access to him were eager to see him; those who had had an interview wanted to see him again. Hence he was, as it were, tossed about by opposite currents, which threw him hither and thither. But, wonderful to relate! pressed and almost suffocated as he was, he ever appeared as an angel of charity and meekness. His features betrayed his excessive fatigue; but never the consequences of fallen nature. Yet a temperament so active, and at the same time so sensitive, must have felt keenly the vexations and worries of each day. He was conscious of the rapid flight of

7. *Petit mémoire,* deuxième rédaction, p. 46.
8. *Procès apostolique continuatif,* p. 816.

time and the real needs of so many souls, though some people would detain him with the same everlasting questions, whilst others would talk to him of some trumpery affair. Such, however, was the patience and sweetness of his charity that everybody went away satisfied.

It happened more than once that when some fifty or more people were crowding round his confessional, he was asked to come into the sacristy. He would obey the summons, and listen without a sign of impatience, even if he had been disturbed for the sake of mere trifles. He has been seen, at a moment when the throng of penitents awaiting their turn was greatest, to come out of the confessional on three separate occasions, to give Holy Communion to three persons who might have presented themselves together. He did it without a murmur, without a remark of any kind. One who witnessed the scene was so enraged at their want of consideration that he left the church, repeating to anyone who cared to listen: "I am angry for M. le Curé, who is not angry!" "Seeing him always so calm," the Abbé Toccanier relates, "I said to him: 'Were the angels in your place, Monsieur le Curé, they would surely get cross: I shall have to be cross myself in your place.'"[9]

One day in 1854, at the conclusion of the catechism, as he was on his way from the church to the presbytery, he was pestered to such an extent—one person endeavored to slash his surplice, another to tear out a few hairs—that some witnesses of the scene gave vent to their indignation, and exclaimed: "Monsieur le Curé, you really should send all these people packing. . . . In your place, I should be in a boiling rage," and so forth. "Good gracious!" the saint replied, "I have spent thirty-six years at Ars; I have never yet been cross, and now I am too old to begin."[10]

Priests were loud in their admiration of such patience. M. Gerin, curé of the cathedral of Grenoble, whom M. Vianney used to call his "cousin," remained for hours

9. *Procès de l'Ordinaire,* p. 102.
10. *Ibid.,* p. 848.

absorbed in the contemplation of his meekness and patience when subjected to the pressure and jostling of the crowds.[11]

"I have watched the servant of God very closely to see whether I could detect in him any sign of impatience," says Chanoine Tailhades, "but never did I succeed in doing so; even in the midst of the greatest importunities I found him always meek, always smiling, always the same. When I commented upon it: 'What can I do?' he said, 'what would be the good of my losing my temper? Oh! how good it is for a priest to offer himself every morning as a sacrifice to God!'"[12]

By far the greatest trial of patience consists not so much in bearing with the importunities of the crowd, as in the daily relations with persons with whom contact is irksome and irritating. Here we have the touchstone of patience and its most splendid triumph. Now the holy Curé, for the space of eight years—from 1845 to 1853—had to tolerate the methods of a priest whom the ingenuous and discriminating Catherine considered as "having been sent by God to try the patience of His faithful servant."[13] From the moment when he was appointed to assist M. Vianney, "he looked upon himself as a guardian rather than as an auxiliary."[14] Yet he was a good priest, very anxious to do his duty. He was twenty years younger than the Curé d'Ars, who had paid his seminary fees. M. Raymond was, however, wanting in tact and judgement. He showed it from the beginning of his stay at Ars. Nothing abashed, he installed himself in M. Vianney's room, the holy man being quite resigned to occupying a dark and very damp room on the ground floor. Thereupon the parishioners protested that they would make a disturbance if anyone presumed to interfere with the customs of their Curé. So the latter returned to his room and M.

---

11. Jean Pertinand, *Procès de l'Ordinaire,* p. 378. M. Gerin died in the odor of sanctity on February 13, 1863. Even to this day at Grenoble he is known only as "the holy curé Gerin."
12. *Procès de l'Ordinaire,* p. 1510.
13. *Petit mémoire,* troisième rédaction, p. 69.
14. Comte des Garets, *Procès de l'Ordinaire,* p. 972.

Raymond took lodgings in the village.

The newcomer, whom M. Vianney himself had asked to have as an assistant, dreamt of nothing less than of supplanting his pastor, of directing the pilgrimage; in fact, of becoming the Curé d'Ars.[15] He failed to realize that with the departure of the saint the village would sink back into its former obscurity. Brusque, obstinate, priding himself on his cleverness and eloquence, he treated the man who had been his benefactor, and was now his superior, "with harshness, without consideration, and without any deference to his years and his holiness."[16] All that can be said to exonerate M. Raymond is that "he did not realize how much pain he could give."[17] He permitted himself, many times, to take the servant of God to task, reproaching him either with not giving him his entire confidence or with not managing the pilgrimage according to his good pleasure; "he even went so far as to contradict him publicly in the pulpit."[18]

It is easy to imagine how painful such proceedings must have proved for the gentle and sensitive soul of M. Vianney. "During the first days," Catherine Lassagne writes, "seeing that his assistant was so much younger and that he himself had had him educated, he made some effort to assert himself, but perceiving that he only provoked him the more, he resigned himself to inform him about things, to consult him frequently, in a word, to give in to him as much as possible." More than that—and this

15. Abbé Beau, *Procès de l'Ordinaire,* p. 1206. M. Raymond's ambitions as regards the parish were a mystery to no one, and the saint himself knew quite well how matters stood. When we examine the parochial registers, we might imagine that those ambitions were an accomplished fact, for M. Raymond speaks like one in authority. Thus, from September, 1845, to September, 1853, he registers all his official acts as *curé soussigné* and he signs: *Raymond, curé.* For the years 1846 and 1847, there is even the aggravating circumstance that he baptized in the parish church of Ars as *curé of the said parish—curé de ladite paroisse. . . .* The Abbé Toccanier, who succeeded M. Raymond in 1853, modestly signs as *assistant priest,* or *vicaire;* but M. Raymond, never. Yet the holy Curé had not resigned his authority into his hands. He baptized on August 15, 1847, and again on September 12, 1848. In the entry of both acts he describes himself as parish priest of the said parish, and signs: *Jean-Marie Vianney, Curé d'Ars.*

16. Baronne de Belvey, *Procès apostolique ne pereant,* p. 213.

17. Chanoine Seignemartin, *Procès apostolique ne pereant,* p. 642.

18. M. Beau, *Procès de l'Ordinaire,* p. 1207.

was a triumph of grace and virtue combined—the Curé d'Ars sincerely loved his assistant. "I have only one regret," the Abbé Raymond was to say later on; "it is that I did not draw more profit from his example; nevertheless, I trust in the tender and fatherly affection that he always showed to me."[19]

M. Vianney would not allow his vicaire to be attacked, and made himself his champion on all occasions. The villagers saw through the schemes of M. Raymond and sided with their parish priest. He, on the other hand, would speak up for the vicaire, adding: "If he is made to suffer we shall go away together." When M. Dubouis was commissioned by Mgr. Devie to inquire into the conduct of M. Raymond, the Curé d'Ars said: "Oh! let me keep him; he is not afraid to tell me the truth about myself!" "How grateful I am to him," he likewise said to some intimates, "without him it would have been difficult for me to know that I loved the good God a little."[20] "You tell me nothing, you do not rebuke me," was the reproach he later on addressed to the good and conciliating M. Camelet, the superior of the missionaries, "I do not feel as happy as before." On October 24, 1848, he wrote to Mgr. Devie to invite him to bless the chapel of the *Providence.* He improved the occasion by putting in a good word for his vicaire:

"I have nothing special to tell your lordship concerning M. Raymond, except that he deserves a warm place in your heart in return for all his goodness to me. Never give credence to those wicked tongues that are everlastingly retailing evil."

But was it not already going too far when a priest connected with Ars furnished matter for justifiable criticism? Some pious persons pointed out to M. Vianney that such a state of things had lasted long enough.[21] So the saint

19. *Procès de l'Ordinaire,* p. 340 (session of January 24, 1863).
20. *Ibid.,* p. 511.
21. Those in the immediate entourage of the holy Curé would not have been sorry had he shown himself stricter towards his assistant. "At first it seemed to me," Frère Jérôme confesses, "that M. Vianney allowed M. Raymond too much scope. However, on looking more closely into the matter, I saw that he acted thus from motives of charity, prudence, and humility." (*Procès de l'Ordinaire,* p. 566).

asked Frère Athanase to write a letter to Mgr. Devie in his name: "He gave me a rough idea of what I was to say," the secretary relates, "and he laid special stress on M. Raymond's claims to a good post. It was Holy Week. I showed the draft of the letter to the servant of God as he was making his way to the back of the altar. He read it, collected himself for a moment, and then tore it in four pieces. 'I was thinking,' he said, 'that Our Lord carried His Cross during these sacred days; surely I can do as He did.'"

A little later he agreed to M. des Garets' speaking of the matter to Mgr. Devie. The interview took place at Bourg. In the meantime the Curé d'Ars had changed his mind. When the Mayor broached the subject, the Bishop produced a letter which he had just received, in which the saint asked that his "beloved M. Raymond" might be left to him for yet awhile.

In the end the impossible vicaire took the initiative and himself asked for a change; he understood at last that he would never supplant his rector who drew the multitudes to Ars. As we have already seen, in 1853, Mgr. Chalandon appointed him to the parish of Polliat. Until the very end M. Vianney treated him with consummate tact. "After my departure," says the Abbé Raymond, "he wrote to me as follows: 'You have been such a help, you have rendered so many services to me that you have riveted my heart to yours!'[22] I had the happiness of seeing him again eight days before his death. I shall never forget the kindness with which he received me, and the generosity that prompted him to present me with a cope. . . . As soon as I heard of his demise I set out for Ars, where I had the consolation of being able to embrace him for a last time."[23] On the very day of the funeral the missionaries begged

22. M. Raymond never knew that the saint himself had thought of getting him appointed to another post. Four years after M. Vianney's death, on January 20, 1863, when he was questioned on the "attempted flight" of 1853, he stated in all seriousness: "I believe that he became excited when the missionary (M. Toccanier) arrived. The latter was to take my place, and M. le Curé felt much affection for me." *(Procès de l'Ordinaire,* p. 277).

23. *Procès de l'Ordinaire,* p. 338.

of M. Raymond to put together his personal recollections of the holy Curé. He did, indeed, begin a *Life of the Curé d'Ars,* but never finished it. Fragments of the manuscript that have been preserved, as well as the depositions of the saint's former assistant at the *process* of canonization, betray the most sincere admiration.

M. Vianney endured the sufferings of the body no less patiently than those of the spirit. He was severely tried by sickness and infirmity. We may be permitted to enumerate some of the afflictions, basing ourselves on the authority of persons to whom he gave his confidence.

He had an open sore on his left arm. At times the pilgrims, as they pressed round him and jostled him, caused him acute pain, so that he would exclaim: "Gently! You are hurting me," though, even so, he showed no trace of annoyance.

"For at least fifteen years he was a prey to rheumatism," says the Abbé Raymond, "which he had contracted whilst sleeping in a damp and cold room at the presbytery, and which caused him severe headaches. 'Oh! how I suffer there!' he often told me, putting his hand to his forehead. The lack of exercise occasioned fainting fits: this obliged him to have himself bled every year. Whilst preaching he contracted a double hernia, which he neglected for a long time. Those who saw him could not understand why, when he came out of the confessional, he was so bent. When the doctor intervened, we at last understood the cause of his sufferings."[24]

He suffered much from toothache. "He asked me to draw several of his teeth with pincers," says Pertinand, the schoolmaster.

But even whilst his poor *corpse,* as he called his body, was enduring the most acute pain, he still retained his liberty of spirit; nothing in his conversation or disposition betrayed his intimate tortures. "Once," says Mme. des Garets, "when he came to bless our buildings, he was in terrible pain. I asked him if he would take something.

24. *Procès de l'Ordinaire,* p. 318.

'Ah!' he replied, with a smile, 'I should never have done were I to take something every time I am in pain.' More than once, during night prayers, he was seen to sink back and disappear in the pulpit, as if he were crushed by his sufferings; but presently he would rise up bravely and preach with his usual fire, as if nothing had happened."

M. Vianney's patience is a marvellous example for all, but of his mortifications we may say that they were more admirable than imitable, for in this respect the soldier of Christ "went as far as human strength could go, if not beyond that limit." "M. Vianney," says Comte des Garets, "was a man who utterly killed the old Adam in him, and who never granted anything to Nature."[25] And the Comtesse adds: "His penance was constant, extreme, universal; it embraced his whole existence. The life of a Trappist cannot be compared to his. I do not think it possible to carry Christian penance any farther. The Curé d'Ars makes us accept as true even the most extraordinary facts related of the Fathers of the desert."[26] "Human wisdom," says M. Dufour, "may wonder at such macerations and deem them excessive, but the man who voluntarily undertook them felt a divine inspiration and assistance." "On the path of penance only the first step costs," the saint himself used to say, but what heroism and what grace are required to make a man take that first step and then to lead him to the heights of so difficult a virtue!

M. Vianney's disciplines and hair-shirt are, like trophies of victory, preserved in the old presbytery of Ars. But the most awful of all his instruments of penance is not there; it has been left in the church: that instrument is his *confessional.*

We may say that the confessional was the instrument of his crucifixion. He was "a martyr of the confessional," says the Abbé Monnin. He might have fled from sinners and have hidden himself in a cloister or in a desert; the

25. *Ibid.*, p. 912.
26. *Ibid.*, p. 977.

love of souls made him stay at Ars. He who had spent his youth in the fields, in the pure atmosphere of his native hills, remained, on days when a serene sky calls men into the open country, riveted to that rude seat, a prisoner of sinners. His was a refined and sensitive heart, and he loved the beauty of Nature. Once upon a time he, too, walked in the smiling vale of the Fontblin where the aspens rustle; even now he was only divided from it by a few houses and the walls of his church. However, of his own will, he deprived himself, for a space of thirty years, of the pleasure of tasting its charm, its pastures, its restful shade!

"A few hours spent in the confessional are enough to break the most robust priest; when he comes out of it his limbs are numbed, his head is congested and incapable of consecutive thought. He loses his sleep and his appetite, and were he to resume such interminable sittings day by day, ere long his courage would fail him."[27] Now, according to the Comtesse des Garets, the Curé d'Ars performed a task that would have worn out six confessors. And the Abbé Raymond, who saw him at his post, exclaims: "That which, to me, has always seemed miraculous and beyond human strength is that a priest, who was subject to so many infirmities and who followed so austere a mode of life, should have been able to spend almost his whole life in the confessional! My own health, thanks be to God, is excellent, but I own that I could not have stood such a life for a week, and I have heard a like admission from priests who were accustomed to hearing Confessions during pilgrimages."[28]

It was, indeed, between those planks, within that anticipated coffin, that the Curé d'Ars underwent his greatest sufferings. In the summer, the church felt like a hothouse, and, as M. Vianney himself admitted, "the heat in the confessional gave him an idea of Hell." He was often compelled to keep a wet towel on his forehead whilst

---

27. Mgr. Convert, *Le Curé d'Ars et les dons du Saint-Esprit,* p. 351.
28. *Procès apostolique ne pereant,* p. 559.

sitting there, because of the tortures his violent headaches caused him—in fact, that was the reason why he had his hair cut short on the forepart of his head. On certain days, when the weather was sultry or the heat excessive, the atmosphere of the small church was so vitiated that the heroic confessor felt sick, and was only able to keep at his task by inhaling vinegar-salts or eau-de-Cologne. On the other hand, in that part of Les Dombes the cold is intense, especially when icy winds sweep down from the Alps. "Several times," says M. Dubouis, "the servant of God fainted, either by reason of the cold or because of his infirmities. 'How can you remain like this for so many hours, in such severe weather, without something to warm your feet?' I asked him.

"'Oh, my friend, I can do so for the good reason that from All Saints' until Easter I do not feel my feet at all.'"[29]

Chanoine Alexis Tailhades, of Montpellier, who spent part of the winter of 1839 with him, relates that the poor priest's feet were in such a state that the skin of his heels stuck to his stockings when he removed them at night.

To soften a little the hard board on which he sat for so many hours, small cushions stuffed with straw were sometimes placed on it, but he pushed them aside. Towards the end of his life, during the winters of 1857 and 1858, it became necessary to resort to cunning in order to warm him in some slight measure: every night, before he entered the church, a foot-warmer was surreptitiously placed under his confessional, which was renewed several times during the day. "It was a long time before he became aware of the trick; but when he discovered it, he allowed it to go on because his health was failing fast. In the sacristy, where he heard the men, he was sometimes reduced to setting paper on fire to restore the circulation in his numbed hands. M. Toccanier only obtained his sanction for the installation of a stove by

29. *Procès apostolique ne pereant,* p. 900.

pointing out that the vestments were becoming moldy in that cold and damp hole. For a long time he went without a fire in his room. Every winter's night, during the last fifteen years of his life, Pertinand, the schoolmaster, or one of the Brothers, tried to get to his room before him and to light a good fire of faggots. 'Unfortunately,' Pertinand relates, 'he no longer succeeded in getting warm, even in his own room, and his sleep was much disturbed in consequence. Hence, on the return of spring it was easy to gather from certain of his expressions, that for our good Curé as for the whole of Nature that season was a time of renewal and refreshment.'"[30]

M. Vianney's assiduity in the confessional and the hardships entailed thereby would, of themselves, have sufficed to raise him to high sanctity. However, he thirsted for mortifications as others thirst for pleasure, and he never had his fill of penance. He laid on himself the sacrifice never to enjoy the fragrance of a flower, never to taste fruit nor to drink, were it only a few drops of water, during the height of the summer heat. He would not brush away a fly that importuned him. When on his knees he would not rest his elbows on the kneeling-bench. He had made a law unto himself never to show any dislike, and to hide all natural repugnances. He mortified the most legitimate curiosity: thus he never expressed so much as a wish to see the railway which passed by Ars at a distance of a few kilometers, and which daily brought him so many visitors.

There was no sin in him, but for forty years he fasted and scourged himself for sinners. We have seen what bloody scourgings he inflicted on himself in the beginning of his ministry, so as to obtain the conversion of his people. When this result was achieved he did not allow his instruments of penance to rust. His physical exhaustion, however, compelled him to use them less frequently and less cruelly: it became necessary to allow his wounds to heal before he could reopen them by another scourg-

30. *Procès de l'Ordinaire,* p. 377.

ing. In 1839, thanks to the complicity of Catherine Lassagne, the Abbé Tailhades "made a scrupulous search of his room." "I ended," he says, "by finding behind the curtain at the head of the bed a discipline made of very strong wire." Frère Athanase made a like discovery later on, and declared that it was plain that the instrument had been in use. Then one day someone purloined it. M. Vianney knew no rest until another was procured for him. And the Brother adds: "I have seen one which he had fabricated himself; it was made of very rough links of a chain, so that each blow must have cut into the flesh."

He had besought a number of persons in succession to buy him some small chains, the destination of which he would not divulge, though they guessed it pretty well. One day when Marie Filliat was going to Trévoux she refused to carry out a commission of this kind. So he was obliged to fall back upon a poor youth—almost a simpleton—who would sometimes say to him: "Oh! Monsieur le Curé, really there are too many!" Under the impression that Jean Picard, the farrier of Ars, would suspect nothing, he ordered from him "a chain with double links, four or five centimeters broad and long enough to encircle the body. . . . I did not then suspect the use to which it was destined to be put," the farrier declared. "I had an idea that it was to be for the church clock, which was undergoing repairs just then. However, one Easter day M. le Curé was taken ill in church and I helped to carry him to his room. When we undressed him to put him to bed I saw my chain round his body."[31]

On each arm he wore a bracelet set with sharp points. "By the awkwardness of his actions, by the manner in which he moved, bolt upright, in the pulpit, at the altar, it was easy to see," says Mme. des Garets, "that his body was covered with hair-shirts and other instruments of penance."[32] At one moment his hair-shirt caused a sore

31. Jean Picard, *Procès de l'Ordinaire,* p. 1312.
32. *Procès de l'Ordinaire,* p. 912.

that gave rise to some anxiety, for it might easily have become gangrenous.

Such penances weakened him greatly, so that it was a wonder he was able to keep going at all, seeing that "he lived on what would have been the death of another." No doubt, after his "youthful follies"—that is, his fasts for two or three whole days, he would resign himself, in view of his weakness and the work he had to do, to take sufficient nourishment. Catherine and her companions counted upon this when, about 1827, they were informed that henceforth M. le Curé would take his meals at the *Providence*. They were doomed to disappointment. If he agreed to eat daily, what he ate was so very little! His long-continued fast suffered no real interruption. As a rule, he returned to the kitchen of the orphanage about noon. In a corner of the hearth a small can of soup or milk was ready for him. Sometimes he did not succeed in taking the whole of it. At other times, on the contrary, he ate a tiny piece of dry bread in addition. For a long time he took nothing whatever in the morning. About 1834, when he felt very exhausted, he was forced to obey Mgr. Devie, who ordered him to take some breakfast. From that time, after his Mass, he drank a little milk, but on fast days he went without it. "During Lent in 1849, 1850, and 1851," says Frère Athanase, "I noticed that he took only one meal a day." On very rare occasions he consented to eat a little dessert after his midday meal; but during the last two years of his life he deprived himself even of that slight indulgence. Until his grave illness in May, 1843, he never took any food at night.

From 1854 until 1859, by order of Dr. Saunier, he was obliged to accept a few mitigations which were judged indispensable. "Now that I am compelled to take more sustaining food, I feel less at ease when I go to Confession," he said, with a sigh. And he accused himself of gluttony! What were those too succulent menus? His "spiritual father" will tell us.

"I have often been present at his dinner," says M. Beau.

"From the time when the Sisters took charge of the *Providence* he was served in his own room. He never sat down. On a bare table stood an earthenware vessel which contained a few vegetables, sometimes two eggs, a little meat if he was more exhausted than usual (he never touched meat unless he had first asked my permission), a jug of water, a bottle of wine, and a piece of bread. In less than ten minutes the meal was over. He ate in such a way as not to perceive the taste of his food. The greater part of the portion served out to him invariably remained in the dish; he drank a little water reddened with wine and ate a few mouthfuls of bread. . . . I was greatly struck by this excessive abstemiousness."[33]

A pound of bread lasted him for over a week. "One day," says M. Camille Monnin, "I noticed in his room a small loaf in which a hole had been dug, apparently by the teeth of a rat. In reality, it was just the piece of bread which the servant of God had taken in order to sustain himself during a great part of the day."

A time came when, owing to a contraction of the stomach, it became impossible for him to take a larger quantity of food than the pittance to which he had grown accustomed. During his first years at Ars, at the dinner which followed the clerical conferences, and which was given by the châtelains, "he ate tolerably well," says Mme. des Garets. Soon, however, he obtained a dispensation from the meal, and he looked upon this as a great favor. To gain the "privilege" he put forward the plea that he was expected in the confessional, and that he was anxious to satisfy *his people.*

The Dowager Comtesse des Garets relates that at a dinner given at the château, in honor of Mgr. Devie, the Bishop wished to have his "dear Curé" by his side, and he obliged him to eat like the rest of the company. The saint obeyed; but he subsequently became very ill, and it was thought that he would die. "His stomach was only used to abstinence," says Jean-Baptiste Mandy. After that

33. *Procès de l'Ordinaire,* p. 1208.

meal, Mgr. Devie gave him full freedom to follow his ordinary régime.

It goes without saying that the Curé d'Ars did not force his own régime upon those to whom he had occasion to offer hospitality. At first the menu of the meals served in the presbytery itself was more than modest, and it was a useful precaution for the guest to bring some provisions with him. After the inauguration of the *Providence,* he entrusted the young directresses with the duty of entertaining his guests. "When my niece was about to be married," says Marguerite Vianney, "she went to see my brother a few days before the wedding. He told Catherine Lassagne to prepare a little meal; he sat at table with the parents, and, on that day, putting aside his usual austerity, he took a little of every dish."

"Whenever we brought him wood, corn, or other provisions for his *Providence*," says Guillaume Villier, "he received and treated us very well indeed; he himself served us with food and drink. He was most courteous; he touched glasses with us, but refused to drink—we never succeeded in making him drink with us."

After 1854, the conference dinner was held no longer at the château, but at the house of the missionaries. "At the very last gathering to take place in his lifetime," says Frère Athanase, "several of the priests who were present said to me: 'We have had the best dinner in the whole canton.' That night M. Toccanier spoke of the satisfaction of the priests to M. Vianney, who had himself ordered the meal. 'So much the better!' the servant of God replied, 'things should always be done like that. When we entertain colleagues, we should do it nobly. That is how M. Balley used to act. At Ecully, when there were only the two of us, we lived on what was forthcoming; anything was good enough; but when we had a guest, he could be sure of an excellent reception. . . . Ah! M. Balley! he was so good!'"

It must be added that whilst the members of the conference were having that dinner of which the Curé d'Ars spoke with so much satisfaction, he despatched his own in five minutes at the small table in his room.

"It cost him terribly dear to arrive at such excessive abstemiousness," says Comte des Garets, who was an eyewitness of that mortified life.

If, in order to appraise the penance of M. Vianney, it is necessary to appeal to a *specialist* in the matter, let us hear the humble admission of a Father of the Grande-Chartreuse: "We confess, we solitaries, hermits, monks, penitents of every description, that we only dare follow the holy Curé d'Ars with wondering eyes, that we are not worthy to kiss his footprints, the dust of his shoes!"[34]

---

34. *Letter* written September 15, 1865, to M. Toccanier by R. P. Maurice-Marie Borel, monk of the Grande-Chartreuse (Isère).

Chapter 26

INTUITIONS AND PREDICTIONS OF THE CURÉ D'ARS

ON September 3, 1856, Comte de Tourdonnet, whose château was in the *département* of Corrèze, came to Ars with one of his maid-servants, who was deaf. Although, like so many men of his period, he had lost the faith, he yet wished to obtain from the alleged wonder-worker the cure of the poor girl. He entered the church, but, wishing to have a personal interview with M. Vianney, he made sign to Marie—for that was the name of the maid—to wait near the main entrance. After a considerable delay he at last saw the servant of God, who, at that hour, was hearing Confessions in the sacristy. "Monsieur le Curé," he asked, "could you cure my servant?" "Ah, yes; you mean *Marie?*" the saint replied. "I *see* her in *the chancel.*" "Excuse me, Monsieur le Curé, *she is at the bottom of the church.*"

Which of these two was mistaken, the little country parish priest who *saw* that person in the chancel, or her master who *knew* her to be at the bottom of the church? True, M. Vianney had called the maid by her name, though M. de Tourdonnet had not mentioned it, but that might have been no more than chance; so many domestic servants are called Marie! . . . The Count was anxious to clear up that point on the spot. He walked down the nave towards the holy water stoup. Marie was not there. He stepped outside; she was not to be found in the throng of pilgrims who were coming and going. Once again he looked in every part of the nave. Where could she have gone to? Finally he decided to go into the chancel, where the Curé d'Ars had *seen* her half an hour earlier. There, indeed, he found his servant, praying behind the high altar, near a confessional, at a spot which M. Vianney could not have seen even from the threshold of the sacristy. The unbeliever was stupefied. He related the occurrence to several people of Ars, notably to the Abbé Toccanier, who wrote it down then and there. "And now, Monsieur le Comte, are you willing to put your signature to these few lines?" the missionary asked.

"Why not, since the thing is true?"

"Eh! How do you explain it?"

"I cannot understand it at all. . . . In any case, *the eyes* of the Curé d'Ars are not made like those of other people."[1]

M. Vianney did not suppose or guess that which remains hidden from other men; by a special grace of God he *saw.* In certain specially gifted subjects phenomena have occurred of extraordinary lucidity, of second sight, or prevision; to these phenomena, which are held to be natural, learned men have assigned a natural explanation. Here we must look for another explanation. The Curé d'Ars possessed that gift which mystical theology calls *intuition.* The crowds that surged around him were not mistaken when they recognized in that amazing fact something preternatural and a mark of holiness.

Père Faivre, who paid frequent visits to Ars, made the following statement: "I have heard many people declare that they had consulted the Curé d'Ars on the subject of their vocation, or about lawsuits, family complications, illnesses, decisions that had to be taken, and that he had invariably answered with admirable appropriateness. He foretold to several persons what was to befall them at a later date. He knew the conscience and interior dispositions of many, so that they wondered greatly. So strong was the general feeling attributing to him supernatural powers that no one ever hesitated to give credence to his words."[2]

However, this intuition was not continuous; all hearts were not for him so many open books. He mostly recom-

1. *Procès de l'Ordinaire,* p. 178.
2. *Ibid.,* p. 1496.

mended nothing more than the means suggested by ordinary human prudence. Yet it frequently happened that, even before people spoke, he revealed that which they wanted to tell him or wished to hide from him. There were those who, on hearing of his gift of intuition, did not dare to appear in his presence, for fear he should make known the state of their soul.

Many times those who were intimate with him endeavored to discover the secret of his supernatural knowledge. In order to foil the inquisitive, but, above all, from a motive of humility, he would answer, "Oh, it is an idea that crossed my mind," or: "Bah! I am like the almanacs: when I hit on it, I hit on it!" One day a young woman from Savoy entered his confessional. Even before she opened her mouth M. Vianney started to talk of the piety of her sisters and of her own attraction towards the religious life. The penitent could not get over it. On leaving the church she fell in with M. Toccanier and told him of her astonishment. "How could you reveal those things to that person, seeing that you did not know her?" the missionary asked the saint. "Eh! I acted like Caïphas; I prophesied without knowing it."

But he did not always jest. At times a sudden question of his interlocutor left him no time to recover from his surprise; in such cases he gave himself away against his will. "On one occasion," says the Abbé Toccanier, "I suddenly asked him: 'Monsieur le Curé, when a man is given a supernatural perception of a thing, is it not somewhat like remembering it?' 'Yes, my friend,' he replied. 'Thus I once told a certain woman: "So it is you who have left your husband in the hospital and who refuse to join him?" "How do you know that?" she said. "I have not mentioned the matter to a soul." I was more surprised than she was: I imagined that she had already told me the whole story.'"

In like manner it has happened that, whilst he was hearing Confessions, he not only admitted that he had extraordinary intuitions, but he even stated the reason why he had them.

A young maid employed by the Cinier family, whose house faced the church, was making her Confession. A big accusation was trembling on her lips. . . . She kept silence, however, putting it off for another time. "But that?" the saint asked—and he specified that which the girl wished to hide—"you do not mention it, yet you have done it."Amazed by this revelation, the penitent asked herself: "How does he know it?" when, replying to that thought which, as a matter of fact, had remained unuttered, M. Vianney added: "Your angel guardian told me."[3]

More than once the prophetic intuitions of M. Vianney were seemingly at variance with the most elementary rules of human wisdom, or contrary to the advice or to the prescience of others reputed to be persons of great prudence. "I think that good Curé is in his dotage," was the remark made to her mother by a girl of Lyons who had just been told that she would one day be the superior of a charitable institution. This issue proved that the man of God had read the future aright. "In the end one felt compelled to acknowledge the sureness of his views and to admit that God Himself enlightened him!"

It would require many pages were we to relate all the extraordinary intuitions attributed to the Curé d'Ars; hence we must perforce be content with merely gleaning a few grains out of too rich a harvest.[4]

The question of the future engrosses and at times torments us all, but especially the young. So, when the fame of M. Vianney went abroad as of a man who could read the heart and lift the veil that shrouded the future, souls eager to know their destiny flocked to Ars.

Mlle. Rosalie Berlioux, of Saint-Étienne, who, as Mère Marie-Saint-Athanase, was to become General of the Marist

---

3. *Documents,* Ball (Archives of the presbytery of Ars).
4. All the facts that we are about to relate bear a serious character of authenticity, whether they were compiled at the time of the *process* of canonization or subsequently. If we abridge, or suppress some names, we do so at the express request of the witnesses. All these various depositions have been controlled by those in charge of the official inquiry, the documents themselves being preserved at the sanctuary of Ars, where we were able to consult them at leisure.

Sisters of Belley, had a younger sister who was very much drawn to the world and did not quite know what to do with her life. She entered the novitiate at Belley, but left it again, for lack of sufficient vocation, as they told her. Thereupon she made up her mind to get married. However, she first wished to have the advice of the saint of Ars. "You want to get married," he told her. "You imagine that in that state you will find nothing but roses; you would find only thorns." The girl came away feeling rather disappointed. On returning a second time, she heard the unexpected decision: "Enter with the Sisters of St. Clare." "And did he assure you that you would be received by them?" her mother asked on her return. A third time the girl journeyed to Ars, and this time the answer she received was a reassuring one: "Yes, my child, you will be received by the Sisters of St. Clare; you will persevere, you will die there, and from there you will go to Heaven." Mlle. Berlioux entered the convent specified by the saint; for twenty-four years she followed its austere rule, and her passing away was the edification of the whole community. "What an enviable death!" exclaimed the mother prioress.

One day, in the year 1855, Mlle. Bossan, sister of the architect of Fourvière, told the Curé d'Ars: "Father, I am to be married soon; will you, please, give me your blessing." But instead of blessing her the saint burst into tears. "O my daughter, how unhappy you will be!" "But then, Father, what shall I do?" "Enter at the Visitation . . . enter, my child, make haste; you will not be given fifty years in which to earn your crown." Mlle. Bossan, as Soeur Marie-Aimé, died whilst holding the office of mistress of novices at the Visitation of Fourvière on August 13, 1880. She had completed her forty-ninth year on July 8.

Mlle. Hedwige Moizin, of Bourg, appeared to have a very pronounced vocation for the cloister. Her family, however, would not hear of it. At the beginning of a new year the poor child went to confide her grief to the ever-compassionate M. Vianney. "Console yourself," he told her; "all your sorrows will have vanished in a year's time." By the end of the year she was dead.

Mlle. Bernard, of Fareins, wished to enter religion. "No," M. Vianney unhesitatingly declared, "you will not be a nun, but your married sister will be one." Shortly after the lady in question became a widow, realized the vanity of the world, and took the veil at the Ursuline Convent of Villefranche, where she died. As for Mlle. Bernard, she remained at home, but fell ill. She begged that the Curé d'Ars might be called to her bedside. He came. "Am I going to die?" she asked. (This was in the first days of June.) "No, my child, not at once; you will last until the Assumption." And she died on that day.

M. Auguste Faure, a professor in a private college of Saint-Étienne, wanted to become a Jesuit. "No, my dear friend," the saint told him; "stay where you are. Life is so short!" Within less than a year M. Faure fell ill with pneumonia whilst he was laboring at the preparation of soldiers for their Easter duties. He expired at the age of twenty-seven, with the *Magnificat* on his lips. At Saint-Étienne he was venerated as a saint.

In 1848, Mlle. Louise Lebon, a girl of Lyons, finished her education with the Benedictine Nuns of Pradines. Her ambition, however, was to return speedily, as a novice, to the convent where she had been at school. She was only seventeen, and the abbess would not receive her. In the meantime she accompanied some of her friends to Ars. In despair of being able to secure an interview with the holy Curé, she wrote to him a letter of four pages, in which she revealed that which she would have liked to tell him by word of mouth. She was fortunate enough to thrust the letter into M. Vianney's own hand as he was returning to the presbytery at noon.

The evening saw the girl once more in church, lost amid a vast congregation. On his way from the confessional to the sacristy M. Vianney crossed the nave. Suddenly he stopped and looked round. At last his penetrating glance rested upon Louise Lebon, and he signed to her to follow him. A minute later she tremblingly knelt at his feet. "My child, it is you who have written to me?" "Yes, Father." "Very well, you must not worry; you will enter your convent. In a few days the mother will write to inform you that she accepts you."

Now, Mlle. Lebon had just had a letter from the abbess as unfavorable as its predecessors. However, ten days after her interview with the Curé d'Ars the girl had the joy of receiving a brief note from the convent: "My dear Louise, the constancy of your desires compels me to say an emphatic *yes.* Come whenever you like." By July 2, 1849, it was an accomplished fact.[5]

Soeur Marie de Jésus, a little novice, saw her profession put off by reason of her extreme youth. In her distress she was allowed to make a pilgrimage to Ars, where she made a general Confession. "O my little one, how happy you are!" the saint exclaimed, as she finished her accusation. "True, Father, I am happy, but I have grievously offended God before I entered religion." "My child, in the world you would have committed so many sins that you would have ended by losing your soul. Be true to your vocation." He wished to see her again before her departure. "O my little sister," he said, "your soul is white, perfectly white. And now, go and make your profession." "But, Father, you know very well that I am supposed to be too young. . . ." "Everything is ready, my child: your cross is made. Go!"

Now, at the very moment when Soeur Marie de Jésus crossed the threshold of the Hospice of Lyons, where she had a commission to execute for her superior, the portress handed her a small parcel. "This is for you, Sister." "May I open it?" "Of course." What was the Sister's emotion when, on undoing the parcel, she found a cross, on the back of which were engraved her name and a date; it was the crucifix of her profession. Urged by a mysterious impulse, the superior had suddenly decided to admit to her first vows the novice who had been condemned to a delay of three years. This was the meaning of the words of the Curé d'Ars: *"Your cross is made. Go!"*

"Yes, my child, you will be a Little Sister of the Poor,"

---

5. These details were given to Chanoine Ball, in 1881, by Mlle. Lebon herself, then Mère Sainte-Beatrix, a Benedictine nun of Pradines.

M. Vianney one day said to Mlle. Ernestine Durand, a girl of Lyons, then eighteen years of age; "yes, yes, you will be a Little Sister. . . . But after having joined the community you will be obliged to leave it again." "Oh, in that case, Father, I prefer_____" "No, no, enter, enter! Three days after your departure from the convent your mother will take you back to it herself." Ernestine obeyed blindly. Having obtained—with much difficulty, it must be admitted—the consent of her parents, she entered as a postulant with the Little Sisters of the Poor of Lyons. She whole-heartedly took up her new life. Presently letters came from her family, full of regrets and even threats: the girl was not yet of age; she had extorted her mother's consent; if need be, recourse would be had to the intervention of the law. As a matter of fact, her brother came to the convent accompanied by a policeman. The postulant was compelled to return home. She was brokenhearted and lost both appetite and sleep. At the end of three days her mother said to her: "Oh, I do not mean to bring about your death; I shall take you back to your beloved companions!" Thus, as the Curé d'Ars had foretold, the child was restored to the convent by her own mother, who, if she were not yet wholly resigned, at least no longer withheld her consent.

Mme. Sermèt-Décroze, of Arbigneux in the Ain, had three daughters. She was anxious that one of them should become a nun, and Josephte, the youngest, a pious, retiring child, seemed just made for a convent. As for the eldest, Anthelmette—they gave children romantic names in those days!—her mother thought her rather worldly. She was certainly fond of finery, so she must be married, and, of course, before her younger sister. In 1856 Mme. Sermèt-Décroze passed through Ars; to M. Vianney she confided the secret of a mother's dreams. "No, my child," he declared, "your Josephte will not be a nun; not she, not she; it will be another of your children, and that sooner than you think."

The good woman could scarcely believe her ears. On her return journey she passed through Lyons, where she bought a beautiful dress for her eldest daughter. "Oh mother," Anthelmette exclaimed when she saw the alluring gift, "I shall have no use for that dress; I want to be a nun." Not long after she entered the novitiate of the Marist Sisters of Belley. As for Josephte, who had never given even a thought to the convent, she was married on February 16, 1857, at the age of seventeen.

The following charming anecdote reveals M. Vianney's "manner." It is related by the Baronne de Lacomble, who was the chief figure in it:

"I was a widow, with two sons. One day I learned that the younger of them had fallen in love with a charming girl of fifteen, he himself being scarcely eighteen years old. Shortly after I received a letter in which my big boy, whilst asking for my consent with affectionate delicacy, declared his determination to follow his inclination. We corresponded, but nothing could shake his resolution.

"I was alone and knew not where to look for counsel. Now, there was much talk of the holiness of M. le Curé Vianney. Having prayed fervently, I resolved to make a pilgrimage to Ars. But that poor little village was so far away! Oh, assuredly this would be no pleasure trip! I was not to be daunted, however.

"At the end of a three days' journey by diligence, I eventually reached Ars. Unfortunately I could only stop for a few hours, and I was told that before seeing M. Vianney it was necessary to await one's turn for an indefinite time.

"I went into the church. From the big door to the confessional there was not one vacant seat. I sat in the very last place, near the holy water basin, and in my disappointment I resolved to depart. Involuntarily my eyes were drawn towards the chapel of St. John the Baptist, in which the Curé was hearing Confessions. Oh, how I prayed!

"What was my astonishment and my emotion when I suddenly beheld a white-haired priest come out of that chapel, and, on entering the nave, walk towards me. He came without stopping anywhere. He looked at me. It was really towards me that he was moving! I was more dead than alive. He stopped, bent down, and whispered into my ear: *'Let them marry; they will be very happy!'*

"Having uttered these words, he straightway returned to his confessional.

"Now, no one knew of my journey, no one could have informed M. Vianney of my arrival, and he had never seen me before.

"Once again God had granted to him, for the sake of a distracted and anxious mother, that marvellous gift of intuition which enabled him to read souls, so that he might comfort them in the midst of their uncertainties and failings."[6]

How many events, both happy and unhappy, M. Vianney has thus known or foreseen!

In March, 1856, meeting for the first time with M. l'Abbé Babey, Superior of the College of Saint-Jean-d'Angély, he asked him with warm-hearted interest: "You have come about young X_____, who is sick?" And, without any hesitation, he mentioned the name of a student who was ill with typhoid fever, on whose behalf the superior had undertaken this pilgrimage. "Very well; tell the parents from me that the child will not die of this illness."As a matter of fact, the boy recovered rapidly.[7]

M. Sébastien Germain, who was born at Mizérieux, was a nephew of Marie Filliat, one of the mistresses at the *Providence.* By reason of this connection he had often, as a boy, served M. Vianney's Mass. He married, had three boys, but was disconsolate at not having at least one daughter. He went to see M. Vianney about the middle of July, 1859. He met him in the square with several rosaries in his hand. Without waiting for M. Germain to state the object of his visit, the saint gave him four rosaries, one after another, saying: "Look, they are for your children."

"But, Monsieur le Curé, I have only three children—three *boys!"*

6. This incident was related by Mme. de Lacomble to Vicomte Anselme de Warren, who in turn related it to Mgr. Convert on May 7, 1918.

7. *Letter* from M. Babey to M. Toccanier, December 13, 1861.

"My Sébastien, the fourth rosary will be for *your daughter.*"

The following year a little girl came to brighten the home of the Germain family, and she herself, now Mme. Jallat, has told us this pretty story. "My father," she said, "did, in fact, give me the modest rosary with its wooden beads and its steel chain. I have it still, as a precious relic."

In the course of March, 1866, Cardinal de Bonald exhibited, at the archiepiscopal residence of Lyons, the plans which he had had drawn up by the architect Bossan for the basilica of Fourvière. This led to so violent a controversy between the admirers of this original style and the partisans of gothic and romanesque architecture that the plans were withdrawn and the Cardinal gave up all hope of collecting the necessary money. The question of rebuilding Fourvière had, perforce, to remain in abeyance.

Now, it so happened that during the summer of 1869, M. l'Abbé Bonnardet, who was to become Vicar-General of Lyons, fell in with M. Bossan in the omnibus which plied between Ars and Villefranche. They spoke of Fourvière, and the priest expressed his profound regret at the total abandonment of what he held to be a wonderful project. "Oh," the architect replied with perfect equanimity, "as far as that is concerned I feel quite happy; the holy Curé d'Ars told me during his lifetime that my church would be built some day, and that in thanksgiving."

Two years later Mgr. Ginoulhiac, impelled by the disasters that had befallen France, pronounced the vow which resulted in the erection of the basilica of Fourvière. M. Vianney had not been mistaken.

Every year the Feast of St. John the Baptist was kept with great solemnity by the parish of Ars, and the Abbé Vianney was in the habit of singing the parochial Mass at the high altar. But on the morning of June 24, 1859, at the very time when the bloody battle of Solferino opened, the holy Curé, contrary to his custom, wished to celebrate at the Lady altar. The people were greatly surprised, but they ceased to wonder when they heard of the battle. "Is my son still alive," a woman asked him in her anguish. "Yes," the saint replied, "but there are many dead."[8]

In 1855, Joanny des Garets, one of the sons of the Mayor of Ars, and a gallant and brilliant young officer for whom M. Vianney felt a very special affection, was about to set out for the war in the Crimea. The holy Curé was asked to come to the château to bless Joanny's sword. The whole family had gathered in the drawing-room. On the threshold the servant of God perceived the officer, who, however, had not noticed his arrival. "Poor little one!" he said softly, folding his hands with an air of infinite compassion; "a ball, a ball!" "Neither my brother nor my mother heard those words," says Mlle. Marthe des Garets, "because there was a certain amount of noise in the *salon,* but my sister, Mme. de Montluisant, and several others heard them quite distinctly. . . . On June 18 our poor Joanny was wounded by a ball, at the storming of the Malakoff Tower, and he succumbed three days later."[9]

On June 10, 1859, Mme. Prat, of Marseilles, happened to be at Ars and to meet M. Vianney. Stopping in front of this person whom he had never seen before, he said to her, in a tone of marked compassion: "O my child, you are going to be struck by a *sudden* blow. Make a novena to St. Philomena." Exactly six months later, on December 10, her husband died *suddenly* of apoplexy at the Bourse at Marseille.

Soeur Marie-François, a young nun of the Third Order of St. Francis of Saint-Sorlin, came with her superior to spend four days at Ars. Just as they were about to leave for home they met M. Vianney. "Take this," the saint said to the superior, at the same time offering her three one-franc pieces; "take this, for you will want it." "But, Monsieur le Curé, I have enough money to pay for the conveyance." "Take it all the same, my child." So she accepted the money. What was the surprise of the nuns when, on reaching Villefranche, they were about to pay

8. Abbé Beau, *Procès de l'Ordinaire,* p. 1218.
9. *Procès apostolique in genere,* p. 312.

the driver! The superior had mislaid her purse, which contained exactly the three francs demanded by the carrier. Fortunately for them, M. Vianney had provided for the emergency.[10]

On another occasion Soeur Marie-François reached Ars at a very early hour. This time she was accompanied by her mother as well as by her superior. M. Vianney noticed the latter as he entered the sacristy to vest for Mass. "Go home quickly," he whispered into her ear. "But, Father, what about Mass?" "No, my poor child, do not wait. One of you is going to be taken ill. If you delay you will not be able to leave for a long time." The superior, very scared, compelled her two companions to start at once for home. "Now," says Soeur Marie-François, "when we were still about two leagues from our house, I was suddenly taken ill, so that I was unable to pursue the journey; my superior and my mother were obliged to carry or drag me along. This was the beginning of a serious illness which kept me in bed for a fortnight."[11]

One summer's morning, in the year 1857, two young women, whom curiosity rather than devotion had brought to Ars, were assisting at M. Vianney's catechism. One of them, the more frivolous of the two, was so disappointed at all she saw and heard that, alluding to the holy priest's simplicity of speech and manner, she had the presumption to say to her friend: "What a caricature! Was it worthwhile to come so far for this?" The preacher overheard the remark. With a smile, not devoid of a touch of irony, he asked the impertinent one: "So you think, mademoiselle, that it is not worthwhile to go so far for the sake of such a caricature?" Having said it, he went on with his catechism.

The confusion of the girl may be imagined. However, she stayed on, and at the conclusion of the instruction, bathed in tears, she went to see M. Vianney in order to offer an apology. Her friend went with her, and the saint received them with his customary kindliness. "Your only

10. *Procès de l'Ordinaire,* p. 1395.
11. *Ibid.*

penance will be to go to Confession today, and tomorrow you will receive Holy Communion." Then, taking apart the friend of the culprit, he said: "On your return journey, keep watch over your companion. Alas! a calamity will befall her. But as she will have received Holy Communion by way of Viaticum, her salvation will not be in jeopardy."

The girls performed their devotions with fervor. Happy in the thought that what had begun as a trip had ended as a pilgrimage, they set out at a brisk pace for their native village. The girl who had been bidden to watch over the other had already forgotten the injunctions of the saint when all of a sudden her companion uttered a scream. An adder had stung her in the leg; the poison took effect at once. The poor child expired there, by the roadside, without it being possible to administer any remedy to her.

Some people, after reading of this incident, will, perhaps, say to themselves: "Surely the Curé d'Ars, instead of merely foreseeing this calamity, should have prevented it." Here we tread on unknown ground. After all, it is possible that the saint, in this instance, was given no more than an intuition of impending disaster, its cause, or the accompanying details being beyond his ken. There were times, however, when God allowed him not only to foresee the peril of others, but likewise how they should be preserved from harm.

Mme. E., the widow of a cavalry officer, relates the following incident: "In 1873, accompanied by my husband and a family of our acquaintance, I went to pay a visit to M. l'Abbé Rousset, curé of a village of La Bresse, the name of which I have forgotten. The good priest, who had known M. Vianney intimately, detained us for lunch, after which he took his guests out to fish. Not feeling very well, I did not go with them, but stayed behind with the curé's servant, a tall woman who, whilst giving me a cup of tea, told me the amazing story that follows:

"'I was nineteen years old and was at the orphanage of the Sisters of Autun. In my eagerness to earn my livelihood I asked for permission to look for a situation at

Lyons. The superior entrusted me to a lady who was about to set out for that town, but who intended making a detour in order to consult the Curé d'Ars.

"'At the moment of our entering the church, M. Vianney was in his catechism pulpit, explaining the lesson of the Sign of the Cross. He noticed me and, interrupting his discourse for a moment, said: "Eh! you big girl over there, come to me in the sacristy after this instruction. I have something to tell you."

"'As soon as the catechism was over I presented myself, "You are on your way to Lyons," he told me, even though I had not spoken a word. "Know, my child, that a great peril threatens you there. When you are in the midst of it, think of me and pray to God."

"'We reached Lyons, and for three days I made futile efforts to obtain a post. Finally I went to a registry office. Two men were there, waiting. I explained my position. "Ah! you are looking for a situation?" one of them said. "It so happens that I am at this very moment looking for a maid." We came to terms, and he added: "My wife must also see you; come to such-and-such an address at three o'clock this afternoon." He lived at La Mulatière.

"'I went there at the appointed time. Dear me, how long the road seemed to be! At length I reached the bridge where the Saône joins the Rhône. There were some boats there, and some workmen. On rounding a bend, however, I found myself in an isolated spot where there stood but one solitary house. On the threshold I beheld the man who had engaged me. He signed to me to come. Suddenly I was seized with an immense terror. Remembering the words of the Curé d'Ars, I called out to God and fled as fast as my legs would carry me. On his part, the wretched man also started in pursuit; he even endeavored to throw a lasso round my neck. He failed, mercifully, and stopped in his pursuit as I drew near the boatmen.

"'I have since learned that I only just missed falling into the hands of the notorious Dumollard, who earned for himself the nickname of the *murderer of servant maids.* When that criminal was brought to justice I gave evidence against him at the assizes. But what would have become of me had it not been for the Curé d'Ars?'"

The reader will have noticed that M. Vianney's perception of things and events that are hidden from the eye of man was spontaneous, effortless, and unaccompanied by any kind of *mise en scène.* In the confessional he read the hearts of his penitents; but his extraordinary power revealed itself on all manner of occasions—in the sacristy, in the pulpit, in the street, in the middle of familiar conversations, even at the altar whilst he was saying Mass. Nor was his intuition invariably connected only with matters of moment; at times it was concerned with very slight matters, and that in the most unexpected way.

"*Ah, here you are at last!*" he exclaimed on beholding at his feet Catherine Bray, a girl of Lyons, who had written to him some time before on the subject of her vocation, but whom he now met for the first time.[12]

To Jean-Baptiste Méthol, Mgr. de Ségur's valet, whom the blind prelate never called by any other name than his surname, the Curé d'Ars gave a small statue of St. John the Baptist, with the words: "Look, my child; take away with you this image of your patron saint, in remembrance of me."

Standing on the threshold of his confessional, and consequently separated from the nave by a thick wall, he said to one of the persons who controlled the crowds: "Please call the woman who is kneeling under the pulpit and who holds a white handkerchief in her hand. I have something to tell her."

In July, 1859, Mlle. Marie Regipas, of Lyons, was the first person to alight from the omnibus which had just stopped in front of the church of Ars. A man who seemed to be expecting her told her at once and without any preamble: "Mademoiselle, M. le Curé wishes to speak to you." "To me?" "Yes, mademoiselle. I am on duty at this moment,

12. *Circular Letters* of the Visitation of Montluel: notice concerning Soeur Marie-Germaine (Mlle. Catherine Bray).

and M. Vianney has just charged me with this commission: 'Go and meet the omnibus which is due now, and ask the young lady who first alights to come at once into the confessional.'" Mlle. Regipas was in a delicate state of health and could only remain in the village for a short time.

One morning, during M. Vianney's Mass, a woman came up to the altar rails with a number of the faithful. Twice the Curé passed her over when giving Holy Communion. As he approached her for the third time, she whispered to him: "Father, you have not given me Holy Communion." "My child, you have taken some food this morning." The lady returned to her place and suddenly remembered that, when getting up, she had eaten a morsel of bread.

In May, 1854, Mlle. Henry, who kept a shop at Chalon-sur-Saône, came to ask M. Vianney for the cure of an aunt who lived at Lyons. "Make a novena to St. Philomena and your aunt will soon be well," was the reply. "Oh, in that case, Father, I am off to Lyons; she will feel so happy!" "No, my child; after my Mass you will take the boat for Chalon. Make haste and go home; whilst you are here *you are being done (on vous coule du plomb)."* Mlle. Henry soon understood the warning. The woman to whom she had entrusted her little shop had not scrupled to waste her goods. As for the sick woman, she was restored to health within a short time.

One day, in the sacristy, a woman of Lyons, accompanied by her daughter aged ten, presented some objects of devotion for the Curé's blessing. Before tracing the Sign of the Cross over them, M. Vianney put aside one of the medals. "I cannot bless that one." The child had stolen the medal as she was passing in front of a stall.[13]

Coming in late for the eleven o'clock catechism, Jean-Claude Viret, a native of Cousance, in the Jura, found no room except behind the little pulpit near the sacristy door. M. Vianney had not so much as noticed his arrival,

13. *Annales d'Ars,* March, 1906, p. 362.

hence he was ignorant, not only of his presence, but likewise of the place where he had settled himself. Now, as the holy Curé's voice reached him only very faintly, Jean-Claude, weary of straining his ears, pulled out his rosary and began to recite it mechanically. But the good man, who was a prosperous farmer, carried away by other thoughts, only fingered his beads in order to reckon up his income. All of a sudden the catechist raised his voice, and this is what the dreaming worshipper heard: "O my children, people come to church and appear before Our Lord, yet they do not realize that they are in His presence, such as, for instance, that man at the sacristy door. He appears to be saying his Rosary, but he is merely reckoning up his income on his fingers. O my children, it makes me tremble to see so little reverence before our Lord!" Poor Viret, feeling that he was meant, could only bow his head in acknowledgement of his guilt.[14]

Mme. Mercier, a pious countrywoman of Bâgé-la-Ville in the Ain, was in the habit of spending annually three or four days at Ars. As soon as she arrived she would go and take her place in the queue near the confessional. M. Vianney was aware of this. On one such occasion he asked her after her Confession: "How long do you intend to stay?" "Until tomorrow, Father." "No, no; leave this very day. There is a snake in your house." The woman, knowing that M. Vianney was enlightened from above, made haste to leave for home. During her absence, and without her knowledge, her husband had taken the mattress stuffed with maize leaves to air it in the sun. When Mme. Mercier reached home she found everything in its place, the rooms clean and polished just as she had left them. She felt somewhat disconcerted, but for fear of being made a laughing-stock, she said nothing about M. Vianney's strange warning. Perhaps she had misunderstood him? Of what kind of serpent was the saint thinking? Whilst she was thus musing she shook her bed, when lo! a big reptile sprang out onto the ground and made for

14. *Mémoire* of Jean-Claude Viret, 111.

the yard, where it was killed by the farm laborers, who had rushed on hearing Mme. Mercier's screams.

In 1845 a widow of the name of Berthier, of La Fouillouse (Loire), had found herself compelled to place her child, a boy of eleven, with a farmer of Saint-Bonnet-les-Oules. Now, it so happened that one day, whilst the child was tending the flocks, a wolf seized one of his sheep. The poor boy was, in consequence, so harshly treated that he fled from the house of his employer; however, not daring to return to his mother, he took to the road. After wandering about for a while he was overtaken by a carriage. The driver, moved to pity, gave him a lift, and the boy, from sheer exhaustion, fell into a heavy sleep. When they reached Montceau-les-Mines the carrier roused the child, but, as he would not reveal his birthplace, he left him there. The little shepherd looked a good boy, so an honest miner agreed to take him into his house, and he employed him in sorting the ore.

When the poor mother learned what had happened at Saint-Bonnet, she gave full vent to her grief, and began to make inquiries in every direction about her son. Alas! she was unable to trace him. After four years of futile efforts she concluded that he must have been either drowned or devoured by wolves. But even so she would not give up all hope. About that time she heard of the Curé d'Ars, and at once sent her daughter to him, charging her to ask M. Vianney for news of the little fugitive.

The girl had hardly uttered a few words when the saint said with decision: "My child, tell your mother that her son is well. He is employed underground by honest folk who are natives of your place, though they live far from here and from your home. But rejoice, both of you; he will come back to you on a feast day."

This astonishing prophecy received a literal fulfillment. Five or six years later a tall young man arrived at La Fouillouse on the evening of the Feast of the Assumption and knocked at Mme. Berthier's door. After the first exclamation of surprise, the first demonstration of affection, the mother wished to ascertain whether her boy had remained loyal to his religion. "Oh yes, mother, I have always fulfilled my duties at Montceau-les-Mines." On hearing this the mother's joy was so great that, whilst thanking God for her happiness, she prayed that He would take her to Himself. She died not long after.[15]

Deeper, far more mysterious than things of earth, are those of the spiritual world. When studying the work of the Curé d'Ars in the confessional, we have seen how he was frequently able to discern amongst the throng such pilgrims as were in a hurry to leave, or sinners who, turning a deaf ear to the promptings of grace, were about to flee from the divine pardon. We shall now give instances of the saint's penetration of the thoughts and consciences of men.

When it was first rumored that M. Vianney possessed the power of reading hearts, a certain skepticism manifested itself among the educated classes. "In the first years," says Mlle. de Belvey, "notwithstanding all that I had been told, I had not the courage to speak to him of something that gave me much pain; I was afraid of being misunderstood, and that his decision would plunge my soul into fresh perplexity, which no one would be able to relieve, since no other priest commanded my confidence to a like degree. As it was not a question of faults that must needs be confessed, I resolved to say nothing. What was my surprise when, on my entering the confessional, M. le Curé answered my thoughts in a manner that would have been impossible even for a person to whom I had given a detailed account of the matter. When I went to him for the first time I was expressly forbidden to make a general Confession. Well, since then I have had countless proofs that he knew my innermost secrets, all the graces that I have had in my life.

"At first he refused to help me to make my Confession; but suddenly he began to question me with regard to this

15. "This incident," M. Ball writes, "was told to me by Soeur Marie, a religious of Saint-Joseph, at Saint-Jacques-des-Arrêts (Rhône), in a letter dated February 6, 1879. This nun not only knew of the incident itself, but was likewise acquainted with *Mére* Berthier and her children."

point or that, yet always about faults that I did not know or that I had forgotten, so that in the end, convinced that he was not mistaken, I never sought to deny anything, even when I was unable to recollect things he pointed out to me. Many people have assured me that he had read their consciences in a like manner."[16]

"You must become a nun, my child," he said one day to Joseline Ballefin, a young milliner of Lagnieu (Ain), at the same time closing the shutter of the confessional. Overwhelmed by this decision, Joseline, who was fond of the world, burst into tears. On the advice of a friend, she came back a second time. "Father," she began, "your words have filled me with sorrow, despair even. Can I trust you? You do not know me." "I not know you, my child? Why, I can read in your soul as if I had been your confessor all your life. Yes, you must become a nun." And once more the shutter was closed.[17]

In 1857, M. Hippolyte Pagès, an architect of Beaucaire, then forty-five years of age, was about to go to Confession to M. Vianney, to whom he had already addressed himself several times, when he suddenly felt a regret for not having become a priest—a regret which had already troubled him and of which he had never spoken to a soul. After listening to his accusations, M. Vianney said: "I know the purely human motives that prompted one of your relations to speak to you about being a priest. If, when I saw you for the first time, I had judged it better for you to become a priest, I should have told you so." In point of fact, a relative of M. Pagès had at one time wished him to enter the seminary, but in this she was prompted by sheer vanity.

Another time the holy Curé said to the same penitent: "Thank you, my child, for your many acts of compassion towards me." In one of his daily prayers the devout architect, having M. Vianney in mind, used this formula: "Lord, be merciful to him, as well as to all my relatives and

16. *Procès de l'Ordinaire,* pp. 251-252.
17. *Circular Letters* of the Visitation of Montluel: notice on Soeur Marie-Hélène Ballefin.

benefactors;" and he then enumerated all those for whom he wished to pray. "You do well," M. Vianney told him, "to mention to God the names of your relations and benefactors, only you name some who are less in want of prayers than others whom you forget." And he added: "Happy is the friend of the father of a pious child!" As a matter of fact, M. Pagès was in the habit of praying every day for M. Claparède, a friend of his father's.[18]

M. l'Abbé Denavit, one of the professors of Saint-Irénée of Lyons, came to Ars, not for the purpose of adding to the tribute of admiration paid to its Curé by the crowds, but rather in the hope of finding him at fault. This priest, for reasons for which it is impossible to account, placed but slender reliance on the decisions of M. Vianney. He waited where the saint would have to cross the short distance between the church and the presbytery, and addressed him as follows: "Monsieur le Curé, I am one of those in charge of the Grand Séminaire of Lyons. I should be grateful if you would give me some advice to help me to acquit myself well."

M. Vianney smiled rather cryptically, looked straight into the eyes of his interlocutor, and, speaking in Latin, so as not to be understood by the bystanders, he said: "*Declina a malo et fac bonum.*"[19] Having said it, he turned his attention to others.

In 1845, M. Dewatine, curé of Mortagne (Nord), visited the village of Ars in the course of a journey. He, too, had his doubts about all he had been told of M. Vianney, and for that reason, at the moment when the latter passed from the church to the presbytery, he left the crowd that was waiting for the so-called *saint.* But what was his amazement when the man of God went out of his way, tapped him on the shoulder, and whispered into his ear: "*Have confidence,* my friend."

A cobbler of Lyons, Antoine Saubin by name, without completely losing his faith—which had been ardent in his youth—had plunged headlong into spiritualistic prac-

18. M. Pagès, *Procès de l'Ordinaire,* p. 447.
19. "Decline from evil and do good." (*Ps.* 36:27).

tices. Soon the most horrible phantoms began to haunt him by day and by night, so that in June, 1859, he made up his mind to visit the Curé d'Ars. On entering the church, he succeeded in securing a place from which he had a view of the altar of St. Philomena. M. Vianney had that very moment knelt down at the shrine to recite some of the Hours of his Office, but his back was turned to Antoine Saubin, who longed to see his face. Time went by; our spiritualist was not the most patient of men, and his hours of leisure were not many. "If that priest had the spirit of God, as it is alleged, he would know that I want to speak to him and that I am in a hurry." Scarcely had he formulated this thought within his mind when M. Vianney, turning round, said: "Patience, my friend; I shall be at your disposal in a moment." Saubin's stupefaction was immense. He had two interviews with M. Vianney. Soon his terrors vanished; he recovered the faith of his childhood, and not long after, under the name of Frère Joachim, he took the habit of a Trappist in the monastery of Notre-Dame des Neiges.

M. Camille Monnin, a solicitor of Villefranche, numbered among his acquaintances a fellow-citizen whom the tyranny of human respect kept away from every religious observance. This poor man found himself one day among the crowd that thronged round M. Vianney. Suddenly the Curé d'Ars, who had never before seen the man, made his way through the ranks of pilgrims, and, stopping in front of him, "O my friend," he said in a winning tone of voice, "it is that head of yours that ought to be cured."[20]

"Whilst giving a mission," M. Camelet relates, "I was struck by the devout attitude of a simple railway servant. 'I was converted by the Curé d'Ars,' he told me. 'When I came into this district I heard so much about that priest that I wished to see for myself. I had no intention of going to Confession; I just wanted to gain information. Well, I was so struck by the man's appearance

---

20. M. Camille Monnin, *Procès apostolique continuatif,* p. 249.

that I conceived a desire to speak to him. I entered the sacristy, and he bade me kneel down in his confessional.

"'"My friend," he asked, "how long is it since you were at Confession?"

"'"Ah! it is such a long time, Father, that I cannot remember."

"'"Examine yourself well. It is twenty-eight years."

"'"Twenty-eight years? Twenty-eight years? Yes, that is it."

"'"And you did not receive Holy Communion; you only had absolution."

"'That was also correct. Upon this I felt a quickening of my faith, and so lively did it become that I believe I made a very good Confession, and I promised God never again to give up my faith.'"[21]

One day, under the pretext of sending him on an errand, the Baronne de Belvey despatched to M. Vianney a hardened sinner, who only set foot in the church at Christmas and Easter. It would seem that he had not been to Confession since his first Communion. "How long is it since you were last at Confession?" M. le Curé asked.

"Oh, forty years."

"Forty-four," the saint replied.

The man took a pencil and made a hasty calculation on the plastering of the wall.

"Yes, it is quite true," he admitted, overcome with amazement. The sinner was converted and died a good death.[22]

In 1851, Mlle. Étiennette Vermorel, of Arcinges (Loire), came to Ars for the purpose of making a retreat, which she was anxious to begin by a general Confession. "Father, I have carefully examined myself." The saint allowed her to make her accusation. At last he said: "Is there nothing else that you can think of?" "No, Father, nothing, absolutely nothing." "Very well, my child. Since you wish to leave the confessional as sinless as you were after your Baptism, go and ask Our Lady of the Seven Dolours to

21. *Procès de l'Ordinaire,* p. 1376.
22. "I myself have seen the numbers written on the wall," says the Abbé Claude Rougemont *(Procès continuatif,* p. 789).

make you see what remains to be confessed, and then come back."

So the girl went into the chapel of the *Ecce Homo,* where there is a statue of the sorrowful Mother. There she remembered three sins, which she hastened to confess. "And is that really all, this time?" the man of God asked. "I think so, Father." "But that last fault, my child, which you have forgotten and of which you have never accused yourself?" And he made known to her that sin with the minutest circumstances of time and place. He added: "It is true, you remember nothing else." As a matter of fact, Mlle. Vermorel was just then vainly searching her memory. "When you pass the spot I have mentioned, it will come back to your mind." The saint gave her absolution, assured her that her vocation was that of virginity, but in the world, and sent her away rejoicing. Now, on the return journey she happened to pass by the place where she had once offended God, and the recollection of it came back to her mind. But her happiness was not dimmed, for she knew that all was forgiven.[23]

The Abbé Toccanier relates the following fact: "A youth of Lyons, whose sincerity is proved by his life and conduct, told me that at the age of fifteen he went to Confession to the Curé d'Ars. Suddenly the saint stopped him. 'My friend, you are not telling everything.' 'Well, Father, will you help me? I cannot remember any other sin.' 'What about those candles which you stole from the sacristy of Saint-Vincent to decorate your little shrine?' He was quite right."[24]

A man of the *département* of La Drôme, whose wife was sick, came to consult the great healer of Ars, as men consult a physician. He was told that he could only see him in the confessional. So into the confessional he went, without much enthusiasm, however. Our pilgrim was slightly disfigured. He had once been mixed up in a case of murder, when he was found wounded, in a ditch. He

23. "I have this account from Mlle. Vermorel herself," says M. Ball. "She is now sixty-three years of age, and I have every reason to believe in her perfect veracity."
24. *Procès apostolique in genere,* p. 174.

was arrested on suspicion and imprisoned whilst awaiting trial. To his utter amazement, the servant of God now recalled to his memory the blows, the ditch, and the imprisonment. The man grasped the fact that he had to deal with no ordinary physician. Moved by those revelations, he became converted and never hesitated to tell his tale to whosoever wished to hear it.

A great many persons were advised by M. Vianney either to embrace religion or to settle in the world, though supernatural intuition was not evident in every decision that he made. Thus many young men—perhaps some sixty of them—were told by him: "Become a Brother of the Christian schools, and you will be the instrument of much good." "He took much interest in our congregation of the Holy Family," says Frère Gabriel, its founder and first superior; "he found for us some forty postulants." He sent, perhaps, as many as twenty to La Trappe, assuring them that this was their real vocation. To one of those youths, who quailed at the prospect of such a sacrifice, he put this question: "Those who are already in the monastery, are they not likewise made of flesh and bones?" He left the penitent to draw his own conclusion. In those various circumstances M. Vianney's natural prudence and his fine judgement may have sufficed to enlighten him. But, as we have seen, in certain instances he was favored with the illumination of a prophet.

The life of the Curé d'Ars coincides with a period when Catholic enterprises underwent a great development. He was consulted about the opportuneness and the chances of success of most of them. Here also he proved a wise counsellor and even a prophet whose previsions have stood the test of time.

In 1848, before founding the monastery of La Pierre-qui-Vire, Père Muard consulted M. Vianney. "Your undertaking is the work of God," the saint told him; "it will certainly succeed. Difficulties must not deter you."

Some time after the Christmas of 1856, which he used to call the *day of his conversion,* Père Chevrier still hesitated to devote himself, soul and body, to the rescue of destitute children. So he took the road to Ars. "O my child," the Curé told him, "your thoughts are inspired by Heaven. You will meet with many difficulties, but if you have courage and perseverance you will reap a plentiful harvest of souls." Père Chevrier understood the message. He persisted, and thus founded—God knows at what cost—the *Providence du Prado,* which is doing untold good.

M. Vianney never met Mlle. Eugénie Smet, who, as Mère Marie de la Providence, was to establish throughout the world the Institute of the Helpers of the Holy Souls; yet every time her name was mentioned in his hearing he used to say: "Oh, I know her!" About 1850 the young woman—she was then twenty-five years of age—conceived the idea of founding an association whose prayers and good works would all be applied to the Holy Souls. She understood from the very start that, to achieve success in such an undertaking, souls were required who were dead to self and wholly given to God. But was it necessary to found a new Order, and must she be its first religious? Mlle. Smet, who was timidity and sensitiveness personified, trembled at the prospect. When she consulted Mgr. Chalandon, Bishop of Belley, he advised her to consult the Curé d'Ars. The saint dictated his answer to M. Toccanier: "An Order for the benefit of the Holy Souls! I have long been waiting for it! Let her establish it as soon as ever she wishes. Yes, let her be a religious and let her found this new Order: it will spread rapidly in the Church."

There were no resources of any kind, however; and then it meant complete separation from beloved parents who obstinately withheld their consent. "Go on with it," was the holy Curé's message; "all will be well; moreover, those tears of too natural an affection will soon dry up." On November 21, 1855, Mlle. Smet unexpectedly secured her mother's consent. For a time she had to feel her way; trials and sufferings were not spared her, but in the end the Helpers of the Holy Souls, even during M. Vianney's lifetime, established themselves firmly in Paris, whence their institute spread to other parts of France, and later on to Belgium, England, Austria, Italy, the Far East, and America. It would seem that M. Vianney had a special love for this religious family, and, under God, it is to him that the Sisters attribute their existence and their success.

From the archives of the sanctuary of Ars we gather that some twenty undertakings—congregations, missions, confraternities, works for the young, pilgrimages, orphanages—owe their creation or their continuation to the inspiration of M. Vianney. "Have a pure intention,"[25] was his advice to founders and superiors. "Be humble. You will prosper in the measure in which you trust in Providence."[26] "Make less noise in the newspapers, but a little more at the door of the tabernacle."[27] Nor was he afraid to dissuade from undertakings of which he foresaw the failure or uselessness. "If every beneficent plan could be sure of his approval," says the Abbé Toccanier, "every project that offered no guarantee of real usefulness he rejected."

One question presents itself before we close this chapter on the intuitions and predictions of the Curé d'Ars. Did our saint predict any events of importance concerning the Church, France, society, such as persecutions or wars? This question has already received several judicious replies. We reproduce one of these, because, after a prolonged study of documents, it adequately expresses what we think on the subject.

In 1904, when the *law* of separation between Church and State was preparing, M. Joseph Vianney wrote as follows:

"If during his lifetime nothing gave rise to so many and varied discussions as the struggles of the Curé d'Ars with the devil, nothing, since his death, has caused greater stir than his predictions. And since people only lend to the rich, many a prophecy that he never made has been fastened upon him. Even today no event of any conse-

25. Words addressed to the Abbé Flèche, founder of a work for youth at Mâcon.
26. Words spoken to Père Chevrier *(Procès apostolique continuatif,* p. 775).
27. To the Abbé Griffon, founder of the orphanage of Seillon.

quence for the Church in France takes place on which he is not supposed to have expressed an opinion beforehand. Thus it comes about that, without realizing how such temerity compromises his memory, people lightly bandy about, as coming from him, utterances of very doubtful authenticity."[28]

When, in the course of the Great War, the struggle became protracted beyond all previous calculation, prophecies were once more circulated as having been uttered by M. Vianney, which, by reason of their definiteness and opportuneness, had every appearance of having been fabricated.[29] One in particular caused a great sensation, for it looked like the promise of a victorious *revanche.* This prophecy, which has since then been explained, amplified, analyzed, and modified in a dozen ways, was attributed to the Curé d'Ars by Frère Gaben, a Lazarist; however, it does not bear a satisfactory guarantee of authenticity.[30]

As regards alleged prophecies, the Curé d'Ars himself was forever recommending caution. "The pilgrims," says the Comtesse des Garets, "were always pressing him to state his opinion on political questions. He kept silence. Yet statements were attributed to him; even totally false prophecies were circulated under his name, to his great distress. 'Poor Curé d'Ars! How they make him talk, though he says nothing!' Things went so far that an imperial police official came from Lyons to question the Mayor of Ars concerning a prophecy attributed to M. Vianney, which had caused no small stir." We know how the inquiry ended. The saint and the commissary of police spoke not of politics, but of very different matters. It would seem that

---

28. *Le Bienheureux Curé d'Ars,* p. 157. "To my mind the servant of God made no real prophecies concerning public events, but he often made known to particular persons events that subsequently happened to them." (Marthe Miard, *Procès apostolique continuatif,* p. 862).
29. *Annales d'Ars,* July, 1921, p. 44.
30. Frère Gaben was born on June 26, 1821, at Boussac (Aveyron). On June 19, 1858, at the age of thirty-seven, he entered the Lazarist novitiate at the mother-house in the rue de Sèvres, where he spent the whole of his religious life, and where he died on March 4, 1881. He had been admitted with reluctance, owing to his complete lack of education, but the Curé d'Ars, whom he visited on two separate occasions in 1858, having assured him that God wanted him there, he insisted so much that the superiors ended by accepting him.

the officer went to Confession; we are justified in drawing such a conclusion from the tears the man shed at the close of that unusual interview.[31]

There were times, however, when M. Vianney gave manifest signs of supernatural knowledge.

M. Jules de Maubou relates that when at Ars in 1849 he met M. Sanchez Remon, an exiled Carlist officer. They conversed whilst walking up and down in the village square. The Spaniard indulged in some violent recriminations against Pius IX, who had just fled to Gaëta. He called him a "*pape libéral*" and reproached him with having received, at the time of his elevation to the Supreme Pontificate, the acclamations of the demagogues. In his opinion, the Pope was no longer worthy to occupy the chair of St. Peter. "I did not share these opinions," says M. de Maubou, "and after about an hour's walk we parted." All this time M. Vianney had been catechizing in the church. When he came out of the presbytery, after his midday meal, the saint saw the nobleman. "O my friend," he observed, "how different are the ways of God from the ways of men! You have been told this morning that when the Pope goes back to Rome he should resign his pontifical authority. Well, you will live to see that Pius IX will be one of the greatest Popes that ever ruled the Church."

That same year M. de Maubou visited Ars in order to seek the Curé's advice. He was being pressed to accept a post of some importance in the public administration. The Prince-President had just restored the Panthéon to Catholic worship; he had appointed a commission to study a law on religious education; in a word, it looked as if Louis-Napoleon—the future Napoleon III—were prepared to set up a Government sincerely favourable to religion. "I asked M. Vianney what he thought of the proposal that had been made to me," says M. de Maubou. "After listening with marked interest, he stopped a moment, with eyes lowered, as if seeking inspiration by reflection and

31. See p. 475 of this book.

prayer. Then, turning abruptly towards me, he said with emphasis: 'No, no, my friend, do not accept office at the hands of the new Government. Louis-Napoleon will one day be an enemy of the Church.'"[32]

"On one occasion"—it was in 1856—says Catherine Lassagne, in her *Petit mémoire,* "in the presence of Frère Jérôme and myself, M. le Curé spoke of the imperial family, but I do not remember the circumstances that led him to do so. Of the little Prince Napoleon, born a short while before, he said: 'Ah! he will be very good, that little prince; he has a fine head.' Yet our holy Curé did not read the newspapers and had not seen the portrait of the child."

If we now examine existing documents in order to discover prophecies of distant events, we find, among others, the following two. The one takes us, so we believe, to the very end of time: "After his illness of 1843," M. des Garets assures us, "M. Vianney told me that he greatly loved the Jesuits and that he felt quite confident that their Society would endure."[33]

The other prediction concerns a Protestant country that once merited the title of the "Isle of Saints." On May 14, 1854, the Curé d'Ars received a visit from Bishop Ullathorne of Birmingham.[34] "I was speaking of prayer for England," the Bishop writes, "and was describing in a few words the difficulties and sufferings of our poor Catholics for their faith, when suddenly he interrupted me by opening those eyes—cast into shadow by their depth, when listening or reflecting—and streaming their full light upon me in a manner I can never forget, he said, in a voice as firm and full of confidence as though he were making an act of faith: *Mais, Monseigneur, je crois que l'Église d' Angleterre retournera à son ancienne splendeur.* ('I believe that the Church in England will recover her ancient splendour'). I am sure he firmly

32. These two incidents are contained in a *Letter* written on September 8, 1878, by M. de Maubou to Canon Ball, at that time curé of Ars.
33. *Procès de l'Ordinaire,* p. 891.
34. These details are taken from a letter written in Lyons on the very evening of May 14, 1854 *(Letters of Archbishop Ullathorne,* p. 52, Burns and Oates).

believes this, from whatever source he has derived the impression."

With regard to Ars, that village so wonderfully transformed by the grace of God, it has been affirmed that its Curé prophesied for it a dark and gloomy future. We read in Émile Baumann's book, *Trois villes saintes,* that M. Vianney predicted that in less than a century after his death Ars would have become what it had been when he arrived in the village.

No letter, no contemporary memoir or statement, no deposition in the process of canonization, hints at the existence of so pessimistic an oracle. At all events, it would require no small amount of good will to recognize a prophecy of this kind in a very obscure passage of the *Petit mémoire* of Catherine Lassagne:

"It was (in 1845) on the day when M. Vianney announced that M. Raymond, curé of Savigneux, was to be his assistant. 'Ars is like a big tree,' he said in his instruction. 'If you cut the root, the tree will fall; or, if you prefer, it is like well-risen dough which subsides and dwindles.' No one understood what he meant!"[35]

Considering the date and other circumstances, only one interpretation seems to fit these words. M. Vianney was not thinking of his own people and their future religious history, but of the ceaseless stream of penitents, the flow of which would cease on the day when he himself should disappear. It is certain that if the Abbé Raymond, who aspired to take his place, had had his wish in 1845, or even later, Ars would have "dwindled"—that is, the village would have lost much of its importance. The *pilgrimage* would have followed M. Vianney wherever he might have fixed himself. This is proved by what happened in 1843, when he "fled" to Dardilly. Since the saint remained at his post to the last, notwithstanding his craving for solitude, the root was not cut and the tree did not fall.

The mighty tree still stands erect in the very midst of

35. *Petit mémoire,* troisième rédaction, p. 102.

Ars. We shall see presently how the pilgrimage survives its founder, even though in another form. As for the parish, up till now it has cherished the teaching of M. Vianney as men cherish the last will of a venerated father.

Chapter 27

THE MIRACLES OF THE CURÉ D'ARS

ONE day—probably in September, 1843—Marguerite Humbert, of Écully, paid a visit to her cousin, the parish priest of Ars. In the course of conversation, M. Vianney remarked that "God is always almighty; He can at all times work miracles and He would work them now as in the days of old were it not that faith is wanting!"[1]

And yet the servant of God was aware that extraordinary things happened in his parish; at times he even admitted that much good was being done there, but he ascribed everything to God and the saints, especially St. Philomena. When describing the beginnings of the pilgrimage, we explained how the Curé d'Ars, amazed at his supernatural powers and disconcerted by the veneration of which he was the object on the part of the crowd, felt happy to bring to the front the youthful virgin martyr and to hide himself under her shadow. However, his success in this respect was never complete. The crowd, no doubt, trusted in the intercession of St. Philomena and hailed her miracles, but many thought that her prayers were only heard when they were mingled with those of the holy Curé. "I do not work miracles," he would protest, "I am but a poor ignorant man who once upon a time tended sheep. Address yourselves to St. Philomena; I have never asked anything through her without being answered." Obviously he forgot that the fact of being invariably heard by Heaven is a guarantee of a high degree of holiness, nor did he notice that many prodigies

1. *Procès de l'Ordinaire,* p. 1325.

took place after his own personal blessings or the laying-on of his hands.

He sought but one thing: the glory of God through the salvation of souls. There was his true mission and he fully realized it. Hence he attached a quite secondary importance to miracles of bodily healing, whereas he greatly esteemed miracles of conversion.[2] "I feel very much inclined to forbid St. Philomena to work miracles on behalf of the body," he said one day. "She must cure souls before all else. This poor corruptible *corpse* is not worth much. But if she must heal the sick, then for mercy's sake let her do so elsewhere." Those visible, material prodigies drew too many people to Ars. The saint's humility suffered from such a concourse.

"Monsieur le Curé," the Abbé Toccanier told him one day, "a rumor, unfavorable to you, is being spread."

"'What is it, comrade?"

"It appears that you have forbidden St. Philomena to work any more miracles here."

"That is quite true," he replied. "It causes too much talk. I have asked the Saint to cure souls here to her heart's content, but to heal bodies elsewhere. This time she has heard me: several sick people have come here to begin their novena; they finished it at home, where they were cured, unseen, unknown!"[3]

It almost looks as if he had made a bargain with his favorite saint. However, unluckily for him, the miracle frequently happened at the very beginning of the novena. In that case he would "scold" the Saint, as for instance, after the cure of a little cripple: "*St. Philomena has broken her word.* She should have cured the child elsewhere!"

Then a sudden change would come over him. His exquisite sensitiveness made him fear lest he should have given

---

2. "Divine power meets with no obstacle when it raises the dead to life, but in the resurrection of a soul it seems to clash with the very laws which its own self gave to free will, since the sinner may refuse to be converted. Hence it is said that the omnipotence of God is shown forth more admirably in the conversion of a sinner than in the creation of the world." (Bl. Raymond of Capua, *Life of St. Catherine of Siena*).
3. *Procès apostolique ne pereant,* p. 288.

pain to the dear Saint. "Why do you forbid her to cure people?" Catherine Lassagne once asked him; "do you imagine that she is pleased?" "Oh! for three nights I did think that something was wrong, that something was missing; St. Philomena seemed to reproach me with forgetfulness, so I promised to pray to her a little more."

When the pilgrims saw the Curé's apparent neglect of St. Philomena, they in their turn had less frequent recourse to her. Then there would be little "scenes" between the saint on earth and the Saint in Heaven, of which only the Angels were the witnesses.

A cure had taken place whilst M. Vianney was saying Mass at the altar of the holy martyr. He returned to the sacristy without having noticed anything out of the ordinary. Whilst he was busy autographing the pictures that had been laid on the vestment press, the Abbé Raymond approached and gave him the news. "Monsieur le Curé," he added, "St Philomena has been resting for quite a while."

"Eh! that is just why I have scolded her during my Mass; I said to her: 'Great Saint, if you perform no more miracles, you will forfeit your reputation!'"[4]

If we examine the numerous depositions that are found in the *process* of canonization, or the documents preserved at Ars, it becomes evident that the prodigies which surrounded the head of our saint with an anticipated radiance were really miracles wrought in conjunction with another—viz., St. Philomena. When he thought that a certain cure was desirable, M. Vianney formulated his wish either by word of mouth or only within his heart, after which he left it to St. Philomena to obtain its realization from God. That is why he was wont to call her his *chargée d'affaires,* his *intermediary,* his *consul with God.* Most of the miracles of Ars seemed to have originated in this way, but there were instances when God, so to speak, did not give the holy martyr time to inter-

4. *Procès de l'Ordinaire,* p. 334.

vene, so that her great friend was unable to attribute to her miracles that he himself had wrought.

We have already mentioned poor Soeur Dosithée, a nun of the *Providence* of Vitteaux.[5] She was consumptive, and the doctor had declared that "she would go at the fall of the leaf." When M. Vianney noticed her in the midst of the crowd, he summoned her to his confessional before her turn. "Sister, why do you wish to be cured?" he asked. She told him why. "Very well, go and ask for your cure in the chapel of St. Philomena; I will pray for you in the meantime." Soeur Dosithée prayed to the saint, and at once became conscious of an improvement. This was in May, 1853, when the Sister was twenty-five years old. She died at the *Providence* of Vitteaux on February 11, 1914, at the age of eighty-six.

During the course of the very serious illness which, in May, 1843, threatened to carry off M. Vianney, Mme. Claudine Raymond-Corcevay, of Chalon-sur-Saône, came to Ars in order to obtain her cure. She suffered from laryngitis and bronchitis and was unable to utter a word without experiencing pains in her throat as acute as if she had been burned with a red-hot iron. Intercourse with the persons around her was only possible to her by writing on a slate. In fact, it was by this means that she addressed herself to M. Vianney on the morning when, as a convalescent, he left his room for the first time to go into the church. "My child," he told her, "earthly remedies are useless to you; far too many have already been applied to you. Yet the good God wishes to cure you; address yourself to St. Philomena. Put your slate on her altar; compel her; tell her that if she is not willing to restore your voice to you, she should give you her own!" "At once," as the lady relates, "I went and prostrated myself at the feet of the little saint, and at the end of my prayer I was cured. I had not spoken for two years, and for six years I had endured atrocious pains. On returning to the house of Mme. Favier, with whom I lodged, I read aloud before

5. See p. 303 of this book.

several people a few pages of a book which treated of confidence in Our Blessed Lady. I was indeed cured." On August 11 of that same year, the feast of St. Philomena, Mme. Raymond caused the church of Ars to resound with the notes of the beautiful voice that had been so wonderfully restored to her.[6]

In 1863, Mme. Gérin, M. Vianney's sister, related the following incident: "My grand-daughter, called, like me, Marguerite, suffered from a growth in the throat. The physicians had acknowledged their failure to cure her. So it was decided to take her to her uncle, the Curé d'Ars. My brother bade us make a novena to St. Philomena; no improvement ensued, however. He told us to make another, and he prayed with us. During the night of the eighth day of the novena the child became very sick. Presently she felt she was cured, and the disease never came back."[7]

A girl from the neighborhood of Charlieu (Loire) was paralyzed on one side. Though she was able to drag herself along, her left arm was quite useless. She was about to relate to the man of God a long tale of woe when he stopped her with the injunction: "Go and talk about all this to St. Philomena!" So she made her way through the crowd, as best she could, to the altar of the saint. "Restore my arm to me," she pleaded, "or give me your own!" She was cured at that instant. She who had been paralyzed so long ran to the *Providence* in order to make her friend Catherine Lassagne the sharer of her happiness.

A young man of Feurs (Loire) of the name of Baron, in consequence of a fall from his horse, had remained doubled up with his head between his knees. He endured agonies. In this pitiful state he was taken to Ars. "Address yourself to St. Philomena," M. Vianney told him. Two of the guardians of the church came each day to fetch the injured youth from the hotel and set him down in the chapel of the virgin martyr. By degrees the youth resumed an erect attitude, and at the end of two months, without

6. *Procès de l'Ordinaire,* p. 1459.
7. *Ibid.,* p. 1026.

any medical intervention, he found himself perfectly cured.

Charles Blazy, of Cébazat (Puy-de-Dôme), could only walk with the help of crutches, his legs being almost completely paralyzed. M. Vianney advised him to make a novena to St. Philomena, which was, however, without result. The man was wanting in faith. With like dispositions he began a second novena. "Father, do you think I shall be able to leave my crutches here?" "Oh! my friend, you have as yet great need of them." But grace was at work in the soul of Charles Blazy. Would the second novena also prove barren? Its very last day fell on the feast of the Assumption—August 15, 1858. After the saint's Mass the poor invalid dragged himself into the sacristy. "Well now, Father, shall I take my crutches to St. Philomena—yes or no?" "Yes, go my friend!" The helpless man stood up. He was cured. In a transport of joy he raised his now useless crutches high in the air and, passing through the crowd of pilgrims who were in astonishment at what had happened, he offered them to his heavenly physician. On September 8, M. Bazin, curé of Cébezat, wrote as follows: "When Charles Blazy returned from Ars, he was able to do the journey of eighteen kilometers on foot and without fatigue, and today he enjoys perfect health." The fortunate man eventually became a Brother of the Holy Family of Belley.[8]

On Ash Wednesday, February 25, 1857, Anne Dévoluet, a poor woman of Saint-Romain (Saône-et-Loire), came to Ars pushing a shabby hand-cart in which lay her little son, a fine boy of eight years of age who was suffering from hip disease. Entrusting little Jean-Marie to the Vernu family, the courageous woman, wishing to make sure of seeing M. Vianney, and regardless of her exhaustion, decided to spend the first hours of the night in the church porch. When the holy Curé saw her, although he had not previously met her, he said: "Come before the others; you are in a greater hurry." Now a strange thing happened:

8. *Procès de l'Ordinaire,* pp. 179, 751.

the woman made her Confession, but, owing, no doubt, to lack of time, she never even mentioned the little cripple. In her distress she came back for the Curé's Mass, accompanied this time by the child. She secured a place close to the sacristy. No sooner had M. Vianney entered, than the attendant came to close the door. *Mère* Dévoluet had resolutely put her foot in the doorway, however, and whilst she was arguing with Frère Jérôme, the Curé said: "Let her come in!" She threw herself on her knees and lifted up her child for the saint's blessing. "That boy is too big to be carried," the saint observed; "get up, my good woman, and set the little one down." "But he is unable to stand!" "He will be able to do so now. Have confidence in St. Philomena." The holy Curé kissed the child on the forehead; he then said: "Go, good mother; go and pray before St. Philomena; she will cure him for you." When Anne Dévoluet was about to take the cripple in her arms once more, he forbade her: "No, no, let him walk!"

With much difficulty, and held by the hand, the child managed to reach the altar of the holy martyr. He knelt down of his own accord, remaining in that attitude for nearly three-quarters of an hour, without apparent fatigue, directing his eyes in turn to the recumbent statue of St. Philomena and to a small prayerbook which his mother had given him. As for the poor woman, she was bathed in tears and quite unable to pray, for she seemed hardly to realize where she was.

At length the child stood up unaided, saying: "I am hungry!" and he began to walk about. His mother seized his hand, but he escaped and ran in his stockinged feet towards the door. He was eager to go outside; unfortunately it was raining. "Now you see, mother, that you should have brought my sabots!" (The child had already asked for them during the journey.) Taking the boy in her arms, the mother carried him to a shop where sabots were sold. The child was so delighted when he saw himself thus shod that he began to skip and jump, and the rain having now ceased, he remained in the street to play with some children of his own age.[9]

Although Ars was well used to miracles, this one caused a great stir in the village, so that an echo thereof came even to the ears of M. Vianney. It was on this very occasion that he accused St. Philomena of breaking her word![10]

It occasionally happened that the Curé d'Ars worked miracles without a previous invocation of St Philomena—at least, without an external one. The following are a few examples.

"A sick woman had come by the diligence from a village, the name of which I have forgotten," Soeur Saint-Lazare relates. "Supporting herself on her crutches, she waited for the moment when M. Vianney would go by. 'Well now, walk!' said the servant of God. She hesitated. 'Walk, since you are told to do so!' added M. Toccanier, who accompanied the holy Curé. Thereupon the woman laid aside her crutches. 'Take them with you!' M. Vianney commanded, when he saw the commotion in the crowd."[11]

Jean-Claude Viret writes as follows in one of his *Mémoires:* "One day, finding myself at Ars, I went to Confession to M. le Curé. It was about five o'clock in the afternoon. I saw him go into the sacristy leading by the hand a little girl of thirteen or fourteen. The child's eyes were covered with a white bandage. She went into the sacristy with the holy Curé and her mother.

"I watched them attentively. Presently the daughter and the mother came out of the sacristy: there was now no bandage over the girl's eyes. I followed them as they left the church and asked: 'What have you been doing in the sacristy with the holy Curé?' 'Oh, monsieur,' the mother replied, 'my daughter has been blind for two years; she could only just see a glimmer of light; since speaking to the Curé d'Ars she sees the crucifix which she is holding in her hands quite clearly.'

"Whereupon I handed her a prayerbook in order to

---

9. This account is according to the depositions of Anne Dévoluet and her son, Jean-Marie, taken on August 9, 1864 *(Procès de l'Ordinaire,* pp. 1414-1425).
10. *Procès de l'Ordinaire,* p. 1160.
11. *Procès apostolique ne pereant,* p. 768.

ascertain whether she could read its title. The girl replied: 'I can see the characters, but for two years I have read nothing whatever.'

"When I related the incident to M. des Garets, the Mayor of Ars, who was standing near the church door, he showed no surprise. He merely remarked: 'Oh! our holy Curé performs many such miracles!'"

One day in 1854, Mathilde Besançon, a little five-year-old girl of Grenoble, was playing with a companion of some twelve or thirteen years of age. The bigger girl seized the little one by the head near her ears, and lifted her up with such violence that the muscles of the neck were torn. The child was no longer able to hold her head erect without support. After many months, realizing that the injury done was irreparable, her parents took her to Ars for the purpose of praying at the shrine of St. Philomena. Their supplications, however, were of no avail. They subsequently assisted at the Mass of M. Vianney, whose prayers they had solicited. Suddenly, in the middle of the silence which marks the moment of the Consecration, the girl stood up, exclaiming: "O mother, I am cured! Look!" As a matter of fact, she was able to move her head in every direction and without any help whatever.

One day in 1855, Mme. Raymond-Corcevay was kneeling in M. Vianney's confessional. Two years previously, as we have seen, she had been cured of laryngitis. "Can I feel assured," she asked, " that St. Philomena will leave me the power of speech until the end?" "Listen, my daughter," the servant of God replied, "only a few days ago a good country-woman came here with a little girl of seven years of age, who had been dumb from birth. The poor mother was making her Confession when all of a sudden she stopped. 'Go on, my child!' I said. 'Ah! Father, I cannot! Think of it! I have never yet heard my little girl speak. Listen! she is here, near the confessional. Oh! what a grace! what a grace!' and indeed the child was dumb no longer; she was speaking quite distinctly. The poor woman was too overcome to go on with her Confession.

All that she could do was to repeat, with many tears: 'What a grace, my God, what a grace!' "[12]

Mlle. Claudine Venet, of Virégneux, a small village of the canton of Saint-Galmier, in the Loire, was taken to Ars on February 1, 1850. In consequence of an attack of brain fever, she had become completely deaf and blind. M. Vianney had never seen her; no one had introduced her to him. On that February 1, she happened to be standing outside the church as he went by. Without speaking a word, he took her by the hand, led her into the sacristy and made her kneel down in the confessional. He had hardly given her his blessing when her sight and hearing returned. It seemed to her that she had awakened from a long dream. After her Confession, the servant of God made the following amazing prophecy: "Your eyes are healed, but you will become deaf for another twelve years. It is God's will that it should be so!" On leaving the sacristy, Claudine Venet felt her ears closing once more. As a matter of fact, she could no longer hear anything.

The infirmity lasted twelve years, as foretold on this February 1, 1850. Calm and resigned, enjoying the sight that had been restored to her, the stricken woman awaited the day of her deliverance. Great was her emotion when, on January 18, 1862, she felt she was perfectly cured.[13]

In 1855, a girl of Montchanin (Saône-et-Loire) of the name of Farnier, came to Ars to beg from M. Vianney the cure of her paralyzed leg. "My child," the saint told her, "you disobey your mother far too often, and answer her back in a disrespectful manner. If you wish the good God to cure you, you must correct that ugly defect. Oh! what a task lies before you! But remember one thing: you will indeed get well, but by degrees, according as you try to correct that defect." As soon as Mlle. Farnier returned home she endeavored to show more obedience and respect to her mother. Her crippled leg, which had

12. Mme. Claudine Raymond-Corcevay, *Procès de l'Ordinaire,* p. 1460.
13. On August 31, 1864, Mlle. Venet made a pilgrimage of thanksgiving to Ars. After praying for a long time at the holy Curé's tomb, she made her deposition in the presence of M. Ball, who asked her to sign the minute, so amazing did her story seem to him. (Archives of the presbytery of Ars).

been four inches shorter than the other, insensibly grew longer, and at the end of a few years her infirmity had wholly vanished.[14]

"In 1856," M. Hippolyte Pagès relates, "I witnessed the cure of a girl who, as the result of a paralytic stroke, had been dumb for three years. When she had made her Confession, in writing, to the servant of God and received Holy Communion from his hand, she discovered during her thanksgiving that the gift of speech had been restored to her. I have conversed with her and personally verified the cure. 'This is how it happened,' she told me. 'During my thanksgiving I understood that I should be able to speak from the motions made by my tongue to follow the prayers from my heart.'"[15]

A lady of Lyons wished to present to the Curé d'Ars a poor child who had a large wen under one eye. The child was to undergo an operation, but it had been decided first to ask the blessing of the servant of God. Now at the very moment when the saint raised his hand over the little one, the mother seized that venerable hand and applied it to the wen, which vanished instantaneously. The occurrence having caused a stir in the village, M. Vianney endeavored to forestall public opinion. That evening, whilst M. Toccanier and Frère Athanase were accompanying him to his room, he turned to them with the remark:

"Oh! comrades, a fine trick—*une belle farce*—was played upon me today. I felt so ashamed that had I seen a hole anywhere I should have tried to hide in it."

"Indeed! and what happened?" the missionary asked.

"Well, whatever people may say, the good God still works miracles. A lady brought me a child who had a large tumor near his eye. She made me touch it, when it all disappeared."

"This time you will not be able to say that it was St.

---

14. *Mémoire* of the Abbé Marcel Gauthey, December 20, 1901, pp. 3-6: "I was six or seven years old when Mlle. Farnier died. I remember having seen her many times; she showed no trace of lameness."

15. *Procès de l'Ordinaire,* p. 450.

Philomena," M. Toccanier observed.

He appeared somewhat taken aback, but ended by remarking: "Oh, well! after all she may have had something to do with it."[16]

From these words of the Curé we might perhaps infer that when it was a question of a cure, he first invoked the Saint, or that he had some mysterious light concerning the role she played on such occasions. However this may have been, it is certain that he took good care to attribute all graces of healing to the virgin martyr, and to Our Lady all graces of conversion.

The *process* of canonization mentions some thirty miracles at least. Since then other witnesses have come forward with their depositions. We likewise know that thousands of sick people besought the holy Curé to deliver them from their sufferings. Out of so vast a number what was the proportion of those whose prayers were heard? Most of them were not restored to health. The saint had gifts of a higher order for them, for he knew the blessings that accrue from sufferings endured in a spirit of Christian patience. "The greatest cross is to have no cross!" he proclaimed. "So much the better, my friend, so much the better! By this means faith is quickened," he said to Frère Athanase, when the latter enumerated his sufferings to him. "Having accompanied him one day on a sick-call," M. Dufour relates, "I heard him say to the sick man: 'O my friend, I do not know whether to pray for your cure or not. One should not take the cross from shoulders that are so well able to bear it.'"[17]

Whenever he was approached by people who sought a cure, M. Vianney demanded before all else and as an indispensable condition, that the suppliant should believe. "O woman, great is thy faith!" Our Lord exclaimed before

16. Frère Athanase, *Procès apostolique in genere,* p. 233. Abbé Toccanier, *Procès apostolique ne pereant,* p. 332. In his manuscript notes, Frère Athanase adds: "The next day Frère Jérôme said to us: 'You should have seen M. le Curé crossing the square after the child's cure! It was really laughable. He pressed his hands to his cheeks and took long strides, as if he had been beaten by someone.'"
17. *Procès apostolique in genere,* p. 346.

He healed the daughter of the Canaanitish woman. (*Matt.* 15:28). The Curé d'Ars demanded no less from those who expected a miracle. "That is not the way to behave for one who desires to be cured," he said to a young man of Marseilles, suffering from epilepsy, who was as wanting in faith as in morals.[18] "Very well, make a novena of prayers," he said to a woman of Montfleur (Jura) who had journeyed to Ars on behalf of a sick relative; "only," he added with a note of uncertainty in his voice, "I do not know if the good God will hear you, for in that household over there, there is no more religion than in a stable." This was only too true. As for the sick man, he died on the last day of the novena.

A citizen of Nantes was a victim to gout. He was about to set out for Paris, where he was to undergo a very expensive treatment, when a friend of his, the excellent M. Sionnet, *trésorier* of the *fabrique* of St. Nicholas, endeavored to convince him that "the prayers of the Curé d'Ars would yield better results than all the consultations of the best physicians."

However, the sufferer argued and wanted to lay down his own conditions. Frère Athanase was written to and requested to explain matters to M. le Curé. The reply from Ars was as follows "M. le Curé, who can suffer no *ifs* or *buts* where the good God is concerned, has just told me that it will be as well to let that man set out for Paris, for one who lays down conditions whilst seeking to obtain a grace, may be quite sure that he will obtain nothing."

Miracles are signs of divine approval, though sanctity may exist without them. Had he wrought not a single miracle, the Curé d'Ars would yet call for our admiration. His life was in itself a daily prodigy. Ribadeneira, writing of St. Bernard in that volume of the *Lives of the Saints* which the Curé d'Ars was forever reading, says

18. From a *Letter,* dated Jannary 19, 1862, to M. Toccanier from Pierre L_____, the young man here spoken of who, if he was not cured, at least resumed the practice of his religion.

that "the Abbot of Clairvaux was himself the first and the greatest of all his miracles." This sentiment of the old hagiographer has been re-echoed with no less felicity by one of M. Vianney's contemporaries—namely, the worthy Jean Pertinand, the village schoolmaster, who was likewise the saint's friend and his occasional nurse. "The most arduous, most extraordinary, and most prodigious work that the Curé d'Ars accomplished was his own life."[19] And his neighbor of Fareins, the Abbé Dubouis, declares that "without supernatural assistance M. Vianney would have sunk under the crushing weight of his work."[20] "It is humanly inconceivable that, for the space of thirty years, he should have been equal to a task under the weight of which any other priest, however strong he might have been, would have quickly succumbed," says Canon Gardette.[21] "He was visibly helped by God," is the attestation of Père Faivre.[22] In conclusion we quote the opinion of one of the physicians who attended the holy Curé: "Knowing, as I do, his mode of life, I look upon his existence as extraordinary and beyond the range of a natural explanation," was the verdict of Doctor Michel, of Coligny.

Hence we may conclude in the words of Paul Bourget: "No, the era of miracles is not over, but to produce them saints are required—and they are too few."[23]

---

19. *Procès apostolique ne pereant,* p. 866.
20. *Ibid.,* p. 902.
21. *Ibid.,* p. 931.
22. *Ibid.,* p. 1495.
23. *Nouveaux pastels, Un Saint.*

Chapter 28

THE GREAT MYSTICAL EXPERIENCES OF THE CURÉ D'ARS

"I WILL come to the visions and revelations of the Lord . . . the signs of my apostleship . . . signs and wonders and mighty deeds." (*2 Cor.* 12:1, 12). In those words of St. Paul we have a graphic description of the life of the Curé d'Ars at the stage of his existence which our biography has now reached. With the help of documents—few in number but of unimpeachable veracity—we shall endeavor to describe some of the extraordinary favors bestowed upon him from above.

Before enumerating the sublime experiences of his interior life, St. Paul apologized to his loyal friends of Corinth. Assuredly, self-glorification was a perilous thing. But he was compelled to break through his natural reserve because his enemies denied his divine commission. The only way to refute a calumny of this kind was to show how God Himself had put the seal of His approval upon his apostolic labors.

True, the Curé d'Ars was not weighed down by "the solicitude for all the churches." (*2 Cor.* 11:28). Hidden away as he was in an obscure village, he met, with silent resignation, attacks that were aimed solely at his own person.

Whenever occasion warranted, he willingly spoke of his struggles with Hell; but he would never disclose the compensations awarded him by Heaven.

"The servant of God never referred to the divine favors of which he was the object. It was obvious that all inquiries relative to such things vexed and wearied him. When thus questioned he would pour out his heart in transports of love for God, or relate some delightful episode he had read in the *Lives of the Saints,* of whom he always spoke as if he had been personally acquainted with them. Hence, if we know anything at all of his mystical life, we owe the information not to himself, but to those around him."[1]

Occasionally, however, the servant of God betrayed himself, for at times he would be carried away by emotion, or he would fall into one of the traps that were set for his humility. Thus he arrived one day at the *Providence* with a radiant countenance, exclaiming, in the hearing of Catherine Lassagne, who stood astounded: "What a grace! What happiness! What a wonderful thing!"

"But where was it?" she asked after a while.

"In the church . . . in the church!"

He could say no more. The great things that God works within His creatures produce of their very nature silence and wonderment, and that something wholly divine which robs us of all power of utterance.[2]

What was it that the holy Curé had seen in his church that day? Maybe it was that "procession of saints" of which he once spoke to Soeur Catherine Lacand, the mere recollection of which thrilled his soul.

Those who were privileged to assist at his Mass often witnessed how at that hour his whole person became, as it were, transfigured. He was himself aware of the fact, so much so that he bade the orphans of the *Providence* not to look at the priest when he was at the altar. His lively faith and seraphic love "enkindled in him a fire that caused his eyes to flash and his countenance to burn whilst he said his Mass."[3] "When serving his Mass I often noticed that his attitude was so recollected as to give the impression of an ecstasy," says André Trève; and Comte des Garets adds that "one instinctively looked at his feet to see whether they still touched the ground."[4]

The servant of God admitted that at times he required

1. *Procès apostolique ne pereant,* p. 992.
2. Bossuet, *Elévations sur les mystères,* 12ème élévation.
3. Words of General des Garets, nephew of Mlle. d'Ars, to M. le Chanoine Coubé *(Panégyrique du B. Vianney,* August 6, 1918).
4. *Procès de l'Ordinaire,* p. 950.

no nourishment other than the Eucharistic Species—an experience he shared with other saints. "Oh! how hungry I felt during Mass," he told Catherine Lassagne one morning. "When the moment of the Communion came, I said to Our Lord: 'My God, feed my body as well as my soul!'—and the pangs of hunger vanished at once." "I think a time will come when the Curé d'Ars will derive his sustenance from the Holy Eucharist alone," a priest was heard to remark.

Was he favored with visions during his Mass? Did he behold Christ in human form? According to the Abbé Toccanier, "it was generally believed at Ars that he enjoyed the sight of Our Lord's presence in the Eucharist."[5] "After the Consecration, when I hold Our Lord in my hands, I am utterly lost to my surroundings," he himself confessed.[6]

If these words are too vague, the following is a more definite admission: "As soon as we pray for sinners, when Our Lord is on the altar during Mass, He casts towards them rays of light, in order to make them see their misery, and so to convert them." "Wait a moment . . . presently . . . after my Mass," he often said to those who consulted him in the early hours of the morning, as if it were incumbent on him to take counsel with the Lord during the Holy Sacrifice. In this way he informed a girl of Rive-de-Gier, who was one day to be Soeur Marie-Gabriel, of the Visitation of Montluel, that in spite of appearances to the contrary, she was called to the religious life. When he met her on leaving the church, his face was radiant as he exclaimed: "O my child, how happy you are! Our Lord has chosen you for His bride."[7]

One day, after the catechism class, he was taking his frugal meal standing at the dresser which did duty as a table. Believing himself to be alone—he had not noticed that Jeanne-Marie Chanay had preceded him into the kitchen—he began to sigh: "To think I have not seen the

5. *Procès de l'Ordinaire,* p. 118.
6. *Ibid.*
7. *Circular Letters* of the Visitation of Montluel: notice on Mlle. Tonine Grodemouge, in religion, Soeur Marie-Gabriel.

good God since Sunday!" He was startled when Jeanne-Marie, who had heard everything, asked: "So before Sunday you were wont to see Him?" Greatly annoyed at having thus betrayed himself the good saint answered not a word.

About the year 1850 he said in one of his eleven o'clock instructions: "You see! we are altogether earthly, and our faith is so weak that we look at things as if they were three hundred leagues away, or as if God dwelt on the other side of the ocean. If our faith were lively we should most assuredly see Him here, in the Blessed Sacrament. *There are priests who see Him daily during the holy Sacrifice of the Mass.*"[8]

If M. Vianney "saw the good God," how did he behold Him? We do not think that he saw an external apparition; only his mind experienced that which must forever remain ineffable and invisible. As a matter of fact, the holy Curé made a fairly definite statement in an intimate conversation with his dear friend the Abbé Tailhades. In an hour of affectionate confidences he went over the first years of his ministry, "a time of extraordinary graces," he admitted. "At the altar I enjoyed wonderful consolations; I beheld the good God."

"You beheld Him?"

"Oh! I would not say that I saw Him with the eyes . . . but what a grace! what a grace!"[9]

In these words M. Vianney points to something higher than even that lofty contemplation to which choice graces had raised him, something more excellent than even that mystical union in which God gathers the soul to Himself, so that it pours itself into His bosom and enjoys an intimate and sweet experience of His presence.[10] Nor was it a bodily ecstasy during which, according to St. Thomas, "contemplation withdraws the soul from the operation of the senses."[11]

---

8. *MSS. de la Bastie,* p. 25.
9. Abbé Tailhades, *Procès de l'Ordinaire,* p. 1516.
10. Mgr. Convert, *Le Curé d'Ars et les dons du Saint-Esprit,* p. 109.
11. *De Veritate,* q. 10, a. 11.

No contemporary evidence is forthcoming to show that, at the time of his Mass, the Curé d'Ars experienced real raptures. It would not seem that in saying it he ever exceeded the usual time. But there were occasions when he certainly received that sublime favor.

Soeur Marie François, of the third Order of St. Francis of Saint-Sorlin, went to Confession to him during Holy Week in 1849 or 1850. Her accusation concluded, she asked: "Father, what is it God wants of me?" "Ah! my child . . ." a faint and gentle voice murmured from behind the grating.

"That was all. After that," the Sister relates, "M. Vianney spoke as if to himself, for the space of five minutes and in a tongue unknown to me; at any rate I could not understand him. In my astonishment I looked into his face. He seemed to be out of himself, and I thought that he beheld the good God. Deeming myself unworthy to remain in the presence of so great a saint, I withdrew, feeling quite overcome with fear."[12]

In March, 1852, at about half-past one in the morning, the Curé d'Ars summoned to the confessional, before everyone else, Soeur Clotilde, a young nun of the Congregation of the Child Jesus. The light of only one candle lit up that corner of the chapel of St. John the Baptist. But when M. Vianney opened the shutter of the confessional, his penitent saw him wholly enveloped in a transparent and unearthly radiance.

The nun was greatly excited, nevertheless she made her Confession. When she had finished, she said: "Father . . ." "Make your Confession," the saint murmured, still resplendent. Once more the poor Sister went through her accusation.

"Father," she ventured to say once more.

"Make your Confession."

"But I have nothing more to say."

A long pause ensued. At last the Curé came to himself. "My child, have you always been exact in the per-

12. *Procès de l'Ordinaire,* p. 1393.

formance of your penances?" he asked.

At these words the Sister suddenly recollected past negligences that had slipped her memory. She humbly acknowledged the fact, was absolved, and withdrew. She had been in the confessional for nearly an hour. When she issued from it the holy Curé had recovered his normal aspect.

In 1849 Mlle. Marie Roch, of Paris-Montrouge, came to consult M. Vianney. She felt convinced that he alone would be able to ease her severe interior trials. After a long delay she finally succeeded in getting close to the confessional; in fact, she was even able to peer into the dark corner where the saint was seated, and this is what she beheld. The holy priest's face seemed to project two fiery rays, his features being completely hidden by the brightness of their light. But was she not the victim of an hallucination? Yet no delusion appeared possible; she was in perfect possession of her senses, nor could this be a mere play of the sun's light.

As if fascinated by that dazzling countenance, Mlle. Roch gazed at it for at least eight or ten minutes, when it still shone with undimmed radiance. In the end she did not dare to enter the confessional and left the chapel of St. John the Baptist. But the saint had read in her heart. The next day, after the catechism—that is, about noon—he passed near her. He stopped and said: "Fear nothing, my child: all will be well."[13]

What did the Curé d'Ars perceive or experience during those moments when he seemed to be no longer of this earth? He alone could have let us into his secrets, but he always refused to do so. Happily, on at least two or three occasions, a third person was favored with similar visions to his own, and these privileged people were less reticent. Thus we possess clear and circumstantial information concerning at least one of those apparitions.

Mlle. Étiennette Durié, who related the incident that follows, was born at Arfeuille, in the *département* of the

---

13. *Annales d'Ars,* May, 1915, p. 383.

Allier. She was an intelligent woman, reserved and worthy of confidence. She devoted her time to collecting money for the furtherance of M. Vianney's charitable undertakings. On the morning of May 8, 1840, she arrived at Ars the bearer of a considerable sum, destined for the foundation of Masses. Calling first at the *Providence,* where she had some food, she went to the presbytery in order to deliver the money into the hands of him for whom it was intended. The following is Mlle. Duriés own account of what happened:

One o'clock had just struck. M. Vianney was alone in his room, and Catherine Lassagne let me into the presbytery. As I was going up the staircase, I heard M. Vianney's voice as if he were in conversation with someone, so I went up softly and listened. Someone said to him in a very gentle tone of voice: "What do you ask?"

"Ah! my good Mother, I ask for the conversion of sinners, the comfort of those in affliction, the relief of my sick people, especially that of one who has long been suffering and pleads either for death or a cure."

"She will get well," the voice replied, "but a little later."

"On hearing these words I hurried into the room, the door of which had remained ajar. I was suffering from cancer, and felt sure that I was the person under discussion. What was my astonishment on beholding, standing in front of the fireplace, a lady of ordinary stature, clad in a robe of dazzling whiteness, on which were scattered golden roses. Her shoes appeared to be as white as snow. On her fingers shone the brightest of diamonds, and around her head was a wreath of stars which flashed like the sun, so that I was dazzled by their brilliance.

When at last I felt able to raise my eyes to her once more, I saw her smile gently. "My good Mother," I exclaimed, "do take me with you to Heaven!"

"Later on."

"Ah! now is the time, Mother!"

"You will always be my child, and I shall always be a

mother to you." After uttering these words she disappeared. For a while I remained dumbfounded, for I was overcome at the thought that such a grace should have been vouchsafed to me. "Is it possible to witness such wonderful things and yet remain so ungrateful?" I said to myself. When I came to, I noticed M. le Curé still standing at his table, with his hands joined on his breast, his countenance radiant, and his gaze fixed. I feared that he was dead, so I approached and pulled at his cassock. "My God, is it you?" he said.[14]

"No, Father, it is I." And as I uttered the words he came to himself and made a movement. "Where were you, Father? What have you seen?"

"I have seen a lady."

"So have I; who is this lady?"

"If you speak of it," M. Vianney said severely, "you shall never again set foot in this room."

"Shall I tell you what I thought, Father? I thought it was Our Lady."

"And you were not mistaken. . . . So you have seen her?"

"Yes, I have seen her and spoken to her. But now you

---

14. In this scene the Curé d'Ars exhibits all the phenomena of a genuine ecstasy, in which the mystical union no longer acts only on the soul, but likewise upon the body: inaction of the senses, inertness of the body, partial or complete cessation of the action of the heart and lungs, and at times even the symptoms of actual death." (A. Poulain).

All this has been admirably described by St. Teresa, in her Life written by herself (ch. xviii): "The soul, while thus seeking after God, is conscious, with a joy so excessive and sweet, that it is, as it were, utterly fainting away in a kind of trance: breathing and all bodily strength fail it . . . the eyes close involuntarily, and if they are open, they are as if they saw nothing. . . . The ear hears, but what is heard is not understood. The senses are of no use whatever . . . for all bodily strength vanishes and that of the soul increases, to enable it the better to have the fruition of its joys . . . (ch. xviii, 14).

"During rapture, the soul does not seem to animate the body, the natural heat of which is greatly lessened; the coldness increases, though accompanied with exceeding joy and sweetness . . . (ch. xx, 2). Then it is as if the body were dead, perfectly powerless. It continues in the position it was in when the rapture came upon it—if sitting, sitting; if the hands were open, or if they were shut, they will remain open or shut . . . and though they (the senses) have no power to deal with outward things, there remains the power of hearing and seeing; but it is as if the things heard and seen were at a great distance, far away. I do not say that the soul sees and hears when the rapture is at the highest." (ch. xx, 23, 24).

"When Our Lord brings a soul on to this state, He communicates to it of His greatest secrets by degrees. True revelations—the great gifts and visions—come by ecstasies . . ." (David Lewis' translation, ch. xxi, 15).

must tell me in what state you were, for I thought you were dead."

"Oh! no . . . but I was too happy at beholding my Mother."

"My dear Father, I owe it to you if I have seen her! When she comes back, consecrate me to her so that she herself may consecrate me to her divine Son."

The servant of God gave me his promise, adding: "You will be cured."

"But when, Father?"

"A little later. Do not ask so many questions."

In a gentler tone he added: "With the Blessed Virgin and St. Philomena we know where we are."[15]

Was the Curé d'Ars not thinking of this amazing scene when he one day said to a distinguished visitor:

"People would not dare to set foot on such and such a flag-stone in this room if they knew what took place there?"

Two features of the above occurrence should be noted: M. Vianney speaks of the Blessed Virgin and of St. Philomena as one who is accustomed to be visited by them; he promises quite simply to consecrate Mlle. Durié to Our Lady, for he feels sure of fresh apparitions. The latter would like to know more, but the man of God cuts short indiscreet inquiries.

He did not show himself any more communicative during the six years which the Abbé Toccanier spent with him. "One day I told him that people said he saw visions," the latter relates. "All I succeeded in getting out of him was this simple avowal: 'Yes, near the head of my bed I once saw someone dressed in white, who spoke softly to me, like a confessor.'"[16]

If we may give credence to Marianne Renard, who, with her mother, lived in a house adjoining the old presbytery, M. Vianney was favored with visions from the earliest years of his ministry. "At the beginning of the

---

15. *Procès de l'Ordinaire,* p. 1447. Mlle. Étiennette Durié was cured of her cancer at Ars itself, three and a half months later, on August 15.
16. Abbé Toccanier, *Procès apostolique ne pereant,* p. 331.

pilgrimage—viz., towards 1828—a woman came to Ars for the purpose of going to Confession to the servant of God. She entered the church very early in the morning. The sacristy door had been left open, and there she saw M. Vianney conversing with a lady dressed in white. Not daring to enter, she waited outside. At length M. Vianney noticed her presence. 'Why did you not come in at once?' he asked. 'Oh! Father, because you were conversing with a lady.' The servant of God remained silent. When the woman entered the sacristy, the lady had disappeared. The penitent, who had not seen anyone leave the sacristy, took it for granted that M. le Curé had been conversing with Our Blessed Lady."[17]

François Bourdin, who, as we have already seen, was a convert of M. Vianney's,[18] should have had a very clear conscience after seven consecutive Confessions. Nevertheless, after an eighth, as he was about to go to Holy Communion at the Mass of one of the missionaries, he suddenly became anxious: "Had he really been absolved? . . . He had no more than a vague recollection; if he had not been absolved, could he believe himself to be in a state of grace? . . ." Instead of approaching the altar rails, Bourdin took the last place among those waiting to go to Confession. He had learned patience during the long periods of waiting during the past week, so he stayed until the evening. At last he found himself quite close to the blessed door. When the man who was before him left the confessional, François Bourdin entered and knelt down. No one besides himself had come into the sacristy.

Now at that moment M. Vianney was no longer seated on the bench where he heard Confessions. With his back turned to the door, he was conversing with a lady somewhat taller than himself and who was likewise standing. She was dressed in pale blue and appeared to be of marvellous beauty. The holy Curé had not noticed the penitent who was just then coming in, but the lady bestowed a kindly look upon the newcomer. The mysterious collo-

17. *Procès apostolique ne pereant,* p. 738.
18. See p. 308 of this book.

quy lasted about half an hour, yet there was no sound of words. All this time Bourdin remained on his knees, on the prie-Dieu, his head in his hands. "He felt as if an immense weight were taken off his chest, and experienced a sensible impression of the presence of grace in his heart."

All of a sudden the priest seized the penitent's arm. Bourdin rose and looked for the apparition. It had vanished, and the sacristy door was still shut. Instead of sitting down to hear him, the holy Curé dismissed him with much kindness: "Go, my friend, go in peace! you are certainly in the friendship of God."[19]

There can be no doubt that stories of this kind circulated in the parish and among the pilgrims. "People were persuaded," says Mme. de Cibeins, "that M. le Curé had visions, and that he enjoyed, in particular, apparitions of the Blessed Virgin Mary."

However, we have heard him himself allude to other visions; for instance, he mentioned St. Philomena. He again spoke of such apparitions towards the end of his life. In May, 1859, he was conversing with the Baronne de Belvey in the little reception room which had been set up at the entrance to the presbytery. The conversation took on a character of great intimacy, and the holy old man became reminiscent. "I was at a loss to know the will of God concerning the new church," he confided to the baronne, whose absolute discretion he knew. "Should I put all our resources into that building and so sacrifice the work of parochial missions? Whilst I was at prayer St. Philomena appeared to me; as she came down from Heaven she looked beautiful, and was enveloped in a bright, white cloud. Twice she told me: 'Nothing is more

---

19. The account, given by M. Joly, curé of Benonces (Ain), which contains these astonishing details, is preserved in the archives of the presbytery of Ars. M. Joly knew François Bourdin quite well, for he lived in retirement in his parish, near the Chartreuse des Portes. In 1900, when this account was drawn up, Bourdin was nearly eighty years of age, but still in possession of all his faculties: "The old man enjoys universal esteem because of his piety and virtue," the Abbé Joly writes; "his testimony is above suspicion." We may note once more that in this vision also M. Vianney's conduct shows all the essential phenomena that accompany ecstasies and raptures.

precious than the salvation of souls.' By this she meant the work of the missions." "Whilst he was speaking," says Mme. de Belvey, "M. Vianney stood erect, his eyes were raised to heaven, and his face was radiant, so enraptured was he by the remembrance of that heavenly visit."

M. Vianney's intimates suspected that he slept but little. On his own confession it was known that the devil often kept him awake. But were those repulsive visits without their compensations? How could the secret be drawn from him? With all his adroitness in this respect, M. Toccanier ascertained but little. "You likewise pray at night?" he remarked in a casual way. "Yes, my friend, if I wake up. I am old now; I have not long to live, and I must make use of every moment. . . ." "You lie on the bare floor and you sleep but little?" *"Oh! one does not always lie on the bare floor. . . ."* An awkward pause ensued: the holy Curé realized that he had said too much. Yet he nearly forgot himself a second time. "Really, Monsieur le Curé," the missionary remarked, "all these missions that you are founding make it quite clear that the good God wants you here." "O my friend, *there is much more besides!"* But there were to be no further confidences that day; M. Vianney quickly changed the subject. This incident took place on November 22, 1856.

Perhaps the mysterious brightness seen in the sky of Ars by a seminarist, who eventually died at Notre-Dame d'Aiguebelle, was but the reflection of the visions that comforted the holy Curé in the hours of the night. However that may be, the young Abbé Tissot—later on Père Marie-Barthélemy—who was spending his vacation at the house of Pertinand, the schoolmaster, on looking out of a first-floor window about midnight, beheld a great brightness over the presbytery; whence he concluded that something unusual was taking place within its walls.[20]

Certain occurrences, which have every appearance of true revelations, seem to show that, by divine favor, the

20. Catherine Lassagne, *Petit mémoire,* troisième rédaction, p. 105.

eyes of the Curé d'Ars more than once gazed into the mystery of the next world. The Comtesse des Garets made the following attestation:

"My personal conviction is that M. Vianney was in direct touch with the dead, and that he knew what was happening in Purgatory. In the Crimean War one of my sons gave his life for France. We no sooner received this sad and glorious news than our holy Curé greatly reassured us with regard to the salvation of our Joanny. A few days later, in his catechism, the following remark escaped him in reference to our beloved boy: 'It is just like that poor little one . . . he is in Purgatory, but for a short time.' Nevertheless, we were not without anxiety; had our child seen a priest before his death? Now, after six months we received a letter from an officer which stated positively that, after being wounded, our son had made his Confession, and that he died an edifying death. My husband hastened to impart the news to M. le Curé, who merely remarked: 'Oh! I am very glad for his mother's sake; but, as for me, that letter does not add to what I have always believed.'"[21]

A young nun of the *département* of Seine-et-Loire, after consulting M. Vianney about her own vocation, wished to know whether her father, who had died in consequence of an accident, was saved. "Yes, my child, but he is very *low down.* Pray much for him."

About the year 1849, Mme. Meunier, of Perreux, near Roanne, came to Confession to the Curé d'Ars. "My child," he told her even before she had uttered a word, "your husband works on Sunday. Tell him from me to give up that bad habit. A time will come when he will feel glad to have listened to me." And he added: "It is wrong to make mutual promises to return after death to give information about the next world, because the good God but rarely grants the power to do so." As a matter of fact, M. and Mme. Meunier had made a promise of this kind to each other. As regards the other matter, the man obeyed

---

21. *Procès de l'Ordinaire,* pp. 901-902.

the injunction of the holy Curé and refrained from work on forbidden days. The following year, on Trinity Sunday, as he was driving home from Vespers, his horse suddenly shied and threw him on the road. He died without the Sacraments and without recovering consciousness.

Seven weeks after the accident Mme. Meunier came to confide to M. Vianney her fears as to the salvation of her husband. He had no sooner opened the shutter than he said: "My child, you think that some members of your family are damned, but I do not think so." "Father, will the person in whom I am interested have to stay long in Purgatory?" "Wait a moment." Having said this, M. Vianney withdrew once more into the recesses of the confessional. The penitent heard him speaking softly to himself, for nearly five minutes, as if he were conversing with someone who remained invisible to her. Then, drawing near to the grate: "Poor bread-winner!"[22] Mme. Meunier had not yet told him that she had five children and that the death of her husband left her penniless. "He only wants a few Masses to get to Heaven. He will be there in three years' time, and you will learn it from one of your children."

Three years later one of the children, still in its tenderest years, died far from Perreux, in the house of an aunt. The night of the child's death, the mother had a dream in which she saw the little one going up to Heaven with his father. Thinking that the child was in good health, Mme. Meunier paid no heed to the dream, but when she heard that the little angel had taken wings, she remembered the prediction of the Curé d'Ars.[23]

People sometimes threw themselves at the feet of the saint when despair had seized upon their hearts. Perhaps one they loved dearly had been taken from them, a sinner, alas! whom they held to be lost forever. But M. Vianney was able to see farther than they.

---

22. "Pauvre père nourricier!"
23. "All that precedes," M. Ball writes at the conclusion of his account, "was related on June 10 (year not given) in the presence of M. Toccanier and Soeur Saint-Lazare, by Mme. Meunier herself, who at that time lived at Montagny (Loire)."

"A pious lady"—such is the only description given of her by the Baronne de Belvey, who relates the story—"had a husband who did not practice his religion. She prayed much for his conversion, for he suffered from acute heart disease and was liable to die suddenly. The lady loved to decorate a statue of Our Lady which she had in her house. Her husband took pleasure in gathering flowers for her, knowing full well to what use she would put them. He died an apparently sudden death and without the Sacraments, and it would seem without having recovered consciousness. His wife's grief was dreadful to behold; she fell ill, and her friends even feared for her reason. At length she was able to go to Ars, though she lived at a great distance from that village. 'Madame,' the holy Curé told her at this their very first meeting, 'have you forgotten the bouquets of flowers that you were wont to offer to the Blessed Virgin?' These words which at first astounded her, reassured and comforted her, and restored to her health of body and peace of mind."[24]

One day the Abbé Guillaumet, for many years Superior of the Immaculate Conception at Saint-Dizier (Haute-Marne), was on his way to Ars. It was in 1855 or 1856. The only subject of conversation in the compartment was the marvels that were taking place in the blessed village; M. Vianney's name was on the lips of all. Seated beside the priest was a lady in deep mourning, who was listening with rapt attention. On reaching the station of Villefranche, M. Guillaumet was about to alight when his neighbor opened her lips to ask: "Monsieur l'Abbé, will you allow me to accompany you to Ars? I may as well go there, as elsewhere. . . I am travelling to distract my thoughts."

The priest consented to act as guide to the stranger when once they had reached the village. The carriage which they took at Villefranche set them down right in front of the church. The eleven o'clock catechism was drawing to a close, so M. Guillaumet led the lady to a

24. *Procès apostolique ne pereant,* p. 234.

place between the church and the presbytery. They had not long to wait. Suddenly the Curé d'Ars appeared, still wearing his surplice. He stopped in front of the lady in black, who, following the example of the crowd, had gone down on her knees. He bent over her and whispered into her ear: "He is saved!" The woman started. M. Vianney repeated: "He is saved!" A gesture of incredulity was the only reply of the stranger. Whereupon the saint, stressing each word, repeated: "I tell you he is saved. He is in Purgatory, and you must pray for him. Between the parapet of the bridge and the water he had time to make an act of contrition. Our Blessed Lady obtained that grace for him. Remember the shrine that you put up in your room during the month of May. Though your husband professed to have no religion, he sometimes joined in your prayers; this merited for him the grace of repentance and pardon at the last moment."

M. Guillaumet could not grasp the purport of these words, though he heard them distinctly, since he was close to the widow. Only on the following day was he informed about the marvellous lights that God vouchsafed to his servant. His sorrowful fellow-traveller spent the hours following upon her interview with M. Vianney in solitude and prayer. Her appearance was changed; she had recovered peace.

When the moment of departure came she went to thank M. Guillaumet. "The physicians prescribed that I should travel for the sake of my health," she told him; "in reality I was in black despair because of the tragic death of my husband. He was an unbeliever, and my one object in life was to bring him back to God. I did not get the time. He committed suicide by drowning himself! I could only think of him as lost. Oh! were we never again to meet? Now you heard what the Curé d'Ars told me more than once: 'He is saved!' So I shall see him again in Heaven! . . . Monsieur l'Abbé, I am cured!"[25]

25. This fact was taken down by Mgr. Convert on July 28, 1922, at the dictation of M. le Chanoine Maucotel, Superior of the Grand Séminaire of Verdun, who had it direct from M. Guillaumet.

Only one solitary case is quoted where M. Vianney seemed to entertain fears for the eternal fate of a dead person. No doubt, if he made other confidences of a like kind, the sorrowful secret will have been well kept. "A certain person from Paris or its vicinity," says M. Hippolyte Pagès, "questioned him about the soul of a relative of hers who had recently died. She received this answer, without further comment: 'He refused to go to Confession at the moment of death.' It was only too true; the dying man had refused the priest, a circumstance which M. Vianney had had no means of knowing beforehand."[26]

Several times, on the other hand, the Curé d'Ars greatly comforted those in grief, by assuring them that the departed soul was already enjoying eternal bliss. "Oh! what happiness to have parents in Heaven!" he said to a girl whose mother had just died. "Your mother practiced great patience during her long illness. God has received her, and she is praying for you."[27]

Mme. des Garets relates the following incidents: "Mlle. de Bar, a relative of ours, had lost her mother, whose life had been one long series of trials. She visited Ars. At the very moment when she entered the sacristy M. Vianney approached her and said: 'O mademoiselle, so you have lost your mother? . . . She is in Heaven!'

"'That is my hope, Monsieur le Curé.'

"'Oh! yes, she is in Heaven.' And when Mlle. de Bar presented her mother's rosary to have it blessed by him, he took it in his hands and kissed it reverently, as he would a relic."

"Having spent her life in the practice of good works, Mlle. de Murinais passed away after a prolonged and painful illness. I asked M. Vianney's prayers on her behalf. 'It is unnecessary to pray for her, my child,' was his reply. And when the sister-in-law of the deceased asked him to say some Masses for the repose of her soul, he refused with the words: 'She has no need of them.'"[28]

26. *Procès de l'Ordinaire,* p. 449.
27. *Ibid.*
28. *Procès de l'Ordinaire,* p. 902.

Other supernatural favors also—such as are met with in the lives of the greatest mystics—fell to the lot of the Curé d'Ars.

Thus he received in a plentiful measure the *gift of tears.* According to St. Teresa, these tears spring from a sentiment of ineffable tenderness towards God, or from the interior martyrdom endured by the soul when it sees God being offended. "Those tears are caused by God and shed in ecstasy," Lacordaire writes. M. Vianney could never speak of sin and sinners without shedding tears. He sobbed all the time he was making the Stations of the Cross.[29] When he distributed Holy Communion, tears would often trickle down upon his chasuble. In the last years of his life in particular, he could never preach about the Eucharist, the goodness and love of God, the happiness of Heaven—those were his favorite topics—without being stopped by his tears. He shed tears before the simplest spectacle of nature if it reminded him of the goodness of God or the obstinacy of sinners. "The other day," he said in a sermon preached in his first years, "as I was returning from Savigneux, the little birds were singing in the woods. I began to weep. Poor little creatures, I thought within myself, the good God has made you to sing, and you sing. And man, who was created that he might love God, loves Him not!"[30]

In the lives of some saints we read that at times a mysterious power raised them above the earth, and that they remained in the air without any natural support, This phenomenon is called *levitation.* At least on one occasion Ars witnessed this spectacle. Canon Gardette, chaplain to the Carmelites of Chalon-sur-Saône, testified to the fact under oath:

"One day my brother, who is curé of Saint-Vincent at Chalon-sur-Saône, came with me to Ars. In the evening, whilst the servant of God recited night prayers, we took up a position facing the pulpit. About the middle of the exercise, when M. Vianney was saying the act of charity,

29. Jean Pertinand, *Procès de l'Ordinaire,* p. 384.
30. *Procès de l'Ordinaire,* p. 775.

my brother, whose eyesight is excellent, saw him rise into the air, little by little, until his feet were above the ledge of the pulpit. His countenance was transfigured and encircled by an aureola. My brother looked round, but witnessed no commotion among the assistants. So he kept quiet, but as soon as we came out of the church he could no longer refrain from speaking of the prodigy he had beheld with his own eyes: he spoke of it to all who wished to hear, and with much eagerness."[31]

Thus the Abbé Gardette not only saw M. Vianney lifted up by an unseen power, he also beheld his forehead encircled by an aureola, that mysterious anticipation of Heaven's own brightness which at times irradiates the saints whilst they are as yet on earth.

Let us penetrate yet farther into the mysteries of God, and see whether we may find in the life of the Curé d'Ars proofs of his having reached, by degrees and after manifold purifications, "that calm and enduring union with God, which is called *transforming union,* which appears to be the last stage of mystical union and the proximate preparation for the beatific vision."[32] *Rapture* is but the passing union of the soul with God—a simple *spiritual espousal.* Beyond it there is that transforming union, which is so intimate, so serene, so indissoluble that, in the language of the mystics, it is called *spiritual marriage.* By this intimate union "the soul is so *transformed,* that she forgets herself so that henceforth she can only think of God and His glory."[33] In that state God completely masters the soul.

---

31. *Procés apostolique ne pereant,* p. 237.
32. Tanquerey, *Précis de théologie ascétique et mystique,* II, p. 920. Père Poulain, on his part, defines *spiritual marriage* as "a state in which the soul is habitually conscious of the divine co-operation in all her higher operations and in the depths of her being. No union of a more intimate nature can be imagined. This grace can be considered under another aspect, which gives a still higher idea of it: in concurring in our supernatural acts God makes them His own; He renders them divine, and shows that He does so. There is, therefore, a *transformation* of the higher faculties with regard to their manner of operation. The soul is aware that in her supernatural acts of intellect, love, or will, she *participates in the divine life, in those analogous acts that are in God.* This constitutes the essence of the spiritual marriage" *(The Graces of Interior Prayer,* XIX, II, p. 287 of English trans.).
33. Tanquerey, *op. cit.,* p. 924.

When we studied the interior life of M. Vianney, we saw that his whole existence was "a continual prayer," that is, an uninterrupted intercourse with God. "Oh! the beautiful life," he exclaimed in one of his catechisms. "Oh! the beautiful union of the soul with Our Lord! The interior life is a bath of love into which the soul plunges. God holds the soul, when she has reached that stage, as a mother embraces the head of her child in order to cover it with caresses. Our Lord hungers after such a soul!"[34] Those words, wrung from his innermost heart, give away the secret of his own soul, wholly surrendered to the divine operations of *transforming union.* "I wish I could lose myself and never find myself except in God!" he exclaimed another time. His dearest wish was now granted: Eternal Wisdom had become affianced to his soul.

Did God give him some external token of this mystical espousal?[35] A curious incident seems to suggest that He did. True, it is only a simple letter written by a devout woman of Villefranche-sur-Saône to one of the saint's successors, but it rings true and testifies to absolute good faith.[36]

"MONSIEUR LE CURÉ,

"I deem it a duty to inform you that I was at Ars on July 2, 1856, and not having succeeded in seeing the saint in the confessional, owing to the crowd of strangers that thronged round it, I promised myself the satisfaction of at least throwing myself at his feet to ask for his blessing. As soon, therefore, as I came into the presence of that wonderful man, I endeavored to grasp his sacred

---

34. Baronne de Belvey, *Procès de l'Ordinaire,* p. 214.
35. The *mystic ring,* of which we are about to speak, is not a necessary adjunct of the *spiritual marriage.* St. Teresa does not as much as mention it in the *Seventh Mansion* of her *Interior Castle,* in which she describes *transforming union.* None the less "it may happen that the spiritual marriage begins with a *ceremony* and rejoicings. But these are passing facts that must not be confounded with the marriage itself, which is a permanent state. For example, in certain *Lives* of saints we read of the interchange of rings, of angelic chants, etc. These circumstances are not necessary . . ." (R. P. Poulain, *op. cit.,* XIX, 22, p. 290 of English trans.).
36. The letter is kept in the archives of the presbytery of Ars—unfortunately it bears no date. It is signed: "Jeanne Clairet, of Villefranche-sur-Saône (Rhône)."

hand so as to kiss it reverently. But he withdrew it, saying to me in a grave yet gracious manner: 'Oh! do not rob me of my ring!'

"At the same moment I saw what I had not noticed until then: on the fourth finger of his left hand there shone a golden ring of extraordinary brilliancy.

"So he had received, because he deserved it, the wonderful favor which other saints have also had bestowed upon them."

The writer of this letter clearly observed, on M. Vianney's finger, a ring invisible to all others: the saint himself mentioned it. No delusion seems possible. Hence we conclude that the Curé d'Ars, united as he was to God by that spiritual marriage of which he wore the symbol, belonged indeed to the line of the great mystics, such as St. John the Almoner, St. Lawrence Justinian, Bl. Henry Suso, St. Catherine of Alexandria, St. Catherine of Siena, St. Teresa, and others. No doubt he thought of the ineffable joys experienced by him in his sublime intimacies with God when, pressed by M. Toccanier's questions concerning his relations with Our Lord and the happiness he derived from them, he let escape the far too vague admission: "Oh! my friend, there is much more besides!"

Chapter 29

THE LAST YEAR OF THE SAINT'S LIFE (1858-1859)

"DURING the last year of M. Vianney's life, at least one hundred thousand strangers visited his church."[1] People flocked to Ars with all haste, for they felt the end of the holy man's life to be drawing near all too quickly. Everyone wished to see him, to hear him, and, if possible, to go to Confession to him. He was now no longer equal to the task; missionaries heard Confessions in the side chapels.[2] The rush was such that those who wished to see him at all costs, found themselves obliged to wait as many as six days for the privilege of approaching him for a few minutes.[3] In order to gain time, therefore, he heard Confessions far into the night, though he had risen one hour after midnight, and sometimes even earlier. "He was like a mariner who, lest he suffer shipwreck, rows with all his strength and hails from afar the harbour for which he so eagerly longs."[4]

But few of the people, who were so eager for pardon and peace, seemed to realize that by their reckless exigencies they were killing a poor old priest "who was already worn out by a life of immolation and incessant toil!"[5] For him there never was as much as one half hour of relaxation and genuine rest.

In March, 1859, barely five months before the saint's

1. Pierre Oriol, *Procès de l'Ordinaire,* p. 758.
2. Pierre Bossan, the architect, had even been commissioned by the saint to make a new confessional. This confessional was only executed after the Curé's death. It now stands in the chapel of the *Ecce Homo* of the old church.
3. During the last six years, the Communions distributed annually in the church of Ars amounted to 30,000, and the Masses that were asked for to the number of 36,000 (Abbé Toccanier, *Procès apostolique ne pereant,* p. 269).
4. Catherine Lassagne, *Petit mémoire,* troisième rédaction, p. 50.
5. *Le Croisé,* of August 20, 1859.

death, a journalist, M. Georges Seigneur, entered his church at about four o'clock in the afternoon.

"The Curé d'Ars," he relates, "was in the confessional. I had scarcely knelt down, when I heard an indescribable sob issue from the confessional. Was it an exclamation of pain? or a cry of love? Every ten minutes the sob was repeated. Sheer exhaustion wrung that plaintive cry from the oppressed heart of the Curé d'Ars; yet this cry of pain became one of love, and the sensible effort of a soul crushed by earth to open for itself a way to heaven."[6]

His *catechisms* were now nothing but a string of exclamations that ended in tears. He could only be heard with extreme difficulty, for his voice had become exceedingly weak and he experienced great difficulty in articulating. From time to time a cough, that sounded more like a cry of pain, betrayed his sufferings, but the love of God and zeal for souls triumphed over his exhaustion.

Everybody lamented that dry and harrowing cough. Everyone pitied him, whilst he only regretted the loss of time caused by this discomfort. He had become so feeble that he was compelled to take a little milk before going to bed. In fact, this was the only alteration he ever made in his régime, and on certain days he took nothing whatever until that late hour.

One day, at noon, he went into the little house adjoining the presbytery occupied by Catherine Lassagne. "Ah! my poor Catherine," he said, "I can do no more!"

"Sit down for a moment, Monsieur le Curé, whilst I prepare a cup of hot milk for you."

"Oh no, do not prepare anything—it is my bed I need."[7]

He left the house to go to his room. Regardless of his prohibition, Catherine at once began to make ready a cup of milk. But, on entering the presbytery, she met M. Vianney on the staircase. He had given up the idea of rest and was on his way to the church. That was too much for Catherine, so she told him boldly: "Monsieur le Curé, take this cup, otherwise you will not be able

6. *Le Croisé,* of August 20, 1859.
7. He meant the short siesta which he took in the afternoon, lying on his pallet.

to hold out till night."

"No, no, I do not want anything."

"Monsieur le Curé, you must drink this milk."

M. Vianney touched his forehead with his finger as if to say that she made his head ache.

"Come, let me go," he said.

"Monsieur le Curé, I shall not move!"

However, an imperative gesture obliged Catherine to let him pass. He succeeded in reaching the yard. Thither Catherine followed him, a cup of milk in her hand. "The pilgrims will see you," the Curé exclaimed. His protestations were in vain—he was forced to yield. And when evening came he confessed to the inexorable Catherine: "I really think that without your cup of milk I should not have been able to hold out until the end of the day."[8]

As early as 1855, seeing his growing exhaustion—"My head gets confused," he sometimes confessed—M. Toccanier, on his own initiative and without the Curé's knowledge, had obtained for him a dispensation from the daily recitation of the Breviary.[9] He nevertheless went on reciting it, almost daily, but he was forced to give up saying it on his knees—a custom dear to him, and one that he had observed from the time of his subdiaconate.

In November, 1858, as he was leaving the room in which the pupils of the *Providence* were gathered, he fell on the staircase and bruised his leg. He neglected the wound so that it became ulcerated and took a long time to heal.[10]

---

8. *Annales d'Ars,* December, 1920, p. 183.
9. Abbé Toccanier, *Procès de l'Ordinaire,* p. 1476. The following is Mgr. Chalandon's answer to the Abbé Toccanier:

"BELLEY,
"*November* 19, 1855.

"MY GOOD FRIEND,

"I hear with much regret of the state of health of our good curé. I forbid him to say his Breviary whenever you refuse to allow him to recite it. I shall say it in his name as well as in my own, and let him offer his sufferings to God for my intentions.

"Sincerely yours *(Tout à vous),*
"GEORGES, Bishop of Belley."

10. In one of the books belonging to his library we came across an "old woman's" recipe for "sores on the legs," to which, no doubt, he paid no attention whatever.

Even now he still took the discipline though he almost swooned in so doing. He bitterly lamented that he was no longer able to punish himself as of old. "A few days before his death," M. Pagès relates, "he sent me to Lyons, and as I was about to set out, he commissioned me to bring him a chain two feet long and a little thicker than a watch-chain. 'If you refuse to obey,' he said, 'I shall have to make use of another which is much sharper.' He used the latter in the morning by way of preparation for the day's work.

"Time was no longer when he could say: 'I have a good *corpse:* when I have taken a little food and slept for two hours, I am able to resume my work.' At present, when he felt most exhausted, he merely remarked: 'We shall rest in the next world!'"

"My good Curé, you must spare yourself," M. des Garets kept repeating.

"Ah! *bast!* my friend, the good God will see to all that," he would reply with a smile.[11]

The short time allotted to his night's rest was spent in turning from side to side on his hard and narrow pallet, whilst his body was bathed in perspiration. Had Frère Athanase not related it, who would have dared to think that it cost him a hard struggle every morning to rise before dawn, and that he went to the church to resume his task with feelings of the utmost reluctance? "I always have to begin all over again!" he groaned.[12]

Notwithstanding these instinctive rebellions of human nature—and in this we see one of the marvels of this wonderful existence—not once would this old man of seventy-three remain in bed "for a rest which was no rest at all."[13] "This morning I should have liked to stay in bed," he said one day, "but I did not hesitate to get up; the salvation of souls is so important a matter!"[14] And thus, though already worn out with fatigue, he entered his confessional at the accustomed hour.

11. *Procès de l'Ordinaire,* p. 972.
12. *Ibid.,* p. 814.
13. *Ibid.,* p. 134.
14. Frère Athanase, *Procès apostolique ne pereant,* p. 1033.

"He owned to me," the Abbé Toccanier relates, "that one day he collapsed four times on the way to the church, and that it was with extreme difficulty that he got up again. Another time, when I told him that he looked very tired, he replied with a smile: 'Oh! the sinners will end by killing the poor sinner.'"[15]

At about four or five o'clock in the morning, as also towards three or four o'clock in the afternoon, he felt an irresistible inclination to sleep. It was in vain that he struggled, that he kept turning between his emaciated fingers his string of rosary beads, at times he did fall asleep. "Considerate people who noticed it paused in their Confessions so as to give him a few moments' rest."[16]

It was at this period of uninterrupted heroism that he gave his beloved "comrade" Toccanier those wonderful answers which are worthy of undying admiration:

"Father," the missionary asked one day, "if the good God gave you the choice, either to go up to Heaven at once or to go on working as you are at present doing for the conversion of sinners, what would be your decision?"

"I should stay on."

"But the saints are so happy in Heaven! No more sufferings, no more temptations!"

"Yes," he admitted, "in Heaven the saints are happy indeed, but they are like men who live on their income.[17] But they have labored well, for God punishes laziness and only rewards work; however, unlike ourselves, they cannot, by their labors and sufferings, win souls for God."

"If God left you here below until the end of the world, you would have plenty of time in front of you; surely, you would not then get up so early in the morning?"

"O my friend, I should certainly always get up at midnight, fatigue has no terrors for me: I should be the happiest of priests, were it not for the thought that I must appear before the tribunal of God in the capacity of curé!"As he uttered the words two big tears trickled

15. *Procès de l'Ordinaire,* p. 134.
16. *Procès de l'Ordinaire,* p. 322.
17. "Ce sont des rentiers."

down his cheeks.[18]

In the meantime his infirmities were on the increase. But like the sun when it reaches the Western sky, his soul shone with ever brighter radiance the nearer it drew to the end of the period of trial. However stricken his poor body may have been, "his spirit was ever free, his countenance calm and smiling. Nothing in him betrayed to the pilgrims the secret of even his keenest sufferings."[19] When he felt he had reached the limit of endurance, he still endeavored to hold out until he should have around him only such persons as knew him and who were, in consequence, acquainted with his infirmities. Then he would allow himself to drop on to a chair, saying gaily: "Ah! really, this is laughable!"[20]

He was still full of activity and even meditated fresh undertakings. At the close of 1858, he had a mission preached in the parish. "This time you will convert us," he said to M. Descôtes, the preacher. At this time, too, he was studying with Pierre Bossan the plans of the "beautiful church" which he wished to build in honour of St. Philomena. He himself settled the architect's fee by presenting him with "a magnificent rosary, the beads of which were corals on a chain of gold wire." However, the new building would cost a great deal of money. On April 2, 1859, he opened a subscription, he himself heading the list with a sum of 1,000 francs. "I shall pray to the good God," he wrote—and these were the last lines he ever traced—"for those who shall help to build a beautiful church in honor of St. Philomena."

At the close of this same month he gathered round his person the men and youths of Ars who had just made their Easter duties. That year Easter fell on April 24. He began by likening himself to Moses calling the people of Israel together for the last time.

"O my children," he said among other things, "what a beautiful deed you have just performed. By fulfilling

18. *Procès de l'Ordinaire,* p. 133.
19. *Ibid.,* p. 161.
20. Jeanne-Marie Chanay, *Procès de l'Ordinaire,* p. 701.

your Easter duties you have prepared, in your hearts, an abode for the good God, and you are about to prepare another for Him by building a beautiful church. On other occasions, my brethren, it was I who came to you; you have never refused me anything. I thank you for it. . . . Today, it is the missionary who calls on you, but that is as if it were myself: my heart goes with him. . . . Ah! there are still some sinners in the parish.[21] It is necessary that I should go so that another may convert them."[22]

This allocution was his lowly *Nunc Dimittis*. And indeed "several people took these words of M. Vianney's as a farewell discourse and drew the conclusion that his death was not far off."[23]

If at times he appeared terrified at the thought of the judgements of God, if he trembled to "die as curé," he no longer felt any misgivings as to his true calling. To use his own phrase "he had clinched his bargain with God."[24] He knew quite well that God alone would relieve him from his post at Ars. Hence his fears were tempered with the most loving confidence. "In the course of the last year of his life," says Mlle. Marthe des Garets, "he came to the château, spoke to us of the love of God, and burst into tears." In the pulpit he sometimes began with another topic, but he invariably came back to Our Lord's presence in the Holy Eucharist. This attraction of his towards the Real Presence sensibly increased towards the end of his life. . . . He interrupted himself, shed tears, his countenance became radiant, and all that he could utter were exclamations of love.

As the result of many struggles he had won for himself an unshakable peace. "At the time of my first illness," he ingenuously confessed, "I was still troubled by a few things; at present I no longer fear anything."[25] On

21. Six or seven of the parishioners of Ars had stayed away from Holy Communion.
22. According to a rough draft written down by M. Toccanier immediately after the allocution.
23. Frère Jérôme, *Procès de l'Ordinaire,* p. 568.
24. *Procès de l'Ordinaire,* p. 813.
25. *Ibid.,* p. 628.

the other hand, the contradictions of men had ceased by now; time was no longer when anyone dared to treat him disrespectfully, and as for his assistant—M. Toccanier loved him as a father. The only thing with which the saint could reproach him and his colleagues of Pont-d'Ain, was an excess of attraction to the poor Curé d'Ars! One day, when he spoke to the missionary in this strain, the latter replied with delightful apropos:

"Honour thy father and thy mother, that thou mayest be long lived upon the land. . . ."

M. Vianney's countenance beamed and he showed himself greatly touched by the answer of his *comrade.*[26]

Loneliness, infirmities, the very weariness of life often end by embittering aged people; they find it more difficult to bear with others; their own troubles seem to them a heavy enough burden. M. Vianney preserved until the very end his exquisite and compassionate kindness.

Five months before his death, two strange visitors came to see him. They were two poverty-stricken women, one of whom was none other than Pauline-Marie-Philomène Jaricot, of Lyons. She was now utterly destitute, worn out, and, withal, in a pitiable plight.[27] They were frozen with cold, for they had travelled on a day when an icy north wind swept over the snow-bound fields. M. Vianney received them in his own room, it being the only one where he could give them a fire. He went downstairs himself to look for some straw and a few sticks. But the wood was wet and the fire went out as soon as it was lit. "I beseech you," Pauline sighed, "do not think of the cold; I am used to it; it will be much better if you warm up my soul with a few sparks of faith and hope."

The saint comforted to the best of his power that soul who had undergone such grievous trials and by whom God had done such great things. Nevertheless the inter-

26. *Ibid.,* p. 150.

27. She had spent large sums on various apostolic and charitable works, but ended by being cheated out of her considerable fortune. Her poverty had become such that, in February, 1855, she was compelled to have herself enrolled among the destitute who were in receipt of parish relief. *(Cf.* Louis Petit, *Pauline-Marie Jaricot,* Vitte, Lyons, p. 50.)

view was brief. Pilgrims were besieging the presbytery and clamoring for their confessor. M. Vianney presented Mlle. Jaricot with a small wooden cross—a silent symbol of resignation to God's Will—and, after blessing the kneeling visitors, he left the room.[28]

---

28. M. J. Maurin, *Le Curé d'Ars et Pauline-Marie Jaricot,* Lyon, pp. 58-65.

Chapter 30

LAST ILLNESS AND DEATH

IT is an incontestable fact that M. Vianney had long had a presentiment not only of the approximate time, but of the exact date, of his death. "Since his last attempt at flight (in 1853)," Catherine Lassagne relates, "our holy Curé hardly ever spoke of going away, unless it were of his departure from this world into the next. He often said: 'We are going; we shall have to die, and that soon.'"

Some time before the Feast of Corpus Christi, of 1858, he was presented with a beautiful scarf. "'It will come in handy for the procession,' I told him; 'it will help you to hold the monstrance.' 'I shall not use it twice,' he replied, with a mysterious smile. As a matter of fact, on the Feast of Corpus Christi of 1859—which fell on June 23—he was so weak that he had not the strength to carry the Blessed Sacrament from one altar of repose to the other; it was placed in his hands only at the moment of the Benediction."

At the approach of All Saints, 1858, he sent Catherine to the château of Cibeins "to draw a pension of twenty sous a day which had been granted to him out of charity." "That will be the last time," he said at first, with some hesitation in his voice; presently he repeated in a firmer tone: "Yes, it will be the last time."[1]

In the course of July, 1859, Mme. Pauze, a pious woman of Saint-Étienne, came to Confession to M. Vianney. She was in the habit, each year, of making on foot and accompanied by her husband, a pilgrimage to La Louvesc. The Curé d'Ars took great delight in talking to her of the good St. Francis Régis, whose tomb he, too, had visited, and to whom he owed so much. Mme. Pauze was under

1. We owe these details to various accounts of Catherine's *Petit mémoire,* troisième rédaction, p. 98; *Procès de l'Ordinaire,* p. 58; *Procès apostolique in genere,* p. 126.

an impression that she would not be able to revisit Ars, so she bade farewell to M. Vianney. "Yes, yes, my child, we shall meet again in three weeks' time!" The pilgrim returned home pondering the meaning of those words. Did the Curé d'Ars expect soon to pass through Saint-Étienne? Mme. Pauze informed her family of a promise which to her seemed unintelligible. Now, "three weeks later the Curé d'Ars and his devout penitent, having died almost at the same time, were able to meet in Paradise."[2]

On July 18—that is, seventeen days before M. Vianney's death—Mlle. Étiennette Durié, who, as we have seen, witnessed one of the saint's ecstasies in his room, returned to Ars after having made a retreat at La Louvesc. When she entered the confessional the following moving dialogue, which seemed to belong already to another world, took place:

"I do not think I made a good retreat at La Louvesc, Father, because I was worried about your health. I thought you were ill."

"It is true," he replied, "that I am not ill at this moment, but my career is at an end. This is my last year. . . . I have told you so on previous occasions in order to baffle an idle curiosity, but this time I tell you what I know: this is my last year. . . . Do not speak of it, my child. I have only a few days to live. I need that time to prepare myself. Were you to betray me, they would all rush to come to Confession, and I should be overwhelmed."

"Oh, you are sufficiently prepared as it is."

"I am only a great sinner; you see, I weep at the thought."

"But then, what will become of me?"

"If I have the happiness of going to Heaven, I shall ask the good God to go on being your guide."

"O Father, ask Him to leave you with us for yet a little while."

"No, I cannot pray for that; the good God would not grant it. I shall soon leave this world."

And, with many tears, he added: "I know not whether

2. *Annales d'Ars,* March, 1903, p. 328.

I have properly discharged my duty."

"If you complain, Father, what about me left behind in the world?"

"What you are doing need not fill you with the same fear with which my ministry as a priest must necessarily fill me."

"Father, your work is so much better than mine."

"Oh, how I fear death! Ah! I am a great sinner!"

"The goodness of God, as you yourself have told me, is greater than all our sins. . . . I wish I were as sure of going to Heaven as you are! But, Father, when are you going to die?"

"If it is not at the end of this month, it will be at the beginning of the next."

"How shall I know the day if you refuse to tell me?"

"Someone will tell you; you will be present at my funeral, and you will spend the night preceding it by my deathbed."

Mlle. Durié would not yet give credence to such a prophecy. However, before giving her absolution, the saint said with emphasis: "Receive, my child, the last absolution of the father of your soul."

When Étiennette Durié had received absolution she returned to the charge: "Of your charity, Father, tell me the day of your death."

"No, my child, you must not know it; you would remain here and would thus have to endure too many vexations; but you will hear of it in due time."

The woman left Ars on July 22 to execute some commissions for M. Vianney. Twelve days later, as she reached Roanne, she fell in with Père Vadon, a religious who told her: "I hear that M. Vianney is ill." Thereupon the saint's words came back to her mind, and she set out for Ars with all speed. She was not to see "the father of her soul" alive. When, at five o'clock in the afternoon, she entered the old presbytery, she was met by the sound of sobs. The saint had died the night before.[3]

The close of July, 1859, was marked by torrid heat.

3. *Procès de l'Ordinaire,* pp. 1451-1452.

Both day and night the atmosphere was heavy and sultry; even in the open the air seemed on fire, but within the little church, now fuller than ever, it was almost impossible to breathe. Every few minutes some pilgrim would leave the church for a breath of air. But the saint remained in his confessional, heroic to the last in his martyrdom of devotion and zeal. "If a priest were to die in consequence of his labors and sufferings for the glory of God and the salvation of souls, it would not be a bad thing!"[4] These were his words. They were to be realized in his own person.

On Friday, July 29, he felt worse as soon as he rose from his bed. For all that, he went down into the church, towards one o'clock in the morning. As soon as he was seated in his confessional he was seized with attacks of suffocation and was repeatedly compelled to leave the church for a few moments' rest in his yard. All this time he was in a burning fever.

At eleven o'clock, before giving his catechism, he summoned to the sacristy M. Oriol, one of his volunteer guards, and asked him for a little wine. When he had taken a few drops out of the hollow of his hand he had strength enough to go up unassisted into the small pulpit; but it was impossible to hear what he said.[5] Nevertheless, the assistants understood that he was speaking of his favorite topic, inasmuch as he kept turning round towards the tabernacle on which he fixed his weeping gaze.

In the evening he returned to the presbytery, bent down and leaning on Frère Jérôme's arm. He looked like death. On the way he met the whole des Garets family. He raised his enfeebled hand over these beloved friends. "This is the last time that he will bless us!" those noble Christians said amid their tears.[6]

When he reached the foot of the staircase he swooned for a moment. The Brother suggested to him to go once more into the open, for perhaps the fresh air would revive

4. *Petit mémoire,* troisième rédaction, p. 100.
5. Pierre Oriol, *Procès de l'Ordinaire,* p. 753.
6. Mlle. Marthe des Garets, *Procès apostolique in genere,* p. 317.

him. Still assisted by Frère Jérôme, he went in the direction of the house of the Brothers. But he returned immediately, for by now he was utterly exhausted. With the greatest difficulty he reached his room, where Frère Jérôme helped him into bed, and, at his reiterated request, he finally left him alone.

At about one o'clock in the morning, feeling frozen with cold, though the heat was stifling, there being no night breeze, he knocked in order to summon assistance. Catherine Lassagne, who, unknown to him, had kept watch in the adjoining room, was first on the scene. "It is my poor end," he whispered; "you must send for M. le curé of Jassans." Summoned by Catherine, Frère Jérôme now entered the room. It was the very latest moment at this time of year—a quarter-past one, or half-past one—when the Curé d'Ars was wont to go into the church. But now he spoke to the sacristan neither of rising nor of saying Mass. He felt he was stricken to death. "It is my poor end," he repeated. "Go and call my confessor."

"I shall also send for the physician."

"It is useless; the doctor can do nothing."

The Abbé Toccanier, in his turn, came hurrying in weeping. "Monsieur le Curé, St. Philomena, who cured you sixteen years ago, will cure you this time, too."

"Oh, St. Philomena can do nothing now!"

The Abbé Louis Beau, curé of Jassans, and Dr. Saunier, of Sainte-Euphémie, arrived almost at the same moment, just as day was breaking. The doctor could but verify the extreme weakness of the sufferer. All power of reaction was gone. "If the weather should get cooler," the physician prognosticated, "we may still cherish some hope; if there be no diminution of the heat, we shall lose him." But the heat grew ever more intense: a thunderstorm was even then gathering over Ars. Great was the distress of the pilgrims, several of whom had arrived during the night, when they learned that M. le Curé would not come down that morning—nay, that perhaps he would never again be seen in his church. They surged round the gate of the small yard. Some, by a permit that must remain inexplicable, unless the saint himself summoned them, even came to kneel by his bedside to finish their Confessions.[7]

He whom it had hitherto been so difficult to take care of had now become "docile as a child." The reader will recollect that, during his illness of 1843, it had been no easy task to make him accept a mattress. Now, during the morning of the Saturday, when one was placed upon his hard pallet, he smiled his thanks. He took every remedy that was administered to him. Only once did he protest, when a sister of St. Joseph, who was tending him, began to brush away the flies which settled on his face, bathed in perspiration. He made a gesture, and those nearby understood him to say: "Leave me with my poor flies. . . . The only vexatious thing is sin!"

"He was perfectly conscious, and remained so until the end," declared his confessor, who was the witness of this sublime death scene. "He made his Confession with his wonted devotion, without anxiety, and without allusion to his suffering state.[8] He uttered no wish to be cured. Nor was the devil permitted to torment him in this supreme hour." "His greatest fear had been lest he should fall into despair at the last." Now the fear of death, of which he had given evidence so often and so strongly, vanished completely.

After tasting to the dregs the bitter cup of this land of banishment, he now relished *the delights of death,* realizing in his own person one of his own beautiful sayings: "How sweet it is to die if one has lived on the cross!"

The progress of the malady was rapid. The servant of God was perfectly calm. No complaint escaped his lips,

---

7. Pierre Oriol, *Procès de l'Ordinaire,* p. 753; Catherine Lassagne, *Procès apostolique in genere,* p. 124.
8. Our account of the death of the holy Curé is taken from various depositions: the first in importance is that of M. Beau, curé of Jassans *(Procès de l'Ordinaire,* pp. 1218-1220); those of Catherine Lassagne *(Petit mémoire,* troisième rédaction, pp. 100-101, and *Procès de l'Ordinaire,* p. 528); that of Frère Jérôme *(Procès de l'Ordinaire,* pp. 571-572); that of Frère Athanase *(Procès de l'Ordinaire,* p. 876); that of Abbé Monnin *(Procès de l'Ordinaire,* pp. 1164-1165); that of Marthe Miard *(Procès apostolique continuatif,* p. 864).

so that it was difficult to realize that he was suffering at all. Priests, brothers, devout laymen, watched by him in relays, though it seemed that he would have preferred to be left alone.

The people of Ars, his own beloved parishioners, and some pilgrims were constantly appearing at the door of his room in order to have pious objects blessed by him, or to ask a last blessing for themselves. He readily complied with these pious wishes, though he never uttered a word. On the very eve of his death, when it had been decided no longer to admit anyone, there were those who forced their way into the room. "We shall go in, in spite of you," they declared, in accents broken by their sobs, to Frère Athanase, who stood on guard at the gate of the courtyard. "He was our parish priest before he became yours!" So the Brother let them pass on condition that they went up the stairs without making a noise. In silence, though they repressed their sobs with difficulty, they knelt down on the threshold of the sickroom. The saint recognized them; someone guided his enfeebled hand, and he traced a Sign of the Cross over them. "I saw him in his bed on the last day of his life," says Guillaume Villier, who must have been one of that group; "he was as calm and gentle as an angel."

The Comte des Garets, who hardly ever left the presbytery during those sorrowful days, summoned his family. The dying saint gazed for a moment on those children in whom he had taken a fatherly interest. He remembered that he had not yet bestowed some small keepsake upon young Marthe-Philomène, so he made a sign to Frère Athanase to fetch him a rosary for her.

In the meantime the pilgrims, massed between the church and the presbytery, were clamoring for their confessor; the latest arrivals asked to be allowed to see him at least once. They were informed that M. Vianney would bless them from his bed. At stated times a little bell was rung, and at the signal those outside fell on their knees and crossed themselves.

Within the church, groups of suppliants pressed round

the altar of St. Philomena, beseeching the "dear little saint" to cure her great friend. Some persons even undertook a pilgrimage to the shrine of our Lady of Beaumont.

All that was humanly possible was done to ease the saintly sufferer. "If the heat diminishes we may cherish some hope," Dr. Saunier had declared. Some of the good people of Ars imagined that they could procure a measure of coolness for the saint by hanging long sheets of canvas from the presbytery roof. M. Pagès and others, climbing on ladders, watered those sheets from time to time. They all vied with one another in devotion to their pastor.

As for the gentle invalid, he seemed to belong to earth no longer. "His lips were not seen to move," his confessor relates, "but his eyes remained firmly fixed on high and gave the impression that he was lost in contemplation. I believe that during those hours something unusual must have taken place within his soul. To the various questions that were put to him he nearly always replied with a simple 'yes' or 'no.'"

As a matter of fact, he spoke only a very few words. In the course of the morning of Tuesday, August 22, Frère Athanase and M. Toccanier took it in turns to watch by his bedside. Whilst the Brother was on duty, the doctor was announced. "I still have thirty-six francs," the saint managed to say; "ask Catherine to give them to M. Saunier. And then let her request him not to return; I should not be able to pay him. . . ." M. Toccanier confided to his holy rector his own fears for the future: "Father, since the Government has refused to sanction the lottery, and, on the other hand, God takes you from this world, it is all up. . . ." "Courage, comrade! It is a matter of three years!"[9]

At about three o'clock in the afternoon of that same day his confessor deemed it prudent to give him the last

9. Abbé Toccanier, *Procès de l'Ordinaire,* p. 182. At the end of three years M. Toccanier had collected sufficient funds to make a start with the construction of the new church.

THE SHRINE OF THE CURÉ D'ARS

Sacraments. In point of fact, he himself had asked for them, nor did he wish to wait until the following morning, as someone had suggested. "How kind the good God is!" he murmured. "When we are no longer able to go to Him, He Himself comes to us!"

The bell tolled whilst the curé of Jassans carried the Blessed Sacrament from the church to the sickroom. Some twenty priests followed in procession, carrying lighted candles. At the sound of the bell fresh tears filled the eyes of the dying saint. "Father, why do you weep?" asked Frère Élie, who was kneeling by his bedside. "It is sad to receive Holy Communion for the last time!" the dying priest whispered.[10]

When he beheld the procession entering his room, he raised himself unaided into a sitting posture. He folded his hands, and his tears flowed copiously. His confessor gave him holy Viaticum and Extreme Unction. "He received both Sacraments with his wonted faith and devotion," says M. Beau. The room being already overheated, the priests had been obliged to put out their candles.

After this moving ceremony the Abbé Étienne Dubouis, *desservant* of Fareins, undertook to keep watch.

"Monsieur le Curé, you are with the good God," the old confrère remarked.

"Yes, my friend," the saint replied with a heavenly smile.

"Today we are keeping the Feast of the Translation of the Relics of St. Stephen," M. Dubouis added. "Whilst still on earth that saint beheld Heaven open."

At these words, the abbé relates, M. Vianney raised his eyes with an extraordinary expression of faith and happiness.[11]

One important matter perturbed the Mayor and the inhabitants of Ars: who should possess the mortal remains of their Curé![12] The last will made by M. Vianney and

10. *Procès de l'Ordinaire,* p. 206.
11. *Procès apostolique ne pereant,* p. 904.
12. There is a first will of his, dated December 2, 1841, which begins thus: *"I give my sinful body to the earth and my poor soul to the three Persons of the Most Holy Trinity and to Mary conceived without sin."*

written by himself—on November 10, 1855—was as follows: *"I leave it to the Bishop of Belley to dispose of my body after my death."* But what would Mgr. de Langalerie decide? Could they feel sure that the prelate would not yield to the demand of the people of Dardilly, who, several times already, had requested their holy countryman to make a will in their favor? As a matter of fact, was it just and reasonable that he to whose holiness Ars owed all its splendor and glory should deprive it of the precious inheritance of his body?

For these reasons, on Wednesday, August 3, at an hour when the attendants were relieved, Maître Gilbert Raffin, *notaire* at Trévoux, entered the sickroom, accompanied by four witnesses. "Where do you wish to be buried?" the notary asked. All present strained their ears, and he was heard to whisper: "At Ars . . . but my body is not much."After that M. Raffin drew up a will, to which the saint was, however, unable to put his signature.[13]

On the same day, "at three o'clock," says M. Beau, "I read the Commendation of the Soul to him, in the presence of several priests. He continued perfectly calm and lost in contemplation. The Abbé Alfred Monnin and

---

A second will, certainly written before that of 1855, is thus worded: *"I wish that after my death my body should be taken to Dardilly, my native place. Such is my will."* The original text of this document is kept in the house in which he was born.

13. This testament is as follows:

"Before Maître Gilbert Hippolyte Raffin, *notaire at* Trevoux, *département* of the Ain, and in the presence of witnesses hereafter to be named, appeared

"M. Jean-Marie-Baptiste Vianney, Curé d'Ars, who, though ill in bed, but having the full use of his faculties, dictated to the said Maître Raffin his testament, which the latter wrote down as it was dictated, as follows:

"I name and appoint as my sole heir M. Joseph Camelet, priest at Pont-d'Ain.

"I will that my mortal remains should repose for ever in the cemetery of the parish of Ars.

"Such is my last will which alone I wish to be executed, all previous dispositions being hereby annulled and revoked.

"The present will was drawn up and read to the testator, in the presence of witnesses, at the presbytery of Ars, on the third of August, one thousand eight hundred and fifty-nine, at an hour of relief, the witnesses being Messieurs Claude-Prosper Garnier, Comte des Garets, landowner and Mayor of the Commune of Ars, where he is domiciled, Pierre Oriol, householder, François Pertinand, carter, Hippolyte-François Pagès, householder, all domiciled at Ars, who have signed together with the notary, not, however, the testator who declared his inability to sign, by reason of his weakness caused by the malady from which he suffers."

(Then follow the signatures: "Comte des Garets, Oriol senior, François Pertinand, Hippolyte Pagès, and Raffin.")

another missionary had arrived a short time before, having hastened to Ars from the parishes where they were giving missions.

August 3 found Mgr. de Langalerie, Bishop of Belley, at Meximieux, where final arrangements were being made for the distribution of prizes which was to take place on the following day. It was there that the prelate learned of M. Vianney's desperate condition. He left the Petit Séminaire without delay and set out for Ars.[14] Full of anxiety, he reached the village at about seven o'clock in the evening. Hurrying breathless to the presbytery, he prayed aloud as he forced his way through the crowd, who fell on their knees as he went by.[15]

The sick man recognized his Bishop perfectly, greeted him with a smile, and endeavored to express his thanks, but could not articulate a word. The Bishop embraced him and told him that he would now go into the church to pray for him. Once more the saint smiled. "This was the only moment of the day when I saw him come out of his union with God," says his confessor, who was present at the interview.

About ten o'clock that night the holy Curé seemed to be near his end. M. Toccanier gave him the last blessing and the plenary indulgence *in articulo mortis.* At midnight the Abbé Monnin gave him his missionary cross to kiss, and once more began the prayers for the dying. He said them slowly, interspersing them with fairly long pauses.

On Thursday, August 4, 1859, at two o'clock in the morning, at the moment when the priest uttered with trembling lips those words, "*May the holy angels of God come to meet him and conduct him into the holy city of Jerusalem,*" whilst a storm broke over Ars, and the lightning flashed and the thunder rolled, St. Jean-Marie-Baptiste Vianney, supported by the arms of Frère Jérôme, "gave up his soul to God, without agony," and fell asleep like the laborer whose task has been well done. M. Oriol

14. The distance between Meximieux and Ars is about forty kilometers.
15. Monnin, *The Curé of Ars,* p. 543 (of English trans.).

had the consolation of closing his eyes. He was seventy-three years, two months, and twenty-seven days old, and he had been parish priest of Ars for the space of forty-one years, five months, and twenty-three days.

About four o'clock M. Beau went into the church to say Mass for him. The sacristan had laid out a black vestment. He who for thirteen years had been the intimate confidant of his soul hesitated at first to put on the vestment of mourning, for, he declared, "M. Vianney's life had been so holy that he did not believe him guilty of a deliberate venial sin."[16]

In the church tower of Ars the bell began to toll. At the first sound the villagers, whose souls had been so long oppressed with anguish, gave vent to the immensity of their grief. With streaming eyes, people said to one another: "Our holy Curé is dead!" "In the neighboring villages," says Mlle. Marthe des Garets, "they shared our sorrow, for the lament of the bells spread the news of our loss." At Savigneux, at Mizérieux, at Trévoux, and even as far as Jassans, the funeral knell was rung. At Savigneux the curé thought it necessary first to consult the Mayor, M. de Bonnepos. "Is that a question to ask when we have lost the Curé d'Ars?" the Mayor replied with some sharpness.

"The news of the holy Curé's death spread with lightning rapidity; the telegraph carried it everywhere."[17] At once the crowds began to march. On the evening of August 4, M. Camille Monnin, notary at Villefranche and brother of the missionary, hastened to Ars. "The road," he related, "was encumbered by pilgrims, both on foot and driving. A considerable crowd was gathered in the village square. Everybody wept. I, too, was overcome with emotion. I fell into the arms of my brother, and we mingled our tears."[18]

---

16. Frère Athanase, *Procès de l'Ordinaire,* p. 1032.
17. Abbé Beau, *Procès de l'Ordinaire,* p. 319.
18. *Procès apostolique continuatif,* p. 263. It was on August 10, by means of the *Univers,* in which Léon Aubineau gave a lengthy account of the death and funeral of M. Vianney, that the news of the great loss became known in the presbyteries of France.

"On that morning, for the first time for many years, the Angelus was rung only at sunrise!"

Mgr. de Ségur, who had been informed by telegram, wrote from Laigle (Orne), to M. Toccanier, on August 7: "So our saint is now in Paradise! Could you possibly render me a twofold service in connection with him? The first would be to get me some autograph of his: I should value it as a true relic. The other is, to give me a few intimate details about his blessed end. . . ."

On August 16, M. du Colombier, brother-in-law of M. des Garets, wrote from his château du Pin to his niece Beatrice: "We can talk of nothing but that poor Curé d'Ars. It is particularly at night, under our lofty limes, that we speak of him. The spectacle of the clear, starry sky, the Milky Way, the beautiful moonlight, everything lifts the soul and mind to the good God, and on that road it is the Curé d'Ars we meet first. What glorious festivals he has had up there since he left his poor church, his confessional, his chapel of St. John (the Baptist), his presbytery, his bare room, his poor pallet; since you began to mourn for him, and the pilgrims wait for him in vain; since the Angelus, which used to ring out at one o'clock in the morning, has begun, as in commonplace belfries, to ring at break of day; since he is no longer among you!"

Chapter 31

IN GLORY

THE saint had no sooner breathed his last than his "poor corpse" became the object of reverent care and attention. M. Vianney had at one time expressed a wish that he should not be undressed after his death;[1] he wanted to keep from the eyes of men the secret of his awe-inspiring penances. The prohibition was nevertheless set aside. With unspeakable emotion the missionaries and the Brothers were thus able to contemplate that most venerable relic, those holy limbs which "exhibited a picture of human emaciation in the last degree."[2]

About five o'clock in the morning the body of the Curé d'Ars, clad in cassock, rochet, and stole, was carried into one of the rooms on the ground-floor. "His countenance was calm and serene, as if he were still alive."[3] From that moment an unending procession began to file past the sacred remains, and it lasted for forty-eight hours. It was necessary to marshal the crowds in the vicinity of the presbytery, and the Mayor, Comte des Garets, was obliged to summon the *gendarmerie* to help in the preservation of order. All wished to approach the servant of God, now asleep in death, to behold once more the beloved face of a father, a friend, a comforter, a shepherd. . . . The crowds were broken up into small groups, each being given time to say one *Pater* and one *Ave.* The Brothers and two pupils from the orphanage stood near the body, and during two days they never ceased from touching the precious relic with pious objects. "All the shops of Ars

1. Jeanne-Marie Chanay, *Procès de l'Ordinaire,* p. 707.
2. R. P. Monnin, *Procès apostolique ne pereant,* p. 995.
3. Abbé Toccanier, *Procès apostolique ne pereant,* p. 337.

were stripped bare," says Marthe Miard; "from my own house women carried away in their aprons pictures, crosses, rosaries, and medals, without even stopping to pay for them."[4]

In vain did Maître Raffin, of Trévoux, put his seals on the presbytery: pious thefts were perpetrated on all sides. Some pilgrims, greatly daring, very nearly succeeded in getting away with the most interesting souvenirs. They managed to reach the first storey, whence they endeavored to penetrate into the saint's own room; they had already cut away so much of the door that, but for the timely arrival of the guardians, they would have achieved their purpose. As for the three elder-trees in the courtyard, they were stripped of all the foliage within reach of the hand.

The march past of visitors was interrupted only for half an hour in the afternoon of August 4. At the moment when the sun burnt his fiercest, the body was moved from the bed of honor, which was adorned with flowers and green branches, and, for the first time, a photographer was able to take a picture of the features of the Curé d'Ars.[5]

The obsequies had been fixed for Saturday, August 6. The night before there was such an influx of visitors into the village, that provisions gave out, and the greater number, having failed to find lodgings, were compelled to spend the night in the open. At eight o'clock an immense procession was formed, made up of three hundred priests and religious and six thousand lay people. The coffin had not yet been closed, so the features of the saint were still

4. *Procès apostolique continuatif,* p. 864. When all the shops had been emptied of their devotional objects, all sorts of things were placed on the remains of M. Vianney. In a notebook of Jean-Claude Viret we find an inventory of all the souvenirs he brought back from Ars between 1848 and 1859. On page 34 of this memoir we read: "Also, you will find *some sugar and tobacco* which were placed on the body of the holy Curé after his death."

5. Three photographs were taken. Jean-Claude Viret has left us, in his own quaint language, the following details of the operation: "I, Jean-Claude, was present when the photographs were taken. The good holy Curé, Jean-Marie-Baptiste Vianney, was taken out of his presbytery and placed in the yard at a moment when the sun was fiercest, and it was necessary to hold an umbrella over the holy Curé to guard him from the sun, and it was I, Jean-Claude, who held that umbrella all the time that it was needed." *(Mémoire MSS.,* p. 33).

visible. As soon as the body was taken out of the house, M. Alfred Monnin relates, there occurred in the crowd one of those spontaneous and irresistible movements which had always taken place whenever the servant of God appeared during his lifetime. All wished to approach the coffin, to gaze for a last time upon the features of the Curé d'Ars. The procession started: for the last time the Curé d'Ars traversed the streets of his beloved village.

This was no funeral procession, but a triumphant progress. Behind the little girls in white and the clergy in choir dress came the heavy coffin of lead and oak, carried in turn by priests, the Brothers of the Holy Family, and the young men of the village.[6] As it was borne past them, the people who lined the route fell on their knees, as if to receive a last blessing. Silent tears flowed from every eye. Among the crowd there were a few men indifferent to religion. One of them was so impressed by all he saw, Frère Jérôme relates, that he exclaimed with deep emotion: "Oh! yes, he was a saint!" and his soul was completely changed. From afar, at intervals, there came the sound of the knell from the belfries of the surrounding district.

The procession halted in the square; the body was laid at the foot of the calvary which stood in its center. On this spot Mgr. de Langalerie, who officiated, pronounced the funeral oration of the servant of God. It was the first panegyric delivered in his honor, and not one of those that were to follow has been more moving, nor, perhaps, more eloquent. It was an anticipated canonization:

"Well done, good and faithful servant . . . enter thou into the joy of thy Lord."[7]

"Keep silence, my brethren! Lend an attentive ear, devout people, whom reverence and grief have drawn in such numbers to this imposing ceremony. I will repeat it once more, that saying of Our Lord in the holy Gospel.

---

6. The curé and the préfet of Trévoux, the Abbé de Sérezin (Canon of Belley), and the Comte des Garets (Mayor of Ars), were the pall-bearers.
7. *Euge serve bone et fidelis . . . intra in gaudium Domini tui* (*Matt.* 25:21).

Tell me, is there one among you who does not feel as if he heard it proceeding from the mouth of God Himself at the moment when the beautiful soul of our holy Curé was at length released from that body which had worn itself out in long continued service of the divine Master? . . . Let us ponder for a few moments, my brethren, that sweet and comforting saying. At the present moment it is our hope and consolation. And I will add that it conveys a wholesome lesson to us, in the name of him who henceforth will never again speak to you, except by the example of his life, and, in all likelihood, by the marvels wrought at his tomb."

Commenting upon his text, the Bishop of Belley drew a rapid sketch of the superhuman existence of the Curé d'Ars, calling it "a marvel of the power and love of God."

"How many years, how many centuries perhaps, since a spectacle such as this has been witnessed—a priestly career passed amid like conditions, so fruitfully, so blessedly, and so continuously occupied and spent in the service of God? . . .

"A Curé d'Ars is not to be replaced. God himself, even in the interest of His glory, refuses to multiply such prodigies of grace and holiness. All France has lost a priest who was its honor, one whom people came from all the provinces to see and consult. . . .

"'Well done, good and faithful servant . . . enter into the joy of thy Lord . . .'—that is to say: 'Your task is done; you have worked, you have toiled enough; come, receive the reward of your labor. . .'

"And know this, beloved and venerated Curé, that the most splendid, the most longed-for day of my episcopate, would be that on which the infallible voice of the Church would allow me to acclaim you solemnly and to sing in your honor: *Euge serve bone et fidelis . . . intra in gaudium Domini tui."*[8]

At the conclusion of the discourse the coffin was carried into the church, into which only the public author-

8. On the following August 18, Mgr. de Langalerie sent his printed discourse to all the clergy of Belley.

ities, the clergy, and the members of the deceased's family were admitted. The gendarmes of Trévoux were posted outside the doors of the church, and it was with difficulty that they kept back the multitude. However, not a sound arose from the crowd, which was massed on the steps leading up to the church and in the narrow street. During the *Requiem* Mass, celebrated by Canon Guillemin, Vicar-General of Belley, a religious silence hovered over the sorrowing village, which had itself become a vast church. The crowd fell on its knees and rose again at the signal given by the bell.

The Absolution was given by Mgr. de Langalerie, after which the coffin was set down in the chapel of St. John the Baptist, in front of the confessional, now empty, alas! in which the servant of God had absolved and comforted so many poor souls. All the time that the coffin remained there, it was watched, day and night, and exclusively by people of the parish. On August 14 the venerable remains were lowered into a vault, which had been constructed in the middle of the church. The tomb was closed with a slab of black marble, on which were carved a chalice and this simple inscription:

CI-GÎT JEAN-MARIE-BAPTISTE VIANNEY, CURÉ D'ARS.[9]

There the remains of the servant of God were to repose from 1859 until 1904—that is, a period of forty-five years.

In the meantime requests for relics came from all quarters. Thanks to the telegraph, Dardilly had learned of the death of M. Vianney on August 4. The following day the Superioress of Notre-Dame des Anges, a boarding school founded in the parish by the Sisters of Saint-Joseph, wrote to the Bishop of Belley, to claim the saint's chalice. Mgr. de Langalerie, on his part, forwarded to the Mayor of Ars a petition of the people of Dardilly, which also bore the signature of the Cardinal-Archbishop of Lyons. If they could not have his body, the saint's countrymen claimed at least his heart! The Comte des Garets

9. This inscription, worn out by the feet of pilgrims, has been completely effaced for a number of years.

persisted in his refusal to comply with the request. "On the day of the funeral," he wrote to the Bishop of Belley, "I told the people of that parish that, later on, when it would be possible to exhume the body, they should have an important relic, but that they must be satisfied with my promise and refrain from repeating a demand which, under the present circumstances, is unseemly, and does not appear to be prompted by genuine devotion. As an old friend of the saintly priest, and as Mayor of Ars, I shall always resist such a violation of his will and his tomb."

A new *pilgrimage* now began. The voice of the people which, for the nonce, was indeed that of God, proclaimed the sanctity of the Curé d'Ars. Henceforth they would visit his church to honor him and to pray to him. The tomb had been surrounded by an iron grille; it was soon covered with flowers and wreaths and used as a candlestand. The missionaries who served the sanctuary removed, without delay, these emblems of devotion and even the grille itself. It was necessary to keep from the tomb all signs of a premature cult, for already the Bishop of Belley held a beatification as possible, and no one had a right to forestall the official sentence of the Church. Nevertheless, it was lawful to invoke the Curé d'Ars privately. Day by day pilgrims came to kneel on the marble slab that covered his remains. One day Cardinal Villecourt, in all the majesty of his purple and his white hair, was seen bending down to the ground to kiss that sacred stone.

In the meantime the diocesan authorities were not idle. On them devolved the grave and sweet duty of furnishing authentic proofs of the holiness of the Curé d'Ars. On November 21, 1862, to the great joy of the faithful, Mgr. de Langalerie constituted an ecclesiastical tribunal, whose duty it was to inquire into the life, virtues, miracles, and writings of the servant of God. Thus began what is called the *Process of the Ordinary.* It required two hundred sittings to collect the depositions of sixty-six witnesses, and the task of the tribunal only ended on March 6, 1865.

A few days after that date Mgr. de Langalerie took to Rome an authentic copy of the *Process*—1,674 pages in folio—and handed it to the Sacred Congregation of Rites. Even before the end of March his Holiness Pius IX appointed as *ponente* of the *Cause of Ars,* Cardinal Villecourt, who resided in Rome,[10] and authorized Cardinal Patrizi, Prefect of the Rites, to open the French in-folios and to have them translated into Italian. Censors were also appointed to examine M. Vianney's writings.

The *Process of the Ordinary* was a preliminary investigation for the purpose of informing the Holy See whether or no the *Cause of Ars* should be taken up. It was followed by the *Apostolic Process.* It was customary to allow ten years to elapse between the two *processes.* By a decree of February 6, 1866, Pius IX set aside that rule, for the great and saintly Pontiff, who knew M. Vianney from hearsay,[11] was himself eager to see that lowly priest honored by the Church. The council of the Vatican, the Franco-German War, the occupation of Rome by the Piedmontese troops, delayed the introduction of the Cause. At length, on October 3, 1872, His Holiness had the satisfaction of approving the "commission," the setting up of which marked the opening of a new era, and indeed, by that very fact Jean-Marie-Baptiste Vianney was declared *Venerable.*

The *Apostolic Process,* which was entrusted to three successive Bishops of Belley—Bishops Richard, Marchal, and Soubiranne—lasted twelve years, from August 3, 1874, till October 12, 1886. Like Pius IX, Leo XIII loved the

10. Cardinal Villecourt died within less than a year of his appointment *as ponente.* His place was taken by Cardinal Pitra, on February 1, 1866.
11. In an audience granted by Pius IX to Frère Gabriel, Superior-General of the Brothers of the Holy Family of Belley, the conversation turned on the Curé d'Ars, when the Holy Father spoke of him most sympathetically. He blessed a rosary expressly destined for M. Vianney. This rosary the saint kept for three months. He treasured it greatly, and "it cost him very much to part with it"; but he was in need of money for his poor, so he exchanged it for a generous alms. (Comtesse des Garets, *Procès de l'Ordinaire,* p. 800; Mlle. Marthe des Garets, *Procès apostolique in genere,* p. 300).

Curé d'Ars. "You must push this Cause," he said in 1889 to Mgr. Luçon, the future Cardinal of Reims, who was at that time Bishop of Belley; "the Curé d'Ars is the religious glory of France." And to the *Postulator* His Holiness declared: "This Cause surpasses all others; it must suffer no delay. I greatly desire to beatify the Venerable Vianney." God denied him that consolation.

To the former parish priest of Sarzano and of Tombolo, who became Pope Pius X on August 4, 1903, exactly forty-four years after the death of the servant of God, it was granted to raise him to our altars. On January 26, 1904, Pius X presided over the *General Congregation* whose duty it was to examine into the miracles of the Venerable Vianney. The tribunal of Belley had put forward seventeen cures which had taken place since his death. From these the advocate of the Cause, M. Morani, selected two which seemed to him sufficient—viz., the curé of Adélaïde Joly and that of Léon Roussat.

These two miracles deserve to be related here. We give the account in the very words of the eyewitnesses. The following is the deposition made on October 10, 1864, by Léonide Joly, the sister of the girl miraculously cured:

"I was born at Saint-Claude on May 8, 1848. Adélaïde is four years younger than I. For five years we have both been in the orphanage kept by the Sisters of Charity, in the parish of Saint-Jean, at Lyons.

"I always dressed my little sister in the morning. One day she complained of pains in her left arm. In September, 1861, the mistress who came to inspect our work noticed that Adélaïde was not working, and that her arm was resting on her knee. She called her a little idler, whereupon we both burst into tears. The child was taken to M. Berne, the head surgeon of the *Charité.* He said that Adélaïde had a white swelling, that her arm was disabled for life, and that she would have to wear a surgical appliance. The appliance was not ordered, for our mistresses wished to try something else. They made us begin a novena to the Curé d'Ars, and as they possessed an old pair of shoes that had belonged to that holy priest, they took one of the laces and tied it round my little sister's arm.[12]

"After the lapse of seven days Adélaïde said to me: Léonide, my arm no longer hurts me.' When I uncovered her arm I saw that she could move it with ease. I ran quickly upstairs to tell the news to our mistress. She scolded me gently for having acted without her permission. On the ninth day of the novena the Sister herself removed the bandages from the arm, which she found perfectly cured. It could be moved freely, and bore the same appearance as the other one, showing no sign whatever of emaciation. The swelling was quite gone. Dr. Berne was astounded at the cure. He made no difficulty when asked to give a certificate, which was sent to the Bishop of Belley. In our great happiness we made a novena of thanksgiving, and ever since we often invoke the Curé d'Ars, who cured my little sister."[13]

The miraculous cure of the boy Roussat was thus told by his father, a baker at Saint-Laurent-lès-Mâcon (Ain), when he gave evidence in the *Process of Beatification:*

"I certify that on January 1, 1862, my son, Léon Roussat, aged six years and two months, was attacked by nervous symptoms, which at first were only slight, but which soon grew in gravity and frequency. We called in Dr. Carteron, of Mâcon, who treated him successively for worms, fever, taenia, and finally for epilepsy.

---

12. That old pair of shoes had a history. "In March, 1862," Soeur Marie-Anne Callamand, Sister of Charity, relates, "a young woman of the parish of Saint-Jean, who had just lost her mother, informed us that the latter had once received from a friend a pair of shoes which had belonged to the Curé d'Ars and that she had given them to a beggar woman. No doubt she had parted with them very regretfully, but she thought that the good Curé would not disapprove of her conduct. The beggar woman, who lodged in an attic on the sixth storey of that lady's house, laid them by in a corner, for they seemed too bad to wear. When she gave up her lodgings she left the shoes behind, and Mlle. Lavie (that was the young lady's name) thought she would give us pleasure by presenting them to us. We were, indeed, happy to acquire them, for they were a precious relic. When we beheld them, we were lost in admiration of the extreme poverty of the holy Curé. Soeur Marguerite felt a sudden inspiration to ask me for one of the laces. 'With this,' she said, 'I am sure that the Curé d'Ars will cure Adélaïde. We shall make a fervent novena and you will see.' I answered: 'Very well, do as you wish,' and I gave her the shoe lace. A Lazarist Father, M. Mellier, superior of the house at Angers, assisted at this scene. Without asking for my permission, he seized the other shoe lace and obstinately refused to give it back to me. 'I, too,' he said, 'may have some use for it.'" *(Procès de l'Ordinaire,* p. 1581).

13. *Procès de l'Ordinaire,* pp. 1590-1591.

"The doctor's prescriptions yielded no result, and the boy grew steadily worse, so my wife and I went to Lyons, where we showed the child to Dr. Barrier, the *major* of the big hospital. He prescribed the use of chalybeate water, a new treatment upon which he placed great reliance.

"The only result was an alarming increase of the number and intensity of the attacks: the boy collapsed on an average as often as fifteen times in a day. When we paid a second visit to M. Barrier he contented himself with giving us a few hints in writing, adding: 'Your child is young; there are some who get over it, others who do not; in any case it is useless to bring him back to me.'

"We were not satisfied with a reception of this kind, and it was with very heavy hearts that we started on the return journey. Now, as we passed through Villefranche, which is close to Ars, I said to my wife: 'We must take our Léon to Ars.' On reaching home we began a novena in honor of the holy Curé. Alas! our prayers were not answered; the hour of grace had not yet struck. The attacks of the poor stricken child were now so intense and so frequent that he collapsed oftener than ever. It even happened that after an attack he remained for two hours like one dead, cold, and frozen. From that time he became quite paralyzed, and lost all power of speech.

"On Easter Monday we wanted to carry him to the tomb of the Curé d'Ars, but M. le curé of Saint-Laurent objected: our pious pastor was afraid—and his fears were only too reasonable—that our child would die on the journey.

"But on May 1 he could keep us back no longer. He himself was going to Ars, where the Bishop of Belley was to lay the foundation-stone of the new church. We set out with him: should we have the misfortune to lose our child, M. le Curé would be there to stand by us!

"We arrived at the close of the ceremony, and had the good fortune to receive the blessing of his Lordship for our dear little sufferer, When the Bishop had entered the house of the missionaries, M. le curé and my wife presented to him Léon, whom he embraced and blessed once more, recommending us to begin a novena to the Curé d'Ars: we were to say one decade of the Rosary each day. Monseigneur was kind enough to promise that he would unite his prayers to ours, and to assure us that the child would be cured.

"From the house of the missionaries we carried the child to the tomb of the saint. On our return to the hotel we had the joy of seeing the little one, who had been quite paralyzed, take his glass with his right hand, drink, and then play with some matches, which he lit and then threw far from him.

"On the way from Ars to Saint-Laurent, which we reached late at night, our dear Léon had only two slight attacks. His sleep was peaceful, and was prolonged until morning. We had to dress him as we had been in the habit of doing: his limbs were still paralyzed; in fact my wife noticed two slight attacks.

"At about ten o'clock we sat down to table. Shortly after, oh joy! Leon asked me by signs to move his chair away from the table. When I had done so he jumped from it and began to run about. He was perfectly cured. True, his speech was still halting, but by the end of our novena, that, too, was restored to him. May everlasting thanks be given to God and His servant, the Curé d'Ars.

"Ever since then the boy's health has been perfect: he has never had a moment's illness. Having witnessed such a prodigy, I could not refuse to give my heart to the good God. I am, and I hope to remain, a convinced Christian."[14]

On February 21, 1904, Pius X promulgated a decree recognizing these two miracles as authentic and valid for the beatification of the Venerable Jean-Marie Vianney. On April 17, Good Shepherd Sunday, a final decree declared that it was safe to proceed to the solemn beatification.[15] "He is a saint!" the crowds had exclaimed of old as the Curé d'Ars went by. Indeed, his holiness seemed as evident as the light of the sun. The Church, ever wise

14. Jean-Marie Roussat, *Procès de l'Ordinaire,* pp. 1549-1551.
15. Decree "*de tuto.*"

and prudent, had taken no fewer than forty-two years to come to a final decision, and her judgement was that of the Christian people. At this news there was great joy in the Catholic world, more particularly in the hearts of priests:

"Nothing more agreeable, nothing more profitable could have happened," Pius X said, on February 2, to some members of the clergy of Paris, "not only to us who for so many years have gladly carried out the duties of the parochial ministry, but to the parish priests of the whole world, than to see this venerable Curé invested with the honour of the Blessed, the more so that his glory will be reflected upon all those whose life is dedicated to the cure of souls."

At last the morning of the great day dawned upon Rome. A radiant sun shone on that Sunday morning, January 8, 1905, which had been set apart for the exaltation of the lowly Curé d'Ars. Mgr. Luçon, Bishop of Belley, whose duty it was to deliver the tickets that would admit their holders into the Vatican basilica, had distributed thirty thousand of them. Over the porch of St. Peter's, a painting by Bottoni and Francisi displayed the figure of M. Vianney dominating the Eternal City. In the portico, above the main door, a picture by Capparoni showed an episode of the pilgrimage of Ars: that of the servant of God passing through the crowd. Within, the basilica wore its festive decoration: the frieze and the pillars were draped with red damask edged with gold. In the apse, where the actual beatification was to be enacted, there floated two large banners, one of which—that on the right hand side—showed the cure of Adélaïde Joly, and the other—that on the left—displayed a picture of the interior of the church of Ars, with little Léon Roussat lying prostrate on the tomb of the new *Beatus*. Between the confession and the altar of St. Peter's Chair, thousands of electric candles sparkled, whilst God's own sun irradiated the mighty dome.

At about ten o'clock the great procession, composed of cardinals, bishops, and heads of Orders, unfurled itself.

Then came the students of the Seminario Pio, the parish priests of Rome, who had decided to assist in a body at this glorification of a curé of France, the Chapter of St. Peter's, all preceding Mgr. Luçon, who was to sing the Mass. Cardinal Rampolla, archpriest of the Vatican basilica, clad in his purple *cappa magna,* closed the procession.

During the reading of the Brief of Beatification, when the words: *"We allow that henceforth the title of 'Blessed' be given to the venerable servant of God, Jean-Marie-Baptiste Vianney"* were uttered, the curtain that covered Bernini's *"gloria"* fell, and all eyes could see, amidst golden clouds encircling the Chair of St. Peter, the picture representing the Curé d'Ars, supported by two angels, taking his flight towards Heaven.

At that moment all the bells of the basilica rang out a joyous peal over the Eternal City. By an instinctive movement of veneration, those present fell on their knees, and many eyes were moist with happy tears. Mgr. Luçon intoned the *Te Deum,* which thirty thousand voices took up with holy enthusiasm. When the hymn was ended the Bishop of Belley, whom this glorious minute amply compensated for so much toil and labor, solemnly censed the relic of the Blessed Vianney now for the first time exposed upon the altar, after which he sang the Church's first prayer to this new and powerful protector. Then the pontifical High Mass began at the altar of the Chair.

Before this altar, at about four o'clock in the afternoon, Pope Pius X came in person to venerate the relics of the Curé d'Ars.[16] On that unforgettable day the Rome of the Popes—Rome, the head and heart of the Church and the mother of souls who, adorned with the purple of the mar-

16. Pius X hoped to be able himself to canonize the Curé d'Ars. Not long after the beatification, at a private audience, Mgr. Olivier, Bishop of Ajaccio, seeing on the Pope's table a statue of the new Blessed, said to the Pontiff: "Holy Father, the presence of such an image before your eyes is a great honour for France." "Ah!" the Pope exclaimed, interrupting his writing and raising his head, "*socius meus,* he is my companion." He then proceeded, speaking in Latin: "Let us pray God to work, as soon as possible, by his intercession, the miracles that will allow us to canonize him." "We very much hope, most Holy Father, that it will be Your Holiness who will perform that canonization." Whereupon the Pope smiled graciously. (*Annales d'Ars,* August, 1906, p. 86).

tyrs' blood, "surpasses in its beauty all earthly beauty," rendered to Blessed Vianney love for love. Rome! In his lifetime he could never hear its name uttered without shedding tears of tender emotion.[17] How he would have loved to know her, to visit her! What happiness it would have meant for him had he been able to cast himself at the feet of the Sovereign Pontiff! "In a few days I shall be with the Holy Father," he was told by Cardinal Pacca's secretary, who had made a pilgrimage to Ars. "Oh! could I but go with you!" the man of God replied with tears of holy envy in his eyes. He professed the most fervent loyalty to Rome and her teaching. "When the question of the Liturgy was first mooted in France, he showed himself at once a partisan of the *Roman Liturgy.*" He was anxious to pray in union with the common Father of the faithful, by making use of the same liturgical forms. He repeatedly expressed a wish to have a *Roman Breviary.*[18] Verily, on January 8, 1905, Rome raised to her altars one of her best and most loving sons.

These Roman solemnities, it will be readily imagined, found an echo in the village of Ars. On the first three days of August a splendid triduum was celebrated there, in which three cardinals, fifteen bishops, and 22,000 of the faithful from every part of France took part. As a matter of fact, the inhabitants of this corner of La Dombes had worked for the space of forty-five years to bring about the glorification of their beloved pastor.

The "beautiful church," which M. Vianney had only beheld in his dreams, was now standing. In order to find the necessary funds, the devoted Abbé Toccanier went on a begging tour, in the course of which he visited all the

17. Abbé Beau, *Procès de l'Ordinaire,* p. 1205.

18. On hearing of the devout and beautiful *legends* of the *Roman Breviary,* M. Vianney stated more than once what happiness it would give him to recite such an Office. Whilst in Paris I bought him a copy. I meant to make him a present of it, with the intention of keeping it as a relic after his death. However, M. Martin, my colleague of Pont-d'Ain, drew his attention to the fact that the *Roman Breviary* was longer than that of Lyons, which had been adopted in our diocese. "M. le Curé," he remarked, "who already found it most difficult to recite the latter—by reason of his infirmities and his unceasing toil—would be better advised if he made no change." The servant of God decided to abide by this opinion. (Abbé Toccanier, *Procès de l'Ordinaire,* p. 1277).

big towns in France.[19] A lottery, in which the two first prizes were the prie-Dieu and the watch of the Curé d'Ars, brought in 100,000 francs. As early as 1862, Pierre Bossan began the erection, at the apse of the old church, of the dome that was to cover the altar of St. Philomena. On August 4, 1865, Mgr. de Langalerie was able to consecrate the altar. Thirty years later, during the administration of Mgr. Convert, the "beautiful church" was completed. Vainly had M. Vianney endeavored, once upon a time, to hide his glory in that of his "dear little saint;" today the basilica of Ars is a hymn in stone in which are blended the name of Jean-Marie Vianney and that of Philomena. In his first plan, Bossan had not foreseen a transept; M. Sainte-Marie Perrin erected one in honor of the holy Curé. There the body of the servant of God now rests.

The reliquary of bronze in which it is enshrined is a gift of the clergy of France. Adorned with lilies and roses, it is an exquisite piece of work. The shrine is surmounted by a statue of St. Philomena, and at the four corners, standing erect, are the ascetic figures of SS John the Baptist, Francis Régis, Francis of Assisi, and Benedict Labre. Through the crystal of the reliquary the pilgrim beholds the mortal remains of the Curé d'Ars.

In view of the impending beatification, the body of the Venerable Vianney was exhumed on June 17, 1904. With joy and wonder it was ascertained that it had remained incorrupt. The skin had indeed grown dark and the flesh had dried up, but the body was intact, only the face, though it remained perfectly recognizable, had suffered somewhat from the ravages of death. The saint's heart was found intact, so that this precious relic could be kept apart.

The precious remains were wrapped in bands of fine linen and clothed in the following vestments: a tunic of

19. M. Toccanier died at Ars on November 7, 1883, his death following closely upon that of Catherine Lassagne, who died on October 13 of the preceding year. "One day," M. Toccanier himself relates, "I asked the Curé d'Ars to 'give me a lift up' when he would be in Paradise. 'Yes, my friend,' he replied, 'I shall tell the good God to let my comrade in.'" *(Procès apostolique in genere,* p. 143).

white watered silk, a black cassock, a rochet edged with fine lace, and a stole of cloth of gold embroidered with lilies and roses of the same material. A rosary of jasper beads was twined round the darkened fingers, and the face was covered with a wax mask which reproduces the features of the servant of God. When, on April 2, 1905, the old men of Ars, who had known M. Vianney well, were shown the relic as it is seen today by pilgrims, they burst into tears and exclaimed with one voice: "Oh, how truly like him!"

The reliquary is placed on a marble altar, under a carved stone canopy supported by columns of cipolin marble. Two large frescoes from the brush of Paul Boret form a framework to the shrine.

One jewel—the fairest of all—was still wanting to the glorious diadem with which earth had encircled the head of the Curé d'Ars. In beatifying him, Holy Church had indeed raised him to her altars, but so far he was only entitled to a restricted cult which could hardly spread beyond the boundaries of France. By a decree of April 12, 1905, Pius X had declared him "the patron of all priests having the cure of souls in France and in the countries subject to France;" but was that incomparable priest not destined to become the patron and pattern of the priests of the whole world? The honors of canonization alone could procure for him so magnificent a privilege.

After the great festivities of Rome and Ars, the authorities of Belley did not remain inactive. Even the war did not interrupt work for the Cause. In 1916, during the episcopate of Mgr. Manier and the pontificate of Benedict XV, the two miracles required for the canonization of Blessed Vianney were examined.

The cure of Soeur Eugène and that of Mathilde Rougeol were held to be proofs of his sanctity.

Soeur Eugène, a religious of Saint-Charles, began to suffer from varicose veins at the beginning of 1905. Before long they started to bleed, and this caused an ulcer six centimeters in length and five in breadth, which made walking impossible for the poor Sister. In August, 1905, some persons of Ronno (Rhône), where Soeur Eugène was stationed, spoke to her of a pilgrimage to Ars. The poor invalid besought them to take her to the village of the holy Curé. She was carried into the church and placed on a chair over the tomb in which M. Vianney had at one time reposed. There she remained for nearly an hour. "Father," she naively told him, "it was my duty to cook for my community—I must do so tomorrow!" Suddenly she felt cured. Standing up, she walked unaided to the hotel where the pilgrims from Ronno were staying. The following day Soeur Eugène resumed her duties as cook.

Mathilde Rougeol was born on September 23, 1878, at Villers-la-Faye (Côte-d'Or). As the result of a severe attack of influenza she developed tuberculous laryngitis on reaching her twenty-eighth year. She lost all power of speech and, realizing that there was no hope, she gave up consulting physicians. In July, 1910, she took part in a pilgrimage to Lourdes, led by Mgr. Dadolle, Bishop of Dijon. The virgin of Massabielle refused to cure her. On the way home the pilgrims stopped at Ars. Mlle. Rougeol put all her trust in the intercession of Blessed Vianney. In his sermon in the church of Ars, Mgr. Dadolle conjured the blessed Curé to work the miracles necessary for his canonization. Before leaving, the pilgrims gathered for the last time in front of the altar to kiss the relic of the heart. Whilst kissing it, Mathilde said within herself: "If you wish it, you can cure me!" When she was once more back in her place, she tried to sing. O marvel! her voice, which she had lost four years earlier, broke forth as of old when she joined in the well-known hymn:

C'est notre saint, notre honneur, notre gloire,
Le Curé d'Ars qu'on acclame en ces lieux. . . .[20]

The cure was instantaneous and complete. It was in a clear and resonant voice that Mathilde Rougeol made two

20. "He is our saint, our honour, our glory,
The Curé d'Ars whom we acclaim on this spot. . . ."

successive depositions, the one on October 4, 1916, the other on September 16, 1920, before the ecclesiastical tribunal in charge of the Cause.

On November 1, 1924, the solemn decree approving these two fresh miracles attributed to the Curé d'Ars was read at the Vatican in the presence of His Holiness Pope Pius XI. On Sunday, December 28, the decree *de tuto,* sanctioning the canonization of Blessed Vianney, was read in the presence of the Pope.

On May 31, 1925, the feast of Pentecost, the lowly priest "whose virtues and miracles have, in the eyes of other nations, covered the whole of France with incomparable glory," received the supreme honors.

It was a festival of Heaven rather than of earth. A fortnight earlier, on Sunday, May 17, Rome had exalted St. Therese of the Child Jesus. To honor the "little queen," St. Peter's had been decorated with unheard-of splendor. The angelic maiden of Lisieux now, so to speak, lent those splendors to the "poor Curé d'Ars"; and priest and nun, both of them the glory of the same century and the same country, were enveloped in the magnificence of a common triumph. Every pillar was adorned with immense purple hangings fringed with gold; the pedestal of every statue was decorated with garlands of laurel leaves whilst from the immense dome there streamed down a flood of light, of gladness, and of glory.

The crowd, from every country and of every tongue—it was a new Pentecost—but where the speech of *douce France* predominated, filled every nook of the vast edifice. Thirty-five cardinals and two hundred bishops escorted the Supreme Pontiff. Enthusiastic acclamations broke forth as the standard of Blessed Vianney advanced under the sparkling vault of the basilica. And when, at about half-past ten, speaking as Head of the Church and infallible Teacher, Pius XI, with his fine voice amplified by loud-speakers, pronounced the liturgical formula: "*We declare to be a saint and we enroll in the catalogue of the saints the Blessed Jean-Marie-Baptiste Vianney,*" the crowd broke into loud applause; the silver trumpets resounded; the bells of St. Peter's and the bells of all the churches of Rome rang out a joyful peal, and every heart beat high with joy.

At nightfall, on the piazza of St. Peter's, a fresh homage was offered to the new saint. The dome thrown up into the sky by the genius of Michelangelo, the façade of the basilica, the colonnade of Bernini, the obelisk itself shone with the brightness of a thousand torches under the star-lit sky of Rome. Unnumbered multitudes streamed in the direction of the Vatican to contemplate a spectacle unique in the world, one which the Eternal City itself had not witnessed for more than fifty years. It was no excessive display, seeing that it was men's way of thanking God for having given to the Church a priest who appeared in the land of France like a burning fire and a light whose brightness shall never grow dim.

INDEX

Apostolic process, 616ff.
Ars, 111; church, 134, 173, 185, 242, 614, 623f.; history, 114ff.
Athanase, Frére, 242, 309,343, 398, 446, 601f.

Balley, M. Charles, 25, 29, 37, 42, 97, 104
Bibost, Mère, 74, 112, 129

Chaffangeon, Père Louis, 197, 247
Chalandon, Mgr., Bp. of Belley, 366, 415, 429
Champagnat, Marcellin, Founder of the Little Brothers of Mary, 79, 82
Chanay, Jeanne-Marie, 210, 389ff., 567f.
Chaneins, 201
Colin, Jean Claude, Founder of the Society of Mary, 82, 428
Combalot, Abbé, 472f.
Concordat, 33
Courbon, M., 89, 92, 102, 173

Dardilly, 3, 12, 16, 24, 28, 41, 438f., 606
Devie, Mgr., Bp. of Belley, 185, 192ff., 226, 282, 294, 295, 359, 383, 390, 393, 415, 428f., 482, 506
Dubouis, Abbé, 493, 506
des Garets, Comte, Mayor of Ars, 368, 372, 381, 434, 462, 488f.
des Garets, François, Vicomte, 120, 170, 177
des Garets, Marie Anne Colombe Garnier, 119, 177, 195, 247f.

Ecully, 5, 13, 25, 26, 38, 48, 97f.

Fayot, Claudine, 60, 102
Fayot, Paul, Mayor of Les Noës, 59
Fesch, Cardinal, 37, 48, 75, 81, 88f., 91ff.
Filliat, Marie, 211, 389
Fourvière, N. D. de, 228, 528

Gardette, Canon, 82, 89, 582f.
Giraud, Maximin, 404ff.
Giraud, Angélique, 404ff.
Grappin, Le, 252ff.
Groboz, M., Vicaire of Ste-Croix, 25, 29, 88

Helpers of the Holy Souls, 544
Humbert, Mme., 26, 41

Immaculate Conception, Dogma of, 423

Jérôme, Frère, 432, 465, 598f.
Jesuits, 548

Labre, St. Benôit, 3, 4
Lacordaire, Père, 489
Langalerie, Mgr., Bishop of Belley, 606, 615
Lardet, Benoîte, 209, 220
Lassagne, Catherine, 207, 209, 233, 391, 394, 430
Leo, XIII, Pope, 616f.
Limas, 201
Loras, Mathias, 43, 73, 175, 274
Louvesc, La, 45
Luçon, Mgr., Bp. of Belley, 617, 622
Lyons, 53, 81

Maissiat, M., 320f.
Marie de la Providence, Mère (Eugénie Smet), 544
Matthieu, Mélanie, 404ff.
Montmerle, 201, 203
Monnin, Abbé, 471f.
Muard, Père Jean Baptiste, O.S.B., 543

Napoleon Bonaparte, 29, 51, 68, 76, 81, 88, 91
Napoleon, Louis, 475, 547
Noës, Les, 57, 69

Paray le Monial, 4
Philomena, St., 103, 278f., 375, 551ff.

Pius VI, Pope, 27
Pius VII, Pope, 51, 88
Pius IX, Pope, 545, 616
Pius X, Pope, 617, 620f., 625
Pius XI, Pope, 627
Process of the Ordinary, 615
Providence, The, 192, 209ff., 388f.

Raymond, Abbé, 275, 371, 378, 381, 406ff., 411f., 504f, 549
Regis, St. Francis, 45
Revolution, The, 15f., 23
Rey, M. Jacques, 12, 33, 37
Robespierre, 24
Robins, Les, 59, 70
Roanne, 54

Saint-Bernard, 201, 204
Saint-Trivier-sur-Moignans, 201, 203
Salette, La, 404ff.
Sisters of St. Joseph, 390

Toccanier, Abbé, 430f., 449, 451, 471, 599
Tournier, Abbé, 37
Trévoux, 201f., 205

Ullathorne, Bishop, 300, 548

Verrières (Petit Séminaire), 73, 75, 81
Vianney, Catherine, 5, 13
Vianney, François, 5, 30, 35, 438f.
Vianney, François (Cadet), 5, 68
Vianney, St. Jean-Marie: birth, 5; baptism, 5; infancy, 6ff; childhood, 16ff.; boyhood, 29ff.; first Confession, 26; vocation, 35; Confirmation, 48ff.; conscription, 51f.; retreat at Les Noës, 57; pilgrimage to La Louvesc, 45f.; education, 24; at Ecully, 39ff., 73; at Verrières 75ff.; at Lyons, 81; failure, departure and return, 85-88; Holy Orders, 90, 94, 96; first Mass, 97; Vicaire at Ecully, 97f.; Curé d'Ars, 105f.; first works, 125; catechism, 136f.; sermons, 140, 182, 201; conversion of Ars, 120f., 136f., 141f., 148ff., 195, 227, 249; trials of early years, 181ff.; calumnies, 185, 282, 289ff.; missions, 201; assaults of the Devil, 252, 272; the pilgrimage to Ars, 274ff., 298; horarium, 340; illness, 371; attempted departures, 370, 379, 385, 430f.; foundation of schools, 399, and of missions, 400; La Salette, 404ff., Franciscan tertiary, 427; last illness, 595ff.; death, 607; funeral, 611f.; declared Venerable, 616; beatified, 620f.; canonized, 627; confessor, 298, 302, 326ff., 509f., 586, and director, 326f., 452; conversions, 305f., 315, 317ff., 321; honors, 415f., 418, 420; humility, 292, 478ff., 481ff.; intuitions, 518ff.; levitation, 582f.; miracles, 189, 217f., 265ff., 306, 400, 413f., 551; mortifications, 130, 285, 356, 468, 491, 499, 502ff.; mystical experiences, 565ff.; poverty, 112, 122, 490; predictions, 520ff.; sanctity, 467ff.; spiritual marriage, 583
Vianney, Jeanne Marie, 5
Vianney, Marguerite (Gothon), 5, 7, 17, 50, 129, 259
Vianney, Marie (*née* Beluse), 5, 9, 66f., 70
Vianney, Matthieu, 5, 36, 39
Vianney, Pierre, 3
Vincent, Jérôme, 60